D0987399

HISPANICS IN THE
U.S. CRIMINAL JUSTICE SYSTEM

Second Edition

HISPANICS IN THE U.S. CRIMINAL JUSTICE SYSTEM

Ethnicity, Ideology, and Social Control

By

MARTIN GUEVARA URBINA, PH.D.

Professor, Criminal Justice
Sul Ross State University–Rio Grande College

and

SOFÍA ESPINOZA ÁLVAREZ

Founder & President
Fundacion Empower Global, A.C.
San Miguel de Allende, Guanajuato, México

CHARLES C THOMAS • PUBLISHER, LTD.
Springfield • Illinois • U.S.A.

Published and Distributed Throughout the World by

CHARLES C THOMAS • PUBLISHER, LTD.
2600 South First Street
Springfield, Illinois 62704

This book is protected by copyright. No part of
it may be reproduced in any manner without written
permission from the publisher. All rights reserved.

© 2018 by CHARLES C THOMAS • PUBLISHER, LTD.

ISBN 978-0-398-09216-0 (paper)
ISBN 978-0-398-09217-7 (ebook)

First Edition, 2012
Second Edition, 2018

With THOMAS BOOKS *careful attention is given to all details of manufacturing
and design. It is the Publisher's desire to present books that are satisfactory as to their
physical qualities and artistic possibilities and appropriate for their particular use.*
THOMAS BOOKS *will be true to those laws of quality that assure a good name
and good will.*

Printed in the United States of America
MM-C-1

Library of Congress Cataloging-in-Publication Data

Names: Urbina, Martin G. (Martin Guevara), 1972- editor. | Alvarez, Sofia
Espinoza, editor.
Title: Hispanics in the U.S. criminal justice system : ethnicity, ideology, and social
control / [edited] by Martin Guevara Urbina, Ph.D., Professor, Criminal Justice,
Sul Ross State University-Rio Grande College, Sofia Espinoza Alvarez, Founder
& President, Fundacion Empower Global, A.C., San Miguel de Allende,
Guanajuato, Mexico.
Description: 2nd edition | Springfield, Illinois: Charles C Thomas, Publisher, Ltd.,
[2018] | Includes bibliographical references and index.
Identifiers: LCCN 2018008517 (print) | LCCN 2018012679 (ebook) | ISBN
9780398092177 (ebook) | ISBN 9780398092160 (pbk. : paper)
Subjects: LCSH: Crime and race--United States. | Discrimination in criminal jus-
tice administration–United States. | Hispanic American criminals. | Hispanic
Americans–Social conditions. | Hispanic Americans--Statistics. | Hispanic
Americans–Legal status, laws, etc. | United States--Race relations.
Classification: LCC HV6194.H57 (ebook) | LCC HV6194.H57 H57 2018 (print) |
DDC 364.3/468073--dc23
LC record available at https://lccn.loc.gov/2018008517

CONTRIBUTORS

Adalberto Aguirre, Jr., PhD, is Professor of Sociology at the University of California, Riverside. His research interests focus on critical race theory, immigration, racial and ethnic inequality, and the death penalty. Dr. Aguirre has published many book chapters and scholarly journal articles in professional journals, and he is the author/coauthor of more than ten books, including *American Ethnicity: The Dynamics and Consequences of Discrimination* (2016); *Structured Inequality in the United States: Critical Discussions on the Continuing Significance of Race, Ethnicity, and Gender* (2007); *Diversity Leadership in Higher Education* (2007); *Racial and Ethnic Diversity in America: A Reference Handbook* (2003); *Sources: Notable Selections in Race and Ethnicity (2001); Women and Minority Faculty in the Academic Workplace* (2000); *Perspectives on Race and Ethnicity in American Criminal Justice* (1994); *Chicanos in Higher Education: Issues and Dilemmas for the 21st Century* (1993); *Race, Racism and the Death Penalty in the U.S.* (1992); and *Experimental Sociolinguistic Study of Chicano Bilingualism* (1978).

David V. Baker, JD, PhD, teaches at the University of South Carolina at Wilmington. He holds a bachelor's degree in political science from California State University at Northridge, a master's degree and doctorate in sociology from the University of California at Riverside, and a juris doctorate in law from California Southern Law School. He has received two National Endowment for the Humanities fellowships for advanced study in American slavery at the University of California at Irvine and immigration policy at the University of California at Los Angeles. He has held visiting lectureships at the University of California at Riverside and California State University at Fullerton and San Bernardino. He has also taught graduate seminars in law and justice studies at Chapman University. His research and teaching interests are in race and ethnic relations with an emphasis on systemic racism in the capital justice system. He has contributed several works to social science journals, law reviews, and coauthored books on the death penalty, structured social inequality, and American social problems. His books include: *Women and Capital Punishment in the United States: An Analytical History* (2016); *Structured Inequality in the United States: Discussions on the Continuing Significance of Race, Ethnicity, and Gender* (2007); *Social Problems: A Critical Power-Conflict Perspective* (2005); *Sources: Notable Selections in Race and Ethnicity* (2001); *Perspectives on Race and Ethnicity in American Criminal Justice* (1994); and *Race, Racism and the Death Penalty in the U.S.* (1992). Professor Baker is an associate editor of *Criminal Justice Studies: A Critical Journal of Crime, Law and Society.*

Charles Crawford, PhD, is Professor of Sociology at Western Michigan University and holds a doctorate in criminology from Florida State University. He has published numerous refereed journal articles and book chapters on a wide variety of criminal justice topics and has served as a consultant or reviewer for the National Science foundation, the Rand Corporation, and other agencies. Some of his articles have appeared in the journals *Criminology; Police Quarterly; Crime, Law and Social Change; Crime, Media, Culture: An International Journal;* and *Police and Society.* He is also the editor/co-editor of three books, *Spatial Policing: The Influence of Time, Space, and Geography on Law Enforcement Practices* (2018); *Federal Law Enforcement* (2018); and *Policing and Violence* (2001).

Robert J. Durán, PhD, is an Associate Professor of Sociology at the University of Tennessee, Knoxville. He earned his doctorate in sociology from the University of Colorado. As an urban ethnographer, his major research interests include supporting various forms of empowerment for marginalized groups, improving race and ethnic relations, critiquing punitive forms of social control, and discouraging colonial and colonized forms of violence. His current research projects have focused on the states of Colorado, New Mexico, Texas, Utah, and the United States-Mexico border. Dr. Durán has published numerous book chapters and refereed journal articles, appearing in scholarly journals like *Aztlán: A Journal of Chicano Studies; Journal of Contemporary Ethnography; Journal of Ethnicity in Criminal Justice; Latino Studies;* and *Social Justice: A Journal of Crime, Conflict and World Order.* His book on gang in America, *Gang Life in Two Cities: An Insider's Journey* (2013), documents the realities and myths of gang behavior, and his forthcoming book, *The Gang Paradox: Miracles and Inequality on the U.S.-Mexico Border* (both with Columbia University Press), he situates criminality within a broader context. Dr. Durán is the recipient of the 2010 Hispanic Faculty and Staff Caucus Junior Faculty of the Year Award at New Mexico State University and the 2011 New Scholar Award from the American Society of Criminology Division on People of Color and Crime.

Christina Ann Medina, PhD, is an Associate Professor of Government and the Director of the Master of Public Administration (MPA) program at New Mexico State University (NMSU). She earned her doctorate in Public Affairs at the University of Colorado at Denver in 2008. Professor Medina's research interests include education policy, immigration policy, program evaluation, and community engagement. Dr. Medina has published articles on public administration, education policy, parental involvement, and on issues regarding higher education, specifically Hispanic serving (HSI) and Minority serving (MSI) institutions.

Alfredo Mirandé, JD, PhD, A native of Mexico City and father of three children, Dr. Mirandé is Distinguished Professor of Sociology and past Chair of Ethnic Studies at the University of California, Riverside, and has also taught at the Texas Tech University School of Law. He received a B.S. from Illinois State University, M.A. and Ph.D. from the University of Nebraska, and a JD, Juris Doctorate, from Stanford University. Professor Mirandé's teaching and research interests are in Chicano sociology, gender and masculinity, constitutional law, civil rights, and law, race, class, and gender. Dr. Mirandé has published numerous journal articles in sociology, law, and ethnic studies, and author of numerous books, including *Behind the Mask: Gender Hybridity in a Zapotec Community* (2017); *Jalos, USA: Transnational Community and Identity* (2014); *Rascuache Lawyer: A Theory of Ordinary Litigation* (2011); *The Stanford Law Chronicles: 'Doin' Time on the Farm* (2005); *Hombres y Machos: Masculinity and Latino Culture* (1997); *Gringo Justice* (1990); *The Chicano Experience* (1989); *La Chicana: The Mexican-American Woman* (1981); and *The Age of Crisis* (1975). Dr. Mirandé is a full-time teacher and researcher, and has a limited, largely pro bono law practice, specializing in criminal law and employment discrimination.

Kathryn D. Morgan, PhD, is Professor of Criminal Justice and Director of the African American Studies Program the University of Alabama at Birmingham. She is also the Affirmative Action and Diversity Officer for the College of Arts and Sciences. Dr. Morgan was awarded degrees in Sociology and Criminology from Texas and Florida State University. Professor Morgan's research and teaching areas include race, crime and social policy, gender issues in criminal justice, correctional practices, and policies. A recently developed line of research focuses on the death penalty and its application both nationally and in Alabama. Dr. Morgan's research has appeared in various scholarly journals, including *Journal of Criminal Justice; Justice Quarterly; Criminology and Public Policy; Criminal Justice Policy Review;* and *Criminal Justice Review.* Recently, she published a book, *Probation, Parole, and Community Corrections Work in Theory and Practice* (2016), designed to prepare students for careers in probation and parole.

Natalie R. Ortiz, PhD, is the Data-Driven Justice Program Manager at the National Association of Counties (NACo), where she works with local governments to develop strategies, technologies, and policies for using data and analytics across health, human services and justice systems to reduce jail populations and improve individual and system outcomes. She was previously a Senior Research Analyst at NACo, establishing the association's criminal justice research agenda, creating county-level datasets, and demonstrating the role of counties in the justice system to federal and state lawmakers. A graduate of the criminology and criminal justice doctoral program at Arizona State University, her research appears in peer-reviewed journals and is cited frequently in national-level policy discussions on reducing the jail population.

Ilse Aglaé Peña, MS, has coauthored book chapters and refereed journal articles. Her academic areas of interest include law and society, capital punishment, ethnic studies, and social justice. Currently, Peña is working on a book, *Hispanic Soldiers: The Latino Legacy in the U.S. Armed Forces,* documenting the role, significance, and contributions of Latinos in the United States armed forces over the years, a project that includes face-to-face interviews with high ranking Latinos in the military, and Latinos who have received the Medal of Honor, the U.S. highest and most prestigious military decoration that may be awarded to recognize U.S. military service members who distinguished themselves by acts of valor, awarded by the President in the name of Congress.

Carlos E. Posadas, PhD, is an Associate Professor of Criminal Justice at New Mexico State University. He earned his doctorate in Justice Studies at Arizona State University. His teaching and research interests include immigration and justice, the U.S.-Mexico border race, gender, and crime. Dr. Posadas has published articles examining issues influencing the judicial and police officer decision-making process, on juvenile justice and disproportionate minority contact (DMC), on issues regarding higher education and the Hispanic Serving Institution (HSI) mission, and the U.S. Border Patrol museum.

Mary Romero, PhD, is Professor of Justice Studies and Social Inquiry at Arizona State University and Affiliate of Women and Gender Studies, Asian Pacific American Studies and African and African American Studies. She received the American Sociology American Section on Race and Ethnicity Minorities 2009 Founder's Award [Recognize career excellence in scholarship and service]. In 2004, she received the Society for the Study of Social Problems' Lee Founders Award 2004, the highest award made by the Society for the Study of Social Problems for a career of activist scholarship. She is a former Carnegie Scholar, Pew National Fellowship for Carnegie Scholars, Carnegie Academy for the Scholarship of Teaching and Learning. Dr. Romero is author of numerous articles and book chapters. And, she is the author/co-editor of numerous books, including *The Maid's Daughter: Living Inside and Outside the American Dream* (2011); *Maid in the U.S.A.* (1992, 2002); *Blackwell Companion to Social Inequalities* (2005); *Latino/a Popular Culture* (2002); *Women's Untold Stories: Breaking Silence, Talking Back, Voicing Complexity* (1999), *Challenging Fronteras: Structuring Latina and Latina Lives in the U.S.* (1997); and *Women and Work: Exploring Race, Ethnicity and Class* (1997). Her most recent articles are published in *Indiana Law Journal; Aztlán; International Journal of Sociology of the Family; Critical Sociology; Contemporary Justice Review; Critical Sociology; Law & Society Review; British Journal of Industrial Relations; Villanova Law Review;* and *Cleveland State Law Review.* She served on the Law and Society Association Board of Trustees (Class of 2008) and the Council of the American Sociological Association (2007-2009). She serves on the international editorial board of Brill's "Critical Studies in Social Science" and National Review Board of Meridians: Feminism, Race, Transnationalism. Her research focuses on the unequal distribution of reproductive labor as a paid commodity and its role in reproducing inequality among families within countries and between nations. Embedded in feminist legal scholarship on caregiving, this research explores questions from a legal perspective: is work primarily an artifact of family law, or should it be examined through the lens of employment law? Her research also includes writings on social inequalities and justice that incorporate the intersectionality of race, class, gender, and citizenship and links the parallels between domestic gendered race relations and immigration and identifies the continuum between racism against citizens and racism against noncitizens.

Rick Ruddell, PhD, the Law Foundation of Saskatchewan Chair in Police Studies, joined the Department of Justice Studies at the University of Regina (Canada) in September, 2010. Prior to this appointment he served as Director of Operational Research with the Correctional Service of Canada, and held faculty positions at Eastern Kentucky University and the California State University, Chico. A graduate of the doctoral program in Criminology and Criminal Justice at the University of Missouri-St. Louis, Dr. Ruddell's research has focused upon policing, criminal justice policy, and juvenile justice. He has published over 100 journal articles and several books, including *Making Sense of Criminal Justice* (2018); *Oil, Gas, and Crime: The Dark Side of the Boomtown* (2017); *Exploring Criminal Justice in Canada* (2017); *Policing Rural Canada* (2016); *Do the Crime, Do the Time: Juvenile Criminals and Adults* (2012); *American Jails: A Retrospective Examination* (2010); *Juvenile Corrections* (2009); *Understanding Correctional Violence* (2009); *Issues in Correctional Health* (2008); *Making Sense of Criminal Justice: Policies and Practices* (2007); *Corrections and the Criminal Justice System* (2007); and *American Behind Bars: Trends in Imprisonment, 1950–2000* (2004).

Gabriella E. Sánchez, PhD, is an Assistant Professor of Security Studies and Associate Director for Research at The University of Texas El Paso's National Security Studies Institute. Her research and teaching interests involve the social ecology of transnational organized crime, of border crossings and human mobility efforts, and of bottom-up resistance and insurgent movements. Prior to joining NSSI she was a Clinical Assistant Professor at The Catholic University of America, a Research Fellow at Monash University's Border Crossing Observatory (Melbourne, Australia), a Visiting Lecturer at Wellesley College, a Fulbright Scholar at the Hebrew University in Jerusalem, and a Post-Doctoral Researcher at START, the University of Maryland's Department of Homeland Security Center of Excellence. An anthropologist by training, Dr. Sanchez has completed field research in over 20 countries on five continents, including transborder research for her recent book, *Human Smuggling and Border Crossings* (2015), emerging from her ethnographic work among human and drug smuggling facilitators. A consultant for federal and state agencies and global NGOs, her professional affiliations include the American Anthropological Association, the American Society of Criminology, the Racial Democracy, Crime and Justice Network, and the University of Oxford's Border Criminologies Research Group. She is also a reviewer for various academic journals.

Claudio G. Vera Sánchez, PhD, is an Associate Professor in the Justice Studies Department at San Jose State University. He earned his doctorate from the University of Illinois at Chicago. His areas of research center on youth justice, policing, and ethnic/racial minorities in the United States. His studies have explored the experiences of young minorities (e.g., Latinos and African Americans) with the police, the perceived legitimacy of the police in underprivileged neighborhoods, and how officers negotiate police work within inner-city neighborhoods. Dr. Vera Sánchez's recent publications analyze diverse topics, including "Immigration, Illegality, and the Law: Governance, Equality, and Justice" (2018); "Latino Police Officers, Policy, and Practice: Positive Police Reform or Reinforcement of Structural Hierarchies"

(2017); "Latino Officers, Policy, and Practice (2015); "Sacrificed on the Altar of Public Safety: The Policing of Latino and African American Youth" (2011); and "Racialized Policing: Officers' Voices on Policing Latino and African American Neighborhoods" (2011). Professor Vera Sánchez is also committed to transformative learning, and he has worked collaboratively with university students to redirect students with previous involvement with the legal system from a "path of prison" to college.

In our quest for knowledge, discovery, and positive transformation, we dedicate this book to all the "crusaders" who devote their careers and lives promoting social change, empowerment, and a universal message of understanding, compassion, equality, justice, and human dignity. We also dedicate this volume to our family, friends, professors, and mentors, who (as noted in the acknowledgement page) have guided, encouraged, and supported us during difficult and uncertain moments.

M.G.U.
S.E.A.

PREFACE

Men fear thought as they fear nothing else on earth—more than ruin—even more than death. . . . Thought is subversive and revolutionary, destructive and terrible, thought is merciless to privilege, established institutions, and comfortable habit. Thought looks into the pit of hell and is not afraid. Thought is great and swift and free, the light of the world, and the chief glory of [people].

—Bertrand Russell

Predating the Constitution, the United States has characterized itself as a country grounded in essential elements, like civility, stability, freedom, democracy, civil and human rights, equality, tolerance, and justice, always progressing, while avoiding ruptures and discontinuities. In truth, contrary to *conventional wisdom,* the United States is more reflective of continued political, economic, and social chaos in the historical fight for expansion, wealth, power, and control than a unified movement for universal freedom, equality, social change, and justice. In effect, while there has been gross inequality and injustice in all major United States institutions, some of the most fundamental discontinuities, inefficiencies, inequalities, and injustices have been generated by the very system, the criminal justice system, that has been designed to govern safety, order, and positive social change. Worse, in the very arena where the machinery of justice is operating and thus efficiency, equality, and justice is supposed to prevail, some of the most catastrophic events and movements are taking place, while strategically and aggressively targeting certain segments of society, particularly Latinos, blacks, and poor whites.

As in the past, today people tend to blindly accept criminal justice policies, especially social control policies and immigration laws, without truly questioning the very essence of American criminal law, beginning with its foundation and the forces driving criminal justice policies. Most notably, in the context of race and ethnicity, as early as 1740, the South Carolina Slave Code, for example, identified

> the people commonly called negroes, Indians, mulattos and mestizos have [been] deemed absolute slaves, and the subjects of property in the hands of particular persons the extent of whose power over slaves ought to be settle and limited by positive laws so that the slaves may be kept in due subjection and obedience (cited in Hall, Wiecek, & Finkelman, 1996:37),

resulting in a legacy of manipulation, marginalization, oppression, and silencing of minorities, while allowing whites absolute control of America's main institutions, to include the economic, educational, and political systems.

Starting with the Declaration of Independence (1776), race has played a central role in defining U.S. laws and how criminal justice policies are applied to blacks. Normally left out from the *pages of history,* Latinos, like blacks, have in fact suffered the indignities of conquest and *de jure* segregation. In the case of Mexican Americans, under the rationale of Anglo-Saxon expansion and Manifest Destiny, premised on the ideology of racial, ethnic, religious, and cultural superiority of white Americans, the Treaty of Guadalupe Hidalgo ended the Mexican-American War in 1848, granting the United States 55 percent of Mexico's territory, an area that now comprises about one-third of the continental United States. Soon after, the 1855 "Greaser Act," an anti-vagrancy law enacted in California defining vagrants as "all persons who are commonly known as 'Greasers' or the issue [children] of Spanish and Indian blood," was a deliberate use of criminal law to specifically target Mexicans based on race and ethnicity (Morín, 2009:16; Urbina, Vela, & Sanchez, 2014). Clearly, as documented by legal scholar José Luis Morín (2009:15), "This history is instructive as to how Latinas/os would be regarded in later years, since persons of mixed racial backgrounds, as many Latinas/os are, have been and often continue to be viewed with disdain, and subject to discrimination by dominant 'White' social structure."

Towards the end of the twentieth century, Jonathan Simon (1997:173) charged that advanced industrial societies were actually "governed through crime," with the overdeveloped societies of the West and North Atlantic "experiencing not a crisis of crime and punishment but a crises of governance that has led [them] to prioritize crime and punishment as the preferred contexts of governance," redefining the limits of criminal laws, while socially reconstructing the confines of race and ethnicity (Dowling & India, 2013; Simon, 2007; Urbina & Álvarez, 2016). Then, at the turn of the century, Tony Fitzpatrick (2001:220) argued that as "global capital becomes apparently unmanageable" and "as the polity and the economic detached after a century of alignment," the state must give itself, particularly its agents, something to do, and so the state "socially and discursively constructs threats that only it can address through . . . punitive responses to the chaos it has [helped facilitate]," as in the case of the war on drugs, the war on terrorism, and most recently, under the Trump administration, the war on immigrants (Alexander, 2012; Salinas, 2015; Urbina & Álvarez, 2017), as documented by Álvarez and Urbina in *Immigration and the Law: Race, Citizenship, and Social Control* (2018). With crime and criminal justice systems becoming increasingly transnational, assisted by advanced technological innovations and a highly charged American media, "at once totalizing and individualizing," such social control strategies congeal in appealing political formations that can govern "all and each" with stealthy precision (Gordon, 1991:3; Simon, 2014; Urbina & Álvarez, 2016, 2017), giving the state a notion of absolute control, legitimacy, and justice, and to a feared and misinformed society, an appearance of global power and solidarity.

In effect, from the early conquest of Native Americans, to slavery, to the conquest of Mexicans, to the conquest and colonization of Puerto Ricans, to the war on terrorism, to the war on immigrants, with its corresponding elements, like racial profiling, public space housing sweeps, police surveillance cameras, and drug/prostitution-free zones, such movements clearly reveal that the U.S. obsession with law and order is just as much about race and ethnicity, as it is about safety, equality, progress, and justice. For instance, as reported by renowned legal scholar David Cole (2001:248), "racial profiling studies . . . make clear that the war on drugs has largely been a war on minorities. It is, after all, drug enforcement that motivates most racial profiling." Invariably, while the overall rate of the inmate population in state and federal prisons increased dramatically in the latter part of the twentieth century (1971 to 2001), Latinos experienced a tenfold increase (Bonczar, 2003), with similar trends in the early part of the twenty-first century (Urbina & Álvarez, 2016, 2017). In fact, by 2004, the rate of Latino incarceration in state and federal prisons was 2.6 times greater than for whites (1,220 per 100,000 compared to 463 per 100,000), according to Paige Harrison and Allen Beck (2005) of the Bureau of Justice Statistics, with the Sentencing Project (2003:1) reporting that "Hispanics are the fastest growing group being imprisoned." Quickly, the ramifications of redefining race, ethnicity, crime, and punishment became gravely pressing in imprisonment rates, as reported by Loic Wacquant (2001:82), "turning over from 70 percent white at the mid-century point to nearly 70 percent black and Latino today, although the ethnic patterns of criminal activity have not been fundamentally altered during that period."

In all, as we witnessed during the 2015/2016 presidential elections and now under the Trump administration, possibly as in no other time in U.S. history is the dominant majority experiencing a more significant "cultural crisis" in that after centuries of *total control* (Álvarez & Urbina, 2018), their ideas about race, ethnicity, gender, and social life are under attack by the intertwining forces of diversity and multiculturalism (Urbina, 2014) as well as political and economic uncertainty (Urbina & Álvarez, 2016). In effect, in part

> because the United States considers itself a 'moral' and 'law-and-order' society, the US has a phobia of the *outsider,* the *different,* and the *stranger.* As an institutionalized state of feeling and thinking, such phobia has manifested itself into ignorance, which in turn has resulted in viciousness and vindictiveness [and] fear of those who threaten our interests or the status quo has manifested itself into low levels of tolerance (Nieling & Urbina, 2008:233),

making the criminal justice system the prime apparatus for suppression, control, and silencing of those who threaten the dominant social structure.

Though, while the disproportionate representation of minorities, particularly blacks and Latinos, in the criminal justice system is well documented, much less analyzed are the historical and contemporary mechanisms, beliefs, and ideologies that govern the minority experience. As such, considering the strategically selective and aggressive tactics of policing minority communities, the punitive movement of the judicial system, and the grossly disproportionate number of Latinos under the con-

xvi   *Hispanics in the U.S. Criminal Justice System*

trol of the legal system, or as some critics characterize it, the *era of mass incarceration* (Alexander, 2012; Hinton, 2016; Ríos, 2006; Simon, 2014; Urbina & Álvarez, 2017; Vallas, 2016), it is of utmost importance that the ways in which ideas of ethnicity, race, gender, and class uphold the supposed "legitimacy" of the criminal justice system be demystified and exposed in the pages of academic literature, a central objective of this revised book, undertaken by some of the most prominent authors from around the country. In this mission, rather than attempting to develop a single explanation for the ethnic experience in policing, the courts, the penal system, and society in general, this updated second edition presents a variety of studies that illustrate alternative ways of interpreting crime, social control, equality, justice, social change, and progress. As in the first edition of this book, the findings reveal that race, ethnicity, gender, class, and several other variables continue to play a significant and consequential role in the legal decision-making process. In short, the authors report sound evidence that testifies to a historical legacy of manipulation, brutality, marginalization, oppression, prejudice, discrimination, power, and control, and to white America's continued fear about racial and ethnic minorities, a movement exacerbated in the twenty-first century with Trump's highly charged anti-immigrant and anti-Mexican political rhetoric. As such, this book presents a variety of studies and perspectives that offer a pathway toward addressing long-neglected but vital topics in the discourse on criminal justice policy and reform.

Martin Guevara Urbina
Sofia Espinoza Álvarez

ACKNOWLEDGMENTS

It would have been impossible to conduct this project and edit this book without the patience and unconditional support of many highly talented, sincere, loyal, and dedicated people, who guided and encouraged us during the entire process. To begin, our most profound appreciation goes to all the contributing authors for not only participating in this project but also being vested in producing creative, refreshing, and captivating original chapters. We are honored for their patience, encouragement, and support during the lengthy and complicated process. This book never would have come to fruition without their assistance, perseverance, and advice throughout the various stages of the project.

We like to acknowledge Dr. Adalberto Aguirre, Jr. (University of California–Riverside), Dr. Tomas Almaguer (San Francisco State University), Dr. David V. Baker (University of South Carolina at Wilmington), Dr. David E. Barlow (Fayetteville State University), Dr. Melissa H. Barlow (Fayetteville State University), Professor Steven W. Bender (Seattle University School of Law), Dr. Charles Ramirez Berg (University of Texas at Austin), Dr. Jorge Castañeda Gutman (New York University), Dr. Leo R. Chávez (University of California, Irvine), Dr. Charles Crawford (Western Michigan University), Dr. Arnoldo De León (Angelo State University), Dr. Joe R. Feagin (Texas A&M University, College Station), Dr. Ruth Gomberg-Muñoz (Loyola University, Chicago), Dr. Ramon A. Gutierrez (University of Chicago), Dr. Peter Laufer (University of Oregon), Dr. Rubén Martínez (Michigan State University), Dr. Alfredo Mirandé (University of California, Riverside), Dr. Felipe de Ortego y Gasca (Western New Mexico University), Dr. Marcos Pizarro (San Jose State University), Dr. Mary Romero (Arizona State University), Dr. Rick Ruddell (University of Regina, Canada), Professor Lupe S. Salinas (Thurgood Marshall School of Law), Dr. Angela Valenzuela (University of Texas at Austin), and Dr. L. Thomas Winfree (Arizona State University) for their words of wisdom, compassion, and support during difficult, uncertain, or tearful moments. We are forever indebted to you for never losing confidence in us and encouraging and inspiring us to continue with our lines of research and publications.

We also extend our profound gratitude to Professor Francisco Roberto Ramírez Ramírez (Universidad de Guanajuato, México) for his guidance and assistance in academic and legal endeavors. To María Aurora Ramírez Padrón, law school director/career coordinator (Universidad de León, San Miguel de Allende, Guanajuato, México), for her kindness, support, and advice. Also, a word of acknowledgment and appreciation goes to Jonathan Stefanonni for his friendship, affection, and everlasting support.

We like to thank the Empower Global Foundation for supporting this project. Illustrating its active role in social reform, transformation, and human rights through discovery and knowledge, the Empower Global Foundation provided funding for the early stages of this project, ensuring that the project would become a reality. Vested in the betterment of our communities, Empower Global creates, designs, supports, and encourages the development of social programs, schemes, proposals, and research based projects to contribute, habilitate, and influence in the empowerment of all individuals without distinction–at all levels of social strata and of all geographical locations. In addition, the Foundation promotes education, knowledge, discovery, and cultural sensibility holistically. Considering that, according to modern times, globalization represents a cornerstone for the growth of society, a central mission of the Empower Global Foundation is to implement progressive actions with positive international impact.

We like to say a special thanks to our publisher, Charles C Thomas, its president, Michael Thomas, and his staff for being extremely patient, supportive, helpful, and understanding throughout the entire publishing process. Their patience, guidance, encouragement, and professionalism have been vital for making this project a reality. And, we like to acknowledge the heroic efforts of all the people who contributed to the making of this book in one way or another. We are well aware that seldom we have the privilege and honor to work with highly talented, honest, and loyal individuals–passionate crusaders for knowledge, discovery, equality, and justice.

M.G.U.
S.E.A.

CONTENTS

SECTION TWO: HISPANICS AND THE JUDICIAL SYSTEM

SECTION THREE: HISPANICS AND THE PENAL SYSTEM

SECTION FOUR: LATINOS, GLOBALIZATION, AND SOCIAL CONTROL

ILLUSTRATIONS

HISPANICS IN THE
U.S. CRIMINAL JUSTICE SYSTEM

Chapter 1

THE LATINO CONDITION IN THE AGE OF MASS INCARCERATION: ETHNICITY, DIVERSITY, CHANGE, AND SOCIAL CONTROL

MARTIN GUEVARA URBINA AND SOFÍA ESPINOZA ÁLVAREZ

[Our] knowledge of everyday life has the quality of an instrument that cuts a path through a forest and, as it does so, projects a narrow cone of light on what lies just ahead and immediately around; on all sides of the path there continues to be darkness.

–Peter L. Berger and Thomas Luckmann

Around the globe, for over 200,000 years, human mobility has been a landmark of social existence and transformation. People are voluntarily leaving, forced to leave, or taken out of their area of origin to different geographical areas, normally with specific objectives, like the relocation of criminals from one country to another, the transportation of slaves to different countries, and the importation or exportation of "immigrants" around the world. In modern times, though, no country in the world has possibly experienced more human mobility, migration, and social transformation than the United States, particularly with the advent of globalization, with its multiple corresponding elements, like the governing dynamics of the educational, economic, political, and criminal justice systems; technology; cultural diversity, and multiculturalism.

Yet while human mobility, expansion, migration, and societal transformation have been historical inner elements of the American experience since the days of the conquistadors, and subsequent conquest, colonialism, slavery, and imperialism, the focus of academic discourse, investigations, and publications has been on Caucasians (whites) and African Americans (blacks), with much less academic dialogue of other ethnic and racial minorities, even though Latinos now constitute the largest minority group in the United States and thus the second largest ethnic/racial group in the country, right behind the white population. In fact, historically ethnic minorities, along with certain racial minorities, like Native Americans and Asians, have either been excluded from the *pages of history,* or all Latinos of various national origins have been treated as a mono-

3

lithic group. Consequently, over the years, there has been gravely scant discourse on Latinos, particularly Mexican Americans, who have historically constituted the high majority of Latinos in the United States, with a similar pattern of neglect experienced by other ethnic/racial minorities. Similarly, as in everyday life, in their engagement with America's institutions, particularly the criminal justice system, as the largest ethnic minority and, overall, as the largest minority group, Mexican Americans and Latinos have not only been less studied, documented, and discussed in academic settings, to include research, publication, and dialogue. In essence, they have been historically manipulated, intimidated, marginalized, oppressed, and silenced.

Therefore, without exploring both the ethnic and racial experience in its totality, from conquest and colonialism to twenty-first-century globalization, the truths and realities of the American experience remain skewed. Latinos and other racial minorities remain in the shadows of the past, keeping the ethnic realities of Mexican Americans and other Latinos hidden from the academic literature and, for undocumented minorities currently living in the United States, in a state of manipulation, intimidation, oppression, marginalization, and silence.

This chapter shows that significant research gaps remain to be bridged if we are in fact going to be more inclusive in academic investigations, and thus generating and disseminating more representative, sound, and objective information, projecting the historical realities of the entire American experience, to include not only whites and blacks, which historically have "represented" the so-called American multicultural society, but also Mexican Mexicans and other ethnic/racial minorities, like Asians and Native Americans. For instance, generally, historians, political scientists, sociologists, psychol-

ogists, criminologists, and other social scientists tend to focus on certain issues, events, or situations while documenting the minority experience, without historically delineating the ethnic experience over time and either minimizing or excluding historical movements that have governed the ethnic (Latino) experience for centuries–providing a story of the Latino, particularly Mexican American, experience without unearthing the historical roots, which originally set in motion the forces that would ultimately shape and reshape the everyday experience for Mexican Americans, other ethnic/racial minorities, and poor whites. For instance, as recently documented by Martin Guevara Urbina, Joel Vela, and Juan Sánchez in *Ethnic Realities of Mexican Americans: From Colonialism to 21st Century Globalization* (2014), one of the most detrimental social movements against Mexican Americans and other Latinos, along with African Americans–for over one and a half centuries–has been the criminalization of Mexican identity. However, while scholars have been documenting the overrepresentation of minorities, especially African Americans and, more recently, Latinos, throughout the American criminal justice system, they have failed to analyze not only the Mexican American experience but the overall ethnic experience by the totality of intertwining historical factors, events, issues, circumstances, cultural diversity, and, most critical, ideologies, which in fact structure the institutional foundations.

This kind of historical, theoretical, and methodological approach is not, on its own, sufficient to fully capture the ethnic realities of Mexican Americans and other ethnic/racial minorities over the years in everyday life or in their engagement with America's main institutions, beginning with the educational system and subsequently in their encounters with the criminal justice system. Consequently, it fails to delineate, in their totality, the forces, contours, and governing dynamics of social control, cultural diversity, and multiculturalism over time. In essence, the ethnic experience begins to rapidly unfold when Mexicans were first joined by whites in then Mexican territory, soon after Mexicans became foreigners in their own land, subsequently beginning a migration cycle that continued for decades and quickly exacerbated a legacy of struggle, brutality, and hate that remains highly charged in the new millennium—exacerbated or bluntly exposed by Republication presidential candidate Donald Trump's anti-Mexican comments on June 16, 2015 when he officially began his presidential race, anti-Mexican rhetoric that we have been hearing daily.

In effect, in modern times, the ethnic experience begins when Mexicans, along with other ethnic/racial minorities, first enter the United States. At times, even before they arrive in the land of the "free," the United States tends to influence people beyond its national borders, especially now with the advent of a modernized form of globalization, a kind of migration in itself, shaping the confines of transnational immigration, diversity, multiculturalism, and social control.

Therefore, researchers, critics, and commentators need to place contemporary ideas, practices, and experiences in the context of the past and of broader ideas about ethnicity, race, cultural diversity, and historical ideologies, which continue to shape and reshape not only the realities of Mexican Americans but also other ethnic and racial groups, including African Americans, Asian Americans, whites, and Native Americans in the twenty-first century. As such, by delineating the historical significance of the Latino experience over the years, providing a critical examination of prior race and ethnic investigations, and introducing the subsequent chapters—followed by 17 detailed chapters—the contributing authors demonstrate a different approach to the contemporary study of race and ethnicity, cultural diversity, multiculturalism, and social control in the United States. By focusing primarily (but not exclusively) on the Latino experience, and paying particular attention to the Mexican American experience as the largest Latino subgroup, we seek to better understand the overall American experience, while trying to provide a *balance* to the existing literature.

THE ETHNIC EXPERIENCE OVER TIME: EMERGING TRENDS AND ISSUES

Contrary to conventional wisdom that ethnic minorities are *new* to America, Latinos were some of the first immigrants in the United States and thus Mexican Americans and other Latinos have been in the United States for centuries. Before the English came to America in 1609, there was a Latino presence in the Southwest, including Texas, and they have been in the present-day U.S. since 1565 in Florida and 1598 in New Mexico, centuries before the Treaty of Guadalupe Hidalgo that ended the Mexican-American War in 1848, in which Mexico lost over half (55%) of its territory to the United States, and, subsequently, further fueling the notion of conquest, expansion, privilege, power, control, and, ultimately, reformulating white supremacy and dominance over ethnic and racial minorities—redefining and solidifying the parameters of cultural diversity, the dynamics of multiculturalism, and law and society, along with social control, over time.

Invariably, normally excluded from popular discourse, *Latino culture has been part of "America" longer than the United States has existed.* Therefore, understanding the Latino experience and the Mexican American heritage is essential for understanding the roots of America's ethnic and racial minorities and their everyday stories, whether it is the cowboy icon, mustangs, barbecue, dollar sign, law, or Texas chili, which is as old as the U.S. Constitution (1787). Contrary to arguments that Latinos are *infiltrating* the supposed Anglo heritage, Spanish culture and language became part of the national fabric when the United States expanded west of the Mississippi River and south of the Carolinas. Mexicans, officially the first Latinos of the United States, joined the American populace through the conquest of Mexico by the United States in 1848. Geographically, Latinos lived in what is now the western and the southwestern United States decades before the first arrivals of non-Latino Europeans at Plymouth Rock in 1620. The area known today as Santa Fe, New Mexico was founded in 1610, and St. Augustine, Florida was founded in 1565 (Weber, 2004). In fact, the oldest records of European explorers and settlers on U.S. territory were actually written in Spanish. The oldest European town, St. Augustine, Florida, was founded by Spain in 1565, 42 years before the founding of Jamestown in the Colony of Virginia. United States law has also been influenced by the Spanish legal tradition, as symbolized by the carving of Castillian monarch Alfonso X, King of Castile, in the United States House of Representatives. The U.S. dollar, a powerful symbol of Americanism, also has Spanish roots. In fact, illustrating the historical ethnic influence, from 1500 until the mid-19th century, the Spanish dollar, commonly known as "pieces of eight," was the de facto currency of international commerce, and it was legal tender in the United States before

Congress approved the Coinage Act of 1857—thus serving as a model for national currencies ranging from the U.S. dollar to the Chinese yuan. Even the dollar sign ($) is widely believed to have derived from symbols connected to the Spanish currency circulating in the American colonies, and stock prices were quoted on the New York Stock Exchange in *eighths* until 1997 (Nadeau & Barlow, 2012).

As for demographic shifts and trends, despite historical mechanisms for population control, and the long legacy of prejudice, racism, manipulation, intimidation, oppression, and hate against Latinos, particularly Mexicans, the Mexican American and overall Latino population continues to grow. This leads to significant demographic changes across the country, with corresponding elements of cultural diversity and multiculturalism, along with changes in America's main institutions. Reviewing figures for the first decade of the twenty-first century, in 2000, 50 percent of Latinos lived in Texas and California alone, but dropped to 46.5 percent in 2010 (Passel, Cohn, & López, 2011). Nationally, 76 percent of Latinos resided in nine states (Arizona, California, Colorado, Florida, Illinois, New México, New Jersey, New York, and Texas) in 2010, in comparison with 81 percent in 2000 and 86 percent in 1990, revealing a significant shifting trend. Narrowing in on the Latino population by region, the West and South were home to the majority of Latinos, along with an increase in the South and Midwest. According to Jeffrey Passel, D'Vera Cohn, and Mark Hugo López (2011), in 2010, 20.6 million Latinos resided in the West, 18.2 million in the South, 7 million in the Northeast, and 4.7 million resided in the Midwest, with rapidly shifting trends across the country.

In effect, a decade into the twenty-first century, Latinos, now the largest minority group and the second largest ethnic/racial group (second only to whites), constituted approximately 16.3 percent (50.5 million) of the total U.S. population (308.7 million in 2010). As one of the two fastest growing segments of the population, Latinos now live in every state of the country and in every major city across America. By 2010, for instance, Los Angeles, the second largest city in the United States (3.8 million in 2010), was 48.5 percent (1,838,822) Latino and 29.4 percent white (in 2009), making the city's racial composition a "minority-majority" (all racial groups included), with people of Mexican origin constituting the largest ethnic group of Latinos with 31.9 percent of the Los Angeles population in 2010, followed by Salvadorans (6.0%) and Guatemalans (3.6%), making Los Angeles the second largest Mexican city in the world, after Mexico City. Within a year, Los Angeles had the largest (4.8 million) Latino population of any county in 2011 and the largest numeric increase since 2010, with Starr County, Texas, having the highest share of Latinos at 95.6 percent—with Mexican Americans, in each area, constituting the largest ethnic population. At the state level, California, District of Columbia (Washington, D.C.), Hawaii, New Mexico, and Texas are already minority-majority states (all ethnic/racial groups included). By July 1, 2011, California had the largest (14.4 million) Latino population of any state, while New Mexico had the highest percentage of Latinos at 46.7 percent. By July 1, 2012, California, Florida, and Texas (along with Hawaii and the District of Columbia) were *minority-majority* states (more than 50% minority), and New Mexico, having the highest percentage of Latinos (47% in 2012), not including other ethnic/racial minorities, was approaching 50 percent Latino, with the majority being Mexican Americans. By mid-2014, Latinos (39%) overtook whites (38.8%) living in California, making the Latino population the largest ethnic/racial group in California.

Within one year, the ethnic demographic trend quickly shifted the ethnic/racial landscape. Nationally, Latinos numbered 52 million (16.7%) in 2011, increasing by 3.1 percent since 2010, with 53 million (17%) by 2012, revealing the rapidly shifting demographics. Regarding ethnic demographics, according to the U.S. Census Bureau, by July 2011, Mexican Americans constituted 10.8 percent of the total U.S. population (311,591,919), comprising 64.6 percent (33,557,922) of all Latinos (51,939,916) in the United States, followed by Puerto Ricans (4,885,294) and Cubans (1,891,014). Today, the United States is home to the second largest Mexican community in the world, second only to Mexico, and comprising nearly 22 percent of the entire Mexican origin population of the world.

As recently reported by the associate director of the Pew Hispanic Center, Mark Hugo López, "in many respects, California looks like the future of the United States demographically" (Alvear, 2013:1). Comparatively, there are currently more Latinos living in the United States than people living in the country of Canada. It has been projected that by the year 2060, 31 percent (about 128.8 million) of the U.S. population will be Latino, and Latino children will become the largest youth population by mid-century, surpassing white children. In 2016, for instance, Mexican American and Latino students comprise 51.3 percent of school-aged children in the state of Texas and projected to reach 67 percent by 2050. Even though Asian Americans are now projected as the *upcoming majority,* for the first time in history, recent demographic trends indicate that ethnic minorities (Latinos) will become the second largest minority group (after Asians), but Latinos could possibly become the majority, considering that Mexican Americans are on track to become the upcoming majority in various states, "revolutionizing

America's multicultural society" (Urbina, 2014:8), clearly revealing the pressing significance of effective, sound, and balanced institutions, beginning with the educational system and criminal justice system. Broadly, these trends also illustrate the importance of having just, diverse, and representative institutions, along with relevant and timely research, publication, and dialogue.

As reported by legendary scholar Felipe de Ortego y Gasca, who taught the first course in Chicano (Mexican) literature in the United States at the University of New Mexico in 1969, Mexican Americans and other Latinos, who are not newcomers to the United States, lack acknowledgment, recognition, and respect in everyday life and in their engagement with America's main institutions, beginning with, as children, the educational system and the criminal justice system, along with public discussions, academ-

ic documentaries, and American textbooks. Worse, American text-books, reports Ortego (2007), have historically reported a highly skewed story of Mexican Americans as well as the overall Latino community in the United States and this has to change. Regarded as the founder of Chicano literary history and theory, Ortego (2007) declares, "TV net-work media and a majority of mainstream newspapers don't have a clue about American Hispanics." Consequently, in plain twenty-first century, the Mexican American and overall Latino story remains incomplete in our fields of modern knowledge, as their truths and realities have been skewed or omitted from the *pages of history* and remain hidden in the shadows of the past, which must be unearthed if we are to capture the essence of the American experience in its totality.

THE LATINO COMMUNITY IN MULTIRACIAL AMERICA: ETHNIC RESEARCH IN HISTORICAL PERSPECTIVE

Understanding the ethnic realities of U.S. Hispanics in their totality, though, requires that we situate the Latino experience within a historical and broader context. Consider, for instance, the current dynamics between blacks and the American police (e.g., shootings of blacks, arresting of young blacks, and unrests across the country). While some critics are characterizing the various unrests as isolated (or detached) events, the current state of policing, as the front agents of the law, is in fact a historical movement—a process. This characterization is grossly incomplete, preventing mainstream America from capturing and understanding the essence of the current relationship between blacks and the police; subsequently, failing to understand why a high percentage of blacks are under the control of the criminal

justice system, in some cases sending more blacks to prison than to universities, where the prison then replaces the educational system for "educating and socializing" our youths. As such, we will briefly utilize police-Latino community relations, as one example, to illustrate the ethnic realities of Latinos over time—as with blacks—policing Latino communities is highly "connected" to multiple intertwining factors, like immigration, economics, national security, and education via the school-to-prison pipeline (Battle, 2015; Goffman, 2015; Urbina & Álvarez, 2015, 2016).

Exploring the experiences of ethnic minorities during the early days in the Americas, scholars document that Latinos, particularly Mexicans, were targets of continuous manipulation, intimidation, oppression, and violence by vigilantes, the KKK, mainstream society, and, more critically, the criminal justice system—via the police and the legal system, with anti-Latino laws, like the 1855 Vagrancy Act, known as the Greaser Act (Acuña, 2015; De León & Del Castillo, 2012; McWilliams, 1990; Urbina, 2012, 2014; Urbina et al., 2014), resulting in a legacy of racism, hate, violence, and oppression that gravely escalated after the Treaty of Guadalupe Hidalgo in 1848 (Almaguer, 2008; Bender, 2003; De León, 1983; Gómez, 2000; Mirandé, 1987; Salinas, 2015; Urbina, 2012, 2014; Urbina & Álvarez, 2015; Urbina et al., 2014). Then, with a legacy of hate already in motion at the turn of the twentieth century, during the height of the Mexican Revolution (1910–1920) fear of violence and an ensuing race war in the United States along the U.S. side of the Rio Grande fueled both vigilante and police violence against people of Mexican descent (Acuña, 2015; Almaguer, 2008; De León, 1983, 1997, 2002, 2009; Gonzáles-Day, 2006; McWilliams, 1990; Salinas, 2015; Urbina & Álvarez, 2015). The high number of lynchings, burnings, and killings of Mexicans by Anglo mobs continued with impunity from 1848 to 1916, as vividly documented by William Carrigan and Clive Webb in "The Lynching of Persons of Mexican Origin or Descent in the US, 1848– 1929" (2003) and Richard Delgado in "Law of the Noose: A History of Latino Lynching" (2009). In fact, in a period of two years (between 1915 and 1916) nearly 300 Mexicans (most of whom were American citizens) were hanged or shot by vigilante groups (Carrigan, 2006; Carrigan & Webb, 2003; Urbina et al., 2014).

Though, the most feared groups were not so-called outlaws, but the very agents of the law—the police, particularly the Texas Rangers (*Los Rinches*). Historical data show that 56 Texas Rangers operating in the area have been characterized as the most powerful and abusive agents in early law enforcement (McLemore, 2004, Urbina & Álvarez, 2015; see also Skolnick, 2011; Skolnick & Fyfe, 1993; Walker 1998), vividly documented by Charles Harris and Louis Sadler in *The Texas Rangers and the Mexican Revolution: The Bloodiest Decade, 1910–1920* (2007). In *Gunpowder Justice: A Reassessment of the Texas Rangers* (1979), Julian Samora, Joe Bernal, and Albert Peña explain how the Texas Rangers continually violated the civil rights of people since 1823 when the Rangers were created (officially in 1835). Describing the Mexican experience, Historian Carey McWilliams (1990) documents that the Texas Rangers participated in lawless executions, and that they considered themselves as the authority to declare an open-season against Mexicans, "terrorizing" Mexicans with impunity. Other atrocious acts in Texas included widespread instances of Mexicans ". . . being subjected to threats, torture, flogging, castration, and thinly disguised murder. Many innocent Mexicanos lost their lives as a result of Ranger policing," including widespread local posse action, shootings, burnings, hangings, lynching, and other mob violence (Meier & Ribera, 1993:116–117; Urbina, 2012; Urbina & Álvarez, 2015; Urbina et al., 2014). In one case, for example, a constable transporting three prisoners to jail was stopped by Texas Rangers and given a receipt for the transfer to their custody, the prisoners were found dead the next day (Hinojosa-Smith, 1986). William Carrigan (2006:175) reports that the highest levels of violence in Texas occurred in South Texas where the Texas Rangers often joined Anglo aggression by taking a "brutal binge of retaliation, summarily killing hundreds of Mexicans without due process of law." Reflecting the historical dynamics of slavery, the lynching of Latinos was indeed a routine practice that created little news interest in how mobs and police officers often removed

Mexicans from jail and executed them (Urbina, 2012; Urbina & Álvarez, 2015; Urbina et al., 2014). For instance, on Christmas of 1917, Texas Rangers and U.S. soldiers took 15 Mexican men from their homes in Porvenir, beat them during questioning, and then shot each one in the head. Abuses of Latinos at the hands of the Texas Rangers continued through the early 1970s when federal judges in *Medrano v. Allee* finally began to apply the provisions of the federal civil rights acts against the Rangers. Of course, encounters with the Texas Rangers is just but one early example of mistreatment of Mexican Americans and other Latinos, with a similar experience taking place in Arizona by the Arizona Rangers and New Mexico by the New Mexico Rangers, exacerbating the already strained ethnic/race relations and community relations across the country. Exploring the police-community relations, Paul Taylor (1931:230) documented:

> One reason the Mexicans carry guns is because of their relations with the police. The latter, especially in Indiana Harbor [East Chicago], shoot the Mexicans with small provocation. One shot a Mexican who was walking away from him, and laughed as the body was thrown into the patrol wagon.

Around mid-century, a series of incidents, like the 1942 Sleepy Lagoon trial and the 1943 Zoot Suit Riots (Pagán, 2003; Urbina & Álvarez, 2015; Weitz, 2010), further fueled the conflictive police-community relations (Morales, 1972). During the Zoot Suit Riots, the police simply followed servicemen at a distance and allowed them to attack Pachucos, who were allegedly attacking sailors. The police essentially watched as service men entered bars, restaurants, stopped public transportation, and even entered private homes in search of zoot suiters. Towards the end of the riot, the police,

including off-duty police officers, had arrested nearly 600 young Mexican American men, even those who were stripped and beaten. By contrast, the police arrested a handful of sailors, many of whom were released. In the last days of the riot, service men were attacking all Mexican Americans and some black residents (Escobar, 1999; McWilliams, 1990; Moore, 1978; Pagán, 2003).

Broadly, despite researchers like Emory Bogardus (1943) and Carey McWilliams (1990) arguing against presumed Mexican inherited tendencies toward criminality, mainstream America, legitimized by some intellectual racists, continued the myth enhancement, with governmental officials like Captain E. Durán Ayres, chief of the foreign relations bureau, proclaiming highly charged statements, like . . . this Mexican element considers all that to be sign of weakness [fistfights], and all he knows and feels is a desire to kill, or at least let blood . . . when there is added to this inborn characteristic that has come down through the ages. . . . (McWilliams, 1990:212). Pragmatically, adverse actions, stereotypes, and racist ideologies tend to establish consequential trends, not only resulting in lasting negative police-community relations, but impacting the entire criminal justice system and all facets of social life in all institutional settings. In effect, after more than 450 years (since 1565) in the making of *brown* people, most notably, Mexican Americans, significant gaps remain in virtually all areas of social life, with police-community relations simply being one of the most *visible,* which, as noted herein, are tied to social control, including the school-to-prison pipeline, as recently documented by Lila Bartolomé, Donaldo Macedo, Victor Ríos, and Anthony Peguero in *Latina/o Students and the School-Prison-Pipeline* (2013), Marquaysa Battle in "12 Heartbreaking Facts About the School to Prison Pipeline that

Every Person Should Know" (2015), and Alice Goffman in "How We're Priming Some Kids for College–and Others for Prison" (2015); ultimately, impacting the entire minority community and eventually the country as a whole, as illustrated by Urbina and Wright in *Latino Access to Higher Education: Ethnic Realities and New Directions for the Twenty-First Century* (2016). Juan Gómez-Quiñones (1990:189), for instance, documents that "As the 1980s unfolded, the Chicano community in the United States was at a historical juncture. Much had been accomplished, new problems had arisen, and past injustices still lingered, as did obstacles to progress." At the end of the twentieth century, Malcolm Holmes (2000:359) remarked, "Tensions between Anglos and Hispanics (nearly all of whom are of Mexican origin) in the Southwest have persisted throughout this century, and those of Mexican origin continue to be seen as threatening dominant group interests." More recently, resonating the historical legacy of hate, in 2015, Donald Trump shared his racist venom during his campaign for the presidential race, charging that "When Mexico sends its people, they're not sending their best . . . they're sending people that have lots of problems, and they're bringing those problems with us. They're bringing drugs. They're bringing crime. They're rapists."

Clearly, contrary to the notion of history as a story composed of a series of events over time, history is in fact a *process,* and subsequently a sound analysis of Latinos and the U.S. criminal justice system not only requires that we situate social control within a broader context, but that it be examined from a historical context–as a process, governed by defined ideologies, influencing the legal system and by extension all other American institutions. All in all, the mere fact that "the *empirical story* does not support America's highly propagated notions, like the *land of the free,* the *land of opportunity,* the *land of equality,* or *Lady Justice* (Statue of Liberty) symbolizing universal justice for all Americans" (Urbina et al., 2014:10), reveals the urgent call to better understand what's in a sense America's most fundamental institution–the criminal justice system, equality before the law.

THE NATURE OF PRIOR INVESTIGATIONS

As earlier, even though ethnic minorities have been in the United States since 1565, bypassing African Americans in the general population in 2000, making them the largest minority group in the United States, the academic literature on Latinos, whose experiences with the criminal justice system differ from those of blacks and whites, remains limited and inconclusive. To this day, most studies that have analyzed the experiences of male or female offenders in the criminal justice system, whether it's in the area of policing, courts, or corrections, have focused almost exclusively on race, following a dichotomous "black-white" approach; that is, African American versus Caucasian, excluding Latinos, or treating them as a monolithic group, without delineating differences within ethnic subgroups, like Cubans, Mexicans, and Puerto Ricans, these three ethnic groups being the largest ethnic groups in the United States.

Most commonly, debates regarding the dynamics of the criminal justice system hinge on whether or not the criminal or juvenile justice system is prejudiced or racist. Authors thus consider whether law enforcement officers target minorities, principally blacks, whether judges, prosecutors, and juries are more punitive when dealing with racial minorities, and whether jail, prison, or probation and parole officers are influenced by the race of defendants. Undoubtedly, social scientists working on these issues provide vital academic information about race and the criminal justice system. Without these empirical investigations, the scope of the now well-documented overrepresentation of minorities, particularly blacks, in all stages of the criminal justice process would remain unresearched, undocumented, and thus unlikely to be resolved.

In the case of ethnic minorities in the criminal justice system, though, scholars have only begun to take a serious and honest quest to better investigate, understand, document, and dialogue the Latino experience. In effect, not too long ago, Professor Robert Sampson of Harvard University and Professor Janet Lauritsen of the University of Missouri-St. Louis (1997:364) observed: "despite the volume of previous research on race and ethnic comparisons, we know very little about criminal justice processing other than for blacks and whites. Quite simply, there is little empirical basis from which to draw firm conclusions for Hispanic [and Asian, and Native] Americans." Moving into the twenty-first century, in a study published in *Criminology,* Darrell Steffensmeier and Stephen Demuth (2001) concluded that the most obvious *shortfall* is the limited attention to the treatment of Latino defendants in the judicial system. In another study, "Latinos/as in the Criminal and Juvenile Justice Systems," published in *Critical Criminology* (2007), the author reports that in comparison to hundreds of studies that have been conducted on race (blacks versus whites), he was able to locate only 53 studies that had analyzed the effects of ethnicity on the lengthy criminal or juvenile justice *process,* which covers a wide and complex range of legal

decision-points. Of the 53 ethnic studies reported by Urbina (2007), 34 treated Latinos as a monolithic group, 15 analyzed the Mexican experience, and four included Puerto Ricans in the analyses, with one of the four Puerto Rican studies also analyzing the Colombian, Dominican, and Cuban experience, clearly revealing the limited focus on Latinos, and more so within ethnic subgroups.

Crucially, a limited investigative approach often unintentionally reifies current essentialist assumptions about race and ethnicity, and thus these concepts are then viewed and treated as static, fixed, and self-evident, even though, as social scientists have documented, ideas of race and ethnicity and about the nature of *difference* are, in fact, socially constructed and historically contingent (Álvarez & Urbina, 2018; Acuña, 2015; Almaguer, 2008; Salinas, 2015; Urbina, 2014; Urbina et al., 2014), with over 450 years (since 1565) in the making of *brown* people, most notably, Mexicans, as documented by Law Professor Laura Gómez in *Manifest Destinies: The Making of the Mexican Race* (2007). In effect, once we begin to analyze the ethnic reality by the totality of historical events, situations, and circumstances, the *empirical picture* does not support, for example, the nondiscrimination thesis in the processing of Latinos in policing, the judicial system, or corrections. In truth, contrary to arguments that the brutal forces of the past have been eliminated, it has become increasingly clear that there are fragile and antagonistic relationships between ethnic minorities and the U.S. criminal justice system, relationships which manifest themselves in numerous ways. Recent studies testing for ethnic effects, for instance, typically indicate differential treatment in favor of whites and, on occasions, blacks (Salinas, 2015; Urbina, 2007, 2012; Urbina & Álvarez, 2015, 2016).

The imbalance of academic literature is further hindered in that the focus of investigations has been primarily on Latinos, giving Latinas limited attention and thus their truths and realities are being hidden in the shadows of the past, as documented by Vicki Ruiz in *From Out of the Shadows: Mexican Women in Twentieth-Century America* (1999). In fact, until recently, few academic studies focused on Latinas in the context of the criminal justice system, in part because female offending in general was not defined as a significant social problem worthy of academic discourse, and because some people assumed that there was little (or no) variation between Latinas and Latinos. The existing literature on minorities and recent studies on the nature of crime and punishment, though, not only demonstrate that there are significant differences between men and women offenders, but that there is significant variation between Latinas and women of other races, like blacks and whites, as well as differences between the Latino subgroups, like Cubans, Mexicans, Puerto Ricans, or people from Central and South America, as reported by Urbina in *A Comprehensive Study of Female Offenders: Life Before, During, and After Incarceration* (2008) and Martha Escobar in *Captivity Beyond Prisons: Criminalization Experiences of Latina (Im)migrants* (2016).

Indeed, although the relationship between ethnicity, race, gender, socioeconomic status, and punishment varies geographically (Ruddell & Urbina, 2007), the widespread overrepresentation of minorities in penal institutions suggests that ideas of ethnicity, race, and difference have shifted from a *driving force to a necessary element* for the criminal justice system, now a multibillion dollar enterprise, to appear functional and progressive (Urbina & Álvarez, 2016). As figures indicate, nowhere is this punitive movement more apparent and repressive than in the United States where the penal population moved beyond two million in 1999, for the first time in history, with detrimental

race and ethnic variation in the distribution of punishment. In effect, by the end of 2005, blacks (39.5%) and Latinos (20.2%) accounted for 59.7 percent, while whites represented 34.6 percent of inmates sentenced to more than one year in prison (Harrison & Beck, 2006), a major population disproportion, where Latinos constituted approximately 15.1 percent (45.4 million) and blacks constituted about 13.5 percent (40.7 million) of the total general population in 2007. More globally, by February 28, 2008, the United States was ranked as the number one incarcerator, with more than one of every 100 adults (2, 319,258) in jail or prison. According to the 2008 report, "For some groups, the incarceration numbers are especially startling," particularly for "black and brown" people, to include minority women, mostly blacks and Latinas (Alexander, 2012; Urbina, 2008), a punitive and aggressive movement that does not correspond with the actual realities of crime, punishment, safety, equality, or justice, as detailed in the following chapters.

Pragmatically, considering the transformations that the criminal justice system, to include law enforcement, the judicial system, and the correctional system, has been undergoing to equate issues like changes in demographics, political and government objectives, ideological motives, community concerns, economic uncertainty, and public fear and demands—a comprehensive examination of ethnic minorities in the criminal justice system is vital to further enhance our understanding of Latinos in their encounters with the police, their appearances in the judicial system, and their experiences in the prison system. Similar to the academic approach, which has focused almost exclusively on the experience of blacks and whites, the criminal justice system, as a whole, has devoted its efforts and resources to male offenders, and, once arrested, indicted, prosecuted, convicted, and sentenced to jail or prison, concentrated on white and black inmates. For instance, given the sharp increase of incarcerated women, female prisoners tend to be enmeshed in a system that is ill-equipped to handle the needs of female offenders, the issues leading to their arrest and subsequent incarceration as well as the challenges that women confront during their imprisonment, much less the specific concerns of Latina inmates, like language barriers, immigration status, gender stereotypes, and culture-related issues.

Together, the existing literature reveals that while various Latino-related issues and concerns–like the hotly debated issue of immigration–have received wide attention in the academic literature and public discussion, the Latino experience in the legal system has not been studied, documented, or dialogued in its totality. Several classic books, though, have been published, serving as a frame of reference for the exploration of various significant areas of investigation which remain to be documented if we are to provide a balance to the existing literature, and thus take the necessary steps toward addressing Latino-related situations and, ultimately, the criminal justice system as a whole. The historical complexity of the matter itself shows the need for additional documentation on the experience of ethnic minorities with the criminal justice system, which involves a lengthy, punitive, and often uncertain process that not only impacts their lives, but the lives of their children and friends who might be residing in the United States or back in their country of origin, a phenomenon normally not relevant to black or white defendants. Logically, providing a balance to the existing literature also requires that a balanced approach be utilized in presenting the Latino experience throughout the many decision-points of the criminal justice system, if in fact we are to have inclusive and

objective dialogue, while providing the foundation to establish mechanisms that will enable us to move the discourse beyond race, ethnicity, gender, and socioeconomic status to a level of decency, efficiency, public safety, equality, and justice for everyone.

As such, considering the selective and aggressive tactics of policing ethnic communities, the punitive movement of the judicial system, and the grossly disproportionate numbers of Latinos under the control of the criminal justice system, it is of utmost importance that the ways in which *ideas* of ethnicity, race, gender, and class uphold the "legitimacy" of the criminal justice system be demystified and exposed in the pages of academic literature, a central objective of this book, undertaken by some of the most prominent authors from around the country. In this mission, rather than attempting to develop a single explanation for differential treatment in policing or the courts, and the overrepresentation of Latinos under some type of formal control by the criminal justice system, this book presents a variety of studies that illustrate alternative ways of interpreting crime, punishment, safety, equality, and justice. It builds a framework of methodological, theoretical, and philosophical analysis within diverse fields of investigation to better understand the various forces, to include historical, financial, structural, political, and ideological, shaping and reshaping the dynamics of crime and punishment, which, with the advent of yet another form of globalization, are becoming transnational, as evidenced by the U.S.-Mexico joint effort against drug cartels and immigration from Central and South America. It is important to understand how policies related to punishment are sometimes contingent upon broader transnational arrangements; that is, crime and punishment that transcend international borders and legal systems. In effect, some emerging social control policies, such as drug laws and anti-terrorism legislation, are the result of collaborative efforts that involve several countries, and are increasingly linked to foreign policy, making some current crime and punishment practices, like many economic and trade policies, global in nature. To accomplish this mission, contributing authors draw on literature from diverse fields of study, including sociology, criminology, criminal justice, feminist theory, critical race and ethnic studies, post-colonial perspectives, and globalization literature.

As for the polemic issue of race and ethnic effects in the criminal justice system, the work of cultural theorist Paul Gilroy, *The Black Atlantic: Modernity and Double Consciousness* (1993), and Lupe S. Salinas, *U.S. Latinos and Criminal Injustice* (2015), provide an expedient point of academic departure. According to Gilroy, ideas and ideologies of race and modernity are historically linked, and race, as we perceive it today, is a social construct dating to the late eighteenth and early nineteenth centuries, an era when the prison was invented and thus moving punishment from out of the public domain to secrecy behind bars, setting the stage for penal power, control, and expansion, vividly illustrated by French philosopher Michel Foucault in *Discipline and Punish: The Birth of the Prison* (1995), Michael Lynch in *Big Prisons, Big Dreams: Crime and the Failure of America's Penal System* (2007), and Martin Guevara Urbina in *Capital Punishment in America: Race and the Death Penalty Over Time* (2012). Chicano Historian Rodolfo Acuña, Sociologist Adalberto Aguirre, and Sociologist Tomas Almaguer have illustrated that historical ideas of ethnicity and modernity are indeed linked, though, actually dating back to the early days in the Americas, a strategy set in placed by movements like colonialism, conquest, slavery, and U.S. imperialism. In the context of the criminal jus-

tice system, Urbina (2012) reports that variation in punishment is largely governed by *threat differentials;* that is, the level of financial, political, or social threat that minority populations presumably pose to white America, especially the *voting class.*

These propositions have consequential implications for the entire American criminal justice system. For instance, what if ideas of race and ethnicity which, as social scientists document, are historically contingent and constructed, are necessary for the criminal justice system, to include law enforcement, the judicial system, and the correctional system, to *survive* and *expand,* a crucial observation in the context of the recent globalization of crime and punishment? Likewise, consider the implications if indeed variation in punishment is governed by threat differentials, also a critical observation in the context of the current *international war on terror.* More globally, could the United States sustain its multibillion dollar criminal justice system, if one out of four black men of a certain age were not under some form of incarceration or surveillance (Alexander, 2012; Austin & Irwin, 2012; Tonry, 2006)? Worse, if current incarceration trends continue, a black male born in 2001 has a one in three chance of going to prison during his lifetime (Bonczar, 2003). Similarly, could the criminal justice system survive and grow without the "new minority," Latinos, who bypassed the black population in 2000? Closer to resembling statistics for blacks, a Latino born in 2001 has a one in six chance of going to prison during his lifetime, while a white male has a one in 17 chance of going to prison (Bonczar, 2003), even though, as illustrated in the following chapters, these figures do not necessarily correspond to crime variation in the context of race and ethnicity.

Beyond male-race variation, could the criminal justice system *survive and continue to grow* without the newly "targeted" population, female offenders, especially black and Hispanic women? The lifetime probability of going to prison among black women (5.6%) is almost as high as for white men (5.9%), but a lower probability for Latinas (2.2%), with white females (0.9%) having a much lower lifetime chance of going to prison (Bonczar, 2003). Ultimately, would the criminal justice system *survive, grow, and prosper* without the "intergenerational connection," minority offenders and their children, especially impoverished minority children, who are now being diverted to imprisonment via the school-to-prison pipeline? With thousands of people joining the work force of the American criminal justice system primarily because of employment and job security, would the system, with an annual budget of 260 billion dollars as of 2010, the latest available figures (a monetary budget bigger than the GDP of some countries), survive economically? Or, frankly, what if young white women and men were being detected, arrested, indicted, prosecuted, convicted, placed on probation, sentenced to jail or prison, or executed at the same rate? Would the American society support such practices by the police, the courts, or the penal system, if the pool of people were coming from white communities and not from the ghettos and barrios of America, or communities of impoverished white people? Would white America be asking for the development of more laws, the implementation of existing criminal laws, the creation of more jails and prisons, and asking government and law enforcement officials to be more punitive on criminal defendants? Evidently, in analyzing the realities of crime and punishment, the connections between modern punishment trends and historical practices of conquest, colonialism, slavery, imperialism, immigration, group identity, and, most recently, globalization must be brought

to light. In short, just as it has been documented that punishment is an expression of historically contingent sensibilities (Garland, 1990), *ideas of race, of ethnicity, of gender, of class, and of difference* play into the type of behavior that Americans define as crime and strategies of when and how Americans respond to criminal behavior.

As such, by giving *voice to a historically marginalized and neglected group* in the United States–mapping major forces, like historical, financial, political, theoretical, and ideological and how they interact with ethnicity, race, gender, class, and punishment, and through documenting the historical interdependence of these concepts–the contributing authors of this book provide a unified, inclusive, and refreshing presentation of the Latino experience in the American criminal justice system. In particular, by exploring essential connections in the realm of modernity and historical ideas between elements like race, ethnicity, gender, class, and punishment–this academic book with original chapters by some of the most renowned authors in diverse fields of investigation–challenges current practices and views of crime and punishment in the United States and abroad, with the central objective of examining the ethnic experience in the criminal justice system, paying particular attention as to how ideas of ethnicity underpin and *legitimize* police, judicial, and correctional practices in the United States. Altogether, this book adds to the current academic literature by expanding on various areas of academic investigation.

First, as noted earlier, this book documents the ethnic experience in mainstream America by analyzing a series of essential factors instead of focusing on a single structural, theoretical, or ideological force like the rancorous debate regarding immigration that have influenced and continue to influence the Latino experience in society, and ultimately serve as the "driving forces" into law enforcement, the judicial system, and, eventually, the prison system. Ideally, the goal would be to study the Latino experience in its totality if we are to provide a truly realistic and objective account of America's people, the criminal justice system, and, essentially, America.

Second, this book details various key decision-points throughout the entire legal *process,* often more detrimental than the actual punishment, instead of limiting the analysis to a selected decision-point, like arrest or conviction, and thus presenting a more holistic profile of Latinos as they encounter the police, the judicial system, or the penal system. Failure to analyze multiple stages (decision-points) of criminal justice processing simultaneously can erroneously lead to a conclusion, for example, of *nondiscrimination* when in reality ethnic disparity may be more pronounced in different stages (Salinas, 2015; Urbina, 2007, 2012). Differential treatment might be present at one decision-point, disappear in the next, and again become noticeable in the following stage of the legal decision-making process. Further, researchers examining a single stage who find that prosecutors, judges, or juries treat Latinos equally, or even more leniently, than whites or blacks may incorrectly interpret this finding as fair and consistent treatment rather than a correction of earlier police misconduct, prosecutorial overcharging, lack of evidence, or errors during the early stages of the judicial process (Urbina, 2007), as recently documented by Nicole Van Cleve in *Crooked County: Racism and Injustice in America's Largest Criminal Court* (2016).

Third, since a key objective is to examine crucial decision-points of the legal process, contributing authors of this book analyze all three major components of the criminal justice system, law enforcement, courts, and corrections, to enhance our understanding of the *cycle of Latino criminality, punishment,* and *justice.* Evidently, obtaining a more realistic picture of the ethnic experience with the criminal justice system enables us to better understand the current state of Latinos, and, more significantly, allows us to gain sight into the future of the already largest minority group in the United States and very likely, the *upcoming majority.* For instance, a prior record, like number of arrests, convictions, and time served in jail or prison, tends to govern whether a person is able to find employment, especially a decent job, and hopefully refrain from committing additional crimes. Unlike blacks and whites, though, a prior record could result in deportation for Latino defendants, leaving behind family and friends and leading to fragile social relations and unstable community ties (Álvarez & Urbina, 2018). Considering the transnational and drastic impact of the "war on drugs" on Hispanic men, women, and children, with the typical offense in the criminal justice system being drug related, a drug conviction not only hinders the prospect of finding legal employment, but getting an education to secure social, political, and, above all, economic stability. In essence, with little or no education, or lack of skills to compete in a competitive and technological job market, crime becomes a survival mechanism for many Latino offenders. Logically, *savage poverty leads to crime,* which in turn leads to arrests, indictments, prosecutions, convictions, probation, jail, prison, or even execution. Combined with a prior record, the criminal stigma then further diminishes the probability of being accepted by the community, getting an education, obtaining employment, maintaining emotional and psychological stability, which in turn further increases the chances of being re-arrested, prosecuted, convicted, and ending back in prison, resulting in a cycle of poverty and crime that gets worse each time a person gets arrested, prosecuted, convicted, and sentenced to jail or prison, as documented by Jeffrey Reiman and Paul Leighton in *The Rich Get Richer and the Poor Get Prison* (2017).

Fourth, seeking to equate the consequential implications of historical gender stereotypes regarding Latinos, the contributing authors of this book are sensitive to gender variation in the context of the criminal justice system. In effect, as reported in the following chapters, Latinas tend to suffer triple oppression because historically they have been victims of gender, ethnicity, and class marginalization and manipulation, often structurally dislocated from major American institutions, like education, finance, telecommunications, and corporate America.

Fifth, the contributing authors also analyze major forces shaping and reshaping public opinion, law enforcement tactics, judicial mechanisms, and penal practices as to how Latinos are treated by the criminal justice system, a process that, for some, actually begins way before a person is arrested, as when foreigners first arrive in the United States and viewed with disdain for accusations like, "they are taking our jobs, they don't pay taxes, or they are committing crimes" (Álvarez & Urbina, 2018). As such, understanding the *root of "social disobedience," the dynamics of arrest and prosecution, and the subsequent march to jail or prison* is essential as Americans strive for public safety, equality, and justice.

RATIONALE FOR WRITING THIS BOOK

As noted herein, even though the criminal justice literature is extensive in detailing the experiences of blacks and whites, the experiences of Latinos are by far less studied and less documented in both academic and public discussion, and thus less known, resulting in a knowledge foundation that is yet to be inclusive and objective. While there are a number of publications documenting the ethnic minority experience in the American criminal justice system, to include law enforcement, the judicial system, and the correctional system, there are only a few comprehensive books available which provide a sense of comparison and foundation for the investigation of Latinos. In effect, although numerous books covering diverse issues have been published, a number of which examine the machinery of justice through the lens of race, ethnicity, gender, class, or other factors, very few books have ever been published documenting the realities of Latinos in the U.S. criminal justice system.

Even though Latinos are now the nation's largest minority group and what we see as possibly the *upcoming majority* group in the United States, publishing institutions have, so far, paid limited attention to the impact of ethnicity in policing, the judicial system, or the penal system (Morín, 2009; Urbina, 2008, 2011, 2012, 2014; Urbina et al., 2014), as recently documented by Lupe S. Salinas in *U.S. Latinos and Criminal Injustice* (2015) and Urbina and Álvarez in *Latino Police Officers in the United States: An Examination of Emerging Trends and Issues* (2015) and in *Ethnicity and Criminal Justice in the Era of Mass Incarceration: A Critical Reader on the Latino Experience* (2017). Notably, just as the devaluing of research and publication on Caucasians deprives whites of the dignity of contributing to theorizing about their lives, failing to document the experiences of Latinos deprives them of voicing their everyday realities, concerns, and experiences. Lastly, considering the high probability of Latinos to encounter the police, the judicial system, or the correctional system at some point in their lives (Álvarez & Urbina, 2018; Morín, 2009; Ríos, 2011; Salinas, 2015; Urbina, 2014; Urbina & Álvarez, 2015, 2016, 2017; Urbina et al., 2014), their experiences with the criminal justice system need to be investigated as finely as possible, if we are to capture the very essence of the nature of crime, punishment, public safety, and, eventually, diminish the cycle of criminality, injustice, ineffectiveness, and inequality in the United States. The chapters included in this book, then, provide a conceptual framework for better understanding the forces shaping and reshaping the Latino experience, and by extension the American experience in its totality. Ultimately, while seeking to provide readers an objective, realistic, holistic, and balanced education, the following chapters also delineate research and policy recommendations for bridging existing gaps in criminal justice policy and practice.

FORMAT OF THIS BOOK

In contrast to most existing publications, this book provides a comprehensive account of the simultaneous interaction of various forces that shape and reshape the experiences of ethnic minorities throughout the entire criminal justice system. As such, seeking to devote specific attention to all three major component of the criminal justice system, this book is structured into three sections, each of which corresponds to a different body of scholarly work on Latinos, with each section containing five chapters. The first section, "Hispanics and the American Police," documents the Latino experience in policing across the United States, the second section, "Hispanics and the Judicial System," details the Latino experience in the mysterious, elusive, and often lengthy judicial process, and the final section, "Hispanics and the Penal System," explores the Latino experience behind bars. The concluding section, "Latinos, Globalization, and Social Control," ties the three sections, from a national and international standpoint, details propositions for bridging existing gaps in policy and practice, provides recommendations for future research, and vents into the future of Latinos and the criminal justice system and society as a whole.

CHAPTER OUTLINE

As this outline demonstrates, this book conjoins theoretical and empirical research about the ethnic minority experience in all three major areas of the U.S. criminal justice system. The first chapter in each section provides a theoretical overview or context that the subsequent chapters either develop or complement through historical documentation, theoretical evaluations, methodological approaches, philosophical thought, or empirical research. The concluding chapters tie the various topics together, providing a frame of reference and a context for future analysis as we seek to better understand both race and ethnic effects in the context of the criminal justice system.

In the first chapter of Section One, "Hispanics and the American Police," Charles Crawford explores the historical dynamics and influence of ethnicity in law enforcement, focusing on how ethnicity impacts policing field practices, such as traffic stops, use of force, and the subsequent actions that police departments have employed to alleviate these problems, while placing the Latino experience within an historical and broader context. In Chapter 3, Robert J. Durán provides an overview of research studies and biographical accounts that have focused specifically on the relationship between Latinos and law enforcement in the United States, with the ultimate objective of exposing the ethnic realities of the Latino experience in policing and everyday life. In Chapter 4, Mary Romero and Gabriella Sánchez provide a detailed examination of the most critical issues facing Latino defendants, from detection to arrest, seeking to better understand the law enforcement process in its totality. In Chapter 5, Carlos E. Posadas and Christina Ann Medina analyze the history of immigration laws as it pertains to Latinos, primarily Mexicans, documenting how Mexicans have been excluded from the United States through strategic anti-immigrants legislation. In the last chapter of Section One, Claudio G. Vera Sánchez explores the ethnic realities of Latino officers, which go beyond street patrol and encounters with the community, as Latino officers, for instance, must cope with structural, political, and ideological issues within their respective departments, community, and the media. Considering demographic shifts and thus the importance of representation, the author illustrates that contemporary organizations and institutions, particularly institutions like the police, must be observed from the vantage point of *colorblindness.* Documenting that colorblind laws, policies, and strategies have fundamentally structured the police institution, the author reveals that it is this system of racially neutral and racially coded strategies that structure the practices and experiences of Latino officers in the American police.

In the first chapter of Section Two, "Hispanics and the Judicial System," David

V. Baker documents the historical forces governing the ethnic experience within the context of the judicial system, focusing on the repressive practice against Mexicans in the southwest that resulted in executions, vigilantism, and mass expulsions of Mexicans. In Chapter 8, Adalberto Aguirre illustrates how the identity construction process in society is rooted in a group's access to privilege and power, reporting the long history of repressive practices by the dominant group against Mexicans in the United States, while focusing on the political climate and legal context for criminalizing Mexican identity. In Chapter 9, Alfredo Mirandé addresses the topic of Latinos and the Fourth Amendment, revealing that in an immigration context the constitutional right of people to be protected against unreasonable searches and seizures has been eviscerated for Latinos, particularly Mexicans and "Mexican-looking" people. Then, in Chapter 10, Mirandé examines the underrepresentation and systematic exclusion of Latinos from grand and petit juries in the U.S. judicial system. In the last chapter of Section Two, Urbina broadens the examination of ethnicity and punishment by exploring the processing of the typical defendant, indigent defendants, in the legal system vis-à-vis the views of practitioners responsible for the daily operation of the *machinery of courtroom justice,* concluding with possible remedies to the existing shortcomings of the court system in processing indigent defendants, most of whom are Latinos or African Americans.

In the first chapter of Section Three, "Hispanics and the Penal System," Sofia Espinoza Álvarez seeks to further analyze not only the prejudice and discrimination thesis, but also the interaction of historical, cultural, structural, social, financial, political, and ideological forces that continue to shape public opinion and criminal justice policies, focusing primarily on the historical and contemporary forces paving the road to prison for Latinos. In Chapter 13, Rick Ruddell and Natalie R. Ortiz explore pressing critical issues confronting Latino prisoners, and placing race and ethnicity within a broader context, to better understand the Latino experience it its totality. In Chapter 14, Kathryn D. Morgan details the historical origins and philosophy of probation and parole as well as the influence of race, ethnicity, and gender. In Chapter 15, Ilse Aglaé Peña and Urbina document the historical legacy of executions in America within the context of race, ethnicity, and gender, making note of executions during slavery, female executions, juvenile executions, and the execution of foreign nationals in the United States. In the last chapter of Section Three, Álvarez and Urbina explores the racial, ethnic, and gender realities of life after prison in the United States. The major roadblocks to community reentry are then detailed, followed by an analysis of the significance of community integration and the importance of building *bridges* between prison and society. It is argued that the most crucial gap to the establishment of social control remains to be bridged: from prison to the community. Otherwise, released inmates are likely to return to prison. Then, recommendations for overcoming state and federal *legal barriers* for reentry are provided, followed by proposi-

tions for community reentry of both male and female offenders, concluding with a series of steps for *making it outside* upon release.

In the concluding chapters, Urbina and Álvarez explore the contours of globalization, and its connectivity to race, ethnicity, ideology, and social control. In particular, Chapter 17 examines the influence of various crucial elements of globalization, focusing not only on the Latino experience, but also equating the white and black experience to delineate race and ethnic variation in the globalization movement within an historical context and, ultimately, placing the Latino experience within a global context. Finally, in Chapter 18, the authors seek to analyze the future of Latinos, projected to become the second largest group in the United States and possibly the *upcoming majority,* in the context of the criminal justice system, in an era of globalization and militarization of social control, and society as a whole, while illustrating the significance of researching and documenting the Latino experience–to bridge existing gaps. Lastly, the authors explores the race and ethnic experience through the lens of science, law, and the American imagination, concluding with policy recommendations for social and criminal justice reform and ultimately *humanizing difference.*

SUMMARY

The following 17 chapters of this book seek to bridge existing gaps in research and publication, while detailing the powerful forces that have *governed* the ethnic experience with the U.S. criminal justice system and with the American society since Latinos first settled in present day United States in 1565, aggravating the situation after 1848 with the Treaty of Guadalupe Hidalgo that

ended the Mexican-American War, which, combined, such forces have actually served as a *foundation* for a venerable legacy of inequality, injustice, hate, intolerance, and ignorance. In the context of the criminal justice system, combined forces have, in some situations, enticed Latino criminality and eventually *paved the road* into the criminal justice system. Invariably, in this volume, we argue that we have to go back to the "roots," as we need to have a deeper and holistic understanding of the Latino experience so that history does not repeat itself and ultimately situate mechanisms for social and criminal justice reform.

Section One

HISPANICS AND THE AMERICAN POLICE

Policemen so cherish their status as keepers of the peace and protectors of the public that they have . . . been known to beat to death those citizens or groups who question that status.

—David Mamet

Crimes were committed to punish crimes, and crimes were committed to prevent crimes. The world has been filled with prisons and dungeons, with chains and whips, with crosses and gibbets, with thumbscrews and racks, with hangmen and heads-men and yet these frightful means and instrumentalities have committed far more crimes than they have prevented . . . Ignorance, filth, and poverty are the missionaries of crime. As long as dishonorable success outranks honest effort-as long as society bows and cringes before the great thieves, there will be little ones to fill the jails.

—Robert Ingersoll

Chapter 2

THE HISTORICAL DYNAMICS OF ETHNICITY IN LAW ENFORCEMENT

CHARLES CRAWFORD

But the fact remains that far too often the police acts like the biggest, baddest gang on the block, with more firepower and the weight of law . . . behind them.

–Luis Rodríguez

Today, as in the past, race and ethnicity shape nearly every part of life in society. Across the globe ethnicity can be a source of pride and celebration, and in different contexts it can engender fear and hatred of others. Our experiences in diverse areas, like housing, religion, education, and social networks are influenced in subtle and sometimes not so subtle ways by the dynamic boundaries of race and ethnicity. Racial and ethnic tensions may surface in various ways in society, as in the form of jokes, fear, or violence. Though, as disturbing as some of the forms of ethnic strife may be, perhaps the most unsettling is the differential treatment of ethnic minorities in the U.S. criminal justice system, beginning with law enforcement, later as they are processed through the judicial system (see Section Two of this volume) and eventually the penal system (see Section Three). In effect, a cursory look at the recent scholarship reveals an abundance of research that examines the detrimental impact of criminal justice actions on racial and ethnic minority communities. Such impact can be seen in early, like bail, and later stages of judicial proceeding (Álvarez & Urbina, 2018; Demuth, 2003; Urbina, 2012; Urbina & Álvarez, 2015, 2017), affirmed in statistics showing that 33 percent of federal inmates are Latino (Federal Bureau of Prisons, 2017), and the disparities found in the application of the death penalty, as documented by Martin Guevara Urbina in *Capital Punishment in America: Race and the Death Penalty Over Time* (2012) and Álvarez and Urbina in "Capital Punishment on Trial: Who Lives, Who Dies, Who Decides–A Question of Justice (2014)?"

These are all criminal justice actions that warrant concern; however, it is the historically troubled minority-police relationships that reveal some of the deepest-rooted social problems in society, dating back to the early days in the United States. Researchers, for instance, have explored issues of excessive stopping of minorities (Higgins, Vito, & Walsh, 2008; Solis, Portillos, & Brunson,

2009), and complaints of excessive force and brutality against racial and ethnic minorities (Durán, 2009a, 2009b, 2009c; Holmes & Smith, 2008). In areas like religion and, to some degree, educational and housing settings, there is some choice for participation. In the context of the criminal justice system, however, contact with law enforcement is frequently involuntary and the ways in which race and ethnicity can influence this interaction often interact with numerous intertwining issues, like politics, class, and justice. This chapter will briefly explore how research has defined race and ethnicity, the impact of race and ethnicity in law enforcement, and finally examine the issues of Latinos working in policing.

DEFINING RACE AND ETHNICITY

Although the terms *race* and *ethnicity* are well entrenched in the social science literature, there is still debate and confusion over their definitions. As such, since ethnicity is central to the discussion of this chapter, I will begin with a brief discussion of these concepts. Race and ethnicity are essentially social constructs, with the distinctions and emphasis placed on these categories being extremely influential, powerful, and often consequential. As Michael Omi and Howard Winant (2014) illustrate, the social sciences began to reject biological notions of race in favor of a social concept in an attempt to refute scientific racism. Martin Marger (2009) describes race as one of the most misused, misunderstood, and dangerous concepts of the modern world, while rationalizing appalling injustices and mistreatment. The term race suggests a biological difference among people, such as facial features, skin color, and other physical traits. From a biological standpoint, though, the differences have been documented as trivial at best, considering that the Human Genome Project has demonstrated that humans actually share more than 99 percent of their genetic makeup (Soo-Jin Lee, 2005). However, the impact of racial division is fundamental from a sociological viewpoint, as presumed variation carries severe implications and ramifications. As reported by University of California-Riverside Sociologists Adalberto Aguirre and Jonathan Turner (2007:2), "when people associate superficial biological differences with variations in psychological, intellectual, and behavioral makeup, they may feel justified in treating members of a distinctive group in discriminatory ways." In diverse societies like the United States, racial or physical differences are noticed as a fact of life, and citizens have become increasingly aware of ethnicity as an additional element of differentiation.

Yet, ethnicity as a concept is relatively new to the discussion on race relations. Prior to the 1960s, most groups that are considered ethnic today were categorized as a distinct race. Further, although there is no one standard definition of an ethnic group, some common elements can be found. Melvin Tumin (1964:243), for example, described an ethnic group as one that essentially exists in a larger social system and claims or exhibits complex cultural traits. Ethnic groups can be considered subcultures with distinct languages, religions, and traits that are somehow different from the larger social group. These distinctions may be minor in some cases or essential aspects of life for the ethnic group. More recently, Wilbur Zelinsky (2001:44) suggested that an ethnic group is one that is constantly undergoing change, its members perceive or are perceived by others as sharing common cultural or historical traits, typically coming into existence due to friction or conflict with others in the same geographical space.

In a sense, ethnicity is broader and more inclusive than race, suggesting a sense of community, with shared characteristics, as in the case of Latinos, the largest ethnic group in the United States. As such, although numerous definitions exist, for this discussion the working definition of ethnicity that will be employed comes from Aguirre and Turner (2007:2-3): "when a subpopulation of individuals reveals or is perceived to reveal shared historical experiences as well as unique organizational, behavioral, and cultural characteristics, it exhibits its ethnicity." This working definition, while helpful, does not fully resolve the complicated debate over the meaning of ethnicity or the ethnic group. Physical features, for instance, are often used to include individuals into an ethnic group. For example, an individual can be labeled Latino, or black, based on skin color, which presumes certain historical experiences and culture to go with this label. In truth, not everyone who possesses the physical trait of brown or black skin color will identify with, nor be included in this group. Another level of complexity can be added when different elements of ethnicity are considered, such as language, bringing up another dilemma for individuals and groups, especially in the Latino community. Concurring with Omi and Winant (1994:14), "the definition of the terms 'ethnic group' and 'ethnicity' is muddy." While disputes over the meaning of ethnicity are likely to continue, few people can deny that serious racial and ethnic divisions exist in the United States, and that however inaccurate these social constructs may be in defining people as different, they continue to be highly influential and consequential not only in everyday social life, but the criminal justice system, most notably from law enforcement, as the first point of contact with the community.

THE RECOGNITION OF ETHNICITY IN LAW ENFORCEMENT

For years, volumes of research literature on race and criminal justice have been published, particularly on the treatment and experiences of black citizens in the United States. Clearly, this focus is warranted given the present levels of incarceration of black offenders and the complaints of mistreatment and heavy-handed law enforcement tactics employed in many black communities. By contrast, little research attention has been given to the criminal justice experiences of Latinos (Álvarez & Urbina, 2018; Urbina & Álvarez, 2015, 2017; Urbina, Vela, & Sanchez, 2014). An analysis conducted on the research retrieved from the Criminal Justice Abstracts between 1968 and 2002 revealed that only 1.3 percent of manuscripts were clearly focused on Latinos (even though there were Latino subjects in the data) supporting the fact we know very little about the Latino experience in criminal justice beyond crime commission (Schuck, Lersch, & Verrill, 2004). Latinos comprise one of the fastest growing ethnic populations in the United States (Álvarez & Urbina, 2018; Urbina, 2014). The U.S. Census Bureau (2017) reports that between 2014 and 2015 the Latino population in the country grew by 1.2 million, which was nearly half of the people added to the nation's total population. Shifts in ethnic demography have significant policy implications for local, state, and federal law enforcement operations, which tend to be further complicated by the politicized nature of immigration, culture and media-fueled fear of crime, particularly along the 2,000-mile border with Mexico, as we have witnessed with the Donald Trump administration, exacerbating the anti-Mexican sentiment with Trump's highly charged political rhetoric.

In the context of the U.S. criminal justice system, the decades-long research focus on race and criminal justice, however, has ignored Latinos, resulting in significant gaps in the literature and leaving questions as to whether this group's encounters with law en-forcement, and later the judicial and penal systems, are different from the experiences of either African Americans or whites. Currently, our understanding of how race impacts police practices is largely informed by the experiences of African Americans, most recently with police shootings. In itself, this research gap demonstrates the need to move beyond the black/white binary to gain insight into the treatment of one of the most diverse minority ethnic groups in the United States.

LATINOS AND CLASHES WITH THE POLICE: A BRIEF HISTORY

While Latinos now live in every state of the United States, as in the past, most of the Latino-police conflict tends to be concentrated in the Southwest (Álvarez & Urbina, 2018; Bender, 2005; De León, 1983; Ramírez, 2010; Urbina & Álvarez, 2015; Urbina & Peña, 2018). In this regard, by examining historic actions in these areas we can gain insight into both law and police actions that are currently taking place. With a legacy of hate already in motion at the turn of the twentieth century, during the height of the Mexican Revolution (1910–1920) fear of violence and an ensuing race war in the United States along the Texas side of the Rio Grande Valley fueled both vigilante and police violence against Mexicans and American citizens of Mexican descent (Acuña, 2015; McWilliams, 1990; Urbina et al., 2014). In fact, between 1915 and 1916 nearly 300 Mexicans (most of whom were American citizens) were hanged or shot by vigilante groups. The most feared groups were not so-called outlaws, in comparison to the 56 Texas Rangers operating in the area. In one case, for example, a constable transporting three prisoners to jail was stopped by Texas Rangers and given a receipt for the transfer to their custody, the prisoners were found dead the next day (Hinojosa-Smith, 1986; Urbina & Álvarez, 2015). In part, these responses were shaped by beliefs of a growing border problem during the massive migration of Mexicans from 1890 through the 1930s and stereotypes about Mexican criminality, both notions persisting in 2018 (Álvarez & Urbina, 2018; Urbina et al., 2014).

Of course, encounters with the Texas Rangers is just one early example of mistreatment of Mexicans and Mexican Americans, with a similar experience taking place in Arizona by the Arizona Rangers, modeled after the Texas Rangers. In effect, a close examination of the Southwest in recent history has shown that the police as well as the courts and correctional institutions have simply held a different standard of justice for Latinos (Urbina & Álvarez, 2015). Early researcher Paul Warnshius working with data collected in the 1931 Wickersham Commission Report on *Crime and the Foreign Born* concluded that Mexican immigrants were disproportionately arrested for public order crimes as a means to keep them in check, and that they were subjected to routine dragnets and brutal field tactics by the police. Revealing the significance of early stereotypes of criminality surrounding both race and ethnicity, a Chicago police sergeant once stated, "Indian and Negro blood does not mix very well. That is the trouble with the Mexican, he has too much Negro blood" (Warnshius, 1931:39).

As a mechanism of social control, fears and stereotypes regarding Latino criminality have been effectively utilized to categorize, marginalize, and oppress ethnic minorities (see Aguirre, this volume), as in the case of the well-documented 1943 "Zoot Suit Riots" in Los Angeles. The zoot suit worn by some young Mexican Americans (*Pachucos*) came to represent hooliganism and gang culture to the media, police, and prosecutors. While, to the tens of thousands of soldiers stationed near Los Angeles leaving for war, the zoot suit represented freedom and individuality they no longer possessed. As Kevin Starr (2002) documents, these young Mexican American zoot suiters were free from the military, dressed in all their glory and flirting with Mexican American girls (Pachucas) resulting in competition for females which was a major source of conflict. Tensions were running high in the city with young soldiers being trained for war amid a culture of defiance with the Pachucos. For instance, just two weeks prior to the Zoot Suit Riots there were 18 serious incidents of violence involving soldiers and sailors and numerous incidents of taunting and fights between military men and zoot suiters establishing a pattern of clashes (Starr, 2002).

What became known as the Zoot Suit Riot lasted from June 3 to June 10, 1943; beginning with a fight between 11 soldiers and young Mexican American men. Quickly, though, a false report of 200 sailors out looking for revenge began to circulate, and local newspapers and the Los Angeles Police Department turned the scuffle into a full-scale riot. In response, off duty officers went into a Mexican American community to arrest young Pachucos who were allegedly attacking sailors. By the next day rumors spread throughout Los Angeles that there would be a full scale counterattack by zoot suiters. Servicemen began to pour into the city searching for zoot suiters. Young Mexican American men were stopped on sidewalks, pulled from street cars and beaten, had their ducktail hair styles cut off, and many were stripped and left naked on the streets (Miller, 2009).

For the Los Angeles Police Department, the problem was not the thousands of sailors that were attacking civilians, but the source of the riot was the Mexican American men. During the riots, the police simply followed the servicemen at a distance and allowed them to attack the Pachucos at will. The police essentially watched as service men entered bars, restaurants, stopped public transportation, and even entered private homes in search of zoot suiters. Towards the end of the riot, the police had arrested nearly 600 young Mexican American men, even those who were stripped and beaten. By contrast, the police arrested a handful of sailors, many of whom were released. In fact, in the last days of the riot service men were attacking all Mexican Americans and some black residents. As J. Mitchell Miller (2009) reports, this failure to protect an entire segment of the population and directly observing lawlessness in brutal action against Latinos may have shaped the relationship between the LAPD and members of the Mexican American community, a relationship that remains fragile today, in 2018.

In the area of immigration, there are also numerous historic events serving as examples of the contentious relationship between the Latino community and law enforcement in the United States. As one of the most aggressive anti-immigrants movement, Congress authorized the Border Patrol to launch Operation Wetback in 1954. The operation gave the Border Patrol blanket authority to stop and search "Mexican-looking" people to check their residence status. As such, between 1954 and 1959 the Border Patrol deported approximately 3.8 million undocumented people and U.S. citizens of Mexican descent to Mexico (Álvarez & Urbina, 2018). Pragmatically and symbolically, anti-immigrants movements like Operation Wetback reinforce the notion that Mexican Americans will always be a marginal group in the United States. Most recently, Trump has promised to build a "big beautiful wall" to keep Mexicans, other Latinos, Syrians, Muslims, and anyone trying to enter the country through Mexico.

Beyond the immediate impact of such historical events, these actions tend to establish consequential trends, resulting in lasting negative police-ethnic community relations. A survey by the Pew Hispanic Center (2009), for example, found that 45 percent of Latinos felt that police officers treat Latinos fairly in their neighborhood, while, by comparison, 74 percent of whites and 37 percent of blacks felt that the police treat whites and blacks equally. Further, nearly a quarter of Latinos reported that they or a close family member had been stopped and questioned by the police, with native-born Latinos reporting that they were more likely to be stopped and questioned by the police than foreign-born Latinos, 32 percent versus 19 percent respectively (López & Livingston, 2009). Evidently, the impact of ethnicity on law enforcement actions does not occur in a social vacuum. Government and law enforcement officials have clearly recognized ethnicity in the past, often associating ethnic status with prejudicial beliefs about character, work ethic, and criminality, which may further fuel anti-Latino sentiments as well as police practices. Cleary, this historic pattern of distinguishing ethnicity provides a context for better understanding actions from the Border Patrol, to racial profiling, excessive stopping, and police brutality in the twenty-first century.

LATINOS AND POLICING PROBLEMS TODAY

Historically, the simultaneous interactions of historical, cultural, political, ideological, financial, racial, and ethnic factors have shaped and reshaped the experience of Latinos in their encounters with the police. As such, in this chapter, the focus will be primarily on two of the most consequential issues confronting both U.S. Latinos and law enforcement: racial profiling, deadly force, and police brutality. There are decades of research on African Americans and whites interactions with police, courts, and corrections, but only scant information on Latinos. However, one of the complicating factors when it comes to assessing Latino experiences with policing is that research on Latino perceptions of criminal justice is still emerging (Urbina & Álvarez, 2015). Nonetheless, what research exists is revealing and shows their perceptions and experiences with police are quite different from other groups (Urbina & Álvarez, 2015).

Racial Profiling

Although the relationship between some minority communities and the police have improved over the decades, serious issues remain and have grown more complex with the realization of how ethnicity can contextualize these encounters, most notably with the controversial practice of racial profiling.

Racial profiling became an appealing research topic during the 1990s, and has resurfaced in light of recently proposed immigration reform and enforcement. Racial profiling can essentially be described as the practice of targeting certain groups based on race or ethnicity and the belief that they are more likely to be engaged in criminal activity. Though, as the topic of racial profiling gained the attention of scholars and the news media, it has focused primarily on the experiences of black motorists to the extent that racial profiling became euphemistically known as "Driving While Black," eclipsing many of the other problems in police-minority relations.

Practically, racial profiling substitutes skin color for probable cause for a traffic stop, questioning, or search. However, although the notion of racial profiling appears to be new, minority communities have long reported excessive stopping and differential police practices that were designed to control what was perceived as dangerous classes ranging from slaves to impoverished ethnic white minorities (Crawford, 2010; Skolnick, 2011; Walker, 1998). In recent history, the practice of racial profiling can be traced to the intense focus on the war on drugs during the 1980s, as drug interdiction policies by federal, state, and local law enforcement took priority and were increasingly defined by race and ethnicity (Alexander, 2012; Urbina & Álvarez, 2017), such as the much publicized Drug Enforcement Administration and Florida Department of Motor Vehicles' *Operation Pipeline* (Glover, 2007).

Already the largest minority group in the United States and as the Latino population continues to grow, police-Latino relations have become pressing beyond the traditional confines of the Southwest, with Latinos now living in every major city of the country, like Raleigh, North Carolina, Tulsa, Oklahoma, and Nashville, Tennessee. Cru-

cially, some studies have found that racial profiling of Latinos is more likely to occur in hyper-growth rural areas. Nationwide, studies examining diverse states like Texas, Pennsylvania, Maryland, and Ohio have found that Latinos are stopped for traffic violations more frequently than whites and at disproportionate rates compared to their population (Mucchetti, 2005). Sylvia Lazos Vargas (2002) reports that Latinos in rural areas of the South and Midwest tend to be more diffuse with fewer legal advocacy groups or investigations into racial profiling. Combined with a lack of fluency in English (Urbina, 2004a; Urbina & Álvarez, 2015), these actions further complicate the interaction and lead to a reluctance to report biased encounters.

In an article, "Driving While Brown" (2005), Anthony Mucchetti reviewed findings from several studies on the disproportionate stopping of Latinos. Among Mucchetti's findings were that in Texas, Latinos were 40 percent more likely to be stopped than whites, 75 percent of Texas law enforcement agencies conducted searches of Latinos at elevated rates; Latinos in Missouri were twice as likely to be searched by the police as any other minority group; and in Iowa Latinos were 10 percent of those that had their vehicles searched during a traffic stop as compared to 2.7 percent of whites. The most revealing finding was that despite these heightened levels of searches of Latino motorists, they were less likely to have contraband than whites, suggesting that this race-conscious policing policy has essentially failed, with detrimental consequences for ethnic minorities.

Racial or ethnic profiling and excessive stopping have a detrimental impact on police and community relations as well as procedural justice. A 2008 police-citizen contact survey revealed that blacks and Latinos that were stopped were more likely to be ticketed, handcuffed, arrested, or reported that the officer threatened them with violence (Eith & Durose, 2011). Beyond the possibilities of being pulled into the criminal justice system, racial profiling exacts a toll that may be difficult to quantify. As documented by Mucchetti (2005), being racially profiled subjects the target to a barrage of questions designed to uncover suspected illicit behavior, even if the stop ends without incident the experience may leave the motorists humiliated, creating hostility within the ethnic community and the general population. Worse, these race-conscious policies further perpetuate stereotypes of criminality and reinforce the idea that Latinos are second-class citizens, essentially permanent foreigners in their own land.

Immigration

While the war on drugs in the United States remains a focus in policing, under the Trump administration, political attention on immigration status has become another source of excessive stopping and racial profiling, as recently documented by Álvarez and Urbina in *Immigration and the Law: Race, Citizenship, and Social Control* (2018). The enforcement of immigration laws is certainly not new in the United States, and the target groups have changed over time. However, America's complex relationship with Mexico and the resurgence of a backlash against immigration has meant that racial profiling has taken on a new form and purpose. Traditionally, immigration enforcement has been under the authority of the federal government, however as a result of the shifting focus on immigration, state and local law enforcement has been pulled into this heated politicized debate. While court cases have been decided prior to 2016 on local law enforcement engaging in immigration issues, under the Trump administration there have

been serious efforts to ramp up immigration enforcement through a patchwork of agreements and executive orders as well as threats to pull federal funding from what are termed sanctuary cities. This has created a new level of fear among immigrants and those who are undocumented.

A 2013 survey of more than 2,000 Latinos in Cook, Los Angeles, Harris, and Maricopa counties shed light on perceptions of the police in the wake of local law enforcement's growing role in immigration enforcement. The survey revealed that there is a pronounced fear of the police due to increased activity in immigration enforcement. More specifically, 44 percent of the Latinos surveyed said they are less likely to call the police if they had been a victim of crime fearing that the police will inquire about their immigration status or the status of people they know. This was 70 percent for undocumented residents. Interestingly, 28 percent of U.S.-born Latinos reported not calling the police due to fear they may inquire about the immigration status of people they know. Furthermore, nearly 40 percent reported they now feel they are under more scrutiny since local law enforcement is engaging in immigration enforcement (Theodore, 2013).

There are serious consequences to these perceptions of the police in the arena of ethnicity, immigration, and society (Álvarez & Urbina, 2018; Urbina & Álvarez, 2015). This fear of police essentially pushes Latinos into the shadows making them vulnerable to crime and unwilling to call the group sworn to protect them. In addition, this can create a form of isolation, as some Latinos are afraid to leave their communities, further exacerbating mistrust of police and withdrawal from society. The withdrawal becomes clear when reported crime is examined. For instance, Houston, Camden, and Los Angeles police departments have all seen noticeable drops in calls for service and reported crimes such as rape, robbery, and domestic violence from Latino communities in 2016 and 2017 (Bever, 2017). Considering that homicide is the second leading cause of death for Latino males between the ages of 15 and 24, and as a group Latinos have a homicide victimization rate twice that of whites, isolation and lack of cooperation with the police due to fear has dire repercussions. While the true numbers of Latino victims may never be known due to the consternation of factors briefly outlined here, the issues of immigration enforcement, fear, and mistrust of the police must be addressed.

Deadly Force and Police Brutality

For decades, scholars have documented police brutality and use of deadly force against minority citizens (Durán, 2013; Escobar, 1999; Marin, 2015; Morales, 1972; Nasser, 2015; Ríos, 2011; Urbina & Álvarez, 2015). Names such as Walter Scott, Philando Castille, and Eric Garner have become synonymous with police targeting African Americans and the deadly consequences of race and perception of minorities as a threat. There have been nationwide protests, and a public awareness of these issues that may be unmatched in history. However, largely absent in this discussion of policing, brutality, and deadly force, are Latinos who may suffer a similar fate (Escobar, 1999; Ríos, 2011; Urbina & Álvarez, 2015). Organizations such as the National Council of La Raza and Black Lives Matter have been trying to raise awareness of this issue and the fact that police killings of Latinos are underreported and do not garner the same media spotlight (Fountain, 2016; Nasser, 2015; Urbina & Álvarez, 2015). The rate of Latinos killed by police is second only to African Americans.

There are complex forces at work that contribute to lack of attention and coverage on police shootings of Latinos. Part of the issue is the lack of identity of victim's ethnicity. Race tends to be the primary factor for media coverage, and a victim may be both black and Latino. In some instances a suspect or victim's ethnicity is simply not recorded. Furthermore, the larger social and research issue is that civil rights and research on police abuse has focused on the black and white binary essentially silencing the voices of Latinos (Downs, 2016; Urbina & Álvarez, 2015). In addition to these concerns, the primary focus for most media coverage of Latino issues centers around immigration and often ignores criminal justice issues. There have been several shootings of Latinos that have drawn only local media attention and fallen from the national debate on this issue (Fountain, 2016; Urbina & Álvarez, 2015). In July 2016, 19 year old Pedro Villanueva was killed by two undercover California Highway Patrol (CHP) officers in Fullerton, California. Villanueva was attending a street car show where dangerous tricks were being performed. The officers followed him and his passenger in an unmarked undercover car that did not have a dashcam for about five miles into a dead-end street in Fullerton, where Villanueva made a U-turn and drove towards the officers. The officers opened fire and he died at the scene. While most major police departments in the United States prohibit firing at a moving vehicle, CHP is one of the few agencies that authorize this risky tactic (Parvini, 2016).

There were 183 Latinos killed by the police in 2016 and Villanueva was one of 27 who were unarmed at the time of their death (*The Guardian,* 2017). Each of these deaths has a context, some may be justifiable, and other cases are highly disputed with witnesses contradicting the official police narrative. I urge readers to conduct their own research and review of these issues from grassroot and newspaper databases. Police shootings of Latinos remain underreported for a variety of reasons and should be center stage in the national criminal justice debate and reform efforts (Durán, 2015; Marin, 2015; Nasser, 2015; Salinas, 2015).

Excessive force and police brutality are perhaps the most historically persistent and disturbing problems in police-minority relations (Escobar, 1999; Morales, 1972; Urbina & Urbina, 2015). Jerome Skolnick and James Fyfe (1993) have documented that police brutality is historically and sociologically related to lynching and other vigilante activities involving the police. Although the analogy by Skolnick and Fyfe may seem hyperbolic, it actually reflects the fact that police brutality serves as a powerful tool for intimidation and oppression. Historian Carey McWilliams (1990) describes "police brutality" as the substitute for the lynching of the past. A wide range of police misconduct such as verbal abuse, racial slurs, and threats may also be viewed as police brutality, but the primary focus of this discussion is on the use of physical force. Logically, the use of force in policing is considered a justified part of the occupation, and officers are allowed to use appropriate force to counter a suspect's resistance or violence. The force applied during a police-citizen encounter must be reasonable, but once the use of force surpasses this basic standard and is greater than what is deemed necessary, it can clearly be characterized as excessive force, or worse, brutality (Dempsey & Forst, 2011; Locke, 1996).

In the context of race variation, perceptions of and experiences with police brutality vary significantly by race and ethnicity. Blacks and Latinos are well aware of police misconduct either through direct experience or awareness of mistreatment of others in their neighborhoods (Durán, 2013; Ríos, 2011). Ronald Weitzer and Steven Tuch (2004) surveyed more than 1,700 residents in cities with populations over 100,000 and found that 39 percent of Latinos and only 13 percent of whites believed that the police constantly used excessive force. The personal experiences of those surveyed were equally revealing, as the authors found that 9 percent of Latinos had excessive force used against them versus 3 percent of whites, and 10 percent of Latinos knew of excessive force used against a member of their household versus 5 percent of whites. In effect, overall, the main finding of their research was that Latinos and blacks were more likely to report personal and vicarious experiences with police brutality, misconduct, and had been victims of repeated police abuse.

These negative contacts with police stem from the fact that Latinos face a heavy-handed law enforcement presence in their communities similar to African Americans. Increasingly these enforcement efforts are conducted with military grade equipment and with similar aggressive tactics (Balko, 2013; Dunn, 1996; Miller & Schivone, 2015; Urbina & Álvarez, 2015; Urbina & Peña, 2018). For example, in 2014 immigration sting operations in New Orleans were carried out with such approaches as the local law enforcement used mobile fingerprinting technology applied in Iraq and Afghanistan. There were raids on Latino businesses and communities, and the information gathered was used to round up those with warrants and deportation orders (Bull, 2014). Another assessment of the aggressive policing tactics employed in Latino communities is the recent expansion of Special Weapons and Tactics Team (SWAT) raids.

The American Civil Liberties Union (ACLU) published an appropriately named report, *When War Comes Home,* in 2014. The report examined 800 SWAT raids in 20 states and found 79 percent were for search warrants (primarily in drug investigations), which was not the intended purposes of SWAT deployments. There was also no standard definition of "high risk" scenarios and frequent unsubstantiated information of an armed suspect, which would warrant a SWAT raid. In Allentown, Pennsylvania 2010–2011, Latinos were more than 29 times as likely to be impacted by SWAT activity as compared to whites (American Civil Liberties Union, 2014). This is an extension of the war on drugs, which has often been a war on people of color (Alexander, 2012; Bosworth & Flavin, 2007; Corcoran, 2006; Urbina & Álvarez, 2017; Welch, 2006, 2009). Sixty-eight percent of the SWAT deployments that were carried out on minorities (African American and Latino) were for drug searches versus 38 percent for whites. As the ACLU report further notes, SWAT deployment drug searches are twice as likely to involve forced entry with the use of battering rams, yet contraband was only found in 25 percent of such entries. This racial gap in the use of SWAT deployment is a clear example of the concentration of military style aggressive policing in communities of color, which further undermines confidence in the police and has had a detrimental impact on community relations.

In sum, excessive force and brutality have existed since the creation of law enforcement agencies in the United States (Acuña, 2015; Skolnick & Fyfe, 1993; Walker, 1998), with racial and ethnic minorities being much more likely to be victimized by this troubling and consequential aspect of police misconduct (Durán, 2009a; Escobar, 1999; Urbina & Álvarez, 2015). While many aspects of police violence have been explored with various theoretical explanations, like minority-threat hypothesis, community account-ability, or individual psychological theories, the evidence from decades of research on the use of deadly force is clear in that minorities are much more likely fired upon by the police (Escobar, 1999; Fountain, 2016; Locke, 1996; Marin, 2015; Meyer, 1980; Urbina & Álvarez, 2015). Yet, despite the frustration of this enduring problem, police departments must continue to operate. This can be a difficult proposition as policies that are successful in one community, improving the relationship with a given minority group, may fail in a different context. Further, while there are various strategies for alleviating the problem of police brutality, a global solution is complicated (Urbina & Álvarez, 2015). For example, James Fyfe (1996) suggests that training/retraining is the primary method for dealing with excessive force, while Wayne Kerstetter (1996) advocates a procedural justice approach in the complaint process, and others such as the ACLU focus on the increased militarization of the police and suggest these paramilitary tactics have no place in contemporary society (American Civil Liberties Union, 2014). Perhaps the most commonly applied approach is to have the police force reflect the community racial and ethnic composition, sometimes willingly and at other times under court order (Dempsey & Forst, 2011; Urbina & Álvarez, 2015). With significant changes in racial and ethnic demographics, police administrators must carefully monitor the communities they serve for rapid changes. Although diversity in hiring police officers, especially Latino officers, tends to lag behind rapid changes or expansion in the community, it is an essential subject that has major implications inside and outside the police department (Urbina & Álvarez, 2015).

LATINOS INSIDE LAW ENFORCEMENT

The recognition of the importance of ethnicity and law enforcement extends beyond the context of police-citizen interactions. As noted herein, the relationship between the police and the Latino community has been tumultuous. Recently Urbina and Álvarez (2015) reported the lack of diversity in many American law enforcement agencies, revealing that in hundreds of police departments across the United States the percentage of whites on the force is 30 percentage points higher than in the communities they serve. At its core, a diverse police force increases a department's legitimacy, which may ultimately enhance community relations. A representative force will be more responsive to community needs, and may alleviate some of the most serious problems in the police-minority relationship. Brad Smith and Malcolm Holmes (2003), for instance, found that the more closely the proportion of Latinos in the police department matches the proportion of Latinos in the community, the lower the incidence of civil rights criminal complaints. More globally, this indicates that a more diverse police force may have benefits for the community, departments, and the criminal justice system.

Although the numbers of Latinos in law enforcement are increasing, they remain an underrepresented group in policing (Urbina & Álvarez, 2015). During the late 1980s, Latinos were less than 5 percent of police officers and by 2013 the percentage of Latino police officers increased to nearly 12 percent. The largest percentage of Latino officers (24.7%) was employed in cities with populations greater than 1 million (Reaves, 2015; Urbina & Álvarez, 2015). As the proportion of Latinos grows in a given community, the need for representation on the force becomes more apparent. As the population grows, so does Latino political presence.

Further, having a political presence may be particularly important as political influence may be used to force departments to address diversity issues in areas with a large Latino population as compared to those with fewer Latinos.

Obtaining a police force that is representative of the community is invaluable not only in the context of law enforcement, but for assisting in the improvements of the judicial process and the penal system, a laudable goal as more Latinos enter the ranks of law enforcement. However, despite their growing numbers in law enforcement, there is little empirical research on the impact of increased numbers of Latino officers on the force (Urbina & Álvarez, 2015). As reported by John Dempsey and Linda Forst (2011), the Latino officers' ability to relate to the Latino community, especially as a communicator in emergency situations, is essential to the operation of the department, police-community relations, and the well-being of the community as a whole. In addition, there may be another important factor at work with having a representative Latino force as officers may be role models. As Tony Chapa, executive director of the Hispanic American Police Command Officers Association points out, police are highly visible in society, and in the Latino community when young people look to see representatives from the government, it is not elected officials they find, it is the officer on the street (Johnson, 2015). However, there are roadblocks to creating a diverse force that police departments may face (Urbina & Álvarez, 2015). For example, the recruitment efforts are not as simple as expanding the application pool. As discussed herein there is a history of abuse and mistrust that must be acknowledged. This may be a hindrance to some considering a career in law enforcement as historically they may view the police as a force not aligned with their best interests. Furthermore, citizenship status, and some police departments' lack of interest in having diversity and other internal barriers may all impact Latino representation on the force (Maciag, 2015; Urbina & Álvarez, 2015). Additionally, there has been little inquiry into how Latino officers view their position and work environment once on the force, which may give insight into the complexities of ethnicity inside the department and patrolling communities that are becoming more diverse.

A recent survey of nearly 8,000 police officers by Pew Research highlights how Latino officers view their work, communities, and issues in law enforcement. The survey revealed that Latino officers held similar views to white officers on matters such as the recent national focus on African Americans killed by the police where 72 percent felt they were isolated incidents and not the symptom of a larger problem. Interestingly, nearly half of the Latino officers said their work nearly always makes them feel frustrated. The issue of immigration enforcement was also relevant in the survey with a majority of Latino (60%) and black (64%) officers responding it should be up to federal authorities to identify undocumented immigrants, while 59 percent of white officers felt local police should take an active role (Pew Research Center, 2017).

Assigning Latino officers to Latino neighborhoods would be a logical and effective choice for departments seeking to diversify their force, corresponding with the demographics of their respected communities. Yet, without strategic planning, such a choice may ignore the subtleties of ethnicity, as wide ethnic diversity may exist in large Latino neighborhoods, as people come from places like Mexico, Cuba, Puerto Rico, and other Central and South American coun-

tries, each of which have distinct cultural practices and use of the Spanish language (Urbina, 2014). In short, there may be great ethnic diversity within the ethnic community, and residents may be quite different from the Latino officers that have been assigned to patrol their neighborhoods. In effect, considering the significance of communication in the criminal justice system (Urbina, 2004b), having Latino officers who do not speak Spanish may further complicate their role, perceptions, and effectiveness within the community and police department, as the Latino community may feel that police departments are not being trained to truly meet community issues, and thus the Latino community continues to be marginalized and neglected (Urbina & Álvarez, 2015).

As for Latino officers, they may experience a type of double marginality, which is not so different from what some black officers confront. Consider, for example, the historic tense relationship between the police and the black community, and then black police officers entering the police force. The problems between the police and the black community are multifaceted, which may lead to calls for an increase in the numbers of black police in predominately white departments and for more black officers patrolling black communities. According to Kenneth Bolton and Joe Feagin (2004), some of the black officers they interviewed felt they had to prove to the black community that they were not sellouts, and that they were trying their best to actually help the African American community. The black officers also felt that they faced a double standard because of the expectations from the black community, and that they must work twice as hard as white officers to be accepted in the department.

In addition, once in the department, black officers faced various types of discrimination ranging from only being allowed to patrol black neighborhoods, the inability to arrest white citizens, to inequities in evaluations, rewards, and discipline, while further complicating the relationship between black officers and the black community. For instance, even though there has been general support of black officers from black citizens, churches, and activist groups, largely due to the adversarial relationship between the police and some black communities, residents have had a difficult time reconciling the role of black police officers and the policing practices of the past in the United States. Bolton and Feagin (2004) conclude that some research has shown a declining impact of racism for black police officers; yet, in the interviews they conducted the officers gave several examples of overt and covert racism they had experienced. Despite these negative occurrences, though, the officers ultimately had pride in their ability to do their job as well as being in a position of authority for the black community.

In the context of ethnic minorities-police relations, in many ways the experiences of Latino officers mirrors those of black police officers. Not unlike residents in black communities, some Latinos have had negative experiences with the police in the United States (Durán, 2009a, 2009b; Escobar, 1999; Fountain, 2016; Marin, 2015; Urbina & Álvarez, 2015), and recent immigrants may have experienced corruption and abuse in their home countries. Once in the United States, these early experiences in their country of origin can engender a mistrust of the police that can make police patrol in Latino communities difficult, and thus difficult to gain confidence. Still, Latino officers fill a critical void as some Spanish-speaking community residents may feel more at ease when Spanish-speaking officers show up, possibly sharing the same culture or country of origin. Then again, similar to the African American experience, this is where the dou-

ble marginality may arise, as Latino officers may feel pressure to do their job differently or more aggressively simply because of their ethnicity. A conflicted situation, as newly immigrated Mexicans, for example, may expect leniency from Mexican American police officers, resulting in role conflict for the officers (Dempsey & Forst, 2011).

One of the heavily touted reasons for having a diverse force is the hope that departments that reflect the community will result in more understanding and efficiency, resulting in fewer incidents of excessive force or brutality (Urbina & Álvarez, 2015). An investigation by Geoffrey Alpert and Roger Dunham (2004) on the use of force revealed a more intricate dynamic in the interactions between minority officers and minority citizens. The authors found that in the Miami Dade Police Department, black officers used force against black suspects more frequently than white or Latino officers (67% versus 40% and 41% respectively), while Latino officers used force against Latino suspects more frequently than white or black officers (35% versus 33% and 17% respectively). Although these results could be a product of patrol deployment and working with citizens of similar backgrounds, the findings suggest that minority officers respond differently to various ethnic groups, and that these officers may feel more comfortable using force against suspects from their own ethnic or racial group.

Together, though the experiences of Latino officers within police departments have not been as well documented as those of black police officers, the existing literature is enlightening. One particular research article that surveyed more than 1,100 patrol officers in the Milwaukee Police Department found that Latino officers were more likely to report negative workplace experiences such as perceptions of bias, underestimating ability, and sexually offensive behavior. Further, both Latino and black officers perceived fewer opportunities for promotion and preferred assignments as compared to whites (Urbina & Álvarez, 2015), revealing clear perceptions of bias and lack of opportunity, resonating the remarks made by controversial Los Angeles police chief Daryl Gates in a 1978 press conference in which he stated that Latinos were not promoted because they were lazy (Skolnick & Fyfe, 1993).

Given the complicated dynamics of diversity and multiculturalism in the United States (Urbina, 2014), issues of race, ethnicity, and perception of bias can be further complicated within police departments once additional issues are analyzed. Consider, for example, the position some Latino officers who appear "white" may find themselves in the course of their duties. These officers may be privy to conversations and comments about Latino and black officers by white officers and citizens who may feel comfortable sharing their thoughts with them based on the officer's white appearance (Dempsey & Forst, 2011). Although minority officers may be recruited and assigned to patrol predominately minority communities, some officers may view these assignments as discrimination, and that they are not receiving the opportunity to work in other areas simply because of their race or ethnicity. This may be perceived as limiting their chances for promotion and recognition within the department and community as a whole. While being bilingual might be considered a positive attribute during the recruiting and hiring process, bilingual Latino officers may find themselves pulled away from their regular duties to serve as translators for others (Dempsey & Forst, 2011; Urbina & Álvarez, 2015), a situation that might be considered as distracting by some police officers. Worse, these issues may take a serious emotional or psychological toll on police officers. In effect, Nnamdi Pole, Suzanne Best, Daniel

Weiss, Thomas Metzler, Akiva Liberman, Jeffery Fagan, and Charles Marmar (2001) studied 655 urban police officers to assess if there were any differences by gender, race, or ethnicity for duty-related symptoms of posttraumatic stress disorder (PTSD). The authors found that after controlling for all relevant variables, Latino officers evidenced greater duty-related PTSD symptoms than either white or black officers.

From a judicial standpoint, some of these negative events have resulted in discrimination or affirmative action lawsuits, and, along the way, the creation of support groups for Latino officers (Urbina & Álvarez, 2015). In this context, the National Latino Peace Officers Association (NLPOA) was founded in 1974 in the state of California with four main objectives: To recruit qualified Latino police officers, assist officers during their probationary period, encourage continued education, and provide assistance during the promotion process. Other prominent support groups include the Hispanic American Police Command Officers Association, The Hispanic National Law Enforcement Association, and the Federal Hispanic Law Enforcement Officers Association, with these organizations playing vital roles in supporting Latino officers at various levels of law enforcement as well as implementing major changes in police departments around the country.

Case in point: The NLPOA along with a Japanese group successfully challenged the height requirement of the California Highway Patrol, which opened the door for women and minorities that were kept out of law enforcement due to stature. Once established, these organizations can provide support and legal assistance when needed by women, minorities, and even whites. Well established organizations, though, are normally found in larger urban departments or in communities with sizeable populations of

Latinos, leaving minority officers from smaller departments with a limited or no support network. As such, this type of limitation can be a crucial situation in small communities, as it can be difficult for Latino officers in small departments to make a stand and emphasize their ethnicity in small institutions, with hostile environments. Ultimately, these officers may find it easier to simply try and blend in, confirming to the established culture of the other officers. Together, while Latinos have made great strides within law enforcement, from reflecting the composition of the community to entering the ranks of upper command and creating new policies, grave problems still persist, from the traditional issues of prejudice and discrimination to the emerging expectations and challenges based on their newly acquired status, all of which demonstrate the dynamics of ethnicity inside police departments in the United States, as documented by Urbina and Álvarez in *Latino Police Officers in the United States: An Examination of Emerging Trends and Issues* (2015).

CONCLUSIONS AND RECOMMENDATIONS

After decades of investigations, it becomes clear that race and ethnicity influence criminal justice process and decisions, beginning with law enforcement and later in the judicial and penal systems, as detailed in the subsequent chapters. Evidently, even though police departments have become more diverse, with some departments enacting legislation and policies seeking to address the problems of mistreatment, racial profiling, and brutality, differential treatment and violence continue, and thus improvements remain to be done.

As noted herein, the experience of Latinos is indeed very different from that of either blacks or whites, and early research on Latinos and policing tended to focus on mistreatment along the border. Considering recent demographic changes, there is a growing need to examine the perceptions of the police, and how law enforcement officials are responding to the growth of Latinos in areas outside bordering states with Mexico, allowing us to not only test for geographical difference, but also expand the test for both ethnic and race effects in the distribution of punishment and justice.

Once we move beyond the traditional binary approach of black and white, crucial research questions must be carefully examined, as we seek to better understand the ethnic experience in law enforcement in its totality. For example, how is recent anti-immigrants sentiment and political rhetoric shaping the contact between Latinos and the police? Is this experience significantly different for native-born versus foreign-born Latinos? How will the recent anti-immigration laws impact the relationship between Latinos and the police in states and cities across the country? Given the changing ethnicity of cities across the country, what do these newly formed communities consider to be effective policing or a representative department? In effect, the issues that were highlighted in this chapter, such as profiling, excessive police force, and the complexities of Latinos working in law enforcement can be further investigated within the context of these research questions, questions which will be explored in the next four chapters.

As detailed in the following chapters of this book, as scholars in criminal justice, we need to broaden our research focus if we are to gain better insight and holistic knowledge of the expectations and experiences of all Americans. Within the context of law enforcement, the incorporation of a Latino focus will ultimately supplement other areas of research, such as criminological theory as well as race and ethic relations. Police studies that focus on ethnicity must continue building on the current knowledge, while taking into account factors like the diversity of country of origin, religion, language, and cultural practices within the Latino community, as each of these distinct features along with the neighborhood environment influence how police officers communicate and deliver service in minority communities. Finally, as the Latino population continues to grow in the United States, challenges are being redefined and new ones are being created inside and outside of policing. Logically, these changes merit a newly energized research agenda to explore the ways in which ethnicity shapes and reshapes law enforcement practices, the objective of the following chapters.

Chapter 3

POLICING THE BARRIOS: LATINOS AND THE AMERICAN POLICE OVER THE YEARS

ROBERT J. DURÁN

When any soldiers go to war, they must have enemies. When cops go to war against crime, their enemies are found in inner cities and among our minority populations. There, in a country as foreign to most officers as Vietnam was to GIs, cops have trouble distinguishing the good guys from the bad.

–Jerome Skolnick and James Fyfe

For all studies on policing, one of the most hidden elements, similar to events unfolding underneath a shadow, from mainstream researchers is how agents of the state enforce criminal laws on Latinos as well as the communities where ethnic minorities live. Historically, U.S. criminal laws tend to benefit those who create them, and thus in this chapter I present various forms of underpolicing (lack of) and overpolicing (aggressive) that challenge issues of equality and due process. Alfredo Mirandé (1987) advocates that understanding the contemporary situation of Latinos in the criminal justice system requires a contextual analysis of history which has maintained a double standard in the judicial system: one standard for Anglos and another for Chicanos (Mexicans), "gringo justice." As for undocumented people, James Cockcroft (1986) utilized the concept of "outlaws" to describe the experience of Mexican immigrants residing in the United States, not in the pejorative sense of bandits, but rather in the literal sense of *outside the law:* laborers without rights.

As such, the historical concepts of *outlaw* and *gringo justice* serve as a foundation for the descriptions developed in this chapter to describe the enforcement of laws in the barrios. Whether migrants or indigenous, the history of each nationality, "Latino" or "Hispanic," is one of colonialism: from the seizure of half of Mexico (Acuña, 2015; Bosworth & Flavin, 2007; Meier & Ribera, 1993; Mirandé, 1987; Spickard, 2007; Urbina & Smith, 2007), to the occupation of Puerto Rico (Malavet, 2004; Monge, 1997), to the embargo against Cuba (González, 2000), or the intensive involvement of the U.S. government in Latin America (Blum, 1995; Herman & Chomsky, 2002). In the process, ideologies were developed and maintained to criminalize Latinos whereas whites have not encountered such magnifying inspection or oppositional legislation.

As noted in previous chapters, there are various reasons for the investigation of ethnic minorities, with at least three essential reasons to focus on Latinos and law enforcement. First, Latinos are one of the fastest growing and largest minority group in the country. Latinos are projected to increase from 15 percent of the population in 2008 to 30 percent in 2050. Figures for the first decade of the twenty-first century show that in 2010, the 50 million Latinos in the United States were mostly composed of five nationalities: Mexico (63%), Puerto Rico (9.2%), Cuban (3.5%), Salvadoran (3.3%), and Dominican (2.8%). Latinos can be found in every state in the country, with the largest populations residing in New Mexico (46%), California (35.9%), and Texas (35.6%), with substantial concentrations in Arizona, Colorado, Florida, Illinois, Nevada, and New York. Second, exploring issues involving Latinos can enhance our understanding of race and ethnicity that moves beyond the traditional *black* and *white binary* approach of research and publication, with a much greater number of scholars exploring the relationship between law enforcement and African Americans. Not captured in binary approaches, for instance, is the fact that Latinos along with other marginalized groups confront lower levels of education and political inclusion and higher levels of poverty and unemployment that have been found to increase differential treatment by law enforcement officials. In effect, Ramiro Martínez (2007) conducted a search of the *Criminal Justice Abstracts* from 1990 to 2006 for the keywords "Hispanic" or "Latino" and "police," resulting in 68 items whereas a similar search using "Black" or "African American" and "police" netted 485 articles on the topic. Third, issues of citizenship expose Latinos, both the 60 percent citizen and 40 percent foreign-born, to immigration law enforcement agents that other racial and ethnic groups rarely encounter.

Researchers have argued that the lack of studies devoted to the investigation of Latinos presents a serious limitation in criminological research (Carter, 1985; Holmes, 2000; Martínez, 2007; Mirandé, 1987; Salinas, 2015; Urbina, 2007, 2012, 2014; Urbina & Álvarez, 2015). The purpose of this chapter, then, is to provide an overview of research studies and biographical accounts that have focused specifically on the relationship between Latinos and law enforcement in the United States, by chronologically following and analyzing the research data by focusing on two time periods: 1823 to 1979 and then 1980 to 2010. In doing so, the ultimate goal will be to bring forth the light that will expose the events unfolding underneath the historical shadows of the Latino experience in the United States.

EARLY HISTORY OF LATINOS AND LAW ENFORCEMENT: 1823 TO 1979

To begin, a central objective is to separate the past from the present in order to examine historical changes in an effort to prevent undue generalizations. One of the most significant components of law enforcement is discretion: the authority given to officers to make independent decisions. In the early history of policing, officer decision-making lacked policies, legislation that limited police authority, with no historical precedent to guide police behavior (Roth, 2011). Shifting notions of sovereignty kept individuals in a state of conflict when enforcing laws definitely became part of a political or economic enterprise. I will begin by providing a brief summary of historical events, some of which have been referenced in previous chapters, for historical context as to how the Latino experience has unfolded over time.

Geographically, in the Southwest, Robert Rosenbaum (1998) reports that Mexicans perceived their treatment by Anglo police officers as "capricious and unjust." The high number of lynching and killings of Mexicans by Anglo mobs continued without punishment from 1848 to 1916, only 100 years ago. Law enforcement officers maintained a standard of "shoot first and ask questions later," a practice being rationalized and justified with the violent *bandito* image. In effect, Latinos were socially constructed as criminals in order to rationalize and legitimize police behavior (Bender, 2003; Martínez, 2002; Mirandé, 1987; Tovares, 2002; Urbina & Álvarez, 2016; see also Aguirre, this volume). Raul Tovares (2002), for instance, explains how the Texas insurrection for independence in 1835, and the Mexican-American War of 1848 created a time frame where stereotypes strategically emerged depicting Mexicans as bloodthirsty savages and greasers, prone to excessive greed and dissocial values. In fact, despite the Treaty of Guadalupe Hidalgo granting Mexicans *white* status, Mexicans were continually characterized as nonwhite and unequal (Acuña, 2015; Almaguer, 2008; De León, 1983; Gómez, 2007; Montgomery, 2002; Nieto-Phillips, 2004; Urbina, Vela, & Sanchez, 2014). Rosenbaum's (1998) archival research found a double standard of laws and punishment, clearly showing the ingrained prejudice and racism of Anglo America. Tomás Almaguer (1994) examined the historical origins of white supremacy in California, and found

that Mexicans were targeted with various laws, like the 1855 Vagrancy Act (or Greaser Act), for being perceived as idle and unemployed. This particular law allowed officers to arrest, fine, imprison, or require labor service for targeted individuals. In all, Almaguer (1994:57) documents that "Although Mexicans were legally accorded the same rights as free white persons, actual extension of these privileges to all segments of the population was quite another matter." Residents continued to face displacement from their land as European newcomers began to use violence, lynching, existing laws, or developed new laws, to seize lands previously held by Mexicans or other indigenous groups.

While often portrayed as brave, heroic, and honorable men, the Texas Rangers were the most powerful and abusive agents in early law enforcement (see Baker; Urbina & Álvarez, Chapter 1, this volume). Julian Samora, Joe Bernal, and Albert Peña (1979) explain how the Texas Rangers continually violated the civil rights of people since 1823 when the Rangers were unofficially created. Operating as a paramilitary force, the Rangers went back and forth into Mexico to retrieve cattle and slaves, with absolute power, authority, and immunity. Describing the Mexican experience, Carey McWilliams (1990) documents that the Texas Rangers participated in lawless executions, and that they considered themselves as the authority to declare an open-season against Mexicans, "terrorizing" Mexicans with impunity. Other atrocious acts in Texas included widespread instances of Mexicanos ". . . being subjected to threats, torture, flogging, castration, and thinly disguised murder. Many innocent Mexicanos lost their lives as a result of Ranger policing," like local posse action, shootings, lynching, and other mob violence (Gonzáles-Day, 2006; Meier & Ribera, 1993:116–117).

The new dividing border between the United States and Mexico quickly became a space where entry into the United States for Mexicans often resulted in brutality or they were forced to participate in a dehumanizing process of fumigation. In 1910, Mexicans protested immigration officials along the Santa Fe Bridge due to abuses committed against them while entering the United States to work (García, 1981). After 1917, crossing the border changed dramatically, as Mexicans were required to strip naked and be disinfected with various chemical agents including gasoline, kerosene, sodium cyanide, cyanogens, sulfuric acid, and Zyklon B before gaining entry into the United States (Romo, 2005). In fact, the risks of the fumigation process included the possibility of death as experienced in 1916 when 50 individuals in the El Paso, Texas jail were stripped of their clothing and bathed in gasoline when they caught fire, killing 27 individuals. Critically, Zyklon B, the fumigation of choice, was later used in Nazi Germany in gas chambers. Further, police officers were accused of taking pictures of naked Mexican women and sharing the photos. Such unequal and brutal treatment led to the 1917 Bath Riots where several thousand individuals protested this practice as dehumanizing and deadly (Romo, 2005). Reporting the experience, the *Texas State Journal of Medicine* (1915–1916:556) cited, "All passengers are not subjected to this treatment: clean, well dressed American or other similar 'first class' have no treatment. . . ."

To further exacerbate the situation for Mexicans, the emergence of the revolutionary war in Mexico from 1910 to 1920 contributed to community fear of raids occurring on the U.S. side of the border. In retrospect, U.S. law enforcement officials felt justified in heightening their level of brutality against both Mexicans and Mexican Americans. As in previous years, highly fused by racist beliefs, there was no stopping of the Texas Rangers. In fact, William Carrigan (2006:175) reports that the highest levels of violence in Texas occurred in South Texas where the Texas Rangers often joined Anglo aggression by taking a "brutal binge of retaliation, summarily killing hundreds of Mexicans without due process of law." Reflecting the historical dynamics of slavery, the lynching of Latinos was indeed a routine practice that created little news interest in how mobs and law enforcement officers often removed Mexicans from jail and executed them. For instance, on Christmas of 1917, Texas Rangers and U.S. soldiers took 15 Mexican men from their homes in Porvenir, beat them during questioning, and then shot each one in the head. Carrigan (2006) further reports that during the eight decades of his study (1836–1916) mob violence was in fact tolerated by local authorities, and that extralegal violence was seen as a just and necessary function of social control.

Outside of Texas, the barrios of East Los Angeles may have served as an early buffer between Mexicans and Anglos. Edward Escobar (1999) conducted an extensive historical study of the Los Angeles Police Department from 1900 to 1945, and found that from 1900 to 1920 there were no conclusive data to suggest that the LAPD *overpoliced* Mexican barrios. In fact, despite the media consistently linking Mexicans with criminality, the police department did not appear concerned with life in the barrios, possibly attributed to protective factors in the barrios, or the fact that whatever crime was taking place was "Latino-on-Latino." There were, however, 17 charges of misconduct filed against the police, but, as usual, the officers were exonerated in all but three cases. Ricardo Romo's (1983:88) research on the creation of the barrio in East Los Angeles, though, supports the possibility of early protective factors in that the barrio offered

Mexicans ". . . at least partial opportunity to make a better life for their families." The hands-off approach of the LAPD, however, drastically changed in following years.

In 1929, the Wickersham Commission (officially known as U.S. National Commission on Law Observance and Enforcement) launched an in-depth study to determine the accuracy of data involving illegal activities by the foreign-born. In their study, "Report on Crime and the Foreign Born," the authors found much prejudice and discrimination directed at Mexicans, but cautioned that other groups have historically encountered similar discrimination (Wickersham Commission, 1931). Writing a section in the 1931 report, "Crime and the Foreign Born: The Problem of the Mexican," Paul Taylor cited that most Americans viewed Mexicans as foreign despite their nativity, resulting in police brutality and deadly force in communities across the country. More globally, citing numerous situations as representative of the Mexican experience, Taylor (1931:230) documented:

> One reason the Mexicans carry guns is because of their relations with the police. The latter, especially in Indiana Harbor [East Chicago], shoot the Mexicans with small provocation. One shot a Mexican who was walking away from him, and laughed as the body was thrown into the patrol wagon.

Along with the physical brutality, Mexicans were often arrested in large numbers based on little or no evidence of wrongdoing. In all, Taylor (1931:243) concluded, "It is clear that Mexicans in the United States, both aliens and citizens, are frequently subjected to severe and unequal treatment by those who administer the laws." As with other similar reports, shortly after its publication, Harry Anslinger, Commissioner for the Federal Bureau of Narcotics, neglected to heed the Commission Report findings. In-

stead, Anslinger pushed for new legislation against marijuana due to its alleged association and enhanced level of violence by Mexican Americans (Reinarman, 2002). Subsequently, associating Latinos with drugs and thus creating new laws defining such behavior as illegal led to even more legislation and ideologies to justify increased targeting of Mexicans, drastically increasing arrest trends.

Then, in the 1940s, the association of Mexicans with criminality once again emerged with individuals who wore the Zoot Suit (see Aguirre; Urbina & Álvarez, Chapter 1, this volume). The flashily dressed Latino youths were creating a new genre of style, but were characterized as being dangerous and anti-American. Escobar (1999) reports that the hostile relationship between Mexicans and the Los Angeles Police Department developed in the early 1940s when race and crime were starting to be intertwined in local police perceptions. Two incidents highlighted this link: The Sleepy Lagoon trial in 1942 and the Zoot Suit Riots of 1943, both events being well documented by researchers (Escobar, 1999; McWilliams, 1990; Moore, 1978; Pagán, 2003). The primary theme to be taken from these incidents is that not only law enforcement officials allowed, but even participated in the beatings of Mexican Americans. In fact, police officers specifically sought out Mexican Americans when determining who to arrest and criminally charge, while neglecting to enforce laws against white assailants.

Despite researchers arguing against presumed Mexican inherited tendencies toward criminality, some continued the myth enhancement including Captain E. Durán Ayres, chief of the foreign relations bureau, by proclaiming highly charged statements, like ". . . this Mexican element considers all that to be sign of weakness [fistfights], and all he knows and feels is a desire to kill, or at least let blood . . . when there is added to this inborn characteristic that has come down through the ages . . . (McWilliams, 1990: 212), resonating characterizations by Adolph Hitler during his extermination of about six million Jews.

The 1940s and 1950s were characterized with emerging conflicts due to style of dress, gang labeling, and drug enforcement, expending beyond Los Angeles. Zoot-suit fears impacted the city of Denver, Colorado, for example, where individuals from Los Angeles were alleged to begin spreading trouble (Durán, 2010). Though, in the beginning, local police representatives at the time downplayed criminal and delinquent involvement despite sensational media headlines. However, as expected, soon the Denver Police Department began aggressively pursuing Spanish-surnamed people with a variety of newly-created legislation and enforcement tactics. There is indication that the police department and its officers discretely condoned harassment and unequal treatment, but at least a small number of officers were definitely racist (Walsh, 1995). The mix of ethnicity and corresponding elements, like culture and language, for Latino groups quickly sparked widespread fear from the general public whereas groups of whites were in fact tolerated for engaging in the same behavior. James Walsh (1995) found a significant increase in the number of arrests from 1941 to 1948 that involved drug violations or vagrancy charges. Joan Moore (1978) documents that after 1947 a similar escalation of drug enforcement was taking place in Los Angeles barrios. Then, with new laws in place, an "increasingly hostile law enforcement attitude toward the gangs appeared . . . ," with law enforcement initiating its first federal mass arrests (and prosecutions) in the Maravilla neighborhood based on a secret federal grand jury (Moore, 1978:73). Pragmatically, the racism by local police officers and federal agents was coun-

terproductive and actually served to strengthen gangs (Moore, 1978).

Nationally, patterns of inequality continued to be demonstrated in police misconduct, jails being used as holding cells for beatings, and government initiatives used to deport Mexicans (Álvarez & Urbina, 2018). Rodolfo Acuña (2015) describes how a 13-year-old named Eugene Montenegro was shot in the back on July 1946 by a sheriff deputy in Monterey Park, California. Another officer, William Keys, of Los Angeles participated in several beatings of suspects and shootings of Mexicans, with the shootings being in the back. On Christmas Eve of 1951, eight drunk police officers took seven young Chicanos out of their cells at Lincoln Heights Jail and beat them (Escobar, 1999). Yet, none of the violations ever received disciplinary action.

In the case of undocumented people, when the labor of Mexicans was no longer desired, the government resorted Mexicans for removal, as with Colorado's illegal martial law of 1936 that resulted in one hundred thousand Latinos escorted from the state by the National Guard, and Operation Wetback in 1954, where allegedly over one million undocumented immigrants were rounded up and deported (Álvarez & Urbina, 2018; Meier & Ribera, 1993).

The 1960s continued the trend of previous decades of law enforcement officials believing in the presumed criminality of Latinos, and thus deserving of second-class treatment by the police and the community. In fact, according to Moore (1970a), much of the "bitterness" revolved around *law enforcement agencies defining Mexicans as prone to crime* (see Aguirre, this volume). In effect, the folklore stereotype of "quick smile and quick knife" perpetuated the highest levels of police administration. In 1960, for example, Chief William H. Parker of the Los Angeles Police Department gave his official view:

The Latin population that came in here in great strength were here before us, and presented a great problem because I worked over on the East Side when men had to work in pairs-but that has evolved into assimilation-and it's because of some of these people being not too far removed from the wild tribes of the district of the inner mountains of Mexico. I don't think you can throw the genes out of the question when you discuss behavior patterns of people. (Moore, 1970a:92–93)

Among ethnic minorities, Moore (1970a) found that Mexicans were particularly targeted for being perceived as violent, dangerous, or illegal (see Aguirre; Álvarez; Posadas and Medina, this volume). As such, Stan Steiner (1970:163–164) reports that people of Mexican descent were shocked by officers' inability to distinguish threats, and thus expected "the police to treat all Mejicanos with the same brutality, without seeing a difference between a wedding party and a brawl in a bar," clearly second-class treatment by law enforcement. Steiner (1970) further found that most white officers, who did not live in the barrio, had little or no knowledge of the lives of Latinos, like language or culture. Alfredo Mirandé (1987) cites that the barrios remained ethnic enclaves where Latinos continued to be physically and socially isolated from Anglo society, allowing for an additional mechanism of social control, marginalization, and negligence. In effect, Mirandé (1987) reports that the role of police officers was to keep Chicanos in their place by enforcing defined isolation. Ian Haney López (2003), for example, describes how a 1972 police-community relations hearing held in East Los Angeles included a former deputy of the sheriff's office who reported that arbitrary stops were the order of the day. The officer testified that physical beatings accompanied an arrest, and then charged the person with assaulting an officer

to secure a conviction in court and, in turn, possibly sentenced to jail or prison.

The U.S. Commission on Civil Rights (1970) tried to find whether there was any factual basis on behalf of Mexican Americans alleging discrimination by law enforcement officials, interviewing 450 people from 1967 to 1968. In its report, "Mexican Americans and the Administration of Justice in the Southwest," the U.S. Commission on Civil Rights (1970:i) cited:

> The Commission reports that there is widespread evidence that equal justice is being withheld; Mexican Americans are reportedly subject to unduly harsh treatment by law enforcement officers, often arrested on insufficient ground, and receive physical and verbal abuse and penalties which are considered disproportionately severe.

Further, there were also problems in other crucial areas, like traffic enforcement, police protection, discourtesy, and use of excessive force, to include both adults and juveniles. The process for remedying illegal police acts was found inadequate and dangerous due to law enforcement retaliation. In all, the Commission described the Latino experience in its report as a "bleak picture of the relationship between Mexican Americans in the Southwest and the agencies which administer justice in those States" (U.S. Commission on Civil Rights, 1970:87).

The information supporting the social distance between law enforcement and Latinos was supported by various other research studies. In 1969, the American Civil Liabilities Union (ACLU) of Southern California documented pervasive hostility and brutality toward Mexicans when they established a center for legal advocacy and data collection in East Los Angeles (López, 2003). Between August 1966 and July 1968, 205 cases were identified where police malpractice occurred with the bulk number of cases involving the LAPD (108) and the Sheriff's Department (76). Of the 205 victims, nearly 80 percent were charged with an offense. The study found that charging an individual with an offense ensured the legitimacy of police misconduct. In actuality, according to Ian Haney López (2003:45), "excessive violence against Mexicans was part of the work-a-day world of law enforcement in East Los Angeles, an accepted and expected part of the job."

In places like Denver, the Latino community shared many of the same obstacles with the barrios of Los Angeles. David Bayley and Harold Mendelsohn (1968) interviewed police officers, community members, and leaders in the community. Spanish-surnamed individuals were more critical than whites or blacks regarding policing in their own neighborhoods. More than one-fourth of the respondents thought their treatment by police was unfriendly or prejudiced whereas only four percent of whites reported similar feelings. The researchers found that despite higher levels of negative interactions and police brutality than whites experienced, minorities were less likely to file complaints because of the belief, by nearly half of the Spanish-surnamed individuals that it would not matter, while only 20 percent of whites thought their complaints would go unsupported. Together, Bayley and Mendelsohn (1968:109) concluded that "The police seem to play a role in the life of minority people out of all proportion to the role they play in the lives of dominant majority." Two years later, Steiner (1970) described similar problems in Denver between Mexican Americans and the police department, where it was claimed by the chairman of a police review board that the yearly "wild-West shooting of minorities by the police" grows worse, not to mention numerous reports of unequal treatment and warrantless searches of automobiles, homes, and people.

Notably, as in previous decades, grass-roots community organizing continued to challenge unequal treatment and misconduct by law enforcement (see Baker, this volume), as vividly illustrated by Ernesto Vigil (1999). Among the various issues of grave concern were how Latinos were often arrested, not charged, but held in jail for long periods of time; and how police shootings of Chicanos tended to be problematic and questionable, with problems often being covered-up by the police department. Such widespread mistreatment led to the creation of the *Crusade for Justice* movement which directly challenged the two primary institutions that normally served the community unfairly (Vigil, 1999): law enforcement agencies and educational institutions. Strategically, the police responded to the challenges to their legitimacy by cooperating with the Federal Bureau of Investigation (FBI) to infiltrate, suppress, and silence leaders of the Chicano Movement, making it seem that they were the "victims" and not the aggressors. Outside Mexican barrios, similar situations were taking place, and other forms of resistance began in places like Chicago in the Puerto Rican communities. Felix Padilla (1987), for instance, describes how the Humboldt Park neighborhood faced a long history of police abuse as well as economic and political marginalization. Gina Pérez (2001) reports that Puerto Ricans were at first perceived as a model minority or, in other words, the "dark-eyed gentle people," and thus not considered a threat due to mostly fighting among themselves, with little involvement in crime. This perception, though, quickly changed in June of 1966 after the Division Street Uprising when residents protested the police shooting of a young Puerto Rican man by a white police officer. Police officers used police dogs to control the crowd, but the uprising lasted for three days. The protest helped to politicize and develop an ethnic consciousness, but it also developed a new image of Puerto Ricans as "dangerous, poor, and culturally deficient" (Pérez, 2001:48). Still, Puerto Ricans became more vocal and oppositional towards the ongoing abuse from law enforcement.

The 1970s began with several relatively ignored protests that often led to a negative police response. In East Los Angeles, residents protested the Vietnam War, unequal schools, and unjustified police behavior (López, 2003; Mirandé, 1987; Morales, 1972). Armando Morales (1972) documents the riots that left five Mexican Americans dead and numerous police officers injured. One of the Mexican Americans killed by police was Ruben Salazar, a former reporter for the *Los Angeles Times* and a strong voice for the Mexican community (Acuña, 2015). Again, as in previous decades, shootings by police officers constantly served as the spark for uprisings. In Texas, Shirley Achor (1978: 64) cites that in Dallas "Police relations have been a major–and corrosive–issue, with accusations of brutality and harassment often corroborated and documented." Normally, mostly due to negligence, the police allowed barrio residents to take care of their own problems, but several incidents demonstrated how the Latino community continued to receive unequal treatment. For example, on July 24, 1973, Officer Darrel Cain was questioning two brothers about an attempted burglary of a soft-drink machine. Both boys denied knowledge, and so Cain took out his .357 magnum handgun and spun the cylinder warning Santos Rodríguez to tell the truth. Rodríguez repeated not knowing, but Cain pulled the trigger, playing the deadly game of Russian roulette. The first time the gun clicked, but the second time the gun fired killing the 12-year-old boy. Officer Cain argued that he thought the gun was

empty, and he was subsequently suspended. However, during the trial proceedings, it was determined that the two brothers' fingerprints did not match the attempted burglary, viewed as grave injustice, the Brown Berets protested in the streets. Surprisingly, Cain was found guilty and sentenced to five years in prison (but served only half of it). Of course, the shooting death of Santos Rodríguez was not an isolated case as researchers have documented numerous shootings of Latinos by police officers (Acuña, 2015; Durán, 2015; Fyfe, 1981; Meyer, 1980; Mirandé, 1987; Sotomayor, 1982; Urbina & Álvarez, 2015; Vigil, 1999). Beyond ethnic minorities, in two separate studies, one in New York City (Fyfe, 1981) and the other in Los Angeles (Meyer, 1980), blacks were found to be the most common victims of police shootings, but Latinos were also overrepresented whereas whites remained underrepresented. Critically, contrary to the popular belief, blacks and Latinos were also more likely to be unarmed when they were shot by the police.

While, presumably, various projects of social change were being implemented under the President Richard Nixon administration (1969–1974) in the 1970s, extra-legal violence continued to plague Latino communities across the country. In East Los Angeles, for instance, in the 1970s lowriders and cruising became popular, and thus police began to apply other forms of social control, like closing Whittier Boulevard and making numerous arrests (Rodríguez, 1997). Roberto Rodríguez, a journalist who captured on film the beating of an individual by the Los Angeles County Sheriff's Department, became a target himself, as he was taking pictures. The police beat Rodríguez, and charged him with attacking an officer with a camera. He pleaded innocent and was found not guilty. Rodríguez then pursued a lawsuit against the Sheriff's Office, and later wrote a book describing the incident, hoping to bring awareness to the community, and, ultimately, so that Latinos would no longer remain silent to police abuse. However, Rodríguez feared that the decline and destruction of civil rights organizations by law enforcement would in fact allow police abuse to become even worse. In effect, Mirandé's (1980) survey of 170 individuals in a barrio showed that 39 percent of Chicanos feared the police, compared to only 5 percent of white respondents. Like Rodríguez (1997), Mirandé (1980:538) cited the lack of justice due to ethnic and racial inequality, as "For Chicanos, justice in the United States has come to mean 'just us.'"

In sum, despite constant crucial challenges, Latinos organized and developed various forms of resistance to unequal treatment, abuse, and brutality by law enforcement. In the early days, violent resistance could occasionally serve a purpose (Rosen-baum, 1998), whereas over time other strategies of activism and nonviolence became more appropriate for an all-inclusive social movement seeking positive change. Among the numerous organizations created in response to police violence include: Unión y Patria (Unity and Nation) led by Jesús Ávila, emerging in the 1920s in Utah (Iber, 2000); the Brown Berets in Los Angeles, California in 1968 (López, 2003); the Community Service Organization led by Edward Roybal (Escobar, 1999); and the Crusade for Justice led by Corky Gonzáles in Denver, Colorado (Vigil, 1999). As in the early days, Latinos attempting to reform or alter the structure of police departments were often specifically targeted by local police officers, sometimes bringing in federal agents, citing fears of foreign influence, particularly communism, as a justification for new laws, aggressive policing, and federal involvement (Muñoz, 1989; Urbina, 2005; Vigil, 1999).

CONTEMPORARY STUDIES OF LATINOS AND LAW ENFORCEMENT: 1980 TO 2010

In the 1980s, some Latino civil rights organizations altered their agendas to focus on other social issues, some were temporarily destroyed, and others ceased to exist. Yet, the multiple issues confronting Latinos did not completely disappear. Juan Gómez-Quiñones (1990:189) documents that "As the 1980s unfolded, the Chicano community in the United States was at a historical juncture. Much had been accomplished, new problems had arisen, and past injustices still lingered, as did obstacles to progress." Coinciding with these events were the increasing numbers of law enforcement officers, the use of incarceration as a *solution* to crime, and the ever-expansive growth of the U.S. criminal justice system (Díaz-Cotto, 2000; López, 2003; Salinas, 2015; Urbina & Álvarez, 2016, 2017; see also Álvarez; Urbina & Álvarez, Chapter 17, this volume).

Though, compared to all the previous decades under white rule, the early 1980s ushered in the era of "Hispanics" or "Latinos" (Acuña, 2015; Gómez-Quiñones, 1990; Muñoz, 1989). Public perceptions shifted away from inequality as the number of minorities increased in higher education, and thus the middle-class. To a degree, the *political tone* of ethnic minorities moved away from activism and militancy, and instead focused on assimilation into the Democratic or Republican parties, seeking to take an active role on the national level (Bender, 2014). However, despite the advancement of greater numbers of Latinos toward the middle-class, large sections of Latinos continued to be isolated in barrios across the country (Urbina et al., 2014). Exploring life in the barrios, Earl Shorris (1992:157) found a disturbing relationship between Latinos and the police:

> In every Latino neighborhood in the United States, with the possible exception of some parts of Miami, police treat all children, especially adolescent boys, as if they are criminals. It is not uncommon in East Los Angeles to see a group of boys and girls kneeling on the sidewalk or in the middle of the street, handcuffed, and responding as best they can to the questions and insults of the police.

East Los Angeles, of course, was not the only barrio to experience this type of treatment, as revealed by analyzing the literature in several regions of the country, a situation that extends into the twenty-first century. Globally, a 2005 nationwide survey found that Latinos and blacks were more likely than whites to be ticketed, arrested, handcuffed, searched, or be threatened to use force against them (Bureau of Justice Statistics, 2007).

Southwest and Southeast

Prior to the 1980s the Southwest received the bulk of research attention regarding Latinos and law enforcement, a trend which has continued until today, 2016. Analyzing the experience of Latinos in the U.S. Southwest, Malcolm Holmes (2000) claims that the percent of Latinos in the U.S. population was positively related to the average annual civil rights complaints from 1985 to 1990, providing additional support to the conclusion that Latinos in the Southwest were targets of aggressive crime control strategies. According to Holmes (2000:359), "Tensions between Anglos and Hispanics (nearly all of whom are of Mexican origin) in the southwest have persisted throughout this

century, and those of Mexican origin continue to be seen as threatening dominant group interests." New Mexico, the longest and most inhabited area of Mexico that became part of the U.S. Southwest reveals the patterns in which racial and ethnic groups are considered a threat. Robert Durán and Carlos Posadas (2010) reviewed seven years (2002–2008) of statewide data involving 182,609 arrests to determine whether disproportionate minority contact existed in the New Mexico juvenile justice system. Latino youths comprised 50 percent of the population, but 63 percent of all arrests whereas white youths comprised only 24 percent of all arrests, while constituting 34 percent of the population. These findings coincided with Lisa Bond-Maupin and James Maupin's (1998) study of a rural New Mexico county where Latinos were found to be under considerable police surveillance.

In California, researchers continued to document law enforcement actions targeted, or, in some cases, negligence against barrios and immigrants (Álvarez & Urbina, 2018). During the 1990s, Daniel Dohan (2003) studied an area where undocumented workers experienced an absence of law enforcement. However, the increasing immigration legislation in California changed this pattern of underenforcement. Guadalupe Vidales, Kristen Day, and Michael Powe (2009) conducted telephone surveys in Costa Mesa, California during two different time periods and found that once a local mayor began utilizing city police to enforce immigration laws, Latinos experienced several changes including an increase in the number of stops, negative attitudes toward the police, less likely to contact the police, and community relations deteriorated as local elected officials continued their anti-immigrant sentiment. In effect, James Diego Vigil's (2002) ethnographic studies found that many law-abiding and impoverished ethnic minority residents in East Los Angeles shared a hostile attitude toward the police due to poor police-community relations.

Dohan's (2003) ethnographic research of two communities revealed pressing differences in law enforcement surveillance between the barrios and neighborhoods recently experiencing a growth of Latino residents, documented or undocumented. In fact, Dohan's (2003) second ethnographic research site was a Mexican American barrio with over five different law enforcement agencies patrolling on foot, in cars, from helicopters, and regularly engaging in roundups with the infamous CRASH units. In another study, Vigil (2007) found that the Los Angeles Police Department stopped youths frequently regardless of gang status whereas those who were gang involved experienced more extreme forms of monitoring. In the projects, though, the police began to fear becoming a victim of violence, and so they often did not patrol certain neighborhoods, resulting in neglect and isolation. When law enforcement officials did engage the community, however, they tended to act aggressively. Celeste Fremon (2005) reports that the police had a special term called NHI or "no human involved" when describing the victimization of perceived gang members. As such, mothers in the barrio began organizing a group called Committee for Peace in the Barrio to monitor the police and improve tranquility (Fremon, 2005). Clearly, these are situations that signify great aggression against Latinos by law enforcement. Yet, Kimberly Belvedere, John Worrall, and Stephen Tibbetts (2005) analyzed 400 police reports in an urban Southern California community and determined that Latinos were less likely to resist arrest than other racial groups. In another ethnographic study, Victor Ríos (2006) illustrates the hyper-criminalization of Latinos and blacks in the San Francisco Bay Area.

As in other areas, many of the youths were arrested for nonviolent offenses, and some were treated as criminals even prior to entering the juvenile justice system. In fact, even community centers became housing locations for probation officers, further expanding criminal justice surveillance.

In Utah and Colorado, Robert Durán (2009a) conducted a 5-year ethnographic study of two cities (Ogden, Utah and Denver, Colorado), and found that in the post-civil rights era the term *gang* was being used to justify and legitimize aggressive policing in Latino communities. As in other parts of the country, despite few individuals actually being gang members, a gang profile was used to stop Latinos for minor driving violations or for some other form of nonviolent behavior to coercively gather intelligence data, while strategically seeking additional funding for presumed gang involvement. Jorge Iber (2000) shows how police officers in Salt Lake City, Utah continued to believe that a Latino-owned tortilla factory was involved in drug distribution despite numerous raids providing counter information, a similar situation occurring in places like Milwaukee, Wisconsin. Yet, Durán (2009b) found that few Latinos filed complaints with police departments, not because of the infrequency of misconduct, but because complaints were consistently regarded by police departments as unsubstantiated or, worse, they were afraid of police retaliation. Essentially, lack of accountability and community protection by police departments led to the development or reorganization of social groups that worked to attain justice for those who were victims of crime. The Latino community also organized groups to protest, provide counter-information, and encourage activism to refute criminal stereotypes.

In Arizona, Cynthia Bejarano (2005) researched a border community where youths reported fear of the Border Patrol due to immigration checks at schools. In fact, children were told to carry birth certificates or face deportation. Among various pressing issues, there were two issues of crucial concern for Latino youths: (1) how being undocumented created a feeling of *no rights* in a supposed democratic country; and (2) how secondary knowledge of English was essential in establishing identity and status. In the words of Bejarano (2005:49), "The mastery of English is profoundly important in claims making and establishing legitimacy in the United States." Bejarano (2005) also found that both Mexicana/o and Mexican Americans along the border were normally seen as noncitizens, with undocumented youths being preoccupied with fears of deportation. In effect, the substantial increase of federal enforcement along the border, and its impact on border communities has been captured by researchers (Álvarez & Urbina, 2018; Andreas, 2003; Dunn, 1996, 2009; Romero, 2006; Salinas, 2015).

Cecilia Menjívar and Cynthia Bejarano (2004:122), for instance, conducted interviews with immigrants from Cuba, El Salvador, Guatemala, and Mexico in Phoenix, Arizona, concluding that "not all immigrants, not even all Latinos, share the same experiences." Their home country influenced perceptions of crime, policing, and socioeconomic status in the United States, conceptualized by the authors as "bifocal lens." For instance, individuals from El Salvador and Guatemala were associated with political violence, Cubans were *defined* as "deserving refugees," and Mexicans were categorized as "illegal aliens" and thus associated with criminality. Such bifocal lens shaped the daily lives of Latinos, especially their *mobility* in the neighborhood, forcing Central Americans and Mexicans into going to great lengths to avoid contacts with the criminal justice system for fear of being detected, arrested, incarcerated, or deported.

Worse, as in other parts of the country, Marjorie Zatz and Edwardo Portillos (2000) found allegations of police use of excessive force, amidst already strained relations between the police and Latino barrios in Phoenix. Then, with several shootings of young men further dividing the community, and, consequently, youths saw themselves as protectors of the neighborhood, and perceiving the police as interlopers (Zatz & Portillos, 2000).

In Texas, David Carter (1983) surveyed a random sample of 500 Latinos, finding that participants felt less safe, perceived police as providing inadequate protection, and they did not believe the police were effective in reducing crime, when compared with the general population. Using the same dataset, Carter (1985) found that Latinos perceived officers to have a "bad attitude," and that officers engaged in discriminatory policing. Malcolm Holmes (1998) conducted phone surveys in El Paso, Texas and found that young Latinos who resided in the barrio were more likely to have seen police abuse. Crucially, El Paso reportedly had a four-to-seven times higher rate of federal civil rights complaints than other cities in the Southwest. John McCluskey, Cynthia Pérez McCluskey, and Roger Enriquez (2008) conducted a telephone survey in San Antonio, Texas to determine community satisfaction with the police. The researchers found San Antonio to be a majority-minority community where Latinos were more supportive of the police than whites. However, consistent with other studies, less acculturated Latinos reported less support for the police, with the level of perceived disorder in the community having the largest impact on whether the police was supported; that is, more disorder, less support for law enforcement. In the city where state laws are defined, Austin, Texas, Ben Chappell (2010) conducted an ethnographic study of Mexican Americans who drove *lowriders*. Similar to police behavior in other parts of the state, despite individuals who drove customized vehicles going to great length to distance themselves from gangs, drugs, and criminality, the police regularly profiled and pulled over these types of cars and trucks, according to the author. In this study, Chappell (2010:30) further stated that the lowrider image carried a barrio association, with corresponding marginalization wherever it went, "Functioning as a flashpoint of ongoing spatial conflicts, lowriders lay bare the processes through which social space is produced and contested, and the relationship of these to the shifting and yet permanently uneven ground of cultural identity." More globally, Chappell (2010) found that police officers were involved in the regulation of public space, and in doing so, served to limit Mexican Americans' position in society.

In reviewing the literature on Latinos and law enforcement, there seems to be some exceptions, though. In a 1997 telephone survey in Odessa and Midland, Texas regarding citizen attitudes' toward law enforcement, Spanish-speaking Latinos reported greater satisfaction, cooperation, and positive attitudes toward the police than whites or English speaking Latinos (Cheurprakobkit, 2000; Cheurprakobkit & Bartsch, 1999). In Reno, Nevada, Mark Correia (2010) found similar results in a phone survey and personal interviews, comparing immigrant and nonimmigrant views of the police. Immigrants reported more favorable attitudes toward police officers, possibly due to little police exposure. In fact, immigrants believed that the police were better prepared, and that they treated people more honestly and fairly than the police in their home country. However, Correia (2010) found that the longer immigrants had lived in the neighborhood, their views of the police became more negative. In all, the

greater the level of exposure to prejudice, discrimination, and encounters with law enforcement, the less positive immigrants became of U.S. law enforcement.

Lastly, Miami, Florida has long held a significant Cuban presence. Roger Dunham and Geoffrey Alpert (1988) studied five neighborhoods of which one contained a high percentage of working to middle-class Cubans who had lived there since the 1960s, a second neighborhood composed of recent Cuban immigrants since 1980, and the other three neighborhoods were black and Anglo. The respondents included high school students, police officers, and county residents, with attitudes toward police practices differing significantly by neighborhood. Of the five neighborhoods, the 1960s Cuban neighborhood viewed police behavior the most positive, followed by whites. Also, while Cubans of both neighborhoods believed the police should primarily control crime, the other neighborhoods disagreed. Cubans gave more support for the use of police discretion, with the more successful Cubans and blacks being against ethnic suspicion.

Midwest and Northeast

In Chicago, which contains a high concentration of Latinos, Felix Padilla (1996:6) found that some Puerto Ricans living in the barrio claimed that "the harassment from the police led many to turn to the gang in search of protection." Describing life in the barrio, one of Padilla's (1996:89) interviewees noted: "There is a war out there; the law has declared war on us. We are targets of abuse from the Chicago police department because they have a license to do what they want. So, if this is how it is going to be, then we have to protect ourselves." In effect, Padilla (1996) found that Latinos were targets of police belittling, and that gang members and nonmembers were often treated very similar, with the police sometimes confiscating drugs for their own use. In a kind of survival situation, gang members reported paying off the police in some cases, according to the author–events and situations that we have been hearing regularly during the last two years (2015-2016), as Chicago has been making national headlines, events recently documented by Nicole Van Cleve in *Crooked County: Racism and Injustice in America's Largest Criminal Court* (2016).

In Missouri, Leigh Culver (2004) examined three neighborhoods, which were newly emergent Latino immigrant communities, using field observations with police, interviews, and focus groups. From Culver's (2004) investigation, four patterns were observed: (1) language barriers, resulting in confusing interactions; (2) fears of the police, due to negative interactions in their home countries; (3) immigration issues, resulting in a nondesire to contact the police due to fear of deportation; and (4) the nature of contacts, the primary method for interaction between the police and the Latino community was through traffic violations, providing an unequal form of interaction to build rapport. In another study, Leigh Herbst and Samuel Walker (2001) used direct observations with police, and they evaluated 911 call centers to determine challenges for serving Latino residents in a Midwestern city. In this particular study, Herbst and Walker (2001) found low levels of interaction and conflict, and that language barriers constituted a small percent of all calls, presenting a minor problem in delivering services.

In New York City, David Brotherton and Luis Barrios (2004) report that among their respondents, they found a generalizable contempt for law enforcement based on negative personal experiences, and widely held views that the role of the police was to protect the white power structure. Brotherton and Barrios (2004) discovered a series of raids against members of a gang who were attempting to reform themselves. In another study, while conducting an ethnographic study in East Harlem, researcher Philippe Bourgois (1995) was repeatedly stopped, searched, cursed, and humiliated by New York City police officers based on the reasoning that there was no reason for a "white" boy to be in the neighborhood unless he was an undercover cop or a drug addict. After five years of researching, Bourgois (1995) found that the hostile attitude by the police did not allow the community the opportunity to reduce drug dealing. In the words of one respondent, "That's terrorism with a badge. That's what that is. The cops look forward to that. They get up in the morning and go. Yeah, Ah'm'a' gonna kick some minority ass today" (Bourgois, 1995:36). In effect, Robert Kane (2002) found that an increase in the Latino population increased police misconduct in New York City from 1975 to 1996. More recently, similar conclusions were reached by Carmen Solís, Edwardo Portillos, and Rod Brunson (2009) in their study of 30 Afro-Caribbean youths (Puerto Ricans and Dominicans) in El Barrio (Spanish Harlem). Reporting that youths claimed differential and aggressive policing, the authors document that the police did not seem to care about Latino communities, or actually wanted to provide the same level of protection to all racial and ethnic groups. In fact, according to the authors, racial profiling, disrespectful treatment, and questions of immigration status were a regular experience for Latinos.

Other studies, using telephone surveys and police data, are consistent with qualitative reports of differential treatment by law enforcement officials in New York City, which like Chicago and Los Angeles, has been making national headlines during the last two years. Michelle Fine, Nick Freudenberg, Yasser Payne, Tiffany Perkins, Kersha

Smith, and Katya Wanzer (2003), for instance, conducted a street survey of 911 New York City urban youths, including 36 in-depth telephone interviews. Here too, Latino youths reported alienation from authority figures and more likely to be picked up in sweeps, with African Caribbean and African American youths expressing more negative attitudes toward the police and security guards within the schools. John Reitzel, Stephen Rice, and Alex Piquero (2004) analyzed telephone poll data conducted by the *New York Times* for New York City residents. Again, Latinos were more likely to report that racial profiling was widespread, and they were more likely than whites to personally have experienced profiling. In another New York City study, Andrew Gelman, Jeffrey Fagan, and Alex Kiss (2007) analyzed 125,000 police stops of pedestrians during a 15-month period, concluding that Latinos and blacks were stopped more often than whites even after controlling for precinct crime variability. Further, the researchers found that stops of whites were more precise in resulting in an arrest whereas stops of Latinos and blacks were broader and less accurate. As for the highly controversial issue of illegal drugs, Andrew Golub, Bruce Johnson, and Eloise Dunlap (2007) reviewed 12 million adult arrests in New York City between 1980 and 2005 to examine disparities involving marijuana smoking in public view. As the most frequent arrest misdemeanor, Latino and black communities were substantially and disproportionately impacted, especially young Latino and black men. More globally, Robin Engel and Richard Johnson (2006) found that despite minority motorists being stopped and searched at higher rates than whites, nationally, minorities were less likely to be found with contraband.

In another study, researchers conducted a focus group in Mount Pleasant, D.C. with men and women from Columbia, Dominican Republic, El Salvador, and Honduras (Hammer & Rogan, 2002). The respondents listed their inability to speak English, and that officers' inability to speak Spanish posed great difficulty in interactions. Therefore, their key strategy when stopped was to deescalate conflict by maintaining good behavior, acting courteous and polite, even in conflicted situations. Finally, given such conflicted situations, Venessa García and Liqun Cao (2005) surveyed residents of a small Northeastern city to determine race and ethnic satisfaction with the police. As in many other places, Latinos had the lowest satisfaction with the police while whites had the highest, a critical situation in that community safety and satisfaction are essential elements for the improvement of race and ethnic relations as well as the development of effective and equitable social control policies.

CURRENT TRENDS IN POLICING: A CALL FOR CHANGE

Two other fundamental trends to the investigation and documentation of Latinos and policing are: (1) the demographics of law enforcement officers; and (2) enhanced federal law enforcement since 9/11 (see Álvarez; Posadas and Medina; Urbina & Álvarez, Chapter 17, this volume). First, sound investigations and documentation on how the demographic composition of law enforcement impacts policing are vital (Urbina & Álvarez, 2015, 2017). Currently, Latinos only comprise 10 percent of all sworn officers. In effect, studies have described a lack of representation of Latinos in the police force (Achor, 1978; Bayley & Mendselsohn, 1968; García, 1981; Pérez, 2001; Vigil, 1999), as recently documented by Urbina and Álvarez in *Latino Police Officers in the United States: An Examination of Emerging Trends and Issues* (2015). Mona Ruiz, for example, provides a vivid biography of how she grew up in the barrio and had to overcome many obstacles, including sexism, to become a police officer (Ruiz & Boucher, 1997). However, while some researchers have found that the inclusion of Latino police officers can make a positive impact (Cheurprakobkit & Bartsch, 1999; Smith & Holmes, 2003), others seem to view structural divisions in society and actual police institutions trumping ethnicity (De Angelis & Kupchik, 2009; Durán, 2015; Holmes, 2000; Vigil, 1999; Wilkins & Williams, 2009), clearly illustrating a need for closer examination of police demographics (see Álvarez & Urbina, Chapter 18; Vera Sanchez, this volume). Second, numerous changes have occurred since 9/11 with federal law enforcement, combined with a wave of anti-immigrant legislation and anti-Latino rhetoric (Álvarez & Urbina, 2018; Johnson, 2005;

Welch, 2006, 2007, 2009). Among the most polemic police trends is the increase in state and local communities attempting to model Arizona's 1070B legislation (see Aguirre; Vera Sanchez, this volume), allowing local police officers to begin enforcing federal immigration laws. Together, these new trends in the U.S. criminal justice system include specific targeting of Latinos with DEA arrests, gang injunctions, mega-prosecutions under the Racketeer Influenced and Corrupt Organizations Act, ICE sweeps, massive deportations, associating Latino gangs with transnational crime or terrorism (Díaz, 2009; Urbina & Kreitzer, 2004), and various demonizing crusades (Hayden, 2005), along with moral panics advocating more policing and mass incarceration (Álvarez & Urbina, 2018; Urbina & Álvarez, 2016, 2017). Again, these modern law enforcement trends attest to the need of a more holistic investigation and documentation of Latinos, and, ultimately, a call for positive social change in law enforcement and society, as documented by Urbina and Álvarez in *Latino Police Officers in the United States: An Examination of Emerging Trends and Issues* (2015).

CONCLUSION

Evidently, the historical relationship between U.S. law enforcement and the Latino community has been uncertain, chaotic, and conflictive. For centuries, abusive and disparate practices have shaped the ethnic experience, and our beliefs of whether "equality and justice" can be accomplished in this country. The barrios, especially Mexican barrios, have borne the brunt force of policing efforts, normally justified with ethnic stereotypes of "criminal" or "illegal," and legitimized by various high ranking government officials and some academic racists (see Urbina & Álvarez, Chapter 17, this volume).

More globally, when such terms are generalized to the entire Latino community, they fail to represent the actual realities of crime and justice, but, instead, turn residents into outlaws. Ultimately, these redefined and legitimized elements become mechanisms for maintaining colonial-type social control, *recreating a system of gringo justice,* in the twenty-first century—beginning with policing, the frontline agents of the criminal justice system.

Beyond law enforcement, mainstream society, for various reasons, has failed to socially, economically, and politically challenge certain inequalities, and, instead, many tend to join the bandwagon for aggressive enforcement against presumed enemies. Still, barrios across the country remain the heart of grassroots resistance, sometimes changing the political advocacy of the past, while continuing to develop future leaders who will speak up not only for Latino residents, but everyone who is fighting to avoid being kept under the shadows, intimidated, oppressed, and silenced. Logically, the structural inequalities facing residents living in the barrios differ from those living in the suburbs or gentrified high-rise apartments, by what Karl Marx (1852:1) identified as "Men make their own history, but they do not make it as they please; they do not make it under self-selected circumstances, but under circumstances existing already, given and transmitted from the past. The tradition of all dead generations weighs like a nightmare on the brains of the living." As such, as in the past, today, and tomorrow, the leaders of the Latino community will face tremendous obstacles debunking stereotypical images, clouding the minds of some government officials, law enforcement, academics, and society as a whole.

Chapter 4

CRITICAL ISSUES FACING HISPANIC DEFENDANTS: FROM DETECTION TO ARREST

MARY ROMERO AND GABRIELLA SÁNCHEZ

Men make their own history, but they do not make it as they please; they do not make it under self-selected circumstances, but under circumstances existing already, given and transmitted from the past. The tradition of all dead generations weighs like a nightmare on the brains of the living.

–Karl Marx

The process, from detection to arrest, for administrative violations, criminal offenses, or detention, is assumed, theoretically, to follow the same guidelines. In particular, to protect Fourth Amendment rights, police officers are expected to establish probable cause and reasonable suspicion prior to stopping suspects (see Mirandé, Chapter 9, this volume). With the objective of ensuring efficiency, while securing public safety, police officers can then use discretion in giving warnings, issuing citations, or making arrests. While the anti-immigrants sentiment has been exacerbating under the Trump administration, even officers working in agencies with 287(g) agreements in place can use discretion in inquiring about an individual's citizenship status. Depending on the person's *legal status* and the reasons for the arrest, some people may be immediately released after they are booked and pay bail (if they can afford it), while others, particularly those unable to establish the legal right to be in the country, may face indefinite detention in immigration facilities, federal prisons, state prisons, or private prisons—a situation that is becoming more complicated and consequential with Trump's punitive social control policies. This chapter ties various issues raised in the previous three chapters, while expanding the examination of pressing disparities in law enforcement, the ramifications of landmark Supreme Court cases, and the consequences of ethnic profiling on Latinos, especially in the war against drugs, the war against terrorism, and, more recently, the war on immigrants.

Seeking to place the Latino experience with law enforcement within a broader framework, and thus better understanding the ethnic-police relationship in its totality, we begin our discussion with an overview of specific landmark cases and legislation impacting the process of detecting and arresting Latinos in the United States. Having laid the foundation of the legal structure that establishes guidelines for arrest and detention, we then present legal and social science research findings on law enforcement practices, discrepancies occurring in Latino-police encounters, and conceptual frameworks that identify the ways Latinos are placed in *harm's way of the law,* a process that actually involves various decision-points, from detection to arrest, and, ultimately, the judicial and penal systems.

LANDMARK SUPREME COURT CASES AND CURRENT LEGISLATION

Understanding the practicality of legal decisions requires insight into the dynamics of U.S. jurisprudence, particularly legal cases that directly, or indirectly, influence the experience of minorities in their encounters with the police. Probably the most infamous Supreme Court cases involving U.S. law and Latinos, which changed the way in which all arrests are now made, is *Miranda v. Arizona* (1966). The case is based on the 1963 arrest of Ernesto Arturo Miranda, which was based on circumstantial evidence connecting him to kidnapping and rape. Miranda was interrogated for two hours without being informed of his rights, and he eventually signed a typed prepared statement claiming: "I do hereby swear that I make this statement voluntarily and on my own free will, with no threats, coercion, or promises of immunity, and with full knowledge of my legal rights, understanding any statement I make may be used against me." The Supreme Court ruling in *Miranda,* based on the Fifth Amendment privilege against self-incrimination, demanded that defendants in police custody must be informed of their right to remain silent and their right to consult an attorney. As such, the "Miranda warning" serves to inform or remind individuals of their constitutional rights. Since then, officers are required to advise suspects interrogated in custody of their right to remain silent and to obtain an attorney. However, subsequent rulings challenging aspects of the original case include statements given without police questioning or police action invoking an incriminating response; that is, statements signifying the meaning of "knowing, intelligent, and voluntary," corresponding with the need for public safety, and thus informally waving the *Miranda* rights. Therefore, as indicated in *Harris v. New York* (1971) and *Rhode Island v. Innis* (1980), statements made prior to being informed of the *Miranda* rights may be used in the defendants' trial. Under a recent case, if suspects under police custody acknowledge that they understand these rights, but the defendants do not explicitly invoke or waive their rights, the acknowledgment may be interpreted as waiving the *Miranda* rights, the Supreme Court ruled in *Berghuis v. Thompkins* (2010).

More directly, from a judicial standpoint, several significant Supreme Court cases succeeding *Miranda v. Arizona* have eroded Latinos' Fourth Amendment rights (see Mirandé, Chapter 9, this volume). In effect, contrary to the presumed color blindness of U.S. laws, in *United States v. Brignoni-Ponce* (1975) the Supreme Court ruled that the Fourth Amendment allows police officers to use "Mexican appearance" as a legitimate consideration when making an immigration stop or questioning people about their citizenship or immigration status as long as racial profiling is not the sole factor. Then, in *United States v. Martínez-Fuerte* (1976), the Supreme Court ruled that the Fourth Amendment was not violated by the Border Patrol when routinely stopping vehicles at checkpoints, relying largely on the basis of the occupants' appearance of Mexican ancestry (Sullivan, 2008). Further, *Martínez-Fuerte* (1976) allowed for the operation of a fixed police checkpoint without the authorization of a judicial warrant. Though, while *United States v. Montero Camargo* (2000) finally identified the harm of profiling people simply on the basis of their appearance (Aguirre, 2004), with demographics in the Southwestern United States being noted and the Court concluding that race should not be used in investigatory stops, it was almost wholly circumscribed a few years earlier by the *Whren v. United States* (1996) decision to include any traffic offense as "legally" sanctioned (Hlawati, 2001; Ramírez, Hoopes, & Quinlan, 2003).

More politically, symbolically, and ideologically than pragmatically, towards the end of the twentieth century, the passage of the 1996 Anti-Terrorism and Effective Death Penalty Act (AEDPA) and the 1996 Illegal Immigration Reform and Immigrant Responsibility ACT (IIRIR) allowed for the detention by immigration authorities of immigrants who in the past had committed crimes that were considered under the new legislation as aggravated felonies, in many cases years after their sentences have been fulfilled. As such, the broadening of the laws transformed offenses like driving under the influence of alcohol or check theft into aggravated crimes (Álvarez & Urbina, 2018; Human Rights Watch, 2007; LaBrie, 1999; Rah, 2001). Then, early in the twenty-first century, with George W. Bush taking over as President of the United States, the September 11, 2001 terrorist attacks on the United States quickly led to a sudden approval of racial and ethnic profiling as a *presumed sacrifice* of civil liberties in order to achieve greater security (Ramírez et al., 2003). Under the name of national security, the establishment

of the U.S.A. PATRIOT Act, the Homeland Security Act (HSA), and the Enhanced Border Security and Visa Entry Reform Act (EBSVERA) combined immigration and criminal law enforcement, obscuring the difference between immigrants, criminals, and terrorists:

> criminal aliens (deportable for their post-entry criminal conduct), illegal aliens (deportable for their surreptitious crossing of the US border), and terrorists (deportable for the grave risk they pose to national security) are all deemed dangerous foreigners for whom criminally punitive treatment and removal are uniformly appropriate and urgently necessary. (Miller, 2005:113)

Under this new movement, immigration enforcement transitioned to aggressively secure the border with Mexico. Strategically, after the passage of the U.S. PATRIOT Act, and largely as a result of unfounded intelligence reports, U.S. authorities expressed concern over the possible entrance of terrorist groups through the Mexican border (Álvarez & Urbina, 2018; Bowers, 2005; Kaye, 2006), with, arguably, the assistance of other presumed anti-American groups, human smuggling gangs, spearheaded by Mexican drug trackers. Crucially, even though such statements were later dismissed, *the punitive tone was set in motion*, with a strong feeling of hate, vindictiveness, and retaliation against certain racial and ethnic minorities. In fact, in the midst of then President George W. Bush's push for immigration reform in 2004 (Hing, 2009), Immigration and Customs Enforcement (ICE) began to engage in work-site raids as well as targeting families in private residents without warrants, unannounced, and at predawn (Álvarez & Urbina, 2018; Lochner, 2007; Lum, 2007; Martínez, 2007). Together, this redefined social control war has resulted in numerous immigration operations, such as Operation

Send Back to Sender (2006), Operation Scheduled Departure (2008), Operation Streamline (2010), and Operation Endgame (2003–2012). Logically, combining the enforcement of immigration and criminal law increased the level of police force, having critical implications for policing and the community (Álvarez & Urbina, 2018; Shahani & Greene, 2009).

While in the past, the conditions of *United States v. Brignoni-Ponce* (1975) only applied to the U.S. Border Patrol, the addition of the 287(g) statute to the Immigration and Nationality Act under the then President William J. Clinton administration (1993–2001) extended the same powers to local law enforcement agencies through the signing of Memorandums of Agreements, or MOA's (ICE, 2008). The new section authorized ICE to enter into agreements with state and local law enforcement agencies to engage in immigration law enforcement. As such, by signing a Memorandum of Agreement, local law enforcement agencies allow for the training and deputizing of their officers to enforce immigration law during their regular law enforcement duties. For immigration officers, like local policing, ICE officers have discretionary power to determine who is released from detention and the conditions of the release, like the amount of the bond to be paid (Amnesty International, 2009).

Once suspects are identified by ICE, or, in the case of 287(g) participating agencies, by the agency itself, as unauthorized to be in the U.S., officers can initiate the process of immigration detention by placing what is known as an immigration hold on detainees, considered of administrative rather than criminal nature. If arrested, the defendants' criminal charges, if any, are processed first. If the investigation into the commission of criminal acts is completed without charges being filed, individuals with a hold are then transported to ICE to handle issues emerg-

ing from their immigration status. Once individuals are placed in immigration detention, they remain detained until adjudication, determination of status by adjudicator, or an immigration hearing before a judge takes place. However, the time frame from the time people are detained to the time they go before an immigration judge in federal court varies, adding more uncertainty to an already complicated and uncertain process. Legal scholars, researchers, and immigrant advocates have documented that the process, which can go for hours, days, months, or even years is indeed arbitrary (Álvarez & Urbina, 2018; Ashar, 2002; LaBrie, 1999), and thus consequential, placing the legitimacy of U.S. immigration law in question.

If immigrants are sent to a county jail, housing is normally determined on the basis of individuals' perceived risk, which is generally assessed on the basis of prior criminal history, nature of charges, mental health issues, physical health, and past drug or alcohol use (James, 1998). Contrary to the popular imagination, though, most people detained for immigration-related offenses have no criminal record or evidence of a violent past, as recently documented by Álvarez and Urbina in *Immigration and the Law: Race, Citizenship, and Social Control* (2018). Yet, detainees facing immigration charges, which are of administrative nature, are often housed alongside those facing criminal charges, sometimes a devastating experience for immigrant children (Álvarez & Urbina, 2018; Salinas, 2015; see Posadas & Medina, this volume).

Immigration court hearings to determine asylum, deportation, or other action are conducted by an immigration judge at federal courts throughout the country, sometimes in remote places, resulting in massive detentions and backlogs, along, of course, with deportations and incarcerations. While some hearings are collective, particularly those where large groups of people involve voluntary departure, some cases involve individual hearings, increasing the detention term for some individuals. Further, some immigrants potentially face criminal charges at the federal level if it is determined that their presence in the country is a result of reentry, as cited in the *reentry of removed aliens* code (8 USC §1326), resulting in thousands of immigrants being incarcerated throughout the country (Álvarez & Urbina, 2018; Urbina & Álvarez, 2017). Once immigrants have completed their sentences, and they are no longer facing additional charges, they are usually

deported to their country of origin, if their country is willing to take them back.

The common practice is to transport immigrants by land or air to a U.S. border to be released, but individuals labeled as violent or dangerous, including juveniles with documented ties to gangs and those with alleged terrorist ties are escorted by immigration agents and flown to their country of origin, or to a country from where they can then be transported or escorted by other authorities to their country of origin, or a country that will accept them.

U.S. POLICING PRACTICES: FROM DETECTION TO ARREST

A critical examination of the policing process, from detection to arrest, is essential in identifying law enforcement practices and immigration legislation that contribute to prejudice, differential treatment, discrimination, intimidation, violence, or profiling in policing, and, by extension, the judicial and penal systems. As noted in the beginning of this chapter, the process from detection to arrest is assumed to follow the same guidelines across all racial and ethnic groups. In truth, the ethnic experience is largely governed by diverse circumstances, which are influenced by issues like citizenship, poverty, lack of healthcare, and educational attainment, as documented by Urbina and Álvarez in *Ethnicity and Criminal Justice in the Era of Mass Incarceration: A Critical Reader on the Latino Experience* (2017). Considering that the majority of people in prison are there for drug-related offenses, obvious inequities include the historical legacy of oppression, injustice, lack of opportunity Latino drug addicts encounter entering rehabilitation centers or when seeking to receive medical assistance for drug-related conditions.

Instead, like drug distribution, drug use by Latinos tends to be criminalized (Walker, Senger, Villarruel, & Arboleda, 2004). Historical stereotypes as well as racial and ethnic profiling, which attribute to the development of criminal laws, continue to be embedded in police practice, making Latinos a target of criminal laws, as illustrated by the uneven police hyper-surveillance between racial and ethnic neighborhoods, especially in low-income residential areas, placing minorities in police view for detection and subsequently arrest, indictment, prosecution, and imprisonment (Chambliss, 1999; Salinas, 2015; Urbina & Álvarez, 2015, 2016, 2017). Practically, racial and ethnic profiling operates within and outside these geographical areas; that is, functioning to limit Latino use of public and private space by creating profiles, and thus categorizing residents as to who belong and who does not belong in certain areas. Latinos, particularly the working poor and lower-middle classes, are targeted by the combination of so-called social control wars, like the war against crime, the war against drugs, the war against gangs, and the

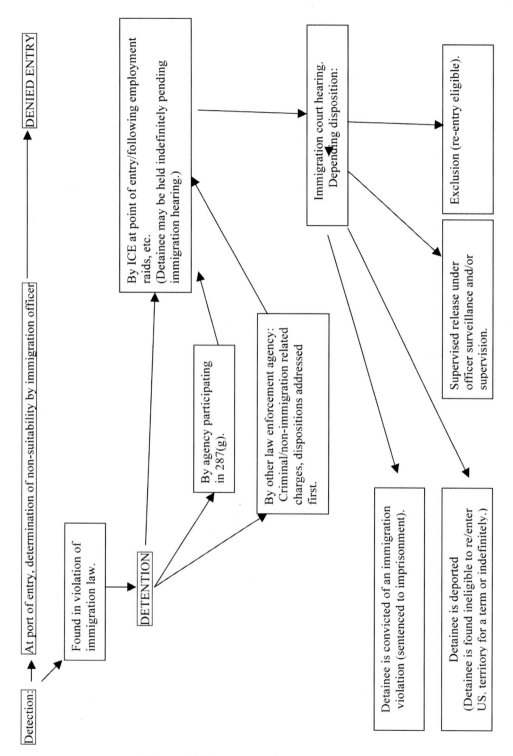

Figure 4.1. Immigration Detention Process.

war against terrorism, which have incorporated immigration law enforcement and local policing (Álvarez & Urbina, 2018; Urbina & Álvarez, 2017; Walker et al., 2004). In the process of fighting these various "wars," local police and highway patrol agencies, as well as immigration agencies, have become highly militarized (Álvarez & Urbina, 2018; Martinot, 2003; Urbina & Peña, 2018). Unfortunately, police training focusing on the use of force rather than community policing, including training on diversity, culture, language, and communication, have created hostile relationships between the police and Latino communities (Urbina & Álvarez, 2015). In all, as an ethnic minority group, Latinos are more likely to experience excessive force and brutality in police encounters, and subsequently have their civil and human rights violated (Salinas, 2015, 2018). Given the highly popularized racial and ethnic stereotypes in the U.S. media (Berg, 2014; Delgado, 2018), police officers are more likely to use excessive force on Latinos, including juveniles, vis-à-vis middle-class whites (Morín, 2009; Salinas, 2015; Urbina & Álvarez, 2015). In short, from detection to arrest, law enforcement officers operate with enormous discretionary powers that have completely different consequences for different racial and ethnic groups in the United States, as highlighted in the following section.

Racial and Ethnic Profiling in Law Enforcement

In these various social control wars, the Latino community is assumed to be implicated, and therefore police use racial and ethnic profiling with great autonomy in their aggressive anti-crime movement, with almost total immunity (Salinas, 2015; Urbina & Álvarez, 2015; see Crawford, this volume).

As reported by David Harris (2003:224), "Police can use color as evidence of criminal involvement, even without any other evidence that points in that direction. This means, in clear and unequivocal terms, that *skin color itself has been criminalized.*" Obviously, racial and ethnic profiling physically marks racialized Latinos as undocumented immigrants or criminal suspects, with socioeconomic status, culture, and language further fusing the *color line.* At the turn of the century, as targets in the war on drugs and even terrorism, police officers have relied on the Drug Enforcement Administration's (DEA) profiles, which include point to point driving, nervous body language, and rented cars (Ramírez et al., 2003), responding with qualifiers such as "not that I know of," owner of vehicle not present, occupants in a car considered mismatched (like a Hispanic male and a white female), car windows not fully opened, and the presence of fast food wrappers, hand tools, cell phones, pagers, receipts, or maps in a vehicle (Getlin, 2001). Crucially, while the same clothing or haircuts, for example, can be replicated by middle-class youth, this same practice by Latinos can be viewed as indicators of gang affiliation, resulting in detection and possibly arrest. In effect, the widely publicized case of New Jersey State Troopers racially profiling blacks and Latinos as drug carriers in the 1990s resulted in a drastic increase in arrests, prosecutions, and convictions, prompting several academic investigations (Lange, Johnson, & Voas, 2005), and most recently Trump has characterized Mexicans and Latinos in general as illegals, criminals, and terrorists–in his words, "bad hombres." Together, studies show that profiles of criminal activity are racially and ethnically constructed and strategically applied to place Latinos, particularly young men, in harm's way of U.S. laws (Álvarez & Urbina, 2018;

Morín, 2009; Salinas, 2015; Urbina & Álvarez, 2017). As such, although there is no clear evidence that Latinos use more drugs than other groups, they are more likely to be arrested for drug-related offenses.

Studies show, including a report by the U.S. Commission on Civil Rights, that racial profiling by law enforcement agents is actually a major problem (Mucchetti, 2005; Serpa, 2000), with policing being extremely notorious for racial profiling in the detection and enforcement of drug and gang control laws (Harris, 2003; Morín, 2009; Urbina & Álvarez, 2015). In essence, as in the well documented case of "driving while Black," "driving while Brown" is yet another reference to "unwritten violation[s] in the state's traffic code" (Mucchetti, 2005; Skolnick & Caplovitz, 2001:418). Once detected, similar to African Americans, while regulations specifying the conditions of detection are based on the Fourth Amendment, Latinos do not receive the same protection against unreasonable search and seizure, in part because the legal mechanisms in place allow racial and ethnic profiling practices (see Mirandé, Chapter 9, this volume). Beyond traffic, searches, and seizures, racial and ethnic profiling is used in pedestrian stops and workplace raids, along with "dragnet" tactics used by local police, county sheriffs, border patrol, and ICE. Further, along with these patrol methods, zero tolerance tactics are used to control movement and behavior by restricting the use of public areas, such as sidewalks, parks, and beaches. As a strategy for intimidation, oppression, and control, repressive policing characterizes the zero tolerance approach of law enforcement that includes stop and frisk campaigns. Worse, along with the "stop and frisk" tactics are the street sweeps that are considered to be brutal and militaristic (Álvarez & Urbina, 2018; Durán, 2009a, 2009b, 2009c; Robinson,

2002; Starr & Fernández, 2009; Urbina & Peña, 2018). Strategically, using these tactics involve much lower standards for probable cause and thus pretextual stops, stop and frisk, and sweeps have become a common practice (Álvarez & Urbina, 2018; Morín, 2009; Salinas, 2015), instilling fear in the Latino community, and, worse, resulting in hostile and fragile community relations (Chávez, 2013; Urbina & Álvarez, 2017; Walker et al., 2004). In effect, legal scholars have demonstrated that the *reasonable man* standard continues to be biased toward white, middle-class heterosexual men (Kaplan, 2009a, 2009b; Salinas, 2015; Urbina & Álvarez, 2017).

In sum, legal scholars (Harris, 1999; Johnson, 2000; Mucchetti, 2005; Salinas, 2015) and social scientists (Adler, 2006; Álvarez & Urbina, 2018; Heyman, 2001; Lugo, 2008; Urbina & Álvarez, 2015, 2017) report that ethnic and racial profiling in both local policing and immigration has indeed been rationalized and legitimized by high ranking law enforcement and government officials as well as some academic scholars; that is, intellectual racists. For example, impoverished and working-class racialized Latinos are likely to receive more police scrutiny based on their clothing, the year and make of the vehicle they drive, and the stores and restaurants they go to. As such, the discretionary use of stopping drivers for minor violations places racialized Latinos, particularly low-income people, in harm's way of immigration and criminal laws. In short, the determination of probable cause and reasonable suspicion are not racial, class, or ethnically neutral (see Vera Sanchez, this volume), but, on the contrary, often marked by prejudice, systemic racism, constant harassment, brutality, violations of civil, statutory, and constitutional rights, and institutionalized discrimination.

Abuse and Brutality in Policing

Once ethnic and racial profiling is institutionalized as a mechanism for police operations, police abuse and brutality become viewed and rationalized as a "necessary approach" to law and order, overshadowing social interactions between the police and low-income Latinos, particularly Latino youth who are frequently characterized as gang members or drug dealers (Durán, 2009a, 2009b, 2009c, 2013; Ríos, 2011; Tapia, 2017; Urbina & Kreitzer, 2004; see also Crawford, this volume). Consequently, Latino families are sometimes forced to alter their way of living to cope with redefined expectations and social conditions. For instance, parents frequently respond to the threat of police violence toward their sons, or daughters, by instructing their children about keeping both hands on the steering wheel at all times, to not move without asking permission, to avoid driving in certain neighborhoods, and to not wear particular colors that might be interpreted as gang affiliation (Durán, 2013; Lee, 1997; Tapia, 2017). As noted herein, when a stop is made, the encounter between the police and the suspect is determined by the police's use of discretionary behavior, which can range from a polite verbal exchange to a brutal encounter, possibly death (Urbina & Álvarez, 2015). Police use of discretion, for instance, includes their tone of speech, gestures, posture, giving a warning, issuing a citation, or making an arrest (Morín & del Valle, 1990; Urbina & Álvarez, 2015). While the degree of force used in making arrests varies, studies consistently find that cases of police misconduct or brutality are higher for Latinos than whites (Amnesty International, 1998; Durán, 2013; Human Rights Watch, 1998; Ríos, 2013; Salinas, 2015; Urbina & Álvarez, 2015). As reported earlier, like African American men, Latinos are frequently characterized as gang members or drug dealers and thus potential criminals (Durán, 2009a, 2009b, 2009c; Romero, 2001; Roy, 2009; Starr & Fernández, 2009). As such, low-income Latino youths have been demonized as super-predators, which in turn *rationalize* and *legitimize* state violence carried out under the so-called war on drugs and gangs (Chávez, 2013; Corcoran, 2006; Tapia, 2017). Investigating the determinants of deadly force, David Jacobs and Robert O'Brien (1998:837) concluded, "Political or threat explanations for the state's use of internal violence suggest that killings committed by the police should be greatest in stratified jurisdictions with more minorities," a situation that extends into the twenty-first century, as documented by Victor Ríos in *Punished: Policing the Lives of Black and Latino Boys* (2011), Robert Durán in *Gang Life in Two Cities: An Insider's Journey* (2013), and Michael Tapia in *The Barrio Gangs of San Antonio, 1915–2015* (2017).

Beyond local policing, complaints against abuses committed by immigration officers highlight the institutionalization of abuse within the agency, as acts of violence committed during the detention of undocumented immigrants are often described by its administration officials as "procedural problems" and not violence or brutality (Bosworth & Flavin, 2007; Rosenbaum, 1994:1; Welch, 2006), giving police officers almost total immunity from accountability. Not surprisingly, documented abuses against Latinos by immigration authorities, which include verbal and psychological abuse, inappropriate and illegal searches, beatings, sexual assaults, and shootings, have further escalated as a result of the war on drugs, immigrants, and terrorism (Álvarez & Urbina, 2018; Rosembaum, 1994; Salinas, 2015; Urbina & Álvarez, 2017). In fact, in June of 2010, the shooting of Sergio Hernández Güereca by a Border Patrol officer in Mexican territory was *justified* by the agency as "self defense," and characterized as a response to the use of force by Hernández (a 14-year-old) and his friends, who arguably were throwing rocks to the officers. Investigations, though, showed that the Border Patrol officer shot at the teenager at least twice, killing the teenager (Reuters, 2010).

Beyond the drastic and, at times, grave impact on individual defendants, the most detrimental impact falls on the most disadvantaged, children, especially the children of undocumented immigrants (Álvarez & Urbina, 2018; National Council of La Raza and The Urban Institute, 2007; Salinas, 2015). In fact, while children of immigrants tend to be U.S. citizens, immigration raids result in children being separated from their parents, experiencing the emotional impact of witnessing their parents being taken into custody, and children are often forced to wait with their parents, during the processing, in prison-like environments (Álvarez & Urbina, 2018; Hing, 2009; National Council of La Raza and The Urban Institute, 2007; Romero, 2008a; Romero & Serag, 2005; Salinas, 2015; Schmall, 2009). An illustration of the implementation of 287(g) raids at predominantly Latino neighborhoods, for example, is the case of Ciria López Pacheco, an undocumented mother of two U.S.-born children. In January of 2009, Pacheco was stopped at nighttime during a crime suppression raid in the town of El Mirage, Arizona for failing to turn her car lights on. A 287(g) officer working with the Maricopa County Sheriff's Office approached her vehicle while wearing a ski mask. López' children started crying, afraid of the masked officer. A records check revealed that López had an outstanding ticket warrant from 2006. In the meantime, the children were asked repeatedly by the officer to be quiet. López was taken into custody, and the children were left in the care of an officer until a neigh-

bor picked them up. While the warrant was eventually dismissed, López remained in custody for several weeks, pending her immigration hearing (*New York Times,* 2009), truly revealing the fear, chaos, and uncertainty not only for the defendant, but, more crucially, their children. Ironically, under Trump's policies, including his travel bans, immigration raids, arrests, incarceration, and deportations, these types of situations have become more consequential, even for those who are supposed to be protected, like the Dreamers.

The Dynamics of Police Discretion

Discretionary enforcement allows police officers to selectively decide their methods of operation, like which individuals to "stop and frisk" or which violations warrant a stop, depending, of course, on geographical area, socioeconomic class of the area, or racial-ethnic composition of the area. Beyond the areas to patrol and the frequency of patrol, police officers have the absolute powers as to which vehicles to pull over. For instance, procedurally, a stop might involve not coming to a complete stop at a stop sign, loitering, or the failure to use a signal before turning; yet, these actions do not always result in a stop. In all, across the country, studies show that Latinos are more likely to be stopped for traffic violations relative to whites (Morín, 2009; Mucchetti, 2005; Salinas, 2015). When stopped, Latinos are more likely to be cited or arrested in comparison to whites (Morín, 2009; Salinas, 2015; Walker et al., 2004). Further, while police officers seldom enforce serious violations in certain areas, like upper-scale neighborhoods (not to mention gated-communities), numerous reports demonstrate that police officers tend to enforce minor violations in low-income and minority communities (Milovanovic & Russell, 2001; Urbina & Álvarez, 2015).

In the case of immigrants, discretionary power enables immigration law enforcement officers the ability to operate with wide discretion and almost total immunity from accountability, shaping not only the procedural experience but also final outcomes (Álvarez & Urbina, 2018; Salinas, 2015). When an individual's immigration detention involves only civil violations, for example, ICE is not obligated to provide access to legal counsel, as in criminal offenses; and thus individuals in deportation proceedings have the "privilege" to secure legal counsel, but at no expense to the government (Álvarez & Urbina, 2018; Amnesty International, 2009). While detainees are sometimes given a list of legal organizations that handle immigration cases, the information provided may be invalid, expired, or unavailable. Consequently, most detainees in immigration detention attend immigration court without an immigration attorney. Once in court, immigration judges have the discretion of determining the amount of bond as well as denying immigrants to be released on bail. As such, Latino immigrants are detained for long periods of time, while seeking to avoid deportation or simply being deported (Álvarez & Urbina, 2018). In a 2009 report, "Jailed without Justice: Immigration Detention in the USA," Amnesty International found that judicial reviews and affordable bonds are being denied, revealing that the use of mandatory detention is arbitrary and, in many cases, in violation of international laws (Salinas, 2018).

While logistically, it is easier to transport detainees to the nearest ICE detention centers, the decision to house immigrants at specific locations while in immigration custody does not always follow specific rules or the most logical choices. This discretion results in detainees being held in locations hundreds or even thousands of miles away from their place of residence, where their young children might be attending school. For example, during the ICE raids at meat packing plants in 2008, detainees from Colorado and Nebraska were transported to Camp Dodge in Iowa, a military base run by the National Guard (Hing, 2009). Then, as if the situation was not complicated enough for family and friends of detainees, the locations of immigration facilities were not publicly released, and there were no permanent depositories of immigration detention information. That is, there was no system in place that would allow relatives to find out the whereabouts of people in immigration facilities. In effect, various sources report that the detention policies resulted in extreme hardship for families, particularly the separation of parents and children (Human Rights Watch, 2007; Salinas, 2015, 2018). In fact, children and spouses were unable to locate family members detained, and thus they had no way of contacting them or providing any kind of assistance. Parents detained feared that they would lose custody of their children if their presence in the United States became known to authorities. In communities where local law enforcement agencies have a 287(g) agreement in place, immigration detainees are kept in local jails, since the agency in charge is authorized to enforce immigration law, which can be a lengthy process until the time the detainees go to court to determine their immigration status, and right to be in the country is determined. Lastly, as an additional barrier in the already complicated and uncertain process, visitation policies may prohibit undocumented immigrants from contacting their relatives while in detention, as they may also face arrest, as in the case of Maricopa County, Arizona (MCSO, 2007).

Violation of Statutory, Constitutional, or International Rights

At the very essence of freedom and democracy, Latinos have historically faced powerful barriers in protecting their basic rights (Salinas, 2018). In the area of law enforcement, unfamiliar with legal protections, like the *Miranda* rule, Latinos do not always fully understand their rights (Romero & Serag, 2005; Urbina, 2004a; Urbina & Álvarez, 2015, 2017), particularly the process for obtaining state appointed counsel (Urbina, 2012; see also Urbina, this volume). In ethnic communities experiencing adverse police relations or when they are being targets of drug or immigration raids using excessive force, encounters and arrests are likely to be intimidating and brutal, sometimes resulting in violation of rights (Álvarez & Urbina, 2018; Durán, 2013; Ríos, 2011; Salinas, 2015, 2018). Under these circumstances, people may be overly cooperative without comprehending the nature of self-incrimination, or they may feel forced into giving or signing a confession. In the case of immigrants and first generation Latinos, they may have limited English-speaking (and reading and writing) abilities that allow them to respond to simple questions, but they are actually unable to truly comprehend the *Miranda* warning (*United States v. Garibay,* 1998), the formal documents, or other constitutional or international rights. Further, monolingual English-speaking police officers are unable to communicate with sole Spanish-speaking suspects, and bilingual officers may not be adequately fluent to speak clearly or fully comprehend regional dialects or localism (Urbina & Álvarez, 2015). Yet, throughout the criminal justice system, Latinos with limited English proficiency encounter the lack of interpreter assistance (Urbina, 2004a), which heightens the level of fear in dealing with police officers, making the criminal justice system somewhat incomprehensible (Lazos Vargas, 2002; Urbina & Álvarez, 2015, 2017; Walker et al., 2004). Together, the lack of adequate interpreters throughout the entire police process (and the judicial process), including the ability to correctly interpret Spanish-speaking 911 calls, threatens the protection of *Miranda* rights for monolingual Spanish-speaking Latinos.

Analyzing the ethnic experience in its totality reveals that, unlike whites and blacks, Latinos are confronted by a mixture of powerful intertwining forces, like skin color, language, accent, citizenship, and culture. Therefore, in targeting people in immigration operations by identifying *Mexican appearance* (see Aguirre, this volume), the assessment of probable cause and reasonable suspicion is legally and morally questionable (see Mirandé, Chapter 9, this volume). Unlike whites who could be from so many different countries, and, possibly, undocumented but able to blend in, skin complexion and other physical characteristics are constructed as representing citizenship status for Latinos. Critically, combined with physical characteristics, class, or cultural attributes, such as Spanish-speaking, speaking English with an accent, or style of dress (Benítez, 1994; Vargas, 2001), occupation and geographical space also shapes the everyday experience for ethnic minorities (Salinas, 2015; Urbina & Álvarez, 2015, 2017). For instance, to quickly capture socioeconomic status, and thus the level of money, social standing, prestige, and power, the opening question by customs agents when people are entering the United States and by local police officers (and even state police officers) tends to be: "What's your occupation?" The reply, straightaway, *sets the tone* for what will transpire, for both process and final outcomes.

Geographically, shopping in areas catering to customers seeking Latino goods, foods, or cultural events also place racialized Latinos at higher risk of being detected and stopped than those identified as white. Consequently, characteristics signifying *Mexicans* place Latinos at a disadvantaged or at risk before U.S. law enforcement agents (Álvarez & Urbina, 2018; Goldsmith & Romero, 2008; Goldsmith, Romero, Rubio-Goldsmith, Escobedo, & Khoury, 2009; Salinas, 2015). An investigation of employment site raids conducted by ICE between 2007 and 2008 reveals that most operations were conducted at businesses known for their reliance on immigrant workers, such as construction and restaurant industries (Salinas, 2015; Schmall, 2009). During a raid in a meat packing plant in Iowa, for instance, workers were separated in two lines, and asked to identify themselves as documented or undocumented. Several people were ordered to move to the "undocumented" line because they "have Mexican teeth" (Hing, 2009:2). Invariably, these raids have resulted in the detention of thousands of U.S. citizens of Latino origin and violations of civil rights (Hing, 2009; Salinas, 2015, 2018), as similar trend that is quickly unfolding under the Trump administration, with hundreds of immigrants being detained, arrested, incarcerated, or deported (Álvarez & Urbina, 2018). As such, targeting neighborhoods and shopping areas by race and ethnicity, equates citizenship with whiteness, and assumes that citizens and immigrants do not reside in the same communities (Álvarez & Urbina, 2018; Romero, 2006, 2008b).

Conditions of Correctional Detention

Once Latinos are detected and arrested, they must then experience the complicated, lengthy, and uncertain judicial process, if indicted by the grand jury or charged by the prosecutor, as detailed in the following section of this book. For individuals indicted, prosecuted, convicted, and sentenced to jail or prison, they must then experience the realities of life behind bars, as reported in Section Three of this book. In the case of immigrants, detainees may experience lengthy or unspecified periods of confinement in immigration facilities or local jails, sometimes under truly oppressive conditions. In a study, Amnesty International (2009) identified numerous detention centers that neither met international human rights standards, or the guidelines established by ICE. For instance, while in detention, people are poorly fed, allow to shower only if the detention center has water (usually cold) installations in place, and often not given enough blankets to cover at night in extremely cold buildings. Further, even though detainees may have access to basic medical service by placing "sick call" slips or "tank orders," which they must complete describing their medical needs before orders are reviewed by a nurse to determine if detainees are in need of medical attention (Human Rights Watch, 2009:28). The process can be complicated. The forms, for example, must be completed in English, a language the majority of immigration detainees do not speak, let alone read or write. In fact, since some detainees are illiterate and therefore not quite able to describe their symptoms, medical conditions often go untreated. Actually, even if basic medical services are available, proper treatment is normally not provided. For instance, medical services are usually given to detainees with signs of chronic emotional distress, determined by psychiatrists who may or may not be competent or full-time employees at the facilities. As such, there are reports of widespread prescription of anti-depressants and tranquilizers to temporarily address mental health issues like anxiety and severe depression. Worse, detainees constantly report intimidation by detention officers, who "downplay" their condition or who mistreat them if they request medical care (Álvarez & Urbina, 2018; Human Rights Watch, 2009; Salinas, 2015), ending up being abused, neglected, and untreated, while their medical condition worsens.

In truth, contrary to *conventional wisdom* that detainees housed in immigration facilities or other correctional facilities might not be receiving the best medical attention but indeed receiving *adequate* treatment, immigrant detainees are among the most abused and neglected (Salinas, 2015). In fact, in plain twenty-first century, over one hundred men and women died while under the agency's custody from 2003 to 2009 (ICE, 2009), largely attributed to the "egregious failures of medical care" (Human Rights Watch, 2009:1). Consider, for instance, the case of Francisco Castañeda. In 2008, Castañeda, an immigrant from El Salvador who had lived in the United States since 1982 died largely as a result of the lack of medical treatment while housed in immigration detentions. Castañeda sustained an injury to his genitals during his booking at a county jail, at which time he was told to secure medical treatment. Once transferred to an ICE detention center, Castañeda was seen by medical staff, but he was told that treatment for his injury was "elective in nature." The extremely painful lesion to his groin went untreated for months. Castañeda was eventually released, to be diagnosed a few days later with cancer, which had extended to the lymph nodes in his groin area. His penis had to be amputated, and Castañeda died a few months later (American Civil Liberties Union, 2010; Moore, 2009).

Finally, at no other time in U.S. history has the government taken such aggressive anti-social control movement. Currently, federal, state, and local governments are increasing punitive and militarized approaches against various groups, while targeting Latinos, especially undocumented immigrants and the impoverished (Urbina & Peña, 2018). In effect, current draconian policies serve as a *call to equality and justice* by all people, not only to immigrant advocates and activists who recognize that the current treatment of people is one of the worst moments in U.S. history. As documented in various studies, the violation of human rights of immigrants and violation of constitutional and civil rights of Latinos are common features in urban and rural areas across the country. Today, while some see him as a twenty-first century *Superman* who is trying to save America from *unwanted and dangerous intruders,* or as he calls them "bad hombres," some of the most egregious violations are exemplified by President Donald Trump's immigration policies. Trump, who is more of a reflection of a modern version of a Ku Klux Klanner than an objective and progressive president, first made international news for his anti-Mexican accusations, the very same day he announced his candidacy for president of the United States. In truth, as a glorious movement to immigration hawks, and blatant violations of human dignity to social justice activists, the anti-immigrants movement by Trump actually goes much further than simply policy or national security, revealing, under this political slogan of "make America great again," the very inner core of America, the legacy of hate, vindictiveness, ignorance, and hypocrisy.

SUMMARY

More globally, critical issues facing Latinos in the law enforcement process from detection to arrest share some similarities to other racialized groups, particularly African Americans and with racialized immigrants in the United States. However, unlike African Americans, Latinos are confronted with citizenship status, a situation that impacts both documented and undocumented Latinos in the law enforcement process. As detailed in this chapter and in the previous three chapters, Latinos have been targeted in every major law enforcement campaign for decades. As identified targets, ethnic profiling of Latinos has become routine in police practices and immigration law enforcement, gravely exacerbating with the Trump administration. As reported in this chapter, several Supreme Court cases have eroded the Fourteenth Amendment rights of Latinos, particularly those condoning racial and ethnic profiling, while lowering the standards for search and seizure (see Mirandé, Chapter 9, this volume). In short, critical issues that place Latinos in harm's way of the law are: (1) discretionary stops based on ethnicity or class; (2) use of intimidation or violence to demean and subordinate people stopped; (3) restricting Mexicans the freedom of movement but not others in the same vicinity; (4) reinforced stereotypes of Mexicans as aliens, foreigners, inferior, and criminals; and (5) limited access to fair and impartial treatment before U.S. laws (Álvarez & Urbina, 2018; Romero, 2006; Urbina & Álvarez, 2017).

The criminal justice process, though, does not end with local, state, federal, or immigration law enforcement. As reported in the five chapters of the following section, once Latinos are detected and arrested, they must then confront the costly, complicated, lengthy, and often uncertain judicial process, if they are indicted by the grand jury or charged by the prosecutor. Then, for Latinos indicted, prosecuted, convicted, and sentenced to a correctional institution, they must then experience the actual realities of living behind bars in jails, public prisons, private prisons, federal facilities, immigration detention centers, or military prisons, as documented in Section Three of this book.

Chapter 5

IMMIGRATION LOCKDOWN: THE EXCLUSION OF MEXICAN IMMIGRANTS THROUGH LEGISLATION

CARLOS E. POSADAS AND CHRISTINA ANN MEDINA

An eye for an eye only ends up making the whole world blind.

–Mohandas K. Gandhi

While observers have suggested that some of the most crucial controversies surrounding immigration reached their climax after the September 11, 2001, attacks on U.S. territory, immigration has always been, though somewhat silent, a crucial and controversial issue confronting ethnic/racial minorities, both documented and undocumented (Álvarez & Urbina, 2018; Acuña, 2004; Almaguer, 2008; Gutiérrez, 1997). The truth is that immigration is, primarily, a financial and political euphemism that normally targets Latinos, especially Mexicans, and highly propagated by the American media. Worse, despite the fact that the majority of Mexicans are legal U.S. residents, the *social construction* of "illegal alien" is normally applied to all Mexicans or Latinos in general (Álvarez & Urbina, 2018; Acuña, 2015; Shorris, 2001; see also Aguirre, this volume). Among the issues not covered in the media or by racially motivated right-wing individuals is the fact that the largest populations of undocumented people in the United States today are probably not Mexicans but non-

Latinos, like Canadians, Irish, Poles, and Russians (Acuña, 2015). Consequently, the public is presented with a skewed and fragmented "picture" of the immigration phenomena, resulting in punitive and selected enforcement of immigration legislation and crime control policies (Welch, 2006; see also Álvarez, this volume).

Historically, as if Gunnar Myrdal's theory of "economic racism" needed additional proof, explicit ethnic statements about Mexicans surfaced during the 1930s Depression years. Then, the Immigration and Naturalization Service's (INS) infamous witch hunt of 1954, referred to as "Operation Wetback," was, again, a product of nativist/racist tradition of blaming the victim for inequality. This all-out assault was directed by retired military generals (similar to the witch hunt of the 1930s), and resulted in the apprehension and repatriation of a reported 1,075,168 Mexicans (Álvarez & Urbina, 2018; Gutiérrez, 1997). Historian Vicki Ruiz (1999:138) documents that Mexicans, many of whom were native U.S. citizens, "were the

75

only immigrants targeted for removal." Along the way, the threat, actual or imagined, and the resulting fear of undocumented people, has been "legitimized" by high ranked government officials (see Urbina & Álvarez, Chapter 17, this volume). As such, the general public has also come to see immigrants as criminals and as a danger to society (Kil & Menjívar, 2006). Like those who favored the return of African Americans to Africa, nativists wish to preserve both their ideological and racial purity. Researchers, however, have found that immigrants actually commit crimes at lower rates than natives (Martínez, 2000, 2002; Martínez & Valenzuela, 2006; Lee, Martínez, & Rosenfeld, 2001; Adelman, Reid, Markle, Weiss, & Jaret, 2017). These negative perceptions, though, create dire consequences for some of the most vulnerable people in society (Díaz, 2011; Gonzales, 2014; Salinas, 2015).

In short, the *ethnic construction* of immigrants, the criminalization of immigrants, and criminal victimization of Latinas and Latinos under the "rationalization of secure borders" (Urbina & Peña, 2018), which reinforce historical stereotypes, pre-existing immigrant notions, and mythical perceptions about the dynamics of immigration laws, need to be well investigated and documented. This chapter, then, explores the history of immigration laws as it pertains to both Latinos, primarily Mexicans, who constitute the largest ethnic minority group of the Latino population, beginning with an historical discussion of Mexican migration to the United States. The chapter also chronicles important immigration policies resulting from the most recent presidencies of Barack Obama and Donald Trump.

HISTORY OF MEXICAN IMMIGRATION

American employers have long courted Mexican immigrants, as Mexican men and women helped build the railroads, worked the mines, worked the fields, worked in factories, and now work in the service industry. This courtship began as early as the 1870s and has continued with varying intensity ever since (Álvarez & Urbina, 2018; Gutiérrez, 1997). In the early part of the twentieth century, the Mexican Revolution (1910–1920) created Mexican refugees who traveled as far north as Chicago (slaughterhouses), Milwaukee (breweries), and Gary, Indiana (steel mills). This marked the beginning of the *migration ritual* in which Mexicans from many villages in Mexico routinely sent their sons to work in the Midwest industries, with many Mexicans traveling to border-states, like Texas and California (Álvarez & Urbina, 2018; Portes & Rumbaut, 1990), essentially, becoming a tradition for many Mexicans.

From Migrants to Immigrants

When Mexico lost all of what is now the U.S. Southwest, it left many Mexicans with a life-altering decision to make: go south to Mexico or stay and accept the United States offer of U.S. citizenship. The largest Mexican communities existed in Texas, New Mexico, and California, and in 1870 the Mexican-born population was estimated at 42,435 (Romo, 1996). By 1900, according to Ricardo Romo (1996:89), the Mexican population had increased to more than 100,000, with Mexicans in the United States still "able to encourage other family members to emigrate. In many of the barrios, one could find neighborhood clusters of extended family and friends from the same homeland town." In a sense, this can be seen as the beginning of the extensive social network system that now exists among Mexican laborers (Posadas,

2007), though now viewed and treated not as migrants but as illegal immigrants.

The next 30 years (1901–1930) experienced the first large migration of Mexican immigrants as over one million, recruited migrants, made their way into the U.S. labor pool. Romo (1996) documents that most of these migrants were unskilled workers who were recruited to work the railroads and mines. Also, while migrants tend to be associated with Mexican men, Romo (1996:89) reports that "men, women, and children arrived at the U.S.-Mexico border and contracted for work" in the labor camps of Texas, California, and other states.

What caused such increase in the number of Mexicans migrating to the United States? Alejandro Portes and Ruben Rumbaut (1990) Ruth Gomberg-Muñoz (2011) document that it was the United States' urgent need for labor and the development of the Southwest that created the migrant system, with recruiters going to Mexico to begin directing labor outflows from Mexico's interior. In fact, labor recruiters brought, literally, trainloads of people from Mexico to accommodate the labor needs of the Southwest development at the time.

Not surprisingly, the 1924 Quota Act that limited European immigration exempted Mexicans, but it allowed for the creation of the Border Patrol, which, from the beginning, turned its primary focus to the U.S.-Mexico border (Hernández, 2010). The Mexican exception was the result of successful lobbying from Southwestern farmers and growers who established Mexicans as the preferred labor source for agriculture in the Southwest (Gomberg-Muñoz, 2011; Romo, 1996). In addition, World War I (1914–1918) created a labor shortage that not only allowed more Mexican immigrants into the United States, but it also allowed Mexican Americans an opportunity to obtain better paying jobs. In fact, the Mexican-born population continued to grow until the Great Depression (1929) when Mexicans began to be repatriated by government officials in communities across the Southwest, with many immigrants, including children and Mexican Americans who were U.S. citizens, being deported (Álvarez & Urbina, 2018; Guerin-Gonzáles, 1994; Romo, 1996).

Juan Ramon García (1996) cites that from 1900 to 1932 Mexican migration to the U.S. Midwest increased the total Mexican population, establishing some of the Mexican barrios that still exist today. Also, while the notion tends to associate Mexican immigrants as agricultural workers, migrants were often destined for farms and other industries in the Midwest and other parts of the country, particularly in the high demand labor industries of large cities, like Chicago and Detroit, where wages were sometimes higher and employment more stable (Gomberg-Muñoz, 2011). During this period, railroads, farmers and growers, and industrial factories competed for *cheap Mexican labor.* With a high labor demand, many immigrants also traveled to the Midwest via the newly created *contract labor,* which served as a prelude to the *bracero* program that followed.

World War II (1939–1945), like World War I, brought another domestic labor shortage that forced U.S. farmers and industrialists to find alternative labor sources. As before, lobbying at the Capitol by powerful interest groups convinced the U.S. government to create the Mexican contract worker program. The Bracero Program, enacted in 1942, became the first migrant program in which both governments tried to administer Mexican migration at the highest level of government. The program lasted 22 years, undergoing several renewals and extensions, allowing over 5 million Braceros to work agricultural and industrial jobs (Gomberg-Muñoz, 2011; Romo, 1996). With the United States entering World War II, many Mexican Americans and Mexicans also joined the war effort, either through military participation or helping alleviate the labor shortage in the mainland.

While the Bracero Program was supposed to ensure humane working conditions, cited in the legal agreement signed by both countries, for Mexican migrant workers, where workers were supposed to "receive free transportation and food, guaranteed wages, safe working conditions, and sanitary living quarters" (Romo, 1996:92), the actual working conditions were everything but humane (Álvarez & Urbina, 2018). In effect, the working conditions of the Bracero Program have been characterized as "a slave labor program" (Magaña, 2003). As such, with many other jobs in demand, this allowed migration to continue, with many migrants not participating in the program to avoid the savage working conditions. With the government occupied in World War II, the Border Patrol in its infancy, and a high labor demand, Mexican migrants could easily cross the border and quickly obtain employment, without having to participate in the Bracero Program.

Braceros, though, quickly discovered that working conditions outside the Bracero Program were just as brutal, as employers took the opportunity to exploit migrant workers without fear of repercussions (Gomberg-Muñoz, 2011). Texas, in particular, was notorious for recruiting non-Bracero workers, and thus the growing number of undocumented workers revived xenophobia and blatant discrimination against workers (García, 1980; Gomberg-Muñoz, 2011), which, of course, migrants were experiencing since the early 1900s before the first repatriation. In fact, beyond savage working conditions, Braceros had to endure segregation, prejudice, racism, discrimination, and violence, an experience confronting Mexicans and Mexican Americans, clearly a *legacy of ex-*

ploitation and oppression that started in the 1830s (Álvarez & Urbina, 2018; Brophy, 1972; Gomberg-Muñoz, 2011; Martínez, 2001; see also Baker, this volume). In retrospect, Mexicans and Mexican Americans mobilized, creating social movements and organizing groups in an effort to challenge intimidation, oppression, and violence (Rosales, 1999; Ruiz, 1987, 1999; Salinas, 2015).

In 1954, after years of purposely allowing, actively recruiting, and encouraging thousands of undocumented workers to cross into Texas and other parts of the country, the then Immigration and Naturalization Service (INS) initiated *Operation Wetback*. Through this federal initiative, the INS, with local law enforcement, repatriated as many Mexican workers as it could, using intimidation, harassment, and conducting sweeps in Mexican neighborhoods and other "Mexican-looking" neighborhoods, which included Native American neighborhoods. The INS used trains, trucks, buses, ships, and airplanes to repatriate Mexican workers. The total number of Mexicans repatriated is estimated at 1.3 million, though disputed by the INS, claiming lesser figures (García, 1980), in addition to hundreds of thousands of immigrants who left before, during, and after Operation Wetback. Among those left in the United States as undocumented were women and children who had migrated by themselves, with families, or husbands.

Still, with high labor demands, the Bracero Program continued until 1964, though, its termination *did not intend to end* Mexican laborers migrating to the United States (Álvarez & Urbina, 2018; Durand, Massey, & Parrado, 1999). By then, the relationships established between laborers, for better or worse, and employers did not mean that their jobs would disappear with the termination of the program. Workers continued crossing to the United States as employers kept actively recruiting and hiring them. Conveniently, an immigration act was passed in 1952 making it unlawful to smuggle aliens into the United States, but the act excluded employers from being criminally charged or fined for hiring undocumented workers. In fact, it was then that the *Texas Proviso* law began its 34-year era of contradicting immigration policy, as employers were told that they could not hire undocumented immigrants, but Texas was exempted. Such exemption continued until 1986, when the Immigration Reform and Control Act (IRCA) legislation was enacted.

Further, ending the Bracero Program did not mean that there would be a decline in Mexican labor demand, as illustrated by the Texas Proviso law. In actuality, the end of the program increased the number of workers who were undocumented, with many more to come to fulfill the U.S. expanding job market, resolve the labor crisis created by the termination of the Bracero Program, and to be with friends or family who stayed behind during the immigration sweeps. The *circular migration,* or seasonal migration, ritual continued unabated until the United States began to drastically increase border enforcement in the 1990s. Though, starting in the 1950s, immigration officials began increasing enforcement, sometimes conducting raids in cities where agricultural workers tend to gravitate (Álvarez & Urbina, 2018; Magaña, 2003), raids which continue today, in 2018.

The Immigration Reform and Control Act of 1986, the last immigration amnesty, granted legal residence to over 2 million Mexican migrants (Durand, Massey, & Parrado, 1999; Hagan, 1994). The 1986 amnesty, combined with increased border enforcement, however, marked the beginning of the end of the circular migration pattern that had existed for nearly 100 years. The provisions of IRCA, in many cases, *required*

undocumented migrants to stop circulating back and forth until their *legal status* was resolved, and thus Mexicans, documented and undocumented, began settling in the U.S. in larger numbers than ever before.

Soon after 1986, two major immigration laws were passed (1990 and 1996), which included increased border controls, revised rules for exclusion and deportation, and new restrictions for immigrants wishing to access social services (Magaña, 2003), to continue the trend of incrementally making it more difficult for migrant workers. The Immigration Act of 1990 was designed to address legal and illegal immigration by increasing the number of immigrants eligible for admission under the "flexible cap," along with resources for increased border enforcement. The 1996 Personal Responsibility Act was created to "end social services afforded to immigrants, both legal and illegal, as well as stricter penalties for smuggling activities," and additional funding for border enforcement (Magaña, 2003:21).

While IRCA was able to bring relief to millions of immigrants, the policy failed to address the slow process of legalizing the status of their families, creating yet another migrant shift, more migration, both documented and undocumented, as it was difficult for families to endure years before reunification with family members who could be thousands of miles away. With the election of President George W. Bush and Mexican President Vicente Fox, the possibility of an immigration amnesty, or guest worker permits, was *seriously* being considered, but the idea was left behind after the September 11, 2001, terrorist attacks on the United States, a situation that further antagonized the anti-immigrant movement, creating stronger anti-immigrant sentiments. It has been almost two decades since 9/11, the economic recession and national security concerns that followed and lingered have left little hope for immigrants, other than enforcement, detention, deportation, or incarceration (Urbina & Peña, 2018; see also Urbina & Álvarez, Chapter 17, this volume).

In sum, Mexican workers were recruited for over 100 years, working under extremely oppressive conditions. As a community, Mexican immigrants and Mexican Americans have been deported, marginalized, abused physically, emotionally, and psychologically, and used as scapegoats during economic crises (Álvarez & Urbina, 2018; Gomberg-Muñoz, 2011; Gonzales, 2014; Salinas, 2015; Spickard, 2007), a situation that continues today. Yet, while efforts for a new agricultural guest worker program were never resumed, increased family separation and human trafficking, including women and children, continued through the Obama and Trump presidencies, despite a series of new immigration policies enacted since 2009. While neither Obama or Trump have pursued immigration reform as aggressively as promised, the policies enacted during their respective administrations have been among the most aggressive enforcers of immigration law in history (Álvarez & Urbina, 2018; Olivas, 2012; Urbina & Peña, 2018). Meanwhile, the lack of comprehensive immigration reform has continued to motivate federal officials and U.S. states seeking to control immigration through strict legislation.

LOCKDOWN THROUGH LEGISLATION

With Mexican migrants continuing to settle throughout the United States, beyond the South, fear of immigrant people, particularly in areas where the white population is decreasing (Johnson & Lichter, 2008), seems to have increased. As such, anti-immigrant people are pushing stringent federal, state, and local legislation (Massey, 2008; Rakesh, Suro, & Tafoya, 2005), as recently documented by Álvarez and Urbina in *Immigration and the Law: Race, Citizenship, and Social Control* (2018). For instance, growing fear and economic concerns have led to anti-immigrant legislation across the United States, from Utah to Georgia, from Arizona to Alabama, aiming to bypass federal law (Álvarez & Urbina, 2018; *Atlanta Journal Constitution*, 2006). Beyond *illegal employment,* states are implementing laws to prohibit social services to undocumented immigrants, along with nativistic "English" only laws, tougher employer sanctions, rental restrictions, and prohibiting undocumented children from being able to receive state financial aid or in-state tuition for college, resulting in *attrition through enforcement.* These initiatives are essentially a lockdown at the local/state level, but similar ones are also taking place at the federal level (Álvarez & Urbina, 2018; Doty, 2009).

As in the past, there is no doubt that the most identifiable targets of undocumented immigrants are people of Mexican heritage (Álvarez & Urbina, 2018; Mohl, 2003; Salinas, 2015), with laws that have clearly continued and renewed nativism that have criminalized Mexican behavior (see Aguirre, this volume), and police enforcement that haunt both Mexican immigrants and Mexican Americans (Urbina & Álvarez, 2015; Urbina & Peña, 2018; see also Durán; Romero & Sánchez, this volume). Therefore, we now turn to a brief review of federal immigration law, noting the nativist and racist tone that immigrants have experienced during last 100 years, followed by a brief review of state laws and local ordinances designed for "cracking down" on undocumented immigrants, particularly people of Mexican origin.

FEDERAL LEGISLATION

Along with major shifts in U.S. immigration laws, there is a long history of nativism and racism, which, in truth, are manifestations of the very same laws (Álvarez & Urbina, 2018; Briggs, 1984; Daniels, 1990; Magaña, 2003; Nevins, 2010; Sadowski-Smith, 2008). Beginning with the Aliens Act and the Alien Enemy Act of 1798, the United States sought to establish how the government would deal with noncitizens, especially during wartime, economic crises, and increased immigration. In fact, as the immigrant population began to increase with non-whites and people coming from places other than Northwest Europe, immigration laws began to directly target different racial groups, beginning with the Steerage Act of 1819, which focused on preventing European poor from coming to the United States, reducing the number of migrants utilizing the "indenture servitude" argument to reach the United States (Sadowski-Smith, 2008). As nonwhites, Asian immigrants were targeted directly through the Act of 1862 that "prohibited the transportation of Chinese 'coolies' on American vessels" (Magaña, 2003:90), the 1875 Page Law banned "involuntarily traveling Orientals" (Sadowski-Smith, 2008:783), and through the Chinese Exclusion Act of 1882, which was not officially repealed until 1943. The Immigration Act of 1917 expanded restrictions to other Asian people while continuing to impose stricter criteria on all immigrants, like literacy and mental health exams.

The year the U.S. Border Patrol was established, the Immigration Act of 1924 established a quota system that heavily favored Northwestern Europeans, while limiting Southeastern Europeans who were more likely to be migrating to the United States (Magaña, 2003). Laws declaring deportable acts and some exemptions to the 1924 law

followed, including the Act of April 29, 1943, that established the first guest worker program for Mexicans, as well as North, South, and Central Americans (Magaña, 2003), eventually serving as the legal rational for the Bracero Program of nearly 20 years (1947–1964). In effect, the Immigration and Naturalization Act of June 27, 1952, consolidated various laws passed from 1924 to 1952, allowing people from all races to be eligible for naturalization and, by extension, aimed to eliminate gender discrimination in immigration proceedings.

The loosening of the strict quota for Asian immigrants began through the Act of September 26, 1961, but it was not until the Immigration and Nationality Act Amendments of October 3, 1965, that the 1924 quota system was officially terminated, and marked the beginning of limits placed on immigrants from the Western hemisphere. Of course, throughout the 1900s, people from all over the world were coming to the United States to work, including Mexican migrants, who endured multiple repatriations and deportations. As noted above, while IRCA in 1986 helped secure legal status for over 2 million Mexican immigrants it did not address the economic, political, or legal elements governing immigration, but instead, set the foundation for the controversial immigration debate we are experiencing today (Álvarez & Urbina, 2018; Mohl, 2003).

However, while these federal laws aimed to restrict, deport, and control immigrants, with the exception of the large-scale repatriation and deportation efforts, their effects have been minimal, and, worse, more detrimental than positive. As for actual enforcement, it was not until the 1990s, when the budget for Border Patrol agents began to increase and more agents allowed for operations like *Gatekeeper* and *Hold the Line,* that border apprehensions increased drastically. Yet, as noted herein, this resulted in more stable migration, especially from Mexico and Latin America, settling in the United States, dramatically increasing the number of undocumented migrants, as their families also arrived or stayed in the United States to avoid being detected during *migration.* By 2009, though, the Border Patrol had 20,000 agents, and thus crossing the border became firmly entrenched as a deadly proposition, with migrants searching for more remote and deadlier paths to the United States (Álvarez & Urbina, 2018; Eschbach, Hagan, & Rodríguez, 2003; Nevins, 2010).

In the 1990s, President Bill Clinton signed the Personal Responsibility and Work Opportunity Reconciliation Act (PRA) and the Illegal Immigration Reform and Immigrant Responsibility Act (IIRAIRA) of 1996. The first immigrant act provided strict guidelines for local benefits and social service available to noncitizens, and the second act offered further immigration regulation and a new mechanism to deport longtime permanent residents convicted of a *felony,* no matter how long ago the offense occurred. However, the "felony" measure included minor offenses, like misdemeanor theft and nonviolent assault, if the punishment carried a one-year sentence, whether the sentence was served or suspended (Rapaport, 2001). Consequently, longtime immigrants with a felony on their record faced the possibility of deportation, even if they had been productive members of society, with no criminal convictions for many years. Though, pardons could be used to remove the *deportable felony* from the immigrants' record, and some states, including Georgia, actually exercised this option. Still, under IIRAIRA, long-term residents, brought to the United States as babies, were deportable if convicted of a felony as adults and have not naturalized their immigration status.

The reality of mixed status families comprised of both undocumented and U.S. citizen members is prevalent today and has resulted in tens of thousands of undocumented students pursuing college educations without federal financial aid and/or little state financial aid more commonly available in only 10 U.S. states with local Development, Relief, and Education for Alien Minors (DREAM) Act legislation granting in-state tuition and financial aid to qualified students. Long-stalled since 2001, the federal DREAM Act would have created a path to citizenship for some immigrants who came to the United States as children and have been admitted to college or the armed forces. Despite their persistence, these students are locked out of entering the professions they have trained for, as they cannot accept employment. This reality prompted immigration reform proponents to call upon President Barack Obama to use the administrative discretion available to him and on the 30th anniversary of *Plyer v. Doe,* the 1982 case in which the U.S. Supreme Court ruled that states could not deny funds for the education of children of undocumented immigrants—the president announced a halt to the deportation of some undocumented immigrants who came to the United States as children and have graduated from high school and served in the military. The president's decision, which uses existing prosecutorial discretion, is the adoption of a "deferred action" policy and while the policy does not grant legal-residency status, as the federal DREAM Act would have, it defers deportation for a renewable two-year period with no limits on how many times it may be renewed. While announcing the policy demonstrated new political will, it does not change existing law or expand available discretion. As a result of Obama's Deferred Action for Childhood Arrivals (DACA) policy, an undocumented person's chances of being deported may be reduced, but without employment authorization and a reasonable opportunity to regularize their status, they continue to live in the shadows—with limited hope.

The Department of Homeland Security (DHS) began taking steps toward DREAM Act goals in June 2011. Director of U.S. Immigration and Customs Enforcement, John Morton, issued a memo announcing that the government would focus on deporting known criminals and urged prosecutors to use their discretion in considering those who would qualify for DACA (Delahunty & Yoo, 2013). Initially, Department of Homeland Security data revealed fewer than 300 applicants had been granted administrative closure as of 2012, a small number given early estimates nearing 800,000 qualified for approval. Since then estimates indicate at least 750,000 dreamers have been impacted but the right to work remains highly regulated today and has been throughout U.S. immigration history.

While the same critics who would further restrict immigration have said the DACA policy has gone too far, others feel it has not gone far enough as deferred action in itself can be a vague and confusing process to navigate. Furthermore, it was the Obama administration that was responsible for the removal and deportation of nearly 400,000 unauthorized immigrants during this same period of time (Álvarez & Urbina, 2018; Olivas, 2012).

In its totality, the most direct impact of IIRAIRA has been on undocumented Mexican immigrants. For undocumented Mexicans, even if they marry a U.S. citizen and have U.S.-born children, they will not be able to regularize their immigration status without leaving the country, or risking a 10-year ban before being allowed to reenter (London, 2010). As such, undocumented immigrants with U.S. citizen spouses and children live in the shadows without legal relief, under the restrictions of IIRAIRA, as many families are unwilling to be divided for years. Lastly, IIRAIRA also eliminated much of the discretion immigration judges had, making it more difficult for undocumented immigrants to find relief once detained. In essence, federal legislation has created an underclass of people *locked down* and *invisible,* in fear of deportation and being separated from their families.

New Deportation Rules with Trump Presidency

New deportation rules following the Donald Trump presidency have claimed many families. Throughout the country Immigration and Customs Enforcement agents have detained families and children, deporting some to countries they fled decades ago to escape violence and persecution. Often families are separated without an opportunity to say good-bye to their loved ones and the new rules governing applications for re-entry into the United States mean long periods of time before any family reunification may be possible.

Following DACA, in 2014, President Obama issued an executive order that would have removed the threat of deportation for millions of undocumented immigrants and allowed them to receive work permits. However, several states challenged the program and a federal judge in Texas while it made its way through the courts. In January 2017, President Trump promised to wipe out all of President Obama's immigration policies and priorities, laying the groundwork for a new wall along the U.S.-Mexico border, and unleashing ICE agents to enforce the law and punish "sanctuary cities" providing immigrants "protection." Further, the Trump Administration deported its first DACA immigrant in early 2017. Memos issued by

Department of Homeland Security Secretary John Kelly on February 20, 2017 gave direction to ICE, Customs and Border Protection and U.S. Citizenship and Immigration Services that implement Trump's executive orders on immigration enforcement.

The memos countermand Obama administration policies that placed enforcement priorities on undocumented immigrants with serious criminal violations and newer arrivals. The memos also encourage detaining immigrants and asylum seekers rather than allowing them to remain in the community while their cases are considered. Recent cases also highlight efforts to deport parents of U.S. citizens, many of whom are minors despite the harm that is caused (Zayas & Bradlee, 2014). Recent studies have also focused on understanding how local immigration enforcement policies have affected the provision and utilization of health services among Latino immigrants (Hardy, Getrich, Quezada, Guay, Michalowski, & Henley, 2012; Rhodes, Mann, Simán, Song, Alonzo, Downs, Lawlor, Martinez, Sun, O'Brien, Reboussin, & Hall, 2015).

Local and State Policies

As detailed above, beyond a few noted cases, prior federal laws had minimal impact reducing the immigration flow; instead, federal initiatives altered immigrant patterns, while creating major barriers and consequences for immigrants and U.S. employers. From the beginning, limited border enforcement and lax enforcement of employer sanctions under IRCA, combined with powerful lobbies on behalf of employers, the federal government had little urgency, certainly not a priority, to truly lockdown documented immigrants, who uphold America's economic system. As for geographical mobility, federal legislation curved the circular migration between the United States and Mexico, but it created migrant mobility (until the Trump administration) within the United States, with about 3.2 million immigrants moving freely and expanding their social networks across the United States, eventually residing in every state.

Furthered fused by the economic, political, and military crises, especially after 9/11, the immigration crisis soon became the primary target of state legislators and law enforcement officials, who seek the opportunity to make news headlines, as in the case of Trump. In effect, state and local laws tried to deter undocumented immigration by denying undocumented immigrants social benefits, not a new strategy but simply better orchestrated across states, with well-defined slogans against immigrants, like "they take our jobs." One of the first state laws was California's Pro-position 187, "Save our State," passed by voters in 1994, and although it was never implemented, it took five years for supporters to finally drop their request for appeal. A central objective of Proposition 187 was to have social service agencies work with the federal government to identify undocumented immigrants and then deny them social benefits and public service.

After 9/11, states, counties, and cities across the United States enacted various types of ordinances to deter undocumented immigrants from living in their communities. Towns like Hazleton, PA; City of Farmers Branch, TX; Prince William County, VA; Cherokee County and Cobb County, GA; Valley Park, MO; Phoenix, AZ; Suffolk County, NY; San Bernadino, CA; and Carpentersville, IL, are just a few of the many places which have passed or attempted to pass ordinances to deter immigrants by targeting businesses by threatening to take away their license for hiring undocumented workers and penalizing businesses who receive city/county funding for hiring undocumented workers, landlords for renting to undocumented tenants, tenants for not having a "residential occupancy license," passing anti-loitering ordinances to discourage day laborers, giving police authority to seize vehicles used by employers hiring day laborers, and requiring all city business to be conducted in English (Álvarez & Urbina, 2018; Kretsedemas, 2008).

The American Civil Liberties Union (ACLU) and the Mexican American Legal Defense and Education Fund (MALDEF), along with other groups, have filed lawsuits that have led to courts striking down local ordinances, or simply local governments repealing the ordinances themselves. Numerous towns have also found that while cracking down on immigrants, they tend to lose economic activity that often leaves their economy worse than before the ordinance passed, causing towns and counties to reconsider their illegal immigrant initiatives (MALDEF, 2008).

Along with city and county ordinance, state governments have also tried to curve immigration through state-wide legislation, while proclaiming that Congress has failed to pass federal comprehensive immigration reform. In 2007 alone, it is estimated that state legislators introduced more than 1,500 pieces of legislation related to immigration, including the highly controversial SB 1070 in Arizona, signed into law in 2010 by Governor Jan Brewer. SB 1070, one of the toughest anti-immigrant laws to date,

> makes it a misdemeanor for noncitizens to be in Arizona without carrying proof of immigration status and it requires Arizona local police to enforce federal immigration laws. Specifically, the act obligates police, during a lawful stop, to determine a person's immigration status if there is a reasonable suspicion that the person is an illegal alien. (London, 2010:180)

Soon after, other states followed, adopting elements of SB 1070, but like Arizona's law, most state immigration laws, in part or in their totality, have been ruled unconstitutional by federal courts.

States have also tried to implement their own employer sanctions, like requiring employers who hire undocumented workers to register and pay fees, denying workers' compensation to certain immigrant workers, requiring state agencies to collect information on those they serve, particularly immigrant status (Álvarez & Urbina, 2018; Kretsedemas, 2008; NELP, 2006; also see Newman, Johnston, Strickland, & Citrin, 2012). In fact, more stringent than Arizona's law, Alabama passed an anti-immigrant law, which was partially upheld by the Federal District Court in Birmingham on September 28, 2011. The Federal District Court upheld provisions in the state law that allow authorities to ask about immigration status to people arrested or detained upon reasonable suspicion that they may be in the United States illegally, while also criminalizing illegal residents for failure to carry alien-registration papers. Alabama's law also nullifies contracts by undocumented immigrants, forbids transactions between undocumented immigrants and agencies of the state, and requires that all elementary and secondary schools collect information regarding the immigration status of their students (Robertson, 2011), quickly resulting in drastic ramifications. For instance, immigrant students stopped attending school. More globally, these laws, as designed, create the conditions for racial profiling, disproportionately affecting ethnic minorities, especially Mexican immigrants (see Crawford; Romero & Sánchez, this volume). Like Operation Wetback, these laws not only affect undocumented people, but the Latino community as a whole, including permanent legal residents and U.S. citizens.

Analysis conducted by Newman and colleagues (2012:177), demonstrates that U.S. states that experienced a drastic proportionate growth in their immigrant population in the years leading up to federal authorization of E-Verify for state usage, so too was there a drastic spike in the state's likelihood of adopting laws requiring or strongly incentivizing the use of the E-Verify system by in-state employers; declaring,

> These findings highlight an interesting disjuncture between the ostensible purpose of the E-Verify system and the interests underlying state policy adoption. While putatively designed to control the amount of illegal workers and immigrants within a state, the size of a states' immigrant population did not serve as a significant basis for E-Verify policy adoption. Rather than reflecting an attempt by states to address economic distress or large absolute sizes in their immigration populations, the results suggest that the adoption of E-Verify laws by states act as more of a policy reaction or backlash to the experience of acculturation.

Considering the economic and legal implications of being able to legally drive; only 12 states (California, Colorado, Connecticut, Delaware, Hawaii, Illinois, Maryland, Nevada, New Mexico, Utah, Vermont and Washington) and the District of Columbia allow unauthorized immigrants to obtain a driver's licenses, impacting both employers and immigrant workers financially and criminalizing immigrants for driving without a license. Utah restricts the use of the license only for driving. New Mexico's two-term governor, Susana Martínez, made "legal driving" a campaign promise to stop the state from issuing driving licenses to undocumented immigrants. Under the notion of border and economic security, politicians and law enforcement officials have strategically utilized political rhetoric to implement anti-immigrant legislation, misconstruing the realities of immigration, including "misperceptions, misrepresentations and misunderstandings" that pit ethnic and racial minorities against each other and misled whites about immigration policies, harming the entire American society (Álvarez & Urbina, 2018; Kilty & de Haymes, 2000:2), and, for individual immigrants, deportation, detention, or incarceration.

IMMIGRANT DETENTION AND ITS CONSEQUENCES

Immigration to the United States may have started as a relatively unregulated journey, but in the late 1800s and early 1900s immigrants began to experience an increase in hurdles, with many being detained in Ellis Island as well as Angel Island. Angel Island was known as the Ellis Island of the West, serving as a detention center during this time (Barde & Bobonis, 2006), but the number of detainees was much smaller than the current number of detainees in detention facilities across the United States. In modern times, IIRAIRA created more immigrants eligible for deportation, but also detention, as many immigrants challenge their deportations, in which case, they are detained, sometimes indefinitely. Similarly, the Antiterrorism and Effective Death Penalty Act of 1996 (AEDPA) and the USA Patriot Act of 2001 both created more categories for which immigrants can be detained (Gryll, 2011).

It's estimated that "From 1994 to 2008, the daily detention population multiplied by almost five times. In 1994, the daily detention population was only 6,785; that number rose to 31,244 by 2008" (Gryll, 2011:1220). In 2008, the Immigration and Customs Enforcement (ICE) agency had 378,582 detainees (Schriro, 2009), increasing to a record high of 383,524 detainees in 2009 (Office of Immigration Statistics, 2010). Mexican immigrants accounted for 58-62 percent of those in detention (Schriro, 2009), supporting the argument that Mexican immigrants are likely to be apprehended and detained, experiencing the consequences of detention. More globally, the current detention trend drastically increases the immigration industrial complex (Álvarez & Urbina, 2018; Díaz, 2011), where the industry of criminalization and incarceration has created an additional and convenient source of revenue: the detention of noncriminals (Urbina & Álvarez, 2016; see Álvarez, this volume).

Among the various consequences, families composed of mixed-status and detained families may be separated when family members are sent to different detention centers, creating confusion and uncertainty. In effect, research shows that the vulnerability of deportation or detention negatively impacts the well-being of Latino immigrants, including the stability of the family household, the mental and emotional state of children, and the children's academic achievement (Brabeck & Xu, 2010). While arrested immigrants have historically experienced brutality (Álvarez & Urbina, 2018; Phillips,

Rodríguez, & Hagan, 2002), detained immigrants are experiencing trauma. Scott Phillips, Jacqueline Hagan, and Nestor Rodríguez (2006), for instance, found that detainees were subject to verbal harassment, more likely to experience the use of force, including excessive force, and procedural restrictions, such as access to telephones and adequate food and water. With immigrant detention centers being subcontracted to for-profit companies like Corrections Corporation of America (Álvarez & Urbina, 2018; Feltz, 2008; Wilder, 2007), the brutality and injustice are not only likely to continue but get even worse, as the element of legal accountability becomes critically vague and thus difficult to enforce.

An increase in noncriminal detainments as a result of President Trump's immigration policy directives has also been seen. According to figures provided by ICE, in the El Paso area of responsibility, which includes New Mexico, there have been 570 arrests between January 20, 2017 through April 29, 2017, that compares with 498 total for all of fiscal year 2016. The percentage of noncriminal arrests has also increased. In 2016, about 29 percent of those arrested were noncriminals. In the first part of 2017, noncriminals accounted for more than 47 percent of arrests.

CONCLUSION

As detailed herein, immigration legislation at all levels has been governed by the simultaneous interaction of powerful force, most notably, race/ethnicity, economics, wars, and labor shortage. Together, despite the argument that the federal government is incapable of controlling undocumented immigration, hundreds of thousands of immigrants are being stopped, processed, detained, and deported every year. In fact, ICE

and the Border Patrol have made millions of apprehensions, drastically increasing detention, six-fold, in the last 15 years, with Mexican immigrants being the largest population managed by the Department of Homeland Security and its agencies, ICE and the Border Patrol. Critically, *inspired* by politicians, advocates of anti-immigrants on the news media, and law enforcement officials, like former Maricopa County Sheriff Joe

Arpaio, who was found guilty of criminal contempt by a federal judge for violating a court order in a racial profiling case targeting Latino immigrants, even citizens are taking the law into their own hands and forming civilian border patrols and minutemen groups to patrol the U.S.-Mexico border (Álvarez & Urbina, 2018; Doty, 2009; Salinas, 2015).

In its totality, the anti-immigrant movement and its laws have been targeting primarily, though not exclusively, Latinos, especially Mexican immigrants. In effect, the hundreds of local ordinances, multiple state laws, and various federal legislative mandates have socially redefined undocumented workers, or as noted by renowned Mexican intellectual Jorge G. Castañeda (2007), *from migrants to immigrants.* Likewise, undocumented workers have been legally redefined, *from migrants to illegal aliens,* suggesting criminality. The *criminalization of immigrants, in turn, has resulted in the criminalization of non-criminals and, in essence, the criminalization of Mexicans and the whole Latino community* (Álvarez & Urbina, 2018; Urbina & Peña, 2018; see also Aguirre; Urbina & Álvarez, Chapter 17, this volume).

Finally, along with broken families, deportation, detention, fear, and uncertainty (Álvarez & Urbina, 2018; Rodríguez & Hagan, 2004), immigrants are being displaced, further marginalized, and racially profiled, impacting not only Mexicans and the Latino community, but the entire American society. Crucially, with ICE conducting more internal enforcement and the Border Patrol making more apprehensions along the border and across the United States, the immigrant lockdown will continue for a long time (Álvarez & Urbina, 2018; Coleman & Kocher, 2011), and for those detained, detention could be indefinite, while politicians, lawmakers, and law enforcement officials tinker with the machinery of justice.

Section Two

HISPANICS AND THE JUDICIAL SYSTEM

This is a court of law, young man, not a court of justice.
                                                    —Oliver Wendell Homes, Jr.

Courts talk like upper-class white men and subordinate those who do not.
                                                    —Paul J. Kaplan

Chapter 6

LATINO POLICE OFFICERS: POLICY, PRACTICE, AND STRUCTURAL HIERARCHIES

CLAUDIO G. VERA SÁNCHEZ

A historical world is a humanly created one. It is composed of people, institutions, practices, and languages that are created by circumstances of human experience and sustained by structures of power.

–Dorothy Ross

With significant shifts in demographic trends, along with ethnic and race effects in both defendants and law enforcement officers, police reform advocates have been advocating for increase Latino representation in the police force under the notion that representation will reduce inequality and injustice. In this chapter, the central premise is to describe how policy shapes the experiences and practices of Latino officers. This endeavor, though, is met with several challenges in that, for example, a narrow body of literature centers on white and black experiences, infrequently incorporating Latino officers (Martínez, 2007; Urbina & Álvarez, 2015). Subsequently, what follows is a tentative framework about Latino officers couched on the existing literature. Eduardo Bonilla-Silva's (1997, 2001) influential framework of race in the United States, which states that the American society is operating within a "post-racial" paradigm, provides the theoretical lens for this chapter.

Bonilla-Silva suggests that the concepts of race in contemporary society cannot be exclusively defined from antiquated, racially explicit, or racially coded perspectives. After the 1960s and with the advent of the Civil Rights Act of 1964, he suggests that contemporary organizations and institutions, particularly institutions like the police, must be observed from the vantage point of *colorblindness.* His focal argument is that colorblind laws, policies, and strategies have fundamentally structured U.S. organizations and institutions, including the police.

As for ethnic minority officers, studies reveal that police organizations have paved the foundation for two distinct yet related realities Latino officers may experience. Police organizations in cities like New York, Chicago, and Los Angeles often operate within a colorblind system that appears race neutral at face value, but in practice imposes considerable costs within Latino and black communities. Impacted by geography and demographics, police organizations in places like Alabama, Arizona, Georgia, and Nebraska often encourage the enforcement of racially coded policies and practices. In effect, although Bonilla-Silva's framework centers primarily on colorblind policies, he acknowledges that racially coded policies remain common in many cities and states. Pragmatically, it is this system of racially neutral and racially coded strategies that structure the practices and experiences of Latino officers in the American police.

DOES IT MATTER IF OFFICERS ARE WHITE, BLACK, OR LATINO?

As noted above, with shifts in demographics, scholars have debated whether hiring more Latino or African American officers will improve interactional barriers between the police and the barrios and ghettos, particularly with inner-city residents (Durán, 2015; Pérez McCluskey & McCluskey, 2004; Smith & Holmes, 2003). A few decades ago, Jerome Skolnick (1975:69) reported, "suggestions have been made to enlist colored policemen for colored neighborhoods, or to bring in trained colored policemen for the Commonwealth." More recently, Ronald Weitzer (2000) wrote an article comparing black and white officers' interactions with residents. He found that pressing differences emerged, just not in expected directions. In some cases, for instance, African American officers were harsher to suspects than their white counterparts (see also Alex, 1969; Cao & Huang, 2000; Leinen, 1984). According to Weitzer (2000), black officers opted to appear impartial to their white partners, often overcompensating by being harsh toward minority residents. One of his interviewees claimed, "[black police] . . . treat you just as bad, and they say 'My brother.' How can you be a brother when you just slammed my head against the car, showing off to the White officer, trying to be like him" (Weitzer, 2000:318)? As for ethnic minority officers, studies have found similar patterns of aggressive treatment by Latino officers on minority residents (Wilkins & Williams, 2009; see also Durán, 2015). These findings are startling considering that even minority officers themselves have perhaps experienced unpleasant encounters with the police at some point (Barlow & Barlow, 2002). For instance, Chicago where African Americans constitute 29 percent and Latinos 17 percent of the police force and New York with 16 percent black and 30 percent Latino officers are known for having some of the most ethnically diverse police forces in the country (Gibson, 2010; Goodman, 2013); yet both cities continue to regularly make national headlines when it comes to aggressive policing (Urbina & Álvarez, 2015; Van Cleve, 2016). In fact, Brad Smith (2003) found that officer diversity had a negligible impact on the number of police-caused homicides, showing that a racially representative police force was no more likely to avert police shootings than a racially homogenous force. Broadly, although hiring Latino or black officers can cosmetically alter the image of police organizations, and can occasionally alleviate police-community tensions (Weitzer, Tuch, & Skogan, 2008), whether proportional representation of minority officers will transform the organizational policies and practices within police departments remains questionable (Smith & Holmes, 2003; Wilkins & Williams, 2008). In *Latino Police Officers in the United States: An Examination of Emerging Trends and Issues* (2015), Urbina and Álvarez detail that with strategic mechanisms in place, including enhanced training and education, police departments may be transformed into more inclusive, representative, and effective institutions.

A growing body of literature reveals that situational contexts have a profound impact on human behavior (Zimbardo, 2008), findings which have been extended to police work (Klinger, 1997; Wilson, 1968). In his influential experiment, for instance, Philip Zimbardo found that after randomly assigning well-adjusted individuals to play the "role" of either guards or prisoners, in less than a week thereafter, those in power (i.e., guards) became abusive. In essence, Zimbardo's famous analogy illustrates that *there are no rotten apples, only rotten barrels.* If individuals are subjected to a rotten barrel, he suggests, the situational exigencies will eventually overwhelm those individuals (in this case, police officers) and transform them into rotten apples. In which case, contrary to conventional wisdom, perhaps it may be trivial to categorize officers as black, white, or brown (Latino), because in actual practice police organizations may convert them all into "blue" (Weitzer, 2000). If this is the case, organizational policy and practice drive the actions of all officers, not just white officers. In an early study, James Q. Wilson (1968) demonstrated that organizational factors structured the styles of policing observed in eight communities, and more recent studies reveal that organizational context can in fact shape the style, practice, and even attitude of Latino officers (Klinger, 1997; see also Durán, 2015). Together, the literature suggests that although many of the policies and strategies that Latino officers are exposed to are not racially coded, they do not need to be—as racially neutral strategies, manufactured by police organizations, can produce aggressive styles of policing and negative experiences with the community irrespective of an officer's race or ethnicity.

Nationally, for years cities and states have adopted racially neutral crime control efforts or organizational strategies that unequivocally transform the landscape of policing (Giroux, 2013). Among various developments, since 1988, the police are becoming exceptionally militarized (Alexander, 2012; Balko, 2006, 2013; Dunn, 1996; Kil, 2011; Kraska & Kappeler, 1997; Michalowski, 2007; Miller & Schivone, 2015; Urbina & Peña, 2018). Recently, Henry Giroux (2013) reported how the militarization of the American police, with leftover weapons from Afghanistan and Iraq, have made their way into police departments across the country, not only changing police roles but also resulting in consequential outcomes (Álvarez & Urbina, 2018; Urbina & Álvarez, 2015). Radley Balko (2006), for example, reports that paramilitary strategies—such as special police units (like gang units and tactical units)—are responsible for countless human rights violations. In one of numerous well-documented individual incidents, Balko (2006:38) reports, "Mini Matos, who is deaf and speech-impaired and has asthma, was handcuffed at gunpoint in front of her children, ages eight and five. Police had the wrong apartment." Assuming "justification" under the supposed war on terror (Bosworth & Flavin, 2007; Welch, 2006, 2009), as questioned by Giroux (2013), once the war on terror subsides, what is the likelihood that military training and tactics by the police will be abandoned? Logistically, unlike historical police strategies, the militarization of the American police is a racially neutral strategy that redefines police organizations and their organizational culture via a set of practices that structure how Latino, white, and black officers will perform their duties. Subsequently, the militarization of the police transforms the culture of the organization from a public safety to a public war model, guaranteeing that aggressive tactics will be launched against inner-city minority neighborhoods irrespective of whether they are necessary or not (Durán, 2009a; Giroux, 2013; Ríos, 2011), as illustrated during the August 2014 Ferguson unrest after the shooting death of a young black by a white officer (Urbina & Álvarez, 2015).

With shifting demographics, the question then becomes, if the organizational culture promotes a war against crime or crime doers, how many inner-city neighborhood residents will be forced to endure the collateral consequences of these aggressive strategies? Dennis Rosenbaum (2006) warns that the tactics and strategies employed in inner-city neighborhoods of color produce early tracking and criminalization. Invariably, if police organizations use contact cards to track every young person in the neighborhood, *wolf packs* (i.e., special units working together) strategize to strike down community disorder, gang units are deploy to locate guns or drugs, mega number of officers are dispatched to poor communities, and officers are rewarded for making arrests, police organizations may *unintentionally* serve a criminogenic function. Though, in "Neoliberalism, Criminal Justice, and Latinos: The Contours of Neoliberal Economic Thought and Policy on Criminalization" (2016) Urbina and Álvarez illustrate that criminalization is not (and never has been) an unconscious or unintentional process, but a conscious, intentional, and strategized governing process (see Aguirre; Álvarez, this volume). Rosenbaum (2006) and other scholars have termed this phenomenon "net-widening," a process of policing that saddles minority youths and adults in the community with criminal records. These organizational strategies have been documented since 1970 (Salinas, 2015; Urbina & Kreitzer, 2004; Urbina & Álvarez, 2015, 2017), when it was discovered that heavy police saturation of Mexican communities in East Los Angeles was greater than middle class areas such as Wilshire Division, despite the fact that crime was greater in the latter (Romero, 2001). In a provoking proposition, Michelle Alexander (2012) invites us to imagine what the arrestee and prison population would look like if instead of raiding inner-city neighborhoods, helicopters and special units raided the houses of lacrosse teams or the dorms at any major university. Undoubtedly, many of those students would be stamped with the label of "drug offender" and may live out the rest of their lives struggling to overcome the consequences born from exclusionary practices, like not completing college, not being able to secure employment, or not being able to vote to have a voice. In fact, officers themselves have expressed dissatisfaction about the pressure to use these tactics, as one minority officer reported, "Numbers, numbers, numbers. It's all about numbers [arrests]. If yours drop, your supervisor will probably have a word about it [get you in trouble]" (Cashmore, 2001:651).

Stop-and-frisk procedures are another seemingly racially neutral, social control method that has become widely accepted in inner-city police departments. The rationale for their induction is that police organizations desperately want to reduce the number of guns and drugs in high-crime areas. In a recent study, Rocco Parascandola, Jennifer Fermino, and Dareh Gregorian (2013) found that 85 percent of people who were stopped under stop and frisk in New York City were minorities. However, contrary to often cited assumptions, only in 1.5 percent of the stops were guns or drugs found. Clearly, not an isolated study, as the high rate of stops versus contraband ratio for minorities is a consistent finding in the literature (Alexander, 2012; Jones-Brown & King-Toler, 2011). More broadly, after reviewing a large database, in 2013, a New York judge found that out of 2.3 million frisks, no weapon was found in 98.5 percent of the cases (Parascandola et al., 2013). The judge terminated stop-and-frisks for being unconstitutional, only to be reintroduced months later because of major objections by police departments. Police organizations, it appears, do not seem to envision police work without such historically situated practices, despite growing evidence questioning their effectiveness. As for ethnic minorities, Latino officers, equipped with stop-and-frisk procedures as a policing strategy, will inevitably stop large numbers of minorities but will negligibly find guns or drugs, though not without consequential implications.

As more ethnic minorities seek to join the police force, what do studies suggest for compassionate Latino officers, whose goal is to dedicate themselves "to protect and to serve" missions and work diligently to assist minority communities, particularly officers who were born/raised in ethnic communities and are now or will be patrolling the barrios, perhaps the streets where they grew up? Early studies suggest that minority officers appear to have intimate knowledge about minority cultures and communities, and thus they tend to show great empathy toward minority issues and concerns (Decker & Smith, 1980; Goldstein, 1977). Realistically, however, good intentions do not get to the root of entrenched historical dynamics nor do they obviate the need for transformation, including sound policy and practice. As the saying goes, *the road to hell is often paved with good intentions*. In policing, not only in a highly televised recent incident, like the Ferguson unrest, but over and over, we have witnessed how good intentions often lead to hellish results, though no one is willing to take responsibility for their hellish results.

A Latino who wishes to pursue a career in law enforcement or is currently housed within a police department must comprehend that police organizations in poor neighborhoods, especially inner-city areas, employ racially neutral strategies that in actual practice are anything but neutral in their application. I once conducted ridealongs in a Latino district in Chicago, a major city with a high concentration of Latinos. When I entered the gang office (outside public view), a sign on the wall read: "Quality comes before quantity only in the dictionary, so go get some heads." There was nothing racially coded about the message, yet the message was clear. The culture of disposability, data-driven strategies, and numerical results outweigh the consequences of these policing strategies and wash off notions of prejudice and racism. Once in the police force, Latino officers, along with other minority officers, must face the stark reality that exists in police organizations within inner-city areas– they will contribute to a seemingly racially neutral apparatus that unintentionally promotes minority confinement (Durán, 2009a, 2009b; Ríos, 2011), along with poor whites who do not have the money to buy their justice, as documented by Jeffrey Reiman and Paul Leighton in *The Rich Get Richer and the Poor Get Prison* (2017).

If tomorrow we were somehow able to locate every troublesome white officer across the nation, and terminated their employment, would racial profiling, aggressive policing, and other questionable police tactics disappear? The policing literature has for too long centered on the race of the officers (normally black/white), racist or prejudicial sentiments, or sensitivity training as central to the reformation of police organizations, police practices, and troublesome policing. Some scholars, however, indicate that it may not matter if police officers are Latino, black, or white, because in practice they may all be "blue" (Weitzer, 2000). This analogy suggests that police organizations in their efforts to enhance public safety, devise racially neutral strategies (e.g., militarized police, stop-and-frisk procedures, gang units, and other special units) that systematically produce astronomical numbers of police stops, unwelcome experiences with the police, and arrests, resulting in a "justified" and legal pipeline to send minorities directly to jail or prison (Bartolomé, Macedo, Ríos, & Peguero, 2013; Ríos, 2011; Urbina & Álvarez, 2015, 2016, 2017). In short, Latino officers must cope with the notion that although they may have the best intentions in mind, and there are many officers who truly wish to protect and serve underserved communities, contemporary strategies and practices in police departments lend themselves to wholesale profiling, harassment, and excessive force; ultimately resulting in a large-scale funneling of minorities through the legal system (Alexander, 2012; Morín, 2009; Salinas, 2015; Urbina & Álvarez, 2016, 2017).

LATINO OFFICERS AND THE ANTI-IMMIGRATION ERA

While Latino officers must confront multiple realities in policing and in their everyday life, perhaps no issue is more significant to Latinos than the hotly debated anti-immigration movement, as it impacts Latino officers and the Latino community, citizens and noncitizens. Along with federal immigration agencies, which include the two largest employers of Latino officers (Urbina & Álvarez, 2015), several cities and states are implementing racially coded laws and policies that target Latino immigrants and their families, as recently illustrated by the supposed "child migrant crisis," another highly televised movement during the summer of 2014 (Álvarez & Urbina, 2018). According to Ediberto Román (2013), discrimination, xenophobia, or racism against immigrants has become acceptable in the American society, making it easier for politicians and law enforcement officials to justify questionable police practices. In the first line of defense, the police stop, arrest, and possibly deport immigrants who are ascribed the label of "illegal," signifying criminality and thus dangerousness (see Aguirre, this volume). David Hernández (2008) reports that immigrant detention has tripled since the 1990s, accounting for 275,000 individuals annually. Analyzing trends for the first decade of the twenty-first century, Yolanda Vásquez (2011) documents that although Latinos represent 53.1 percent of immigrants residing in the United States, Latinos account for 94 percent of the total number of noncitizens deported. Further, consistent with other studies, Vásquez (2011) finds that immigrants are not being stopped, detained, and deported for serious crimes, but instead the majority of offenses are limited to traffic violations. According to Nancy Walker, J. Michael Senger, Francisco Villarruel, and Angela Arboleda (2004), even though immigrants constitute the largest growing prison population, only 1.5 percent of immigrant prisoners were sentenced for violent offenses in comparison to U.S. citizens (15%), trends which continue to this day (Álvarez & Urbina, 2018; Salinas, 2015). Worse, as if the Latino community needed additional surveillance, in June of 2012, the U.S. Supreme Court ruled in *Arizona v. United States* that a provision of SB 1070 was constitutional, authorizing officers to stop anyone they suspect resides in the country illegally. Clearly, while perhaps under good intentions, the Supreme Court, by de facto, institutionally legitimized racial profiling.

Scholars have amply documented the racial profiling, intimidation, harassment, roundups, arrests, detention, and deportation of immigrants by the police (Álvarez & Urbina, 2018; Brabeck & Xu, 2010; Fussell, 2011; Golash-Boza, 2012a, 2012b, 2015;

Salinas, 2004, 2015; Welch, 2006, 2009). Mary Romero (2006), for instance, found that in many cases police targeted Latinos during raids and demanded immigration "papeles" or "papers" (e.g., green card) irrespective of citizenship status. According to Romero (2006:23), none of the stops were motivated by criminal activity, but rather "citizenship is visibly inscribed on bodies in specific urban spaces rather than 'probable cause'." Combined with the current political climate and society's anti-immigrants sentiment, these racially coded strategies represent challenging dilemmas for Latino officers working in those cities and states (Urbina & Álvarez, 2015). Consider, for example, the ambivalence of officers when encountering mixed-status families (Romero, 2008b). When children are documented, but parents are undocumented, how should officers enforce laws such as SB 1070? Officers must deport the parents, but not the children in this common and consequential scenario. In effect, Vásquez (2011) found that in 1.6 million families separated from 1996 to 2007 by the police and immigration officials, children routinely experienced psychological, educational, and economic effects. Today, with the nation's Capitol still being far from resolving the immigration situation, with Obama's immigration reform plan receiving a split decision by the U.S. Supreme Court on June 23, 2016, the outcome of these racially coded strategies is that Latino officers are dissolving families, whose only crime is often remaining in the country past their visa expiration or who have been unsuccessful resolving documentation issues.

With the advent of various social control policies such as SB 1070, which allow and in a sense encourage racial profiling as a legitimate policing strategy, Latino officers will have to roundup, arrest, and deport individuals who share their ethnic background, from where they grew up to religion, to customs and traditions. Latinos, of course, constitute a highly diverse ethnic group, and thus there is no guarantee that the arrest, detainment, and deportation of those ethnically similar will result in cognitive dissonance or perceived as an injustice. Josiah Heyman (2002), for instance, found that Latino immigration officers did not self-identify as Latino, but instead as U.S. citizens. In other studies, Latino officers strongly self-identify as Latino, but in other cases they identified themselves as Anglo/white (Irlbeck, 2008). In effect, officers either ascribed to nationalism (i.e., American label) or ethnic identity (e.g., Latino or white), suggesting a complex racial identity that may not be compatible with undocumented immigrants who are being policed (Urbina & Álvarez, 2015).

While we often hear about the Arizona anti-immigrants movement, Arizona is not alone in its crusade to banish Latino immigrants, using the police and the law as an apparatus to stop people who appear Latino for questioning. Policies such as Alabama HB 56, Florida HB 7089, Georgia HB 87, and Nebraska 5165, what some scholars have coined as *crimmigration* (Beckett & Evans, 2015; Hartry, 2012; Hernández, 2015; Stumpf, 2006, 2013; Vásquez, 2011), along with policies of 22 other states, are racially coded policies that often target immigrants and revive the specter of a racialized past (Acuña, 2015; Almaguer, 2008; Álvarez & Urbina, 2018; Bender, 2003; De León, 1983; McWilliams, 1990; Mirandé, 1987; Salinas, 2015). For example, Nebraska 5165, which prohibits renting to immigrants, bears remarkable similarities to Jim Crow laws and restrictive covenants which once prevented renting apartments or selling homes to blacks in white areas. Or, consider HB 56 in Birmingham, Alabama, which targets immigrant children with the objective of expelling them from public schools, the law resonates with the policies of the South that unequivocally maintained educational exclusion for African Americans. Or, similar to Arizona SB 1070, requiring police officers to stop any person suspected of being undocumented, HB 7089 in Florida, punishing a person with 20 days of jail for failure to present documentation, resembles the *slave codes* of the South which required slave patrols to apprehend anyone in the countryside who was suspected of not having their *freedom* papers or still being a slave. Just as slave patrols were once required to distinguish between black freedmen and slaves, officers must differentiate between undocumented Latinos and documented ethnic minorities. Broadly, Latino communities categorized as undocumented become susceptible to aggressive anti-immigrant policies (Álvarez & Urbina, 2018; Bacon, 2009; Castañeda, 2007; Gutiérrez, 1997; Kubrin, Zatz, & Martínez, 2012; Perea, 1997; Salinas, 2015).

Strategically, racially coded policies are often justified by verbose political rhetoric and inflammatory charges that immigrants are taxing the economy, appropriating all the jobs, and undermining educational opportunities of U.S. citizens (Chomsky, 2007; Golash-Boza, 2015; Gomberg-Muñoz, 2011; Gutiérrez, 1997). Critics, however, report that the data does not support the rationale for the enforcement of these policies (Álvarez & Urbina, 2018; Gomberg-Muñoz, 2015; Gonzales, 2014; Salinas, 2015; Sulzberger, 2010). For instance, in Nebraska where it has become illegal to rent to or hire immigrants, the state registers as the third lowest in the nation for unemployment (4.6%); clearly, the claim that immigrants are hoarding all the jobs in Nebraska appears unsubstantiated. In fact, according to a report by the Center for American Progress (2011), Alabama's anti-immigrant law will cost the state 40 million dollars in revenue (and approximately 130 million dollars in taxes) if the 10,000 undocumented immigrants stop

working. Georgia, the third largest producer of watermelons in the country, reports that many crops rotted during the labor shortages after anti-immigrants laws were implemented. Consequently, Latino officers' experiences stand to be partly circumscribed by racially coded policies that target Latino immigrants and Latino nonimmigrants, their children, as well as their families, based on empirically unsupported claims (Brabeck & Xu, 2010; Human Rights Watch, 2015; Press, 2006; Román, 2013).

More broadly, racially coded policies not only undermine the efforts of well-meaning officers but entire police organizations, and further disrupt conflictive relationships between the police and Latino communities. Some officers hold reservations about targeting immigrants, or suspected immigrants, or pursuing controversial types of police work, like ethnic and racial profiling. Claudio G. Vera Sánchez and Dennis Rosenbaum (2011) found that some officers perceive immigrant neighborhoods as hardworking and as less prone to law breaking, and therefore not interested in policing them aggressively. In fact, one of the first lawsuits against Arizona SB 1070 was filed by a 15-year-old veteran of the Tucson Police Department (*America's Voice,* 2011). Other police officers echo the sentiment of Sheriff Clarence Dupnik, "[I have] no intention of complying. I think the law is one of the worst pieces of legislation I've seen in 50 years. [It's] racist, disgusting and unnecessary" (*America's Voice,* 2011). Retired Police Chief Arturo Venegas charged, "[The law] essentially legislates racial profiling, putting police in the middle of the train tracks to face an onslaught of civil-rights violations lawsuits. No other law in the country allows citizens to sue a government agency for not arresting enough people" (*America's Voice,* 2011).

In sum, racially coded policies not only weaken fragile historical relations between the police and minority communities, but they are also likely to place officers in danger. Immigrants who fear losing everything by being deported might resort to noncompliance to free themselves, endangering their lives and those of the officers. Evidently, racially coded policies, combined with their aggressive enforcement, actually promote law-breaking behavior and threaten meaningful community *engagement* with the police, a fundamental element of community-oriented policing (Byxbe, Urbina, & Nicosia, 2011). Subsequently, some of the nation's leading police chiefs have expressed their opposition to new state laws that require police officers to act as immigration officers. Nationally, with rapid shifts in demographic trends, in areas that have longstanding legacies of racism, Latino officers will not only have to enforce racially coded laws and policies, but also tolerate organizational contexts where racist sentiments appear to be permanent features in policing institutions, a subgroup of the community and society at large. Ellis Cashmore (2001:650), for instance, reports how black officers routinely had to endure their partner's brazen prejudice,

I was on a job with this officer . . . we were chasing these Black guys and he shouted at them, 'you f***ing niggers, we'll have you.' And when we got back to the station, he never said a word about it. It was like he didn't even know I existed.

Not an isolated case, as this "invisibility" described by minority officers has been documented in other works (Morash & Haar, 1995), prompting feelings of social distance (Haarr, 1997). In one of the few studies seeking to understand the experiences of Latino police, an officer stated, "Because you're a police officer, Anglo's think you're one of them, not Latino, just a police officer" (Irlbeck, 2008:482). Alternatively, black officers have been exposed to racist jokes, name-calling, slurs, petty harassment, and racist cartoons (Bolton, 2003), situations that carry implications and ramifications. Scholars, for instance, document that Latino and black officers report more negative workplace experiences than white officers (Hassell & Brandl, 2009; Morris, 1996); clearly, revealing the need for the transformation of the American police (Urbina & Álvarez, 2015).

DISCUSSION AND CONCLUSION

In all, Latino officers may face two distinct yet related experiences within the domain of policing. In places like New York, Chicago, and Los Angeles, where a high concentration of Latinos reside, police organizations have designed and adopted "racially neutral" strategies to address social control movements. During the last few decades, for example, operating under the assumption of neutrality, the militarization of the police, aggressive policing strategies, and controversial social control methods are often rationalized under the banner of public safety and, more recently, under the slogan of "national security" (Balko, 2013; Dunn, 1996; Welch, 2006, 2009; Whitehead, 2013). With highly charged media propagated images, even inner-city communities themselves have accepted these practices, and some perceive them as inevitable and desirable public safety initiatives (Meares & Kahan, 1999), a critical movement as demographics continue to shift and more Latinos join the police force. Perhaps more than any other time in U.S. history, police officers, as agents of the law, will be operating within institutionalized racially neutral strategies, and thus Latino officers will unintentionally

contribute to overpolicing and disproportionate minority confinement. Well-inten-
tioned Latino officers, with a strong sense of
justice, who aspire to intervene on behalf of
minority communities, will become engulfed
by the leviathan of strategies and policies
that appear to be racially neutral at face
value but in actual practice promote the
criminalization of Latino communities (De
León, 2014; Urbina & Álvarez, 2016; see also
Durán, 2015). As reported by Cashmore
(2001:657),

> The pressure to produce results has, according
> to some officers, inclined police officers to tar-
> get ethnic minority groups in certain areas,
> particularly inner cities. Racial profiling, in
> this conception, is much more to do with po-
> lice practice than bigotry or xenophobia. It
> highlights how the racist behavior of individu-
> als may be addressed in terms of institutional
> imperatives.

Critically, the consequences associated with
targeted policing, aggressive tactics, arrests,
and criminal records are not only devastating to individual offenders, but entire communities and society at large (Alexander,
2012; Salinas, 2015; Urbina & Álvarez, 2015,
2016, 2017).

In terms of policy implications, these
racially neutral and racially coded policies
and strategies not only foster distrust and
promote unwelcome experiences with the
police, but they also threaten the stability of
police and other criminal justice agencies.
Under the unfolding net-widening social
control movements, police organizations will
be required to make numerous stops, arrests,
and warehouse thousands of individuals,
while diverting attention from more sustain-
able crime control efforts, like well-designed
community-oriented policing initiatives
(Byxbe et al., 2011; Urbina & Álvarez,
2015). Nationally, particularly in anti-immigration cities and states, Latino officers will

also be instructed to enforce racially coded
strategies, further marking the convergence
between immigration law and criminal law
(Álvarez & Urbina, 2018; Cox & Miles, 2013;
Salinas, 2015), and thus some police organizations will be at the forefront of such collaborative policing efforts.

However, the blame should not exclusively fall on the police, as police organizations are not known for advancing sustain-
able social change or critically questioning
or reforming institutionally driven strategies
or practices (Walker, 1998). As reported by
various scholars, police organizations have
traditionally reinforced instead of challenged
the status quo (Platt, Frappier, Ray, Schauffler, Trujillo, & Cooper, 1982; Skolnick, 2011;
Urbina & Álvarez, 2015, 2016). As a historical reminder, we must keep in mind that
some early police organizations were created, in part, to enforce *Slave Codes, Black
Codes,* or *Jim Crow* laws (Alexander, 2012).
Revisionist historians often proclaim that
these officers were men and women of their
time, and hence their actions were justifiably
compatible with those time periods. Officers
overlooking the torture and lynching of
African Americans (Garland, 2005) or the
lynching of Mexican Americans (Carrigan,
2006; Carrigan & Webb, 2003; Delgado,
2009; Gonzáles-Day, 2006; Urbina, 2012;
Urbina et al., 2014), as opposed to safeguarding their lives, arguably, reflects nothing more than the unfortunate racial temper-
ature of the era. To be sure, typically rationalized with slogans like "that's the way it
was back then," such arguments are limited
in that there were other individuals, like the
Grimke Sisters or Charles Sumner of Massachusetts, who were also operating within the
same timeframe; yet actively opposed injustice against blacks even when they faced persecution. Notably, the same police organizations that maimed or overlooked violence
against slaves, arrested freedmen during

Reconstruction, water cannoned black children and unleashed police dogs against protestors in the 1960s, launched teargas against mostly peaceful protestors during the Occupy Wall Street Movement in 2011, participated in the aggressive and militarized policing during the 2014 Ferguson unrest, or unleashing the dogs during the Dakota pipeline protest in September 2016 (Alexander, 2012; Giroux, 2013; Urbina & Álvarez, 2015), will enforce laws and policies that target immigrants and their families. If the historical cycles of policing continue in the twenty-first century, Latino officers will unquestionably enforce the racially-coded laws and policies that continue to surface in an era of immigrant mass hysteria, moral panic, aggressive policing, and mass incarceration.

Lastly, as documented herein, for too long, the literature has centered on sensitivity or cultural training, hiring more minority officers (Cashmore, 2002; Lasley, Larson, Kelso, & Brown, 2011), or making police more accountable, as vital to reforming police organizations and reducing historical interactional conflicts between the police and minority communities. Such strategies, however, attempt to reform police organizations by focusing on the symptoms, instead of the underlying causes of questionable police practices, like overpolicing, ethnic/racial profiling, police brutality, or militarized policing. Therefore, *without transformation of the entire police force* (Urbina & Álvarez, 2015), Latino officers will succumb to organizational pressures, and they will be compelled to enforce seemingly neutral strategies in cities and states where police organizations operate within a colorblind paradigm and racism appears to be unacceptable. With shifting demographic trends and as more Latino officers join the force, racially neutral strategies, as well as racially coded ones, will systematically guarantee that more Latinos will be stopped, frisked, arrested, and pipelined to jail or prison (Urbina & Álvarez, 2016, 2017). Globally, as vividly documented by legendry Judge Lupe S. Salinas (former civil rights attorney, prosecutor, assistant to the U.S. Attorney General, judge, and now law professor) in *U.S. Latinos and Criminal Injustice* (2015), the historically strategized system of laws and policies that Latino officers stand to enforce whether racially neutral or racially coded remains one of the most dangerous threats to Latino communities in a supposed post-racial society.

Chapter 7

HISTORICAL AND CONTEMPORARY FORCES GOVERNING HISPANIC CRIMINAL (IN)JUSTICE

DAVID V. BAKER

Our nation was born in genocide when it embraced the doctrine that the original American, the Indian, was an inferior race. Even before there were large numbers of Negroes on our shore, the scar of racial hatred had already disfigured colonial society. From the sixteenth century forward, blood flowed in battles over racial supremacy. We are perhaps the only nation which tried as a matter of national policy to wipe out its indigenous population. Moreover, we elevated that tragic experience into a noble crusade. Indeed, even today we have not permitted ourselves to reject or feel remorse for this shameful episode. Our literature, our films, our drama, our folklore all exalt it. Our children are still taught to repsect the violence which reduced a red-skinned people of an earlier culture into a few fragmented groups herded into impoverished reservations.

–John F. Kennedy

Understanding the Mexican and Latino experience over the years requires that we delineate the governing dynamics of the U.S. criminal justice system; that is, the simultaneous interactions of historical and contemporary forces shaping and reshaping the Latino experience with the criminal justice system and in everyday social life. This chapter brings into sharper focus the historical and social forces affecting the criminal justice experience of Mexicans in the borderlands, focusing on internal colonialism and Mexican repression, Mexican executions, Mexican lynchings, and Mexican expulsions.

REPRESSIVE PRACTICES AGAINST PERSONS OF MEXICAN DESCENT IN THE BORDERLANDS OF THE AMERICAN SOUTHWEST, 1848–1929

Criminal justice researchers and legal scholars have largely overlooked the malicious persecution of Mexican people in the southwest borderlands in the second half of the nineteenth century and the early twentieth century as an outcome of Anglo-American colonial interests (Delgado, 2009; Goméz, 2000; Gonzáles, 2009; Mirandé, 1987; Mocho, 1997; Urbina, Vela, & Sanchez, 2014). Despite scholars' concerns in providing "a wider and more expansive view" of criminal justice history, researchers have overlooked the Mexican presence in the borderlands during the period (Oliver & Hilgenberg, 2006; Urbina et al., 2014). Interestingly, there is more scholarship on the administration of justice history in the southwest borderlands in the first half of the nineteenth century when Spain and Mexico controlled the region (Acuña, 2015; Almaguer, 2008; Bender, 2003; De León, 1983; De León & Del Castillo, 2012; Heizer & Almquest, 1971; McWilliams, 1990; Mirandé,

1987; Saunders, 1995). Scholars have also documented the experiences of Mexicans with the administration of justice in the southwest after 1930 (Alfieri, 2004; De León, 1997, 2002, 2009; Goméz, 2000; López, 2003). To correct for the oversight in the criminal justice record regarding the experience of Mexicans from the post-bellum decades (1866–1913) to the Mexican Revolution (1910–1920), this chapter focuses attention on the repressive practice against Mexicans in the southwest from 1848 to 1929 that resulted in executions, vigilantism, and mass expulsions of Mexicans. These practices were critical features of a virulent repressive campaign initiated by a dominant Anglo population to divest Mexicans of their land, social position, and ultimately their lives.

INTERNAL COLONIALISM AND MEXICAN REPRESSION

Critical scholars use internal colonialism as a theoretical framework to assess the objective historical reality of ethnic relations in the United States (Feagin, 2000, 2006; Heffernan & Koenig, 2000; Olivas, 2000; Urbina et al., 2014; Yinger, 1985). Internal colonialism explains that the structure of ethnic relations is rooted in a history of exploitation and subjugation (Almaguer, 1971, 2008; Barrera, 1979; Blauner, 1969, 1972, 1987, 2000; Casanova, 1965; Gutiérrez, 2004; McWilliams, 1990; Mirandé, 1978, 1985; Moore, 1970b; Rosenbaum, 1990). Social control of subordinate groups is essential to societal systems accenting intergroup domination and oppression. In an internal colonial structure, the dominant group implements repressive institutional strategies to control conquered groups. In effect, the *law is a repressive institution that utilizes criminal justice as a systematic tool for maintaining differ-*

ential power relations between the dominant group and conquered populations (see Aguirre, this volume). State sanctioned violence is integral to the control, domination, and exploitation of conquered populations in an internal colonial structure. That is, the state uses violent legal repression to ensure the economic, political, and social control of conquered groups (Quinney, 1974, 1977). As Alfredo Mirandé (1985:73) explains, "[t]he legal and judicial system, rather than serving as an objective and impartial institution, became a vehicle for advancing the [colonial] interests of Anglo-Americans." As such, the official task of police, prosecutors, judges, juries, and even state executioners is to protect against subjugated individuals who victimize members, interests, or institutions of the dominant group. It follows, then, that the dominant group defines as *criminal* those activities of subordinate group members that the dominant group perceives as a threat to its interest (Chambliss & Seidman, 1971; Quinney, 1970; Staples, 1975; Turk, 1969). In short, the law, and its repressive use of criminal justice practices, perpetuates a structuration of inequality that criminalizes individuals of marginalized groups (Friedman, 1993). Ethnic violence, widespread lawlessness, and increased marginalization accented Mexican life in the borderlands during the post-bellum decades:

After the Mexican war the list of skirmishes is a long one: the San Antonio Cart War in 1857; the Corinista uprising in 1859; a Mexican invasion of Corpus Christi in 1875; the El Paso Salt War in 1877; anti-Mexican riots in Alpine and Laredo, Texas in 1886; lynching and burnings in Rio Grande City in 1888 and in Brownsville in 1894; riots in Beeville and Laredo in 1894 and 1899; and the Catarina Garza war in 1892; [and the] uncounted lynching and murders by the Texas Rangers, the Wolf Hunters and other vigilante groups. (Del Castillo, 1985: 136)

MEXICAN EXECUTIONS

Arguably the most turbulent period in borderland history, justice officials executed more Mexican capital offenders from 1848 to 1929 than in any other period in American history (Allen & Clubb, 2008a, 2008b; Espy & Smykla, 2004; Urbina, 2012; see also Peña & Urbina, this volume). Arizona, California, New Mexico, and Texas hanged more than 200 Mexican prisoners in the period, comprising *two-thirds* of Mexican prisoners executed historically in the United States. California outpaced other borderland jurisdictions in executing Mexican prisoners in the period, as state authorities hanged roughly 40 percent of executed Mexican prisoners. The condemned were mostly young, marginalized, impoverished, and unskilled construction and railroad workers, miners, common laborers, and ranch-hands. Officials executed Mexican prisoners mostly for killing Anglos, but hanging Mexican prisoners for killing other Mexicans was not uncommon. In many cases, drunkenness often accompanied impulsive violence between friends and acquaintances that involved killings in response to verbal insults. There, the cultural value of "machismo" demanded Mexican men defend their honor when "provoked by humiliation or injured

pride" (McKanna, 2007:57). There were relatively few Mexican executions for spousal killings when troubled romantic and marital relations ended in murder. More often, juries were sympathetic to Mexican husbands who were provoked into killing an unfaithful wife, "a provocation recognized by the law as being sufficient to arouse the passion, and thus to reduce the crime to manslaughter" (McKanna, 2007:59). A scarcity of Mexican hangings for raping white women in the period belies the Anglo notion of Mexican men as "rapacious and hot-blooded creatures who wantonly lusted after white women" (Almaguer, 1994:62). Horse stealing and cattle rustling were frequent crimes committed by Mexicans, though executions for these offenses accounted for a negligible share of Mexican executions. Whipping, beating, and branding Mexicans were more prevalent than executions for theft crimes.

Assessing ethnic disparity regarding the execution of Mexican prisoners is feasible given available census estimates of the Mexican population in the southwest borderlands in the post-bellum decades leading to the Mexican Revolution (Gibson & Jung, 2006; Gratton & Gutmann, 2000; Martínez, 1975; Nostrand, 1975). Dissimilarities in proportionate representation of Mexican executions to Anglo executions support the notion that justice officials discriminated against Mexicans in imposing the death penalty. Mexicans comprised slightly more than 10 percent of the borderland population on average throughout the post-bellum period, but they represented more than 21 percent of regional executions. These figures reveal that Mexican prisoners were more than *twice* as likely to be hanged for capital crimes relative to their proportionate representation in the borderland population. The overrepresentation of Mexican executions for capital crimes means that justice officials excessively executed Mexican offenders. The overrepresentation of Mexican executions contrasts with the underrepresentation of Anglo executions. Anglos averaged about 81 percent of the borderland population throughout the period, but were about 41 percent of regional executions, with Anglos hanged for capital crimes *less than twice as often* as one would predict from their proportionate representation in the region's population.

Comparative execution rates controlling for population differences between Anglos and Mexicans provide another measure of Mexican capital justice inequality in the borderlands. Mexican execution rates far exceeded Anglo execution rates throughout the post-bellum decades, as justice officials executed Mexicans at an overall rate nearly *five times* the rate of Anglo executions in the period. Mexican execution rates *by decades* reveal that Mexican execution rates far exceeded those of Anglo execution rates. In the 1910s, for instance, Mexican execution rates were *tenfold* the execution rates of Anglos. Though borderland authorities hanged nearly twice as many Anglo prisoners as Mexican prisoners for capital offenses, disparities in Mexican execution rates relative to Anglo execution rates given each population's proportionate representation in the borderlands suggest severe ethnic discrimination in executing Mexican prisoners.

There is considerable anecdotal evidence of ethnic bias and discrimination in borderland capital justice systems that amplified the vulnerability of Mexicans to execution. Virulent Anglo racism accented a double standard of capital justice that disadvantaged Mexicans. Anglos dominated the justice system as sheriffs, police officers, state prosecutors, and judges. These justice officials did not necessarily deem the killing of a Mexican a criminal act, "the evidence is convincing that the dominant white society and its law really meant white man, white justice" (De León, 1983; McKanna, 2007:95–96). State prosecutors recurrently refused to indict Anglos who perpetrated capital offenses against Mexicans (McKanna, 2007). Jurisdictions tried Mexicans largely before biased Anglo juries and judges whose distorted and mean-spirited cultural views toward Mexicans influenced trial outcomes (Rosales, 1999). The "whiteness" of the justice system afforded Anglos far greater prospects of acquittal and dismissal of their capital cases than Mexicans, especially in cases involving Anglo defendants with Mexican murder victims.

Mexican defendants often pleaded guilty to murders because Anglo judges frequently expressed open courtroom disdain for Mexicans (Rosales, 1999). Even if authorities afforded Mexican defendants jury trials, judicial officers rarely provided Mexican defendants with Spanish interpreters to ensure that Mexican defendants with limited or no understanding of English were aware of judicial proceedings and courtroom testimony (Aguirre & Baker, 1989; see also Urbina, 2004b). Drastic results occasioned Mexican defendants who spoke only Spanish and faced capital trials without understanding the legal proceedings where judges denied defendants' access to an interpreter. One such victim was Simón Ruíz, a young Mexican national from Jalisco who pleaded guilty to killing his Anglo employer while burglarizing his employer's home. A California jury convicted Ruíz of the murder and the trial judge sentenced him to hang at San Quentin Prison. At his sentencing hearing, Ruíz did not learn that the judge had sentenced him to death because he did not have an interpreter. Ruíz reportedly learned of his looming execution only after a fellow bilingual inmate revealed to Ruíz that he was on death row. Ruíz was overcome with "shrieks of horror." Fortunately for Ruíz, the state's governor commuted his sentence to life in prison after repeated appeals to the state's governor from the Mexican consulate and women's groups interested in sparing the young man's life (*Oakland Tribune,* 1921a, 1921b, 1921c).

Many Anglos had available resources for effective legal counsel "who knew how to work the system," but most Mexicans did not have adequate resources for competent legal representation (Urbina, 2012; Urbina et al., 2014). There were few Spanish-speaking lawyers in the southwest and Anglo lawyers were largely indifferent to Mexican defendants. Apathetic and ineffective lawyers made it difficult for Mexicans to defend against capital indictments. There is also a long history of jury exclusion and the barring of courtroom testimony in the southwest that further disadvantaged Mexican defendants (Sheridan, 2003; see also Mirandé, Chapter 10, this volume). Likewise, impoverished Mexican defendants found appellate courts largely inaccessible, to the point that well over *two-thirds* of Mexican capital defendants did not seek appellate review of their convictions and death sentences (Urbina, 2011, 2012). In a few cases, women's groups raised funds for appeals of convicted Mexican defendants and at times solicited Mexican consulates to apply diplomatic pressure to state governors for stays of execution (McKanna, 2007).

Anglos engaged in widespread lawlessness along the border in the post-bellum period, but government authorities more strongly focused their anger and animosity on Mexican banditry (Rosales, 1999). Scholars explain that "brigands" are often conquered minorities victimized by exploitation and racism "whose oppressed status is the source of their criminality" (Gonzáles, 2009:89). Criminalizing Mexican liberators from colonial oppression as political insurgents accented Anglo repressive strategies to control Mexicans in the southwest. *Political insurrection* accentuated the capital justice experience of Mexicans in the borderlands. Anglo racism and deliberate repudiation of the provisions in the Treaty of Guadalupe Hidalgo (1848) safeguarding Mexicans' rights to land and culture in the southwest gave rise to an insurgency of *los pobres Mexicanos* as social bandits (Mirandé, 1985). Anglo criminalization of Mexicans as *bandits* or *bloodthirsty outlaws* was a response to Mexicans moving deliberately and decisively against Anglo conquest, occupation, and political and economic repression (see Aguirre, this volume).

The Anglo population reduced Mexican "resistance and struggle against dispossession and oppression to the image of a violent, barbarous, and ferocious bandito" (Romero, 2001:1090). Mexicans used violent political resistance "as one means for retaining some measure of *self-determination* in the face of an increasingly oppressive new regime" (Rosenbaum, 1990:16). Robert Rosenbaum's (1990:16) typology of political resistance in the borderlands includes *social banditry,* "the most basic and constant expression of hostility that was carried out by individuals who refused to submit and who enjoyed the support of their general communities."

Social bandits were typically victims of Anglo cruelty and injustice though admired, respected, and supported by impoverished Mexicans (Mirandé, 1987; Urbina et al., 2014). Executing Mexican insurgents proved an effective retort to a community countering the brutality of Anglo oppression. Though mythology surrounds much about "Mexican banditos," Mirandé (1987:74) explains that developed legends "appear to have been little more than a smokescreen to mask injustices and atrocities perpetrated against Mexicans."

Despite the folklore, one pronounced feature of the lives of many impoverished rebellious Mexicans in the borderlands was "to go outside of the law and defend rights and property that should have been legitimately theirs" (Mirandé, 1985:73). Some of the more notorious political insurgents who Anglos labeled as *bloodthirsty outlaws* in early California included Joaquín Murieta, José Barrillo, Luciano Tapia, and Tiburcio Vásquez. Juan Flores, for instance, was the leader of the Flores-Daniels gang that operated in California between San Luis Obispo and San Juan Capistrano in the mid to late 1850s. Flores led some 50 to 70 Mexicans compatriots rustling cattle and committing robberies and murders against Anglo settlers. The vigilantes condemned Flores to the gallows after lynching many of his compatriots, hanging him in February 1857 before a crowd of some 3,000 people. Mexican insurgents often hanged in jail courtyards after trials calculated to assure their executions, while many others died in gun battles with state police and vigilante possess or murdered outright by law enforcement. In early October 1868, for instance, a posse of five armed men pursued José Claudio Alvitre for arrest because he was a *desperado* who belonged to a gang of horse thieves. One of the posse men shot and killed Alvitre (*The Upper Des Moines,* 1868). Arizona officials

condemned Augustine Chacón as "one of the blackest hearted villains that ever operated in the southwest" (Cleere, 2006; *Hutchinson Daily News,* 1897:2; Wilson, 2004). Insurgentes in Texas included Juan Nepomuceno Cortina, José María Méndez, Francisco Barela, Catarino Garza, Gerónimo Parra, Gregorio Cortez, and José Córdova. In New Mexico, brothers Juan, Pablo, and Nicanor Herrera, and Vicente Silva violently challenged the transformation of communal Mexican land to private Anglo cattle enterprises (Rosenbaum, 1990).

Beyond the social banditry of individual insurgents, entire Mexican communities joined in organized rebellions that challenged the dominant order resulting in still more Mexican executions. Rosenbaum (1990:16) refers to such insurgent *community upheavals* as "when tensions became sufficiently high and widespread to precipitate a spontaneous outbreak." Community upheavals took place throughout the borderlands. In New Mexico, for instance, Mexicans openly rebelled against American occupation. One insurgency began in Taos when Mexican rebels killed the territorial governor. Though the rebellion spread quickly, the American military swiftly and mercilessly crushed the revolt killing some *three hundred* Mexican insurgents and ruthlessly demolished their towns and villages. Officials charged Pablo Montoya and Tomás Romero as leaders of the rebellion, Montoya standing trial and hanged in February, but guards shot and killed Romero during an escape attempt. In Santa Fe, a grand jury indicted Antonio María Trujillo, Pantaleon Archuleta, Trinidad Barcelo, and Pedro Vigil as principals in the revolt. Juries acquitted all but Trujillo who was hanged for high treason. Officials held another 40 captured prisoners in Taos and ultimately indicted most of them for the governor's murder, including leaders Polio Salazar and Francisco Ulibarri.

A jury acquitted Ulibarri and several others, but Polio Salazar, José Manuel García, Pedro Lucero, Juan Ramon Trujillo, Manuel Romero, and Isidro Romero were hanged for the governor's murder as well. Another 11 unnamed rebels were hanged within months (Torréz, 1996).

Anglo homesteaders and merchants in New Mexico disrupted the traditional way of native rural life when they appropriated communal Mexican lands and fenced off open ranges for commercial cattle enterprises and cut off water supplies and grazing land from New Mexican sheepherders. Under the auspices of a clandestine organization known as *Las Gorras Blancas* or "The White Caps," hundreds of poor Mexican farmers responded to Anglo encroachment with midnight raids to intimidate Anglos. The insurgents tore down fences, burned barns and haystacks, scattered livestock, and burned thousands of railroad ties and damaged railroad trestles (Correia, 2010). Pablo Herrera, one of the political insurgents that led Las Gorras Blancas was shot to death by a county sheriff while walking along the street. Officials never prosecuted the sheriff for Herrera's murder. Vincente Silva was one of the more violent members of Las Gorras Blancas who, along with about 60 men, engaged in violent assaults of Anglos and their ill-gotten property.

Anglo violence accounted for the deaths of more than 5,000 Mexicans during the decade of the Mexican Revolution, 1910 to 1919 (Hill & Sadler, 1990). Besides the outright murder of Mexicans, the Anglo community executed one of the highest numbers of Mexican prisoners in the decade since 1848. From 1915 to 1916, one of the more violent community upheavals took place when Texas Anglos discovered an armed Mexican insurrection called *The Plan of San Diego* (Harris & Sadler, 1978; Johnson, 2003; Sandos, 1992). The Mexicans involved with the insurrection were associated with revolutionaries in Mexico. A captured manifesto proclaimed the execution of Anglo males over the age of sixteen, freedom for all oppressed people, and the separation of South Texas as an independent state. The revolutionaries killed Anglos, dislocated thousands of people, and destroyed bridges, railroads and other infrastructure until authorities suppressed the insurgency by summarily executing Mexicans.

MEXICAN LYNCHINGS

Sociologist Oliver Cox (1945:578) distinguished lynchings in the United States "as an act of homicidal aggression committed by one people against another through mob action for the purpose of suppressing either some tendency in the latter to rise from an accommodated position of subordination or for subjugating them further to some lower social class." An important feature of Cox's definition of lynching is the association between the *deadly violence of mob action* and *class oppression*. Scholars isolate the connection between *mob action* and *social oppression* as maintaining *social control* over subordinate populations through terrorism; suppressing subordinate competition for economic, political, and social rewards; and stabilizing the class structure and preserving the privileged status of a superordinate population (Tolnay & Beck, 1995). Borderland scholars have extended lynching theory to people of Mexican descent in the southwest from 1848 to 1928. William Carrigan and Clive Webb's seminal work reveals the brutality associated with Anglo mob violence and class oppression in the southwest at rates that rivaled black lynchings in the Deep South. These scholars emphasize that Mexican lynchings are more than an addendum to U.S. ethnic history, as many criminal justice researchers have dealt with the matter, but accent "a critical chapter in the history of Anglo western expansion and conquest" (Carrigan, 2006; Carrigan & Webb, 2003; Gonzáles-Day, 2006).

Mexicans suffered the wrath of Anglo vigilante terrorism more than the violence of state executions. The borderlands account for most of the nearly 600 Mexican lynchings in the period, three times the number of Mexican executions (Carrigan & Webb, 2003). California and Texas account for a preponderance of Mexican lynchings, with more than 48 percent of Mexican lynching taking place in Texas, followed by California at slightly more than 32 percent. Large numbers of vigilante groups formed in California, New Mexico, and Texas between 1849 and 1896 (Brown, 1969), but it was Texas that had the bloodiest record of vigilante violence in the region, particularly in the 1860s (Friedman, 2005; Zimring, 2011). Much of the lynching carnage in California and Texas resulted from Anglos depriving large numbers of Mexicans to gold mining claims and land settlements. The discovery of gold in California lured Mexicans miners in the late 1840s through the 1850s. The bitter resentment Anglos held toward the success of Mexican miners in extracting the precious metal accented Mexican lynching in the mining camps of early California.

Borderland mobs lynched Mexican women as well. While Anglo men venerated upper-class Mexican women, they marginalized lower-class Mexican females as "sexually promiscuous women of ill-repute" (Almaguer, 1994:62). The Anglo perception of impoverished Mexican women incited anti-Mexican sentiments and legitimated California's only female hanging in the period, that of young Juanita (Gonzáles-Day, 2006; Rojas, 2007). Juanita was hanged for the stabbing death of an English miner in a small mining town in the mountains of northeastern California after an intense argument. Anglos hanged Pablita Sandoval in New Mexico while it was still a territorial possession of the United States (Gilbreath, 2002; Tórrez, 2008). Pablita was hanged for the murder of her married boyfriend, Juan Miguel Martin, after a makeshift trial. Chipita Rodríguez was the earliest female hanging for murder in Texas. She strangled to death at the end of a noose after another person confessed to the murder, rendering Chipita's hanging a wrongful execution (Pittman, 1998). Chipita's wrongful hanging resulted from an irregular trial involving a bigoted judge, virulent Anglo racism, and an apathetic defense lawyer. For additional detail on the executions of these Mexican women, see Álvarez & Urbina (2014), Urbina (2012), and Peña and Urbina, this volume.

Mexican lynchings in the southwestern borderlands were violent manifestations of Anglo bigotry in the postbellum period to the Mexican Revolution. Anglo mobs did not limit their violent aggression toward Mexicans to hanging, but frequently included shooting, burning alive, physical mutilation, and other forms of murderous persecution of Mexicans (Johnson, 2003; Urbina et al., 2014). One of the more horrific killings took place in November 1910 when an Anglo crowd burned alive Antonio Rodríguez, a young Mexican ranchhand in Rock Springs, Texas, after he confessed to raping and murdering the wife of Clem Anderson, an Anglo rancher in Edwards County, because she was rude when he asked for food. The extremists took the young Rodríguez to a site just outside of the county jail yard and tied him to a mesquite tree, and when the funeral pyre was large enough, one Anglo "splashed the contents of a five-gallon can of kerosene on the prisoner and the brush. A match was lit, and the crowd watched silently while Rodríguez turned into a charred corpse." Anglos living in the area approved of Antonio's lynching believing ranchers' wives were in danger of Mexican male ravages. Mexican rioting in response to Rodríguez's murder intensified Anglo fear along the border. A company of Rangers and some armed Anglo ranchers moved into the area to restore calm. Riots and assaults on Americans broke out as far away as Mexico City and armed Mexicans crossed the border in response to Rodríguez's killing. Rodríguez had a wife and young daughter living in Mexico (*New York Times,* 1910). Similarly in 1953, west Texas Anglos engaged in a "sadistic mutilation" killing of young Raul Arevalo for his interest in a young Anglo girl (De León, 1983:105).

Dispelling the notion that lynching substituted for the lack of formal justice, Anglos often lynched Mexicans near jails and courtrooms "when vigilante mobs could not wait for formal justice to proceed" (Acuña, 2005; Delgado, 2009; Urbina et al., 2014). Mexican lynching often involved vigilante committees denying formal justice, as "[m]ost were summarily executed by mobs that denied the accused even the pretense of a trial" (Carrigan & Webb, 2003:416). Some scholars caution, however, that much of the story on Mexican lynching is lost in the pages of Spanish-language newspapers no longer in existence, such as *El Clamor Publico* published in Los Angeles from 1855–1859 (Acuña, 2005; Sanchez, 2016; Urbina et al., 2014). Similar to black lynchings in the postbellum South, accounting for Mexican lynching overlooks the vast numbers of killings where "disappearance is shrouded in mystery, for they are dispatched quickly and without general knowledge. In some swamp a small body of men do the job formerly done by a vast, howling, blood-thirsty mob" (McMillen, 1989:252).

Land dispossession was a major factor in the economic, political, and social conquest of the borderlands. Anglo access to courts that legitimated suspicious claims facilitated the process of Mexican land dispossession (Acuña, 2015; Leyva, 2000; Urbina et al., 2014). As explained by some scholars,

> Mexican landowners, often robbed by force, intimidation, or fraud, could defend their holdings through litigation, but this generally led to heavy indebtedness, with many forced to sell their holdings to meet necessary legal expenses. With depressing regularity, Anglos generally ended up with Mexican holdings, acquired at prices far below their real value. (Estrada, García, Macias, & Maldonado, 1981:105)

In some cases, Anglo officials looted archives and burned legitimate deeds to ensure the legal dispossession of Mexicans from their land. Anglo landowners used Texas Rangers to terrorize and murder Mexican landowners to acquire land titles (Pérez, 2006). Texas Rangers account for much of the violence and brutal oppression of Mexicans though officials rarely prosecuted Rangers for their criminality against Mexicans (Looney, 1971; Pérez, 2006; Samora, Bernal, & Peña, 1979; Urbina & Álvarez, 2015), as vividly documented by Charles Harris and Louis Sadler in *The Texas Rangers and the Mexican Revolution: The Bloodiest Decade, 1910–1920* (2007).[1] Historians estimate that Texas Rangers murdered thousands of Mexicans, as reported by David McLemore in "The Forgotten Carnage 89 Years Ago, Rangers Singled out Hispanics, and Thousands Died" (2004). Carrigan and Webb (2003:416–417) explain that "Their brutal repression of the Mexican population was tantamount to state-sanctioned terrorism."

One of the more notorious instances of Texas Rangers' cold-blooded killing of Mexicans took place in Presidio County at Porvenir in southeast Texas in early 1918. There, some 40 Anglo ranchers, a company of Texas Rangers, and troopers of the U.S. Eighth Calvary, rousted 20 Mexican small farmers and ranchers, including teenage boys. Mexican marauders apparently had killed several Anglos at a nearby ranch, stole some horses, and robbed the ranch store (a trading post). The posse of ranchers, Rangers, and soldiers shot 15 of the rousted Mexicans execution style, including two young boys 16 and 17 years old, and muti-lated their bodies with knives under the pretext that the Mexicans were the bandits who had plundered the ranch. The disfigured bodies were so defaced with bullet and knife wounds that they were virtually unrecognizable (Davis, 2007). As an 11-year-old boy and one of five survivors of the massacre, Juan Bonilla Flores remembered crying while holding his dead father's body and his nearly bullet-severed head in the aftermath of the massacre. In an interview decades later, Flores recalled, "They killed us for our land and because we were Mexicans." Flores died in Odessa, Texas, in March 2007 at 101 years old (Rosales, 1999).

MEXICAN EXPULSIONS

Besides the lethal violence of lynchings and executions, borderland Mexicans endured the brutality of mass expulsions. *Expulsion* refers to the forced removal of subordinate groups from discrete geographical regions. Scholars link expulsions inextricably to "forms of physical and symbolic violence" that serve "to cleanse the body politic of undesirables." As a form of deliberate violence, researchers assert that it is impracticable to separate expulsions from ethnic cleansing, which itself fuses with deportation and genocide (Hernández, 2010). Recent scholarship lays bare the extreme misery marginalized groups have suffered from expulsion in the United States historically. Jean Pfaelzer (2007), for instance, paints a disturbing portrait of Chinese suffering the murderous acts of Anglo mobs during purges and racial cleansing in western states, where Anglos engaged in some 200 roundups designed to eliminate the Chinese population. Elliott Jaspin (2007) examined the crisis of racial cleansing of violent Anglo mobs purging blacks from townships and rural counties across the country that remain ex-clusively white today. Other researchers describe the ethnic cleansing accenting the brutal campaigns and genocidal carnage of Anglos against American Indians in Texas (Anderson, 2005; Gibson, 1980; Stannard, 1992).

Anglos engaged in ethnic cleansing of Mexicans when they forcibly removed Mexicans from regions within the borderlands in the wake of ethnic conflicts. In bringing renewed attention to the omission in the historical record of Mexican repatriation in the United States, social historian José Ángel Hernández has chronicled two waves of Mexican expulsions from regions in the southwest (Hernández, 2010). Hernández traced the *first wave* of Mexican expulsions to include Anglo retaliation for the casualties suffered in the Texas Revolution in 1836, in 1842, and in the 1850s. A *second wave* of Mexican expulsions occurred in the second half of the nineteenth century and the early twentieth century when Anglos perceived increased Mexican immigration to California and Texas as threatening their economic, social, and political interests.

The Texas Revolution culminated from Texans' perceptions that they were "in danger of becoming the alien subjects of a people to whom they deliberately believed themselves morally, intellectually, and politically superior" (Estrada et al., 1981:104). In the 1820s and 1830s, the Mexican government encouraged Anglo settlements by issuing land grants to foster population growth and promote commercial development in the region. As a result, large numbers of Anglo farmers, mostly from southern slave states armed with "white racial framing and stereotypes," migrated into the region making it increasingly more difficult for Mexico to control the dominant Anglo population (Feagin & Feagin, 2011). Settlement conditions imposed by the Mexican government required new arrivals to declare their political allegiance to Mexico and convert to Catholicism, or at least concede not to practice Protestantism. Troubled by Mexico's efforts to enforce the settlement conditions, Anglo settlers assembled conventions in 1832 and 1833 to draft resolutions proclaiming Texas' autonomy despite Mexico's rejection of an independent Texas.

Anglos began a bloody campaign for independence hastening a dark revolutionary period of fierce battles in 1835 and 1836. In early October 1835, Texans stormed Mexican troops at the Battle of Gonzáles, overtook the presidio at Goliad, and defeated a large garrison of Mexican troops at the Battle of Concepcion at San Jacinto. In March 1836, some 1,600 Mexican troops slaughtered 189 Texans at the Alamo and outright executed another 342 Texas troops at Goliad. Leaving Texans ever more resolved to independence was the Mexican massacre of Anglo farmers in Cherokee County in October 1838 and the discovery of a Mexican and Indian conspiracy against Anglos in 1838. In the aftermath of these events, Mexican families living in Victoria,

San Patricio, Goliad, Refugio, and Nacogdoches "were driven from their homes, their treasures, their cattle and horses and their lands, by an army of reckless, war-crazy people [who] distrusted and hated Mexicans, simply because they were Mexicans" (Hernández, 2010:121–122).

The Texas rebellion for independence culminated in the Treaty of Velasco signed by Mexican President Antonio López de Santa Anna. The Mexican government refused the claim, however, believing that Texans had intimidated the jailed Santa Anna into signing the treaty. Throughout 1842 and into May 1843, the Mexican Army made several unsuccessful attempts to recapture Texas when it sent troops into San Antonio. Because of Mexico's ill attempt to reconquer Texas, Anglos "initiated yet another round of intense expulsions of those Mexicans unfortunate enough to be residing in that territory, even if they had fought for independence from Mexico" (Hernández, 2010:123). Texas remained an independent republic until the United States annexed the territory as a state in December 1845. Once Anglos situated themselves in a position of dominance they expelled Mexicans "from Austin in 1853 and again in 1855, from Seguin in 1854, from the counties of Matagorda and Colorado in 1856, and from Uvalde in 1857" (Hernández, 2010:124–125). Anglos expelled Mexicans "under the penalty of death" after discovering a conspiracy of some 200 slaves in Colorado County in 1850. In Seguin, for instance, Anglos prohibited Mexicans from entering Guadalupe County "because of their alleged sympathy with the bond people" (De León, 1983:50). Mexican expulsions occurred again in the 1880s after raiders crossed the U.S.-Mexico border and "wreaked havoc on populations as far north as McCulloch." County officials ordered all noncitizen Mexicans out of the county. In the early 1890s, Mexicans left

Cisco, Texas, out of fear of summary execution by Anglos. One of the largest mass deportations of Mexicans took place in the aftermath of the Plan of San Diego in 1915 (only about 100 years ago) when "Anglo-American fear and vengeance proved to be effective in intimidating Mexican residents . . . the roads leading to the border were congested with lengthy wagon trains of fleeing Mexicans" (McCay, 2011).

In California, the success of Mexicans in the gold fields accented an emboldened Anglo public opinion to expel the Mexican competitors (Gonzáles, 2009).[2] The state passed several mandates excluding Mexicans from the state's economic, social, and political life. The Foreign Miners' License Act of April 1850, for instance, forced a $20 monthly fee on Mexican miners that effectively reduced Mexican competition with Anglo miners. Some 4,000 Mexican miners protested the tax, but the legislation had its intended effect when more than *two-thirds* of the 15,000 Mexican miners in several mining counties "packed their belongings and departed," and returned to Mexico (Gonzáles, 2009:87). Rioting, marauding, the burning of Mexican mining camps and the lynching of Mexican miners forced most to abandon their mining claims (Mirandé, 1987). By 1860, vigilante violence had forced roughly 80 percent of Mexican miners to leave the state (Pfaelzer, 2007). California passed other so-called "Greaser Laws" to purge Mexicans from the state. Immediately after gaining statehood in 1851, for instance, California forced counties with large Mexican populations to pay property taxes at a rate *five times* that imposed in other regions of the state. Many more Mexicans left California because they could not afford the extra tax. In fact, the first state constitution reserved voting rights entirely to Anglo males, with the denial of suffrage to Mexicans effectively excluding their inter-

ests early on in the state's commercial development. The Anti-Vagrancy Act of 1855 imposed slave-like sanctions on Mexicans. The act pertained to "all persons who are commonly known as 'Greasers' or the issue of Spanish and Indian blood . . . and who [went] armed and [were] not peaceable and quiet persons" (Takaki, 1993:10). Officials under the statute imposed fines on Mexicans guilty of vagrancy and forced violators "to pay either in cash or through temporary labor service" (Almaguer, 1994:57). Anglos thereby forced more Mexicans from the state.

Economic contractions and expansions in the early to mid-decades of the twentieth century in the United States had a direct effect on Mexican expulsions *vis-à-vis* immigration policies (Álvarez & Urbina, 2018). Economic decline in the early twentieth century effected the deportation of hundreds of Mexican workers back across the border (Hernández, 2010). World War I (1914–1918) interrupted the flow of European immigrants to the United States leaving much of the developing economy in the southwest without workers. As a result, commercial interests recruited Mexicans to fill commercial labor needs. In the decades of the 1920s, roughly a half-million Mexicans entered the United States to satisfy labor shortages. However, in the midst of the Great Depression, which started in 1929, federal agents deported thousands of Mexican workers after nativist anti-Mexican sentiment reached a *feverous pitch* blaming Mexicans for rising unemployment, lower wages, and affecting a drain on entitlement programs (Balderrama & Rodríguez, 1995; Johnson, 2005). Under *Operation Deportation,* borderland states expelled a half-million Mexicans from the United States, many of whom were citizens of this country. Scholars explain,

Local agencies, saddled with mounting relief and unemployment problems, used a variety of methods to rid themselves of "Mexicans": persuasion, coaxing, incentive, and unauthorized coercion. Special railroad trains were made available, with fare at least to the Mexican border prepaid; and people were often rounded up by local agencies to fill carloads of human cargo. In an atmosphere of pressing emergency, little if any time was spent on determining whether the methods infringed upon the rights of citizens.

After the depression and the onslaught of World War II (1939–1945), commercial interests in the southwest recruited thousands of Mexican nationals under the *Braceros Program* to fill labor shortages. Yet, under *Operation Wetback* in the 1950s, the federal government again apprehended and repatriated hundreds of thousands of Mexican workers (Hernández, 2010; Gutiérrez, 1997).

DISCUSSION AND CONCLUSION

This chapter brings into sharper focus the historical and social forces affecting the criminal justice experience of Mexicans in the post-bellum decades (1866–1913) up to the Mexican Revolution (1910–1920). The ethnic violence experienced by Mexicans living in the borderlands was rooted in Anglo *reigns of terror* against Mexicans. Centuries later, the social relations between Mexicans and Anglos in the borderlands have not changed in the modern era, an era characterized by Anglo domination of Mexicans. That is, the *culture of violence* that has characterized for more than 150 years the lives of Mexicans living in the borderlands continues unabated (Álvarez & Urbina, 2018; Escobar, 2016; Salinas, 2015; Urbina et al., 2014).

In the modern era of capital punishment, borderland jurisdictions have put to death nearly 100 Mexican (and over 100 Latino) prisoners since 1976 (Álvarez & Urbina, 2014; Urbina, 2004a). For a complete list of executed Mexican nationals, Mexican Americans, and other Latinos in modern times, see Peña and Urbina, this volume, and see Urbina (2012) for a complete list of all executed people in the United States, post-1976.

As we entered the twenty-first century we would expect equality in the administration of justice by the American criminal justice system, particularly after centuries of supposed reform. However, Mexicans continue to face a discriminatory capital justice system (Álvarez & Urbina, 2014; Urbina, 2004a, 2012). For instance, justice authorities are *three times* as likely to execute Mexican prisoners convicted of murdering Anglos than Anglo prisoners convicted of murdering Mexicans (Fins, 2011). In fact, as we entered the new millennium, nationally, Mexicans were victims of homicide at a rate 47 percent higher than that of the general population, yet less than four percent of executions involve Mexican murder victims (Rennison, 2002). The violent crime victimization rate for Mexicans is higher than that for Anglos and blacks (Pew Center on the States, 2009). Mexicans are not immune to the systemic ethnic bias in capital sentencing accenting prosecutorial discretion in selecting capital cases; the unlawful prosecutorial use of peremptory challenges that systematically exclude marginalized Mexicans from juries in capital cases; the unrelenting prosecutorial misconduct; the exploitation of capital defendants' mental incapacities; the indifference and ineffectiveness of defense lawyers; and the wrongful convictions due to prosecutorial lawlessness and false confessions (Álvarez & Urbina, 2014; Amnesty International, 2003; Equal Justice Initiative, 2010; Lee, 2007; Urbina, 2012). For instance, in a recent capital trial involving a Mexican defendant, Texas prosecutors offered "expert" testimony that Mexicans are more worthy of the death penalty than Anglo murderers (Vázquez, 2000). Such a prevailing mindset may be one explanation why official reports reveal significant increases not only in the Mexican death row population but also in nondeath penalty cases over the last decade (Álvarez & Urbina, 2014; Snell, 2010; Urbina, 2012). There, a presiding judge sentenced Juan Raul Garza to death for the murder of three drug traffickers and officials executed Garza by lethal injection in June 2001 (Álvarez & Urbina, 2014; Death Penalty Information Center, 2001). What's more, authorities have botched Mexican defendants' executions (Álvarez & Urbina, 2014; Urbina, 2012). In the case of Genaro Ruiz Camacho's lethal injection killing in August 1998, officials delayed the execution for nearly two hours while prison executioners found a suitable vein in Camacho's arm (Radelet, 2010).

The execution of *foreign nationals* in the borderlands attests to patterns of unlawful Mexican executions (Álvarez & Urbina, 2014). In the context of capital punishment, foreign nationals are noncitizens under a sentence of death. Pursuant to the 1963 Vienna Convention on Consular Relations and Optional Protocols, local arresting authorities are required to notify detained foreign nationals immediately of their right to communicate with their respective consular representative. Borderland officials fail to honor treaty obligations; detained foreign nationals learn of their consular rights most often from attorneys and other prisoners and not local

arresting authorities (Álvarez & Urbina, 2014). Failure to give foreign nationals access to consulates violates international law and a binding order of the International Court of Justice, ICJ (Álvarez & Urbina, 2014; Amnesty International, 2011a). In this regard, Mexico sued the United States in 2004 in the ICJ at the World Court claiming that American authorities denied consular rights to 51 Mexican nationals (Fleishman, 2003; *International Law Update,* 2005; Macina, 2003; Schiffman, 2000; Sloane, 2004; Steinmark, 2004; Young, 2005). The ICJ ordered new hearings for the death row prisoners but the Texas Court of Criminal Appeals rebuffed the World Court. Texas has put to death several Mexican foreign nationals without immediate consular notification (Álvarez & Urbina, 2014; Death Penalty Information Center, 2011; Donald, 2005; Dow, 2005; Urbina, 2004a, 2012). Texas executed Mexican national Irineo Tristan Montoya, for instance, knowing that arresting authorities had not informed Montoya of his consular rights. Had Texas authorities given Montoya access to the Mexican consulate to ensure his fair treatment, state officials may not have forced Montoya to sign an English written confession despite his inability to read and write the language (Álvarez & Urbina, 2014; Amnesty International, 2011b; Urbina, 2012).

Individual and collective violence remain intrinsic to Mexican lives. Mexicans are a significant percentage of hate crime targets where ethnicity or national origin motivates the crimes. The growth of hate groups has more dramatically increased in borderlands states, which have become highly militarized (Álvarez & Urbina, 2018; Balko, 2013; Dunn, 1996, 2009; Salinas, 2015; Tirman, 2015). Anti-Mexican hate crimes have increased dramatically in California since 2009 (Potoc, 2011; Salinas, 2015). Often hate crime results in homicides where ethnicity is the motivation of offenders (Federal Bureau of Investigation, 2010). Official figures on anti-Mexican hate crimes are troubling since Mexican victims are often reluctant to contact law enforcement given its long history of maltreatment of Latinos (Urbina & Álvarez, 2015). Much of the hate violence against Mexicans may stem from the "demonization" and "criminalization" of Mexican immigrants fueled by the mass media and such national figures as Bill O'Reilly, Sean Hannity, Ann Coulter, Lou Dobbs (Markert, 2010; Schumacher-Matos, 2009) and political figures like Donald Trump.

Besides individual acts of violence, considerable criminal justice and legal scholarship show a myriad of violent police practices against Mexicans in the southwest that are reminiscent of the brutality waged against Mexicans by the Texas Rangers and other hate groups of decades past (Dunn, 2009; Durán, 2009a; Escobar, 1999; Urbina & Álvarez, 2015; see also Whitehead, 2013). Police aggression is systemic to Mexican communities and often involves "injustice shootings, severe beatings, fatal chokings, and rough treatment" (Álvarez & Urbina, 2018; Dunn, 2009; Human Rights Watch, 1998; Romero, 2006; Salinas, 2015). Hundreds of complaints by Mexican migrants, for instance, reveal that local, state, and federal law enforcement agents patrolling the U.S.-Mexico border violate civil rights of immigrants, including illegal searches of people and private property, verbal, psychological and physical abuse, child abuse, deprivation of food, water, and medical attention, torture, theft, excessive force, assault and battery, and murder (Álvarez & Urbina, 2018; Dunn, 2009; Huspek, Martínez, & Jimenez, 1998; Salinas, 2015, Tirman, 2015).

In effect, Mexican expulsions continue today (Álvarez & Urbina, 2018), as recently documented by Martin Guevara Urbina and Ilse Aglaé Peña in "Policing Borders: Immigration, Criminalization, and Militarization in the Era of Social Control Profitability." With increased militarization of the U.S.-Mexico border and under the guise of legitimate immigration policy, federal authorities expel thousands of Mexicans back across the border annually. Increased criminalization of immigrants over the last few decades has resulted in a substantial increase in the deportation of unauthorized immigrants, most of whom are Mexicans. The tens of thousands of Mexican nationals deported by federal authorities do not include Mexican people apprehended by the U.S. Border Patrol while crossing into the United States unlawfully. Mass deportations of the 1930s depression era continue today. Under the auspices of *Operation Restoration,* for example, local police and federal agents in Chandler, Arizona,

> stopped, questioned, and detained persons of Mexican ancestry–including many U.S. citizens–in an effort to rid the area of undocumented immigrants; police staked out public places believed to be frequented by undocumented immigrants and questioned people who spoke Spanish, and who fit a crude profile of the undocumented immigrant. (Johnson, 2005:11)

Several U.S. Supreme Court cases have found the law enforcement tactics used in the Chandler and similar incidences unconstitutional. Yet since the *Chandler Roundup,* hundreds of other less publicized law enforcement campaigns have resulted in the mass deportation of Mexican immigrants (Álvarez & Urbina, 2018; Beckett & Evans, 2015; Golash-Boza, 2012a, 2012b, 2015; Human Rights Watch, 2015; Robelo, 2014; Salinas, 2015). One recent study documented effects on the children of parents arrested in work-site raids, forced entry of their homes, and operations by local police officers. The effects of these deplorable law enforcement tactics on immigrant children include eating and sleeping disorders, crying and feeling afraid, as well as anxiety disorders, withdrawal and clinginess. Finally, the findings of the study speak volumes about a society that has lost its moral compass and fails to ameliorate the physical and psychological torture of innocent immigrant Mexican children (Chaudry, Capps, Pedroza, Castañeda, Santos, & Scott, 2010), as documented by Urbina in a recent study, "Migrant Children: Exposing Tales and Realities," of migrant children from Mexico, Central America, Syria, and other parts of the world.

Chapter 8

CRIMINALIZING MEXICAN IDENTITY: PRIVILEGE, POWER, AND IDENTITY FORMATION OVER TIME

ADALBERTO AGUIRRE, JR.

What sets worlds in motion is the interplay of differences, their attractions and repulsions. Life is plurality, death is uniformity. By suppressing differences and peculiarities, by eliminating different civilizations and cultures, progress weakens life and favors death. The ideal of a single civilization for everyone, implicit in the cult of progress and technique, impoverishes and mutilates us. Every view of the world that becomes extinct, every culture that disappears, diminishes a possibility of life.

−Octavio Paz

Seeking to further ascertain the continuous oppression of ethnic minorities in modern times, this chapter argues that the identity construction process in society is rooted in a group's access to privilege and power in U.S. society. Those groups with access to privilege and power occupy a position of dominance; while those groups with limited access to privilege and power occupy a subordinate position in society. In effect, as noted in previous chapters (and subsequent chapters), privilege and power differentials have historically situated ethnic minorities, Latinos, in a subordinate position. For in-stance, the limited access of Mexicans, the largest ethnic group in the United States, to privilege and power situates them in a subordinate position within the civic culture and its institutions. Ultimately, the *criminalization* of Mexican identity by the dominant group, Anglos, is a repressive practice that silences Mexicans and obstructs their access to the opportunity structure in society. Given the long history of repressive practices by the dominant group against Mexicans in the United States, then, the focus of this chapter will be on the political climate and legal context for criminalizing Mexican identity.

CRIMINALIZATION OF ETHNIC IDENTITY

History in the making, it is the 1960s; you are sitting on the sofa in the living room watching your favorite television program. The program breaks for a commercial. The television screen comes alive with a cartoon featuring a band of Mexican banditos. The leader of the band is a Mexican bandito with a thick mustache, crossed bandoliers on his chest, a large sombrero, and a cigar sticking out of the corner of his mouth. The announcer's voiceover in the commercial says, "He loves *crunchy* Fritos corn chips so much he'll stop at nothing to get yours. What's more, he's cunning, clever and sneaky! Citizens! Protect yourselves!" And, if by chance you were out of the living room while the commercial played, you might have seen this one commercial during another commercial break:

> Emerging from a cloud of dust appears a band of horse-riding ferocious-looking Mexican banditos. They are called to a halt by their sombrero-covered, thick-mustached, fat-bellied leader, who, upon stopping, reaches with the utmost care for a small object from his saddle bags. He picks up the object, lifts up his underarm, and smiles slyly–to spray Arid deodorant. (Martínez, 1973:521)

One might be tempted to regard television commercials featuring Mexican banditos as humorous, as simply entertaining. However, the two commercials reflect popular thinking in American culture about Mexicans; especially, fears associated with their identity as criminal threats (Romero, 2001). The two commercials communicate the message that "citizens," implying U.S. citizens, must protect themselves from Mex-ican criminals, especially smelly ones. As a result, the *bandito* became the archetype for Mexican identity in the Eurocentric culture of the United States. Interestingly, before the Mexican bandito appeared in U.S. television commercials, there was *Speedy González,* a mouse with the ability to outrun cats, especially Sylvester, as he crossed over from Mexico into the United States to raid for cheese. In the twenty-first century, the archetype Mexican bandito is the *narco-terrorist* who raids the United States for valued resources (see Álvarez; Urbina & Álvarez, Chapter 17, this volume).

As such, the primary purpose of this chapter is to discuss the criminalization of *Mexican identity* and its effects on the social relations that characterize Mexican Americans and other Latinos in the United States. For the purpose of discussion, I use the term *Mexican identity* in reference to people of Mexican-origin in the United States. The term Mexican identity is also inclusive of Mexican-origin people born in the United States and those born in Mexico. An assertion in this chapter is that popular thinking about Mexicans in the United States does not differentiate between persons born in the United States from those born in Mexico because from the perspective of the dominant Eurocentric culture in the United States, "all Mexicans look the same" (Aguirre, 2004). What follows is a discussion of the social construction of identity, an examination of the social construction of a criminal identity for Mexicans, an analysis of the political climate for criminalizing Mexican identity, and, lastly, an evaluation of the legal context for criminalizing Mexican identity.

THE SOCIAL CONTRUCTION OF IDENTITY

People use language in their everyday life to initiate and maintain social identities in social interaction with other people; social identities which in fact are nested in perceptions and beliefs associated with people's behavior. The perceptions and beliefs, in turn, construct a set of expectations for people's behavior so that others may interpret its situational and societal appropriateness. On a group level, language operates on a discursive level through such as an institution as the mass media to project images into the public mind that typify the social identities of groups based on their status characteristics, such as sex, race, ethnicity, or age. The process of identity construction in social interaction and the projection of identities in society facilitate the constitutive structure of social relations in society. From a general sociological perspective, people involved in social interaction are constructing and performing identity. In particular, the role of the *other* in the construction and performance of identity increases the likelihood that a person's identity will be socially congruent with the social context (Branaman, 2001; Cooley, 1907; Mead, 1934).

One can observe that the role of the other in the narration of identity in social interaction creates the opportunity for social identity to be constructed as an external process by people for others. That is, the role of the *other* in the narration of identity is not a neutral activity because the *other* has the responsibility of providing the appropriate feedback to people so that their identity conforms to the social situation. Of importance to the discussion in this chapter is the argument that at a group level, groups in positions of privilege and power assume the role of the *other* for groups with less privilege and power. One outcome is that groups with privilege and power in society construct identities for groups with less privilege and power that portray them as a threat to valued resources in society.

I argue in this chapter that privilege and power are central to the construction and performance of social identities at a group level that maintain social relations in society. The *Frito bandito,* for example, is an externally constructed identity based on the stereotypical belief that Mexicans are thieves and a threat to U.S. citizens. The depiction of Mexicans as *banditos* in the Eurocentric culture of the United States reinforces the relative lack of privilege and power Mexicans have in U.S. society. Manuel Castells (1997) argues that identity is a source of meaning for people that is derivative of a social construction process marked by power relationships. Castells (1997) describes three forms of identity construction: (1) *legitimate identity* promoted by dominant institutions in society to legitimate their power over persons, (2) *resistance identity* promoted by persons in powerless positions to challenge ideologies of dominance, and (3) *project identity* promoted by persons to redefine their new position in society. Of relevance to this chapter is the notion of legitimate identity because of its utility to an examination of how dominant groups and dominant institutions construct identities for subordinate groups in order to marginalize them in society.

THE SOCIAL CONSTRUCTION OF A CRIMINAL IDENTITY

The social construction and representation of identity in society within the interplay of privilege and power has differential effects, negative versus positive, on groups based on their access to privilege and power in society. Groups with greater access to privilege and power can construct identities for themselves that legitimate their dominant position in society. In contrast, groups with less access to privilege and power are subject to identities constructed by dominant groups that legitimate their subordinate position in society. That is, the construction and representation of identity in society is a relational process based on differential access to privilege and power that has either inclusionary or exclusionary outcomes for group participation in society (Bhabha 1996; Hall, 1997; Woodward, 1997).

Regarding the sociological study of criminality, Jane Schneider and Peter Schneider (2008) note that the Chicago school of sociology in the 1930s identified a prevailing association in public thinking between criminality and marginalized groups, suggesting that powerless groups were the "usual suspects" in popular thinking regarding criminal behavior. As an historical example, during the 1940s in Los Angeles, Mexican American youths wearing zoot suits were identified by Anglo society and police agencies as criminals, as anti-American during wartime. The zoot suit's

> symbolic power did not rest on its wide shoulders, but on the cultural capital that came to individuals who wore the distinctive garb. The suit had an element of resistance . . . the suits existed in clear opposition to military uniforms, and they became an object of hate, a substitute for the distant enemy. (Howard, 2010:114–115)

The *Sleepy Lagoon* (1942) incident in Los Angeles fueled police attacks on Mexican American youths wearing zoot suits because the mainstream media portrayed the zoot suit as an indicator of "criminality" (Mazón, 1984; see also Durán, this volume). The *Sleepy Lagoon* incident was a clear indication that Mexican identity, especially one shrouded in a zoot suit, was associated with criminality in a public mind fueled by newspaper stories and images.

In his classic study of *Braceros* in the United States, Jorge Bustamante (1972) used labeling theory to illustrate how the identities of Mexican undocumented workers were stigmatized and criminalized as "wetbacks." Prior to the Border Patrol's creation on May 28, 1924 (Hernández, 2010), Mexican immigrants had been entering the United States as seasonal laborers via a fairly open U.S.-Mexico border. However, after the Border Patrol's creation, institutional interventions, such as work permits, were employed to label Mexican immigrants not meeting the Border Patrol's rules as *wetbacks;* that is, as people here illegally. As a result, the Border Patrol constructed a criminal social identity, *wetback,* in order to legitimate its institutional identity, and the application of enforcement practices that benefited the dominant group in the United States.

Kelly Lytle (2003:5) argues that the war on drugs led to the militarization of the U.S.-Mexico border, and a change in focus from *wetbacks* to *border violators:* ". . . the day of the Wetback was over . . . the day of the border violator, a fugitive in a foreign country had arrived . . . the beginnings of rhetoric within the U.S.-Mexico borderlands that criminalized undocumented Mexican immigrants." As Mexican immigrants became more noticeable to the American public in the

1920s, the term "dirty Mexican" was also used to identify them as undesirable and unhealthy in U.S. society (Ngai, 2003). According to Clare Sheridan (2002:6),

> the common term 'dirty Mexicans' could refer to the work that Mexicans did, the diseases they were supposed to be carrying, or the corruption of the ballot by ill-informed laborers . . . The racialization of Mexicans was based on cultural characteristics thought to be rooted in heredity. These characteristics were used to paint Mexicans not only as inferior, but also as racially unfit for democratic life.

Ironically, congressional bills were introduced in the 109th Congress, the Border Protection, Antiterrorism, and Illegal Immigration Control Act of 2005 (HR 4437) and the Securing America's Borders Act (S 2454), that would make the unauthorized presence of aliens in the United States a criminal offense (García, 2006; Stumpf, 2006). In short, such legislation sought to control the U.S.-Mexico border by targeting "Mexican identity" as a criminal offense.

Consider, for instance, the Samantha Runnion case. Samantha was lured from her front yard by a man that told her he was looking for his dog in July 2002. Samantha was kidnapped, strangled, and sexually abused. Her body was found by two hang gliders in Riverside County, California. The prime suspect in the Runnion case was described as an "Americanized Hispanic" that made most Mexican males "suspect."

Rather than focus on specific features of the suspect, such as accented English or Spanish language use, skin tone, or eye color, to construct a realistic composite portrait of the suspect, law enforcement authorities decided to use the suspect's *identity* as the primary descriptor (Salinas, 2002). The Runnion case illustrates how in fact law enforcement widens the net of potential suspects by criminalizing an *identity* that is readily associated with criminality in the public's mind. During the search for Samantha Runnion's killer Mexican people underwent greater public scrutiny because "law enforcement officials said anyone vaguely resembling the suspect could expect to face scrutiny from the massive dragnet designed to catch Samantha's killer" (Stanton & Brown, 2002:A1).

Lastly, the preceding examples illustrate how Mexican identity has been criminalized by dominant groups and institutions in U.S. society. The association of Mexican identity with negative perceptions and behaviors in the public's mind is instrumental in restricting Mexicans from access to privilege and power. More importantly, the association of Mexican identity with criminality legitimates dominant ideologies that portray Mexicans as threats to U.S. civic culture and the safety of U.S. citizens, as carriers of diseases harmful to Americans, as in the 2009 case of "Mexican swine flu" (H1N1), and as narco-terrorists intent of destroying U.S. communities (Aguirre, 2002; Hernández, 2010; Lacey & Jacobs, 2009; Molina, 2010; Rosas, 2010).

THE POLITICAL CLIMATE FOR CRIMINALIZING MEXICAN IDENTITY

As a status characteristic, Mexican identity is associated in U.S. society with negative expectations in social relations. The negative expectations, in turn, promote public fears reflected in a political and legal climate that treats Mexican identity as a violation of so-cial norms, resulting in *a perceived need by the public* to control and supervise Mexican people in U.S. society. As a result, Mexican identity is used as a tool for constructing a framework for determining who belongs in society, a framework, in essence, rooted in the belief that Mexican identity is associated with social problems, like drug smuggling, and violations of civic culture, such as undocumented immigration, that threaten order in American society (Johnson, 1997; Romero, 2006). In effect, according to Kevin Johnson (2000:677–678), the profiling of Mexican-origin people as undocumented immigrants in the United States:

> deserves special scrutiny because it dispropor-tionately burdens persons of Latin American ancestry in the United States, the vast majori-ty of who are U.S. citizens or lawful immigrants. Generally speaking, whether they are U.S. cit-izens, lawful immigrants, or undocumented aliens, persons of Latin American ancestry or appearance are more likely than other persons in the United States to be stopped and interro-gated about their immigration status.

The Arizona legislature approved SB1070 (Support Our Law Enforcement and Safe Neighborhoods Act) in April 2010. While the act appeared to be global in nature, the primary purpose of SB1070 was to constrain the movement and presence of undocument-ed immigrants, principally Mexican immi-grants, in Arizona. SB1070 made it a state crime to be in the United States illegally and empowered police officers engaged in a law-ful stop, detention or arrest, to ask about a person's legal status when reasonable suspi-cion existed that the person was in the Unit-ed States illegally (Archibold, 2010a, 2010b; Riccardi & Gorman, 2010). In fact, SB1070 resulted in the public's perception of all Mexicans in Arizona as being undocument-ed immigrants and narco-terrorists. In truth, though, SB1070 emerged from a politically fueled climate of hate *pregnant* with images of Mexican drug lords invading Phoenix neigh-borhoods to kill and kidnap defenseless citi-zens (Rodríguez, 2010).

Carefully analyzed, SB1070 did little to alleviate public opinion, primarily Anglo public opinion, in Arizona that Mexicans were a threat to the state's civic culture. In-stead, SB1070 served as a platform for use of the state's initiative process to craft legisla-tion that would further diminish the pres-ence of Mexicans in Arizona. Within one month of SB1070's approval, the Arizona legislature passed HB2281 placing restric-tions on the teaching of Mexican American Studies classes in Arizona's public schools (Acuña, 2015; Grado, 2010; Lewin, 2010; see also Urbina & Álvarez, Chapter 17, this vol-ume). HB2281 outlawed classes that pro-moted the overthrow of the U.S. govern-ment, promoted resentment toward a race or class of people, focused on a particular eth-nic group, and advocated for ethnic solidari-ty. In by-passing classes in Asian Studies and African American Studies, the state's focus on Mexican American Studies only served to enhance the precarious position of Mexi-can people in Arizona's civic culture. The state legislature's passage of both SB1070 and HB2281 was indeed a clear signal that Mexicans were not welcome in Arizona.

One can consider SB1070 as an egregious use of public policy to constrain the move-ment and presence of Mexican immigrants in Arizona; that is, *criminalizing* Mexican identity in Arizona and setting the "tone" for further criminalizing in other states, which in fact quickly followed in Alabama, Georgia, Indiana, and Utah. However, it can also be seen as the culmination of a series of ballot initiatives passed by Arizona voters designed to criminalize Mexican people. Six years be-fore the passage of SB1070, Arizona voters approved Proposition 200 (Arizona Taxpay-er and Citizen Protection Act) in 2004, mod-eled after California's Proposition 187 (Save Our State), to restrict the access of undocu-mented Mexican immigrants to the state's health care and education services. A special feature of Proposition 200 was the imple-mentation of voter identification and citizenship verification procedures that required all people to provide proof of U.S. citizenship in the voter registration process.

In fact, two years after the passage of Proposition 200, Arizona voters in 2006 passed three propositions targeting undocumented Mexican immigrants. Proposition 100 (Bailable Offenses Act) amended the state's constitution to prohibit undocumented Mexican immigrants charged with a felony from being eligible for bail. Proposition 102 (Standing in Civil Actions Act) prohibited undocumented Mexican immigrants from receiving punitive damages in state lawsuits filed in Arizona. Proposition 300 (Public Program Eligibility Act) required verification of immigration status from people applying for state-funded services, such as child care and adult education. The passage of these three propositions suggests that there was increasing public concern with the presence of undocumented immigrants in Arizona. More importantly, the term *undocumented immigrant* was used by state legislation to cloak its purpose of profiling Mexican identity as a crime.

The passage of Propositions 100, 102, 200, and 300 served as a catalyst for the passage of SB1070, and thus SB1070 was the cumulative outcome of public policy initiatives that criminalized Mexican identity in Arizona. Further, the sharing of a border separating Arizona and Mexico transformed Mexican individuals into the most likely suspects in the criminalization of border and state identities. One result was that the propositions did not only criminalize Mexican identity, but they also criminalized the geography of the Arizona-Mexico border (Aguirre & Simmers, 2009). Essentially, similar to the efforts by California voters to use the ballot initiative process as a vehicle for passing anti-immigration legislation (Proposition 187), Arizona voters *used the ballot initiative process to pass anti-immigration legislation guised as judicial, educational, and political reform.* In short, the state of Arizona used the ballot initiative process to enact omnibus anti-immigration laws that for all intents and purposes were anti-Mexican in their design. Together, SB1070 is an anti-immigrant and anti-Mexican juggernaut focused on criminalizing Mexican identity in Arizona's social and cultural institutions.

Lastly, SB1070 has also served as a platform for legislation that challenges the Fourteenth Amendment's definition of *birthright citizenship* (Del Puerto, 2011). The principal sponsor of SB1070 has proposed SB1308 and SB1309 that would deny birth certificates to children born in Arizona to parents who are not U.S. citizens; effectively preventing the children from becoming U.S. citizens. Both SB1308 and SB1309 are disingenuous pieces of legislation that directly link U.S. citizenship to the citizenship of parents. Realistically, both propositions are harmful to children born in the United States of undocumented Mexican immigrant parents because it *criminalizes* children at birth, transforming *birthplace* into a nexus of contested political terrain.

THE LEGAL CONTEXT FOR CRIMINALIZING MEXICAN IDENTITY

On the evening of March 11, 1973, U.S. Border Patrol agents operating a checkpoint on Interstate 5 south of San Clemente, California pursued and stopped a "suspicious" vehicle. The agents questioned the three passengers in the vehicle about their citizenship status. The agents learned that two passengers did not have the necessary documentation to be in the United States. The driver of the vehicle was arrested for transporting illegal immigrants, and the passengers were arrested for illegal entry into the United States. At trial, the agents testified that they labeled the vehicle as "suspicious" because the occupants appeared to be of "Mexican" descent.

The U.S. Supreme Court ruled that the stop of the defendant's vehicle violated the Fourth Amendment because Border Patrol agents based their reason for stopping the vehicle only on the "perceived" Mexican ancestry of the vehicle's occupants (see Mirandé, Chapter 9, this volume). In *Brignoni-Ponce* (1975), the Supreme Court, however, noted in its ruling that Border Patrol agents may stop individuals "only if they are aware of specific attributable facts, together with rational inferences from the facts, that reasonably warrant suspicion that the vehicles contain aliens who may be illegally in the country." In effect, in his writing of the Court's opinion in *Brignoni-Ponce* (1975), Justice Lewis Powell constructed the "legal" context for using social identity as a basis for profiling Mexican-origin people: "The likelihood that any given person of Mexican ancestry is an alien is high enough to make Mexican appearance a relevant factor, but standing alone it does not justify stopping all Mexican-Americans to ask if they are aliens."

Despite its ruling that Mexican ancestry, or Mexican identity, alone is not sufficient to justify stopping Mexican people, the Supreme Court did suggest in *Brignoni-Ponce* (1975) that there is "likelihood" that Mexican-origin people are aliens. Based on a review of immigration cases after *Brignoni-Ponce* (1975), Kevin Johnson (2000) argues that *Brignoni-Ponce,* in actuality, opened the door for the U.S. Border Patrol to increase its use of Mexican appearance as the sole basis for stopping Mexican-origin people. Important to our discussion is the fact that *Brignoni-Ponce* actually serves as a tool that

legitimates the processing of Mexican identity by organizations that are instrumental in constructing and promoting perceptions of people based on group characteristics in public life. As such, in this case, the Supreme Court created the opportunity for the U.S. Border Patrol to use Mexican identity as a tool for profiling and criminalizing Mexican-origin people.

Evidently, a dilemma posed by *Brignoni-Ponce* is that it identifies social contexts, such as immigration stops, in which Mexican identity can be used as a construct for criminalizing Mexicans. In effect, David Strauss (1995:9) notes that *Brignoni-Ponce* ruled:

> law enforcement officers may use Mexican American ancestry as a 'relevant factor' . . . in determining whether there is reasonable suspicion . . . it seems reasonably clear that Brignoni-Ponce represents a category of cases in which the courts would allow race or national origin to be used as a basis for classification . . . Thus the prohibition on the use of racial generalizations is not as absolute as the cases suggest.

The ruling in *Brignoni-Ponce,* then, creates an over inclusive category for Mexican-origin people that is premised on the expectation that "Mexican identity" is associated with a negative evaluation outcome, most notably, criminal; subsequently, placing Mexican/Latino communities under siege by the police.

Years after *Brignoni-Ponce* (1975), the generalized use of Mexican identity in establishing reasonable suspicion stops by law enforcement agencies remains a legal controversy in the courts (see Mirandé, Chapter 9, this volume). For instance, ruling in a case similar to *Brignoni-Ponce,* the ninth Circuit Court of Appeals ruled in *United States v. Montero-Camargo* (2000) that the U.S. Border Patrol could not consider "Hispanic appearance" in making immigration stops. The Appeals Court argued that population changes had taken place in the southwestern states since *Brignoni-Ponce* resulting in the noticeable presence of Mexican-origin people. The Appeals Court noted that in some areas of California and Texas Mexican-origin people had become the single largest group. As a result, in *Montero-Camargo* (2000), the Appeals Court stated in its ruling that "in an area in which a large number of people share a specific characteristic, that characteristic casts too wide a net to play any part in a particularized suspicion determination." That is, the increased number of Mexican-origin people in the U.S. population makes *Mexican identity* of little use to law enforcement agencies in their efforts to determine who is, precisely, a criminal alien. As a result, the Appeals Court wrote in its ruling (*Montero-Camargo,* 2000) that "Hispanic appearance is, in general, of such little probative value that it may not be considered as a relevant factor where particularized or individualized suspicion is required."

As such, the ninth Circuit Court of Appeals ruling in *Montero-Camargo* is essential because it identifies the harm from criminalizing people simply on the basis of their identity, Mexican appearance. In effect, the Appeals Court ruled in *Montero-Camargo* (2000) that,

> Stops based on race or ethnic appearance send the underlying message to all our citizens that those who are not white are judged by the color of their skin alone. Such stops also send a clear message that those who are not white enjoy a lesser degree of constitutional protection, that they are in effect assumed to be potential criminals first and individuals second. It would be an anomalous result to hold that race may be considered when it harms people, but not when it helps them.

The Appeals Court, then, appears to be making a significant statement about institutional practices and social relations that result in some people being treated less equally or equitably than others.

In sum, the Court's statements in *Montero-Camargo* (2000) have the following implications for *Mexican identity* in the United States. First, selecting and sorting people on the basis of "Mexican identity" marginalizes Mexicans in U.S. society because it makes them vulnerable to public perceptions associated with negative evaluations. Second, the use of *Mexican identity* as an evaluative construct by the criminal justice system increases the risk of exposure for Mexican people to repressive and depersonalizing institutional practices. Consequently, the use of *Mexican identity* by state and federal judicial agencies as a basis for determining a person's right to belong in U.S. society underscores the limited access to privilege and power of Mexicans relative to the dominant, Anglo, population. In all, *Mexican identity* is subject to greater scrutiny in American public life than other social identities, especially the identity of white people, simply because it is nested in state and federal judicial practices that reinforce its precarious position in U.S. civic culture and social institutions.

DISCUSSION AND CONCLUSION

The social identity formation process is, in reality, an ideological tool driven by group access to privilege and power in society. Groups with more access to privilege and power in society are able to construct social identities for groups with less access to privilege and power to marginalize their participation in society. That is, people's access to privilege and power will determine where they belong in society, a dominant versus a subordinate position. Implicit in this chapter is the notion of "ideology" as an organized set of values that structures social identity in society. Broadly conceived, ideology structures social identity such that people are able to interpret the social relations that situate them in the social structure; that is, ideology provides people with a social and cultural map for their social identity, dominant versus subordinate, in society.

The idea of "criminalization" posits that dominant groups in society are able to manipulate public perceptions that criminalize the social identities of people occupying subordinate positions in society. The personification of *Mexican identity,* for example, as the *Frito bandito* exploits the subordinate position of Mexicans in U.S. society by allowing a dominant group rooted in a Eurocentric culture to exercise its privilege and power in society. As a result, the dominant group, specifically the Anglo population, actualizes the privilege and power associated with its social identity to sort and select social identities for who belongs in society. Therefore, *the criminalization of Mexican identity is used, strategically and effectively, as an ideological tool by the dominant group to optimize its access to privilege and power in society.*

Of course, Mexicans are not the only group subject to criminalization in U.S. society. The criminalization of African Americans, for example, has become popularized into the phrase "Driving While Black" (DWB). The imposition of criminal social identities on African Americans by law enforcement agencies is based on the assumption that they are more likely to commit crimes or to use their vehicles for transporting drugs (Aguirre, 2004; Harris, 2003). Coincidentally, Mexican people are also subject to a similar practice by law enforcement agencies referred to as "Driving While

Brown" (Mucchetti, 2005). The identifiability of black or brown people, as drivers or passengers in a vehicle, by law enforcement agencies as "potential criminal suspects" increases their exposure to vehicle searches and/or bodily searches. As reported by David Harris (2003:224), "Police can use color as evidence of criminal involvement, even without any other evidence that points in that direction. This means, in clear and unequivocal terms, that *skin color itself has been criminalized.*" In effect, police experts charge that "driving while Black," "driving while Brown" is yet another reference to "unwritten violation[s] in the state's traffic code" (Skolnick & Caplovitz, 2001:418). Consequently, law enforcement agencies use African American and Mexican identities as a tool for criminalizing them in society because, presumably, the carriers of those identities are *suspects* that commit (1) more crimes than white people, (2) crimes with greater impact on society than those committed by white people, and (3) more crimes than white people that involve weapons and/or illegal contraband (Rudovsky, 2002; Russell, 2001).

The subordinate positions Mexicans and African Americans occupy in U.S. society is not only a precarious one, it is also a position that exposes each group to criminalization processes and identities constructed by the dominant group. While one might argue that it makes sense to target groups more likely to commit crimes, it does so at the risk of exposing groups to harmful effects or unintended consequences. Consider how quickly the U.S. public targeted people of "Middle Eastern appearance" as potential terrorists without regard to the harmful effects or unintended consequences for American citizens who appear to look Middle Eastern (Akram & Johnson, 2002; Ashar, 2002). The imposition by the dominant group of criminal identities or suspect identities on subordinate groups is, as noted herein, possible because subordinate groups are less likely to occupy positions of power and privilege in U.S. society that shield them from aggressive and intrusive public scrutiny. In effect, despite the Enron, World Com, and Wall Street financial scandals, and their harmful effects on the American economy, the dominant group is unwilling to profile white male corporate executives as criminals, or at least to increase public scrutiny over their management of financial resources, because they occupy positions of power and privilege that shield them from the imposition of criminal identities, as documented by Jeffrey Reiman and Paul Leighton in *The Rich Get Richer and the Poor Get Prison: Ideology, Class, and Criminal* (2017).

In order to understand the reasoning underlying the imposition of criminal identities by the dominant group on subordinate groups one needs to consider the argument that the structuration of social relations for subordinate groups in the American society is designed to fabricate *deviant or criminal identities* for them. The social relations that contextualize the life experience of subordinate racial and ethnic groups in U.S. society is shaped by social forces, such as prejudice and discrimination, that constrain their participation to social contexts, such as poor crimeridden neighborhoods, that impute their social identity with deviant or criminal images (Aguirre & Turner, 2010; Appiah, 2000). Norman Denzin (1998), for instance, argues that the "hood and barrio" movies of the 1990s created an image of violent minority youths that served to privilege whiteness in the American society. That is, the deviant or criminal identities constructed by the mass media industry serves to reinforce the subordinate position of minority youths in society while promoting the dominant group's privilege and power to marginalize minority youths in society.

In essence, the deviant or criminal identities imposed on subordinate groups by the dominate group create a set of societal expectations for their behavior in society. The societal expectations are rooted in assumptions that criminalize the behavior of subordinate groups based on interpretive filters, such as the mass media, that process subordinate group behavior as a threat to society. That is, *subordinate group behavior is "criminalized" because societal expectations are based on deviant or criminal identities that can only be attributed to subordinate groups; and, as a result, "criminal" behavior can only be understood as "subordinate group" behavior.* Ironically, the interpretive filters used to criminalize the social identity of subordinate groups are social constructions produced by the hegemonic values, beliefs, and practices that protect the dominant group's position in society.

Finally, the increased numbers of Mexican-origin people in U.S. society, coupled with their identification in the public's thinking with social problems, such as drug smuggling, undocumented immigration, disease, or terrorism, has created an opportunity for the dominant group's ability to criminalize Mexican identity as a threat to U.S. civic culture and its values (Aguirre, Rodríguez, & Simmers, 2011). In retrospect, the use of federal and state legislation, such as Arizona's SB1070, is reflective of a political climate that transforms the voter initiative process into a repressive social practice that allows dominant groups to express their privilege and power in society (see Álvarez; Urbina & Álvarez, Chapter 17, this volume). In its expression of privilege and power, the dominant group exposes the precarious position of Mexicans and other Latinos in U.S. society, their vulnerability to the social construction of identities that label them as "usual suspects" for the social ills U.S. society faces, and their utility as a *target of opportunity* for a white hegemonic structure intent on exploiting the social identity of racial and ethnic minorities in the American society. In the end, by constructing their identity as *criminal,* the dominant group silences Mexicans and other Latinos in U.S. civic culture and in its social institutions, and obstructs their access to society's opportunity structure.

Chapter 9

LATINOS AND FOURTH AMENDMENT PROTECTION AGAINST UNREASONABLE SEARCH AND SEIZURES

ALFREDO MIRANDÉ

The right of the people to be secure in their persons, houses, papers, and effects, against unreasonable searches and seizures, shall not be violated, and no Warrants shall issue, but upon probable cause, supported by Oath or affirmation, and particularly describing the place to be searched, and the persons or things to be seized.
–Fourth Amendment, United States Constitution

This chapter addresses an important and largely neglected topic, namely whether Latinos in the United States have a Fourth Amendment right to be protected against unreasonable searches and seizures. I argue that in an immigration context the fundamental right of the people to be protected against unreasonable searches and seizures has been eviscerated for Latinos. In this chapter, I discuss a series of cases where the U.S. Supreme Court has slowly but systematically eroded or limited this fundamental right for Mexicans and "Mexican-looking" people.

SEARCH AND SEIZURE: HISTORICAL BACKGROUND

The Fourth Amendment protection against unreasonable searches and seizures was adopted by the founders of the United States Constitution date as a response to wholesale violations of the right to privacy carried out by the British government against American colonists. Writs of Assistance were used to conduct searches of homes of private citizens, primarily as a way of discovering violations of strict British customs laws and limiting criticisms of the King. These abuses resulted in increased sensitivity by the founders to limiting the power of the government to engage in unwarranted searches and seizures and to stifle political dissent against the King and his ministers.

The origins of the Fourth Amendment can be traced directly to seventeenth and eighteenth century English common law and more precisely to public response to three high profile cases in the 1760s, two in England and one in the American colonies. The two English cases, *Wilkes v. Wood,* 19 Howell's State Trials 1153 (C.P. 1763) and *Entick v. Carrington,* 19 Howell's State Trials 1029 (C.P. 1765), dealt with pamphleteers charged with seditious libel for criticizing ministers of the King and, indirectly, the King himself. In both cases, agents of the King had issued a warrant authorizing the search and ransacking of the pamphleteers' homes and seizure of their books and papers. Wilkes and Entick each sued for damages, claiming that the warrants were void and that the searches were therefore illegal (Stuntz & Kahan, 2002). Wilkes and Entick both prevailed and powerful opinions were issued by Lord Camden who presided over both cases.

In the third case, British customs inspectors were issued Writs of Assistance, which permitted them to search any place where they felt that smuggled goods might be found. Such Writs also empowered the inspectors to compel private citizens to assist them in carrying out the searches. The Writs of Assistance were first introduced in Massachusetts in 1751 in order to bring about strict enforcement of the Acts of Trade, which regulated commerce in the British Empire. Many merchants, however, developed creative ways of evading the Acts of Trade and were skillful in smuggling contraband items. The Writs of Assistance were general warrants, which authorized government officials to inspect not only shops and warehouses but private residences as well.

James Otis was Advocate General of Massachusetts when the Writs were issued. Otis promptly resigned his post when asked to represent some Boston merchants who sued in the Massachusetts Superior Court. Otis sued on behalf of the merchants in

1761, drawing great attention by arguing that the Writs violated the natural rights of the colonists and thus unconstitutional and invalid. Although the merchants lost, Otis delivered a powerful five-hour speech, and his argument and eloquent defense of the individual's right to privacy further intensified opposition to British rule. The Writs of Assistance drew public attention once again with the enforcement of the Townshend Duties in 1767. However, courts continued to uphold the constitutionality of the orders during the 1770s, and as time passed and public passions intensified, officials became increasingly reluctant to use them.

Carefully explored, there is general consensus that the Fourth Amendment was designed to affirm the results of *Wilkes* and *Entick* and to overturn the Writs of Assistance cases. In effect, three principals appear to be contained in the Fourth Amendment. First, the government should not be permitted to search, absent of some compelling justification and substantial reason to believe that the place being searched contains evidence that is being sought. Second, searches, particularly of private homes, should be limited and should not go beyond their justification. Third, the government should be prohibited from issuing blanket warrants. In fact, under English common law it was a trespass to invade someone's home without some kind of authorization, but the warrants in Wilkes and Entick and the Writs of Assistance appeared to have been designed to evade the common law.

Wilkes v. Wood (C.P. 1763), was a civil action of trespass in which the defendant, Wood who had served the Write of Assistance in entering Wilkes' home, had first pleaded not guilty and then gave a special justification (Kurland & Lerner, 2000). The Lord Chief Justice Camden summoned the evidence of the whole, stating that it was an action of trespass and then went through the particulars as to the justification, the King's Speech, libel No. 45. The Lord Chief Justice noted that if the jury was of the opinion that every step was properly taken as represented in the justification, they must find for the defendant. On the other hand, if they found that Wood was a party in the affair they must find a verdict for the plaintiff, with damages.

After presenting the evidence, the Lord Chief Justice noted that if the jury found that Wilkes was the author and publisher of No. 45, it would be filed, stand upon record in the Court of Common Pleas, and would be produced as proof in the criminal case. The jury deliberated for a half hour and found upon both issues for the plaintiff, with a thousand pounds in damages.

Entick v. Carrington (C.P. 1765), was also an action in trespass brought by Entick against Carrington. The plaintiff declared that on November 11, 1762, defendants with force and arms broke and entered the dwelling house of the plaintiff and continued there for hours without his consent and against his peaceable possession thereof. He further alleged that the defendants broke open the doors to the rooms, the locks, and iron bars. Once inside, they broke open boxes, chests, drawers, and other items of the plaintiff, and they broke the door locks, searching and examining all the rooms and all the boxes in his dwelling house, whereby his secret affairs were wrongfully discovered and made public. Both Wilkes and Entick brought actions in trespass against the defendants and both won verdicts, with powerful opinions issued by Lord Camden who was the presiding judge in both cases.

As such, the Fourth Amendment was clearly drafted to address the issues raised by *Wilkes* and *Entick* and the Writs of Assistance (Amar, 1994, 2002). As cited in the Fourth Amendment of the U.S. Constitution, the opening clause, for example, declares that people have a right to be "secure in their persons, houses, papers, and effects, against unreasonable searches and seizures," focusing precisely on infringements that were viewed as being especially intrusive in *Wilkes* and *Entick.* In fact, per the last clause of the Fourth Amendment, "no Warrants shall issue, but upon probable cause, supported by Oath or affirmation, and particularly describing the place to be searched, and the persons or things to be seized."

Yale University Law Professor Akhil Reed Amar (2002:848) notes that contrary to popular opinion, the Fourth Amendment does not require warrants for all searches and seizures, "or indeed for any search or seizure." Warrants were not required but limited, so that "No Warrants shall issue, but upon probable cause . . . ," as reported in the Fourth Amendment. The failure of the Fourth Amendment to include a warrant requirement is not surprising, perhaps, because warrants were "friends" of the government and not of the people who were searched (Amar, 2002). The only thing actually required by the Fourth Amendment is that all searches and seizures be "reasonable" (Amar, 1994: 771). As for specificity of reasonableness, although the founders did not specify what they meant by reasonable, overly broad warrants were presumptively unreasonable and thus unconstitutional.

The next issue is how the Fourth Amendment was to be enforced. Although modern courts focus on the exclusionary rule, or suppression of illegally seized items, as the primary remedy for Fourth Amendment violations, *Wilkes* and *Entick* were clearly not cases subject to the exclusionary rule (Amar, 2002). In effect, England has never had an exclusionary rule and American courts did not implement the exclusionary rule for the first one hundred years after independence. Indeed, during colonial times the federal government authorized outrageous and incredibly intrusive searches. Nevertheless, as in *Wilkes* and *Entick,* citizens could bring suit against the officers for civil trespass and seek compensatory and punitive damages (Amar, 1994).

It is noteworthy that none of the three cases, which gave impetus to the Fourth Amendment, were traditional criminal law enforcement cases like murder, rape, or burglary. Instead, they were cases that focused on violations of the rights of political dissidents who were strongly opposed to the laws they were accused of disobeying. Further, none of these cases involved searches by people that we would consider as law enforcement officers because police forces as we know them in modern times did not exist either in England or in the United States until the nineteenth century (Conser, Russell, Paynich, & Gingerich, 2005).

LATINOS AND THE 4TH AMENDMENT

Over time, the U.S. Supreme Court has carved out various exceptions to the Fourth Amendment's reasonableness requirement. There are, for example, exceptions for searches carried out subsequent to arrest, searches carried out under exigent circumstances, and there are also plain view[3] and "plain feel" exceptions,[4] as well as a poor people's exception (Slobogin, 2003). These exceptions have led some commentators to conclude that the exceptions may have "swallowed" up the rule and other critics to claim that Fourth Amendment jurisprudence is a doctrinal "mess." Akhil Reed Amar (1994:757) quotes, for example, "The Fourth Amendment today is an embarrassment. Much of what the Supreme Court has said in the last half century-that the Amendment generally calls for warrants and probable cause for all searches and seizures, and exclusion of illegally obtained evidence-is initially plausible but ultimately misguided."

Unlike the Fifth and Sixth Amendments which are protections provided to an individual or to an accused person, the language of the Fourth Amendment clearly ascribes the right to "the people" rather than to a particular individual or an accused person.

United States v. Verdugo-Urquidez

In some instances, however, the U.S. Supreme Court has narrowed the class of people protected by the Fourth Amendment to exclude certain groups (Saltzburg & Capra, 2010), including the impoverished and homeless people (Slobogin, 2003). There have also been a number of cases that have eroded the Fourth Amendment rights of Mexicans and "Mexican-looking" people. In *United States v. Verdugo-Urquidez* (1990), for example, a citizen and resident of Mexico was apprehended by Mexican police and transferred to the United States for trial on drug charges. After U.S. and Mexican officials carried out a joint warrantless search of his two residences, the Supreme Court ruled that he was not one of the people protected by the Fourth Amendment.

Specifically, Rene Verdugo-Urquidez was suspected of being the head of a major organization that smuggled drugs into the United States. Mexican officials, after consulting with U.S. Marshals, apprehended Verdugo-Urquidez and took him to the U.S. Border Patrol station in Calexico, California. United States Marshals then arrested Verdugo-

Urquidez and moved him to a correctional center in San Diego where he remained until his trial. Three days after the arrest, DEA agents working in conjunction with Mexican authorities carried out warrantless searches of two of Verdugo-Urquidez's residences in Mexico, seizing documents and other items which were said to implicate him in drug trafficking. Among the items seized was a tally sheet, which the government maintained reflected the quantities of marijuana smuggled into the United States.

The District Court granted Verdugo-Urquidez's motion to exclude the illegally seized evidence, concluding that the Fourth Amendment protects people against unreasonable searches and seizures, and that the DEA agents could not justify why they searched the premises without a warrant.[5]

The Ninth Circuit Court of Appeals similarly held that these searches were in violation of the Fourth Amendment, but the U.S. Supreme Court reversed the rulings, citing that the Fourth Amendment does not apply to the search of the residence of a nonresident alien in a foreign country. The Supreme Court reasoned that the phrase "the people" was a "term of art" in contrast to the words "person" or "accused" in the Fifth and Sixth Amendments and "suggests that 'the people' refers to a class of persons who are part of a national community or who have otherwise developed sufficient connection with this country to be considered part of that community." Verdugo-Urquidez, who had been transported to the United States three days prior to the search, was deemed to have "lacked sufficient connection to the United States to be one of the people protected by the Fourth Amendment." In looking at the history of the Fourth Amendment, Chief Justice William Rehnquist concluded that it was designed to protect the people of the United States from abuses by their government and that it could not be interpreted to

limit government actions against aliens outside of the country.

The Rehnquist majority added that there was no indication that the Framers of the Constitution intended the Fourth Amendment to serve as a restraint on actions by the federal government against aliens outside the United States or in international waters.[6] In fact, in 1798, just seven years after the amendment was ratified, Congress passed an act to "protect the Commerce of the United States," which authorized the President of the United States to "instruct the commanders of the public armed vessels which are, or which shall be employed in the service of the United States, to subdue, seize and take any armed French vessel, which shall be found within the jurisdictional limits of the United States, or elsewhere, on the high seas."

In a dissenting opinion, joined by Justice Thurgood Marshall, Justice William Brennan maintained that it was wrong for the United States to require aliens outside the border of the United States to obey federal law and then to refuse to abide by its own law in investigating the extraterritorial activity that the government has criminalized. Justice Brennan argued that the Fourth Amendment is an "unavoidable correlative" of the state's power to enforce criminal law. Justice Brennan further maintained that "the people" applied to anyone to whom the government's power extends, concluding that an alien subjected to criminal prosecution in the United States is by definition, therefore, one of the people.

Crucially, three points are worth noting. First, Verdugo-Urquidez was in custody in the United States when the warrantless search was carried out, and not on foreign soil or in international waters. Second, Verdugo-Urquidez was in the United States legally, but against his will. Third, the Supreme Court did not decide the question of whether an undocumented alien residing in the United States would be extended Fourth Amendment protections, although an undocumented person residing in the United States would presumably have the connection to this country that is required to be deemed one of the people.

INS v. López-Mendoza

In contrast, in *INS v. López-Mendoza* (1984), the Supreme Court decided that Fourth Amendment protections were extended to undocumented aliens living in the United States, but at the same time held that the exclusionary rule need not be applied in civil deportation hearings. In these two cases, two Mexican citizens, Adan López-Mendoza and Elias Sandoval-Sánchez, were ordered to be deported by an immigration judge in two separate proceedings. The orders were based on admission made by each respondent to the Immigration and Naturalization Service (INS) that they had entered the country illegally, *INS v. López-Mendoza* (1984). The respondents challenged the deportation orders claiming that their arrests by INS officials were illegal and therefore in violation of the Fourth Amendment. During the hearing Sandoval-Sánchez moved to have his admission suppressed because it was the fruit of an illegal search. Although López-Mendoza did not move to have his admission struck from the record, in each instance the presiding judge held that the legality of the arrest was not relevant to the determination of the person's deportation status. On administrative appeal, the Board of Immigration Appeals (BIA) affirmed the orders and noted that deportation hearings are civil proceedings and "the mere fact of an illegal arrest has no bearing on a subsequent deportation hearing," *INS v. López-Mendoza*. The BIA also found that the application of the exclusionary rule in deportation proceedings was inappropriate. The Ninth Circuit Court of Appeals, though, reversed the judgment, holding that the arrests were illegal and the result of unlawful search and remanded the case to see if the arrest was in fact the product of an illegal search.

López-Mendoza worked at a transmission repair shop in San Mateo, California. In response to a tip, INS agents arrived at the shop shortly before 8:00 a.m., but they failed to obtain a warrant to search the premise. The manager of the shop firmly refused to permit the agents to interview his workers during business hours. Despite his refusal, while one agent engaged the proprietor in conversation, another entered the shop through the rear and approached López-Mendoza. In response to the agent's questioning, López-Mendoza provided his name and revealed that he was from Mexico and had no close ties in this country. The agent placed López-Mendoza under arrest. After undergoing additional questioning at INS offices, López-Mendoza admitted he was indeed born in Mexico, was a citizen of that country and that he had entered the United States without inspection by immigration authorities. The agents proceeded to prepare a "Record of Deportable Alien" (Form I-213) and an accompanying affidavit, which López-Mendoza executed, admitting his nationality and illegal entry into the United States.

The U.S. Supreme Court stated that a deportation proceeding is purely a civil action used to determine whether a person is eligible to remain in this country, not to punish an unlawful entry, although entering or remaining unlawfully in this country is itself a crime. The deportation hearing seeks to determine whether a person has a right to remain in this country in the future, not to punish the person for a crime. As such, past conduct is only relevant if it sheds light on a person's right to remain in this country. The only issue before an immigration judge is whether the person entered the United States illegally and nothing more. Therefore, consistent with the civil nature of deportation hearings several protections that apply in criminal proceedings, including the exclusionary rule, do not apply. The "body" or identity of defendants in criminal or civil proceedings, for example, is never suppressible, even if it is the fruit of an unlawful arrest. The respondents are given a reasonable opportunity to be present at the proceedings, but if they do not avail themselves, hearings may proceed without the defendant. In many deportation hearings the INS must show identity and alienate and the burden shifts to the respondents to prove the time, place, and manner of entry.

Similarly, a decision of deportability is not based on evidence beyond a reasonable doubt as it is in criminal proceedings, but on "reasonable, substantial and probative evidence." The BIA (1984) standard only requires evidence of deportability that is "clear, unequivocal and convincing." The U.S. Supreme Court noted that the Court of Appeals has similarly held that the absence of *Miranda* warnings does not preclude the admission of an otherwise voluntary statement made by respondents, with the Supreme Court concluding that "the purpose of deportation is not to punish past transgressions, but rather to put an end to a continuing violation of the immigration laws."

For these reasons, Justice Sandra Day O'Connor concluded in the majority opinion that the Court of Appeals reversal as to López-Mendoza must itself be reversed, adding that the respondent had objected only to the fact that he had been summoned to a deportation hearing subsequent to an unlawful arrest and not to the evidence offered against him. The Supreme Court also held that the BIA (1979) correctly determined that "[t]he mere fact of an illegal

arrest has no bearing on a subsequent deportation proceeding," in *re López-Mendoza.*

Further, the Supreme Court declared that respondent Sandoval-Sánchez had a more substantial claim than López-Mendoza in that Sandoval-Sánchez objected not to the fact that he was compelled to attend the deportation hearing but to the evidence offered at the hearing. In criminal proceedings through statements and other evidence obtained as a result of an unlawful warrantless arrest are suppressible if the link between the evidence and the unlawful conduct is not too attenuated.

Although the Supreme Court had never decided whether the exclusionary rule applied in deportation proceedings, in *United States v. Janis* (1976), it suggested a framework for deciding whether the exclusionary rule is appropriate. The *Janis* test requires that the Supreme Court weigh the likely social benefits of applying the exclusionary rule against the likely costs. However, the primary and perhaps only benefit of applying the exclusionary rule is to deter future unlawful conduct by the police. However, the cost is the loss of what is often probative evidence and all of the ensuing costs that result from a less accurate and more cumbersome adjudication. In effect, the Supreme Court stated that in the long history of the exclusionary rule the Court has never applied the rule to exclude evidence from a civil proceeding.

The Supreme Court held that the exclusionary rule does not apply in civil deportation hearings or that respondents' admission of illegal entry after their unlawful arrest be excluded from evidence at their deportation hearing. Using the balancing test in *United States v. Janis,* the "balance" works against applying the exclusionary rule in civil deportation hearings, as a number of factors significantly decrease the deterrent value of applying the rule in such proceedings. First, regardless of how the arrest of illegal aliens is made, evidence not directly derived from the arrest is likely to result in deportation. Second, statistics show that over 97.7 percent of undocumented aliens agree to voluntary deportation without requesting a formal hearing, so that Immigration and Naturalization Service (INS) agents know that arrestees are not likely to challenge the lawfulness of their arrest in formal hearings. Third, the INS has its own scheme, which is used to deter Fourth Amendment violations. Finally, alternative remedies for Fourth Amendment violations decrease the deterrent value of the exclusionary rule. In retrospect, the social costs of applying the rule would be high in that it would compel courts to release from custody people who are illegally in this country. Invariably, paraphrasing Justice Benjamin Cardozo's famous quote, Justice O'Connor reasoned that "[t]he constable's blunder may allow the criminal to go free . . . , but he should not go free within our borders."

I.N.S. v. Delgado

In *I.N.S. v. Delgado* (1984), a case decided during the same term as *López-Mendoza,* the Supreme Court held that factory surveys, or questioning people regarding their citizenship, did not result in an illegal detention or seizure in violation of the Fourth Amendment. In a majority opinion authored by Chief Justice William Rehnquist, the Supreme Court held that since the INS agents simply questioned the workers, these encounters proved to be classic consensual encounters and not Fourth Amendment violations.

In this particular case, acting on two warrants, INS agents conducted a survey of the Southern California Davis Pleating Company. The warrants had been issued on a showing of probable cause that a number of illegal immigrants were working at Davis Pleating, although neither warrant identified or named any particular alien.

Several agents positioned themselves near the exits of the building, while others were dispersed throughout the factory and questioned most, but not all employees at their workstations. The agents displayed badges, carried walkie-talkies, and were armed, although at no point of the "survey" (raid) were weapons drawn. The agents moved systematically throughout the factory and questioned people as to their citizenship, asking one to three questions regarding their citizenship. If people gave a credible response, the questioning ended, but if employees gave an unsatisfactory response or admitted that they were aliens, they were asked to produce their immigration papers.

The respondents were four employees of the Davis Pleating Company questioned in one of the three surveys who argued that their Fourth Amendment right to be free from unreasonable searches and seizures and the equal protection component of the Fifth Amendment Due Process clause were violated during the survey. Using the standard first articulated by the Supreme Court in *United States v. Mendenhall* (1980), the Court of Appeals reversed the District Court, concluding that the entire workforce was seized during the duration of the survey which lasted from one to two hours because by stationing agents at the doors to the buildings meant that "a reasonable worker 'would have believed that he was not free to leave,'" quoting *United States v. Anderson* (1981). The Ninth Circuit Court of Appeals held that INS agents could not question individual employees, unless the agents had a reasonable suspicion that individual were illegal. The Supreme Court, though, reversed and held that the surveys did not result in an illegal seizure or detention of the entire workforce under the Fourth Amendment.

In the majority opinion, Chief Justice Rehnquist claimed that the Fourth Amendment does not proscribe all contact between the police and citizens. Instead, the Fourth Amendment is designed "to prevent arbitrary and oppressive interference by enforcement officials with the privacy and personal security of individuals," *United States v. Martínez-Fuerte* (1976). Obviously not all contacts between citizens and the police are seizures under the Fourth Amendment. It is "Only when the officer, by means of physical force or show of authority, has restrained the liberty of a citizen may we conclude that a 'seizure' has occurred," as cited in *Terry v. Ohio* (1968).

The Supreme Court rejected the claim that the entire workforce was seized during the duration of the two surveys when the INS placed armed agents near exits of the factory. While the surveys caused some disruption, including the effort of some workers to hide, the record shows that workers were not prevented from moving around the factory. This conduct should not have given respondents any reason to believe that they would be detained if they gave truthful answers to the questions, or simply refused to answer. "If mere questioning does not constitute a seizure when it occurs inside the factory, it is no more a seizure when it occurs at the exits." In short, the Court held that these were classic consensual encounters and that reasonable persons would have known that they were free to leave.

U.S. v. Martínez-Fuerte

In *U.S. v. Martínez-Fuerte* (1973), the Supreme Court upheld the Border Patrol's routine stopping of vehicles at permanent checkpoints located on a major highway away from the Mexican border for brief questioning of the vehicle's occupants as constitutional and consistent with the Fourth

Amendment, even absent of any particularized suspicions that a particular vehicle contained illegal aliens, with Justice Lewis Powell delivering the opinion for the Court.

The cases in *Martínez-Fuerte* (1973), involved criminal prosecutions for offenses related to the transportation of undocumented Mexican aliens, as each defendant was arrested at a permanent Border Patrol checkpoint away from the U.S.-Mexico border and each defendant sought exclusion of certain evidence seized, claiming that the checkpoints were in violation of the Fourth Amendment. The issue of whether or not the Fourth Amendment was violated, then, was whether a vehicle may be stopped at a fixed checkpoint for brief questioning even though there was no reason to believe that particular vehicles contained undocumented aliens. The Supreme Court held that such stops were consistent with the Fourth Amendment, affirming that the operation of a fixed checkpoint need not be authorized in advance by a warrant.

The respondents in case No. 74-1560 were defendants in three separate prosecutions that resulted from arrests at the permanent immigration check-point on Interstate 5 near San Clemente, California, the principal highway between San Diego and Los Angeles, and some 66 miles from the Mexican border.

At the checkpoint, the point agent standing between the two lanes of traffic visually inspects all northbound vehicles, which come to a virtual stop at the checkpoint. While most motorists are allowed to continue without questioning, a relatively small number of vehicles are subjected to a secondary inspection, when the point agent determines that such questioning is warranted. These cars are directed to a secondary checkpoint where occupants of the vehicle are asked additional questions about their citizenship and immigration status. According to the Government (428 U.S. 543, 547), the average length of these secondary inspections is between three and five minutes, as cited in Brief for United States 53. While the decision to subject a vehicle to a secondary checkpoint could be based on reasonable suspicion, the Government admitted that none of the stops cited in No. 74-1560 was based on any articulable suspicion.

In the stops involved in No. 74-1560, respondent Amado Martínez-Fuerte approached the San Clemente checkpoint driving a vehicle which contained two female passengers who were illegal Mexican aliens who had entered the San Isidro border crossing using false documents and then rendezvoused with Martínez-Fuerte and were transferred northward. At the checkpoint, the vehicle was directed to a secondary checkpoint. Martínez-Fuerte produced documents showing him to be a lawful resident alien, but his passengers admitted being present in the country unlawfully. Martínez-Fuerte was charged with two counts of illegally transporting aliens, a federal violation. Prior to the trial, Martínez-Fuerte made a motion to suppress all evidence resulting from the stop because the stop was in violation of the Fourth Amendment. The motion to suppress was denied, and Martínez-Fuerte was subsequently convicted on both counts after a jury trial.

Another respondent, José Jiménez-García attempted to pass through the checkpoint while driving a car with one passenger. The passenger had been smuggled across the border and was picked up by Jimenez-García in San Ysidro by prearrangement. As a result of questioning at the secondary check-point, the illegal status of the passenger was ascertained and Jimenez-García was charged with two counts of illegally transporting an alien and conspiring to commit that offense. His motion to suppress the evidence derived from the stop was granted.

The other respondents, Raymond Guillen and Fernando Medrano-Barragan, approached the Border checkpoint with Guillen driving and Medrano-Barragan and his wife as passengers. Questioning at the secondary checkpoint revealed that while Guillen was a U.S. citizen, Medrano-Barragan and his wife were undocumented aliens. An ensuing search of the car also uncovered three other undocumented aliens in the trunk of the car and that Medrano-Barragan had led these aliens across the beach near Tijuana, where they met up with Guillen. Guillen and Medrano-Barragan were jointly indicted on four counts of illegally transporting aliens, four counts of inducing the illegal entry of aliens, and one conspiracy count. The District Court granted the defendants' motion to suppress.

Martínez-Fuerte appealed his conviction, while the government appealed the granting of motions to suppress in the respective prosecutions of Jimenez-García, Guillen, and Medrano-Barragan. The Court of Appeals for the Ninth Circuit consolidated the three appeals, which presented the common question of whether routine stops and interrogations at checkpoints are consistent with the Fourth Amendment. The Court of Appeals held, with one judge dissenting, that these stops violated the Fourth Amendment, concluding that a stop for inquiry is constitutional only if the Border Patrol reasonably suspects the presence of illegal aliens on the basis of articulable facts. It reversed Martínez-Fuerte's conviction, affirming the orders to suppress in the other cases. The Supreme Court, though, reversed and remanded the cases.[7]

The Supreme Court noted that the Ninth Circuit and the Fifth Circuit are in conflict as to the constitutionality of law enforcement stops that are considered important by law enforcement personnel who are in charge of policing the borders of the United States.

Notably, the Fourth Amendment places limits on search-and-seizure powers to prevent arbitrary and oppressive interference by law enforcement officials, as illustrated in *United States v. Brignoni-Ponce, United States v. Ortiz,* and *Camara v. Municipal Court.* In establishing such constitutional safeguards the Supreme Court has seek to balance the public interest and the individual's Fourth Amendment interest, *United States v. Brignoni-Ponce* (1975) and *Terry v. Ohio* (1968).

Almeida-Sánchez

In *Almeida-Sánchez* (1973), the Supreme Court addressed the question of whether a roving-patrol unit could search a vehicle simply because it was in the vicinity of the border. Almedia Sánchez, a Mexican citizen and holder of a valid work permit, challenged the constitutionality of a warrantless search of his automobile by the Border Patrol some 25 air miles from the Mexican border. The search which was conducted without either probable cause or consent resulted in the discovery of marijuana, which was used to convict him of a federal crime. While recognizing that important law enforcement interests were at stake, the Supreme Court held that because such searches infringed significantly on Fourth Amendment privacy interests that a search of a car without consent could not be conducted without *probable cause* that the car contained undocumented aliens, absent of a judicial warrant authorizing random searches by roving patrols in a designated area. In *United States v. Ortiz* (1975), the Supreme Court held that these same restrictions applied to vehicle searches conducted at permanent checkpoints. The Court held that the Fourth Amendment forbids the Border Patrol absent of consent or probable cause from searching private vehicles at traffic checkpoints away

from the border and its functional equivalent.

In *Martínez-Fuerte* (1973), the Supreme Court distinguished between border checkpoints and roving patrols, holding that while routine traffic stops at fixed checkpoints are technically seizures within the meaning of the Fourth Amendment, they entail minimal intrusion. In balancing the interest at stake, the Supreme Court held that "[w]hile the need to make routine checkpoint stops is great, the consequent intrusion on Fourth Amendment interests is quite limited." The Supreme Court further held that it was constitutional to refer motorists selectively to secondary inspections at the San Clemente checkpoint based on criteria that would not satisfy a roving-patrol stop.

United States v. Brignoni-Ponce

In this particular case, the U.S. Supreme Court made defining rulings regarding the treatment of people of Mexican heritage:

> Thus, even if it be assumed that such referrals are made largely on the basis of apparent Mexican ancestry, we perceive no constitutional violation, Cf. *United States v. Brignoni-Ponce,* 422 U.S., at 885-887. As the intrusion here is sufficiently minimal that no particularized reason need exist to justify it, we think it follows that the Border Patrol (428 U.S. 543, 564) officers must have wide discretion in selecting the motorists to be diverted for the brief questioning involved.

In *Brignoni-Ponce* (1975) the U.S. Supreme Court addressed the question of whether the Border Patrol is authorized to stop automobiles in areas near the border. The San Clemente fixed checkpoint was closed because of inclement weather, as two officers were parked on the side of the road and were observing northbound traffic. Since the road was dark they used the car's headlights to illuminate the road, and they pursued and stopped the respondent's car, later indicating that the only reason for the stop was that the occupants appeared to be of Mexican descent. The Border Patrol agents questioned the occupants of the car and discovered that the respondent and his two passengers had entered the country illegally. The three were arrested and the respondent was charged with two counts of knowingly transporting illegal immigrants in violation of the Immigration and Nationality Act. At his trial, the respondent moved to suppress the testimony regarding the stop and questioning of the occupants of the car, claiming that such evidence was the fruit of an illegal seizure. The trial court denied the motion, the aliens testified at the trial, and the respondent was convicted on two counts of transporting illegal immigrants, with the Supreme Court distinguishing this case from *Almeida-Sánchez*, because the Border Patrol was not claiming authority to search cars but only to question the occupants about their immigration status.

The respondent's appeal was pending in the Court of Appeals for the Ninth Circuit when the Supreme Court announced its decision in *Almeida-Sánchez* (1973), holding that the Fourth Amendment prohibits searches conducted by roving patrols in the vicinity of the border, absent of a warrant or probable cause. The Ninth Circuit, sitting *en banc*, held that the stop in this case more closely resembled a roving-patrol stop than a stop at a fixed check-point, and thus the Ninth Circuit held that the Fourth Amendment as interpreted in *Almedia-Sánchez* forbids stopping a vehicle, even for the limited

purpose of questioning the occupants, unless the officer has "founded suspicion" that the occupants are aliens who are illegally in the United States, and therefore the motion to suppress should have been granted.

The government did not challenge the Court of Appeal's conclusion that the stop was a roving-patrol stop rather than a checkpoint stop, nor did it challenge the application of *Almeida-Sánchez*. The only issue before the Supreme Court was whether a roving-patrol may stop a vehicle and question its occupants when the only basis for the stop is that the occupants appear to be of Mexican ancestry. The Supreme Court affirmed the decision of the Court of Appeals.

As such, the decision in *Brignoni-Ponce* had the effect of limiting the authority of Border Patrol agents to question people in the vicinity of the border. In effect, except at the border or its functional equivalent, officers on roving-patrol may stop vehicles "only if they are aware of specific articulable facts, together with rational inferences from those facts that reasonably warrant suspicion that the vehicles contain aliens who may be illegally in the country." A number of factors may be taken into account in deciding whether there is reasonable suspicion, such as information about recent illegal border crossings in the area, the driver's behavior, driving patterns, and obvious attempts to avoid detection. The Supreme Court concluded that "the likelihood that any given person of Mexican ancestry is an alien is high enough to make Mexican appearance a relevant factor, but standing alone it does not justify stopping all Mexican-Americans to ask if they are aliens."

SUMMARY AND CONCLUSION

As cited in the U.S. Constitution, the Fourth Amendment protects "the people" against unreasonable searches and seizures of "their persons, houses, papers, and effects." The roots of the Fourth Amendment can be traced to English common law and to abuses by the British crown of the rights of political dissidents and to American Colonists who sought to evade strict British custom laws. Therefore, the Fourth Amendment was adopted by the founders in response to widespread violations of the right to privacy carried out by the British government against British subjects and American colonists who were critical of the King or his ministers. Writs of Assistance were used to conduct searches of homes of private citizens, seeking to enforce strict British customs laws and stifle political dissent.

While the primary remedy used to deter the police from violating Fourth Amendment rights is the exclusion or suppression of evidence that is the fruit of an illegal search or seizure, the exclusionary rule was not applied to police action for the first 100 years after its adoption. Under Common Law it was considered as a trespass with civil remedies, including compensatory and punitive damages.

Despite common misconceptions, the Fourth Amendment does not require a warrant under most or any circumstances. Based on the Fourth Amendment of the U.S. Constitution, what it does require is that searches be reasonable and that "no Warrants shall issue but upon probable cause, supported by Oath or affirmation, and particularly describing the place to be searched, and the persons or things to be seized."

However, in recent years the Supreme Court has systematically limited the reach of the Fourth Amendment, particularly as it pertains to Mexican and "Mexican-appearing" persons. In *Verdugo-Urquidez* (1990), for example, the Supreme Court held that a Mexican national who was a suspected drug dealer and was apprehended and brought across the border against his will in a joint venture between United States and Mexican police was insufficiently connected to the United States to be considered "one of the people," thereby upholding warrantless searches of his two residences in Mexico carried out jointly by United States law enforcement and Mexican authorities.

In *Martínez-Fuerte* (1973), the Supreme Court held that routine checkpoint stops of automobiles by the Border Patrol on major highways away from the Mexican border for brief questioning of occupants was consistent with the Fourth Amendment, absent of any individualized suspicion that particular vehicles carry illegal aliens. In his dissent, Justice Brennan remarked that "Today's decision is the ninth this Term marking the continuing evisceration of Fourth Amendment protections against unreasonable searches and seizures," as the decision virtually emptied the Fourth Amendment of its reasonableness requirement. Justice Brennan added that by abandoning any requirement of a minimum of reasonable suspicion or even articulable suspicion, the Supreme Court made meaningless the *Brignoni-Ponce* (1975) holding that Mexican appearance alone does not justify stopping all Mexican-looking people to ask if they are illegal aliens. Consequently, without requiring any objective standard in making a stop, Border Patrol agents will undoubtedly target motorists of Mexican appearance because they share the same "suspicious" physical and grooming characteristics of illegal Mexican aliens. Finally, the U.S. Supreme Court concluded: "Every American citizen of Mexican ancestry and every Mexican alien lawfully in this country must know after today's decision that he travels the fixed checkpoint highways at the risk of being subjected not only to a stop, but also to detention and interrogation, both prolonged and to an extent far more than for non-Mexican appearing motorists."

Chapter 10

A SEPARATE CLASS: THE EXCLUSION OF LATINOS FROM GRAND AND PETIT JURIES

ALFREDO MIRANDÉ

At the heart of the American paradigm is the perception that law and its agents . . . are colorblind and thus justice is impartial, objective and seeks la verdad (the truth). But, la realidad (reality) differs . . . decision makers are often more guided by their environment than by objectivity.

–Martin Guevara Urbina

In 1951, Pete Hernández, a local farm worker, got into a ballroom fight and heated argument in Edna, Texas with Joe Espinoza, after Espinoza had insulted Hernández. Hernández left the bar and returned with a gun, shooting and killing Espinoza. Hernández was indicted by an all-Anglo (white) grand jury in Jackson County, Texas and convicted by an all-white petit jury. Arguing that people of Mexican descent were barred from the jury commission that selected grand juries, and from petit juries that tried and convicted Mexicans, his attorneys filed a timely motion seeking to quash the indictment.[8] On the verge of trial, Hernández also tried to quash the petit jury panel because people of Mexican descent were in fact excluded from jury service in the case. Given that people of Mexican origin had not served on grand or petit juries in over 25 years, Hernández argued that people of Mexican ancestry were discriminated, as a special class, in Jackson County but the trial court denied the motions. Hernández was convicted and sentenced to life imprisonment, but the conviction was overturned by the United States Supreme Court.

Although Hernández was subsequently retried and convicted, *Hernández v. Texas* (1954) became a landmark decision in American jurisprudence, marking the *first time that people of Mexican origin were recognized as a distinct legally cognizable entity, separate and apart from whites and blacks.* The decision was an essential step in Latino struggle for civil rights, and it paved the way to further challenges of discrimination in other areas of American law, such as employment, education, housing, and voting rights. This chapter, then, focuses on an important but largely neglected topic: the underrepresentation and systematic exclusion of Latinos from grand and petit juries in the U.S. judicial system.

HERNÁNDEZ V. TEXAS: THE FORGOTTEN LANDMARK CASE

Hernández v. Texas (1954) was decided in the same Supreme Court term as *Brown v. Board of Education* (1954), and it is, arguably, as important for Latinos as *Brown* for African Americans in the struggle for equality and justice. It is, therefore, surprising that so little is known about the historical, social, and legal significance of the case, as detailed below. In affirming Hernández's conviction, the Texas Court of Criminal Appeals concluded that "Mexicans are . . . members of and within the classification of the white race as distinguished from members of the Negro Race," rejecting Hernández's contention that Mexicans in the United States were a "special class" and subject to protection under the Fourteenth Amendment, noting that "so far as we are advised, no member of the Mexican nationality" has challenged their classification as white or Caucasian. The Texas Supreme Court affirmed the verdict, arguing that Mexican Americans were in fact considered to be legally white.

The petitioner appealed to the U.S. Supreme Court, asserting that the exclusion of this class deprived Hernández of the *equal protection* law guaranteed by the Fourteenth Amendment of the United States Constitution. Though, an allegation that the trial court erred in denying the motions to quash was the sole basis of Hernández's appeal. On appeal, Hernández had a dual burden in substantiating his claim of group discrimination. First, he had to prove that people of Mexican descent constitute a separate class in Jackson County, Texas, distinct from "whites." Hernández did this successfully by showing the attitude of community members. Testimony by responsible officials and citizens indicated that residents of Jackson County clearly distinguished between "whites" and "Mexicans." The participation of people of Mexican origin in business and community groups was shown to be minimal, and until recently Mexican children had attended segregated schools for the first four grades, and at least one restaurant prominently displayed a sign that said "No Mexicans Served." Finally, at the courthouse itself at the time of the hearing, there were two men's bathrooms, one was unmarked and the other said, "Colored Men" and "Hombres Aquí" (Men Here).

No substantial evidence was presented to rebut these facts or the existence of Mexicans as a separate class. After establishing the existence of a *class,* the petitioner had the burden of proving discrimination in jury selection, relying on the pattern of proof established in *Norris v. Alabama* (1935). In *Norris,* the petitioner showed that Negros made up a substantial portion of the population in the area, that some were qualified to serve, and that none had been called to jury service over a substantial period of time. This was taken as *prima facie* proof that blacks had been systematically excluded from jury service. This rule is often termed the "Rule of Exclusion" and can be used to show proof of discrimination against any delineated class.

Hernández proved that 14 percent of the Jackson County population consisted of people with Mexican or Latin American surnames. The County Tax Assessor testified that about 6 or 7 percent of the freeholders on the County rolls were people of Mexican origin, and the state of Texas stipulated that "for the last twenty-five years there is no record of any person with a Mexican or Latin American name having served on a jury commission, grand jury or petit jury in Jackson County." The parties also stipulate that "there are some male persons of Mexican or Latin American descent in Jackson County who, by virtue of being citizens, householders, or freeholders, and having all other legal prerequisites to jury service, are eligible to serve as members of a jury commission, grand jury and/or petit jury."

The petitioner met the burden in Norris showing prima facie evidence of discrimination. In an effort to rebut the presumption of discrimination and denial of equal protection, the State, Texas, presented five jury commissioners who testified that they had not discriminated against people of Mexican or Latin American descent, saying that their only objective was to select those who were best qualified, but the testimony was not sufficient to rebut the petitioner's case. As noted in the Norris case:

> That showing as to the long-continued exclusion of Negroes from jury service, as to the many Negroes qualified for that service could not be met by mere generalities. If, in presence of such testimony as defendant adduced, the mere general assertion by officials of their performance of duty were to be accepted as an adequate justification for the complete exclusion of Negroes from jury service, the constitutional provision . . . would be but a vain and illusory requirement. (*Norris v. Alabama,* 1935)

In *Hernández v. Texas,* the U.S. Supreme Court reasoned that circumstances or chance could well result that no Negro would be appointed on a particular jury or during a particular period, "but it taxes our credulity to say that mere chance resulted in their being no members of this class among the over six thousand jurors called in the past 25 years. The result bespeaks discrimination, whether or not it was a conscious decision on the part of any individual jury commissioner." The Supreme Court, therefore, concluded that the judgment of conviction must be reversed, acknowledging for the first time, the existence of Mexicans as a separate class with corresponding historical, legal, and social implications.

STRAUDER V. WEST VIRGINIA: ESTABLISHING THE PRECEDENT

The first time that the U.S. Supreme Court addressed the issue of racial discrimination in jury selection was in *Strauder v. West Virginia* (1880). Under the laws of West Virginia no colored man was eligible to serve on grand or petit juries, whereas white men were eligible. The West Virginia law was enacted on March 12, 1873 (Acts of 18778:102), stating: "All white male persons who are twenty-one years of age and who are citizens of this State shall be liable to serve as jurors, except as herein provided."

The issue before the Supreme Court, then, was whether the law barring colored citizens from jury service was a violation of the equal protection clause of the Fourteenth Amendment. The Supreme Court held that the West Virginia statute, which denied colored men the equal protection of the law, was unconstitutional. As an historical reminder, the Fourteenth Amendment of the U.S. Constitution was one of three so-called Civil War Amendments designed to secure a recently emancipated race, which had been held in slavery for generations, the superior rights enjoyed by the dominant race. The Thirteenth Amendment outlawed slavery, stating "Neither slavery nor involuntary servitude, except as a punishment for crime whereof the party shall have been duly convicted, shall exist within the United States," and the Fifteenth Amendment gave people of color the right to vote. The Fourteenth Amendment in turn not only gave citizenship and the privileges of citizenship to people of color, but it also stated that no state shall deny any person life, liberty, or property without due process or the equal protection of the law.

As for the *Strauder* case, Strauder, a black man, was indicted for murder in the Circuit Court of Ohio County in West Virginia on October 20, 1874, and he was tried, convicted, and sentenced. The case was appealed and affirmed by the State Supreme Court. Strauder claimed that at the trial in state court, he was denied rights to which he was entitled under the Constitution and he petitioned that the case be moved to the nearest federal Circuit Court pursuant to Section 641.

On appeal, the opinion delivered by Justice William Strong of the U.S. Supreme Court held that the Virginia statute was unconstitutional, as it denied Strauder the equal protection of the law. The Supreme Court affirmed motions to quash the venire "because the law under which it was issued was unconstitutional, null, and void," and the subsequent motions challenging the constitution of the panel for a new trial and in arrest of judgment were overruled and made part of the record. As such, in *Strauder,* the Supreme Court set the standard for discrimination in jury selection which continues today, stating that the question before the Court was not

> whether a colored man, when an indictment has been preferred against him, has a right to a grand or a petit jury composed in whole or in part of persons of his own race or color, but it is whether, in the composition or selection of jurors by whom he is to be indicted or tried, all persons of his race or color may be excluded by law solely because of their race or color, so that by no possibility can any colored man sit upon the jury.

The Supreme Court further noted that at the time that colored citizens were incorporated into the Constitution, it was predictable that those "who had been regarded as an inferior and subject race would . . . be looked upon with jealousy and positive dislike, and that laws might be enacted or enforced to perpetuate the distinctions that had before existed." The Supreme Court also saw the colored race as "abject and ignorant"–unfit of those who had "superior intelligence," for their training had made them "mere children" who "needed the protection which a wise government extend to those who are unable to protect themselves," especially against hostile actions from the states where they resided.

When the Fourteenth Amendment was enacted it was designed to ensure the colored race the enjoyment of all civil rights under the law enjoyed by *whites.* As such, there was error in denying Strauder's petition to move the case to federal court, as Section 641 provides that when any civil or criminal prosecution is commenced in any state court "for any cause whatsoever against any person who is denied, or cannot enforce, in the judicial tribunals of the State, or in the part of the State where such prosecution is pending, any right secured to him by any law providing for the equal rights of citizens of the United States" can upon oath and affirmation be removed before the trial into the next Circuit Court of the United States? Clearly, the petition filed by Strauder in state court before the trial, made a case for removal into the Federal Circuit Court, under Section 641, if, by constitutional amendment and section 1977 of the Revised Statutes, he was entitled to immunity from discrimination against him in the selection of jurors because of their color.

Lastly, the U.S. Supreme Court concluded there was error, therefore, in proceeding to the trial of the indictment against him after his petition was filed, as also in overruling his challenge to the array of the jury, and in refusing to quash the panel, and thus ruled that the judgment of the Supreme Court of West Virginia be reversed, and the case remitted with instructions to reverse the judgment of the Circuit Court of Ohio, setting historical precedent in U.S. jurisprudence.

THE EVOLUTION OF THE BATSON STANDARD

To begin, as ruled in *Strauder v. West Virginia* (1880), the very fact that colored people are singled out and expressly denied by statute the right to participate in the administration of laws, as jurors, because of their color, though they are citizens, and may be in other respects fully qualified, is practically a brand upon them, affixed by American law, an assertion of inferiority, and a stimulant to the prejudice of the white race, which is an impediment to colored people for securing equal justice, which the law aims to secure to all people. The very idea of a jury as a group of men composed of peers or equals of the person whose rights are selected or summoned to determine; that is, of his neighbors, fellows, associates, people having the same legal status in society as that which he holds signifies the essence of legal parameters.

In effect, *Strauder* established the standard for discrimination in jury selection, but it did not guarantee the right to a jury containing members of one's race. What it did guarantee was that states could not use race, color, national origin, or other impermissible grounds to exclude people from juries. That is, it guaranteed the right to a jury selected "without discrimination" against people of a person's race or color. Therefore, the question decided in *Strauder* was whether "in the composition or selection of jurors by whom he is to be indicted or tried, all persons of his race or color may be excluded by law, solely because of their race or color." The Supreme Court further stated that the same principle would apply if white people were excluded from juries, adding, "Nor if a law should be passed excluding all naturalized Celtic Irishmen, would there be any doubt of its inconsistency with the spirit of the amendment."

Before discussing *Batson v. Kentucky* (1986), which dealt with discrimination in peremptory jury challenges, one must distinguish between two types of challenges which can be made during jury selection or *voir dire* (questioning of prospective jurors), *for cause* and *peremptory challenges.* For cause challenges are unlimited and, as the term implies, prospective jurors are excluded by the court for presumed bias or reasons that make it unlikely that the individuals can be fair and objective jurors. A request that prospective jurors be dismissed "for cause" is made when there is specific and forceful reason to believe the individuals cannot be fair, unbiased, or capable of serving as jurors. Causes include acquaintanceship with either of the parties, one of the attorneys or a witness, and the potential jurors' expression during voir dire. Specifically, jurors may be challenged for reasons such as their inability to be unbiased due to prior experience in a similar case such as having been convicted of drunk driving or being a battered wife in a domestic violence case, or any obvious prejudice, or inability to serve, such as being mentally disturbed. The judge determines if individuals shall be dismissed for cause.

Challenges and dismissal for cause differ from peremptory challenges, where each side may use the peremptory to dismiss potential jurors without specifying any reason. In most jurisdictions each side has a limited number of peremptory challenges.[9]

However, since a party does not have to articulate a reason for exercising a peremptory challenge, it's obviously open to the possibility that the challenge could be used to exclude people based on their race, color, or national origin.

In *Batson v. Kentucky* (1986), the U.S. Supreme Court reexamined that portion of *Swain v. Alabama* (1965), as to the evidentiary burden placed on a criminal defendant who claimed that he had been denied equal protection through the state's use of peremptory challenges to exclude members of his race from the petit jury. Batson, a black man, was indicted in Kentucky on charges of second-degree burglary and receipt of stolen goods. On the first day of the criminal trial in Jefferson District Court, the court conducted voir dire examination of prospective jurors and excused some jurors for cause. The prosecution, in turn, used its peremptory challenges to exclude all black jurors from the venire, resulting in an all-white jury. The defense moved to dismiss the jury, arguing that the prosecution's removal of all blacks from the jury violated the defendant's rights pursuant to the Sixth and Fourteenth Amendments to a jury selected from a cross-section of the community, and under the Fourteenth Amendment to equal protection of the law. Without ruling on the petitioner's right to a hearing, the trial judge denied the motion and Batson was tried and subsequently convicted by the selected jury.

In upholding the conviction, the Kentucky Supreme Court noted that it had recently, in another case, relied on *Swain v. Alabama* (1965), which had held that defendants alleging lack of a fair cross-section must demonstrate systematic exclusion of a group of jurors from the venire as a whole. The U.S. Supreme Court, though, overturned the conviction, reaffirming the principle announced in *Strauder v. West Virginia* (1880), that a state denies a black defendant

equal protection when it puts him on trial before a jury from which members of his race have been purposefully excluded.

Although *Strauder* held that defendants do not have a right to a petit jury composed in whole of people of their own race, the Equal Protection Clause guarantees the defendant that the state will not exclude members of their race from the jury venire because of race or color, or on the erroneous assumption that members of their race as a group are not qualified to serve as jurors. By denying people participation in jury service on account of their race, the state also unconstitutionally discriminates against the excluded jurors. Consequently, selection procedures that purposefully exclude black people from juries undermine public confidence in the fairness of the United States system of justice.

Invariably, *Batson* was significant in ruling that the same equal protection principles governing whether there is discrimination in selecting the venire govern determining whether there is discrimination in the use of peremptory challenges, and rejecting the portion of *Swain v. Alabama* concerning the evidentiary burden placed on defendants claiming they had been denied equal protection through the state's discriminatory use of peremptory challenges. *Swain* erroneously held that people could make a prima facie case of purposeful discrimination only if they could show that the peremptory system as a whole was being perverted. The Supreme Court, though, held that the burden placed on *Swain* of having to demonstrate that prosecutors in the jurisdiction as a whole were striking black jurors beyond the facts on his case, is in fact inconsistent with equal protection standards, which were subsequently developed in decisions relating to selection of the jury venire. Defendants may make a prima facie showing of purposeful racial discrimination in selection of the venire by relying solely on the facts concerning its selection in their case.

The question of whether there is discrimination in selecting the venire also governs the use of peremptory challenges in striking individual jurors. Prosecutors are usually entitled to exercise peremptory challenges for any reason, as long as that reason is related to their view concerning the outcome of the case, but the Equal Protection Clause forbids prosecutors from challenging potential jurors solely on account of their race or on the assumption that black jurors as a group will be unable impartially to consider the state's case against black defendants.

After *Batson,* defendants may establish a prima facie case of purposeful discrimination solely on evidence concerning the exercise of peremptory challenges at the defendant's trial. *Batson* set forth a 3-prong test for making a prima facie case. First, defendants must show that they are members of a cognizable racial group, and that prosecutors have exercised peremptory challenges to remove from the venire members of the defendants' race.

Defendants may also rely on the fact that peremptory challenges constitute a jury selection practice that permits those who discriminate those they wish to discriminate. Finally, defendants must show such facts and any other relevant circumstances that raise an inference that prosecutors used peremptory challenges to exclude people from the petit jury on account of their race. Once defendants make a prima facie showing, the burden shifts to the state to come forward with a neutral, or nonracially based explanation for challenging black jurors. Prosecutors may not rebut a prima facie showing by stating that they challenged the jurors on the assumption that the jurors would be partial to the defendants because of their shared race, or by affirming their good faith in individual jury selections. The final burden is on the defendants to rebut the prosecutions' race neutral explanation for the exclusion of prospective jurors, and show that there is prima facie evidence that the exclusion was motivated by race.

HERNÁNDEZ V. NEW YORK: THE EXCLUSION OF BILINGUAL JURORS

While *Strauder* (1880), *Batson* (1986), and other case law have clearly established that defendants have a right to be protected from racial discrimination in the selection of grand and petit juries as well as peremptory challenges, it is not clear whether the same protection applies to the exclusion of potential jurors based on language discrimination, the question decided in *Hernández v. New York* (1991).

In 1986, Dionisio Hernández was charged with attempted murder, assault, and criminal possession of a weapon arising out of an incident in which he allegedly attempted to kill his fiancée, Charlene Calloway, and her mother, Ada Saline. Two patrons at

a restaurant were also injured in the incident. Saline was expected to testify in Spanish as a key prosecution witness. The trial was held in the New York Supreme Court. Jury selection was held during November 3–7, but no transcript of the voir dire examination was created. After 63 prospective jurors were questioned and nine empaneled, defense counsel objected that the prosecution had used four peremptory challenges to exclude all potential Latino jurors. Two of the excluded jurors had brothers who had been convicted of crimes.[10]

Once Hernández raised his *Batson* objection, the prosecutor did not wait for a ruling on whether the petitioner had established a

prima facie case of racial discrimination under *Batson v. Kentucky* (1986), and volunteered
his reasons for striking the jurors in question:
"Your honor, my reason for rejecting the–
these two jurors–I'm not certain as to whether they're Hispanics. I didn't notice how
many Hispanics had been called to the panel, but my reason for rejecting these two is I
feel very uncertain that they would be able
to listen and follow the interpreter." After an
interruption by the defense counsel, the
prosecutor added:

> We talked to them for a long time; the Court
> talked to them, I talked to them. I believe that
> in their heart they will try to follow it [the
> interpreter's translation], but I felt there was a
> great deal of uncertainty as to whether they
> could accept the interpreter as the final arbiter
> of what was said by each of the witnesses, es-
> pecially where there were going to be Spanish-
> speaking witnesses . . . I didn't feel, when I
> asked them whether or not they could accept
> the interpreter's translation of it, I didn't feel
> that they could. They each looked away from
> me and said with some hesitancy that they
> would try, not that they could, but that they
> would try to follow the interpreter . . . I feel
> that in a case where the interpreter will be for
> the main witnesses, they would have an undue
> impact upon the jury.

The trial court rejected Hernández's
claim and the decision was affirmed by the
state appellate courts. On appeal, Justice
Anthony Kennedy, joined by the Chief
Justice, Justice Byron White, and Justice
David Souter, announced the judgment of
the U.S. Supreme Court, holding that the
prosecutor did not use peremptory challenges in a manner that was racially discriminatory or violated the Equal Protection
Clause. Under Batson's 3-step process for
evaluating an objection to peremptory challenges, the outcome seems "questionable,"
but because the prosecutor offered an expla-

nation for the peremptory challenges, and
the trial court ruled on the ultimate question
of intentional discrimination, the preliminary issue as to whether Hernández made a
prima facie showing of discrimination is
moot.

Because the prosecutor offered a race-
neutral basis for his peremptory strikes, the
issue before the U.S. Supreme Court is the
facial validity of the prosecutor's explanation, which needs to be based on something
other than race. Although the Supreme
Court noted that the criterion for exclusion
of whether jurors might have difficulty in
accepting the interpreter's translation of
Spanish language testimony could well have
an adverse disproportionate impact on the
exclusion of prospective Latino jurors, it
held that it is proof of racially discriminatory
intent or purpose that is required to show a
violation of the Equal Protection Clause, as
further noted in *Arlington Heights v. Metropolitan Housing Development Corp* (1977).

The Supreme Court reasoned that it need
not address Hernández's argument that Spanish-speaking ability bears such a close relation to ethnicity that exercising a peremptory challenge on the former ground violates
equal protection,

> since the prosecutor explained that the jurors'
> specific responses and demeanor, and not
> their language proficiency alone, caused him
> to doubt their ability to defer to the official
> translation. That a high percentage of bilingual
> jurors might hesitate before answering ques-
> tions like those asked here and, thus, would be
> excluded under the prosecutor's criterion
> would not cause the criterion to fail the race
> neutrality test.

As such, the Supreme Court concluded that
the trial court did not commit clear error in
ruling that the prosecutor did not discriminate on the basis of the Latino juror's ethnicity.

The implications of *Hernández v. New York* (1991) are substantial, and thus need to be addressed. Although *Strauder* (1880), the first case involving invalidation of a statute based on the Fourteenth Amendment, and the Fourteenth Amendment focused on discrimination against African Americans, the Supreme Court has found that all disadvantaging classifications based on race or ethnicity are subject to protection and are viewed as suspect (Gunther & Sullivan, 1997). Indeed, the Supreme Court in *Strauder* mentioned a law focusing on "all naturalized Celtic-Irishmen" as falling within the purview of the Fourteenth Amendment. However, the Supreme Court in *Hernández* clearly distinguished between race and ethnic discrimination and language discrimination, noting that it was not clear whether some of the jurors were Latino. The Supreme Court stated that the prosecutor focused on the specific jurors "responses and demeanor," rather than their race, ethnicity, or even language proficiency.

An important implication of *Hernández v. New York* (1991) is that it legitimates the use of language as a proxy for race-ethnicity.[11] After *Hernández,* crafty prosecutors are free to exclude Latino jurors from the voir dire, and argue that they were not excluded because of their race or ethnicity, or because of the fact that they are bilingual and Spanish language testimony is going to be offered in the case as long as they can articulate a racial neutral explanation or say that they were not convinced that the jurors would be able to disregard the testimony which they heard in Spanish and abide by the official translation rendered by court interpreter, even if they disagreed with the translation.

Together, I argue that the Supreme Court was wrong in holding that the exclusion of bilingual venire people from juries is not racial discrimination. First, *Hernández* is wrong because the decision is based on an erroneous interpretation of the *Batson* standard. Second,

it assumes that, for bilingual people, language can be divorced from ethnicity or national origin. Third, *Hernández* incorrectly treats bilingualism as behavior that can be altered or changed at will. Although language is certainly learned and can be "unlearned," I propose that once people become bilingual, language is largely an immutable characteristic over which they have little, if any, control; much like race or skin color is an immutable characteristic for other groups. Therefore, language should receive strict scrutiny because bilingual people do not have full control over the language they speak. Fourth, the decision is wrong because it is based on the prevailing liberal model of equality, which defines *equality as sameness.* Finally, *Hernández* is wrong in concluding that the presence of bilingual jurors will detract from the truth-seeking function of juries. I suggest that rather than having a detrimental effect, the presence of bilingual jurors may be necessary to maintain the truth-seeking function of juries.

Hernández is Based on a Narrow and Erroneous Reading of Batson

The *Hernández v. New York* (1991) decision erroneously applied the *Batson* standard. Once a prima facie case is made, the burden shifts to the prosecutor to articulate a race-neutral explanation for striking the prospective jurors. The Supreme Court in *Hernández* concluded that a neutral explanation meant an "explanation based on something other than the race of the juror." This interpretation of *Batson* is so vague that as long as prosecutors give a reason other than race, almost any explanation meets the burden. However, the Supreme Court has consistently held that "[a] racial classification, regardless of purported motivation, is presumptively invalid and can be upheld only upon an extraordinary justification," *Personnel Administrator v. Feeney* (1979).

Hernández Wrongly Assumed that Language Can be Divorced from Race or Ethnicity

Although the prosecutor's explanations need not rise to the level of use to justify a challenge for cause, neither can it be based on assumptions made by the prosecutor that arise solely from the jurors' race or ethnicity, or simply by affirming his "good faith" intention in making the jury selections, as stated in *Batson*, which is essentially what the prosecutor did in *Hernández*. In fact, as the Supreme Court held in *Batson*, the prosecutor "must articulate a neutral explanation related to the particular case to be tried."

Further, *Batson* established that the prosecutor may not rebut the defendant's prima facie case of discrimination "by stating merely that he challenged jurors of the defendant's race on the assumption—or his intuitive judgment—that they would be partial to the defendant because of their shared race." In this case, the peremptory challenges were not based on the assumption that jurors would be biased in favor of the defendant but on the prosecutor's "intuitive judgment" that bilingual jurors would not be able to abide by the official translation. To the extent that bilingual Spanish-speaking ability is linked to being Latino, jurors are thus being excluded on the basis of assumptions, which arise solely from their race or ethnicity. The justification that jurors were excluded not because they were Latino or because they spoke Spanish, but because they might not be able to abide by the official translation which would be insufficient to rebut the presumption of racial/national origin discrimination, particularly because the jurors in question said that "they would try" and the prosecutor believed that "in their heart they will try to follow" the interpreter's translation. An analogy might be the exclusion of whites from a jury trial where African Americans would be

testifying because the prosecutor feared they might not understand African American English or Ebonics. In *Hernández*, the jurors were ostensibly not excluded because they spoke Spanish but because the prosecutor "feared" that they would have difficulty abiding by the official translation, even though they indicated that they would try to abide by it. Lastly, if the reluctance of the Spanish-speaking jurors inheres in their bilingual ability, as I suggest later, they are in effect being excluded because of their race, ethnicity, and language competence, since monolinguals would have little problem abiding by the official translation provided by the interpreter. Notably, the issue of whether one can or would abide by the official translation is one that arises only for bilingual jurors.

Hernández is Based on a Model that Treats Equality as Sameness

Like traditional conceptions of *sex equality*, English-only rules and the use of peremptories to exclude bilingual venire people are derived from a liberal model that seeks to attain equality by treating bilingual and monolingual speakers alike, a model that *equates equality with sameness*. The truth, however, is that bilingual people are different, not the same, as bilinguals are not simply the sum of two monolinguals.

A basic flaw in the traditional model of equality and bilingualism is that it assumes that bilingual employees deliberately "choose" to disregard English-only employment rules or that bilingual jurors somehow "refuse" to accept the official translation as the final arbiter and to disregard Spanish language testimony that they have already heard. This model emanates from a mono-lingual model of language use and is based on additive conception of bilingualism which treats bilingual people as two separate monolingual English and monolingual Spanish speakers. In effect, if we think of language as a faucet, the monolingual English speaker is the "cold" handle of the faucet, and the monolingual Spanish speaker is the "hot" handle, or vice versa. Under this conception of bilingualism, a bilingual person can completely "turn off," or "turn on," one or the other handle at will. An added assumption of the theory of bilingualism employed by the prosecutor in *Hernández* is that bilinguals can turn off both handles and become momentarily bilingual.

In short, the prosecutor in *Hernández* rejected the prospective Latino jurors because he was not convinced from their response during voir dire that they could listen to the Spanish language testimony and then completely disregard it and accept only the English testimony. Since this is a simultaneous translation, the expectation is unrealistic, requiring that jurors have an extraordinary ability to turn the English and Spanish handles "on" and "off" at will. Research on bilingualism and experience of bilinguals suggest that this is not possible, especially for bilinguals who are used to interacting with other bilinguals and to code-switching both between sentences and within them.

Bilingual Classifications Should be Subjected to Strict Scrutiny Because They Are Based on an Immutable Characteristic

The argument in *Hernández v. New York* (1991) that the jurors were not excluded because they were Latino is unpersuasive, given that most Latinos speak Spanish and that about 97 percent of all bilingual Spanish speakers in the United States are Latino and most Latinos claim some knowledge of Spanish.[12] In addition, regardless of language competency, the fear that Latinos will not abide by the official translation can be used as a pretext for excluding them from juries, and thus participation in the judicial process,

with outcomes being governed by only those who are selected for participation.

It should be noted that the prosecutor in *Hernández* did not question non-Latinos about their knowledge of Spanish or whether they would have difficulty abiding by the official translation. The prosecutor also assumed the language competency of the two excluded jurors without first assessing it. Therefore, *Hernández* sets a dangerous precedent because the decisions will likely lead to the wholesale exclusion of Latinos from juries and, by extension, participation in the judicial system. In fact, the holding in *Hernández* was subsequently extended by the Third Circuit Court of Appeals, which held that the "Equal Protection Clause does not prohibit a trial attorney from peremptorily challenging jurors because of their ability to understand a foreign language, the translation of which will be disputed at trial," *Pemberthy v. Beyer* (1994). In *Pemberthy,* the prosecutor used five peremptory challenges to strike Latinos who spoke Spanish because the translation of wiretap tapes would be contested at trial. The defendants moved to suppress all of the wiretap evidence, "arguing, among other things, that the interceptions had not been properly minimized due to the monitors' deficient knowledge of Spanish."

In sum, in *Hernández,* the prosecutor maintained that the jurors were not excluded because they were Latino or because they spoke Spanish but because of their hesitancy in answering whether they would abide by the official interpretation. However, based on bilingualism research, I argue that the excluded jurors in *Hernández* answered in the way that any reasonable honest bilingual person would have answered. I further argue that available research on bilingualism and the experience of bilingual speakers supports the conclusion that bilingualism is largely an immutable trait over which individuals have little, if any, conscious control. In addition to research, which suggests that language processing occurs automatically among bilinguals, postmortem studies of polyglot brains provide evidence that knowledge of more than one language has anatomical consequences (Albert & Obler, 1978:95).

Lastly, bilingual Latinos are different not only from monolinguals but from protected classes for whom language is not a primary basis of difference, identity, or discrimination. Like race or national origin, bilingual children learn the language or languages that are spoken in the home and have little choice or control over the acquisition of language. As such, I argue that if equality is to be attained, law and equal protection analysis must take into account this difference. Otherwise, the *Hernández* equal treatment analysis is bound to perpetuate inequality.

THE EAST LA THIRTEEN AND COMMON SENSE RACISM

In March 1968 thousands of high school students in East Los Angeles engaged in a massive protest and walkout of school seeking to radically revise the school curriculum so that it would reflect the history, heritage, and culture of Chicanos (Stavans, 1996). Two months later, 13 of the organizers of the protest were arrested and charged on 16 counts of conspiracy, a felony, and each faced 45-year prison sentences (Stavans, 1996). Oscar "Zeta" Acosta, an inexperienced Chicano lawyer and creative writer agreed to take the case and represented all of the defendants. This was Acosta's first major case and his first criminal case. Acosta who had served as a legal aid lawyer, once "started dropping acid and staying stoned most of the time and doing all kinds of odd jobs–construction work and washing dishes–and, within about three months my head was

clear" (Stavans, 1996:8). Acosta arrived in Los Angeles in February 1968 to write a story about the Chicano Movement, "intending to stay for a few months, write an article about it and then get out" (Stavans, 1996:8). In fact, when Acosta first arrived in Los Angeles, he stated, "I had no intention of practicing law or of pitting myself against anyone" (Acosta, 1973:22).

The 13 defendants were indicted by the Los Angeles grand jury and charged with *conspiracy to disrupt the schools* (Acosta, 1973). Acosta moved to quash the indictment arguing before the California Court of Appeal that the method for selecting the grand jury was discriminatory and led to the underrepresentation of and denied Chicanos the equal protection of the law (Stavans, 1996). Although the 1968 *East LA Thirteen* case occurred almost a century after *Strauder v. West Virginia* (1880) and 14 years after *Hernández v. Texas* (1954) the motion to quash was denied and the judgment was upheld by the Court of Appeals.

At the time one million Mexicans resided in Los Angeles and constituted the largest minority in the country's most populous county (Stavans, 1996). Yet, in a span of ten years, 178 Superior Court Judges, who nominated grand jurors in Los Angeles County, nominated 1,501 people and only 20 (1%) of the nominees were Spanish surnamed (Stavans, 1996). In fact, 96.1 percent of the judges had never nominated a Spanish surnamed person (Stavans, 1996), with the actual grand jurors being selected at random from the list of nominees. As a result, only four of the 210 (1.9%) grand jurors had a Spanish-surname and one of these individuals was black (Stavans, 1996).

From the testimony of the 30 judges who were subpoenaed by Acosta one can construct a demographic profile of the 1959–1968 grand jurors:

He is wealthy, of independent financial means. He is comparatively advanced in years. He is, or was, a business owner, executive, or professional—or married to one. He is a close personal friend, occasionally once removed, of a Superior Court Judge. He is of the White race . . . In a word, as characterized by an Appellate Judge: WASP. (Stavans, 1996:285)

All but one or two of the subpoenaed judges reported that they did not nominate any Mexicans for the grand jury, because they did not know who was qualified and that they did not feel personally obligated to take affirmative steps to find people who were qualified among the several minorities in the area (Stavans, 1996). In retrospect, "The trial court denied the motion to quash because since in its opinion there was no showing of intentional discrimination, since in each of the last ten years *at least one Mexican was nominated*" (Stavans, 1996:285). This conclusion contradicts the Supreme Court's conclusion in *Hernández v. Texas* (1954) that "it taxes our credulity to say that mere chance resulted in their being no members of this class among the over six thousand jurors called in the past 25 years. The result bespeaks discrimination, whether or not it was a conscious decision on the part of any individual jury commissioner."

University of California-Berkeley Law Professor Ian Haney López (2003:109) notes that in analyzing the testimony presented in the *East Los Angeles Thirteen* case it is clear that "most judges engaged in widespread discrimination without forming intent to do so." In effect, all of the judges denied being prejudiced or that they intended to discriminate against Mexicans or other racial minorities in making their nominations for the grand jury (López, 2003). In fact, López (2003) dismisses the notion that the lawyers were lying or simply trying to cover up their racism and suggests that they probably genuinely believed that they were not racist or biased in

making their nominations. In order to explain the judges' behavior and the contradiction between their professed lack of intent to discriminate, López (2003) turns to the idea that much of our racial beliefs and behavior can be explained by what we simply see as *common sense.* In which case, the type of racism exhibited by the judges is not the old fashioned overt racism, but one that is subtle, covert, and unknowing. According to López (2003:110), while some judges may have harbored animus against Mexicans, "the era and general social context of the cases, though, make it unlikely that the majority of the judges intentionally embraced and acted on racial hatred."

As such, recognizing that it would be difficult to prove intentional discrimination, Acosta told the court: "I am not suggesting arguing that the Judges wake up every morning and say, 'I'm not going to look for any Mexicans today. I'm not going to submit any Mexican Names today" (López, 2003:110). While Acosta insisted that the judges did in fact discriminate, he focused on the results of a discriminatory system, reporting that "We are talking about facts; we are talking about the results of a system" (López, 2003:110).

Clearly, one can see the *power of common sense racism* in jury nominations by analyzing the extent to which the judges tended to completely disregard the criteria given to them for the selection of grand jurors. The 1968 California Code of Civil Procedure, which was provided, listed five prerequisites for grand jurors but only two focused on the personal capacity of prospective jurors. Jurors were expected to possess: "sufficient knowledge of the English language" and were required to be "of ordinary intelligence" (López, 2003:113). Logically, given these minimal requirements, almost any citizen would qualify to serve on a grand jury.

Several U.S. Supreme Court decisions also governed nomination practices, and the

Supreme Court had held that officials selecting grand juries "*must not* simply draw on their acquaintances," cautioning that "Where jury commissioners limit those from whom grand juries are selected to their own personal acquaintances, discrimination can arise from commissioners who know no negroes as well as from commissioners who know but who eliminate them" (López, 2003:114). In another case, the Supreme Court ruled: "The statements of the jury commissioners that they chose only whom they knew, and that they knew no eligible Negroes in an area where Negroes made up so large a proportion of the population, prove the intentional exclusion that is discrimination in violation of . . . constitutional rights" (López, 2003:114). Further, Superior Court judges were issued yearly administrative directives from the presiding judge, consisting of a letter on selecting grand jurors with the following instructions: "The Grand Jury should be representative of a cross -ection of the community. Each judge must therefore be mindful of the need for making nominations from the various geographical locations within the County, and different racial groups, and all economic levels" (López, 2003:114).

In actuality, despite these Supreme Court decisions and directives calling for the selection of grand juries from a cross-section of the population and admonishing judges from simply nominating their acquaintances, judges continued to nominate their friends and acquaintances and largely failed to nominate Latinos, blacks, or members of other racial minority groups. Yet, when confronted by Acosta on the witness stand, they insisted that they simply nominated people who were competent without regard to race or national origin, resonating on the Thomas theorem that *if men define situations as real, they are real in their consequences.*

Although it is hard to understand how the judges could have interpreted the relevant Supreme Court decisions and the cross-sectional directive issued by the presiding judge as legitimating the selection of their friends as grand jurors, this is precisely how many of the judges interpreted these directives. Judge William Levit, for instance, responded to Acosta's admonishment that the grand jury should be representative of a cross-section of the community: "I have no quarrel with that. I would assume that with a hundred and thirty-four Judges, selected as they are and each one given the right to nominate up to two people, that this would be what I would consider a cross-section of the community, broadly defined" (López, 2003:117). Many of the judges felt that they had selected a cross-section of the community in making their individual selections and interpreted the presiding judge's directive as commending, rather than condemning the practice of nominating their friends and acquaintances. For these judges nominating their friends was part of a powerful script, or commons sense (López, 2003). The "pick your friends" script was not only routine practice but assumed a normative character (López, 2003:119).

When pressed by Acosta on the stand as to the cross-sectional requirement, most judges defended their nominations using the "qualifications card." One judge, for instance, said "It wouldn't make any difference who came before me if they are *qualified* as a nominee, but I don't want to nominate people I don't know" (López, 2003: 123). Another judge said, "I think it is the duty of each judge to pick a nominee who he feels is *qualified* for the position, regardless of what race, nationality, or religion he may be" (López, 2003:123-124).

The common sense script carried a strong, unstated implication, not only that grand jurors should be qualified but that "qualified persons were white, non-whites were unqualified," as illustrated by the testimony of Judge Richard Fildew. When Acosta asked

Judge Fildew whether he believed that the grand jury should be represented by the various racial and ethnic groups, he responded: "If the people are qualified, definitely; if they are not qualified, no" (López, 2003:125). Frustrated by Judge Fildew's response, Acosta pressed the issue:

> **Q.** I am assuming that the Grand Jury is eventually composed of qualified people. Now, my question is: Do you believe that the ultimate result of any Grand Jury should be that it be composed generally of a cross-section of the community?
>
> **A.** It would be fine if it could, and I will agree with that, that it would be very nice if it could, but if you are going to impair the quality and get on people just because they are of certain races, then I am not in favor of it (López, 2003:125).

Judge Fildew added:

> **A.** Well, if you are going to get somebody who isn't Qualified just because he is an American Indian or an Eskimo, because you have to have an Eskimo on the Grand Jury, but this fellow isn't qualified, I am Against that . . . (López, 2003:125-126).

Notably, two things are clear from the testimony of the Superior Court Judges subpoenaed by Acosta. First, they justified by the nomination of their friends and acquaintances to the grand jury by saying that they nominated people who were qualified and their friends were qualified. Second, they conflated race and qualifications, so that whites were qualified and people of color were not. What is perhaps most interesting about the judges' emphasis on qualifications is that the criteria for serving on a grand jury are minimal and entail simply "sufficient knowledge of the English language" and that one be of "ordinary intelligence." This means that most citizens of the United States, including most Mexicans and other Latinos would be qualified to serve on the grand jury, for surely there are members of this category who have sufficient knowledge of the English language and are of ordinary intelligence. Essentially, *an indirect and pernicious implication of the testimony of the judges was that Mexicans were inferior and not qualified to serve on grand juries.*

As a consequential rupture to continuity in jurisprudence, in response to the evidence presented before the California Court of Appeals in *Salvador Castro v. Superior Court* (1969), the District Attorney presented no evidence to rebut the presumption of discrimination based on the figures presented before the court. Instead, he argued that there was no evidence to show intentional discrimination against Mexicans and that "since the Mexican population was disproportionately young, alien, non-English speaking, economically disadvantaged and educationally inferior, 'the raw population figures and percentages [would be] utterly meaningless'" (Stavans, 1996:287). Symbolically and pragmatically, Chicanos "interpreted the D.A.'s argument to say that the Mexican was perhaps too stupid and too poor for service on the Grand Jury of Los Angeles" (Stavans, 1996:288).

CONCLUSION

Juries are a hallmark of the legal and judicial system of the United States and one of the cornerstones of our justice system is the right to a trial by a jury of one's peers. The Sixth Amendment provides that one has a right to a speedy and public trial by an impartial jury and the Fourteenth Amendment notes that no state shall "deny to any person within its jurisdiction the equal protection of the law."

In *Strauder v. West Virginia* (1880), the Supreme Court invalidated the conviction of a black man who had been convicted by an all-white jury because of a specific statute that limited jury service to "All White male persons who are twenty-one years of age and who are citizens of this State." Strauder had unsuccessfully sought to have his case moved to federal court and the Supreme Court held that removal should have been granted and that the law was a violation of the Fourteenth Amendment and thus unconstitutional.

In *Swain v. Alabama* (1965), however, the Supreme Court held that it was not a violation of equal protection for a prosecutor to use peremptory challenges to strike all blacks from a jury pool: "[To] subject the prosecutor's challenge in any particular case to the demands [of equal protection] would entail a radical change in the nature and operation of the challenge" given that the "essential nature of the peremptory challenge is that it [is] exercised without a reason stated, without inquiry and without being subject to the court's control." Twenty-one years later, however, *Swain* was overturned in *Batson v. Kentucky* (1986), which held that the equal protection clause "forbids the prosecutor to challenge potential jurors solely on the basis account of their race or on the assumption that black jurors as a group will be unable impartially to consider the State's case against a black defendant." *Batson* further held that a defendant can make a prima facie case of purposeful racial discrimination by relying solely on the facts concerning jury selection *in his case.*

Finally, *Hernández v. Texas* (1954) recognized Mexicans as a distinct and cognizable entity, separate and apart from blacks and whites and struck down discrimination in jury selection against Mexicans in Jefferson County, Texas. Unfortunately, despite these U.S. Supreme Court rulings and precedents, Mexicans and other Latino groups continue to be discriminated against and are grossly underrepresented in both grand and petit juries (Forde-Mazrui, 1999).[13] Arguably, most of this discrimination is not *de jure,* or formally and legally mandated, purposeful discrimination, but covert, indirect discrimination, or what has been termed *common sense racism* in the American judicial system.

Chapter 11

INDIGENT DEFENDANTS AND THE BARRIERS THEY FACE IN THE U.S. COURT SYSTEM

MARTIN GUEVARA URBINA

Where laws are so stated that people of all classes are equally likely to violate them, the lower the social position of the offender, the greater is the likelihood that sanctions will be imposed on him. When sanctions are imposed, the most severe sanctions will be imposed on persons in the lowest social class.
—William Chambliss and Robert Seidman

Students learn in the U.S. school system that the American legal system is based on equality, fairness, and justice, with the picture of *Lady Justice* serving as a powerful symbol of universal justice. Unfortunately, though, American government and history textbooks in the school system offer a simplified or skewed version of law, courts, lawyers, and trials, and, sometimes, outright lies. Contrary to the *popular imagination*, law is not simply a body of rules enacted by public officials in a logical, equitable, and legitimate manner and backed by the authority of the government, as commonly defined in textbooks.

THE DYNAMICS OF AMERICAN CRIMINAL JUSTICE

To begin, working definitions of law deliberately exclude reference to justice because there is no precise legal or scientific meaning to the term. Since law often clashes with abstract concepts like morality and culture, there is no uniformity in U.S. criminal law, leading to crucial variation from practitioner to practitioner and from jurisdiction to jurisdiction. In the application of criminal law, courtroom officials tend not to function so much as an *adversary system* that is fully vested in *due process,* the principal legal doctrine for limiting arbitrariness under the Fifth, Sixth, Eighth, and Fourteenth Amendments, but as a *semi-autonomous social organization,* operating with great discretion and immunity (Salinas, 2015; Urbina & Byxbe, 2011). Suggesting that law is not fixed but flexible, Joycelyn Pollock (2010:374) quotes, "Far from being absolute or objective, the

159

law is a dynamic, ever-changing symbol of political will." Internationally renowned legal Historian and Law Professor Lawrence Friedman (1984:2) documents that "[law] is a word of many meanings, as slippery as glass, as elusive as a soap bubble."

The emblazoned phrase across the front of the federal building that houses the U.S. Supreme Court, notably the most visible icon of American jurisprudence, reads: "Equal Justice Under the Law." Yet, historically, the judicial system has been rampant with inequality and injustice, with economics being a major barrier, as vividly illustrated by Jeffery Reiman and Paul Leighton in *The Rich Get Richer and the Poor Get Prison* (2017) and Lupe S. Salinas in *U.S. Latinos and Criminal Injustice* (2015). Years before the current *crises of drugs* and *terrorism,* William Chambliss and Robert Seidman (1971) observed an inverse relationship between social class and punishment. In effect, the typical defendant is impoverished, young, uneducated, male, and either black or Latino, with most Latinos being Mexicans (Tonry, 2006; Salinas, 2015; Urbina & Álvarez, 2017). Logically, in the context of the judicial system, the situation gets further complicated for indigent defendants, especially minorities and undocumented people, during social, political, or economic instability, as we have witnessed during the 2015–2016 presidential elections, exacerbating quickly after Trump was inaugurated on January 20, 2017. Particularly, during economic uncertainty, political rhetoric and societal concerns about crime focus on criminal courts, with judges, prosecutors, and even defense attorneys being blamed for

"presumed" high crime rates, independent of whether crime is up or down, within an historical context (Urbina & Álvarez, 2016, 2017).[14] Political and public sentiment turns on those who are perceived as a social threat to public order and economic stability, with the biggest impact falling on the impoverished, minorities, and immigrants (Álvarez & Urbina, 2018; Durán, 2009a, 2009b; Kong, 2010; Romero, 2001, 2008b; Salinas, 2015; Urbina & Álvarez, 2017).

The primary objective of this chapter, then, is to broaden the examination of ethnicity and punishment by analyzing the nature of punishment outside the typically studied geographical locations, an area with rapid mobility and a high concentration of Latinos. By exploring the processing of the typical defendant–indigent defendants–in the legal system vis-à-vis the views of practitioners responsible for the daily operation of the *machinery of courtroom justice,* we will gain insight into the fundamentals of punishment and, by extension, capital punishment, a sanction that has historically been used to control and silence minorities, particularly Mexicans and blacks (Álvarez & Urbina, 2014; see also Baker; Peña & Urbina, this volume). Judges, prosecutors, and public defenders in Wisconsin were asked to express their views and concerns regarding the experience of indigent defendants. As for specific issues, the focus is primarily (but not exclusively) on five critical issues confronting the typical defendant, most of whom are either Latinos or blacks: economics, education, social environment, citizenship, and language.

INTERTWINING FORCES IN AMERICAN CRIMINAL LAW

Economics

Historically, in the functioning of the U.S. machinery of justice, no two issues have received more attention than the "influence" of race/ethnicity and economics. Arguably, the more favorable outcomes are tilted toward those who have greater financial, political, and social resources, while limited resources tend to disadvantage the impoverished, especially minority poor. The unspoken reality in the U.S. legal system, as in almost everything else in life, is that money changes almost everything and the larger the amount of money, the bigger the change (Acuña, 1998; Reiman & Leighton, 2017).

For instance, decisions to release offenders, especially for violent crimes, on their own recognizance or on unsecured bonds are based primarily on the level of social standing in the community, determined largely by employment and home ownership, favoring property owners and those with "respectable" employment over impoverished defendants who live in areas that might be view as disorganized, drug infested, and violent. Worse, the longer the judicial process, the more pressing resources become, especially during trial delays and retrials, as in the case of capital punishment (Urbina, 2012).

The *economics discrimination thesis* in legal jurisprudence continues to be in question in the twenty-first century, with some scholars reporting that extralegal factors in interaction with legal factors are influential at each stage of the legal process (Salinas, 2015). Reiman and Leighton (2017), for example, document that socioeconomic status is one of the most influential characteristics shaping final outcomes in the legal system, with minorities being more likely to be harshly penalized. In the context of legal rationality,

understanding the dynamics of bail decisions, for example, enhance our understanding of how defendants come to be differentially situated at later stages of the judicial process, especially since limited resources to hire a competent criminal defense attorney will govern both the process and final dispositions. Further, the *economics discrimination thesis* seems to significantly interact with race and ethnicity (Urbina, 2007; Urbina & Álvarez, 2016, 2017). Some investigators report that political and economic resources are disproportionately unavailable to Latinos, with the possible exception of Cuban Americans (Urbina, 2007, 2011; Urbina & Álvarez, 2017). In effect, according to one researcher, as a community, "Hispanic defendants suffer a triple burden at the pretrial release stage as they are the group most likely to be required to pay bail to gain release, the group that receives the highest bail amount, and the group least able to pay bail" (Demuth, 2003:873).

Economics and Capital Punishment

Former Supreme Court Justice William Douglas once cited that "one searches our chronicles in vain for the execution of any member of the affluent strata of this society," comparing American capital punishment to ancient Hindu law, where rich defendants who hire legal counsel are immune from execution, or, as Brahmans, are immune from execution by law. Indeed, along with the "power of money," incidents of incompetent appointed counsel abound (which is influenced by money), as defense attorneys have been caught asleep in court, drunk during court proceedings, and on occasions offering no defense during the punishment face of capital trials, as documented by Álvarez & Urbina in "Capital Punishment on

Trial: Who Lives, Who Dies, Who Decides—A Question of Justice (2014)?" In effect, analyzing death penalty cases for defendants indicted for murder in Harris County (Houston), Texas from 1992 to 1999, one study found that legal counsel (appointed vs. hired) does influence final dispositions; that is, getting the death penalty, with the author concluding, "legal counsel shapes death sentences" (Phillips, 2009a:745). In a wellknown and highly publicized case, if O. J. Simpson had been working a minimum wage job (approximately $14,000 a year before taxes), no celebrity, social, or political status, chances are that the trial would of lasted a few days and the case would have resulted in: *guilty,* and given the sentence of death and in states like Texas, possibly executed. Lastly, the powerful influence of economics takes multiple dimensions in criminal justice polices (Urbina & Álvarez, 2016), clearly noted in death penalty cases (Álvarez & Urbina, 2014; Urbina, 2012; see Baker; Peña & Urbina, this volume). In another Texas study, also analyzing cases indicted for homicide in Harris County, Texas from 1992 to 1999, the author found that the death sentence was "more likely to be sought and imposed on behalf of high-status victims who were integrated, sophisticated, conventional, and respectable" (Phillips, 2009b:807).

Race and Ethnicity

As documented in previous chapters, even though Latinos have been in the United States since 1565, a high majority of prior studies have focused almost exclusively on blacks and whites. Still, independent of academic investigations, in the processing of ethnic defendants, court officials must make decisions in each stage of the judicial process, and more so in death penalty cases, which involve bifurcated (two-staged) trials. Celesta Albonetti (1991) has characterized

sentencing decisions as "bounded rationality," where judges (and prosecutors) may resort to stereotypes of dangerousness that rest on ideas of individual characteristics, like race, ethnicity, gender, sexuality, unemployment, legal status, and language (Salinas, 2015; Urbina, 2003a, 2004a, 2007; Urbina & Álvarez, 2017; Urbina & Smith, 2007). Further, since judges and prosecutors normally do not have enough information to adequately evaluate offenders' culpability or dangerousness, they develop "perceptual shorthand" based on perceptions of stereotypes, which are highly propagated by the American media (Hawkins, 1981; Steffensmeier, Ulmer, & Kramer, 1998; Urbina, 2005; Urbina & White, 2009). In fact, African Americans, particularly young men, tend to be portrayed by the American media in negative roles, like deviant, dangerous, and dysfunctional, and labels like *school dropouts, criminals, drug addicts, street-smart dudes, welfare pimps,* and *criminals* are widely use to *psychologically intoxicate* a misinformed society, crucially, with some of these community members serving on juries, including death penalty juries. Similarly, studies report that Latinos, like blacks, are perceived by mainstream America to be impoverished, lazy, uneducated, unintelligent, undocumented, and violent (Álvarez & Urbina, 2014, 2018; Salinas, 2015). Edwardo Portillos (1998:156) documents that "the assumption frequently made is that if you are a young Latino, and especially a Hispanic male, you are a gun-wielding, drug-selling gang banger unless proven otherwise," an observation supported by recent studies (Durán, 2009a, 2009b, 2009c; Salinas, 2015; Urbina & Álvarez, 2015, 2016, 2017). Worse, the conceptualization of crime as a minority or "lower-class" social problem fuses the development and reinforcement of race and ethnic stereotypes, with the biggest impact of stereotyping falling most heavily on the impoverished and powerless (Bacon, 2009; Bender, 2005; Berg, 2014; De Génova, 2004; Kappeler & Potter, 2004).

Indeed, beyond race and ethnic stereotypes, Latinos face many of the same social disadvantages confronting African Americans, like poverty, unemployment, and a failing educational system, in addition to various specific issues influencing the ethnic experience, to include language, citizenship, lack of knowledge of the legal system, and fear of deportation. Further, with a long history of antagonism and hatred towards ethnic minorities for arguably representing a social, cultural, financial, political, and criminal threat, in some cases Latinos receive much harsher treatment in the court system than whites and African Americans (Urbina, 2012). In effect, in nondeath penalty cases, some studies show Latinos being disadvantaged at the sentencing stage (Engen & Gainey, 2001; Spohn & Holleran, 2000; Steffensmeier & Demuth, 2000, 2001). As for ethnic effects in different stages of the judicial process, see Urbina (2007, 2012) for a review of nondeath penalty and death penalty studies. Stephen Demuth (2003), for instance, found that Latinos are more likely to be detained than whites, with race and ethnic variation being most pronounced in drug cases. Of course, in some geographical areas, studies show significant difference between racial groups. For example, one study found that, on average, blacks had 20 percent longer sentences than whites in Maryland, with Latinos also experiencing differential treatment (Bushway & Piehl, 2001). In the case of capital punishment, Urbina (2012) found that Latinos who were under the sentence of death in California, Florida, and Texas from 1975 to 1995 were less likely to have their death sentences declared unconstitutional by the U.S. Supreme Court or State Supreme Court, or overturned by an appellate court than both blacks and whites. The findings

also showed that Latino inmates were less likely than blacks and whites to have their convictions overturned by an appellate court (see Baker; Peña & Urbina, this volume).

Language

From a constitutional standpoint, rights are of utmost importance, to ensure fairness, justice, and, ultimately, the protection of democracy and freedom. As reported by Urbina (2004a), in the processing of criminal defendants, legal rights are conveyed in words, indicating that, in essence, defendants have no rights if they are not able to understand their granted statutory, constitutional, or international rights. Judges, for example, inquire whether defendants understand the nature of the charge and the possible sanction upon conviction, whether any threats were made during the arrest process, if they are satisfied with the defense counsel, and whether defendants realize that a plea waives the constitutional right to a jury trial (*Boykin v. Alabama,* 1969), issues which are extremely pressing in criminal cases, and more so in death penalty cases.

Unfortunately, studies show that language is one of the most consequential barriers currently confronting non-English speakers, particularly Latinos in the U.S. court system (Álvarez & Urbina, 2014; Urbina, 2004a, 2004b). One early ethnic study reports that decision-making is unique to Latinos due to cultural stereotypes, which intertwine with language barriers (Zatz, 1984). More recent studies document that defendants with limited English and defendants unable to understand, read, or write English are less prepared and unable to present a strong criminal defense (Álvarez & Urbina, 2014; Molvig, 2001). Unfamiliarity with the U.S. judicial system, combined with cultural difference and fear of retaliation by immigration authorities, might force undocumented

Latinos to be less forthcoming with court officials, which in turn might be perceived as more "deserving" of severe punishment (Brown-Graham, 1999; Messier, 1999). Investigating the minority experience in the Wisconsin legal system, Derrick Nunnally (2004:B1) notes that "cultural differences can create intimidating barriers." To further complicate the judicial process for non-English speaking defendants, judges have the authority under *Alford v. North Carolina* (1971) to accept guilty pleas while claiming innocence, a procedure that sometimes results in devastating ramifications (Urbina, 2004b), like execution in capital punishment cases (Álvarez & Urbina, 2014; Urbina, 2011, 2012; see Baker; Peña & Urbina, this volume). Invariably, for non-English speaking defendants, the novel standard of "equal justice" clashes with reality, with the "equal justice doctrine" being replaced by the "most affordable justice" standard in American jurisprudence.

Citizenship

Within an historical context, citizenship has always been a sensitive and polemic issue (Almaguer, 2008; Castañeda, 2007; Chacón & Davis, 2006; Meeks, 2007; Oboler, 2006; Welch, 2006), as recently documented by Álvarez and Urbina in *Immigration and the Law: Race, Citizenship, and Social Control* (2018). Typically, combined with their "indigent status," the representation of undocumented defendants in criminal proceedings poses consequential challenges for the court system and those vested in the equity of legal jurisprudence. Among the various safeguards, court officials must guard against prejudice due to national origin and cultural differences, preconceived notions of criminality based on ethnic stereotypes, deficiencies in language interpretation, and detrimental consequences of possible deportation in criminal proceedings (Álvarez & Urbina, 2018; De Génova, 2004; Romero, 2008a).

Under the Immigration Reform Legislation of 1996, noncitizens can lose their legal resident status, be deported, or unable to seek naturalization if convicted of a "felony." However, the legal definition of "aggravated felony," which, under immigration law, is a deportable offense, is vague and misleading (Kong, 2010; Motomura, 2010; Salinas, 2015). Further, even if a case is not considered for deportation, the legal definition of a crime is fundamental in how it is perceived in the *popular imagination,* shaping and reshaping *conventional wisdom.* Some people, for instance, to include jury members, might not know that various crimes that are classified as misdemeanors under federal or state law could be classified as aggravated felonies under U.S. immigration law, possibly resulting in deportation (Kong, 2010; Romero, 2001; Salinas, 2015).[15]

Logically, then, defense attorneys should consider possible ramifications when analyzing legal strategies during criminal proceedings, including whether or not to plead guilty, plea bargain negotiations, whether to go to trial, and the dynamics of the trial process, a process that requires broad knowledge of both United States and International Law. If the defense opts for a trial, for example, a motion for post-conviction relief when the defendants are in "removal" proceedings will probably not help them because the government does not delay deportation for collateral attacks, only for direct appeals. The legal process is further complicated for undocumented defendants in that immigration law is controlled by federal statutes whereas state defense attorneys typically specialize in criminal law (see Posadas & Medina, this volume), with the majority of attorneys never trying a death penalty case in their entire career.

To control for possible miscarriages of justice, some states have enacted statutes requiring trial courts to inform undocumented defendants of potential deportation and the consequences of a guilty plea (see Romero & Sánchez, this volume).[16] However, most courts rarely find defense counsel ineffective for neglecting to inform immigrant defendants of possible legal ramifications. Even though the U.S. Supreme Court has ruled that defendants must be fully aware of the consequences of a guilty plea, U.S. courts have found that this does not include awareness of collateral immigration consequences (Motomura, 2010; Salinas, 2015; Welch, 2002, 2006). In actuality, from a moral, ethical, and legal standpoint, the duty of trial courts to inform defendants lies in the fundamental principles of legal jurisprudence, regardless of whether it is a constitutional mandate or not.

Lastly, even though immigrants of all races have experienced multiple obstacles in the judicial process, the harshest cruelties and injustices seem to have fallen on Latinos, particularly Mexicans (Álvarez & Urbina, 2018; see also Posadas & Medina; Romero & Sánchez, this volume). The *threat* posed by the growing number of Latino immigrants centers around contentious issues, such as competition for jobs (even jobs that have traditionally been labeled as "Mexican labor"), the primacy of the English language, as noted by English-only movements and legislation, the preservation of Anglo-American culture, and whether immigrants are a tax and welfare burden on U.S. citizens (Álvarez & Urbina, 2018; Chomsky, 2007; Fox & Rivera-Salgado, 2004). Worse, Latinos may be "judged" as a greater *flight risk* or possibly more dangerous due to their noncitizen status (see Álvarez, this volume). Reaffirming the Thomas' theorem that if people define situations as real, they are real in their consequences, the assumption that

Latinos are more likely to be noncitizens or undocumented immigrants, particularly from Mexico, results in Latinos being detained and harshly sanctioned simply because of their legal status, combined with a lack of community ties and limited resources (Álvarez & Urbina, 2018; Cobas, Duany, & Feagin, 2009; Demuth, 2002; see Crawford; Durán; Posadas & Medina; Romero & Sánchez, this volume). In effect, in 1969, after the advent of the civil rights movement and Chicano movement, Judge Chargin of Santa Clara, California remarked during juvenile court proceedings of a Mexican youth:

> We ought to send you back to Mexico. You belong in prison for the rest of your life for doing things of this kind. You ought to commit suicide. That's what I think of people of this kind. You are lower than animals and haven't the right to live in organized society-just miserable, lousy, rotten people . . . Maybe Hitler was right. (Hernández, Haug, & Wagner, 1976:62–63)

This clearly resonates the historical legacy of hate and, worse, indicating the possible ramifications in legal proceedings, including death penalty cases (see Baker; Peña & Urbina, this volume).

Education

In *Latino Access to Higher Education: Ethnic Realities and New Directions for the Twenty-First Century* (2016), Urbina and Wright document that in twenty-first century America, education is in fact the most powerful and consequential *border* in the pursuit of fairness, equality, freedom, and democracy. In the context of the judicial system, with limited or no education, it's almost impossible to post bail, hire competent legal counsel, retain counsel during lengthy trials, understand the abstract terminology of legal proceedings, understand whether constitutional rights and international legal treaties are being upheld, or obtain decent employment. As such, considering that the great majority of those arrested, prosecuted, convicted, sentenced to jail/prison, or executed are uneducated, education is one of the biggest barriers confronting indigent defendants in the U.S. court system (Austin & Irwin, 2012; Reiman & Leighton, 2017; Tonry, 2006; see also Urbina & Álvarez Chapter 17, this volume).

Together, as cited herein, there is indication that the amount of granted justice in U.S. jurisprudence is highly governed by the simultaneous interaction of various social, cultural, financial, political, and ideological factors. Notably, with limited resources, es-

pecially money, education, and community ties, the *iron cages of justice* continue to lock primarily impoverished defendants, with the majority of executed inmates being uneducated and impoverished (Álvarez & Urbina, 2014; Urbina, 2011, 2012; see Baker; Peña & Urbina, this volume). Though, while the majority of those sent to jail or prison will eventually be released (with the exception of those on death row), the majority will soon be back behind bars in large part because of their inability to find a job due to their criminal record, no education, and, for immigrants, the perception that they pose an economic or social threat to law and order.

RESEARCH FINDINGS FOR WISCONSIN

The Influence of Economics

The objective of this section is to explore the significance of one of the most influential barrier confronting indigent defendants, economics, through a series of financial related questions. Consistent with prior investigations, the majority (42 or 80.8%) of the 52 participating court officials reported that of all defendants who are processed by the legal system, most offenders are indeed "indigent" defendants. In regards to approximately how many defendants, in general, who enter the legal system have a "steady" job at the time of their court appearance (or shortly before their arrest), 39 (75.0%) participants reported that "few" defendants and 11 court officials estimated that approximately half of the defendants have steady but low paying jobs. Of those who have jobs at the time of their court appearance or shortly before their arrest, 39 (75.0%) court officials noted that very few defendants actually have *decent* jobs, with 10 respondents estimating that the majority of defendants' earnings are around

the poverty line. Notably, while 20 (38.5%) respondents documented that *few* defendants, in general, do not qualify for a public defender due to the $250 a month legislative requirement, almost the same number (19 or 36.5%) stated that *most* defendants do not qualify for a public defender. However, of those who do not qualify for a public defender, the majority (43 or 82.6%) of practitioners claimed that most defendants are "barely making it" financially.

Interestingly, while 21 (40.3%) respondents estimated that about half of all indigent defendants are able to obtain *outside* assistance, 20 (38.5%) court officials noted that few indigent defendants are able to secure needed assistance, especially resources that will assist in their defense, like enough money to pay for a lie detector test, a preliminary test used by the defense. Considering the influence of economics on indigent defendants, court officials were asked to assess the monetary fines currently being imposed as a form of punishment. Surprisingly, 16 (30.7%) respondents characterized the fines as "about right," but 34 practitioners stated that the fines are "way too high" for the typical defendant. Considering that court officials are the ones imposing fines, most (39 or 75.0%) respondents reported that the majority of indigent defendants are not able to actually pay the fines imposed by the courts, especially if the fines are substantial, suggesting that fines are more symbolic than pragmatic. More crucially, 18 (34.6%) participants estimated that approximately half of the indigent defendants are able to post bail for minor offenses, with over half (29 or 55.8%) of the participating court officials noting that few indigent defendants are actually able to post bail in criminal court.

The Influence of the Social Environment

Some investigators have documented that the typical indigent defendant grows up in poverty areas, often in chaotic environments, where various illegal vices are in abundance, but with limited opportunities in areas that will actually help people succeed, like education and employment (Bourgois, 1995; Díaz-Cotto, 2006; Mirandé, 1989; Rodríguez, 1993; Ruiz, 1999; Salinas, 2015; Urbina & Wright, 2016). As such, court officials were asked to voice their views as to how influential the social environment is on final outcomes, like conviction and sentence. Of those who responded, 12 believed that indigent defendants growing up in poverty areas does not influence final outcomes in court, but most (33 or 63.5%) court officials, though, reported that where indigent defendants live influence final dispositions. Similarly, while seven respondents stated that indigent defendants growing up in a chaotic environment does not influence outcomes, 38 (73.2%) court officials claimed that living in a chaotic environment influence court dispositions in one way or another. Further, 12

participants noted that living in broken homes does not influence dispositions, but 34 (65.4%) court officials indicated that living in broken homes does indeed influence court outcomes. Likewise, 13 respondents believed that living in single-parent homes has no influence on outcomes, while 33 (63.4%) practitioners reported that living in single-parent homes influence final court dispositions.

The Influence of Education

In a 2004 article, "Language Barriers in the Wisconsin Court System: The Latino/a Experience," Urbina reports that not only are non-English speaking defendant being denied equal access to the law because of language barriers, but that defendants in general tend to have little understanding of the judicial process, with little knowledge of their statutory and constitutional rights and lack of understanding of their rights under international treaties, like Article 36 of the Vienna Convention on Consular Relations. In this context, court officials were questioned on a series of education related issues. Of the participants who responded, 33 (63.5%) estimated that most indigent defendants understand their constitutional and statutory rights, with 15 court officials noting that few defendants actually understand their rights. More specifically, the majority (37 or 71.1%) of respondents felt that most indigent defendants understand the constitutional right of trial by jury, with 14 court officials claiming that few defendants actually *understand* the dynamics of jury trials, some adding that defendants might know that they have such right, but do not actually understand the logistics or implications. Similarly, 44 (84.6%) court officials reported that most indigent defendants understand that a plea waives the right to a jury trial, with seven court officials stating that defendants may know that they have such right but that the great majority do not understand the benefits or ramifications of waiving a jury trial, a critical observation since a high majority of cases are plea bargain. More crucially, while 12 respondents believed that *most* indigent defendants know that they can rely on post-conviction review, half (26 or 50.0%) of the court officials reported that *few* defendants are in fact aware of post-conviction remedies, like filing a habeas petition in federal court once appeals have been exhausted. Lastly, over half (32 or 61.6%) of the responding court officials noted that the mere fact that *the typical indigent defendant is ignorant of the law* influence the judicial process and final dispositions.

The Influence of Citizenship

While citizenship has not received the same level of attention in the criminal justice system, this polemic issue has historically been a major and rancorous debate among the general public, politicians, law enforcement, legislatures, and the media (Álvarez & Urbina, 2018; Acuña, 2015; Almaguer, 2008; Bender, 2005; Chávez, 2013; Meeks, 2007; Oboler, 2006; Salinas, 2015). As such, participating court officials were asked about the possible influence of legal status in the judicial process, as legal status appears to be a significant factor in drug-related cases and even death penalty cases (Álvarez & Urbina, 2014; Urbina, 2012; see Posadas & Medina; Romero & Sánchez, this volume). First, over half (33 or 63.5%) of the respondents estimated that, contrary to the *popular mentality,* few defendants are undocumented; that is, not having the proper documentation to reside in the United States. However, while 32 (61.5%) respondents cited equal treatment, 20 (38.5%) court officials reported that undocumented defendants, particularly Mexicans, processed by the U.S. legal system are

not receiving the same treatment as their U.S. citizens (and legal residents) counterparts. According to one court official, "most judges and lawyers cannot relate to cultural differences" in multiracial or multiethnic communities (see Urbina, 2005; Urbina & Kreitzer, 2004; Urbina & White, 2009). Some court officials noted that even though most undocumented people tend to experience difficulties, especially if they are not fluent in English, Latinos, most notably Mexicans, and Asians, particularly Hmong, are the ones experiencing the greatest challenges in the judicial system. Additionally, 20 court officials claimed that once undocumented people are arrested and required to attend court, they run the risk of being deported to their country of origin. More globally, 27 (51.9%) participants stated that undocumented people are not at a disadvantage in the criminal justice system, but 23 (44.2%) court officials reported that undocumented defendants tend to be at a disadvantage from arrest to appeal in one way or another (Álvarez & Urbina, 2018; Salinas, 2015; see Posadas & Medina; Romero & Sánchez, this volume).

As a whole, combined with citizenship, the primary reasons for differential treatment, according to some court officials, include language barriers, cultural differences, economics, stereotypes, race and ethnic prejudice, fear of crime, and lack of interpreters, especially for uncommon languages like Hmong. As cited by one court official, undocumented people "are seen as not belonging here in the first place so constitutional protections of citizens are not always applicable to them." In the words of one judge: "in the eyes of some people, immigrants are not viewed as deserving of equal treatment." Consequently, as quoted by another court official, "illegal aliens in general probably have the least amount of protection because they have an additional consequence, potential deportation, making it hard to advise them and what legal strategy for the defense to take."

The Influence of Language

As argued by Urbina (2004a), statutory and constitutional rights, verbal and written, are conveyed in words, indicating that if defendants cannot understand their rights, they, in essence, have no rights. In this context, participating court officials were inquired on the possible influence of language. Most (41 or 78.8%) court officials documented that few defendants do not speak English, but that a higher number of defendants have limited English skills, particularly Latinos and Hmong. More critically, the majority of such defendants are indigent with little or absolutely no formal education. Further, 13 participants claimed that most defendants have a "good understanding" of both the judicial process and their legal rights, but over half (30 or 57.7%) of the participating court officials noted that *few* defendants *actually understand* their rights or the judicial process, with some respondents indicating that the legal terminology is so complex that some attorneys confuse state law and federal law, with limited knowledge of immigration law, which is governed by federal statutes. Worse, most (44 or 84.7%) participants estimated that the majority of defendants who do not understand their rights or the judicial process are in fact indigent defendants, particularly Latinos. However, some court officials reported that some black and white defendants speak English, but that they cannot truly understand the legal terminology and often have poor comprehension, which impedes effective communication during court proceedings.

Presenting a provoking challenge to legal theory and judicial rationality, 10 court officials claimed that court interpreters are not always provided to non-English speaking defendants, placing the *distribution* of judicial justice in question, as noted in Urbina's investigation of court interpreters. In effect, the majority (47 or 90.4%) of participating court officials believed that more interpreters are needed in the court system, an observation consistent with prior investigations (Urbina, 2004a). Lastly, most (39 or 75.0%) court officials remembered experiencing situations in which they had difficulties communicating with defendants because of language barriers, putting the defendant at a disadvantage. As such, according to one participating judge, "Unfamiliarity with institutional barriers and no agility to advocate successfully within the system, non-English speakers are definitely receiving less protection, not to mention Deaf and hard of hearing people." Worse, as cited by another court official, "The translation and explanations of court concepts lose the meaning of justice." Again, like the various issues mentioned above, this is another situation that puts the notion of *equality under the law* into question.

MAKING SENSE OF AMERICAN JURISPRUDENCE

In all, the findings suggest that a significant gap remains to be bridged between legal theory and the actual application of criminal law. To ensure continuity, legal reform must equate the judicial process in its totality, but particular attention to various pressing broad issues is warranted, to include the globalization of crime and punishment, as crime and punishment, including death penalty cases, transcend geographical borders and justice systems, as reported by University of Regina (Canada) Professor Rick Ruddell, a leading penal expert, and Martin Guevara Urbina (2004, 2007) in their cross-national studies of imprisonment and capital punishment in 140 countries, and in their study of imprisonment rates in the richest 100 nations.

First, the court system must not only be responsive to bail reform efforts, as defendants are about to enter the judicial system, but also sensitive to the rough economic cycles as well as social and political shifts, as illustrated during the 2015–2016 presidential elections, exacerbating quickly upon the inauguration of Donald Trump. Pragmatically, bail is one of the most important elements during the initial court appearance, setting the stage as to how their experience will unfold. While most defendants have the right to post bail, most defendants are in fact too impoverished to do so in which case they must remain in jail awaiting trial. Consequently, detained defendants are at a disadvantage during pretrial preparation, plea bargaining, trial, and sentencing. For instance, jailed defendants are more likely to be convicted and, once convicted, more likely to be sentenced to prison than those who have obtained pretrial release. As illustrated by Jeffrey Reiman and Paul Leighton in *The Rich get Richer and the Poor Get Prison* (2017), those who are rich enough can buy their freedom and await trial on the streets, but the impoverished await trial in jail, with a higher probability of ending up in prison, a critical situation for those facing the sentence of death, with capital punishment being the most expensive penal process (Urbina, 2011, 2012), as documented by Álvarez and Urbina in "Capital Punishment on Trial: Who Lives, Who Dies, Who Decides–A Question of Justice?" (2014).[17]

Second, the *assembly-line justice* principle, where excessive workload is resulting in de-

cisions being made with such speed and impersonality that defendants are treated as objects rather than individuals, needs to be adjusted to reduce injustices and corresponding ramifications, as evidenced by current DNA discoveries. Clearly reflecting *routine* administration of case dispositions, the principal goal now is disposing cases in a manner that corresponds with the *popular imagination* of a misinformed society. As such, judges, like prosecutors, are by and large elected by voters, the *voting class,* whose views in regard to the nature of crime and punishment clash with reality.[18]

Third, critical characteristics of prosecutors are broad discretion, autonomy, and freedom, arguably to effectively handle a diverse society in a just and efficient manner. In recent years, though, the U.S. Supreme Court has expressed repeated concern about prosecutorial misconduct. As noted above, with the usage of DNA, convictions, including death penalty cases, have been reversed because prosecutors (and, at times, judges and juries) were too zealous in their advocacy of law and order. Unfortunately, the Supreme Court has also ruled that prosecutors have absolute immunity from civil lawsuits when acting as courtroom advocates even in cases of egregious rule-breaking, and there are few checks or monitors on their behavior (Elliott & Weiser, 2004; Urbina & Byxbe, 2011). Simply, if, for example, medical doctors are not immune from medical malpractice, why continue with this historical tradition of absolute sovereignty in U.S. jurisprudence? Not only should court officials be supervised and monitored, they should be exposed to outside review and accountability.

Fourth, the primary purpose of trial by jury is to prevent oppression by the government, and thus provide the accused safeguards against the possibility of prosecutorial bias, prejudice, discrimination, or corruption, and against a possible politically motivated, prejudiced, or tyrant judge. Carefully explored, this novel constitutional protection is more symbolic than pragmatic in that the few defendants who go to trial are processed by practitioners whose truth and reality sharply clash with the everyday life of the accused (King, Johnson, & McGeever, 2010; Salinas, 2015; Urbina & Álvarez, 2017; Ward, Farrell, & Rousseau, 2009), including death penalty trials (Álvarez & Urbina, 2014; Urbina, 2012; Sommers, 2007). For example, laws require jurors to be U.S. citizens, residents of the locality, of a certain minimum age, and able to understand English (see Mirandé, Chapter 10, this volume). While these requirements might sound logical, how do they apply to the thousands of non-English speaking defendants and hundreds of undocumented defendants, who often are viewed with disdain by the local community (Álvarez & Urbina, 2018; Salinas, 2015)? In the words of one participating judge and former prosecutor, "The criminal justice system in its entirety has failed to take into account language and cultural barriers in how criminal offenders, especially poor defendants, are treated. The courts have failed to provide competent lawyers, interpreters, and social workers; nonetheless understand illegal aliens." Addition-ally, as quoted by another participating judge, "Post 9/11 enforcement of immigrant laws is at all-time high, and virtually any criminal offense can result in deportation." According to one participating prosecutor, "Deportation is a real possibility, creating fear in the immigrant community . . . and if deported, they will be taken into custody by immigration authorities, limiting their interaction with their counsel, and no opportunity to pursue appeal." Further, even though the United States continues to advocate diversity, the typical profile of judges and prosecutors:

white, male, middle-class, Protestant, and better educated than the average American (Urbina, 2004a, 2005; Urbina & Kreitzer, 2004; Urbina & White, 2009). Obviously, diversity must go beyond mere publicity and rhetoric to actual social change, this includes the hiring of more female and minority judges, prosecutors, and defense attorneys, as charged by Urbina and Delgado in a forthcoming book, *Latinos and the U.S. Legal System: Laws that Wound–A Call for a Balanced System*.

Lastly, the *quality of justice* depends on the quality of practitioners, like judges, prosecutors, and defense attorneys, who dispense it, which is governed by personnel selection, *judicial education,* practice, and experience. Realistically, though, the majority of American lawyers never actually try a case and judges know relatively little about each case, a situation that is difficult to comprehend by beginning students of criminal law. In the case of capital punishment, the majority of attorneys in America never try a single death penalty case in their entire career, clearly indicating that the issue of competent counsel is much more global. Together, in the lower courts where the majority of cases are processed, "one central conclusion stands out: a few judges do not fulfill minimal standards. A few are senile, prejudiced, vindictive, tyrannical, lazy, and sometimes corrupt" (Neubauer, 2005:182). Consequently, what often looks like an unbeatable criminal case to a law professor seems difficult and unpredictable to an experienced lawyer. In order to be effective legal professionals, practitioners must know all the facts of a case and be up-to-date on the dynamics of criminal law, which might include going back to school, in the same way that other professionals are going back to school to be on the forefront of their respective fields.

CONCLUSION

Some legal scholars characterize the U.S. judicial *process as the punishment* and others characterize *the final outcome as the punishment.* In the case of indigent defendants, particularly foreign nationals, they are in fact receiving not the best but the worst of both worlds: punishment within a procedural and final outcome context, with limited due process. As cited by one participating judge: "Immigrant defendants face the prospect of deportation. Hispanics face stereotypes. African Americans deal with institutionalized racism within the police department, correctional system, as well as judges, prosecutors, and some defense attorneys." Beyond the legal boundaries of justice, indigent defendants experience the unspoken manifestations of the judicial process: coerced condemnation to a life of *street survival* and, ultimately, a life of savage poverty *becomes* the punishment in that they are now unable to find employment (Urbina, 2008; Urbina & Álvarez, 2016, 2017). If deported, undocumented people run the risk of losing their ties to friends and family in the United States, they might no longer be able to apply for U.S. residency, and possibly experience a lifetime of economic hardship and injustice (Álvarez & Urbina, 2018).

Finally, Americans tend to advocate "equal justice" in principle, but normally do not make it a priority to provide needed resources to make it a reality, placing the whole legitimacy of the court system and its distribution of justice, equality, and fairness in question. With some people being socially, politically, and economically "bankrupt" since birth (Urbina, 2008), the wide gap between legal rhetoric and reality becomes more consequential for indigent people, a nightmare for immigrant defendants, and possibly a tomb for inmates facing the sentence of death. Realistically, as noted above, money changes almost everything, with the larger the amount of money, the bigger the influence. Again, if rich people like O. J. Simpson had been represented by an incompetent public defender, chances are that the murder trial would of lasted a few days and the case would have been closed, with a single line in the news: *guilty,* sent to death row and possibly executed. Indeed, justice in the U.S. judicial system has a high price! In essence, the historical record reveals that American law can be either a mechanism of manipulation and oppression or a defined instrument of justice, with judges, prosecutors, and defense attorneys as upholders of the law. With the advent of the globalization of knowledge, let's hope that the pendulum of law shifts towards "equal justice for all."

Section Three

HISPANICS AND THE
PENAL SYSTEM

As one reads history, not in the expurgated editions written for schoolboys and passmen, but in the original authorities of each time, one is absolutely sickened, not by the crimes that the wicked have committed, but the punishments that the good have inflicted; and a community is infinitely more brutalized by the habitual employment of punishment than it is by the . . . occurrence of crime.

—Oscar Wilde

The most absurd apology for authority and law is that they serve to diminish crime. Aside from the fact that the State is itself the greatest criminal, breaking every written and natural law, stealing in the form of taxes, killing in the form of war and capital punishment, it has come to an absolute standstill in coping with crime. It has failed utterly to destroy or even minimize the horrible scourge of its own creation.

—Emma Goldman

Chapter 12

LATINOS AND THE U.S. CRIMINAL JUSTICE SYSTEM: THE ROAD TO PRISON

SOFÍA ESPINOZA ÁLVAREZ

What to do with those whom society cannot accommodate? Criminalize them. Outlaw their actions and creations. Declare them the enemy, and then wage war. Emphasize the differences–the shade of skin, the accent in the speech or manner of clothes. Like the scapegoat of the Bible, place society's ills on them, then 'stone them' in absolution. It's convenient. It's logical. It doesn't work.

–Luis Rodríguez

America's first prison was built by the Quakers at the end of the eighteenth century as an alternative to corporal and capital punishment, with the objective of rehabilitation through hard work, religious study, and penitence. Two hundred years later, the United States is facing an unprecedented binge in prison construction, to the point that it now has the highest number of people under the control of the criminal justice system among "first-world" countries. Imprisonment rates stayed relatively constant from 1920 to 1970 (around 100 per 100,000 but quickly increasing to five times this rate within a few decades), with a slight increase in the late 1930s/early 1940s, but a gradual shift began in 1970, with 380,000 people in prison by 1975 (McCrary & Sanga, 2012). With neoliberalism gaining momentum in the early 1970s, the new era marked the beginning of rapid changes not only in

economic policy but also in both criminal law and policing (Parenti, 2008; Urbina & Álvarez, 2016, 2017; Wacquant, 2009). Quickly, starting in the 1970s, the U.S. legal system underwent a drastic shift by incarcerating more offenders and placing more people under surveillance for longer periods of time. By the end of 2005, nearly 2.2 million adults were incarcerated in state and federal prisons or jails, an equivalent of one in every 136 residents. Overall, 2,320,359 people were incarcerated by the end of 2005: 1,446,269 in state and federal prisons (excluding state and federal prisoners in local jails); 15,735 in territorial prisons; 747,529 in local jails; 10,104 in facilities operated by the Bureau of Immigration and Customs Enforcement; 2,322 in military facilities; 1,745 in jails in Indian territory (midyear 2004); and 96,655 in juvenile facilities (as of 2003). Further, at the end of 2005, there were 4,162,536 adult men and women on probation and 784,408 people on parole. Including people in jails, prisons, probation, and parole, approximately seven million people (1 in every 32 adults or about 3.2% of the adult population) were under correctional control at the end of 2005 (Harrison & Beck, 2006), though experiencing a decline in 2010, for the first time since 1972. As for people behind bars, by the end 2014, the United States held an estimated 1,561,500 prisoners in state and federal correctional facilities (from 300,000 prisoners in 1972), with a decrease of approximately 15,400 prisoners (down 1%) from December 31, 2013, as shown in Table 12.1.

Such draconian shift in incarceration, however, has been strategically orchestrated to target minorities, particularly Latinos and blacks, and impoverished whites (Alexander, 2012; Reiman & Leighton, 2017; Ríos, 2011; Salinas, 2015; Urbina, 2008, Urbina & Álvarez, 2015, 2016, 2017). In effect, reviewing data for the first decade of the twenty-first century, if incarceration rates continue, an African American male born in 2001 has a one in three chance of going to prison during his lifetime, and a Latino born in 2001 has a one in six chance, while a white male has a one in 17 chance of going to prison. The lifetime probability of going to prison among black women (.056) is almost as high as for white men (.059), Latinas (.022), and white females (0.009) have a much lower lifetime chance of going to prison (Bonczar, 2003). Analyzing imprisonment rates over time, Bruce Western, a leading expert in criminal justice, emphasizes three key factors, history (discussed in previous chapters) education (discussed in subsequent chapters) and race (discussed throughout this book) influencing incarceration rates.[19]

In fact, regarding the "race/ethnicity factor," Latinos are the fastest growing group being imprisoned. From 1985 to 1995, the number of Latinos in state and federal prisons rose by 219 percent, with an average annual increase of 12.3 percent (Mumola & Beck, 1997), increasing from 10.9 percent of all state and federal inmates in 1985 to 15.6 percent in 2001 (Harrison & Beck, 2002). Similarly, other figures reveal that Latinos were four times as likely as whites to end up in prison, with one in three people incarcerated in federal prisons being Latino during this era (Bonczar & Beck, 1997). By 2001, for instance, four percent of Latinos in their twenties and early thirties were in jail or prison, compared to 1.8 percent of white males (Beck, Karberg, & Harrison, 2002). According to Paige Harrison and Allen Beck (2006), by 2005, Latinos comprised 20 percent of the state and federal prison population, an increase of 43 percent since 1990–a rate in which one in every six Latinos and one in every 45 Latinas born during this era were likely to be imprisoned in their lifetime. In fact, in 2005, the national incarceration rate for whites was 412 per 100,000 residents, compared to 742 for Latinos and 2,290 for blacks; subsequently, 0.7 percent of all Latinos (nearly double that of whites) and 2.3 percent of all blacks were incarcerated, compared to 0.4 percent of whites. Figures show that Latinos were incarcerated at nearly double (1.8) and blacks at nearly six (5.6) times the rate of whites. By mid-2009, Latino men were incarcerated at a rate nearly 2.5 times that of whites, 1,822 per 100,000 compared to 708 per 100,000, respectively (West, 2010). With a slight decline in 2010, Latinos were incarcerated at 1,258 per 100,000 and black men were incarcerated at a rate of 3,074 per 100,000 residents, while white men were incarcerated at 459 per 100,000 residents (Guerino, Harrison, & Sabol, 2011). In 2011, the prison population was composed of 21 percent Latino, 38 percent black, and 35 percent white (McCarthy, 2013); Latinos

Table 12.1
PRISONERS UNDER THE JURISDICTION OF STATE OR FEDERAL
CORRECTIONAL AUTHORITIES, DECEMBER 31, 2000–2014

Year	Total	Federal[1]	State	Male	Female	Sentenced Prisoners[2]	Imprisonment Rate[3]
2000	1,391,261	145,416	1,245,845	1,298,027	93,234	1,331,278	478
2001	1,404,032	156,993	1,247,039	1,311,053	92,979	1,345,217	470
2002	1,440,144	163,528	1,276,616	1,342,513	97,631	1,380,516	476
2003	1,468,601	173,059	1,295,542	1,367,755	100,846	1,408,361	482
2004	1,497,100	180,328	1,316,772	1,392,278	104,822	1,433,728	487
2005	1,525,910	187,618	1,338,292	1,418,392	107,518	1,462,866	492
2006	1,568,674	193,046	1,375,628	1,456,366	112,308	1,504,598	501
2007	1,596,835	199,618	1,397,217	1,482,524	114,311	1,532,851	506
2008	1,608,282	201,280	1,407,002	1,493,670	114,612	1,547,742	506
2009	1,615,487	208,118	1,407,369	1,502,002	113,485	1,553,574	504
2010	1,613,803	209,771	1,404,032	1,500,936	112,867	1,552,669	500
2011	1,598,968	216,362	1,382,606	1,487,561	111,407	1,538,847	492
2012	1,570,397	217,815	1,352,582	1,461,625	108,772	1,512,430	480
2013[4]	1,576,950	215,866	1,361,084	1,465,592	111,358	1,520,403	477
2014[5]	1,561,525	210,567	1,350,958	1,448,564	112,961	1,508,636	471

1. Includes inmates held in nonsecure privately operated community corrections centers and juveniles held in contract facilities.
2. Counts based on prisoners with sentences of more than 1 year under the jurisdiction of state or federal correctional officials.
3. Imprisonment rate is the number of prisoners under state or federal jurisdiction with a sentence of more than 1 year per 100,000 U.S. residents.
4. Nevada did not submit 2013 National Prisoner Statistics (NPS) data, and Alaska did not submit sex-specific jurisdiction counts to NPS in 2013, so data for these states were imputed.
5. Total and state estimates include imputed counts for Alaska, which did not submit 2014 NPS data.
Source: Data for 2000–2003 (Guerino, Harrison, & Sabol, 2011:2) and data for 2004–2014 (Carson, 2015).

and blacks comprising 59 percent of the imprison population. As such, in 2011, about 1.2 percent of all Latinos and more than 3.0 percent of all black men were imprisoned, compared to 0.5 percent of all white males. In fact, in 2011, Latinos and blacks were imprisoned at higher rates than whites in all age groups for both male and female inmates (Carson & Sabol, 2012). Revealing a continued trend, on December 31, 2013, the United States. held an estimated 1,574,700 people in state and federal prisons–22 percent Latino, 37 percent black, 32 percent white inmates (Carson, 2014), with Latinos and blacks constituting 59 percent as in 2011. About one percent of Latinos (1,134 per 100,000) and almost three percent of black male residents (2,805 inmates per 100,000 black male residents) of all ages were imprisoned on year-end 2013, compared to .05 percent of white males (466 per 100,000).

By 2014 (the latest available data), an estimated 516,900 black males were in state or federal prison at year-end 2014, accounting for 37 percent of the male prison population, white males made up 32 percent of the male prison population (453,500 prison inmates), followed by Latinos (308,700 inmates or 22%). As a percentage of residents of all ages at year-end 2014, 2.7 percent of black males (or 2,724 per 100,000 black male residents) and 1.1 percent of Latino males (1,090 per 100,000 Latino males) were serving sentences of at least one year in prison, compared to less than 0.5 percent of white males (465 per 100,000 white male residents), according to E. Ann Carson (2015) of the U.S. Bureau of Justice Statistics. However, while the disproportionate representation of Latinos in the criminal justice system is well documented, much less analyzed are the mechanisms and beliefs that govern the Latino experience. The focal question, then, in twenty-first century America, beyond high race and ethnic variability in arrests, charging, prosecutions, convictions, sentencing, and time served in jail or prison: "What are the forces *paving the road to prison* for Latinos?"

This chapter seeks to further analyze not only the prejudice and discrimination that is evident, but also the *interaction* of historical, cultural, structural, social, financial, political, and ideological forces that continue to shape public opinion and criminal justice policies. Crucially, practices of social control not only need defined ideas of race and ethnicity to exist and expand, but also to legitimize penal policies as well as broader social elements, like savage poverty, structural marginalization, exploitation, and isolation, eventually leading to destructive personal choices, which, ultimately, result in the very phenomena that we are, arguably, trying to prevent: criminal behavior and consequent imprisonment (Bourgois, 1995; Durán, 2013; Reiman & Leighton, 2017; Ríos, 2011; Rodríguez, 1993; Salinas, 2015; Urbina, 2008, Urbina & Álvarez, 2015, 2016, 2017). As such, this chapter explores historical and contemporary forces paving the road to prison for ethnic minorities, most of which are people of Mexican descent, in relation to their ethnic counterparts and white counterparts. For instance, while elements of criminality might be similar for African Americans, whites, and Latinos, the dynamics, like political rhetoric, for Latino offenders is quite different (Álvarez & Urbina, 2018; Martínez, 2002; Salinas, 2015; Urbina & Álvarez, 2017; see also Aguirre, this volume), as illustrated by Donald Trump's anti-Mexican rhetoric since the day he declared his candidacy for president of the United States. Often characterized as the "Mexican problem," Mexicans are accused of taking jobs from Americans and abusing the educational system, healthcare, and welfare state (Álvarez & Urbina, 2018; Castañeda, 2007; Chávez, 2013; Chomsky, 2007; Golash-Boza, 2015; Gomberg-Muñoz, 2011; Gonzales, 2014). In essence, it is easier to politically, legally, and morally rationalize and legitimize the harsh treatment of people who are essentially viewed as "outsiders," and more so if they are perceived as "illegal aliens." In reality, the war between Mexico and the United States ended 168 years ago, but, clearly, the grudges remain, as indicated by the rancorous debate regarding the high-tech "virtual fence" spear-

headed by the administration of former President George W. Bush (2001–2009) and a major political "weapon" during the 2008 presidential elections–a political strategy once again utilized by Trump's promise, if elected president, to build a "big beautiful wall" along the U.S.-Mexico border to keep Mexicans out.

AN HISTORICAL REMINDER

Colonialism and Conquest

Understanding the "march" to prison for ethnic minorities requires that one equates the development of the original American legal paradigm, including its foundation, ideology, mechanisms, and forces defining and shaping the everyday experience of Latinos within the American society. As documented by various scholars, "fueled by notions of colonialism, slavery, conquest, stereotypes, hate, and the perception of threats, the history of race and ethnic relations in the United States has been vicious, vindictive, and bloody" (Acuña, 2015; Almaguer, 2008; De León, 1983; De León & Del Castillo, 2012; Gómez, 2007; Urbina, 2008:206), shaping and reshaping criminalization and penal practices for minorities (Agozino, 1997; Alexander, 2012; Bales, 2004, 2005; Ríos, 2011; Urbina & Álvarez, 2016, 2017). In the case of Mexicans, the largest ethnic group in the United States, the historical roots of conquest and colonialism continue to remain institutionalized in the American society, culture, and mentality (Berg, 2003; Gómez, 2000; Spickard, 2007; Urbina & Smith, 2007; Urbina, Vela, & Sanchez, 2014). As noted above, the Treaty of Guadalupe Hidalgo in 1848 ended the Mexican-American War, but it did not stop the bitterness between Mexico and the United State (Acuña, 2015;

Almaguer, 2008; Gómez, 2007; Urbina et al., 2014), but, instead, it gave birth to a *legacy of hate* (Acuña, 2015). Consequentially, "the conquest set a pattern for racial antagonism, viciousness, and violence, justified by the now popular slogans such as 'Remember the Alamo'" (Urbina, 2011:109)! To this day, as Earl Shorris (1992) points out, the Alamo has been a shrine to anti-Mexican sentiment, the ultimate symbol of the glorious victory of the moral character of "white" over "brown."

Deeply rooted in colonialism and conquest, structural mechanisms, including criminal justice policies (Bosworth & Flavin, 2007; Gómez, 2000; Hernández, 2012; Urbina & Smith, 2007), have been intentionally and strategically designed and implemented to prevent the advancement of minorities in America's main institutions, like educational, financial, and political systems (Acuña, 1998, 2011; Barrera, 1979; Feagin, 2012; Mirandé, 2005, Moore, 2007; Pizarro, 2005; Reclamation Project, 2014; Urbina & Wright, 2016). For instance, with little education, lack of skills to compete in a highly competitive and technological job market, crime becomes a survival mechanism for many Latino offenders (Durán, 2013; Ríos, 2011; Rodríguez, 1993; Urbina & Wright, 2016). Logically, savage poverty leads to crime (Western, 2002), which in turn leads to arrests, indictments, prosecutions, convictions, and prison (Morín, 2009; Salinas, 2015; Reiman & Leighton, 2017; Urbina & Álvarez, 2016, 2017). Imprisonment then diminishes the probability of obtaining employment, especially well-paying jobs, upon release, which in turn further increases the probability of ending *back* in prison, resulting in a vicious cycle of poverty and crime that gets worse each time a person gets arrested, prosecuted, convicted, and sentenced to prison, eventually impacting the entire Latino community financially, socially, politically, and, ultimately, *silencing* Latinos due to their inability to vote, as a result of a criminal record. Together, with a life-long history of suppression, manipulation, marginalization, neglect, and isolation, Latinos are *enslaved* in a system that has become *self-governing* because Americans, including ethnic minorities, have been socialized and psychologically indoctrinated, vis-à-vis the educational system, media, politicians, and criminal justice officials, to view and treat the American legal system as *normal,* without truly seeing the profound ramifications of such state of normalization, which includes participation in their own victimization, criminalization, imprisonment, and, ultimately, self-destruction.

The Origins of Race and Ethnicity

As documented by Paul Gilroy (1993), ideologies of race and ethnicity are historically linked, and race, as we perceive it today in the context of the criminal justice system, is a reified social construct dating back to the late eighteenth century when the prison was invented (Bosworth & Flavin, 2007; Foucault, 1995). Historically contingent and constructed, ideas of race and ethnicity are inevitably necessary not only for

the criminal justice system to appear objective, necessary, and legitimate, but also to survive and expand, as it seeks to control minorities and impoverished whites, a control mechanism since colonial days. In essence, the United States would have difficulties sustaining its current criminal justice system, with, as of 2010, an annual budget of over "$260 billion dollars" (compared to $82 billion in 1982), most of which goes to salaries of government agents operating the system, if a high percentage of Latinos and black men were not under some form of incarceration or surveillance (Urbina, 2008; Urbina & Álvarez, 2016:43, 2017; see also Austin & Irwin, 2012; Oboler, 2009; Ruddell, 2004; Tonry, 2006). Additionally, the criminal justice system would have difficulties surviving and expanding without the "new minority," Latinas (and black women), who are now being swept under the net of the penal system as a result of the war on drugs, as documented by Urbina in *A Comprehensive Study of Female Offenders: Life Before, During, and After Incarceration* (2008). Above all, the prison system would struggle to survive, expand, and prosper without the "intergenerational connection," minority offenders and their children (Salinas, 2015; Urbina & Álvarez, 2016, 2017). In short, just as it has been documented that punishment is an expression of historically contingent sensibilities (Garland, 1990), ideas of race, of ethnicity, of difference, and of "other," play into our strategies of when and how we respond to behavior government officials have *defined* as "criminal." In this context, what if young white women and men were being imprisoned at the same rate? Would the American society support such draconian practices of confinement, including executions?

REASONS FOR AN ACCELERATED TRIP TO THE PENAL SYSTEM

In addition to historical ramifications of conquest and colonialism and ideas of race and ethnicity, the road to prison for ethnic minorities is further complicated by contemporary ideas of crime and punishment in the general population as well as character and dynamics of courtroom officials, like judges, prosecutors, and defense attorneys, who determine not only the nature of judicial proceedings and final outcomes, but, indirectly, influence the level of policing (Urbina, 2005; Urbina & Kreitzer, 2004; Urbina & White, 2009). As the *deciders* of guilt or innocence, juries, which until recently were all-white by law, are also influential in shaping the judicial process, often a punishment in and of itself, and, of course, final outcomes (see Mirandé, Chapter 10, this volume). The judicial process for minorities is further complicated by politicians, who historically have been conservative, bias, and prejudice (Bender, 2003; Delgado, 1995; López, 2006, Mata, 1998). Then, as an additional barrier for ethnic minorities, the American media has traditionally brutalized Latinos (Berg, 2002, 2014; Galindo & Vigil, 2006; Yosso, 2002).

The American Mentality: Ideas of Crime and Punishment

While the mentality of the criminal justice system is *power, control,* and *expansion* (Urbina & Álvarez, 2016), the mentality of the American public can be described in one phrase: "lockem-up." However, this view is more a reflection of manipulation by politicians and criminal justice officials, shaping the popular imagination, than what people actually favor once they learn about the realities of crime and punishment. Our ideas about crime and punishment are further distorted by the media with a preoccupation on violent crimes, with myths of crime being propagated in television programs like *Cops* and *America's Most Wanted,* playing a significant role in shaping public perceptions about the nature of crime (Berg, 2014; Goode & Ben-Yehuda, 1994). In effect, even though crime remains essentially constant, television coverage of crime on the evening news has increased significantly, creating the notion that crime is out-of-control, and instilling fear in the community (Kappeler & Potter, 2004). As such, some policymakers seek to rationalize their punitive laws by arguing that they are simply responding to the public's fear of crime, a position that is not always supported by public opinion surveys (Beckett, 1997; Beckett & Sasson, 2003). Indeed, even though the media portrays the notion that we are facing a crime wave, most citizens report that they "feel safe" in their communities and still view rehabilitation as a primary objective of corrections, preferring community-based sanctions instead of prison for offenders who do not represent a serious threat to public safety, when informed of the actual nature of crime and punishment (Chesney-Lind & Pasko, 2004).

While the mentality of society is somewhat ambivalent, one thing we can be certain of is the fact that Americans' perceptions toward ethnic minorities and their roles in society have changed in ways that are detrimental to the entire community. In the context of the criminal justice system, we have been experiencing a shift from what some researchers call "the old penology, which emphasized individual responsibility, diagnosis, and treatment, to a new penology concerned with the identification, classification, and management of dangerous groups" (Kruttschnitt, Gartner, & Miller, 2000:685), or what Malcolm Feeley and Jonathan Simon (1992:449) refer to as "the actuarial considerations of aggregates," with impoverished whites and minorities being the main target of the criminal justice system. Historically being socially, emotionally, politically, and financially *bankrupt,* many young Latinos are now further displaced in society, from a very young age. As they grow older, encounters with the juvenile and criminal justice systems tend to push them even sooner and faster into the periphery of society (Bourgois, 1995; Durán, 2009a, 2009b, 2013; Ríos, 2011; Rodríguez, 1993). Then, already in the margins of society, ethnic minorities are being further attacked by the latest series of events occurring in the last several years, events which are changing the perception of Americans, particularly policymakers, law enforcement officials, and court officials, as to how ethnic offenders should be treated by the criminal justice system, and, by extension, changing reporting practices, Latino portrayal in the media, our perceptions of crime and punishment, and the ways we respond to ethnic deviance and criminal behavior.

The New Logic of The Criminal Justice System

To place the American prison system in a global context, the United States not only has the largest prison population and the highest rate of imprisonment in the world, but the gap in relation to other countries continues to widen sharply. As noted earlier, reviewing figures for the first decade of the twenty-first century, by the end of 2005, one in every 32 adults was in prison, jail, on probation or parole, with more than 7 million people being under the control of the criminal justice system, with nearly 2.2 million (approximately 1 in every 136 U.S. residents) being in jail or prison (Harrison & Beck, 2006). China, with a population of approximately 1 billion people, ranks second with 1.5 million prisoners, followed by

Russia with 870,000 prisoners, indicating a significant gap. Crucially, the United States has 10 times the population of its northern neighbor, Canada, yet about 35 times the prison population (Bureau of Justice Statistics, 2004a, 2004b). Similarly, the United States has the highest imprisonment rate, with 737 per 100,000 people, followed by Russia with 611 and St. Kitts and Nevis with 547. According to Ethan Nadelmann of the Drug Policy Alliance, the United States has approximately 5 percent (300 million in 2006) of the world's population (over 6.87 billion in 2006), but about 25 percent of the world's incarcerated population (*Time,* 2006; Walmsley, 2009; Vicini, 2006), revealing significant geographical variation in policing and punishment, which now transcends borders and justice systems.

Logically, to truthfully justify the passage of various criminal laws, which have made the United States the country with the highest prison rates in the developed world (Urbina, 2008; Urbina & Álvarez, 2017), a focal question must be answered: *have crime rates increased significantly in modern times?* From a race and ethnicity standpoint: is the American society experiencing a shift in ethnic criminality? That is, are more Latinos committing crime? Are Latinos committing more crimes? Are ethnic minorities committing different types of crimes? Or, is the current *imprisonment binge* simply a change in criminal laws, law enforcement practices, judicial process, or crime reporting practices? In truth, even though crime statistics are influenced by law enforcement tactics, court response to ethnic criminality, and reporting practices, crimes rates have stayed relatively constant, clearly indicating that ethnic minorities are not getting worse, but that the criminal justice system is becoming more punitive on minorities, especially for drug-related offenses. In fact, according to various sources (including the Brookings Institute, the Pew Research Center, and Uniform Crime Reports by the FBI), crime rates, including violent crime, have actually dropped during the last few decades (Cohn, Talyor, López, Gallagher, Parker, & Maass, 2013; Federal Bureau of Investigation, 2014, 2015; Howe, 2015). In effect, today, the most frequent encounter with the police and the courts seems to be drug-related: distribution, possession, or usage.

An honest analysis reveals that ethnic minorities are not necessarily imprisoned at much higher rates simply because they are more prone than whites to commit crime (Alexander, 2012; Morín, 2009; Reiman & Leighton, 2017; Salinas, 2015; Urbina & Álvarez, 2016, 2017). In effect, during the early part of the twenty-first century, Latinos were generally less likely to be involved in violent crime "than their non-Hispanic counterparts" (Walker, Senger, Villarruel, & Arboleda, 2004:4). Of Latinos who were sent to prison, the overwhelming majority were convicted for relatively minor, nonviolent offenses, or they were first-time offenders, with Latinos being more likely than whites to be arrested and charged for drug-related offenses even though they were not more likely than other groups to use illegal drugs, and they were actually less likely to use alcohol (Bender, 2003; Walker et al., 2004; see also Durán, this volume). As cited by Professor José Luis Morín (2009:20), "Contrary to conventional perceptions, Latinas/os have not been shown to be any more inclined to engage in illegal drug activity than Whites."

With crime rates staying relatively constant, while imprisonment rates continue to increase, the ultimate question becomes: do American criminal laws actually make a significant difference in reducing crime? The answer to this question, as documented by Michael Lynch in *Big Prisons, Big Dreams: Crime and the Failure of America's Penal System*

(2007:23), we can look at a testable hypothesis stating that *as prisons get bigger and more people are incarcerated, crime should decline in society,* by definition. Realistically, the fact that incarceration has expanded almost each and every year from 1973 through the present has not led to a steady downward crime trend, as reported by Rick Ruddell in *America Behind Bars: Trends in Imprisonment, 1950 to 2000* (2004) and Elizabeth Hinton in *From the War on Poverty to the War on Crime: The Making of Mass Incarceration in America* (2016). Instead, criminal laws have resulted in the grave warehousing of thousands of people, with the majority of prisoners being Latinos, blacks, impoverished whites, and uneducated people. Living in prison conditions, which according to legal scholars, are fundamentally cruel and inhumane–ultimately, mass incarceration is inherently unconstitutional–resonating Michelle Alexander's *The New Jim Crow: Mass Incarceration in the Age of Colorblindness* (2012). In short, "the modern logic of the U.S. correctional system can be summed in one word: *imprisonment,*" though, "the new logic becomes a leading force in the very same problem we are trying to solve: crime" (Urbina, 2008:209–210), with detrimental implications and ramifications, as recently documented by Jonathan Simon in *Mass Incarceration on Trial: A Remarkable Court Decision and the Future of Prisons in America* (2014).

Juries, Politics, and the American Media

Criminal laws, once passed by state legislatures or U.S. Congress, are filtered through the lens of those who operate the everyday machinery of justice. In this regard, American jurisprudence is commonly *viewed* as a "legal arena" composed of objective and colorblind judges, prosecutors, defense attorneys, and jurors engaged in a ferocious *battle to find the truth,* acting, almost, like robots, without emotions, bias, or prejudice (Urbina, 2003a). A deeper examination of America's jurisprudence, though, reveals that legal theory and reality clash. As noted by James Levine (1992), juries, often the *final* decision-makers, not only tend to be political, but they are heavily influenced by their preconceived notions of crime and punishment as well as the American media (Kappeler, Blumberg, & Potter, 2000; see also Mirandé, Chapter 10, this volume). In the case of ethnic minorities, perhaps more than with African Americans, the relationship between juries, politics, and the American media is crucial for Latinos, especially Mexicans, given the close proximity to Mexico, with a 2,000-mile border that has fused highly charged political rhetoric, controversy, antagonism, draconian policies, as vividly illustrated by situations like the 2009 H1N1 flu pandemic, the so-called war on drugs, the war on terrorism, and the current anti-immigrant movement, spearheaded by President Donald Trump.

As documented in previous chapters, in seeking to comprehend the Latino judicial experience by its totality requires that one explores the foundations of American jurisprudence (Urbina & Álvarez, 2017). Tracing the history of court process demonstrates the resilience of ethnic conditioning despite changes in the legal system. If one concedes that justice, like lynching, burnings, and hangings, without trials were precursors to the mechanics of modern justice (see Baker, this volume), then juries were founded on a premise that accepted and infused *ethnic, divided, and compromised justice* (see Mirandé, Chapter 10, this volume). Under the Slave Codes and Black Codes established in the 1690s, as a general rule, blacks could not bring charges or testify against whites, in addition to other restrictions, like preventing slaves from carrying weapons, owning prop-

erty, or traveling without an appropriate pass. In effect, it was not until 1954 in *Hernández v. Texas* that the U.S. Supreme Court, three weeks before the famous *Brown v. the Board of Education* (1954) case, struck down the practice of excluding people of Mexican descent from service as jury commissioners, grand jurors, and petit jurors. The legacy of using law to suppress ethnic minorities, though, was blatantly voiced in *Hernández v. New York* (1991), where the U.S. Supreme Court held that a prosecutor's use of peremptory challenges during jury selection to exclude all bilingual, English and Spanish-speaking Latino jurors was constitutional, even if the exclusions resulted in all potential Latino jurors being excluded from juries (see Mirandé, Chapter 10, this volume).

Pragmatically, though, the propagated images of Latinos by the American media suggest that law practitioners and juries, which are composed of the general population, are *socially and psychologically conditioned* to equate *brownness* with danger, deviance, and criminality (De León, 2014; see also Aguirre, this volume). For instance, historically, the typical role of ethnic minorities in the American media normally revolves around notions that support the mentality of mainstream America, with phrases like "the Mexican problem, bandido, illegal alien, dirty, lazy, maid, greaser, wetback, non-English speaker, or criminal" (De León, 2014; see also Aguirre, this volume). In a more fundamental level, as noted by cultural critic Stuart Hall (1980:117), the media is a "major cultural and ideological force, standing in a dominant position with respect to the way in which social relations and political problems [are] defined and the production and transformation of popular ideologies in the audience addressed," with media employees operating with a "professional code," which functions to legitimize hegemonic ideologies through its adherence to the value of *objectiv-*

ity, and thus, subsequently, reproducing the dominant American white male ideology. As a subpopulation of the general population, court officials, to include judges, prosecutors, juries, and even defense attorneys, subsequently *rationalize* overcharging, questionable convictions, lengthy prison sentences, and executions to arguably maintain social order, even under a context of moral illegitimacy and irrational justice.

Further, considering the significance of voting, a powerful force within the legal system, it was a long struggle before women and minorities were allowed to vote, with African American men being allowed to vote in 1869, Native Americans receiving U.S. citizenship in 1924, and women getting the right to vote in 1920. In the case of ethnic minorities, even though Mexican Americans were supposed to obtain the right to vote under the Treaty of Guadalupe Hidalgo in 1848, it was not until 1975 that all Mexican Americans were allowed to vote (Urbina et al., 2014).

The Globalization of Crime and Punishment

A comprehensive analysis of the nature and motive of incarceration also requires an appreciation of international forces shaping modern judicial and imprisonment practices, for structural, political, cultural, and ideological forces governing criminal laws, the criminalization process, and punishment intertwine with the globalization movement, to include the *war on drugs,* the *war on illegal aliens,* and the *war on terror* (see Álvarez, this volume). Richard Bennett (2004), for example, reports that globalization altered the dynamics of crime that transcends international borders, motivating justice systems to mobilize in transcending borders and boundaries (Ruddell & Urbina, 2004, 2007; Urbina & Álvarez, 2016, 2017). Together, these elements have paved the road to prison for ethnic minorities, have accelerated the march to prison, and, once in prison, have resulted in a rapid shift away from the rehabilitative and therapeutic goals that distinguish traditional corrections from imprisonment in the twenty-first century (Alexander, 2012; Hinton, 2016; Simon, 2014; Urbina, 2008). In effect, ". . . the new U.S. government foreign policy at the turn of the 21st century, the local neighborhood dark brown American male has become a villain of global proportions," with brown bodies becoming ". . . the nexus at which domestic law enforcement practices converge with U.S. international political and military objectives" (Olguin, 2008:162). What follows, then, is a discussion of vital legal sanctions that are contributing to the thousands of Latinos, blacks, and impoverished white Americans being sent to prison, and, ultimately, silencing the Latino (and black) community.

A CONTINUUM OF LEGAL SANCTIONS

Philosophically, there are six crucial reasons as to why the inmate population is critically high, and continues to increase, with most of the incoming prisoners being Latinos, or African Americans. First, even though the average prison sentence of two years served by inmates has remained relatively constant since 1923, the public tends to believe that correctional institutions have a "revolving door," in which inmates serve far shorter sentences than before, and thus contributing to the notion that crime is out of control. Though, according to a report by the Pew Center on the States, the average prison stay grew 36% during the last two decades. That is, inmates released from prison in 2009 spent an average of 2.9 years (or 36 percent) longer behind bars than offenders released in 1990. Second, the high inmate population is partially attributed to the perception that incarcerating more offenders and keeping more offenders under surveillance for longer periods of time will significantly reduce crime rates. Third, people believe that rehabilitation no longer works, and thus inmates need to be incarcerated for longer periods of time. Fourth, political pressure for quick fixes has led to an increase in the incarceration industry. Fifth, the public's fear of crime has also contributed to the influx of new prisoners, at a much faster pace. Sixth, analyzing the historical evolution of the political economy of crime and the nature of social control to better ascertain the historical profitability of race (blacks) and ethnicity (Latinos), Urbina & Álvarez (2016) charge that with *great profits to be made in human capital* an unspoken governmental strategy is to carefully monitor the "investment potential" of human capital in unemployed people and inmates versus the investment potential of human capital in criminal justice personnel and services provided. While, on one side, the criminal justice system has been a total failure (Lynch, 2007), "the other side shows great benefits and profits of punitive criminal justice policies, with the notion of failure being used as a strategic political argument for even more punitive policies . . . achieving what it was designed to accomplish, human profitability or, more precisely, ethnic [and racial] profitability" (Urbina & Álvarez, 2016:42, 50).

Historically, but especially since the early 1970s, we have witnessed the evolution of multiple criminal laws. Beginning in 1970 with the passage of the Racketeer Influenced and Corrupt Organizations Act (RICO) to the passage of anti-terrorism legislation after the September 11, 2001, attacks on the

United States, not only have changes in the nature of law have unfolded, but crime perception has been redefined and, subsequently, the treatment of lawbreakers has taken a different approach (Cole, 2003; Corcoran, 2006; Salinas, 2015; Urbina & Álvarez, 2017; Urbina & Kreitzer, 2004; Welch, 2006, 2007, 2009; see also Blazak, 2004). Together, the general response to the perceived dangerousness, potential threat, and fear of crime has been the modification and implementation of punitive and polemic laws, such as laws for controlling drugs, guns, drinking, sentence enhancement laws, gang suppression laws, anti-gang-loitering ordinances, juvenile waiver laws, adjustments in age limits in juvenile legislation, mandatory minimum sentences for nonviolent offenders, and changes in the statute of limitations for appeals on criminal convictions, a trend that continues to gain momentum as international efforts to modify and implement social control policies become more pressing, with the objective of creating a global impact. In short, the mentality, "lock them up and throw away the key," of Americans in combination with large increases in law enforcement, mandatory sentencing laws, and longer sentences have led to larger inmate populations across the country. Practically, the following eight factors have been among the most influential in the latest social control movement; that is, the "legal weapons" use to achieve historical and contemporary objectives, which in reality serve as a mechanism of power, control, expansion, and, ultimately, a mechanism to silence Latinos, blacks, and impoverished whites.

Anti-Drug Laws

No other offense has received more attention than drug-related crimes in the last four decades. Starting with the passage of the RICO law in 1970 by Congress, whose primary objective was to prosecute criminal organizations by adopting heavy mandatory fines and lengthy sentences, state and federal agencies have taken an aggressive approach against drug offenders in the United States and abroad, *setting the foundation for future laws and staging a punitive movement* that would eventually target Latinos, blacks, and poor whites. In effect, drug statutes, like RICO and those that were implemented in the 1980s, especially after the introduction of crack cocaine into poor neighborhoods, have had a net-widening effect to include those simply "guilty by association." Further, coded by elements of race and ethnicity from the onset, the RICO law has become a favorite prosecutorial weapon by prosecutors to target race and ethnic minorities, like Mexicans, Puerto Ricans, blacks, and even Asians (Urbina & Kreitzer, 2004). Then, "the global and aggressive effort to apprehend and prosecute individuals for drug-related offenses has shifted the focus of RICO from the prosecution of domestic drug offenders to that of foreign drug traffickers such as Mexicans and Colombians" (Urbina & Kreitzer, 2004:301). More recently, with terrorism coming of age, this wide-arching statute is taking a new shift to focus on the prosecution of terrorists, as court officials and law enforcement need to stay busy (Dowling & Inda, 2013; Simon, 2007; Urbina & Álvarez, 2016), especially since traditional organized crime has been diminished. Jonathan Simon (1997:173) claims that advanced industrial societies are actually "governed through crime," with the overdeveloped societies of the West and North Atlantic "experiencing not a crisis of crime and punishment but a crisis of governance that has led [them] to prioritize crime and punishment as the preferred contexts of governance," redefining not only the limits of criminal laws but also the parameters of social policies and programs, while socially

reconstructing the confines of ethnicity, race, and gender. Tony Fitzpatrick (2001:220) declares that as "global capital becomes apparently unmanageable" and "as the polity and the economy detached after a century of alignment," the state must give itself, particularly its agents, something to do, and so the state "socially and discursively constructs threats that only it can address through . . . punitive responses to the chaos it has [helped facilitate]," as in the case of the *war on drugs,* along with the *war on terrorism,* the *war on immigrants* (with provoking phrases like "illegal aliens" and "narco-terrorists"), and various other aggressive social control movements, which as delineated by Urbina & Álvarez (2016) are directly connected to the annual multibillion economic enterprise.

Together, people who traditionally received *immunity* from prosecution, particularly women, such as girlfriends, wives, mothers, grandmothers, and other relatives, friends, or associates, are now being caught in the net of the new laws. Consequently, the war on drugs has led to a huge increase in both state and federal prisons (Carson, 2015; Currie, 1985; Lynch, 2007; Urbina, 2008; Walker, 2005). In fact, by the end of 2005, drug offenders accounted for approximately 2 million of the 7 million people under the control of the criminal justice system (Harrison & Beck, 2006), with the inmate population being drastically disproportionally Latino and African American.

Mandatory Sentencing Laws

Considering that conventional wisdom tends to be formed from media-propagated images, stories, and highly charged talks by politicians and law enforcement officials, the typical conversation, whether it is taking place in a coffee shop, bus station, executive office, or even classroom about the nature of crime tends to conclude with one policy implication: high crime rates are a direct result of indeterminate crime control polices, which allow criminals to go free to further victimize the community. As such, some policymakers have argued that the only way to increase public safety is by putting an end to the "revolving door" of corrections, to include a shift from probation to imprisonment. Under intense pressure by the media, politicians, law enforcement officials, and the "voting class," state legislatures and Congress support strict mandatory sentencing laws to include a wide array of offenses, such as drug-related crimes, crimes committed with a gun, and sex-related offenses. As a result, mandatory sentencing laws, which require prison sentences for certain offenses and specify a minimum number of years offenders must serve before release, have had a large impact on inmate populations throughout the country. Logically, since ethnic minorities are a target of law enforcement practices, Latinos, blacks, and impoverished whites are experiencing the consequential effects of such legislation, as illustrated by imprisonment statistics.

Three Strikes and You're Out Laws

Under the notion that offenders do not learn their lesson during their first encounter with the criminal justice system but instead continue to commit crime, states have also implemented sequence-type laws, requiring lengthy mandatory sentences, including laws to lock up repeat offenders for life without parole. First, the notion was that even though drug laws were being modified or implemented, offenders were either not receiving lengthy sentences or they were not serving their entire sentence. Second, due to some highly publicized violent crimes, or what Samuel Walker (2005) reference as "celebrated cases," with provoking and intimidating images of Latinos and blacks committing

crimes during crucial times, like election years, some policymakers began to advocate that the only vital solution to reduce recidivism was to implement lengthy jail and prison sentences.

As such, since 1993, the federal government and over 20 states have implemented some form of the popular "three strikes and you're out" laws, with significant variation across states in regards to crime severity, race, and ethnicity. California's "three strikes" policy, for instance, is even harsher in that it provides for doubling of sentences on a second felony conviction. The state of Georgia implemented a "two strikes" law. These new laws, however, have a consequential amplification effect, truly devastating to minorities, "unworthy" whites, and impoverished defendants. For example, during the early stages of these laws, Jerry Williams was convicted of a third strike for armed robbery of a slice of pizza. Since Williams had two prior robbery convictions, he was sentenced to 25 years to life under California's law (Slater, 1995), and the sentence was upheld on appeal by the U.S. Supreme Court in *Rummel v. Estelle* (1980), pointing to the shift in mentality of the American society and the redefined logic of the criminal justice system.

Truth in Sentencing Legislation

As with other criminal laws, ideas (real or imagined) of violence, recidivism, and rehabilitation have reshaped truth in sentencing legislation. The truth in sentencing approach has become a politically appealing mechanism to slow the presumed *revolving door correctional leak* (Urbina, 2008:25), which actually resulted from events like overcrowding and various court-imposed institutional changes. Ideologically, the voting class needs to believe that their elected (or appointed) politicians and law enforcement oficials are doing something significant to reduce crime rates by increasing the certainty and severity of criminal penalties. While state prisoners serve an average of two years for decades, they have been serving longer sentences during the last several years and federal prisoners are also serving longer terms after the passage of the Sentencing Reform Act of 1984. The modern idea of truth in sentencing normally requires that prisoners serve a minimum of 85 percent of their original sentence, a devastating situation for people convicted of minor offenses or first-time offenders. This is a significant increase from the average 48 percent of a sentence that violent offenders served in 1992, subsequently changing the demographics of the penal system, with devastating implications and ramifications for minority communities.

State and Federal Sentencing Guidelines

Partially attributed to the various changes of existing policies as well as the adoption of numerous complex laws, states and the federal government opted to implement sentencing guidelines to, arguably, avoid chaos, confusion, subjectivity, arbitrariness, and ensure uniformity. Realistically, while sentencing guidelines have been advocated as a logical and efficient prosecutorial tool, they have not proven to be the "ideal model" of prosecution, and, in some situations, according to one court official, the "Federal Sentencing Guidelines are the real problem because of the lack of discretion they allow to judges" (Urbina & Kreitzer, 2004:315). With the exception of atypical cases, sentencing guidelines, designed to provide clear and uniform standards for punishment, have reduced judicial discretion in legal proceedings. Still, U.S. Supreme Court decisions such as *U.S. v. Booker* (2004) and *U.S. v. Fanfan* (2004) have given judges discretion to depart from sentencing guidelines. However, criminal cases do not only differ with regards to legal and extra-legal factors, but there is often great variation in the history and ideology behind each case. Consequently, groups of offenders who traditionally did not end up being prosecuted and subsequently in prison are now being arrested, indicted, prosecuted, convicted, sentenced, and many are now behind bars. In effect, in a study of the RICO statute, "The Practical Utility and Ramifications of RICO," Urbina and Kreitzer (2004:315) report: "RICO may be used politically to go after a non-politically favored group" or people who "have no political clout and are unpopular," to include traditional organized crime and contemporary criminal syndicates, like Columbians and Mexicans, and street gangs in minority communities across the United States.

Immigration Laws

From the time the first settlers set foot on present day United States, immigration has been a hotly debated issue, normally leading to racist policies, political rhetoric and manipulation, struggle, brutality, and harsh penal sanctions for targeted groups (Álvarez & Urbina, 2018; Bacon, 2009; Castañeda, 2007; Chacón & Davis, 2006; Doty, 2009; Golash-Boza, 2012a, 2012b, 2015; Gutiérrez, 1997).[20] Immigration laws, historically shaped and reshaped by various social, racial, ethnic, cultural, political, and ideological forces, have been used to control not only population rates and public safety, but also elements like culture, language, and identity (Álvarez & Urbina, 2018; Chávez, 2013; De León, 2014; Espino, Leal, & Meier, 2008; Fox, 1997; Gonzales, 2014; see also Aguirre, this volume). Logically, one of the most powerful forces has been economics (Bean & Bell-Rose, 1999; Golash-Boza, 2015; Gomberg-Muñoz, 2011; Gutiérrez,

1997; Massey, Duránd, & Malone, 2003). As such, during harsh economic cycles or when the supply of labor exceeds the demand, immigration laws are strategically and selectively used to control the labor population, at times by placing immigrants under the aggressive control of the criminal justice system (Álvarez & Urbina, 2018; Castañeda, 2007; Chacón & Davis, 2006; De Génova & Ramos-Zayas, 2003; Golash-Boza, 2012a, 2012b; Gonzales, 2014; Salinas, 2015).

Currently permeated by what has been the worst economic crises, starting in 2007, since the Great Depression of 1929, the latest anti-immigrants movement has been targeting and demonizing immigrants, with Latinos being aggressively and viciously hunted by immigration officials, especially along the 2,000-mile border with Mexico. For some Latinos who manage to enter the "promised land," their experience could be a nightmare if they are detained because their country of origin might refuse to take them back, or because immigration authorities refuse to deport one (or few) at a time, with thousands of undocumented foreigners being housed in Immigration and Customs Enforcement (ICE) detention centers for no crime other than entering the country without proper documentation (Álvarez & Urbina, 2018; Salinas, 2015). At the turn of the twenty-first century, June 30, 2002, 88,776 noncitizens were in the custody of state or federal correctional authorities, housed in 15 detention facilities around the country, with eight facilities being directly operated by ICE and the rest contracted out to for-profit private companies (Álvarez & Urbina, 2018; Salinas, 2015). Worse, it's common for unaccompanied minors who immigrate to the United States to be immediately institutionalized, and, in some cases, incarcerated until they can be reunited with family members, placed in foster care, or returned to their country of origin, as recently documented by

Urbina in "Migrant Children: Exposing Tales and Realities." More globally, even though the war on "illegal aliens" seems to target people of all races and ethnicities, the immigration debate and corresponding immigration laws truly tend to focus on Latino immigrants, particularly Mexicans, as evidenced by hundreds of laws and multiple operations, like Operation Gatekeeper, Operation Hold the Line, Operation Jobs, Operation Repatriation, Operation Return to Sender, Operation Safeguard, Operation Streamline, and Operation Wetback (see Posadas & Medina, this volume).

In effect, while there has always been an anti-immigrants movement, since the advent of the war on terrorism, along with the war on drugs, there has been an aggressive anti-immigrants movement, including stepped-up deportations, workplace raids, and the passage of more than 300 state laws and local ordinances restricting access to employment, housing, driver's licenses, education, access to hospitals, public assistance (like food stamps), and even library cards (Rumbaut, 2008), along with issues like racial profiling, violence, and violations of civil rights (Dunn, 2009; Johnson, 2000; Romero, 2006; Romero & Serag, 2005; see also Posadas & Medina, this volume). During the last several years, for instance, we have witnessed federal immigration authorities staging factory raids across the country, resulting in arrests, deportations, and separated families (Golash-Boza, 2015; Román, 2013; Salinas, 2015; Tichenor, 2002), while leaving employers scrambling to fill "immigrant jobs" to avoid an economic downfall. Consider, for instance, Arizona's "Support Our Law Enforcement and Safe Neighborhoods Act," signed into law on April 23, 2010, by Governor Jan Brewer, but later a federal judge, Susan Bolton, issued an injunction blocking the law's most controversial provisions. The law instructs police to demand documentation for anyone with "a reasonable suspicion" of being an illegal immigrant and to arrest Americans who stop their cars to pick up day laborers. In reality, the law, which would not only target Mexicans, but Latinos in general (undocumented and documented), is symbolically and pragmatically just like the German Nazi laws that made Jews scared to go out on the streets, with these laws becoming a much more powerful demon in the stillness of the night, resonating the days of the slave patrols and later the KKK.

For immigrants who end up staying in the United States, their new life experience quickly unfolds as labels associated with the manner in which they arrived in the United States, like *refugee, political asylum, wetback,* or *illegal immigrant,* begin the process of identification, categorization, stigmatization, isolation, marginalization, and subsequent criminalization associated with their existence in America (Álvarez & Urbina, 2018; see also Aguirre, this volume). As an ethnic community, the degree of criminalization and subsequent imprisonment will then be governed by the force of intertwining elements, like their political, financial, social status, and stereotypes, as well as America's relationship with their country of origin (Urbina & Álvarez, 2016, 2017). As documented by some ethnic scholars, the "myths and stereotypes about immigrants and crime often provide the underpinnings for public policies and practices and shape public opinion and political behavior" (Rumbaut, Gonzáles, Komaie, Morgan, & Tafoya-Estrada, 2006: 84), resulting in selected arrests, prosecutions, convictions, imprisonment, and executions (Álvarez & Urbina, 2014, 2018; Salinas, 2015; Urbina & Álvarez, 2015, 2016, 2017; Welch, 2002, 2007, 2009).

As if current immigration laws were not enough to hunt immigrants down, anti-terrorism laws have made immigrants ideal tar-gets of arrest, prosecution, and imprisonment (Bosworth & Flavin, 2007; Corcoran, 2006; Welch, 2006, 2007, 2009), as reported by Kevin Johnson in "The Forgotten 'Repatriation' of Persons of Mexican Ancestry and Lessons for the 'War on Terror'" (2005). The Department of Homeland Security (DHS) came into effect on March 1, 2003, and in April 2003, Attorney General John Ashcroft ruled that undocumented immigrants (including asylum seekers) "who have no known links to terrorist groups can be detained indefinitely . . . to address national security concerns" (Swarns, 2003). On April 29, 2003, the U.S. Supreme Court ruled that *legal* immigrants could be detained indefinitely and without bail during deportation proceedings, if they had a criminal conviction, no matter how minor, in their background (Stout, 2003). By early 2004, over 60,000 immigrants (mostly legal residents) had been held for over two years, and up to 70 percent of them were deported for immigration violations unrelated to terrorism (Jonas & Tactaquin, 2004). Essentially, the various laws directly or indirectly attacking immigrants, to include the *Street Terrorism Enforcement and Prevention Law of 1988,* the 1994 *Omnibus Crime Bill, Illegal Immigrant Reform and Immigrant Responsibility Act of 1996,* and the *Anti-Terrorism and Effective Death Penalty Act of 1996,* not only demonize immigrants, but they perpetuate a consequential false conscious among the general public. For instance, contrary to conventional wisdom, immigrants in the United States have lower incarceration rates than other groups in the population due to the nonviolent nature of their offenses and less criminal activity (Butcher & Piehl, 2005), as shown in another study by Professor Robert Sampson of Harvard University. Further, in addition to findings that noncitizen Latino immigrants are actually less likely to commit crime than American citizens, "by other measures of

well-being–including smoking, alcohol con-
sumption, drug use, and pregnancy outcomes–Mexican immigrants are generally
found to do well and sometimes better than
citizens" (Álvarez & Urbina, 2018; Grogger
& Trejo, 2002; Hagan & Palloni, 1999:630–
631). In effect, "Whites are actually three
times more likely to be victimized by Whites
than by minorities" (Dorfman & Schiraldi,
2001:4; Morín, 2009; Salinas, 2015; see also
Durán, this volume). Worse, what some people do not realize, though, is that once the
government begins to strip away statutory,
constitutional, and international rights of the
most vulnerable and undesirable communities, the spillover effect is very rapid and
dangerous for all immigrants and other
noncitizens, and eventually for U.S. citizens
as well (Jonas & Tactaquin, 2004), as recently illustrated by John Whitehead in *A Government of Wolves: The Emerging American Police
State* (2013).

Anti-Terrorism Laws

The September 11, 2001, terrorist attacks
on the United States gave advocates of "law
and order" what they had been anticipating
for years: a rationalization for punitive and
draconian social control legislation. In fact,
under the guise of yet another war on crime,
following former President Richard Nixon's
"Crusade Against Crime" in the 1960s and
former President Ronald Reagan's "War on
Drugs" in the 1980s, the U.S.A. Patriot Act
(Uniting and Strengthening America by Providing Appropriate Tools Required to Inter-
cept and Obstruct Terrorism), signed into
law six weeks after the 9/11 attacks on the
Pentagon and the World Trade Center and
quickly ratified by Congress, the subsequent
Patriot Act II, and the 2006 Military Com-
missions Act provided an ideal opportunity
for a global war on terrorism and greater
militarization, including the militarization of

the police (Álvarez & Urbina, 2018; Balko,
2006, 2013; Dunn, 1996; Hill & Beger, 2009;
Kil, 2011; Kraska & Kappeler, 1997; Urbina
& Álvarez, 2015, 2016; Whitehead, 2013), as
vividly documented by Michael Welch in
*Scapegoats of September 11th: Hate Crimes and
State Crimes in the War on Terror* (2006) and in
*Crimes of Power andStates of Impunity: The U.S.
Response to Terror* (2009). Realistically, though,
the consequences are detrimental. Law Professor David Cole (2003), for instance, documents that after 9/11 the United States continued its long historical practice of ethnic
profiling by socially constructing "enemy aliens" and "enemy races" which served to
undermine the country's legitimacy by creating double standards. Additionally, further
militarization of the police tends to encourage an explicit "means justifies the ends"
mentality and eventual ideology in which
due process and justice are subverted to
"necessity and expediency," and miscarriages of justice are *rationalized* under the
name of national security and hidden under
"secrecy" (Hills, 2001; Kraska & Cubellis,
2004; Welch, 2006, 2009; Whitehead, 2013).
Further, as reported by Stephen Muzzatti
(2005:120), through legislation like Patriot
Act I and II and the Homeland Security Act,
the war on terrorism has become a "catchall
category" used by the police to criminalize a
"wide range of nonviolent political and social activists committed to progressive social
change." Fundamentally, quotes Stephen
Hill and Randall Beger (2009:34), "A combination of ignorance and uncritical acceptance of police militarization has increasingly undermined democratic policing."

Indeed, beyond the target of foreign terrorists, the motive of terrorism legislation
was clearly intended to be much broader to
go after "unwanted individuals and groups,"
creating a global movement against the least
protected. As such, the director of the newly-
created Office of Homeland Security coordi-

nated military units, federal law enforcement, and other intelligence-gathering agencies assigned to detect and destroy terrorism not only abroad, but in the United States as well, with state governments quickly creating their own homeland security agencies, mimicking initiatives of federal authorities (Álvarez & Urbina, 2018). With passion, fear, and uncertainty running high because of safety concerns and a global economic crisis, the *devil quickly changed color* and law violators were now viewed as "the enemy, devilish, or foreigner," prompting politicians and law enforcement officials to quickly turn the war on terror into yet another war on ethnic and racial minorities, impoverished whites, and immigrants. Suddenly, arguably, *immigrants became terrorists and they are entering the United States through Mexico, and Mexicans too became terrorists,* fueling the passions of immigration hawks, as we have been hearing since Donald Trump announced his candidacy for president on June 16, 2015.

As such, the war on terrorism is unquestionably not only an international military effort, but a policing strategy to locally control immigrants, minorities, and impoverished white people. In effect, the questioning of "suspects" quickly led to the arrest and detention of as many as 1,200 noncitizens, although the precise number is unknown due to the government's unwillingness to release complete information. Of those arrested, 752 were charged, not with terrorism-related crimes but with immigration violations. Reports show that a total of 762 "illegal" immigrants were detained in the weeks and months after the attacks, but most of the 762 immigrants were not charged as terrorists or deported. Worse, U.S.A. Patriot Act, Section 215, enabling the FBI to monitor foreigners without establishing probable cause, signifies that noncitizens are no longer protected by the constitutional rights granted to citizens. The FBI, for instance, no longer has

to establish probable cause, or have any reason, to look through people's possessions. U.S.A. Patriot Act, like Section 215, Section 412 indicates that noncitizens are no longer protected by the U.S. Constitution. Further, immigration officials now have the power to denaturalize nonnative-born U.S. citizens convicted of certain crimes, and to indefinitely detain deportable aliens even if there is virtually no chance that their country of origin will allow their return. Crucially, just as the vast majority of *street terrorists* arrested are young and impoverished minority men, predominantly Latino, African American, and Southeast Asians, international terrorists are predominantly young Muslin men from the Persian Gulf region, South and Southeast Asia, and Muslim countries of Africa. Unfortunately, current anti-terrorism laws "are fueled as much by the expression of popular anger and the desire for revenge as by the honest attempt to develop and implement mechanisms of reducing crime and the fear it creates" (Urbina, 2008:220).

Even though there is a wide range of sentencing options that can be used to punish those who are a threat to society, the most politically popular options tend to be the laws cited herein, all leading the way to prison. Other options, like probation, restitution and fines, community service, substance abuse treatment, day reporting, house arrest and electronic monitoring, halfway houses, and boot camps are also being used across the country, but these sanctions are not highly favored by the punitive mentality of the American society, particularly law enforcement officials and politicians during election years (Lynch, 2007; Tonry, 2006; Urbina & Álvarez, 2016, 2017), who prefer draconian laws that will ensure imprisonment, in their pursuit of victory, honor, glory, and, possibly, landing in the White House, as in the case of Donald Trump.

The School-To-Prison Pipeline

With the collapse of public education in the world's richest nation (Urbina & Wright, 2016), with little consideration for negative structural flaws in neoliberal economic policy (Urbina & Álvarez, 2016), a *school-to-prison pipeline* has been developed over the last four decades, as recently reported by the *Association of Mexican American Educators* in a special issue, "Latina/o Students and the School-Prison-Pipeline" (Bartolomé, Macedo, Ríos, & Peguero, 2013). Clearly, there is a grave link between education, socialization, and incarceration (Urbina & Wright, 2016). Almost three decades ago, Rodolfo Acuña (1990:B7) reported, "today's entering Latino kindergartner is as likely to go to jail as to meet the admission standards of state universities." Two years later, Earl Shorris (1992:212) observed, "twelve years after the class picture was taken, more of the children will have died or been killed than graduated from a four-year college."

In the twenty-first century, a 2007 government report revealed that *Latinos (and blacks) are more likely to live in prison cells than college dorms,* with 2.7 inmates for every Latino in college housing, with more than twice as many whites living in college dorms than prison or jail (not including students living off campus). Indeed, "as government leaders, law enforcement officials, and some scholars are profiting handsomely from the fruits of neoliberal policies" (Urbina & Álvarez, 2016:39), states like California "are spending more money on corrections than education and states like New York are sending more minorities to prison than to universities" (Urbina, 2008:205; Urbina & Wright, 2016). According to a recent report by the U.S. Department of Education (2016a), from 1980 to 2013, local and state spending on public schools doubled (from $258 billion to $534 billion), but spending on prisons increased by more than four times (from $17 billion to $71 billion). Not surprisingly, at the same time that state and local spending on prisons and jails has risen more than three times faster than spending on schools since 1990, the number of people incarcerated in local and state prisons more than quadrupled. For instance, in 1990, prison spending was a sixteenth the size of education, but now the combined local and state prison budget is over an eighth the size of the school budget. Further, while prison spending has increased three times as quickly as school spending nationally, there is wide and grave variation in spending on schools and prisons among individual states. For example, total corrections spending grew 149 percent in Massachusetts, compared with 850 percent in Texas. Therefore, in Texas (a minority-majority state), where the disparity is greatest, prison spending grew nearly eight times the rate of school spending. Spending disparities between prisons and higher education are even wider. Figures show that since 1990 state spending on colleges and universities has remained relatively flat (in inflation-adjusted dollars), but spending on prisons has nearly doubled. Today, 18 states spend more on jails and prisons than they do on colleges and universities, illustrating a clear shift in priorities.[21]

In fact, considering the importance of mentoring young children, according to a recent study, the country's largest school districts have more police officers than counselors (Barnum, 2016). Nationally, according to a 2013–2014 study by the U.S. Department of Education (2016b), 850,000 high school students did not have access to school counselors, while 1.6 million (K to 12th grade) students attended a school that employed law enforcement officers but no counselors, and 24 percent of elementary schools and 42 percent of high schools had law enforcement officers. Critically, among high schools where more than 75 percent of students were Latino or black, more than half had officers patrolling schools. In fact, figures show that between 1997 and 2007, there was an almost 40 percent increase in the number of school resource officers.

According to another study, about one in 10 young male high school dropouts is imprisoned, compared to one in 35 young male high school graduates (Dillon, 2009; see also Urbina & Wright, 2016). Further, minority students face harsher punishments in school than their white peers, resulting in a higher number of minority youths incarcerated. Latino and black students, for instance, represent more than 70 percent of those involved in school-related arrests or referrals to law enforcement (Adams, Robelen, & Shah, 2012; U.S. Department of Education, 2016b), *paving the road to prison—contributing to the school-to-prison pipeline.* Once incarcerated (juvenile detention center, jail, or prison), the political economy of *ethnic* (Latino) and *racial* (black) *illiteracy* within the U.S. correctional system replaces the school as the state

institution for socializing the thousands of young minorities (men and women) entering the penal system (Urbina & Álvarez, Chapter 17, this volume).

All together, "underneath it all," these laws serve to reinforce the ideology and practice of conquest, slavery, and colonialism, with the criminal justice system being a mechanism of power and control through imprisonment, penal expansion, and executions. As with the various laws intentionally passed to suppress and control blacks during the slavery era and thereafter, these additional laws are more of a reflection of a new form of power, control, domination, suppression, and subordination than they are of safety, equality, or justice. Ultimately, these laws are being selectively and strategically used to prosecute more race and ethnic minorities and impoverished defendants of all races and ethnicities, while, as statistics show, sending more Latinos to prison, keeping the Latino community in a *slavery-type* status, with the ultimate objective of silencing ethnic minorities.

THE MARCH TO PRISON

Beyond the dynamics of the various forces explored herein, understanding the road to prison also requires that people explore what Urbina (2008:45) characterizes as "the survival triangle": *the link between the home, the streets, and prison* (see Álvarez & Urbina, Chapter 16; this volume). That is, for the ethnic minority community, with a long history of being socially, culturally, politically, financially, and emotionally bankrupt, life at home for many Latinos during their childhood can be quite confusing, uncertain, and even violent (Bourgeois, 1995; Durán, 2013; Escobar, 1999; Ríos, 2011; Rodríguez, 1993). Under adverse cir-

cumstances, young Latinos are forced to run away and live in the streets, often forming gangs in their quest for protection, recognition, respect, and identity, which can serve as *group solidarity;* yet, violent, unpredictable, and deadly (Durán, 2009a, 2009b, 2009c, 2013; Ríos, 2011; Wilkinson, 2004). With limited opportunities, especially in education and employment (Urbina & Wright, 2016), and, in essence, with little to lose, young Latinos are then coerced into illegal behavior, as a means of coping with the cruel realities of their everyday lives (Ríos, 2011; Rodríguez, 1993). As noted by a young Latino during the 1992 Los Angeles uprising, "Go ahead and kill us, we're already dead. . . ." (cited in Rodríguez, 1993:247).

Together, research indicates that dimensions of ethnic criminality also include structural dislocation, deviant and criminal associations, and labeling and processing as status offenders and eventually as adult criminals (Durán & Posadas, 2009, 2013; James & Glaze, 2006; Ríos, 2011; Urbina, 2005, 2007; Urbina & White, 2009). Case in point: The 1992 Chicago Gang Congregation Ordinance, the subject of the famous *Morales* case heard by the Illinois State Supreme Court in October 1997, then by the U.S. Supreme Court in 1999, gave law enforcement exceptionally broad powers to disperse suspected gangsters from selected public areas, with the police issuing more than 89,000 dispersal orders and making more than 42,000 arrests in just three years (Strosnider, 2002).[22] Realistically, though, more than a measure of public safety, gang-loitering ordinances aim to control communities by dismantling residential housing projects and channeling people, particularly Latinos, blacks, and impoverished whites, into specific activities and sections of the city, resulting in confrontations, brutality, arrests, prosecutions, convictions, incarceration, and relocation of people to less valuable, more run-down and decaying residential neighborhoods. Of course, only certain individuals are more likely to be arrested under these laws, like those who are perceived as a threat, according to the subjective assessment of police officers enforcing what is already ethnically and racially coded laws (Roberts, 2001; see also Vera Sanchez, this volume).

Once the process of young ethnic criminality is set in orbit, deviance becomes a norm (a way of life), which serves as a survival mechanism in a world of neglect, abuse, violence, brutality, fear, and uncertainty. Likewise, prison, like the violent streets, becomes normalized among some minority lawbreakers in the sense that it provides a shelter, an "escape" from the lethal and chaotic life in the streets, and a refuge from an intolerant, unforgiving, and even vindictive society. In sum, in a free-market economy where cut-throat competition and institutionalized greed are the norm and in the face of structural dislocation, oppression, manipulation, exploitation, prejudice, and discrimination, delinquency and criminal behavior become a defense and survival mechanism early in life for some young, impoverished, uneducated, and unemployed ethnic and racial minorities and poor whites, as masterfully documented by Victor Ríos in *Punished: Policing the Lives of Black and Latino Boys* (2011).

CONCLUSION

On the surface, the American experience for ethnic minorities seems to be destined by the paths they intentionally take, with the road to prison being paved by the forces of evil, with crime being the driving force. Once one digs a little deeper, though, we unearth troubling evidence revealing the continuation of America's brutal, prejudice, racist, and vindictive past, and white America's continued suspicion, fear, and anger against Latinos, particularly Mexicans, and blacks. We also find that along with science, law has always been a powerful and strategic tool for establishing the confines of order and defining identity, belonging, and exclusion (De León, 2014; Kaplan, 2009a; see also Aguirre; Urbina & Álvarez, Chapter 17, this volume), equating darkness with terror to redefine the limits of crime and punishment: "both are dark, both are outside the boundaries of society, and both are monstrous" (Sánchez, 2007:176). More globally, since Latinos are now being perceived as a possible social, cultural, economic, or political threat to white America (Urbina & Álvarez, 2016, 2017), the racist and essentialist ideologies that permeate Americans are once again being manifested in the very fabric of the criminal justice system: American criminal law. At the end, as in colonial times, race and now ethnic minorities have become *the grease that keeps the wheels of justice turning,* and the "fuel" that keeps the criminal justice system expanding, controlling, and silencing *los de abajo,* the ones at the bottom (see Urbina & Álvarez, Chapter 17, this volume). Lastly, since ethnic minorities have been deemed insignificant as a worthy topic of investigation, minority defendants have received limited attention in criminal justice research and publication, and thus until recently the truths and realities of Latinos had been buried in the darkness of the past. Worse, as recently documented by Urbina and Wright in *Latino Access to Higher Education: Ethnic Realities and New Directions for the Twenty-First Century* (2016), with few Latino scholars in the privilege world of higher education, students of criminal justice, policymakers, and the public have viewed the Latino experience through the lens of "white male" ideology.

Chapter 13

HISPANIC PRISONERS: ETHNIC REALITIES OF LIFE BEHIND BARS

RICK RUDDELL AND NATALIE R. ORTIZ

Man is born free, and everywhere he is in chains.

–Jean-Jacques Rousseau

While America imprisons more people per capita than any other nation, there are some emerging developments. On December 2015, for example, the total correctional population was 8 percent lower than it was in 2000 (Kaeble & Glaze, 2016). Yet, the number of residents under some form of correctional supervision still represented 6.7 million people, with slightly over 4.6 million of those serving probationary or parole sentences in the community and the remaining 2.17 million individuals held in local jails or state prisons (Kaeble & Glaze, 2016). These numbers essentially mean that one in every 37 U.S. residents was under the supervision of the correctional system. There were an additional 51,000 juveniles incarcerated in locally or state-operated facilities in October 2014 (Hockenberry, Wachter, & Sladky, 2016). With the exception of about one-half million juvenile and adult jail detainees awaiting their *day* in court, the remaining individuals had pled guilty or were convicted on some type of offense.

While a tough-on-crime agenda has resulted in high rates of incarceration, one discouraging development is that state and local justice systems have paid comparatively less attention to the rehabilitation of offenders once incarcerated, or made little attempt reforming the individuals "housed" in their custody. As a result, many prisoners are returned to the community more damaged and face more barriers than when they were admitted to juvenile halls, jails, state-training schools for juveniles, or adult prisons. This inattention to address the unmet needs of these populations, though, has critical consequences not only for these individuals, but also for the well-being and safety of society.

As noted in previous chapters, Latinos are overrepresented in correctional populations. According to a study by the Bureau of Justice Statistics, Latinos represented 20.2 percent of the federal and state prison population on December 31, 2015 (Carson, 2016). In terms of juvenile corrections, the *Census of Juveniles in Residential Placement,* conducted in 2013, showed that 23 percent of incarcerated youths were Latinos (Hockenberry et al., 2016), which was up considerably from the 9 percent in 1979 (Smith, 1998). Todd Minton and Zhen Zeng (2016) report that Latinos represented 14.3 percent of the jail population on December 31, 2015, which was representative of their proportion of the national population, and this has been a relatively stable estimate since 2000, when Latinos represented 15.1 percent of the U.S. jail population (Minton & Zhen, 2016).

National-level statistics, however, tend to mask local or state differences in the use of imprisonment. The Urban Institute (2016) reports that differences in whether ethnicity data is collected and reported in a state's correctional system not only means that no one knows how many Latinos are incarcerated, but inflates the number of whites in prison and masks the severity of racial disparities (Urbina, 2007). In some jurisdictions, ethnic minority populations can be overrepresented. As mentioned in earlier chapters, the sources of this overrepresentation are often difficult to pinpoint due to a variety of factors, from differential practices in reporting crime to the police or bias and profiling by law enforcement, to courtroom and sentencing-based disparities and higher involvement in crime, or some combination of these factors (Urbina, 2007). Regardless of the reasons, the fact is that once incarcerated, inmates' options in terms of self-determination are severely restricted by correctional authorities.

Prisoners, regardless of their race, ethnicity, gender, or age, face a series of challenges in correctional settings. Many of these factors are beyond the control of inmates, such as where the facility is located (e.g., whether it is located close to family members), the organizational mission and commitment of the institution's staff to rehabilitation, exposure to negative or anti-social attitudes, staff professionalism, and the impact of correc-

tional violence. Latino inmates may be further disadvantaged as many come from impoverished backgrounds, which may mean less economic support from their families if incarcerated, and the economic situation of their families may prevent visits and their ability to provide other forms of social support, like phone calls, while their relative is incarcerated. Further, if inmates are not legal U.S. residents, they could be separated from their families because of the fear of deportation (see Posadas and Medina; Romero and Sánchez, this volume).

The challenges are increased when ex-inmates return to the community and must confront the same conditions that led to their arrest: gang activity and antisocial associates in their neighborhoods, the temptation of alcohol and substance abuse, and lack of legitimate opportunities for employment. The prisoners' family can also play an important role during reentry, either helping or hindering the process (see Álvarez & Urbina, Chapter 16, this volume). Rebecca Naser and Nancy La Vigne (2006) indicate that males released from prison expected a great deal of support from their families pre-release and, once released, their expectations for support were likely to be met or exceeded. Latinos in their sample, however, were significantly less likely to have their expectations met or exceeded in comparison to whites. Jane Lee and her colleagues (2016), however, found that families were important resources for the reentry of Latino men from prison to the community. Those supports may be important in overcoming some of the challenge that Latino ex-convicts express, including the strain produced by job searches, the stigma of a criminal conviction, separation from family, and overcoming their experiences with the justice system (Paat, Hope, López, Zamora, & Salas, 2017).

Returning with a criminal record also creates barriers to community reentry as opportunities for education, employment, and public housing can be restricted (Mauer & Chesney-Lind, 2003; Visher & Travis, 2003). While most prisoners believe that their reentry into the community will be successful, many lack the social capital, such as a network of friends, family members, or acquaintances that can lead to legitimate opportunities. Other inmates lack the vocational skills to obtain jobs or the interpersonal skills to restore their damaged relationships with friends and family members, and, as a result, return to prison for violating the conditions of their release or for committing new offenses. An additional challenge for Latino prisoners reentering society is that some are members of "mixed" status families (those with authorized and unauthorized immigration status) and this can add to stress and uncertainty for the entire family, including those returning to the community (Chávez, Englebrecht, Lopen, Viramontez Anguiano, & Reyes, 2013).

All things considered, there are a number of issues that have an influential impact upon the institutional experience of juvenile and adult inmates, and we have identified four that are of key importance: (1) receiving appropriate levels of physical and mental healthcare while incarcerated; (2) accessing meaningful opportunities for rehabilitation while incarcerated and post-release; (3) living in safe correctional environments, and; (4) minimizing exposure to negative values or coping mechanisms that increase the risk of correctional misconduct or reoffending once released. Failure to address these issues while individuals are incarcerated may in fact increase the likelihood of recidivism.

Considering the influence of race and ethnicity, a number of conditions may place Latino prisoners at a greater vulnerability. A history of poverty, social isolation, and society's stereotypical views of Latinos make it difficult to make healthy adjustments to custody, survive the correctional experience, and reenter the community upon release. These experiences are worsened if inmates have unresolved medical or mental health problems, which are often a function of being marginalized and living in poverty. Contrary to law enforcement and the judicial system, which partially operate within public view, the penal system operates in a more closed fashion. Therefore, in this particular chapter, instead of focusing almost exclusively on the Latino incarceration experience, we globally explore four critical issues, placing race and ethnicity within a broader context, as we seek to understand the Latino experience in its totality.

CORRECTIONAL HEALTHCARE

Inmates tend to have a high level of needs in terms of healthcare, in both juvenile and adult populations (Fiscella, Beletsky, & Wakeman, 2017; Maruschak, Berzofsky, & Unangst, 2015). In effect, this is a serious problem because of the interconnectedness between correctional and community health, and the "revolving door" of corrections results in arrestees and offenders being admitted and discharged from juvenile facilities, jails, and prisons without rehabilitation. Todd Minton and Zhen Zeng (2016) report that there were an estimated 10.9 million jail admissions in 2015 (one person could be admitted more than once) and 641,000 inmates are released from prison in 2015 (Carson & Anderson, 2016). If these individuals are returned to the community with untreated physical and mental health conditions, it is likely that their health problems will have a negative impact on community health.

The increased need for healthcare in correctional populations is a result of many factors. Access to community-based healthcare is one factor. According to the Kaiser Family Foundation (2013) and The Commonwealth Fund (2015), Latino/as account for the largest share of the nonelderly uninsured population, even after passage of the Affordable Care Act (ACA), which aims to improve the availability, affordability, and access to healthcare. The uninsured rates for Latinos are even higher in states that did not expand eligibility for Medicaid coverage under ACA to low income individuals and families (The Commonwealth Fund, 2015). Latinos enrolled in Medicaid have greater access to medical care and are more likely to visit the doctor than uninsured Latinos (Kaiser Family Foundation, 2011). Among criminal justice populations, ACA may contribute to increased access to care, providing stability for conditions that may contribute to a cycle of incarceration (Kaiser Family Foundation, 2014).

People admitted to short-term incarceration facilities, such as juvenile detention (juvenile halls) or adult jails have often come from "life on the streets," and they have neglected their care while engaging in risky lifestyles, like substance abuse, unprotected sex, or thrill-seeking behaviors. Often arrestees have been abusing substances, as nearly two-thirds of convicted people in jails, for example, were under the influence of alcohol or drugs at the time of their offense (James, 2004). Other individuals are injured, either prior to their arrest (e.g., accidents), or in confrontations with gangs or law enforcement, often the case in Latino communities (Bourgeois, 1995; Durán, 2013; Ríos, 2011; Rodríguez, 1993; Tapia, 2017). Since the majority of inmates are indigent (see Urbina,

this volume), they often have poor histories of dental or healthcare, and, for some juveniles, their first exposure to preventative healthcare might occur in a correctional setting. Prisoners also tend to have higher than average rates of chronic health conditions, such as hypertension (high blood pressure) or diabetes, which are worsened by poor diets and substance abuse (Maruschak, Berzofsky, & Unangst, 2015). Furthermore, many female inmates have significant needs surrounding reproductive health, and some are pregnant when admitted to correctional facilities (Sufrin, Clarke, & Mullersman, 2016; Urbina, 2008).

Inmates also tend to have higher than average rates of communicable diseases, including sexually transmitted infections. The Centers for Disease Control and Prevention (2017) estimated that the prevalence of HIV in correctional populations is five times greater than in the community (non-correctional) population. One challenge for correctional administrators and public health officials is to prevent the occurrence of further cases, and this can be accomplished by providing opportunities for testing, providing education about risky behaviors, and referring those who test positive for HIV for treatment. A more controversial method of reducing the spread of HIV is to provide condoms for jail and prison inmates.

People admitted into juvenile detention or adult jails are also likely to suffer from some form of psychological disorder. A study by the Urban Institute found "An estimated 56 percent of state prisoners, 45 percent of federal prisoners, and 64 percent of jail inmates have a mental health problem" (Kim, Becker-Cohen, & Serakos, 2015:v). Residents of juvenile detentions also have comparatively high rates of mental health problems. Lee Underwood and Aryssa Washington (2016:3) observe that "of the youth involved in the juvenile justice system, estimates suggest that approximately 15% to 30% have diagnoses of depression or systhymia (pervasive depressive disorder), 13% to 30% have diagnoses of attention-deficit/hyperactivity disorder, 3%-7% have diagnoses of bipolar disorder and 11% to 32% have diagnoses of posttraumatic stress disorder." As for the role of race and ethnicity, investigators found that 70.4 percent of the Latinos in their study of psychiatric conditions of juveniles in detention had at least one disorder and that proportion increased to 75.9 percent with Latina youths (Teplin, Abram, McClelland, Mericle, Dulcan, & Washburn, 2006). Researchers found even higher proportions of psychiatric conditions in detention populations, reporting the prevalence of at least one disorder in 98 percent of Latinos and 100 percent of Latinas (Karnik, Soller, Redlich, Silverman, Kraemer, Haapanen, & Steiner, 2010).

The placement of such high proportion of people with mental health problems in correctional settings reflects the lack of community-based services for these populations and sporadic contact and coordination across services when they are provided. Because there are so few alternatives, the behavior of these individuals is sometimes criminalized, as when the police charge people with an offense, in order for them to be placed in a safe setting or simply *out of public sight.* The problem, however, is that criminalizing the behavior of people with mental health problems can further their penetration into the criminal or juvenile justice system, and once entangled in the penal system it becomes difficult to get out. Additionally, a criminal conviction can create lifelong barriers to employment, as well as restricting voting (Chung, 2016) and access to social programs such as public housing or welfare benefits (Mauer & McCalmont, 2013).

There are about 1.4 million state and federal prisoners, all of whom are serving more

than one year (Kaeble & Glaze, 2016). These inmates typically have higher rates of illness than the general public (Binswanger, Krueger, & Steiner, 2009). In a national study of inmate health, Laura Maruschak, Marcus Berzofsky, and Jennifer Unangst (2015) report that one-half (50%) of state or federal prisoners had a chronic health condition such as high blood pressure or heart-related problems, and that over one-fifth of these prisoners had some infectious disease such as tuberculosis or a sexually transmitted infection. Some of the health concerns were very serious, according to Maruschak (2008) who found that while high blood pressure and arthritis were the most prevalent ailments for federal and state prisoners (30.2 and 15%, respectively), 14.9 percent had asthma, 9.8 percent had heart-related problems, and nine percent had diabetes. In all, these rates of illness are much higher than those in community populations. Worse, the long-term nature of incarceration results in some prisoners dying while in prison. In 2014, for example, about 3,000 federal and state prisoners died as a result of illness or AIDS (Noonan, 2016a, 2016b). As for race and ethnic variation, Latinos accounted for 19.8 percent of the state prison population, but represented 10.6 percent of deaths from all causes in 2014 (Noonan, 2016a, 2016b).

While providing appropriate healthcare for prisoners represents a significant burden for correctional administrators, it is in fact their responsibility to comply with federal law. The Eighth Amendment of the U.S. Constitution prohibits cruel and unusual punishment, and people who are incarcerated can seek remedies for constitutional violations, typically through litigation. In *Estelle v. Gamble* (1976), the U.S. Supreme Court established that when correctional officials fail to provide appropriate healthcare, they are in violation of federal law, under Title 42 U.S. Section 1983. In effect, in a national study of inmate lawsuits Margo Schlanger (2003) found that healthcare was the leading source of inmate litigation in large jails and state prisons.

Critics argue that given the long-term nature of imprisonment, and the unmet health needs of many prisoners, the delivery of medical and psychological services represents a significant cost to prison systems, impacting rehabilitation. The California Department of Corrections and Rehabilitation (CDCR), for example, spends $21,582 annually for each prisoner's medical care; that total includes pharmaceuticals, mental, and dental healthcare (Legislative Analyst's Office, 2017a). Costs increase significantly for inmates who are having a mental health crisis and require intensive treatment, and the annual cost to keep an inmate in a specialized mental health bed is $345,000 per year (Legislative Analyst's Office, 2017a, 2017b)

Taken together, while providing good quality healthcare to incarcerated people is expensive, the cost of neglecting their care is higher. When inmates are returned to the community, society has a stake in ensuring that they are healthy, both physically and mentally, as untreated conditions have an impact on public health. Lastly, individuals who have untreated conditions may be less able to pursue employment, education, or other rehabilitative endeavors. Consequently, they may be more likely to reoffend, which in turn jeopardizes community safety, and places inmates in the "revolving door" back to the institution; again, *creating an ongoing ending cycle of crime and imprisonment.*

MEANINGFUL REHABILITATIVE OPPORTUNITIES

The inmates' access to correctional programming typically depends on where they are incarcerated. The programs within juvenile detention as well as adult jails are designed for short-term placements while residents are awaiting their court appearance or serving short sentences, normally sentences under a year for adults. Minton and Zeng (2016) report, for instance, that the weekly turnover rate in jails, where the number of admissions was equal to the number of discharges, was 57 percent. In other words, most jail inmates are only incarcerated for a few days and as a result, providing rehabilitative programming in correctional facilities is a secondary concern compared to providing a "safe" environment. Jails, for example, typically provide few rehabilitative programs. One study found that while most jails offered mental health service, a smaller proportion offered job opportunities, educational courses, or specialized life-skills programs

such as drug counseling or religious/spiritual service (Appelgate & Sitren, 2008). These investigators also found that as the size of the county decreases, the likelihood of the facility offering more comprehensive programs also shrinks. In a Bureau of Justice Statistics report, James Stephan and Georgette Walsh (2011) found that about 10 percent of these programs offered alcohol or drug treatment.

Juveniles placed in most youth detention facilities share a similar lack of service, and this also reflects the short-term nature of their placement. A review of the latest *Census of Juvenile Residential Placement,* for instance, shows that in 2013, the median length of detention was 22 days, which means that one-half of all residents were released after serving 22 days (Hockenberry et al., 2016). As a result, the type of programs that most juvenile halls offer are consistent with short-term stays, and almost all (96%) U.S. juvenile facilities offered substance abuse education although individual, family, and group counseling programs were also commonly offered. Youths who serve a longer period in a detention facility–such as those who are awaiting their court dates on serious charges–may have less access to rehabilitative programs than their counterparts who are serving a disposition in a long-term facility. Andrea Sedlak and Karla McPherson (2010a), for example, found that detention facilities have the lowest degree of specialization in programming service.

Adults and youths placed in long-term facilities, require a different approach to programming. First, most inmates in state prisons (52.9%) have been convicted of violent offenses, while the remainder constitute property (19%), drug (15.7%), and public order (11.6%) offenses (Carson & Anderson, 2016). Most juveniles placed in long-term placements, by contrast, are nonviolent offenders. A federal government study found that 37 percent had been committed for a violent offense, 24 percent for property, 7 percent for drug, and 11 percent for public order offenses, such as possession of weapons or driving under the influence of alcohol (Hockenberry et al., 2016). The remaining juveniles were held for technical violations of probation or parole, or status offenses.

As stated in earlier chapters, most people who come into contact with the criminal justice system come from lower economic classes (Reiman & Leighton, 2017; see also Urbina, this volume), and the majority have poor educational backgrounds and limited work histories. The National Center for Education Statistics (2016) reports that the average literacy score for a sample of U.S. prisoners was 249 (on a scale of 500), which was less than an average U.S. household score of 270, and the average for Latino imprisoned populations was 239. Scores for numeracy were very similar in that prisoners had a lower numeracy score, and Latino prisoners had a lower score than the average U.S. inmate. Moreover, the National Center for Education Statistics reports show that prisoners also have less formal education and most were not fully employed prior to their imprisonment.

As noted above, a substantial proportion of inmates have significant needs for psychological and physical healthcare. Many inmates also have some form of disability, as defined by the Americans with Disabilities Act (ADA), including learning difficulties, emotional or mental health problems, or physical impairments. Though, since the ADA definitions are fairly broad, the number of juvenile inmates and adult prisoners with disabilities can be quite high. Rebecca Vallas (2016:1) estimates that "incarcerated persons are at least three times as likely to report having a disability as the nonincarcerated population." In some states, such as California, prison advocates have launched lawsuits to challenge the lack of services provided to prisoners, and this has led to an expansion in the services to these inmates.

Further, specialized programming is required for specific categories of inmates, such as sexual offenders. In fact, in some cases, treatment is mandated as part of the prisoner's sentence. Altogether, inmate populations have significant needs, and these needs may in fact accumulate in the Latino population, because of the influence of impoverished backgrounds and limited access to medical or psychological service, remedial education, and a tight labor market.

One of the best correctional rehabilitation models is based on the risk, needs, and responsivity (RNR) approach, with the following key features (Bonta & Andrews, 2016):

- **Risk principle:** Match the level of service to the offender's risk to reoffend.
- **Need principle:** Assess criminogenic needs and target them in treatment.

- **Responsivity principle:** Maximize the offender's ability to learn by matching the rehabilitative intervention to that person's learning style and needs.

This strategy is based on assessing the offender's risk and then targeting higher risk offenders for needs-based treatment. Offenders who have been evaluated as having a low risk receive no specific treatment, as prior studies show that intervening with these individuals may actually increase their likelihood of recidivating (Bonta & Andrews, 2016). Risk is determined by assessing the prevalence of static and dynamic risk factors, the latter of which can be targeted for intervention as criminogenic needs. Although definitions of these needs may vary, they typically include: (1) employment/education (a lack of job experience as well as conflict with supervisors and co-workers); (2) family/marital relationships (whether the inmate has positive relationships and their attachment to family members); (3) substance abuse; (4) community functioning (which includes unstable residential histories, debt, the lack of a bank account, and a poorly maintained residence); (5) personal/emotional functioning (the individual's coping skills, hostility toward others, interpersonal skills, impulsivity, and conflict resolution); (6) associates (having mostly criminal friends and acquaintances, being socially isolated and unattached to community groups), and; (7) attitude (which includes the negative values that offenders hold toward the justice system, as well as placing little value on rehabilitation, basic life skills or employment).

The RNR approach maintains that treatment or intervention must be responsive to the individual's needs. These strategies are based on a cognitive behavioral approach that helps inmates restructure their thinking through problem-solving exercises, positive reinforcement from the correctional staff and the disapproval and sanctioning of negative behaviors (Bonta & Andrews, 2016). Realistically though, a single approach may not be successful with all offenders, as an individual, for example, with a learning disability caused by a traumatic brain injury may require that service be provided in a different manner. As a result, "the responsivity principle must take into account the strengths, learning style, personality, motivation, and biosocial (e.g., gender, race) characteristics of the individual" (Bonta & Andrews, 2007:1). Therefore, with changes in demographics, rehabilitative approaches used with Latino populations might take into account the different strengths and cultural values of the ethnic community. Alternatively, some correctional interventions may be delivered in Spanish to increase awareness, understanding, effectiveness, and prevention.

Unfortunately, while sound correctional programming has been shown to decrease recidivism, most correctional systems spend a small percentage of their budget on the delivery of rehabilitative programs, critically impacting the institutional experience for Latinas and Latinos. It is difficult to accurately assess the proportion of correctional funding that goes directly to rehabilitation, but a few years ago the Florida Office of Program Policy Analysis and Government Accountability (2007) indicated that only 1.7 percent of their correctional budget was spent on rehabilitative programs. In California, the Legislative Analyst's Office (2017a) estimates that $2,437 of the annual cost of imprisonment of $70,812, or only 3.4 percent goes to rehabilitation.

The recession that started in 2007-2008 led to long-term cutbacks in correctional spending on rehabilitative programs (Turner, Davis, Fain, Braithwaite, Lavery, Choinski, & Camp, 2015). According to the Vera Institute (Scott-Hayward, 2011), the majority of the 37 state corrections departments they surveyed eliminated or significantly reduced the amount of institutional and community corrections programs available to offenders, with correctional systems reacting in a similar manner, as in the past, with nine states cutting educational, vocational, and substance abuse treatment during the 2001–2002 budget crisis (see Wilhelm & Turner, 2002). In fact, even before the current state budget crisis, many inmates received limited treatment service. Petersilia (2011:1) notes that when she co-chaired an expert panel on California corrections in 2007, "50 percent of all prisoners released the year before had not participated in a single program," a critical situation for Latinos, who tend to be marginalized before, during, and after incarceration (Urbina & Álvarez, 2017).

Though, in contrast to their adult counterparts, there has been more emphasis in providing higher levels of treatment service for juvenile offenders in state training schools. It is a major challenge, however, to ensure that residents in these facilities receive meaningful educational, vocational, and life-skills programming. Some states, such as Missouri, have been leaders in the development of rehabilitative programs in their juvenile justice systems. Beth Huebner (2013) reports that officials in that state reinvented their youth correctional system to focus on continuous case management, small

facilities that rely upon small groups of residents who provide peer support, and a rehabilitative model focused on restorative justice.

In sum, while correctional practitioners and social scientists have made significant strides in developing rehabilitative interventions that respond to the unmet needs of inmates, there has not been a willingness to fund these programs for the long haul. This approach results in a "revolving door" as inmates are being released from juvenile facilities and correctional systems with few new skills to cope with the challenges of community reentry. In fact, many of these inmates are returned to the community worse than when they were incarcerated, as their unmet needs have not been addressed and their educational, employment, and family lives have been disrupted by the correctional experience. Lastly, some individuals are actually returned to the community more vulnerable due to the violence they experienced or witnessed during their incarceration, and, in the case of Latinos, further marginalized with the combination of pressing issues like stereotypes, ethnic profiling, community fear, disdain, hate, their inability of obtaining an education or employment due to a criminal record, and the possibility of being deported (Álvarez & Urbina, 2018; Urbina & Álvarez, 2017).

VIOLENCE REDUCTION IN CORRECTIONS

Part of understanding the consequences of incarceration requires that attention be given to the social experience of being imprisoned (Urbina, 2008, 2016). In the past decade, there has been increased interest in better understanding the prevalence, causes, and outcomes of violence in the penal system, where rehabilitation is suppose to take place. To date, we have been more successful in reporting how much violence occurs, but less successful in knowing the situations that contribute to violence, or responding to the short and long-term impact of violence on inmates and correctional staff. While it is comparatively easy to document the physical aftermath of assaults, less attention has been placed on the psychological harm that inmates experience when witnessing violence or when they have been victimized. Andy Hochstetler, Daniel Murphy, and Ronald Simons (2004:448) found that "prison victimization contributes to the occurrence of depressive and posttraumatic stress symptoms" and that "prison victimization adds to the pains of pre-existing events." In effect, victimization leads to various emotional reactions, including anger, and contributes to high levels of stress that may be manifested in sleep disorders and nightmares (Wolff & Shi, 2009). Victimization may be even more detrimental on those who are struggling with overcoming addictions, suffer from poor physical or mental health and have a history of family dysfunction, an inability to cope with stress and interpersonal conflict.

There are aspects of correctional violence that differentiate it from other forms of assault. It has long been recognized that correctional settings are stressful environments, which are crowded, noisy, drab, depriving, and dehumanizing (Foucault, 1995; Shammas, 2017; Sykes, 1958; Urbina, 2008). Violence, or the threat of violence, adds to these pains, and unlike assaults that occur in the community, prisoners who have been assaulted by other inmates or correctional officers might face those people every day, a critical situation for inmates confined for long periods of time.

Violence behind bars can also have an impact on those who witness correctional violence. In effect, investigators report that being victimized or witnessing another person's victimization can lead to posttraumatic stress disorder and depression, have physical effects, as well as an increased use of medical facilities and recidivism (Blevins, Listwan, Cullen, & Jonson, 2010; Urbina, 2008). Paul

Boxer, Keesha Middlemass, and Tahlia Delorenzo (2009:793), for instance, report that "in general, individuals who were witnesses, as well as victims, of violent crime [in jail or prison] showed the poorest adjustment post-release." Evidently, in addition to stress and depression while incarcerated, negative consequences of correctional violence extend beyond the individual's time in corrections and into the community (see Morgan, this volume).

There may be some gender differences related to exposure and experiences of violence. Susan Friedman, Stephanie Collier, and Ryan Hall (2016) summarized a series of studies describing the prevalence of PTSD for incarcerated women in the United States, and they found that between 29 and 51 percent of women inmates were suffering from this disorder. Like other mental health disorders, it is sometimes difficult to disentangle whether the PTSD occurred prior to their placement in custody, or whether the disorder occurred or worsened after their admissions.

The acknowledgment of the harm of correctional violence has resulted in correctional practice and policies that have decreased the number of assaults. Few state prison systems report the number of assaults, but the U.S. Bureau of Prisons does report the rates of assaults on federal inmates. With respect to less serious assaults, there were about seven assaults for every 5,000 inmates in 2017, and less than one serious assault (0.50) for every 5,000 prisoners (U.S. Bureau of Prisons, 2017). While the number of less serious assaults has been increasing, the rate of serious assaults has been decreasing somewhat. Inmates living in medium security housing seem to be at higher risk of both types of assaults. It is likely that these numbers represent only the "tip of the iceberg," as many assaults actually go unreported as inmates may perceive that correctional officials will not act upon their allegations, or in fear of retaliation by the inmates who assaulted them. Further, these totals would not include acts of coercion, such as threats, that can still result in considerable stress for the victims (Listwan, Colvin, Hanley, & Flannery, 2010).

Each year the Bureau of Justice Statistics presents the results from their *Deaths in Custody* series, showing improvements over the last few years. According to Margaret Noonan (2016a, 2016b), in 2014, 25 jail inmates and 83 state and federal prisoners were murdered. Placed in context, the murder rate in local jail facilities was three murders for every 100,000 jail inmates. When it comes to prisoners, the murder rates were somewhat higher, and in 2014, seven prisoners were killed for every 100,000 state prisoners and eight federal prisoners for every 100,000 federal inmates. The changes in murder rates in jails and prisons between 2005 and 2014, as shown in Table 13.1, revealing that while the rates of jail homicides have been fairly stable over time, the rates of state prisoners have been experiencing an uptick over time.

While homicides in correctional facilities are accurately reported, there had been comparatively limited data on sexual assaults, which are more common, but less likely to be counted. The *Prison Rape Elimination Act,* signed into law in 2003, mandates that statistics on prison sexual violence be collected by the U.S. Bureau of Justice Statistics. The most recent reports show that prison rape is less prevalent than once estimated. Ramona Rantala, Jessica Rexroat and Allen Beck (2014) collected information from adult correctional facilities from 2009 to 2011, and they found there were 2,002 alleged incidents of serious inmate-on-inmate sexual acts (e.g., such as rape) in all U.S. federal and state prisons, and 133 of these acts were substantiated. These investigators also found allegations of 1,028 abu-sive sexual contacts–such as inappropriate touching–and 161 of these acts were substantiated (Rantala et al., 2014). Inmates also alleged that staff engaged in sexual misconduct or harassment, although very few of these acts were substantiated: 207 acts of misconduct and 45 harassment incidents (Rantala et al., 2014).

Juveniles are, however, at much higher risk of being sexually victimized than their adult counterparts. Information collected by the Bureau of Justice Statistics shows that rates of sexual victimization in juvenile facilities are much higher than rates in adult jails or prisons and their study shows there were more substantiated cases of misconduct carried out by staff members than inmate-on-inmate assaults. Rantala and Beck (2016) found there were 15 nonconsensual youth-on-youth incidents, such as rape, but 21 substantiated cases of staff-on-youth sexual misconduct (which involves intentional touching or other sexual acts) for the entire nation in 2012. There were about three times as many cases of youth-on-youth abusive sexual contact than the more serious assaults. These investigators found that occurrences of sexual violence increase in facilities that are understaffed and have more gang violence.

Further, rates of assaults that occur in juvenile corrections are typically higher than in adult facilities. In effect, juveniles tend to be more impulsive and this translates into a higher involvement in assaults in both community and correctional settings. Sedlak and McPherson (2010b:3) found that 68 percent of juveniles in custody reported being "easily upset," while another 61 percent "lost [their] temper easily or had a short fuse." Involvement in gangs can also increase a youth's involvement in violence, although studies have not shown a conclusive link between these factors (Scott & Maxon, 2016).

One of the limitations in our knowledge is that there is little research that tells us about

Table 13.1
MURDERS IN U.S. PRISONS AND JAILS, 2005 TO 2014*

Year	State Prison Murder Rate (100,000 inmates)	Federal Prison Murder Rate (100,000 inmates)	Jail Murder Rate (100,000 inmates)
2005	4	9	3
2006	4	5	5
2007	4	7	3
2008	3	8	2
2009	4	4	3
2010	5	10	3
2011	5	5	3
2012	7	3	3
2013	7	7	4
2014	7	8	3

*Source: Noonan (2016a, 2016b).

the prevalence of violence in detention or long-term youth facilities. In one of the few studies of violence in U.S. juvenile facilities, investigators found that "the assault rate (per 100 juveniles) increased from 13.5 in August of 2002 to 15.5 in November of 2003" (Vásquez, Vivian, Chengalath, & Grimes, 2004: 6). For instance, the juvenile assault rate in Arizona in 2002–2003 was about three times the adult rate in California's Department of Corrections and Rehabilitation in the same year. This comparison, however, must be interpreted with caution, as only a single year was compared, and reporting rates in juvenile corrections may be higher due to a greater staff to resident ratio as well as the fact that reporting require-

ments and definitions in these two systems could differ (Mason & Fearn, 2009). Lastly, it is also important to acknowledge that the data reported were from ten years ago, and much could have changed since then. Many juvenile correctional systems, including the Arizona Department of Juvenile Corrections, are participating in the Performance Based Standards (PBS) initiative, which has proven successful in reducing violence rates in juvenile facilities (PBS Perspective, 2016).

Altogether, the results of the research on sexual violence conducted by the Bureau of Justice Statistics, as well as comparisons of juvenile and adult assaults, suggest that confinement can be a dangerous experience. Some of that risk, as noted by researchers, comes from staff members who work in these facilities (Rantala & Beck, 2016). However, it is also important to recognize that youths confined in detention or long-term residential facilities are more apt to act impulsively than their adult counterparts, so rates of violence tend to be higher for inmate-on-inmate assaults.

As for the influence of race and ethnicity in the context of correctional violence, the literature shows that some marginalized youth may be more vulnerable to victimization, highly attributed to issues like culture, language, stereotypes, and immigration status. Undocumented Latinos, for instance, might be reluctant to report victimization for fear of deportation, or retaliation by correctional staff. There is, however, limited data about the effects of this violence, both in terms of institutional conduct, like are these inmates later engaged in higher levels of misconduct, self-harm, or suicide as a result of their victimization, as well as after their release into the community, like are they apt to have higher rates of reoffending?

The evidence, though, suggests that prison inmates are now less likely to be murdered while serving their sentence than three decades ago. Furthermore, levels of sexual victimization, whether reported by correctional officials or jail and prison inmates, are far less than previously estimated by some scholars and advocacy groups. However, we have comparatively less information about inmate-on-inmate violence. One of the challenges that prison administrators must confront is an increase in murders in federal and state facilities, and throughout 2016-2017 there were an increased number of riots reported in the press, although it is too early to determine whether that is part of a longer-term trend. In the meantime, correctional officials have taken some meaningful steps to reduce violence in correctional institutions over the past few decades, and these mechanisms must be sustained and sensitive to race and ethnicity in order to enable residents of juvenile correctional facilities, as well as adult jails and prisons to serve their time without incident and return to the community without the additional burden of victimization.

PRISON CULTURE

Regardless of whether correctional institutions house juvenile or adult inmates, or males or females, residents in these facilities quickly form their own subculture, or culture within a culture. These correctional subcultures are less conventional than the set of standards or principles held by most community members. Often the values expressed by inmates are based on the exploitation and deception of others, as well as anti-authoritarian, oppositional, and pro-criminal (Elliot & Verdeyen, 2002). To some extent, these values are shaped by the type of facility in which inmates are housed (like jail or prison), the security levels (maximum

security prisons tend to be more violent), the size of the gang population, the perceived legitimacy of the justice system, the region in which the facility is located, and the efforts of correctional officials to create a pro-social environment.

A number of factors also influence the degree to which prisoners adopt these negative beliefs. A week's detention in a juvenile facility or adult jail, for instance, is unlikely to result in many changes in the individuals' core values. A 10-year penitentiary sentence, by contrast, is apt to have a much more profound change on individuals and their outlook toward life due to the length of sentence that they are serving and their long-term interactions with other prisoners. Moreover, the degree to which individuals are attached to the mainstream social system, such as having a history of employment, sound family relationships, and a stable home environment, will also influence their degree of socialization into the correctional environment. Inmates admitted at older ages who have supportive families and a solid plan for community reentry may be less vulnerable to negative socialization. It is also likely that people who had a positive outlook prior to their incarceration will retain those values throughout their incarceration. Additionally, inmates who are engaged in the community, such as those pursuing an education or involved in a religious organization, may also moderate the negative influence of the correctional environment.

The values that inmates hold may also reflect changing social values. The Nebraska Department of Corrections (2016:1, 12), for example, reports that there has been a "shift in the inmate population as more demanding, disrespectful of authority, and violent" and that inmates are "uncooperative and noncompliant," and "more confrontational and push rule limitations." Benjamin Steiner and John Wooldredge (2016) contend that if inmates view authorities as legitimate and they do not feel dehumanized, they are more likely to act respectfully toward correctional officers and abide by the prison's rules. Here too, the influence of race and ethnicity seems pressing, as minority communities may develop an oppositional culture due to their histories of involvement with justice systems. As noted in previous chapters, the overenforcement of everyday activities in some Latino communities can result in considerable tension between community members and law enforcement (Durán, 2009b, 2009c; Ríos, 2011; Salinas, 2015; Urbina & Álvarez, 2015, 2017). Some criminologists, for instance, have identified how the crimes of the poor, Latino, and black populations are disproportionately enforced (Reiman & Leighton, 2017; Ríos, 2011), particularly against people of Mexican heritage (Álvarez & Urbina, 2018; Durán, 2009a; Urbina & Álvarez, 2016; see also Aguirre; Baker, this volume). In effect, the development of an oppositional culture, in some places, may in fact be a manifestation of the realities of life before or during their incarceration (Urbina, 2008; Urbina & Álvarez, 2017).

In all, regardless of the source of these values, the outcomes of negative socialization can be disastrous for inmates. Some inmates leave correctional facilities with visible "markers," like crude jailhouse tattoos, that broadcast to the world that they were incarcerated. Other inmates adopt the correctional facilities' language and terminology, which may identify them as ex-inmates long after they return to the community (Ross & Richards, 2002; Urbina, 2016). Lastly, some inmates join gangs, often along racial and ethnic lines, while incarcerated, with a growing number of prisoners being susceptible to radical political ideologies (Marchese, 2009).

The process of adopting the values of the penitentiary, *prisonization,* was recognized over 70 years ago (Clemmer, 1940), which starts with the inmates' admission (e.g., a "fresh fish" in prisons) and continues until their release. Victor Hassine (2009:190) identified five stages of institutional adjustment, including fear, adaptation, anger, compliance, and institutionalization, when inmates "resign themselves to complete dependence on the prison system." In fact, every inmate will adapt to the correctional environment in one way or another, and their adaptation is the result of a complex interplay of institutional conditions, in which inmates can exert little control, governed by elements like their history, strengths, and weaknesses.

In actuality, it is important that inmates understand the subculture of prisons, as it enables them to survive the correctional experience. Every institution, for example, has written rules established by correctional authorities, as well as informal or unwritten expectations that guide the actions of correctional officers and inmates. In prior eras, this was called the "convict code," although the term is rarely used today (Hassine, 2009). Correctional facilities can be dangerous places for inmates unaware of the informal rules, like borrowing from other inmates, joining gangs, gambling, showing the proper degree of respect to other inmates, and interacting with correctional staff (Santos, 2004). As such, inmates must walk a careful path, as they learn the norms of the institution that will enable them to survive their sentence and reduce their likelihood of victimization, while avoiding the negative socialization that may result in a higher likelihood of recidivism.

Kimberly Collica (2013:25) observes that men and women experience imprisonment differently and "female inmates tend to recreate family while male inmates enlist as gang members." In the paragraphs that follow we describe these different adaptations to prison life for women offenders, and that is followed by a discussion of men in gangs. A major theme that emerged in correctional research during the 1960s and 1970s was that incarcerated women developed and participated in "pseudo" or "make believe" families (Giallombardo, 1966; Ward & Kassebaum, 1964), although family-like groups in women's prisons were identified by prison sociologists as early as the 1930s (Koscheski, Hensley, Wright, & Tewksbury, 2002). Critics note, however, that researchers' understanding of the function of pseudo-families evolved between the 1960s and 1990s, shifting from how they are formed out of sexual needs to how they provided emotional support, friendship, and stability during incarceration (Collica, 2013; Huggins, Capeheart, & Newman, 2006; Urbina, 2008).

Katherine Maeve (1999) suggests that the need for supportive interpersonal relationships is important to women inmates because many have been left isolated by their relatives and friends before incarceration. In a study of pseudo-family groups in Texas prisons, Huggins and colleagues (2006) found that 29 percent of women were in pseudo-family groups, and report that women in these relationships reported experiencing fewer adverse events and disciplinary infractions than women who were not members of pseudo-families. Although correctional staff in women's prisons believed that women joined these groups for the sake of love and support, they in fact overestimated the prevalence of membership and a majority viewed inmate involvement in these relationships as primarily driven by sexual needs. Custodial staff generally viewed such relationships as detrimental to prisons and inconsistent with self-reported accounts of these family members, and they perceived these women as more likely to be involved in disciplinary actions (Huggins et al., 2006). However, in all, although pseudo-families have been identified for several generations, we have comparatively limited data on whether the involvement of women in these relationships has a positive or detrimental impact on their experience while in custody or their reentry into the community (Wulf-Ludden, 2016).

The family-oriented nature of social groups in women's prisons is quite different from the security threats that appear in men's correctional facilities. One of the most destructive steps that inmates might take is to join gangs after their admission to correctional facilities. For example, a survey of correctional administrators revealed that over one-half of gang members were thought to have joined gangs after their admission to prison (Winterdyk & Ruddell, 2010). Respondents said that inmates joined gangs for fear of other inmates, to gain a sense of belonging, to increase their status, gain access to contraband, or control of the "underground" prison economy (Winterdyk & Ruddell, 2010). In fact, according to Jeffrey Ross and Stephen Richards (2002:127), "some penitentiaries are literally run by gangs. In those pens, if you don't join one faction or another, you may not be able to defend yourself." The problem, however, is that gang membership actually increases peoples' likelihood of victimization (Ruddell & Gottschall, 2011), contributes to a higher involvement in institutional misconduct (Drury & DeLisi, 2010; Griffin & Hepburn, 2006; Reidy & Sorensen, 2017), and leads to higher levels of recidivism once released (Dooley, Seals, & Skarbek, 2014; Huebner, Varano, & Bynum, 2007). Further, in addition to increasing levels of institutional misconduct and violence, gangs tend to heighten racial and ethnic tensions in facilities (Hassine, 2009; Trulson & Marquart, 2002), which, in turn, have an impact on all inmates.

The significance of race and ethnicity is evidenced by the fact that gangs tend to form along racial and ethnic lines. Here too, for Latinos, this can have devastating consequences. One particular study of gang members in federal prisons found that Latinos had a higher involvement in violent offenses than non-Latinos (Gaes, Wallace, Gilman, Klein-Saffran, & Suppa, 2002), with similar results being found in a study of violence in one state prison system (Berg & DeLisi, 2006). Though, due to the secretive structure, purpose, and activities of Latino gangs, whether they are in community or correctional settings, it is difficult to understand their nature in its totality. Such complexity is illustrated in an examination of deterrence-based law enforcement strategies in California, as reported by Anthony Braga (2008:336),

> Conflicts among Hispanic gangs mainly involved a very violent rivalry between Norteño gangs (associated with criminal groups and gangs in northern California) and Sureño gangs (associated with criminal groups and gangs in southern California). While Norteño and Sureño gangs were united in their fight against their common rivals, however, they also had ongoing conflicts within their loose alliances.

In respect to gang involvement, the boundaries between prison and community gangs are becoming increasingly seamless and frequent movement of individuals between the two systems suggests that threats in prison parallel with those in the community.

However, although gangs are often associated with crime, Robert Durán (2009a:143) documents that "equating gangs as synonymous with crime allows for differential policing that no longer emphasizes criminal acts, but rather perpetual criminal people," which in turn leads to profiling, the overenforcement of noncriminal activities, and demeaning treatment of Mexican American communities. Durán's (2009a) ethnographic research also reveals that these interactions create a divide between residents of Mexican American communities and law enforcement, contributing to feelings of oppression and thus supporting the development of oppositional values that may be further reinforced in correctional settings.

Juveniles are especially vulnerable to joining gangs as gangs can provide a sense of belonging and support that is sometimes missing from their lives. Scott Decker and Barrik Van Winkle (1996) explain that joining gangs comes from both "pushes" (fear or a need for safety) as well as "pulls" (for excitement), a highly prone situation for Latinos who are often forced to live on the margins of society (Bourgeois, 1995; Durán, 2013; Ríos, 2011; Rodríguez, 1993; Tapia, 2017). In effect, Sedlak and McPherson's (2010a:8) national-level survey of confined juveniles found that "nearly one-third of the custody population professes some gang affiliation," and that "a majority of youths in custody (60%) report that there are gangs in their facilities."

Regardless of the reasons for joining, juvenile gang members pose as many problems for correctional staff as their adult counterparts, including being at higher risk of institutional misconduct than noninvolved juveniles (Colon, 2004). Further, gang members contribute to an oppositional culture where they undermine staff authority as well as the elements of rehabilitation in the facility (Colon, 2004). Similarly, Sedlak and McPherson (2010a) found that increased gang populations were associated with a greater amount of contraband within the facility, less cordial inmate-staff relationships, and an increased use of pepper spray.

Like their adult counterparts, gang members in facilities are also associated with increased violence (Scott, 2014).

Lastly, admissions to correctional facilities are never desirable outcomes as these places are often large, drab, and dangerous, and thus inmates have to adapt in order to survive the experience. In some ways, this process is even more difficult for female inmates, particularly Latinas and African Americans, compared to their male counterparts due to their histories of abuse, neglect, and special needs (Díaz-Cotto, 1996, 2006; Urbina, 2008). Adapting to these environments, however, places inmates at risk of being socialized into a culture that is often antisocial. Consequently, the longer inmates are incarcerated, the higher the risk of adopting beliefs and values that may place them at, yet, higher risk of institutional misconduct, and, worse, reducing their likelihood of successfully reintegrating into the community; again, *creating an ongoing cycle of crime and imprisonment.*

CONCLUSION

While recent figures indicate that the imprisoned population has slightly decreased, the United States has been on an incarceration binge for several decades. There is little doubt that incarceration is an expensive proposition. In California, for instance, it cost $70,812 to house an adult inmate in the state's prison system in 2016-2017 (Legislative Analyst's Office, 2017a), and that cost triples for a juvenile held in a California training school. While people can debate the costs and benefits of incarceration as it relates to crime control, it is likely that incarceration rates will remain high for the foreseeable future, and the social harm caused by mass incarceration will not only continue but possibly get worse (Clear, 1994; Lynch,

2007; Urbina & Álvarez, 2016), as recently documented by Urbina and Álvarez in *Ethnicity and Criminal Justice in the Era of Mass Incarceration: A Critical Reader on the Latino Experience* (2017).

Although the use of incarceration in the United States is much more extensive than in other countries, about 98 percent of prisoners are eventually returned to the community (Travis, 2005). Their success in community reentry is tied directly to public safety, to the extent that they are able to successfully reintegrate (which in fact may be partly facilitated by the service they receive to address the needs that resulted in their criminal activity to begin with), governing the probability of reoffending (see Álvarez &

Urbina, Chapter 16, this volume). In effect, the lack of rehabilitative opportunities for many juvenile and adult inmates in addition to the neglecting of their physical and psychological care contributes to higher levels of recidivism. Whether people are housed in juvenile facilities or in adult prisons, both are subjected to and vulnerable to correctional violence and the high possibility of being socialized into a negative or oppositional institutional culture that contributes to reoffending. As for ethnic/race variation, Latinos (and other ethnic and racial minorities) may be more vulnerable to some of these factors, partly due to the complex history of race relations, which carry into the penal system (Díaz-Cotto, 1996; Oboler, 2009; Urbina, 2008, 2016; Urbina & Álvarez, 2017).

The difficulties of inmates returning to the community have long been recognized (Phillips, 1917), but only in the past two decades has this issue been prioritized in academic and policymaking agendas (Urbina, 2016). Unfortunately, in spite of our acknowledgement of the importance of rehabilitation and needs-based programming, the first cuts to correctional funding have been at the expense of rehabilitative programs, including programs offered in conjunction with community supervision (Scott-Hayward, 2011; Urbina, 2016), which, logically, is a short-sighted practice.

Mark Cohen and Alex Piquero (2009:25) estimate, for example, that saving one high-risk 14-year-old from a life of crime could save society $2.6 to $5.3 million dollars in the long-term, including a reduction in harm to victims, costs of the criminal justice system, and reduces the barriers to opportunity and losses in productivity that result from the incarceration of offenders. Follow up studies have produced similar results about the benefits of saving an individual from crime (Piquero, Jennings, & Farrington, 2013). Finally, American correctional policies based on "warehousing" inmates, while providing only the basic service for their survival (Feeley & Simon, 1992; Urbina, 2008), is not a cost-effective strategy for the long-term management of corrections. If incarceration has to be used, individuals should be returned to the community less damaged than when they were admitted to a juvenile or adult facility.

One of the challenges for correctional systems, however, is that even when an inmate leaves a facility with a greater education, enhanced job skills, or a better work ethic, opportunities for employment in a highly technological and competitive job market are few. Many ex-prisoners have to overcome the stigma of their criminal convictions in their re-entry to the community. Thus, a lack of meaningful work opportunities is a crucial barrier for these ex-prisoners. During times of economic crisis, there tends to be less public and political support for programs that are seen as "helping" inmates, but, realistically, there are serious consequences for inmates, their families, and communities when inmates are unprepared for such transition. In effect, if we do not believe in extending these services out of compassion, we should acknowledge that when these people are healthier and better prepared for community reentry, then inmates will be less likely to engage in behavior that originally leads to imprisonment, and, ultimately, *preventing the vicious cycle of crime and imprisonment.*

Chapter 14

PROBATION AND PAROLE:
CAPTIVITY BEYOND PRISONS

KATHRYN D. MORGAN

These failure rates on probation, parole and community corrections are having just as much effect on driving prison growth as anything passed by the Legislature.
–Christie Donner

The United States has the highest incarceration rate in the world. Reportedly, at the end of 2010 there were approximately 6.5 million (6,493,027) adults under correctional supervision. Approximately 1.6 million were incarcerated in federal and state prisons (Guerino, Harrison, & Sabol, 2011) with an additional 4.8 million adults supervised on probation or parole (Glaze & Bonczar, 2011). Figures for 2017 show that 2.3 million people are incarcerated in the nation's jails and prisons making the United States the world's leader in incarcerating its citizens. The United States incarcerates 700 individuals per 100,000 people in the U.S. population (Sentencing Project, 2016), with approximately 60 percent of those incarcerated being either black or Latino (Carson, 2015; Urbina & Álvarez, 2017). Subsequently, much of the controversy regarding racial disparity has focused on correctional sentencing, particularly the imprisonment of young ethnic and racial minorities.

In fact, broadly, one of the most controversial issues in criminology and criminal justice is the issue of the disparate treatment of racial and ethnic minorities in the criminal justice system. There has been a proliferation of empirical studies that suggest that race and ethnicity impact the decision-making process at every level of discretionary decision-making in the criminal justice system. Several studies have concluded that police are more likely to profile, harass, arrest, and verbally and physically abuse racial and ethnic minorities (Lynch & Groves, 1989; Mann, 1994; Urbina & Álvarez, 2015; Walker, Spohn, & DeLone, 2018). Several studies report that blacks and Latinos are most likely to be detained prior to trial and less likely to receive a nonfinancial release, more likely to be denied bail, and more likely to be deained because of the inability to raise money for bail (Demuth, 2003; Demuth & Steffensmeier, 2004; Katz & Spohn, 1995; Walker, Spohn, & Delone, 2018). As for female defendants, Latinas and blacks are more likely to be detained than white females because of the inability to post any amount of bail. Jailed Latinas and black women, who make up 15 percent and 44 percent of the female jail population, are at the bottom of the economic ladder and lived below the poverty line before being jailed (Alexander, 2012; Salinas, 2015; Urbina, 2008; Urbina & Álvarez, 2016, 2017). Therefore, women may be detained in jail for up to 70 days for being unable to pay bail, which could be as low as $500 but also much higher (Swavola, Riley, & Subramanian, 2016). To further complicate matters, pretrial detention results in disadvantages. Those who remain in jail prior to trial, plead guilty more often, and receive a more severe sentence. Pretrial detainees, denied bail or cannot raise bail money, are punished more severely, usually with a prison sentence, are more likely to receive longer prison terms, and are more likely to reoffend, resulting in higher recidivism rates.

The more recent and acute disproportionality can be trace to the early 1980s when the implementation of punitive policies such as *the war on drugs, the war on immigrants,* and *the war on terrorism* significantly influenced the nature, dynamics, and functions of the U.S. prison system and the criminal justice system as a whole. Indeed, while our fixation on imprisonment has impacted many people, minorities have been disproportionately affected. Imprisonment rates, however, "are only the tip of the iceberg" (Steinmetz & Anderson, 2015:2), as the majority of people under the control of the criminal justice system are supervised through probation and parole. To be sure, while one in 110 people in the United States are incarcerated, one in 62 are on probation, with approximately one in 35 blacks and one in 90 Latinos on probation (Glaze & Kaeble, 2014; Steinmetz & Anderson, 2015). Yet the one penal stage affecting the most offenders proceed through the system has yet to be analyzed by its totality is the less mentioned probation and parole system, particularly the wide-arching implications and ramifications, or what Urbina and Álvarez (2017) characterize as "captivity beyond prison." Therefore, this chapter details central elements of the probation and parole system, placing probation and parole in the context of the past and more expansive ideas about race, ethnicity, gender, and various other pressing factors that shape and reshape the criminal justice experience for women, African Americans, Latinos, and impoverished whites.

PROBATION: PRACTICE AND PROCESS

Since the early twentieth century, there has been a proliferation of programs that embodied the major ideas of the rehabilitative ideal that refocused the emphasis from punishment of offenders to the rehabilitation and reform of offenders. Under this model, probation has been one of the most popular rehabilitation programs developed from the rehabilitation philosophy, and it continues to be the most common community-based correctional program and alternative to incarceration. However, while the probation process has remained similar to its beginnings, there have been changes in this alternative to incarceration.

History of Probation

Several historical practices helped to lay the foundation for probation as we know it today in the United States. Benefit of clergy, judicial reprieve, pardon, and release on recognizance were practices that granted benefits to the accused by minimizing the effects of punishment, providing an alternative to incarceration or relieving the liabilities associated with a conviction. The work of John Augustus, Father of Probation, laid the foundation for our modern probation practices. Augustus, a Boston shoemaker, would approach the judge in a Boston courtroom requesting permission to bail a defendant out of jail, supervise him for a period of time in the community, and return to court to report on his progress. If the defendant was able to refrain from further criminal activity and maintain employment, the defendant would receive a fine instead of a commitment to the House of Corrections (Abadinsky, 1997). Augustus was the first to use the terms *probation* to define his work and *probation officer* to identify his volunteer role. For almost 20 years, Augustus worked as a volunteer probation officer to supervise approximately 2,000 offenders in the community (Lindner, 2007). In 1878, Massachusetts passed a probation law authorizing the mayor of Boston to hire the first probation officer, Captain Savage, who was supervised by the superintendent of police. The officer's primary responsibility was to investigate cases and recommend probation sentences for all offenders who could possibly be "reformed" without punishment; that is, going to jail or prison (Champion, 2008).

Throughout the early twentieth century, adult and juvenile probation programs spread throughout the United States. Probation officers were volunteers who were untrained and used their homes as reporting offices for probationers under their supervision (Abadinsky, 1997). Invariably, the history of probation as a correctional alternative has faced various criticisms about leniency and its ability to deter and rehabilitate offenders under supervision, diminishing resources that required probation departments to do more

with less, questions about racial disparity and discrimination, and twenty-first century challenges from private probation agencies, who wish to maximize profits (Urbina & Álvarez, 2016). In effect, although crime rates have remained relatively constant, probation as a correctional option remains a popular "alternative" for social control. At the end of 2015, probationers comprised 3.8 million (81%) of the 4.6 million offenders under community supervision (Kaeble & Bonczar, 2016).

Probation Process

Following conviction or a guilty plea by the defendant, decisions are made regarding the sentence to be imposed by the court. Probation, a sentencing option and, arguably, alternative to prison, allows offenders to remain in the community in lieu of incarceration. Probation is granted by the presiding judge after a review of the presentence investigation report and a consideration of other factors including the severity of the offense, the seriousness of the prior criminal history, sentencing guidelines, the defendant's age, rehabilitation potential, attitude, and the relationship with his or her family. Defendants who have been convicted of multiple offenses, were on probation or parole at the time of the offense, are addicted to drugs, have a history of violent behavior, seriously injured the victim, or used a weapon in the offense are less likely to be candidates for probation supervision.

Defendants who are granted probation must sign a Probation Order that specifies the conditions that probationers must follow while under supervision. The probationer's signature on the Probation Order indicates an agreement with the court-ordered conditions and the willingness to comply with the requirements of supervision known as *conditions of probation*. Standard conditions are imposed on all probationers with the goal of reducing the risk of recidivism. These conditions include such requirements as maintaining employment, refraining from future criminal behavior, supporting dependents, and reporting to the probation officer as required. Special conditions may include treatment conditions and may be punitive. Punitive conditions usually reflect the seriousness of the offense and they are intended to increase the punishment of the offender. Such conditions include community service, home confinement, restitution, and mandatory drug testing. Treatment conditions are designed to help offenders with problems that might be factors in criminal behavior. The presentence investigation reports serve as the source for many of the treatment conditions of probation.

When probationers violate the conditions of probation either by committing a new offense or violating the administrative rules of probation, they face the possibility of revocation of probation. Probationers may plead guilty to violations or may choose to plead not guilty. If the probationer denies the charges, a revocation hearing is scheduled. Because of the possible loss of conditional freedom, probationers are typically represented by counsel and receive all of the due process protections of defendants in a criminal trial. After both the defense attorney and the prosecution have presented arguments, the judge makes the decision to either continue or revoke probation. The judge may select from several options when making a decision about revocation. These options include: (1) reprimanding the probationer and restoration to probation; (2) returning the probationer to probation supervision with an amended probation order, in which case the amended order may include requirements to serve jail time, receive additional drug/alcohol treatment, and pay additional fees; and (3) revoking probation and imposing a prison term. When probation is revoked, probationers lose the privilege of conditional freedom. Probation may or may not be required to serve the original sentence, and revoked probationers may be given credit for "street time" (Morgan, 2016).

PAROLE: PRACTICE AND PROCESS

Although the United States incarcerates more people than any other nation, 95 percent of those incarcerated will return to the community through a prison release channel at a rate of 600,000 per year or 1,600 per day (Petersilia, 2004). In effect, at year-end 2015 (the latest available figures), an estimated 4,650,900 adults were under community supervision in the United States; that is, about one in 53 adults under community supervision (Kaeble & Bonczar, 2016). There are three mechanisms of release from prison. *Discretionary parole release* is conditional release granted by the parole board after inmates have served at least one-third of the sentence. *Mandatory release* is granted after inmates have served the full sentence minus good time. Currently, it is used by the federal government and states operating under a determinate sentencing structure (Clear & Cole, 2000). *Unconditional release* is granted to offenders who are released with no further correctional supervision because they have completed their sentence, received a pardon, or had their sentences commuted (Clear & Cole, 2000). Traditionally, discretionary parole has been the most common correctional strategy for, notably, releasing offenders and returning them back into the community.

The emergence of parole is associated with the emphasis on rehabilitation and the development of indeterminate sentences. It is a correctional strategy that grants early release to inmates prior to the expiration of the prison term. Under the indeterminate sentencing structure, the sentencing judge assesses a minimum and maximum sentence, leaving it up to the parole board to determine the actual length of the sentence. Following release, parolees serve the remainder of the sentence under supervision in the community.

Historically, parole functioned to release inmates at a time when conditional release was most beneficial, prevent further internalization of the prison subculture and thus reducing the likelihood that former inmates would return to a life of crime, and assist in the rehabilitation and reintegration of offenders back into society. Like probation officers, parole officers were first volunteers, then clinical agents of rehabilitation who used their expertise to assist parolees. However, although used mainly as a rehabilitation technique for offenders, parole has also served other functions. As early as 1893, California, for instance, used parole for nonrehabilitative functions, such as minimizing the use of clemency and correcting for sentences that were considered excessive (Messinger, Berecochea, Rauma, & Berk, 1985). In modern times, with great controversy surrounding the functions and objectives of parole, recent studies have examined the changing parole process and the nonrehabilitative functions of parole. Some critics report that institutional and political objectives such as efforts to control prison population overcrowding (Champion, 2005) or remedy sentencing disparities for inmates who have been sentenced unfairly because of race/ethnicity, gender, or social class (Hofer, 1999) have taken priority over rehabilitation issues. Jonathan Simon (1993), however, docu-

ments that the transformation of the parole process has been governed by shifts in economic and political ideology. Taken together, Simon (1993) concludes that rehabilitation interests have been strategically replaced by management objectives—*social control beyond the prison system.*

History of Parole

The historical development of parole can be traced to the transportation programs of America, Australia, and Great Britain. In the early seventeenth century, Great Britain experienced high unemployment rates, an increase in crime rates, and prison overcrowding. When given a choice of execution or being transported to the American colonies where there was a labor shortage, most of the English prisoners chose transportation to America. After being pardoned by the English government, prisoners were transported by independent contractors to America to work as indentured servants (Abadinsky, 1997). Initially, there were no conditions attached, and thus felons would avoid transportation or would return to England (Abadinsky, 1997). The Transportation Act of 1718 imposed conditions and specified that the pardon would be nullified if convicts failed to comply with the rules and regulations (Champion, 2005). When the Revolutionary War ended the transportation to America program, the English government again searched for a solution to its increasing crime rate and overcrowded convict population. This search resulted in the implementation of the Transportation to Australia program under the leadership of Superintendent Alexander Maconochie, who is knowned as the "Father of Parole." Maconochie instituted many reforms, the most important being the "mark system" where inmates could accumulate marks for hard work and good behavior and use those marks to earn early release (Abadinsky, 1997). Under Maconochie's leadership and service as superintendent, over 1,400 convicts were released, many of them did not reoffend (Champion, 2005).

In 1853, England passed the Penal Servitude Act, which allowed convicts to be released on a *ticket-of-leave* under the supervision of police. Sir Walter Crofton became the administrator of the Irish prison system. Similar in philosophy to Maconochie, Crofton believed that sentences and time served in some way should be related to rehabilitation (Abadinsky, 2009). In 1854, he implemented the ticket-of-leave program in Ireland. This Irish system consisted of four stages that culminated in release of prisoners: (1) strict imprisonment and forced solitary confinement; (2) placement in a special prison to work with other inmates earning marks to progress to the third stage; (3) transportation to an open institution where they could earn release on a ticket-of-leave; and (4) release on the ticket-of-leave under the supervision of police who would help them seek employment (Champion, 2008).

In the United States, the first parole system was implemented at the Elmira Reformatory that opened in 1876 under Zebulon Brockway, Elmira's first superintendent (Abadinsky, 2009). Brockway, a penologist from Detroit, Michigan, had previously attempted to implement the indeterminate sentence for Michigan first-time offenders. Even though the Michigan Legislature passed the statue, the courts later reversed the legislation. At the Elmira Reformatory for adult males in New York, Brockway introduced the indeterminate sentence and recommended that young male offenders be given indeterminate sentences not to exceed the maximum recommended by law. Additionally, he introduced the "mark system" where the accumulation of marks could be used for early release. Once inmates accumulated

enough marks, inmates were conditionally released and supervised in the community for six-month parole periods by appointed guardians. Parolees were required to report to the guardian once monthly and give an account of their conduct and situation. If there was actual or potential criminal behavior, parolees could be returned to prison. By 1900, the foundation for parole in the United States had been laid with three underlying principles: (1) indeterminate sentences; (2) reduction of prison sentences based on good behavior; and (3) release of parolees and supervision in the community. The use of parole as a correctional practice spread throughout the United States in the early 1900s, and by 1944, all states had implemented some form of conditional release (Abadinsky, 2009).

Parole was the most common form of release until the 1970s when criminologists, policymakers, and legislators questioned the effectiveness of rehabilitation programs, rejected indeterminate sentencing in favor of determinate sentencing structures, and introduced the *idea* of "just deserts"; that is, criminals deserve punishment for their crimes and harm caused to society. These challenges resulted in many states abolishing parole as a rehabilitative mechanism. Several years later, with the passage of the Federal Sentencing Reform Act of 1984, the federal government abolished parole and implemented *truth-in-sentencing* for federal offenders that required convicted federal offenders to serve 85 percent of their court-imposed sentences. By 1999, 14 states (Arizona, Delaware, Florida, Illinois, Indiana, Kansas, Maine, Maryland, Minnesota, Mississippi, North Carolina, Ohio, Oregon, Washington, Wisconsin) had completely abolished discretionary parole board release for all offenders (Ditton & Wilson, 1999). Soon after, 16 states abolished discretionary parole for all offenders and four additional states abolished it for violent offenders (Hughes, Wilson, & Beck, 2001). Reportedly, some of the reasons for abolishing discretionary parole include: (1) the failure of indeterminate sentencing and rehabilitation to reduce recidivism rates; (2) abolition of parole fits the ideology of the get tough on crime movement; and (3) the lack of transparency in the parole board process (Abadinsky, 2009). However, coinciding with the exacerbation of neoliberalism in the early 1970s, some critics point to the enormous *profits* of punitive criminal justice policies, which have expanded the criminal justice system into a multibillion dollar enterprise; or, more precisely, the historical *profitability* of racial (black) and ethnic (Latino) minorities via wide-arching social control laws and imprisonment (Urbina & Álvarez, 2016, 2017).

Process of Parole

Inmates may be considered for parole after serving one-third of the sentence if inmates are not prohibited from parole. Inmates who have been sentenced under a determinate sentencing structure, have a sentence of life in prison without the possibility of parole, and former death row inmates whose sentences have been commuted to life in prison are not eligible for parole consideration (Champion, 2008; Urbina, 2012). Some states give incoming inmates a presumptive parole date. In fact, all inmates who are not excluded by law from getting parole are given advance notice of parole, and thus inmates will be released, unless there are major problems (Clear & Dammer, 2000). However, when the Comprehensive Crime Control Act of 1984 was passed (Public Law 98-473, October 12, 1984), one provision mandated the elimination of parole at the federal level by 1992. The legislation also specified that offenders sentenced

under a determinate sentencing structure would be granted a 15 percent reduction in sentence for good behavior, and post-release supervision would be called *supervised release* rather than parole (United States Parole Commission, 2003).

While less examined, the State Parole Board is an important part of the parole process. Although the number of board members and the length of service on the board vary across states, Board membership is a political appointment and board members serve at the pleasure of state governors, who tend to be highly "political" in their aspirations for reelection or higher office. The Parole Board functions to award good time, set initial and subsequent dates for parole hearings, and make decisions about granting or denying parole. However, critics of parole boards cite the lack of transparency regarding the decision-making process and the limited knowledge and education of parole board members to make informed decisions as contributors to the skepticism about parole board effectiveness (Gottfredson & Ballard, 1966; Morgan, 2016).

The parole process begins when the inmate's name appears on a computer-generated list indicating eligibility. Victims and trial officials are notified and the list is sent to the institutional parole officer. Institutional parole officers interview the inmate, prepare case files for board members' review and assist inmates in the preparation of the pre-parole release plan. The pre-parole release plan is an important component of parole release consideration. It details the inmate's plans for employment, living arrangements, and treatment if released. Before the plan can be included as part of the case file for review, field parole services must verify the information. Parole boards often will not approve release if there is no pre-parole plan that has been verified by field parole services. In addition to reviewing the information contained in the inmate's case file, the parole board schedules a parole release hearing where the inmate, the inmate's family and supporters, the victim, the victim's family, and others who may oppose or support the parole release request will speak to the parole board. These hearings are not adversarial and the inmates are not entitled to counsel. The inmates do not have interests that must be protected by the presence of an attorney. Therefore, it is not required that an attorney is present to represent inmates, and thus most jurisdictions do not permit legal counsel. During the release hearing, parole board members consider several things, such as the seriousness of the crime, the length of time served, inmate's age, prior criminal history, alcohol and drug use, and the institutional record. They also consider opposition from police, the district attorney, and the victim or victim's family (Morgan, 2016). If the parole board votes to release, a release certificate is prepared, victims are notified and the inmate is released within two weeks of the decision. If the vote is to deny parole release, the reason for denial is not given to inmates. Instead, inmates may be provided with a new case review date or an order to "serve all" of the sentence (Abadinsky, 2003:247). Once inmates are released on parole, they are given conditions of parole and are supervised by Field Parole Services. Violation of parole conditions may result in the revocation of parole and a return to prison to serve the remainder of the sentence.

The revocation process includes two hearings: a preliminary hearing and a revocation hearing. The objective of the preliminary hearing is to determine if there is enough evidence to show that the parolee violated parole conditions. Parolees are entitled to legal counsel, but the state is not required to provide an attorney. During the preliminary hearing, the parolee's attorney has the right to confront and cross-examine witnesses, challenge the charges, and present evidence. The parolee's adjustment while under parole supervision may be considered during this time. It is also an opportunity to show that parolees did or did not comply with the rules such as reporting, participating in treatment programs as ordered, or maintaining suitable employment. After all the witnesses have been interviewed and evidence presented, the hearing officer decides if there is enough evidence to support a finding of probable cause.

If there is a finding of probable cause, the hearing officer prepares a report for the board and the revocation hearing is scheduled. The objective of the revocation hearing is for the board to decide if the violations are serious enough to revoke parole and return parolees to prison. In making a decision, the parole board will consider adjustment under supervision, other problems, mitigating circumstances surrounding the violations and the recommendation from the hearing officer. The board members vote for or against revocation. At the end of the revocation hearing, the board may decide to:

- Restore the parolee to supervision.
- Restore the parolee to supervision with an amended order that requires participation in a treatment program, jail time or transfer to a halfway house or treatment facility.
- Revoke parole and return the parolee to prison.

RACIAL, ETHNIC, AND GENDER DISPARITIES
IN PROBATION AND PAROLE

Probation: The Influence of Race, Ethnicity, and Gender

While advocates of punitive social control tend to passionately and sometimes aggressively argue that prejudice, disparities, and discrimination are things of the past, studies reveal that there is disparity at every level of the legal decision-making process. These studies suggest that while legal variables such as offense seriousness and prior criminal history impact decisions, extralegal variables also influence decisions made by court officials, including judges. Invariably, the question becomes, does race, ethnicity, gender, or class influence decisions to place convicted offenders on probation (or in prison)? At the end of 2015, there were 4.6 million offenders under community supervision, approximately one in 53 adults in the United States. Of that number, 3.7 million were under supervised probation (Kaeble & Bonczar, 2016). Those numbers indicate that since 2000, there has been a consistent increase in the number of women on probation. In 2000, female probationers comprised 22 percent of the population, by 2008 and 2009, the percentage of women had increased to 24 percent, increasing to 25 percent in 2014-2015. Some scholars document that these trends are more reflective of social ills, a punitive criminal justice system, and political insensitivity, than significant increases in female criminality (Escobar, 216; Urbina, 2008; see also Álvarez, this volume). For instance, this increase may reflect the increase in the number of females arrested for minor offenses, the nature of female poverty, abuse, neglect, and substance abuse, and the fact that women are more likely to be sentenced to probation for property and minor

drug related offenses (Glaze & Bonczar, 2010), as a result of the war on drugs.

However, the most pressing and thus controversial punishments have been racial and ethnic disparities in sentencing decisions that result in more Latinos and blacks being sentenced to prison. Several studies of sentencing patterns at the federal and state level reveal that Latinos and blacks are sentenced more harshly than whites. In 1996, federal court data for United State District Courts indicated that 74 percent of white convicted defendants were sentenced to prison while 82 percent of convicted black defendants and 85 percent of convicted Latino defendants were sentenced to prison (U.S. Department of Justice, 1998). In particular, Latinos and black male offenders who are young and unemployed are more likely to be sentenced to prison and for longer periods than white males who are young and unemployed (Morín, 2009; Salinas, 2015; Spohn, 2000).

Sentencing decisions result in a higher percentage of Latinos and blacks receiving prison terms and fewer defendants being granted probation or placement in similar discretionary community programs. In 2015, whites comprised 55 percent of those on probation, while Latino and black probationers made up 13 percent and 30 percent of the probation population, respectively (Kaeble & Bonczar, 2016). Danielle Kaeble and Thomas Bonczar (2016) further report that this number of Latino and black probationers has remained relatively constant since 2005. In effect, several years ago, Joan Petersilia (1985) found that in California, 71 percent of whites convicted of a felony were placed on probation compared to 65 percent of Latinos and 67 percent of blacks convicted of a felony. Addressing the notion that

Latinos and blacks receive harsher sentences because of crime seriousness and severe criminal histories, Ojmarrh Mitchell and Doris McKenzie (2004) found that even after controlling for these legal factors, Latinos and blacks receive more severe sentences than white defendants.

Studies have found that Latino and/or black probationers are at a greater risk for probation revocation, rearrest for new offenses, and technical violations compared to whites (Gould et al., 2011; Leiber & Peck, 2013; NeMoyer et al., 2014; Sims & Jones, 1997; Steinmetz & Henderson, 2016a, 2016b). For instance, one study found that both Latinos and blacks were more likely to have their probation revoked or adjudicated and less likely to be discharged early compared to whites (Steinmetz & Henderson, 2016a). Studies have also found differential race and ethnic effects based on probation outcomes (Gray et al., 2001; Johnson & Jones, 1998; Leiber & Peck, 2013; Olson & Lurigio, 2000; Piquero, 2003). NeMoyer and colleagues (2014:587) found that Latino juveniles were more likely to not receive a mandatory school requirement for noncompliance, a finding that "many indicate that judges are taking inappropriate extralegal factors . . . into account when imposing probation conditions." Leiber and Peck (2013) found that Latino and black juveniles generally received more severe probation outcomes. More recently, Kevin Steinmetz and Jamilya Anderson (2015) tested for race and ethnic effect across four types of probation failure/success (administrative failure and revocations resulting from technical violations, new felonies, and new misdemeanors) through two analyses of 14,365 probation cases, using logistic regression analysis. Across both models, racial/ethnic categorization were found to be significantly and positively associated with probation failure outcomes, and the standardized coefficients

indicated that the Latino and black categories presented a moderate to strong effect sizes across outcomes studied.

For some critics, though, the historical legacy of prejudice, discrimination, and oppression has "disappeared" somewhere along the way, and thus racial/ethnic bias by decision-makers does not result in more severe sentencing outcomes for racial or ethnic minorities. For them, the answer is simple and straightforward, Latino and black defendants are sentenced more harshly because they commit offenses that are more serious and have more severe criminal histories. Other critics argue that even when racial disparities exist, they are not the result of systematic racial bias but the *unintended consequences* of punitive but well-intended crime control policies, like the war on drugs, designed to reduce crime and protect society. These "get tough" policies, they argued, have resulted in the unintended consequences of higher arrests, prosecutions, and incarcerations of minorities who are disproportionately affected (Kleck, 1981; Wilbanks, 1987).

Other observers, however, document that prejudice and discrimination continue to be *endemic* in the criminal justice system, exacerbating under the Trump administration, which has made Latinos a target, particularly immigrants, to include Dreamers (students) and military veterans. At the turn of the century, Todd Clear and George Dammer (2000) reported that there is bias operating in the selection process for discretionary community programs such as probation that results in the exclusion of Latinos and blacks. To be sure, after centuries of continuous exclusion from America's main institutions, like education, Latino and black offenders are likely to be young, poor, uneducated, unskilled, and have a more complicated criminal history than their white counterparts. Therefore, Latinos and blacks are viewed as less suitable for probation or other community and even prison programs (Clear & Dammer, 2000). Empirical studies further show that typically presentence reports have been drafted (historically written by white men) to favor whites resulting in many judges (who are mostly white) granting probation to white defendants more than minority defendants (Carroll & Mondrick, 1976; see also Mauer, 2006; Urbina & Kreitzer, 2004).

More severe sentencing may also be the result of cumulative disadvantages that Latino and black defendants experience throughout the criminal justice process (Urbina, 2007, 2012; Urbina & Álvarez, 2015, 2017). Many of these disadvantages are related to the defendants' socioeconomic status and class bias that exists in the criminal justice system, as documented by Jeffrey Reiman and Paul Leighton in *The Rich Get Richer and the Poor Get Prison* (2017). While police officers are seldom seen in upper-scale communities, police patrolling practices mandate more intense patrols in *visible* crime areas populated largely by lower-class minorities. Combined with poverty, these often decaying communities have a higher percentage of both offenders and victims and higher police visibility. Subsequently, to further aggravate life in these communities, residents are profiled, stopped, frisked, harassed, and arrested more often (Bourgeois, 1995; Durán, 2013; Ríos, 2011; Rodríguez, 1993; Urbina & Álvarez, 2015, 2017).

In effect, documented evidence reveals the effect of race/ethnicity on pretrial release decisions. Once arrested, minority residents are vulnerable to the money bail system and unlikely candidates for nonfinancial release such as recognizance or release to a treatment facility. Pricing minorities out, the money bail system discriminates against the poor, who are mostly minorities, and distinguishes between the poor and the affluent. Studies report that Latinos and blacks are

more likely to be detained prior to trial and less likely to receive a nonfinancial release, more likely to be denied bail, and more likely to be detained because of the inability to raise required money for bail. Further, poor defendants who remain in jail prior to trial, plead guilty more often, are punished more severely (usually with a prison sentence), are more likely to receive longer prison terms, and pose a higher risk for recidivism (Morín, 2009; Salinas, 2015; Urbina & Álvarez, 2015, 2017; Walker, Spohn, & Delone, 2018). Many of these same defendants use court-appointed attorneys and are tried by juries composed mostly of whites because of racial discrimination in jury selection (see Mirande, Chapter 10, this volume), and the fact that many minorities from lower-class neighborhoods are less likely to report for jury duty, in part because of complicated factors, like their lack of understanding (education) of the judicial process, lack of transportation, distance, and inability to take the day off from work, fear of losing their job, or reduced paycheck. Some evidence also points to the fact that many practicing attorneys are inadequate and unwilling to devote enough time to the preparation of cases involving minorities and indigent people (see Urbina, this volume). In fact, instead of providing an adequate defense, they often encourage defendants to plead guilty (Mann, 1994; Urbina, 2004; Walker, Spohn, & Delone, 2018). In one sentencing study, Cassia Spohn (2000) concluded that retaining a private attorney decreases the likelihood of defendants receiving a severe sentence, revealing the "price of justice" in a supposed *equality before the law* criminal justice system.

Parole: Race and Ethnicity

The racial disparity controversy has recently focused on the issue of granting parole to incarcerated inmates. To begin, of the

2.3 million people in state and federal prisons in the United States, approximately 60 percent of those incarcerated are minorities, Latino or black (Carson, 2015). Beyond the prison system, 856,900 adults were under parole supervision in 2015, of which 44 percent were white, 38 percent black, and 16 percent Latino (Kaeble & Bonczar, 2016).

While some evidence is ambiguous regarding the impact of race on discretionary parole decisions and some studies attributing the disparity in sentencing and parole releases to legal variables rather than racial discrimination (Elion & Megargee, 1978; Scott, 1974; Wilbanks, 1987), other studies conclude that race significantly influences parole release decisions. For instance, results of Petersilia's (1985) study of racial discrimination in three states revealed three significant findings: (1) Latino and black defendants received more severe sentences than white defendants who had similar criminal records and were convicted of similar crimes; (2) Latinos and blacks also consistently served longer sentences than whites sentenced to prison; and (3) black inmates served longer sentences, were less likely to receive parole, and often had additional criteria to satisfy. More recently, other studies have reported similar findings (Hughes, Wilson, & Beck, 2001; Morgan & Smith, 2005).

RACIALIZED EFFECTS OF CRIMINAL JUSTICE POLICIES

The Impact of a Changing Philosophy on Probation and Parole

While questionable, the rehabilitative ideal provided the philosophical foundation of various rehabilitation programs of the early twentieth century. As noted herein, probation and parole were two correctional programs developed from the rehabilitation philosophy that emphasized reforming offenders instead of incarcerating people without rehabilitation. Probation allowed convicted offenders to remain in the community and maintain community ties to family, employment, and social institutions that were beneficial to rehabilitation. By placing offenders on probation, they avoid interaction with hard-core criminals and a prison culture characterized by bitterness, violence, hostility, and stigma that hinders reintegration and social adjustment upon release. The probation philosophy also included elements of community protection and offender rehabilitation. In effect, probationers were supervised by agents of the courts or a probation agency. As trained personnel having dual roles, probation agents were present to ensure that the conditions of probation were fulfilled and provide counseling and assistance in community reintegration. In all, as with all types of community-based corrections, it was generally agreed that rehabilitation of offenders was more realistically possible in the *natural environment* of a free community than behind prison walls. Similarly, the parole model supported rehabilitation and reintegration back into society because it permitted inmates to be released at a time when they could benefit most from conditional release. Thus, inmates avoided further internalization of the prison subculture and reduced the risk of the inmate's return to crime.

In the 1970s, however, a changing correctional philosophy affected probation and parole practice and processes (Urbina & Álvarez, 2016). As crime rates increased during the 1960s and 1970s, there was growing awareness that crime prevention and reha-bilitation programs had not worked. Robert Martinson (1974) and colleagues published a controversial study in which he reviewed 231 evaluations of rehabilitation programs, reporting that "the program shows no appreciable effect on recidivism" and concluding that *nothing works.* Quickly, criminologists began to challenge the rehabilitation philosophy that had dominated criminal justice policy for over 70 years.

Following Martinson's controversial study about rehabilitation programs, Charles Murray and Louis Cox (1979) published *Beyond Probation* also challenging the belief that rehabilitation and treatment efforts reduced future criminal behavior. Instead, they suggested that punishment, not treatment, was more effective in reducing recidivism (Murray & Cox, 1979). During the 1970s and 1980s, James Q. Wilson, who, like Charles Murray, is sometimes characterized as intellectual racist, published his controversial book, *Thinking About Crime* (1983), promoting a new approach to thinking about crime that suggested that criminals are cold calculators with a low stake in conformity who are willing to commit crime for the perceived benefits. Passionally charging, "Wicked people exist. Nothing avails except to set them apart from innocent people" (Wilson, 1983:260).

Subsequently, as a result of the aggressive conservative attack on rehabilitation in the 1970s, under the argument that *nothing works,* get tough advocates attempted to abolish or minimize the use of rehabilitation programs in favor of tougher crime control policies and strategies. Advocating that crime rates could be reduced, not through rehabilitation but through punishment that imposed more pain on offenders than benefits derived from crime, the new philosophy emphasized a return to the classical emphasis on punishment and deterrence while minimizing the focus on rehabilitation.

Concurrent with the neoliberal movement, the *nothing works* cynicism quickly ushered in a period of punitive policies and practices. With high political and economic profits to be made (Urbina & Álvarez, 2016), politicians and law enforcement officials aggressively waged a war on crime by shifting criminal justice policies and practices that reflected a "get tough" on crime agenda (see Álvarez, this volume). Under the neoliberal agenda, laws were passed that instituted "sentencing guidelines," set mandatory sentencing for certain offenses, and mandatory prison sentences for drug offenders (Tonry, 1995; Urbina & Álvarez, 2017). For instance, "three strikes and you're out" polices were popularized as a get tough mechanism that required repeated offenders convicted of three offenses to receive a mandatory sentence of "life without parole" (Champion, 2005:134). The United States Supreme Court also demanded harsher treatment of ordinary street crime, limited rights for those arrested for crimes, limited last minute appeals by death row inmates, and mandated the execution of violent teenage killers (Álvarez & Urbina, 2014; Urbina, 2012). The view that increased incarceration of convicted criminals was an important strategy for deterring criminals and reducing crime rates was further exacerbated by the *war on drugs*–having a major impact on Latino and black offenders, with collateral damage on minority communities (Alexander, 2012; Salinas, 2015).

Drug policies associated with the "war on drugs" quickly resulted in longer sentences for drug users, mandatory sentences for possession of crack cocaine and reclassifying misdemeanor drug possession of crack cocaine for felony possession resulted in more Latinos and blacks being targeted, detected, arrested, prosecuted, convicted, and incarcerated. For instance, while whites constitute the majority in the general population, in the first part of the twentieth century they made up only 36 percent of those in prison for drug charges, with the high majority being either Latino or black (Urbina & Álvarez, 2016, 2017; Walker, Spohn, & DeLone, 2018). Research by Stephen Demuth (2003) indicates that judges, who may have implicit biases especially about the recent anti-Latino immigration policies, tend to sentence Latinos more harshly for drug and nondrug offenses, with similar trends found in recent studies (Álvarez & Urbina, 2018; Urbina & Peña, 2018).

While youth gangs have existed for centuries, the modern drug-trade has created many opportunities for the distribution of drugs and, by extension, guns to carry out their operations in the underworld; presumably, operating primarily in the barrios and ghettos of America. As such, the *target* of the war on drugs has been on racial and ethnic minorities, particularly Mexicans (Alexander, 2012; Álvarez & Urbina, 2018; Salinas, 2015; Urbina & Álvarez, 2017). In effect, studies show that Latinos and blacks are routinely and strategically detected, arrested, indicted, prosecuted, convicted, and sentenced to prison at higher rates and for longer prison terms than whites for the same crimes, while reducing their chance of being placed on probation or released on parole (Alexander, 2012; Álvarez & Urbina, 2018; Reiman & Leighton, 2017; Ríos, 2011; Salinas, 2015; Urbina & Álvarez, 2017).

More broadly, the incarceration rate for Latinos and blacks rose significantly during the past decades, compared to whites, a punitive movement that started in the early 1970s and escalated in the 1980s with the war of drugs, combined with the interacting forces of gangs and guns, with more than half of those arrested for drug offenses being Latino or black. Once arrested, Latinos and blacks are more likely to be sentenced to prison than placed on probation. In fact, by yearend 2010, Latinos (22.3%) and blacks (37.9%) comprised 60.2 percent of the prison population (Guerino, Harrison, & Sabol, 2011), with a disproportionate rate of minorities on death row (Álvarez & Urbina, 2014; Urbina, 2012). Further, for individuals who committed minor nonviolent offenses, instead of keeping them in the community under some type of community program, probation remained a core component of corrections. To be sure, in keeping with the changing get-tough philosophy, probation departments added intensive probation supervision conditions and later programs that emphasized punishment, intensive supervision and surveillance, community service and electronic monitoring—in a sense, extending imprisonment into minority communities.

As for parole, several states including the federal government carried out a similar trend, abolished discretionary parole, passed truth in sentencing legislation, and mandated that offenders serve all of their sentences minus good time (Dickey, 1993; MacKenzie, 2001; Salinas, 2015; Urbina & Álvarez, 2017). As several states toughened sentencing laws and replaced indeterminate sentencing with determinate sentencing, parole was impacted in three major ways: (1) it reduced the use of the indeterminate sentence, thereby minimizing judicial discretion; (2) it limited the power of the parole board and changed discretionary parole; and (3) it limited or eliminated the authority of the parole board to grant early release. Clearly, the changing psychology of social control has resulted in shifting trends and the emergence of pressing issues.

PROBATION AND PAROLE OVER TIME: TRENDS AND ISSUES

Demographics of Imprisonment, Probation, and Parole

Analyzing data for the first part of the twenty-first century, the demographics show shifting trends but they are not indicative of a positive profile. As previously stated, by yearend 2009, over two million (2,292,133) adults were incarcerated in state or federal prisons or jails, followed by a decline (1,605,127) at yearend 2010 (Guerino, Harrison, & Sabol, 2011). Beyond the prison system, almost 5 million offenders have been under community supervision, with the great majority being probationers or parolees (Glaze & Bonczar, 2010, 2011), as shown in Table 14.1.

As for race and ethnicity, by 2009, Latinos comprised 20.6 percent of the total prison population, while constituting only 16.3 percent of the general population (Humes, Jones, & Ramirez, 2011; West, 2010). In effect, by midyear 2009, the disproportionate number of Latinos in prison, on parole, or probation continued, with over 3.7 percent of Latinos and 9.8 percent blacks between the ages of 20 and 24 being in prison, compared to 1.6 percent for whites (West, 2010). As for specific demographic characteristics, Latino probationers and parolees tend to be young, single, with limited or not job skills, have low levels of education, high unemployment rates, no income, alcohol/drug additions, no health insurance, and poor (Morgan, 1995, 2016; Urbina & Álvarez, 2017). A report by the Substance Abuse and Mental Health Services Administration (2011), for example, documents that in 2008, the majority (76.6%) of probationers and parolees were male, never married (63.1%), and between the ages of 18 and 44 (81.3%), with nearly one-third

(29.7%) aged 18 to 25. More critically, over one-third (39.6%) of probationers and parolees had less than a high school education. The majority (36.8%) of probationers and parolees were unemployed, 26.2 percent were not in the labor force, and 30.8 percent reported no source of income. While Medicaid was the most common type of health insurance coverage reported by probation and parole officials, the majority (74.9%) of all probationers and parolees reported having no health insurance.

Shifts in Probation and Parole Populations

As other components of the U.S. criminal justice system, the parole institution has undergone significant changes in the last several decades. States vary in their approach to parole, with some states eliminating or diminishing the authority of parole boards, while others retaining it as a significant function of prisoner reentry. Specifically, the first major element of parole, the decision to release offenders, has also shifted over time, whether it is discretionary (traditional function of the parole board) or mandatory (mandated by law) release. The criminal justice system has moved away from the practice of indeterminate sentencing by judges, which granted parole boards considerable flexibility in deciding offenders' sentence length. Further, the legislative branch is increasingly dictating the release of offenders by establishing mandatory sentencing and rigid release laws.

In all, three major parole trends have occurred over time. First, the authority of parole boards in determining the release of offenders has declined in favor of mandatory releases. In fact, by the end of 2010, 16

Table 14.1
ADULTS UNDER COMMUNITY SUPERVISION ON PROBATION OR PAROLE, 2005–2015*

Year	Total	Probation	Parole
2005	4,946,600	4,162,300	784,400
2006	5,035,000	4,236,800	798,200
2007	5,119,000	4,293,000	826,100
2008	5,093,400	4,271,200	826,100
2009	5,019,900	4,199,800	824,600
2010	4,888,500	4,055,900	840,800
2011	4,818,300	3,973,800	855,500
2012	4,790,700	3,944,900	858,400
2013	4,749,800	3,912,900	849,500
2014	4,713,200	3,868,400	857,700
2015	4,650,900	3,789,800	870,500

*Source: Kaeble and Bonczar (2016).

states had abolished parole board authority for releasing all offenders, and another four states had abolished parole board authority for releasing certain violent offenders. The second major trend lies in the growth of the parole population, with a never ending cycle of imprisonment, release, and reincarceration. Tracing reentry trends of inmates returning to the community after serving time in prison, Timothy Hughes and Doris James Wilson (2002) of the Bureau of Justice Statistics reported that at least 95 percent of all state prisoners would be released from prison at some point, with nearly 80 percent of offenders released on parole supervision, compared to 60 percent in the 1960s. Third,

the proportion of parole violators as a percentage of the total prison population has increased over the years; though, typically for nonviolent offenses or not being able to meet the condition of parole. As for individual characteristics of parolees and probationers, Tables 14.2 and 14.3 show a constant trend in terms of race, ethnicity, and sex.

The punishment of people found in violation of parole and probation has also altered the composition of the prison population, creating a distinct and increasingly common pathway back to prison for former inmates. Parole failures are classified as technical violations (violating a condition of release), or the commission of new crimes, in which case

Table 14.2
CHARACTERISTSICS OF ADULTS ON PAROLE, BY SEX, RACE, AND ETHNICITY*

Characteristic	2005	2014	2015
Male	88%	88%	87%
Female	12	12	13
White	41	43	44
Black/African American	40	39	38
Hispanic/Latino	18	16	16
American Indian/Alaska Native	1	1	1
Asian/Native Hawaiian/Other Pacific Islander	1	1	1
Two or more races	0	–	–

*Source: Kaeble and Bonczar (2016).

Table 14.3
CHARACTERISTSICS OF ADULTS ON PROBATION, BY SEX, RACE, AND ETHNICITY*

Characteristic	2005	2014	2015
Male	77%	75%	75%
Female	23	25	25
White	55	54	55
Black/African American	30	30	30
Hispanic/Latino	13	13	13
American Indian/Alaska Native	1	1	1
Asian/Native Hawaiian/Other Pacific Islander	1	1	1
Two or more races	–	–	–

*Source: Kaeble and Bonczar (2016).

parolees are arrested, charged, and convicted of new offenses. For instance, in 2010 the rate of violating probation conditions stood at 5.7 percent, a slight increase from 2000 (5.5%), while the rate of violating parole conditions dropped from 16 percent in 2000 to 13 percent in 2010 (Glaze & Bonczar, 2011). Revealing the implications and ramifications of parole and probation violations and revocation, according to some figures, more than one-third of incoming prisoners are incarcerated for parole violations—again, showing not only a never-ending cycle of crime and imprisonment but also a net-widening of social control.

Issues in Probation and Parole

Despite the shifts in mandatory release laws and recent attempts to abolish parole, parole populations have continued to increase annually, and as incarceration rates increased, probation populations have been decreasing. Therefore, while there has been a declining probation population since 2002, the parole population has shown slight increases (see Table 14.1). Although federal parole was phased out by 1992, federal offenders may be granted supervised release by the federal courts and the number of federal offenders under supervised release have also contributed to the increase in the parole population (Maruschak & Parks, 2012). Further, prison overcrowding and pressure on state correctional systems to remedy unconstitutional conditions in facilities across the United States, combined with trends toward mandatory prison sentences for drug traffickers, the penal system, including probation and parole, has continue to undergo inevitable change (including objectives, process, and outcomes) in the twenty-first century. Therefore, ultimately, the central question becomes, how effective is probation and parole? Some law and order advocates

argue that probation and parole are necessary and effective mechanisms of social control. However, there is no national standard for measuring the parole or probation success rate, making it difficult to measure the utility of probation and parole in their totality. The U.S. Bureau of Justice Statistics defines *success* as the completion of the terms of supervision without parolees returning to prison or absconding. This definition (expectation), however, does not capture the complexity of the multiple issues surrounding probation and parole.

Effectiveness

As noted above, as the use of probation increases, concerns about outcomes and effectiveness of probation as a correctional alternative also increase. Early studies report high probation failure rates; that is, rearrested, reconvicted, and sent to prison after being on probation (Petersilia, 1985; Vito, 1987; Whitehead, 1991). As for parole, analyzing data for the late twentieth and early twenty-first centuries, a similar failure trend is observed. For instance, in 1983 the Bureau of Justice Statistics reported that 63 percent of released offenders were rearrested within three years, increasing to 68 percent in 1994 (Beck & Shipley, 1989; Lanagan & Levin, 2005), revealing that a high number of parolees do not complete parole supervision. In fact, at the end of the twentieth century, statistics showed that parolees constituted 35 percent of all prison admissions (Beck & Mumola, 1999), and in 2004, 187,000 parolees were revoked and returned to prison as the result of violation of parole rules or commission of a new offense (Glaze & Palla, 2005), suggesting high recidivism rates. Recidivism, however, is difficult to measure. For example, parolees and probationers are often arrested for technical violations, or if the police suspect involvement in crime, or if probationers or parolees live within close proximity to where a crime has been committed. In many of these cases, individuals are never officially charged with any crime, but they are in violation of program conditions which stress that offenders should not be rearrested (Morgan, 1995); again, creating a never-ending cycle of "crime" and imprisonment, while the *control net* continues to get wider and wider.

Probation and Parole: Reentry

In the current era of mass imprisonment with 2.3 million incarcerated in state and federal prisons, with 95 percent of those entering prison eventually released back into the community, another central question becomes: how realistic is reentry for the typical parolee and probationer? A substantial number will be release unconditionally or under mandatory release guidelines without the benefit of pre-release risk assessment or post release custody and supervision. Those released from prison are likely to be over age 35, served longer prison terms, have previous criminal convictions and probation or parole terms, addicted to drugs and alcohol, suffer from various health issues, uneducated, unskilled, and unprepared for jobs that will enable them to "survive" in a competitive and highly technological job market (Urbina, 2008; Urbina & Álvarez, 2017; see also Álvarez & Urbina, Chapter 16, this volume).

Therefore, parolees (and those on probation upon release) returning to the community face many challenges. For instance, although inmates are treated for illnesses while incarcerated, parolees often return with physical and mental health problems, particularly depression and drug addiction, and they lack access to services and treatment after release (Hammett, Roberts, & Kennedy, 2001; Morgan, 2013; Petersilia, 2004; Urbina, 2008; see also Álvarez & Urbina, Chapter 16, this volume). As one of the most critical conditions of probation and parole, employment is one of the toughest challenges for parolees (and those on probation) who have dismal prospects for securing employment. The lack of education, skills, and prospective employers' unwillingness to hire "ex-cons" make getting and keeping employment a complicated issue not only for parolees, but also their family and community. With a prior record, a criminal stigma, poverty, and constant frustration and uncertainty, people are likely to be further push to the margins of society, fueling family violence, crime, and substance abuse. Additionally, probationers, parolees, and other returning prisoners may experience homelessness, loss of voting rights, exclusion from housing areas and professions, and a return to socially disorganized neighborhoods with limited opportunities to succeed, high crime rates, and criminal activities. To address reentry problems and promote public safety, some communities are strengthening supervision of parolees through supervision teams, implementing state and federal reentry programs and collaborating with police departments to assist in finding and providing services to inmates while making parolees accountable (Morgan, 2016; Schmalleger & Smykla, 2011). However, reentry, as a highly complicated and consequential issue, requires strategic planning, innovation, and appropriate funding for programs and services, as detailed in Chapter 16 of this volume.

Due Process Concerns: The Right to Privacy

Beyond the various legal, economic, and social barriers confronting probationers and parolees, as a condition of parole or probation, they must agree to forfeit their Fourth

Amendment right to privacy and allow to be randomly *searched.* This procedure, arguably, provides the criminal justice system with information to determine whether parolees and probationers are possessing drugs, weapons, or committing crimes. Presumably, probation and parole searches not only help in protecting the public, but they enhance rehabilitation efforts since probationers and parolees are less likely to commit crimes if they know that they can be searched at any time, and, if arrested, back to prison, sometimes permanently, under criminal laws like Three Strikes Laws. The Texas Court of Appeal, for instance, quotes that parole (and probation) searches tend to ". . . minimize the risk to the public safety inherent in the conditional release of a convicted offender."

Considering not only the presumed utility of probation and parole searches, but also the implications, manifestations, and ramifications, it is imperative that one understands the conditions and process in which searches and seizures are conducted. To begin, probationers and parolees must agree in writing to be subject to searches or seizures by parole, probation, or police officers at any time of the day or night, with or without a warrant, and with or without probable cause. Typically, officers must have probable cause or reasonable suspicion to believe that a search is warranted before carrying out the search. However, because one objective of parole searches is to insure that parolees (and probationers) are not in possession of the *fruits or instrumentalities* of crime, officers are not required to justify their decision to search.

The requirements for probation or parole searches include: (1) officers must have knowledge that the suspect is on probation or parole; (2) the search must be motivated by a legitimate law enforcement or rehabilitative interest; and (3) the search must be reasonable in its scope and intensity. Most

critically, the courts have expressed that probation and parole searches must not be arbitrary, capricious, or harassing. Legally, the scope of search and seizure is the same for all parolees, a basic rule in all states. The Texas Code, for example, states that officers may search parolees, their residence, their vehicle, and any property under their control. In contrast, the scope of probation searches may vary somewhat because it depends on the terms of the sentencing judge's probation order. Still, the majority of probation searches are essentially the same as the scope of parole searches. This method is sometime called the "four-way" search in that the person, the home, the vehicle, and property under their control are all subject to random searches.

Technically, the search of a home or vehicle is permissible (without consent) if officers have "reason to believe" that the probationer or parolee lives in the residence, either alone or with others. Officers should enter premises in a "reasonable" manner. It appears, therefore, that in most cases officers will comply with the *knock and announce* notice requirement, unless compliance is excused for *good cause.* Officers may search the probationer or parolee's bedroom, all common areas, and all other areas in which the parolee or probationer has exclusive or joint control or keyed access. As for all other rooms, it is prudent to assume that the protective sweep doctrine is permitted if officers reasonably believe that someone inside poses a threat to them. Given the nature of vehicle or home searches, officers may use trained K-9s to assist in the search. In actuality, there are in fact no formal restrictions on what items officers may look for when conducting parole searches, which also applies in most probation searches, normally searching for drugs, weapons, and stolen property. Therefore, if, while conducting a parole or probation search, officers develop probable cause to believe that an item in *plain view* is evidence of a crime, they may seize the item. Lastly, officers searching a parolee or proba-tioner, though, may conduct a "full" search, but it must not be extreme, patently abusive, or destructive.

EVIDENCE-BASED STRATEGIES FOR PROBATION AND PAROLE

As we progress in the twenty-first century, probation and parole, along with imprison-ment, rates continue to be central social con-trol strategies, impacting not only individual offenders but entire communities and soci-ety at large. As such, critics charge that inno-vative mechanisms must be strategically situ-ated to reduced imprisonment, probation, and parole rates, and better manage the pro-bation and parole population, while provid-ing the adequate resources in the areas of ed-ucation, training, healthcare, employment, and supervision.

To begin, we must acknowledge that in the current era of mass incarceration, the expectation has shifted to "effective manage-ment and supervision with fewer resources" (Morgan, 2016:268). Broadly, there are three trends likely to define both probation and parole in the twenty-first century: the re-emergence of rehabilitation, community partnerships, and community justice. Dating back to the 1990s, the awareness that some offenders had special mental health and sub-stance abuse needs and the reentry of pris-oners who were addicted to drugs, mentally ill, or lacking vocational skills fueled an interest in rehabilitation in an attempt to im-prove and return people to society (Reisig, 1998). Therefore, reentry programs were implemented to facilitate prisoners' return to the community and drug courts, mental health courts, and specialized caseloads emerged to address offenders' special needs (Reisig, 1998).

Emphasis has also been placed on strate-gies that work in parole supervision or evi-dence-based practice. One of the effect evi-dence-based strategies for parole supervision has been the use of supervised caseloads. This approach involves placing parolees with special needs in a single caseload that is much smaller than regular caseloads. Some offenders that may be better served through specialized caseloads, like mental health of-fenders, drug and alcohol offenders, sex of-fenders, and domestic violence offenders. Officers supervising these specialized case-loads target the special needs of offenders. However, specialized caseloads go beyond simply placing offenders with similar prob-lems into one caseload. Many of these offi-cers supervising special caseloads develop expertise over time and engage in partner-ships with professionals and treatment spe-cialists to provide offenders more compre-hensive services (Burrell, 2005; Morgan, 2016). Additionally, officers are encouraged to engage in the community and involve the community in the supervision process, and use community-oriented strategies to super-vise offenders, with minimal "intrusion" to avoid, for example, that employed proba-tioners or parole lose their job as a result of unprofessional work visits by officers (Reinventing Probation Council, 2000).

While parole agencies have always col-laborated with community organizations such as police departments, drug treatment centers, employment agencies, and mental health counselors, those partnerships did not become *formal* until recent years (Burrell, 2005; Morgan, 2016). For example, a recent collaboration between probation and parole departments and law enforcement has been Project Safe Neighborhoods, an initiative that promotes collaborations between local, state, and federal law enforcement agencies, corrections, the prosecutor, and the community with the goal of reducing gun crime and violence (Thornton, 2005).

Considering that probation and parole rates are unlikely to reduce *significantly* in the coming years, twenty-first century planning for probation and parole should include greater reliance on technology and specialty courts. Technology can alleviate the problem of prison overcrowding, and provide a better solution to the lack of qualified and trained case managers to deal with the ever-increasing population of probationers and parolees. In fact, with the inclusion of technology and properly trained personnel, one probation officer can care for and track thousands of clients in the same amount of time it takes to monitor 20 people. The cost of monitoring and outfitting a probationer or parolee with a GPS monitoring device, the basic ankle-monitoring bracelet, costs about $9.00 a month to monitor and the newer GPS monitoring device costs about $15.00 a month. The initial cost of a three-part GPS system which includes the ankle bracelet with a radio transmitter, the home unit linking the home phone and ankle bracelet, and the cell phone with GPS antenna is approximately $2,000, much less costly than housing a nonviolent inmate for over $20,000 annually. Probation and parole officers can then use their time more productively, like addressing specific needs of each client and making sure that individual offenders receive the treatment needed to help them when they are no longer under state supervision.

In recent years, *specialty courts* have also emerged as problem-solving courts to address the complex social and psychological problems in cases before the court. These courts (drug courts, domestic violence courts, and mental health courts), developed as a means to provide individuals with a punishment that includes "treatment," normally not provided through the standard criminal justice system. Specialty courts are able to prevent the *bottlenecking* of the judicial system, while giving courts flexibility to sentence offenders based on their specific problems, allowing offenders to receive specific treatment and counseling. The initial cost for creating specialty courts is high, but, in the end, they are in fact effectively preventing people from reentering the criminal justice system, ultimately outweighing the initial high cost. Therefore, as noted by Judge Sergio Gonzalez, who manages a drug specialty court in Del Rio, Texas, specialty courts should be made a priority.

CONCLUSION

Analyzing historical and contemporary trends in imprisonment, probation, and parole, the punitive social control era of criminal justice has definitely emphasized punishment as the primary force for targeting offenders that has resulted in the disproportionate confinement and control beyond the prison of Latinos, blacks, and poor whites. Punitive policies and aggressive enforcement, including *three strikes laws,* mandatory sentencing, the war on drugs, the war on immigrants, and the war on terrorism, have not only significantly increased the correctional population, including probation and parole, but have also resulted in lawsuits and court mandates. Yet, in the era of mass incarceration (Urbina & Álvarez, 2017), some critics question the *severity* of probation and parole, arguing that the punishments are too lenient or little more than a "slap on the wrist" for offenders (Clear & Dammer, 2000), or offenders "getting off" with no punishment.

Other critics question key factors of probation and parole, like the decision-making process, due process, recidivism, monitoring, and rehabilitation (Morgan, 2016; Solomon, Kachnowski, & Bhati, 2005). Other observers are critical of the implications and ramifications of probation and parole, particularly charges of inequality, prejudice, discrimination, and abuse against women as well as ethnic and racial minorities. Senator Edward Kennedy (1979), for instance, once noted that sentencing disparities are compound by parole, since it encourages some judges to impose the kind of harsh sentences that the community expects, exacerbating the disproportionate and negative treatment of Latinos and blacks. Senator Kennedy (1979) remarked that if "flat" or determinate sentencing policies were adopted, parole (and probation) would not be needed to control the offender population where the great majority of offenders are in fact on probation or parole for nonviolent crimes.

Taken together, these differences in probation and parole are likely to result from various forces, organizational and administrative factors, stereotyping, more subtle and indirect forms of prejudice and discrimination, like cognitive bias, and "cumulative discrimination" (Steinmetz & Anderson, 2015: 15). As discovered in other studies testing for race and ethnic effects (Stolzenberg, D'Alessio, & Eitle, 2013; Urbina, 2007, 2012), since most studies analyze race and ethnicity in a singular step (stage) in the criminal justice process, a focus on "episodic discrimination" may not fully capture discrimination at the various stages of the decision-making process. Broader social and structural forces may also impact final outcomes for ethnic and racial minorities. Mexicans, for instance, who make the majority of Latinos in the United States have been

drastically impacted by historical structures and practices that have left a lasting legacy in regards to their economic, political, cultural, and social positioning in the American society, as documented by Urbina and colleagues in *Ethnic Realities of Mexican Americans: From Colonialism to 21st Century Globalization* (2014). As a historically marginalized population, Latinos have been transformed into scapegoats for emerging social ills, including crime, unemployment, economic crises, and various other issues. In fact, we cannot overlook the long history of manipulation, oppression, violence, and hate resulting from the legacy of colonial domination and control. Therefore, economic and social marginalization, oppression, and neglect help shape the material circumstances facing many Latinos, which, in turn influence their experience in, out, and through the criminal justice system–policing, courts, and corrections, including probation and parole.

More recently, under the Trump administration, fears of drug smugglers, immigrants, and terrorism have amplified xenophobia and security concerns, particularly along the U.S.-Mexico border, "prompting" President Trump to build a "big beautiful wall" along the border (Álvarez & Urbina, 2018). Consequently, making ethnic and racial prejudice and discrimination a high priority in public discourse has been a long and complicated endeavor, as a result of various intertwining forces, primarily what Bonilla-Silva (2006) terms "color-blind racism" and what Urbina and Álvarez (2016) characterize as the "historical ethnic and racial profitability of minorities," which has transformed the system into a multibillion enterprise, while some political pundits and intellectual racists passionately act to discredit assertions of racial/ethnic inequality in our alleged post-racial society (Urbina, 2014).

As for the future of probation and parole, considering the current national and transnational punitive movement, which has been expanding the confines of social control, probation and parole will continue to be used as a strategic net-widening mechanism for controlling the offender population—*captivity beyond prisons.* It its totality, let's hope that the probation and parole system will in fact "change lives" through rehabilitation, training, education, employment, healthcare, and appropriate community resources, and not, ultimately, evolve into what has already been characterized as a new form of slavery for blacks and Latinos, with responding collateral consequences for individual offenders, their families, community, and society. Therefore, policymakers, the correctional system, probationers, parolees, the community, and those vested in positive social transformation need to *engage in positive change* for the betterment of the community as a whole. As a starting point, for reintegration to be successful (see Chapter 16, this volume), when inmates are released into the community, the community needs to acknowledge that most of these people are no longer criminals, but individuals who are paying for their past behavior, trying to get rehabilitated, and, in a sense, looking for a *second chance.*

Chapter 15

THE LEGACY OF CAPITAL PUNISHMENT: EXECUTING MEXICANS AND OTHER LATINOS

ILSE AGLAÉ PEÑA AND MARTIN GUEVARA URBINA

Capital punishment turns the state into a murderer. But imprisonment turns the state into a gay dungeon-master.

–Jesse Jackson

As we progress in the twenty-first century, the influence of race, ethnicity, gender, and class in crime and punishment continues to be a pressing issue. In fact, as detailed in previous chapters, with various anti-social control movements, particularly under the Trump administration, the nature of crime and punishment is once again being redefined nationally and abroad. As in the past, this new punitive cycle of social control has revived what seems to be the sanction of last resort when, arguably, all things fail: capital punishment. A closer analysis, though, reveals that executions and capital punishment in general are in fact not directly governed by crime trends, but by the simultaneous interaction of historical and contemporary legacies, conflictive race and ethnic relations, and the influence of various extra-legal factors, like citizenship, nationality, language, and economics. In effect, the history of the death penalty in the United States is a story shaped and reshaped by the race and

ethnicity of the offender and victim, and further fused by various other intertwining factors at different points in time and geography (Baker 2016; Urbina, 2012). However, as a result of traditionally adopting a dichotomous black-white approach of investigation and publication, little is actually known about the ethnic realities of executed Mexicans and other Latinos. This chapter, then, seeks to determine the exact *ethnicity* of Latinos executed in the United States from 2013 to 2017, while focusing on all Latino executions, post-*Gregg* (1976–2017), to better understand the ethnic experience in the current punitive anti-social control movement, including the aggressive anti-Mexican political rhetoric by President Trump. More globally, seeking to better understand the role of ethnicity and race in crime and punishment, in its totality, this chapter also makes note of executions during slavery, female executions, juvenile executions, and the execution of foreign nationals in the United States, dating back to 1608. Invariably, findings in this chapter indicate that the influence of ethnicity and race in the distribution of punishment continues in the twenty-first century.

HOW MANY MEXICANS IS A HORSE WORTH?

While fictitious, the following story illustrates the dynamics of race and ethnicity in the United States by, strategically asking a polemic question. That is, in his novel, *George Washington Gómez* (1990:178–179), renowned Mexican American author Americo Paredes shows the experience of living with conflicting and consequential historical legacies (like conquest, colonialism, slavery, and immigration), while trying to illustrate the influence of race and ethnicity in crime and punishment using a mathematical experiment, where the minor character of Orestes is an immigrant son of an exiled revolutionary intellectual living in a fictitious town called Jonesville in the Rio Grande Valley (Texas) during *la chia,* the Great Depression. Orestes poses the question to his best friend, the novel's protagonist George Washington Gómez, whom everyone calls Gualinto:

[*Orestes:*] "By the way, you know how many Mexicans a horse is worth?"

[*Gualinto:*] "What kind of trick are you setting me up for?"

"No trick. I was just reading the paper, and I figured it out . . . Two men were sentenced in court yesterday here in Jonesville. A Mexican for stealing old man Osuna's prize Arabian stud and a Negro for killing a Mexican in a fight over the price of a bottle of tequila . . . The Mexican got ten years, the Negro two . . . So you would think that before the law in this town a horse is worth five Mexicans."

"It figures."

"But wait. The stolen horse was recovered safe and sound from the Mexican who stole him. Not a scratch on his hides even. While the Mexican the parna [black] killed is stone cold-dead. No way of getting him back to life. What if the Mexican who stole the horse had killed it? He would have got at least twenty years. So you can figure then that the horse is worth ten Mexicans."

"You always were good at arithmetic."

"But that's not all. You know that in murder cases Mexicans and Negros get double the sentence a white man would get. So what if the Mexican had been killed by a Gringo? The Gringo would have got off with a year. One divided into twenty: a Mexican then is worth one-twentieth the value of a horse. But that isn't all of it . . . Chances are that the Gringo's sentence would be suspended. Then how much would a Mexican be worth? What's one-twentieth of zero? Ask El Colorado [red-man, Indian]. He's studying bookkeeping, he ought to know. And shake his hand for me."

THE COLOR OF JUSTICE

The influence of race and ethnicity in crime and punishment continues to be a pressing issue in America, with the distribution of capital punishment being governed by the simultaneous interaction of historical legacies, conflictive race and ethnic relations as well as the influence of *color and economics* (Álvarez & Urbina, 2014; Urbina, 2011, 2012). In effect, the history of executions in the United States is a story shaped and reshaped by race and ethnicity of the offender and victim, and further fused by various other factors at different points in time and space (see Baker, this volume). As such, to further debunk historical myths about the effects of race and ethnicity in capital punishment in the United States, one needs to document the Mexican experience (and, of course, the experience of other ethnic and racial groups), which has been left out from the *pages of history*.

As noted by some scholars, like Adalberto Aguirre and David Baker, for a more holistic examination of capital punishment in America, particularly as we seek to provide a sound interpretation of executions, one needs to look beyond the traditional "black/white" approach, which excludes not only Mexicans, but also the specifics of the various ethnic groups, like Cubans and Puerto Ricans, that constitute the Latino community. Consequently, as a result of adopting a dichotomous approach of theorizing, investigating, and publishing, little is actually known

about executed Mexicans and Latinos in general in the United States since states started executing under the 1976 *Gregg* decision (Urbina, 2004b, 2011, 2012). Of what ethnic group, for instance, were those Latinos who were executed from 1976 to 2017? What were the experiences and characteristics of the individuals executed during this time period, the most crucial death penalty era in modern times? Based on capital punishment studies and the conflictive history of race and ethnic relations between whites and Mexicans (Álvarez & Urbina, 2014; Urbina, 2011, 2012), we would expect that most, if not all, of the Latinos who were executed from 1977 to 2017 were of Mexican heritage. Further, considering the historical legacy of hate in Texas, the "capitol" of capital punishment, we would predict that most, if not all, of the post-*Gregg* executions took place in Texas. Therefore, the main objective of this chapter is to go beyond the black/white traditional approach by disaggregating the group of Latinos who were executed from 1977 to 2017 in the United States, focusing primarily (but not exclusively) on Mexicans and the selected issues that tend to influence the dynamics of capital punishment over time.

CAPITAL PUNISHMENT OVER TIME

An Historical Reminder of Crime and Punishment in America

While sensitive and provoking, to better capture the essence of crime and punishment in modern America, one must obtain an appreciation for the transformations of the United States, which have in one way or another influenced the nature of crime and punishment. After conquest in 1848, for example, violence and brutality against

Mexicans eventually escalated into racial and ethnic oppression comparable to that of African Americans in the Jim Crow South (Urbina, Vela, & Sanchez, 2014; Sanchez, 2016; see Baker, this volume). However, although widely known in the Mexican community and among some scholars, the history of mob violence and lynching, or so-called "illegal" executions, of Mexicans remains relatively unknown to the general public (Acuña, 2015; Allen, Lewis, Litwack,

& Als, 2000; Almaguer, 2008; De León, 1983; Delgado, 2009; Dray, 2002; McWilliams, 1990; Urbina et al., 2014). In fact, despite the recent flourishing of academic investigation, publication, and dialogue on lynching, scholars continue to overlook anti-Mexican violence, with the majority of information focusing on lynching against African Americans. More globally, while people normally tend to hear or associate historical brutality with African Americans, the realities of Mexicans and Latinos in general have been twisted or omitted in both public dialogue and academic discourse, sometimes releasing outright lies (Mirandé, 2005; Noboa, 2005; Pizarro, 2005), eloquently explored by Wendy Leo Moore in *Reproducing Racism: White Space, Elite Law Schools, and Racial Inequality* (2007), Tukufu Zuberi and Eduardo Bonilla-Silva in *White Logic, White Methods: Racism and Methodology* (2008), and Joe R. Feagin in *White Party, White Government: Race, Class, and U.S. Politics* (2012).

Some elements of race and ethnicity in crime and punishment have been traced by some scholars. In one of the few early studies exploring the lynching of Mexicans, Tony Dunbar and Linda Kravitz (1976) found that "For a Mexican living in America from 1882 to 1930, the chance of being a victim of mob violence was equal to those of an African American living in the South." More recently, in a provoking study, "The Lynching of Persons of Mexican Origin or Descent in the United States, 1848–1929" (2003), William D. Carrigan and Clive Webb document "that the danger of lynching for a Mexican resident in the United States was nearly as great, and in some stances greater, than the specter of mob violence for a black person in the American South." More recently, in "The Law of the Noose: A History of Latino Lynching" (2009), constitutional scholar Richard Delgado documents that viciousness, brutality, and hated against La-

tinos, where lynching was strategically used to intimidate, oppress, control, and silence Mexicans and other Latinos.

As for so-called "legal" executions, exploring the impact of race and ethnicity in executions from the late nineteenth century to the later part of the twentieth century (1890 to 1986), Aguirre and Baker (1989, 1997) found that 773 prisoners were executed in the Southwest, with 105 (14%) of the executed people being of Mexican heritage. Then, documenting the role of race and ethnicity in capital punishment for a large part of the twentieth century, reporter Don Reid (1973:109), who witnessed some 190 executions in Texas between 1923 and 1972, the year *Furman* was decided by the U.S. Supreme Court and thus temporally stopping executions, until *Gregg* was decided in 1976, cited:

> it took no study for me to accept that simple, ignorant men committed more crimes of violence than did sophisticated men of means. And, it took but little time to realize that when sophisticated men of means did commit crimes of violence, they seldom were executed for them. Those who were electrocuted were the blacks, Mexican-Americans, the poor whites and whites out of favor in their communities for one reason or another, having nothing to do with the criminal allegations for which they died.

This observation regarding the influence of race and ethnicity in crime and punishment is consistent with Giardini and Farrow (1952), who found that Mexicans constituted the third largest group of individuals under the sentence of death in Texas from 1924 to 1952. In effect, of the 506 men who were placed on death row in Texas between 1924 and 1964, 361 eventually died in the electric chair: 229 blacks, 108 whites, and 23 Mexicans (*San Antonio Express News,* 1999). Together, these investigations reveal the influence of race and ethnicity in capital punishment up until the *Furman* (1972) and *Gregg* (1976) decisions, which set a new era of capital punishment and actual executions (Álvarez & Urbina, 2014; Urbina, 2011, 2012), and thus Latino executions are examined in this chapter.

Mexicans/Latinos Executed, 1977–2017

First, the focus of this chapter on executed Latinos from 1977 to 2017 in the United States is because no one was actually executed between 1973 and 1976 as a result of the *Furman* (1972) decision by the Supreme Court. In fact, the first post-*Gregg* (1976) execution took place on January 17, 1977, with the last on November 8, 2017, during the time frame of this study.

Second, of the 1,465 individuals who have been executed in the United States since *Gregg* (1976), 545 were executed in Texas, followed by Virginia (113) and Oklahoma (112), constituting a high percentage of executions nationwide. Of the 1,465 nationwide executions from *Gregg* to 2017, 122 were Latino executions, identified as "white" or "black" Latino men. As noted in Table 15.1, of the 122 Latino executions nationwide, the majority (103) of Latinos were executed in Texas. As such, of the 122 executed Latinos in the United States from 1977 to 2017, 115 were executed in states (Texas, Florida, and Arizona) containing a high concentration of Latinos, and thus accounting for the majority of Latino executions nationwide. As for the exact ethnicity of Latinos executed from 1977 to 2017, the great majority were of Mexican heritage, as reported in Table 15.1.

Table 15.1
LATINOS EXECUTED IN THE UNITED STATES, 1977–2017

#	Name	Date of Execution	State of Execution	Defendant/Victim Race-Ethnicity	Method of Execution
1.	Jesse de la Rosa	May 15, 1985	Texas	Mexican/Asian	Lethal Injection
2.	Henry Martinez Porter	Jul. 09, 1985	Texas	Mexican/White	Lethal Injection
3.	Rudy Esquivel	Jun. 09, 1986	Texas	Mexican/White	Lethal Injection
4.	Richard Andrade	Dec. 18, 1986	Texas	Mexican/Latino	Lethal Injection
5.	Ramon Hernandez	Jan. 30, 1987	Texas	Mexican/Latino	Lethal Injection
6.	Elisio Moreno	Mar. 04, 1987	Texas	Mexican/White	Lethal Injection
7.	Dale Pierre Selby*	Aug. 28, 1987	Utah	Unknown/3 White	Lethal Injection
8.	Aubrey Adams*	May 04, 1989	Florida	Unknown/White	Electrocution
9.	Carlos de Luna	Dec. 07, 1989	Texas	Mexican/Latino	Lethal Injection
10.	Ignacio Cuevas	May 23, 1991	Texas	Mexican/2 White	Lethal Injection
11.	Joe Angel Cordova	Jan. 22, 1992	Texas	Mexican/White	Lethal Injection
12.	Jesus Romero	May 20, 1992	Texas	Mexican/Latino	Lethal Injection
13.	Carlos Santana	Mar. 23, 1993	Texas	Dominican/Latino	Lethal Injection

continued

Table 15.1–*Continued*

#	Name	Date of Execution	State of Execution	Defendant/Victim Race-Ethnicity	Method of Execution
14.	Ramon Montoya Facunda	Mar. 25, 1993	Texas	Mexican/White	Lethal Injection
15.	Leonel Torres Herrera	May 12, 1993	Texas	Mexican/Latino	Lethal Injection
16.	Ruben Cantu	Aug. 24, 1993	Texas	Mexican/Latino	Lethal Injection
17.	Jessie Gutierrez	Sep. 16, 1994	Texas	Mexican/White	Lethal Injection
18.	Mario S. Marquez	Jan. 17, 1995	Texas	Mexican/Latino	Lethal Injection
19.	Esequel Banda	Dec. 11, 1995	Texas	Mexican/White	Lethal Injection
20.	Luis Mata	Aug. 22, 1996	Arizona	Mexican/Latino	Lethal Injection
21.	Joe Gonzales	Sep. 18, 1996	Texas	Mexican/White	Lethal Injection
22.	Pedro Medina	Mar. 25, 1997	Florida	Cuban/Black	Electrocution
23.	Davis Losada	Jun. 04, 1997	Texas	Mexican/Latino	Lethal Injection
24.	Irineo Tristan Montoya	Jun. 18, 1997	Texas	Mexican/White	Lethal Injection
25.	Mario Benjamin Murphy	Sep. 17, 1997	Virginia	Mexican/White	Lethal Injection
26.	Jose Jesus Ceja	Jan. 21, 1998	Arizona	Mexican/Latino, White	Lethal Injection
27.	Angel Francisco Breard	Apr. 14, 1998	Virginia	Paraguayan/White	Lethal Injection
28.	Jose Villafuerte	Apr. 22, 1998	Arizona	Honduran/Latino	Lethal Injection
29.	Pedro Cruz Muniz	May 19, 1998	Texas	Mexican/White	Lethal Injection
30.	Leopoldo Narvaiz	Jun. 26, 1998	Texas	Mexican/4 White	Lethal Injection
31.	Genaro Ruiz Camacho	Aug. 26, 1998	Texas	Mexican/Black	Lethal Injection
32.	David Castillo	Sep. 23, 1998	Texas	Mexican/Latino	Lethal Injection
33.	Javier Cruz	Oct. 01, 1998	Texas	Mexican/2 White	Lethal Injection
34.	Roderick Abeyta*	Oct. 05, 1998	Nevada	Unknown/White	Lethal Injection
35.	Martin Vega	Jan. 26, 1999	Texas	Mexican/Latino	Lethal Injection
36.	George Cordova	Feb. 10, 1999	Texas	Mexican/Latino	Lethal Injection
37.	Andrew Cantu	Feb. 16, 1999	Texas	Mexican/3 White	Lethal Injection
38.	Jose De La Cruz	May 04, 1999	Texas	Mexican/Latino	Lethal Injection
39.	Joseph Trevino	Aug. 18, 1999	Texas	Mexican/Latino	Lethal Injection
40.	Ignacio Ortiz	Oct. 27, 1999	Arizona	Mexican/Latino	Lethal Injection
41.	Jose Gutierrez	Nov. 18, 1999	Texas	Mexican/White	Lethal Injection
42.	Paul Selso Nuncio	Jun. 15, 2000	Texas	Mexican/White	Lethal Injection

continued

Table 15.1–*Continued*

#	Name	Date of Execution	State of Execution	Defendant/Victim Race-Ethnicity	Method of Execution
43.	Jesse San Miguel	Jun. 29, 2000	Texas	Mexican/White	Lethal Injection
44.	Juan Soria	Jul. 26, 2000	Texas	Mexican/White	Lethal Injection
45.	Oliver Cruz	Aug. 09, 2000	Texas	Mexican/White	Lethal Injection
46.	Miguel Flores	Nov. 09, 2000	Texas	Mexican/White	Lethal Injection
47.	Edward Castro	Dec. 07, 2000	Florida	Mexican/White	Lethal Injection
48.	Adolph Hernandez	Feb. 08, 2001	Texas	Mexican/Latino	Lethal Injection
49.	Juan Raul Garza	Jun. 19, 2001	Federal	Mexican/3 Latino	Lethal Injection
50.	Jose Santellan	Apr. 10, 2002	Texas	Mexican/Latino	Lethal Injection
51.	Rodolfo Hernandez	Apr. 30, 2002	Texas	Mexican/Latino	Lethal Injection
52.	Johnny Martinez	May 22, 2002	Texas	Mexican/White	Lethal Injection
53.	Javier Suarez Medina	Aug. 14, 2002	Texas	Mexican/Latino	Lethal Injection
54.	Rigoberto Sanchez-Velasco	Oct. 02, 2002	Florida	Cuban/Latino	Lethal Injection
55.	Leonard Rojas	Dec. 04, 2002	Texas	Mexican/1 White, 1 Latino	Lethal Injection
56.	John Baltazar	Jan. 15, 2003	Texas	Mexican/Latino	Lethal Injection
57.	John William Elliott*	Feb. 04, 2003	Texas	Unknown/Latino	Lethal Injection
58.	Juan Chávez	Apr. 22, 2003	Texas	Mexican/Latino	Lethal Injection
59.	Andrew Flores	Sep. 21, 2004	Texas	Mexican/Latino	Lethal Injection
60.	Peter Miniel*	Oct. 06, 2004	Texas	Unknown/White	Lethal Injection
61.	Anthony Fuentes	Nov. 17, 2004	Texas	Mexican/White	Lethal Injection
62.	Alexander Martinez	Jun. 07, 2005	Texas	Mexican/Latino	Lethal Injection
63.	David Aaron Martinez	Jul. 28, 2005	Texas	Mexican/White	Lethal Injection
64.	Luis Ramirez	Oct. 20, 2005	Texas	Mexican/Latino	Lethal Injection
65.	Jaime Elizalde	Jan. 31, 2006	Texas	Mexican/2 Latino	Lethal Injection
66.	Robert Salazar Jr.	Mar. 22, 2006	Texas	Mexican/Latino	Lethal Injection
67.	Jackie Barron Wilson*	May 04, 2006	Texas	Unknown/White	Lethal Injection
68.	Jesus Aguilar	May 24, 2006	Texas	Mexican/2 Latino	Lethal Injection
69.	Angel Maturino Resendiz	Jun. 27, 2006	Texas	Mexican/Latino	Lethal Injection
70.	Richard Hinojosa	Aug. 17, 2006	Texas	Mexican/White	Lethal Injection
71.	Angel Diaz	Dec. 13, 2006	Florida	Puerto Rican/White	Lethal Injection

continued

Table 15.1–*Continued*

#	Name	Date of Execution	State of Execution	Defendant/Victim Race-Ethnicity	Method of Execution
72.	Carlos Granados	Jan. 10, 2007	Texas	Mexican/Latino	Lethal Injection
73.	Robert Perez	Mar 06, 2007	Texas	Mexican/2 Latino	Lethal Injection
74.	Vincent Gutierrez	Mar. 28, 2007	Texas	Mexican/Latino	Lethal Injection
75.	Lionell Rodriguez	Jun. 20, 2007	Texas	Mexican/Asian	Lethal Injection
76.	Gilberto Reyes	Jun. 21, 2007	Texas	Mexican/White, Latino	Lethal Injection
77.	John Joe Amador	Aug. 29, 2007	Texas	Mexican/White	Lethal Injection
78.	Jose Ernesto Medellin	Aug. 05, 2008	Texas	Mexican/1 White, 1 Latino	Lethal Injection
79.	Heliberto Chi	Aug. 07, 2008	Texas	Honduran/White	Lethal Injection
80.	Michael Rodriguez	Aug. 14, 2008	Texas	Mexican/White	Lethal Injection
81.	Virgil Martinez	Jan. 28, 2009	Texas	Mexican/4 Latino	Lethal Injection
82.	Ricardo Ortiz	Jun. 29, 2009	Texas	Mexican/Latino	Lethal Injection
83.	David Martinez	Feb. 04, 2009	Texas	Mexican/2 Latino	Lethal Injection
84.	James Edgard Martinez	Mar. 10, 2009	Texas	Puerto Rican/ 2 White	Lethal Injection
85.	Luis Cervantes Salazar	Mar. 11, 2009	Texas	Mexican/Latino	Lethal Injection
86.	Michael Rosales	Apr. 15, 2009	Texas	Mexican/Black	Lethal Injection
87.	Yosvanis Valle	Nov. 10, 2009	Texas	Cuban/Latino	Lethal Injection
88.	Michael Sigala	Mar. 2, 2010	Texas	Mexican/2 Latino	Lethal Injection
89.	Samuel Bustamante	Apr. 27, 2010	Texas	Mexican/Latino	Lethal Injection
90.	Rogelio Cannady	May 19, 2010	Texas	Mexican/Latino	Lethal Injection
91.	John Alba	May 25, 2010	Texas	Mexican/Latino	Lethal Injection
92.	Peter Cantu	Aug. 17, 2010	Texas	Mexican/2 White	Lethal Injection
93.	Humberto Leal	July 7, 2011	Texas	Mexican/Latino	Lethal Injection
94.	Martin Robles	Aug. 10, 2011	Texas	Mexican/2 Latino	Lethal Injection
95.	Manuel Valle	Sep. 28, 2011	Florida	Cuban/Latino	Lethal Injection
96.	Frank Martinez Garcia	Oct. 27, 2011	Texas	Mexican/2 Latino	Lethal Injection
97.	Guadalupe Esparza	Nov. 16, 2011	Texas	Mexican/Latino	Lethal Injection
98.	Rodrigo Hernandez	Jan. 26, 2012	Texas	Mexican/White	Lethal Injection
99.	George Rivas	Feb. 29, 2012	Texas	Mexican/White	Lethal Injection

continued

Table 15.1–*Continued*

#	Name	Date of Execution	State of Execution	Defendant/Victim Race-Ethnicity	Method of Execution
100.	Jesse Joe Hernandez	Mar. 28, 2012	Texas	Mexican/Latino	Lethal Injection
101.	Samuel López	Jun. 27, 2012	Arizona	Mexican/Latino	Lethal Injection
102.	Ramon Torres Hernandez	Nov. 14, 2012	Texas	Unknown/Latino	Lethal Injection
103.	George Ochoa	Dec. 04, 2012	Oklahoma	Mexican/2 Latino	Lethal Injection
104.	John Quintanilla	Jul. 16, 2013	Texas	Mexican/Latino	Lethal Injection
105.	Robert Garza	Sep. 19, 2013	Texas	Mexican/4 Latino	Lethal Injection
106.	Arturo Eleazar Diaz	Sep. 26, 2013	Texas	Mexican/White	Lethal Injection
107.	Edgar Tamayo	Jan. 22, 2014	Texas	Mexican/White	Lethal Injection
108.	Juan Chávez	Feb. 02, 2014	Florida	Cuban/White	Lethal Injection
109.	Ramiro Hernandez	Apr. 09, 2014	Texas	Mexican/White	Lethal Injection
110.	Jose Villegas	Apr. 16, 2014	Texas	Mexican/3 Latino	Lethal Injection
111.	Miguel Paredes	Oct. 28, 2014	Texas	Mexican/2 Latino, 1 White	Lethal Injection
112.	Arnold Prieto Jr.	Jan. 21, 2015	Texas	Mexican/2 Latino, 1 White	Lethal Injection
113.	Manuel Vasquez	Mar. 11, 2015	Texas	Mexican/Latino	Lethal Injection
114.	Manuel Garza Jr.	Apr. 15, 2015	Texas	Mexican/Latino	Lethal Injection
115.	Daniel Lee López	Aug. 12, 2015	Texas	Salvadoran/White	Lethal Injection
116.	Alfredo Rolando Prieto	Oct. 01, 2015	Virginia	Salvadoran/ 2 White	Lethal Injection
117.	Juan Martin Garcia	Oct. 06, 2015	Texas	Salvadoran/Latino	Lethal Injection
118.	Licho Escamilla	Oct. 14, 2015	Texas	Mexican/White	Lethal Injection
119.	Gustavo Julian Garcia	Feb. 16, 2016	Texas	Unknown/White	Lethal Injection
120.	Pablo Lucio Vasquez	Apr. 06, 2016	Texas	Guatemalan/Latino	Lethal Injection
121.	Rolando Ruiz	Mar. 07, 2017	Texas	Mexican/Latino	Lethal Injection
122.	Ruben Ramirez Cardenas	Nov. 8, 2017	Texas	Mexican/Latino	Lethal Injection

Latino executions by state and jurisdiction: Texas (103), Florida (7), Arizona (5), Virginia (3), Nevada (1), Oklahoma (1), Utah (1), and Federal (1).

Mexican:	99	Honduran:	2	Guatemalan:	1
Cuban:	5	Puerto Rican:	2	Paraguayan:	1
Salvadoran:	3	Dominican:	1	Unknown:	8

*Classified as unknown because it was not possible to trace them to Latino heritage, or trace their exact ethnicity.

National Origin, Citizenship, and Ethnic Identity

Again, unlike blacks and whites, establishing ethnic identity, citizenship, or national origin is critically complicated largely because of how information is collected and compiled (Urbina, 2007), combined with social changes, like diversity and multiculturalism and emerging trends in imprisonment, as documented by Urbina *Twenty-First Century Dynamics of Multiculturalism: Beyond Post-Racial America* (2014) and Urbina and Álvarez in *Ethnicity and Criminal Justice in the Era of Mass Incarceration: A Critical Reader on the Latino Experience* (2017). Among the various issues, we will make note of some of the more pressing issues in the data gathering process, utilizing a few selected death penalty stories to illustrate the complexity of delineating ethnic information; that is, discovering the exact ethnicity of executed Latinos, as we seek to better understand the role of ethnicity in capital punishment.

As for ethnic identity, one of the Mexican defendants, for example, executed on December 11, 1995, was once identified by a Yaqui-Mexican as part Yaqui Indian and part Mexican (Hayes, 1999a), making it difficult to determine if indeed he was Mexican.[23] As for citizenship, some of the Mexican defendants could have been U.S. citizens, but actually classified themselves as "Mexican" in formal documents or verbal dialogue (Álvarez & Urbina, 2014), resulting in possible confusion as to whether they were U.S. citizens or foreign nationals. In regards to national origin, some of the executed Mexicans were in fact Mexican nationals (Álvarez & Urbina, 2014).

As an illustration of the complexity of establishing ethnic identity, citizenship, or national origin, consider the story of two executed Latinos. For these two individuals,

the evidence indicates that one person was executed (apparently under the identity of a "white" Latino) in Florida in 1989 and the other (apparently under the identity of a "black" Latino) in Utah in 1987. We, however, were unable to find evidence tying these individuals to a specific ethnic group or to Latino heritage. These two individuals, though, are worth noting for several reasons, especially the fashion in which they were treated by the media and the criminal justice system.

According to one observer, who lived approximately 30 miles from where the Florida murder was committed, and who attended the trial for several days, the defendant, Aubrey Adams, was born in New Mexico but moved to Florida as a child (Hayes, 1999b). Hayes (1999b) found that the Florida school and state employment records had "white-Hispanic" and "white-non-Hispanic" on the forms then, but everything in his records indicated strictly "white"; that is, Caucasian and not "white" Latino (or "white" Mexican), as Mexicans are "white," by law, an intriguing historical element, as vividly documented by Ian F. Haney López in *White by Law: The Legal Construction of Race* (2006). Hayes (1999b), who also followed the proceedings of this particular death row inmate in various newspapers found no evidence of Latino heritage for this Florida execution, revealing the difficulty of locating information containing explicit ethnicity, and thus the complexity of conducting research on Latinos.

The death row inmate, Dale Pierre Selby, executed in Utah in 1987 is also worth noting. Based on the inmate's data file (including appeals), Selby was born in Trinidad, and there is some indication that "he MAY have been 'Indian [and] Black' but nothing to indicate that he was in any way Hispanic" (Hayes, 1999b). Kinder (1982:81) notes that

Selby was once identified by an air force official as a "young black airman, a twenty-year-old Trinidadian named." In effect, Kinder (1982) found that Selby was born in the isle of Tobago, which lies in the azure waters of the Caribbean east of Venezuela, and lived there until three. Twenty miles to the southwest of Tobago is Trinidad, where Dale, who often received a "good licking" grew up (Kinder, 1982:238).[24] There are, however, three important caveats regarding this particular inmate. First, Dale spoke some Spanish and while in San Antonio, Texas he "managed to fall in love with a Mexican" (Kinder, 1982:250). This could have led to the "Latino" identification. Second, the charge to the county by his attorneys was "perhaps the lowest fee in the state's history for a case of this magnitude" (Kinder, 1982:290), bringing into question the influence of money, or lack of. Third, suggesting the role of race/ethnicity in crime and punishment, while a note was passed to a juror that read "hang the niggers," the judge denied a mistrial and he was convicted by an all-white (Caucasian) jury (*Chicago Daily Law Bulletin,* 1992:1), bringing into question the "color of justice," and, more fundamentally, the legitimacy of American justice.

As such, since it was impossible to trace these two individuals to a specific ethnic group or to Latino heritage, these two inmates were classified, along with six other individuals whose exact ethnicity was not possible to identify, as "unknown" Latino origin. As for these two noted inmates, executed in Florida and Utah, this conclusion is supported by Culver (1992:59) who claims that "Texas is the only state to have executed Hispanics" between 1977 and 1990. In all, while the task of locating the exact ethnicity of executed Latinos from 1977 to 2017 was tedious and laborious, only eight had to be classified as unknown because of the inability to locate their ethnicity. Again, as report-

ed in Table 15.1, of the 122 executed Latinos, 99 were Mexican, 5 Cuban, 3 Salvadoran, 2 Honduran, 2 Puerto Rican, 1 Dominican, 1 Guatemalan, 1 Paraguayan, and 8 of unknown ethnicity.

Characteristics of Executed Mexicans and other Latinos

As documented in previous chapters, the experience of blacks, whites, Mexicans, and other racial and ethnic groups tends to be shaped and reshaped by various historical forces. In the area of crime and punishment, here are some of the more pressing characteristics of executed Latinos from 1977 to 2017; or, more precisely, analyze the characteristics of Mexican death row inmates since the great majority of executed Latinos were of Mexican heritage. First, considering the often cited fear by white America, the majority of victims were actually Latino, with the rest being non-Latino, black, Asian, or white, indicating that most homicides were Latino-on-Latino, as reported in Table 15.1. Second, most death row inmates had prior criminal records, which, of course, is part of the typical profile of people who get arrested, indicted, prosecuted, convicted, sentenced, sent to jail or prison, and, in capital punishment cases, executed. Third, while some defendants remained under the sentence of death for only a few months before the execution was carried out, most stayed on death row for several years before they were executed, which is also typical of the majority of all executions in America, putting the utility of executions in question.

Fourth, every executed Latino, especially the Mexican defendants, had non-professional jobs, if they were employed prior to their arrest, with the majority of defendants being young at the time of the crime, uneducated, and sometimes their income was "just barely enough to get by" (Álvarez & Urbina,

2014), revealing that if defendants were not indigent at the time of their arrest, they were soon indigent due to resource considerations. In effect, according to an attorney who witnessed one of the executions: "I think it [capital punishment] is at best extremely arbitrary, at worst extremely discriminatory against the poor" (*New York Times,* 1995:24).

Fifth, in American jurisprudence, an essential legal element in judicial proceedings is the defendant's ability to be "competent" to stand trial. Yet, based on social history, where information was available, some of the defendants were "mildly mentally retarded" or some suffered from "severe brain impairment" (Álvarez & Urbina, 2014), a common element found among the incarcerated population (Urbina, 2008). For instance, Mario Márquez, a Mexican executed in Texas for killing his 18-year-old wife and 14-year-old niece, had an IQ below 70, which is considered mentally retarded (Álvarez & Urbina, 2014). In fact, it's reported that Márquez "had an IQ estimated at 65, with adaptive skills of a 7 year old" (Keyes, Edwards, & Perske, 1999:3). Charged with rape and murder, Miguel Ángel Flores, another Mexican, was represented by a court-appointed lawyer who was unable to speak Spanish, with the defense final argument at the sentencing phase taking less than ten minutes, when normally it can take up to three hours. The defense attorney actually argued against Miguel's only hope of avoiding a death sentence, and the jury never learned of Miguel's mental impairments. Critically, even the prosecution objected to the defense "speech" as a misstatement of the law.

Sixth, executed Latinos tend to have a lengthy history of chronic alcohol abuse and extensive drug use (Álvarez & Urbina, 2014), also a common trait among incarcerated people, situations that seem to worsen stress and depression, which in turn led to suicidal thoughts and even suicide (Urbina, 2008).

Seventh, some Latino defendants did not show signs of remorse, which in part contributed to the execution (Álvarez & Urbina, 2014; Urbina, 2004b). Perhaps more than a sign of viciousness, the lack of remorse could be due in part to the very nature of Latino criminality and punishment, as in the case of Henry Martínez Porter, a Mexican executed in Texas for the slaying of Fort Worth police officer Henry Mailloux: ". . . I shot a man who shot me first" (*San Diego Union-Tribune,* 1985:4). More globally, "acceptance of criminal responsibility," or remorse, varies by race and ethnicity. In effect, considering powerful historical forces, including American criminal law, combined with various other reasons, like cultural standards of appropriate behavior, quality of legal representation, and intercultural and legal miscommunication (Urbina, 2004b), black and Latino defendants are thought to be less likely to express remorse than Caucasian defendants.

Eighth, of the 122 Latinos executed from 1977 to 2017, several death row inmates claimed innocence. For instance, the final words of Lionel Herrera, a Mexican executed in Texas for killing a police officer, were: "I am innocent, innocent, innocent. Make no mistake about this. I owe society nothing. I am an innocent man and something very wrong is taking place tonight" (*Houston Chronicle,* 1993a:1), not an unrealistic claim in that a significant number of death row inmates have now been found innocent through the application of DNA and other investigative techniques (as in the case of Illinois during the last few years), not to mention the number of innocent people who have been executed. In this regard, several Mexican nationals currently on death row in Texas claim innocence (Álvarez & Urbina, 2014; Urbina, 2012). As such, Mexico and some other countries have not extradited fugitives on some occasions unless the death sentence was waived in the United States

(Álvarez & Urbina, 2014; Urbina, 2011, 2012), as illustrated by the highly publicized Florida case involving José Luis Del Toro, who fled to Mexico after committing a murder in Florida.[25]

Lastly, some of the executed Mexicans were not only represented by inadequate counsel, but at times no Mexican American or other minority jurors served on the petitioner's trial jury (Álvarez & Urbina, 2014), an historical situation significantly influencing the role of race and ethnicity in crime and punishment (López, 2003, Urbina, 2012; see Mirandé, Chapter 10, this volume). For instance, Rudy Esquivel was sentenced to death by an all-white jury and executed in Texas in 1986, and Ramon Mata died on death row in Texas in 2000 after 15 years under a death sentence imposed by an all-white jury. Their frustration was summed up by Henry Porter of San Antonio, Texas, executed in 1985 after being on death row

for nearly eight years: "They call it equal justice, but it's your justice . . . a Mexican life is worth nothing" (*New York Times,* 1985:11), in a sense, resonating the essence of the question in the beginning of this chapter, "How many Mexicans is a horse worth?" More globally, Pat Clark, executive director of Death Penalty Focus, made the following observation: "it's interesting that many folks consider the United States a more civilized country than Mexico and yet Mexico doesn't have such a barbaric penalty" (*San Francisco Chronicle,* 1993a:15).[26] In all, even though it's difficult to mathematically quantify the role of race and ethnicity in crime and punishment based on this descriptive information, executed Mexicans (and the other executed Latinos) seem to have defining characteristics, distinguishing them from both black and white death row inmates facing execution or receiving a commutation, as reported below.

THE SIGNIFICANCE OF COMMUTATIONS IN CAPITAL PUNISHMENT

As in executions, the possible influence of race and ethnicity in commutation decisions ought to be examined to control for possible race and ethnic effects. Indeed, in a battle against time and the government to avoid execution, commutations have been viewed by some as "hope," as a last "possibility" of not losing an additional life, or as some would say, another murder in the hands of the state. However, while there was widespread pressure for the commutation of several Latino defendants, especially Mexican nationals, based largely on claims of ethnic discrimination, violation of civil rights, violation of international treaties, innocence, lack of adequate financial and legal representation, mental illness, youth at the time of the offense, irreversibility of mistakes, or a history of chronic drug abuse and neglect of the

defendants, the executions were carried out, particularly in Texas.

In exploring the significance of race and ethnicity from an international context, it seems that the majority of foreign nationals, most of them being Mexican (Álvarez & Urbina, 2014; Urbina, 2011, 2012), sentenced to death in the United States from 1977 to 2017 have been convicted in violation of their rights (Article 36) under the Vienna Convention of 1963 (Álvarez & Urbina, 2014; *Amnesty International,* 1999; *National Law Journal,* 1998; Urbina, 2004b, Vandiver, 1999; Warren, 1999). Article 36, which requires authorities in the country where people are arrested to notify their country (e.g., consulate, State Department) within 12 hours of the arrest, of the Vienna Convention on Consular Relations is an international treaty that became U.S. law in 1969.

However, some legal experts claim that the United States has followed a double standard in the application of international law. For instance, Robert Brooks, a Virginia attorney who represented Mario Benjamin Murphy, a Mexican national executed in Virginia for the murder-for-hire slaying of a U.S. Navy cook, reports that "the State Department maintains a double standard when applying Article 36" (Halperin, 1997:6). According to Brooks, while the "State Department insists on being notified whenever Americans are jailed abroad and that while failure to comply with Article 36 within 12 hours of an arrest is grounds for diplomatic protest, it allows the law to go unheeded when foreign nationals are arrested in the United States" (Halperin, 1997:6), an issue that tends to bring out the passion, hatred, and hypocrisy of some people when the situation involves Mexico and the United States (Álvarez & Urbina, 2014; Urbina & Smith, 2007). In effect, critics report that "People are going to death in violation of every article . . . in every case; Mexican consulates were not notified until after their citizens had been convicted and given the death sentence" (Halperin, 1997:6). Contrast this with the 1994 caning of Michael Fay, an 18-year-old male from Ohio who was lashed four times on his bare buttocks with a rattan cane in Singapore for vandalizing cars. Before the sentence was carried out, there was an enormous outcry from Americans expressed in the U.S. media; again, a common reaction in the United States when something happens to Americans in Mexico, while thousands of abuses are routinely taking place against Mexicans in the United States, with many such abuses implemented by the very agents of the law (Álvarez & Urbina, 2018; Urbina & Álvarez, 2017).

Notably, during the 40 years under study, 1977–2017, when Mexican nationals approached their execution date, the Mexican government (including the President and state governors), protestors on both sides of the border, organizations like the League of Latin American Citizens, religious groups, and international organizations called on the governor to commute the sentences (Álvarez & Urbina, 2014; Urbina, 2004b), often citing the effect of race and ethnicity in capital punishment.

The Story of Three Mexican Nationals on Death Row

Ramon Montoya Facunda, executed in Texas in 1993 for killing a Dallas police officer, was the first Mexican citizen executed in the U.S. post-*Gregg* (1976). Montoya spent more than a decade on death row without any contact with the Mexican consulate. When Mexican authorities finally learned of his case, Montoya's legal appeals were nearly over and the only remaining option was to appeal for clemency. Being the first Mexican national to be executed in Texas in 51 years, there were worldwide protestations, as cited by various news stories. On behalf of Montoya, the Mexican National Human Rights Commission, the Vatican, as well as the National Network of Civil Rights Organizations made up of more than 30 Mexican groups called for a reprieve, not challenging his guilt, but only objecting to the death sentence, which was viewed as prejudiced, racist, repugnant, and barbarous (Álvarez & Urbina, 2014).

Irineo Tristan Montoya, executed in 1997 for apparently killing South Padre Island businessman John Kilheffer, was the second Mexican citizen executed in the United States since Ramon Montoya was put to death in 1993. Notably, "after a lengthy police interrogation conducted without the beefit of counsel," Tristan, who was 18 at the time of the crime, "reportedly signed a four-page confession in English, a language he did not speak, read, or write." As such, a director of Comité Nacional de La Raza expressed his concerns about the mechanics of capital punishment in America:

> This is the global aspect–not only are we trying to save the life of an innocent man and how he was used as a scapegoat–but it's also a protest of the justice system that is discriminatorily used against people of color. (cited in Álvarez & Urbina, 2014:280)

Reporting Tristan's execution, "Today, They Killed Him," reported a Mexico City newspaper, while the headline in *La Jornada,* a leading Mexico City daily newspaper, read: "Indignation!"

In the case of a third Mexican national, José Ernesto Medellin, executed in 2008 for the murder of Jennifer Ertman and Elizabeth Peña, Medellin gained international notoriety when Mexico sued the United States in the International Court of Justice on behalf of 51 Mexican nationals indicating that the United States had violated Article 36. Originally, the U.S. government argued that Mexico's suit was "an unjustified, unwise and ultimately unacceptable intrusion in the United States criminal justice system," but reversed its position shortly. The U.S. Supreme Court agreed to hear the case on May 1, 2007, but dismissed the case to allow Texas to comply with the U.S. government directive. The Texas Court of Criminal Appeals refused to change its decision, with one judge accusing the White House of an "unprecedented, unnecessary and intrusive exercise of power over the Texas court system." In response, the George W. Bush administration (2001–2009) asked the U.S. Supreme Court to overturn the Texas court's decision, with the U.S. government telling the justices that the Texas court's decision, if not reversed, "will place the United States in breach of its international law obligation" to

comply with the International Court of Justice's decision and that it would "frustrate the president's judgment that foreign policy interests are best served by giving effect to that decision." The Court rejected the Bush Administration's arguments and on July 16, 2008, the International Court of Justice asked for a stay of execution on behalf of Medellin and four other Mexican nationals whom they claimed did not receive a fair trial. However, on July 17, 2008, a spokesperson for Texas Governor Rick Perry said that the state would continue with the execution and that "The world court has no standing in Texas and Texas is not bound by a ruling or edict from a foreign court. It is easy to get caught up in discussions of international law and justice and treaties. It's very important to remember that these individuals are on death row for killing our citizens." Again, these cases not only illustrate the complexity of executions and the global nature of capital punishment, but also defined elements and characteristics of Mexican inmates.

Of course, such characterizations are not only related to the situation of Mexican nationals, but also Mexican Americans and Latinos in general. For instance, the case of Leonel Herrera, a Mexican American executed in 1993, also brought national and international protestations on the grounds of innocence (Álvarez & Urbina, 2014), with elements paralleling cases involving Mexican nationals.

Together, independent of nationality and over the protestations of the Mexican government and national and international organizations, Mexican citizens and Mexican Americans have been executed, often under extremely questionable circumstances, with some cases receiving wide publicity, while in others, total silence (Álvarez & Urbina, 2014). In the case of Ramon Montoya, for example, outside the Texas prison unit where the execution took place, protestors held candles and chanted in Spanish, "Justice! and "Life, not death!" The demonstration was the largest in several years for a Texas execution (*Houston Chronicle,* 1993b). At other times, though, "there were no conferences . . . no Hollywood stars speaking out for [death row inmates] . . . no international attention riveted on [their] case . . . no speeches . . . no rallies" (Álvarez & Urbina, 2014; Urbina, 2004b; *Washington Post,* 1993:9).

At the end, for some death row inmates of Mexican heritage, the bold headline across the front page of *La Jornada* summarized the end result after the death sentence of Ramon Montoya, for instance, was carried out in one word: **"EXECUTED."** Other Mexico City newspapers, like El Nacional, made similar statements and criticized the execution on various grounds, but, primarily, the influence of race and ethnicity in crime and punishment. In the United States, Ramon Montoya's lawyer made the following observation of the action by the Mexican government on behalf of Montoya and other Mexicans on death row: "they have done everything you could ask a Government to do . . .

unfortunately, to use the vernacular of Texas, Mr. Montoya is a wetback who killed a white cop" (*Los Angeles Times,* 1994; *New York Times,* 1993:19), resonating the role of race and ethnicity in capital punishment in America (Urbina, 2012).

Foreign Nationals on Death Row in the United States

As reported in cross-national studies, in this new era of crime and punishment, capital punishment has truly become a legal sanction that transcends borders and justice systems, with race and ethnicity being central elements in the judicial process (Ruddell & Urbina, 2004, 2007). In effect, with the globalization of crime and punishment, the current trend of executing foreign nationals and the ethnic profile discussed above is likely to continue. As of December 23, 2017, there are 135 foreign nationals currently under the sentence of death in the United States, and while there are people from 35 different countries, most (86) of those under the death sentence are from Latin countries, with the majority coming from Mexico (54), followed by Cuba (9), and El Salvador (8).

DEADLY MISTAKES IN CAPITAL PUNISHMENT: A QUESTION OF JUSTICE

In the 40 years (1977–2017) since the U.S. Supreme Court reinstated executions under *Gregg,* 1,465 people have been executed and the number of death row inmates has drastically increased into the thousands (Álvarez & Urbina, 2014; Urbina, 2012). A focal question, then: How many death penalty cases end in false convictions? And, by extension, do race and ethnicity play a role in cases resulting in false convictions or, worse, executions? In truth, nobody knows how many

may be innocent, but research, through forensic science like DNA, strongly indicates that some death row inmates are innocent. Some critics claim that at least ten innocent people have been executed since *Gregg,* others estimate that about 1 percent of death row inmates who are executed are innocent, while still others cite that the figure is much higher because once a person is executed the case is normally closed, and the majority of cases are never reviewed for possible error once the person is convicted and given the sentence of death. In fact, one study found that from 1976 to 1998 at least 75 people were wrongly sentenced to die (McCormick, 1998). Invariably, contrary to the popular legal standard of guilty beyond a reasonable doubt, at least 39 people have been executed in the face of strong evidence of innocence or grave doubt about being guilty of the charges, as in the case of some inmates of Mexican heritage. More recently, a new study, "Rate of False Conviction of Criminal Defendants Who are Sentenced to Death" (Gross, O'Brien, Hu, & Kennedy, 2014), reported that about one in 25 (4.1%) sentenced to death in the United States are innocent.

The next question, then, would be: how do innocent people get wrongfully convicted and executed? The list of factors is long and complicated, but a possible factor is the influence of race and ethnicity, governed by police officers and court officials, like judges, prosecutors, juries, and even defense attorneys. A second driving force of wrongful convictions is inexperienced, incompetent, or unprepared lawyers for the defendants, as judges tend to assign death penalty cases to inexperienced lawyers. Further, not only is capital punishment one of the most complicated legal sanctions, but also one of the most expensive (Álvarez & Urbina, 2014; Urbina, 2012). Yet, not too ago, Alabama was paying lawyers $20 an hour, up to a cap of $1,000, to prepare for a death penalty case, and $40 an hour to litigate in court. In Texas, one lawyer delivered a 26-word statement at the sentencing trial: "You are an extremely intelligent jury. You've got that man's life in your hands. You can take it or not. That's all I have to say," and Jesus Romero, Mexican, was executed in 1992 (McCormick, 1998).

More recently, an investigation by the *Chicago Tribune* found that of 131 death row inmates executed in Texas under George W. Bush, who claimed fair trials throughout his tenure as governor (1995–2000), 43 included defense attorneys publicly punished for misconduct, either before or after their work on the given death penalty cases; 40 involved trials where defense attorneys presented no evidence or had only one witness during the sentencing phase of the two-stage trial; 29 included a psychiatrist who gave testimony that the American Psychiatric Association condemned as unethical and untrustworthy; 23 included jailhouse informants, considered to be among the least credible witnesses; and 23 included visual hair analysis, which has been proven to be unreliable. Finally, suggesting the possible role of race and ethnicity in capital punishment judicial proceedings, "expert" witnesses for the state have actually told jurors in several trials that blacks, Mexicans, and Latinos in general, are more likely to be dangerous in the future than whites (see Mirandé, Chapter 10, this volume).

The Story of Clarence, Ricardo, and Christopher: The Quest for Justice

For the betterment of the criminal justice system, defendants, and society at large, the current capital punishment era is being redefined with modern technological advances. As for the possible influence of race, Clarence Brandley, an African American janitor, was accused of killing a white girl in Texas in 1980. A police officer, apparently, told Brandley and a fellow white janitor that one of them would be executed for the crime then looked at Brandley, saying: "Since you're the nigger, you're elected." Later, it was discovered that prosecutors suppressed evidence, and he was freed after 10 years in prison.

As for possible role of ethnicity, Ricardo Aldape Guerra, a Mexican national wrongfully convicted and sentenced to death in

1982 for the murder of a Houston police officer, was released on April 15, 1997, after spending nearly 15 years on death row in Texas. Soon after his arrest, Mexican consular officers worked closely with volunteer lawyers representing Aldape, obtained affidavits from witnesses in Mexico in 1991–1992, and continued working closely with the defense counsel in state post-conviction proceedings. During this time, the Mexican government funded travel expenses for two of Aldape's lawyers, who traveled to Mexico to obtain previously undiscovered evidence. Then, in 1992, the Houston Consul General was instrumental in obtaining new counsel for Aldape from the prestigious law firm of Vinson & Elkins. After spending millions of dollars on Aldape's defense, lawyers convinced a federal judge that Aldape was innocent of all charges, with an appellate court judge upholding a federal court ruling that cited police and prosecutorial misconduct in the homicide investigation (Ampudia, 2010). After Aldape's release, the attorney who led the law firm's efforts stated that he would have never represented Aldape had it not been for the involvement of Mexican consular officers and the Mexican government.

At the turn of the century, Christopher Ochoa, a Mexican American, was released from prison in 2001 after serving 12 years on death row in Texas for a rape/murder he did not commit. In his defense, Ochoa was assisted by the Wisconsin Innocence Project, housed at the University of Wisconsin Law School and run by law professors and students. Headed by well-known criminal defense lawyers Barry Scheck and John Pray of the Wisconsin Innocence Project, the defense, using DNA testing, showed that Ochoa could not have murdered an Austin woman during a Pizza Hut robbery in 1988. In effect, in this new era of capital punishment, for innocent people on death row across the United States, the Wisconsin Innocence Project has become one of the most sophisticated and leading *defenders* of those who are presumed innocent, a symbol of hope for those who may have been wrongfully convicted.

FEMALE EXECUTIONS IN THE UNITED STATES

Perhaps because, in comparison to men, few women have been executed in the United States, their experiences have received minimal attention in academic investigations and public dialogue, making it difficult to explore the role of race and ethnicity in capital punishment in its totality. To begin, since no records were kept and there was no media during the early days in America, with newspapers not becoming common until the mid-1800s, it's difficult to know the exact number of executed women in the United States. Worse, in the case of minority women, little attention was given to the execution of slaves and Mexican women during the seventeenth and eighteenth centuries, with some states keeping no records of executions, and thus making it difficult to examine the experience of the executed women, as vividly documented by David V. Baker in *Women and Capital Punishment in the United States: An Analytical History* (2016). Still, it's estimated that 505 women were executed in the United States between 1608 and 1900, with 306 being verifiable cases. Among the executed women, at least seven girls were hanged. Native American Hannah Ocuish, aged 12, was probably the youngest female execution, publicly hanged in Connecticut on December 20, 1786. Rebecca Nurse, aged 71, was the oldest, hanged for witchcraft on July 19, 1692 (Baker, 2016; Urbina, 2012).

In all, it's estimated that 575 (as of December 31, 2017) women have been executed in the United States since 1632, constituting about 3.6 percent of the estimated 15,931 executions, and, as of April 1, 2017, 53 women are currently on death row, including nine Latinas. Finally, possibly more so than with black and white women, the experiences of executed Mexican women and Latinas in general are difficult to investigate and thus seldom mentioned in academic discourse, due in part to the unavailability of data, a smaller number of Mexican women executed, and no Latinas being executed in over a century. The cases of two Mexican women, though, illustrate the experience of executed women in the early days in America, characterized by Baker (2016) as an American system of patriarchal domination and female subordination.

The Story of Juanita and Chipita

The Fourth of July in 1851 was being celebrated in Downieville, California when a drunken miner, Fredrick Cannon, went to the house of Josefa "Juanita" Loaiza-Segovia, a petite, beautiful, and young Mexican girl, kicking her cabin door open, harassing her, calling her a prostitute, and trying to rape her. She was pregnant at the time. Cannon was chased away, but the next day on July 5, 1851, he returned and Juanita fatally stabbed him. Quickly, a lynch mob formed. She was apprehended, dragged out, and a trial was held in the main town plaza with a hastily selected judge, a jury of 12, and lawyers for both sides. During the 4-hour trial, every statement for Juanita was ignored, and the person given the testimony on her behalf was harassed and beaten by the angry mob. Juanita refused to speak on her own behalf; though, she did request to see a priest, but

was denied. Juanita was declared guilty, taken to her home, and given two hours to get ready for death. As Juanita was about to be hung on the Jersey bridge, she adjusted the rope around her own neck, letting her long hair fall free, her arms and clothes tied down, and a cap over her face, with her final words: "Adios Señores." William Ballou who witnessed Juanita's hanging wrote, "I arrived in Downieville on July 5, 1851, the mob took her out and hung her. It was the first woman I ever saw hung, and it was the most degrading sight I had ever seen." Indeed, Juanita is often cited as the first "legally" executed female in California, occurring soon after the Treaty of Guadalupe Hidalgo which ended the Mexican-American War in 1848.

As another historical illustration of female oppression: Josefa "Chipita" Rodríguez, Mexican American, was convicted for murder and hanged from a mesquite tree in San Patricio, Texas on November 13, 1863, reportedly the first female executed in Texas. Her last words were: "No soy culpable" (I am not guilty). A century later, the Texas Legislature passed a resolution noting that Chipita did not receive a fair trial. Clearly, these are situations that have possibly influenced the dynamics of capital punishment in the context of race, ethnicity, and gender (Baker, 2016; see Baker, this volume).

Notably, while multiple Latinas, mostly Mexicans were lynched, hanged, or "legally" executed before the twentieth century, no Latinas were executed in the United States during the twentieth or early part of the twenty-first century. In fact, of the 54 women (18 blacks and 36 whites) executed in the last 117 years, no Latinas have been executed from 1900 to 2017 (Álvarez & Urbina, 2014; Baker, 2016; Urbina, 2011, 2012).

SUMMARY OF COMMONALITIES AMONG EXECUTED LATINOS

- **Drug Usage:** Drug or alcohol abuse was common among prisoners, with indication that some inmates were able to access illicit drugs even while in prison.

- **Mental Illness:** Mental illness seems to be common among death row inmates from the time they enter prison.

- **Low IQ:** A common trend among executed Latinos, in addition to mental illness, seems to be a low IQ.

- **Ineffective Counsel:** Inexperienced, incompetent, or unprepared counsel was common and detrimental, especially for foreign nationals.

- **Claim of Innocence:** Several defendants claimed innocence.

- **Religious Beliefs:** During their lengthy stay on death row, inmates seemed to find hope in God, especially as they waited for their execution date.

- **The Human Side of Death Row Inmates:** Some prisoners acknowledged their wrongs, became humble, and asked for forgiveness.

- **Final Words of Faith:** In some cases, as inmates were about to be executed, they accepted Jesus Christ as their Lord and Savior.

Consider, for instance, the final statement of Henry Martínez Porter, executed in Texas:

I want to thank Father Walsh for his spiritual help. I want to thank Bob Ray (Sanders) and Steve Blow for their friendship. What I want people to know is that they call me a cold-blooded killer when I shot a man that shot me first. The only thing that convicted me was that I am a Mexican and that he was a police officer. People hollered for my life, and they are to have my life tonight. The people never hollered for the life of the policeman that killed a thirteen-year-old boy who was handcuffed in the back seat of a police car. The people never hollered for the life of a Houston police officer who beat up and drowned José Campo Torres and threw his body in the river. You call that equal justice. This is your equal justice. This is America's equal justice. A Mexican's life is worth nothing. When a policeman kills someone he gets a suspended sentence or probation. When a Mexican kills a police officer this is what you get. From there you call me a cold-blooded murderer. I didn't tie anyone to a stretcher. I didn't pump any poison into anybody's veins from behind a locked door. You call this justice. I call this and your society a bunch of cold-blooded murderers. I don't say this with any bitterness or anger. I just say this with truthfulness. I hope God forgives me for all my sins. I hope that God will be as merciful to society as he has been to me. I'm ready, Warden.

THE MACHINERY OF AMERICAN JUSTICE: WHO LIVES, WHO DIES, WHO DECIDES?

Among most scholars, for several decades it has been a settled matter that death penalty decisions, including final outcomes (i.e., executions) are disproportionately more frequent for blacks and, as demonstrated during the last decade, Mexicans and other Latinos (Álvarez & Urbina, 2014; Urbina, 2012). But, WHY? Death penalty advocates, of all political stripes, argue passionately, enthusiastically, and often aggressively that *disproportionality* occurs because certain races unequally commit crimes for which the death penalty and executions apply. On February 20, 2013, for instance, Federal Judge Edith Jones of the Fifth U.S. Circuit Court reportedly remarked that certain "racial groups like African Americans and Hispanics are predisposed to crime," and that they are "prone to commit acts of violence" and be involved in more "heinous" crimes than people of other races. Judge Jones allegedly charged that Mexicans would prefer to be on death row in the United States than serve prison time in their native country, and that it's an insult for the United States to consider laws of other countries, such as Mexico's. Apparently, Judge Jones claimed that the defendants' argument of innocence, arbitrariness, racism, and violations of international laws and treaties are just "red herrings" used by opponents of capital punishment, and that claims of "mental retardation" by capital defendants disgust her. Appointed by President Ronald Reagan, Jones was one of the final candidates President George H.W. Bush considered nominating to the U.S. Supreme Court (Álvarez & Urbina, 2014).

These notions, however, have historically missed critical facts. American laws and the criminal justice system, from their initial foundation to the twenty-first century have been established and largely controlled by white males, strategically laboring to oppress and dominate ethnic and racial minorities,

who do not pass such laws (Acuña, 2015; Almaguer, 20009; Álvarez & Urbina, 2018; Bender, 2003, 2015; De León, 1983; Mirandé, 1987; Urbina et al., 2014; Urbina & Álvarez 2017). For many decades lynching, burnings, and hangings—which were common from the late eighteenth century to the mid-twentieth century (1960s)—were *strategically* utilized not to prevent or reduce crime, but to brutally intimidate, oppress, and silence blacks and Mexicans (Alexander, 2012; Urbina & Álvarez, 2016, 2017); effectively excluding ethnic/racial minorities from America's main institutions, particularly the economic, political, and educational systems (Acuña, 1998, 2011; Álvarez & Urbina, 2018; Salinas, 2015; Urbina & Wright, 2016)

Historically excluded from America's main institutions, blacks and Mexicans have been, in a sense, socially, politically, and economically *bankrupt,* and thus comparatively poorer (Urbina, 2014; Urbina & Wright, 2016); subsequently, they are less able to obtain "dream-teams" to defend them in criminal proceedings when charged with a crime (Álvarez & Urbina, 2018; Urbina & Álvarez, 2017). Further, historical analysis *unearths* unyielding past prejudice and discrimination against ethnic and racial minorities, particularly blacks and Mexicans (Alexander, 2012; Molina, 2014; Salinas, 2015; Urbina et al., 2014), which continue to influence contemporary economic, political, and educational differences (Urbina & Wright, 2016). In the twenty-first century, so-called *legal* executions (and mass incarceration) have replaced burnings, lynching, and hangings with the unspoken mission of maintaining absolute power, dominance, and control.

THE GLOBAL NATURE OF (CAPITAL) PUNISHMENT

Understanding the role of race and ethnicity in capital punishment in its totality also requires acknowledgement of the global nature of crime and punishment, and, while polemic, the price of American justice. To begin, some experts argue that while the presumed "dangerousness" of offenders has been a focal point of discourse, especially in anti-social control movements, like the war on drugs, anti-terrorism, and anti-immigrants, the actual dangerousness has been far from the truth of the unspoken motives of social control policies (Álvarez & Urbina, 2018; Lynch, 2007; Molina, 2014; Reiman & Leighton, 2017; Urbina & Álvarez, 2016, 2017; see Urbina & Álvarez, Chapter 17, this volume). As for the influence of race and ethnicity, according to some critics, from the advent of the war on drugs, blacks and Mexicans have been a prime target of politicians, government officials, law enforcement, and immigration hawks (Alexander, 2012; Bender, 2005; Molina, 2014; Urbina & Álvarez, 2015, 2016, 2017). In fact, at about the time that people were talking about the introduction of crack cocaine into the ghetto, and thus the criminalization of African American ghettos in the mid-1980s, Marjorie Zatz (1984:165) found that prior record, suggesting dangerousness, was "used primarily against Chicanos [Mexicans], perhaps because they are seen as specializing in drug trafficking from Mexico," a trend that extends into the twenty-first century (Álvarez & Urbina, 2018), with *dangerousness simply serving as rationalization and legitimization for expansion and control* (Durán, 2013; Salinas, 2015; Urbina & Álvarez, 2017), as recently documented by Álvarez and Urbina in *Immigration and the Law: Race, Citizenship, and Social Control* (2018). Today, Mexicans, particularly Mexican immigrants, are being target of law enforcement—sending thousands of Mexicans and other Latinos to prison, as reported in *Ethnicity and Criminal Justice in the Era of Mass Incarceration: A Critical Reader on the Latino Experience* (2017).

Other critics report that beyond the presumed dangerousness that characterizes Mexicans, impoverished Latinos, blacks, and whites have limited financial resources to defend themselves in criminal proceedings (Alexander, 2012; Álvarez & Urbina, 2018; Reiman & Leighton, 2017; Salinas, 2015; Urbina & Álvarez, 2017), particularly in death penalty cases, which are extremely complicated, lengthy, and expensive. For instance, with limited resources, it is difficult for defendants to hire a private attorney, especially experienced and competent lawyers, and thus some defendants must depend on public defenders or court-appointed attorneys, who may not be highly skilled in death penalty cases (see Urbina, this volume). In reality, with the majority of public defenders trying their respected death penalty case for the first time, the great majority of defendants find themselves represented by attorneys that are learning the logistics of capital cases for the first time in their career, putting into question the very essence of American criminal law; that is, equality under the law. As such, there might be some truth to the saying, "if you do not have the capital, you will get the capital punishment," a situation that impacts not only individual defendants, but entire communities. Situating capital punishment within a broader context, the higher the rate of arrests, indictments, prosecutions, convictions, and imprisonment (along with executions), for instance, the lower the probability of getting an education or securing employment, not to mention the consequences of losing the right to vote—in a sense, back to slavery.

SYMBOLIC JUSTICE

In exploring the role of race and ethnicity in crime and punishment, including executions, other critics question whether the *expansion, power, and control thesis* is more symbolic than pragmatic. That is, arguably, executions serve as a symbol of insult not only toward executed Mexicans, but to all Mejicanos of the world, especially when Mexicans are executed close to major Mexican holidays, or, as in the case of Jessie Gutiérrez, actually executed (or, perhaps, sacrificed) on September 16 (Mexico's Independence Day). In fact, to some observers, the execution of a Mexican is not only an act against the individual, but the execution is carried out against Mexico, its people, its culture, and Mexico's governmental policy that forbids executions (Mexico abolished the death penalty in 1929). According to anthropologist Tony Zavaleta, for example, whichever way one puts it, the end result is clear: when executions take place, especially when race-ethnicity is influential or in violation of international law, the state is "shedding Mexican blood on American soil . . . [it is] like slitting the throat of a sacrificial lamb" (Halperin, 1997:4-5).

CAPITAL PUNISHMENT IN AMERICA: UNDERNEATH IT ALL

Finally, probably just as polemic as the influence of race, ethnicity, gender, or economics, lies what could possibly be *underneath it all,* the things we would rather not hear or write about. To begin, executioners no longer wear sheets and hoods to hide their identities, but hide behind a curtain, with three prison guards administering the lethal chemicals comprising of Sodium Thiopental, Pavulon, and Potassium Chloride to stop the heart. Showing the brutal attitude of executioners, in an April 1998 Texas execution, Joseph Cannon, white, was strapped down to a gurney awaiting death with needles in his arm, but then the executioners pumped up the injection apparatus to a degree that the deathly chemicals were released with such a force that Cannon's vein blew and formed a hematoma, requiring 15 minutes before another vein could be found. Witnessing the savage spectacle, his mother reportedly collapsed. In another Texas execution, the parents of inmate Pedro Cruz Muñiz, Mexican, were told that they would be allowed in the viewing room to see Muñiz die by lethal injection. Upon noticing that Muñiz's family was of mixed race and ethnicity, apparently Mexican, black, and a red-haired white-skinned person, the rules suddenly changed and Pedro's family members were told that they would have to wait out in the street while Pedro was being killed, indicating that the influence of race and ethnicity in Texas extends to family members of inmates. When Pedro's death was announced, Texas Department of Corrections guards who were congregating in the streets were reported to be laughing boisterously within sight of Pedro's family, in a sense, showing gross disrespect for human dignity.

At a more profound level, in *Capital Punishment and Latino Offenders* (2011) and in *Capital Punishment in America: Race and the Death Penalty Over Time* (2012), Urbina argues that the historical demon of discrimination is not only deeply rooted in American history and culture, but that it's in the inner core of the American psyche. Once capital punishment in America is analyzed in its totality over time, Urbina (2008:179) bluntly states:

Capital punishment in the United States persists mostly for historical, political, ideological, religious, economical, and social reasons—having little to do with safety or practicality. Fundamentally, capital punishment is one of the biggest demons that the world has ever invented. Now, what is the driving force behind this demon? The most powerful single driving force is *indifference.*

Executions are brutal, vicious, expensive, irreversible, like an everlasting struggle against cancer that continues to get worse and worse. And, at the very bottom of its motive, there lies an historical mystery. As the harshest criminal sanction, capital punishment has been promoted by promising political language, which is designed to make lies sound truthful, government action logical and honorable, murder by the state legal (with a notion of legitimacy and justice), and to a fragile, feared,

and malinformed society, an appearance of global power and solidarity.

The executioners are part of the legal system and its laws, which are assumed to be unalterable, like the word of God. The executioners are serving the state, which has the power to absolve them from this elusive demon. Yet, they do not even know why they are executing. But, of course, they are *not* supposed to. The executioners accept the law almost as they accept the weather, which is, of course, unpredictable by nature. When questioned, the executioners are likely to reply with: "respect for constitutionalism and legality!" No one would support capital punishment if one were not psychologically and emotionally driven on by some powerful demon whom s/he can neither resist nor understand its truth and reality.

CONCLUSION

The evidence shows that 99 of the 122 Latinos executed from 1977 to 2017 were of Mexican heritage, with 103 of the 122 Latino executions taking place in Texas. Based on the results, it appears that while Mexicans have been classified as "white," through the give and take of treaty making in In *re Rodríguez* (1897), final outcomes are quite different, with race and ethnicity, or more precisely racism, continuing to play a role in crime and punishment. In the case of capital punishment, it seems that Mexicans and Latinos in general have received the worst of both worlds: punishment without due process, putting in question the legitimacy of American criminal laws, with *equality under the law* becoming more pressing when Mexican nationals are executed. On numerous occasions, the Mexican government's call for "fair trials" and formal requests, like Mexico "would like the sentences of . . . Mexicans condemned to death in the United

States to be commuted to life imprisonment," were to no avail (*San Francisco Chronicle,* 1993b:4).

Notably, for Mexicans on death row, protestations do not seem to be entirely the byproduct of the release of one Mexican on death row or the execution of another. According to Tony Garza, former Texas Secretary of State, ". . . from the sense of the left and right, Mexico was being scapegoated" (Halperin, 1997:3), a notion supportive by Trump's aggressive and vindictive anti-Mexico political rhetoric, with slogans like "build the wall," while characterizing Mexicans as illegal, criminal, and dangerous—in his words, "bad hombres." Today, in 2018, we could possibly say that the war between Mexico and the United States ended 170 years ago, but the long legacy of hate and vindictiveness remains, particularly under the Trump administration. In essence, Mexicans and other Latinos are now being perceived as a political, economic, cultural, and social threat to the white power structure, the white America who has been in total control for over 500 years. Internationally, with the globalization of crime and punishment and thus newly defined borders, "it is easier to rationalize the harsh treatment of persons who are essentially 'out-siders'" (Blalock, 1967:206). To Nieling and Urbina (2008:233), in part

> because the United States considers itself a 'moral' and 'law-and-order' society, the U.S. has a phobia of the *outsider,* the *different,* and the *stranger.* As an institutionalized state of feeling and thinking, such phobia has manifested itself into ignorance, with in turn has resulted in viciousness and vindictiveness. Likewise, fear of those who threaten our interests or the status quo, has manifested itself into low levels of tolerance.

In sum, the data show that the experiences of Mexicans (and Latinos in general) on death row differ from the experiences of blacks and whites. Ultimately, then, the central objective of this chapter would be that this information will facilitate the development of data sets that will eventually enable us to quantitatively test the effects of race (blacks, whites, and other racial groups) and ethnicity (Mexicans and other ethnic groups) in capital punishment. More globally, Mexicans and the various ethnic groups within the Latino community constitute a separate group, distinct from blacks and whites, and thus must be treated accordingly in academic research, publication, and dialogue.

Chapter 16

LIFE AFTER PRISON: RECOMMENDATIONS FOR OVERCOMING LEGAL BARRIERS, COMMUNITY REENTRY, AND STEPS FOR MAKING IT OUTSIDE

SOFÍA ESPINOZA ÁLVAREZ AND MARTIN GUEVARA URBINA

I have almost reached the regrettable conclusion that the Negro's great stumbling block in the stride toward freedom is not the White Citizen's Council or the Ku Klux Klanner, but the white moderate who is more devoted to "order" than to justice; who prefers a negative peace which is the absence of tension to a positive peace which is the presence of justice; who constantly says "I agree with you in the goal you seek, but I can't agree with your methods of direct action"; who paternalistically feels he can set the timetable for another man's freedom; who lives by the myth of time and who constantly advises the Negro to wait until a "more convenient season."

–Rev. Martin Luther King

As detailed in previous chapters, when it comes to criminal defendants, the focus of the criminal justice system, research and publication, and those vested in community safety or social justice has been on formal proceedings, from arrest to once people are released from prison. In the current era of law and order, though, over 50,000 people leave prison every month, and more than 650,000 inmates are released from state and federal prisons every year, the biggest number in the history of the U.S. penal system. Further, in the twenty-first century, prisoners who are being released are serving longer sentences than inmates of earlier decades, and they are less likely to have received an education or job training behind bars and less likely to be rehabilitated. During the 1980s and 1990s, as jails and prisons filled to overcrowding and a tough-on-criminals movement prevailed, states significantly reduced rehabilitation programs. As such, prisoners typically return home carrying their *old* liabilities, like additions, limited education, unskilled, and poor work habits, in addition to new ones, like a damaged relationship with family and friends, a criminal record, a criminal stigma, and often no place to go. Worse, since most exiting inmates are Latino or African American, minority prisoners must also *confront the influence of being Latino or black.* Together, the central question becomes, how do ex-prisoners fare on the outside, in the community? And, by extension, how do communities fare in incorporating former prisoners?

This chapter, then, provides a discussion of "life after prison" for the typical adult male and female offender, which involves not only the experience of Latinos and blacks but whites as well. After noting the methods of release, the major roadblocks to community reentry are detailed, followed by an analysis of the significance of community integration and the importance of building *bridges* between prison and society. It is argued that the most crucial gap to the estab-lishment of social control remains to be bridged: from prison to the community. Otherwise, with limited resources, a chaotic environment, and a hostile community, re-leased inmates are likely to return to prison (Urbina, 2016). Then, recommendations for overcoming state and federal *legal barriers* for reentry are provided, followed by proposi-tions for community reentry of both male and female offenders as well as a series of steps for *making it outside* upon release. The chapter concludes with a discussion of major challenges facing reformers in the twenty-first century, as we seek to create a more understanding, tolerant, and forgiving soci-ety, while securing public safety and nation-al security.

METHODS OF RELEASE

To begin, the combination of tougher sen-tences has led to a drastic increase in the incarceration of both male and female offenders, and inmates are serving longer prison terms for a wider array of criminal activity (see Álvarez, this volume). Yet, most prisoners are eventually released back into the community because the majority of offenders are incarcerated for nonviolent crimes, normally drug offenses. With the exception of those serving life or death sen-tences, incarcerated people are released from prison to the community, usually under parole supervision through various means, depending on federal or state laws. These categories include discretionary release, mandatory release, expirational release, or some other form of conditional release. A very small percentage of people are "rem-oved" from prison as a result of escapes, exe-cutions, or deaths (Urbina, 2012).

Once offenders have been punished for their crimes, served their sentences, and re-leased from prison, they are back in the community, normally in their "old" neigh-borhoods, to begin a new life, with the expectation that they will never return to prison. Nonetheless, about 75 percent of in-mates return to prison. In this context, there are several essential questions that must be addressed to facilitate *reentry planning* for those who are still in prison to avoid recidivism upon release, and thus reduce the probabili-ty of inmates returning to prison. Morally, what will become of male and female offend-ers once they are released from prison? Will inmates be able to find legal employment with the skills they learned while incarcerat-ed? Considering the wide range of problems facing both male and female offenders, will they be able to pay for their basic needs, like healthcare, and not return to illegal activities like drugs or prostitution? If inmates do not have the necessary skills, will they be able to acquire credentials and qualifications that will allow them to survive in a highly com-petitive and technological job market? Will ex-prisoners be able to reunite with their children, partner, spouse, friends, or other loved ones? Will released prisoners be accepted by the community? Or, will they be treated with mistrust, disdain, rejection, or hostility? Ultimately, what is the probability that those released from prison will end up back in the correctional system?

LEGAL ROADBLOCKS TO COMMUNITY REENTRY

As noted above, more than 630,000 people are released from state and federal prisons every year, a population equal to that of most major cities, and hundreds more are released from local jails. Critically, though, rather than helping released inmates successfully transition from prison to the community, many current state and federal laws have the opposite impact, legal barriers which are significantly interfering with the obligations, rights, and expectations of full citizenship in nearly every aspect of people's daily lives. In effect, current state and federal laws diminish rehabilitation efforts, community reentry and stability, and public safety, and they undermine the presumed commitment to equality and justice. Together, as designed and applied, existing laws are creating legal roadblocks to basic necessities for thousands of people who are trying to rebuild their lives, support their families, and become productive members of their communities.

Further, while legal barriers to community reentry have only recently been critically analyzed, for more than 30 years the federal government and various states have drastically increased the range and severity of civil penalties for people with criminal convictions, and, in some cases, applying legal barriers to people who have never been convicted of a crime (Salinas, 2015; Urbina & Kreitzer, 2004). In fact, for three decades Congress and state legislatures have created new restrictions for the eligibility of various necessities, including public assistance, food stamps, public housing, drivers' license, and student loans, while further expanding legal barriers to crucial social issues, such as parenting, employment, and voting.

Consequently, as a result of such explosive increase of legal roadblocks during the last three decades, successful reentry into society after inmates have been released is much more difficult for people who have been arrested or convicted of crimes, especially for drug offenses, and those who have multiple convictions or incarcerations, even if they can demonstrate that they are rehabilitated, qualified to work, and willing to participate in society. As for ethnic and race variation, because Latinos and African Americans are arrested, indicted, prosecuted, convicted, and sentenced to prison at significantly higher rates than whites, minorities are disproportionately harmed by these state and federal legal barriers, leading to widespread social, economic, and political disenfranchisement of Latinos and African Americans. In effect, a two-year study by the Legal Action Center (2004:7) found that "people with criminal records seeking reentry face a daunting array of counterproductive, debilitating and unreasonable roadblocks in almost every important aspect of life." While obstacles are numerous and complicated, the following are ten of the most influential legal barriers facing released prisoners when they attempt to reenter society and become law-abiding and productive citizens.

Public Housing

Considering that the majority of male and female offenders are indigent (Reiman & Leighton, 2017; Urbina, 2008; Urbina & Álvarez, 2017), with many of them having spent years behind bars, the most immediate concern upon release is a place to stay, especially if they are no longer allowed in their old house or apartment. If released prisoners are not able to stay with family or friends, they either seek public housing or low-income housing, or live in the streets. Federal laws, though, give local housing agencies leeway in most situations to decide whether to bar people with criminal convictions from public housing premises, even if arrests never led to conviction, creating a difficult situation for inmates who have no other place to stay. National data show that:

- In a majority of states, public housing authorities make individualized determinations about an applicant's eligibility that include considering the person's criminal record, as well as evidence of rehabilitation.
- Many public housing authorities consider arrest records that did not lead to conviction in determining eligibility for public housing (Legal Action Center, 2004:16).

Public Assistance and Food Stamps

Along with shelter, released prisoners must also cope with actual survival, and if they do not have a place to stay, they are also likely to lack money and food, especially those who are unable to quickly find employment. As such, released prisoners often look for public assistance. The 1996 federal welfare law, however, prohibits people convicted of drug-related felonies from receiving federally funded food stamps or cash assistance, known as Temporary Assistance for Needy Families (TANF). Further, considering that drug offenses have become the focal target of the criminal justice system, most states now restrict people with drug convictions from being eligible for federally funded public assistance, including food stamps and cash (Legal Action Center, 2004). As a lifetime ban, applied even if people have completed their sentence, overcame addictions, earned a certificate of rehabilitation, or been employed but they got laid off, such prohibition significantly hinders community reentry for thousands of released prisoners.

Employment

Upon being released from prison, people are confronted with multiple expectations, like obeying the conditions of parole, not engaging in criminal activity, and quickly finding employment. In effect, employment is not only one of the most crucial expectations, but one of the most essential in that it signifies social and economic stability, it provides people a physical address, it enhances the chances of securing housing, and it enables people to afford basic necessities, like clothing and food. This expectation, though, is hindered with employment obstacles in that:

- Employers in most states can deny jobs to people who were arrested but never convicted of any crime.
- Employers in most states can deny jobs to, or fire, anyone with a criminal record, regardless of individual history, circumstances, or "business necessity."
- States have the power to offer certificates of rehabilitation but few issue them (Legal Action Center, 2004:10).

Access to Criminal Records

While released prisoners have spent their time behind bars for the crime they committed, upon being released they are not immune from the stigma or legal obstacles of a criminal record. Officially, states have the authority to allow the sealing or expungement of arrest records that never led to conviction as well as conviction records after the elapse of an appropriate period of time. Yet, considering the influence of a criminal record on housing, public assistance, employment, and other social, economic, and political activities, national data show that:

- Most states never expunge or seal conviction records but do allow arrest records to be sealed or expunged when the arrest did not lead to a conviction.
- Virtually anyone with an Internet connection can find information about someone's conviction history online without his or her consent or any guidance on how to interpret or use the information (Legal Action Center, 2004: 15).

Drivers' Licenses

Possibly more than any other formal document, a driver's license has become a necessary element for *everyday functioning,* ranging from driving to opening a bank account. To further complicate matters for released prisoners, many inmates do not have a place to stay and thus no physical address, which is essential for obtaining a driver's license. Moreover, in 1992, Congress enacted legislation withholding 10 percent of highway funds unless states enact laws revoking or suspending driver's license of people convicted of drug offenses for at least six months after the date of the conviction. More recently, in addition to federal legislation restricting the limits of drivers' licenses to people with criminal records, states have passed or attempted to pass laws restricting, revoking, or suspending drivers' licenses for undocumented people, targeting Latinos, especially Mexican immigrants. In 2011, for instance, New Mexico Governor Susana Martinez tried to repeal a law granting drivers' licenses to undocumented people. In fact, some states have attempted to restrict the limits of drivers' licenses to *legal immigrants,* including Texas under Governor Rick Perry. Truly, if implemented, these laws led to consequential obstacles for both illegal and legal immigrants who are being released from state or federal prisons. In short, restricting the ability to drive makes it more difficult to be employed, participate in addiction treatment, obtain an education, get job training, and it restricts people in many other areas of everyday life. In all, national statistics show that:

- 27 states automatically suspend or revoke licenses for some or all drug offenses; 23 states either suspend or revoke licenses only for driving-related offenses or have opted out of the federal law.
- Many states make restrictive licenses available so individuals whose licenses would otherwise be suspended can go to work, attend drug treatment, or obtain an education (Legal Action Center, 2004:17).

Surveillance

In addition to monitoring inmates released on parole to ensure that they meet the conditions of parole, the criminal justice system indirectly or directly monitors those who have committed felonies, even if the offenses are not classified as violent, as well as immigrants waiting for their immigration status to be determined by immigration officials

(Álvarez & Urbina, 2018). However, in the aftermath of the September 11, 2001, terrorist attacks on the United States and the continued international war on drugs, constant surveillance on those suspected of terrorist or narcotics connections is now being conducted by state and federal law enforcement agencies, a critical situation for Latinos who are already associated with narcotics trafficking and even terrorism, or worse, narco-terrorists (Urbina & Álvarez, 2016, 2017, 2018). While surveillance monitoring seems to make sense in ensuring public safety, intrusive surveillance adds to the legal barriers facing released prisoners, as the criminal stigma of being under constant surveillance makes it more difficult to reintegrate into society and live a *normal* life.

Deportation

In the current era of law and order, immigrants, particularly Latinos, are once again a primary target of anti-immigrants legislation, politicians, law enforcement officials, immigration hawks, and society (Álvarez & Urbina, 2018). As such, when released from prison, people who are not U.S.-born citizens face the possibility of deportation, this includes undocumented people, legal residents, people who legally reside in the country with some type of visa, and even naturalized U.S. citizens (Álvarez & Urbina, 2018; Salinas, 2015). Realistically, the impact is not only on those who get deported, but also their families, as young children might be left in the United States if they are U.S.-born, creating chaos, fear, and uncertainty for many people and, in a sense, the entire Latino community (Álvarez & Urbina, 2018), as we have witnessed since June 16, 2015 when Trump first declared his candidacy for president of the United States, escalating after November 8, 2016, and gravely exacerbating after January 20, 2017.

Student Loans

As noted in previous chapters, the typical male and female offender is impoverished and uneducated, making it difficult to obtain education and training that enables them to compete in the job market. As such, those who wish to pursue an education or specialized training are forced to seek financial assistance. However, here too, ex-prisoners are confronted with yet another formal obstacle in that the Higher Education Act of 1998 makes students convicted of drug-related offenses ineligible for grants, loans, or work assistance. Consequently, since this federal legal barrier cannot be altered by states, and the fact that the majority of offenders are convicted for drug-related offenses, the great majority of all released prisoners are not eligible for education financial assistance, significantly impacting Latino offenders (Urbina & Álvarez, 2016, 2017). In effect, while the range of criminal offenses is wide, no other offense results in automatic denial of federal financial assistance.

Adoptive and Foster Parenting

To further complicate reentry, long-term community reintegration, and the opportunity of living a normal life, released prisoners who wish to be law-abiding citizens, be productive members in their communities, and have a stable family are confronted with an additional obstacle in that the federal Adoption and Safe Families Act of 1997 impedes people with certain convictions from being foster or adoptive parents, impacting the everyday life of not only ex-prisoners, but children in need of a family. Though, national statistics show that most states do make individualized determination on the applicants' suitability to be adoptive or foster parents, while considering people's criminal record and evidence of rehabilitation.

Voting

Beyond the daily legal obstacles confronting released prisoners, states have absolute power to decide whether people with a criminal record are allowed to vote, impacting not only individual ex-inmates but the entire community, particularly Latino and African American communities. In fact, all but two states place restrictions on the right to vote for people with felony convictions. According to some figures, about 70 million Americans have a criminal record, making it difficult to get a job, vote, or participate in society (Brown & Douglas-Gabriel, 2016).

In sum, these ten legal barriers not only hinder reentry, long-term community reintegration, and stability and continuity over time, but these obstacles counteract the very purpose of the criminal justice system, rehabilitation, public safety, and justice. Worse, since the great majority of those who get detected, arrested, indicted, prosecuted, convicted, sentenced to jail or prison, and placed on death row are either Latino or African American, the inability to engage in civil activities, like voting, pushes ethnic and racial minorities further into the margins of society, ultimately silencing the entire minority community. Together, the central question of the current model of arrest, incarceration, and release becomes: are ex-prisoners actually being integrated into the community? Or, are they simply being *placed* back to survival days?

COMMUNITY INTEGRATION OR BACK TO SURVIVAL DAYS?

Theoretically, male and female offenders should be able to *regain* their lives once they are released from prison, arguably inmates should not be worse than when they entered the prison system. In fact, if inmates took advantage of supposed *available resources* while in prison, they should be in a better position (than those who did not) to begin the community (re)integration process. Practically, though, "life after prison is more a reflection of 'back to survival days,' than it is of 'community (re)integration'" (Urbina, 2008:189).

Released prisoners are in fact not provided with a smooth transition from prison to their next living shelter. Likewise, the existing mechanisms do not provide a smooth transition back into the community. To begin with, when inmates are released, often in the middle of the night, the typical ex-prisoner is confused, scared, has no belongings, and has little idea about what lies ahead. Normally, offenders express concerns as to whether they will be able to turn their lives around after being released, especially if they spent several years behind bars. For female offenders, the situation is even more complicated in that stable housing and employment are essential to regain custody of their children as well as a permanent address and transportation for legal employment to avoid the temptations of the streets, continuation of healthcare, and substance abuse treatment after release. In effect, the majority of women not only suffer from health conditions like depression, but 60 to 70 percent of women released from prison have nowhere to go. In essence, the typical male and female offender "leaves prison economically, politically, socially, and morally bankrupt" (Urbina, 2008:191).

Economically, upon release, the typical inmate has no place to go, limited resources, and has little knowledge of whatever resources might be available in the community. Independent of how long they were in prison, their level of education remains low, lacking the skills to compete in a highly competitive and technological job market. When unemployment is high, the situation is even more drastic for ex-prisoners who are perceived by society as undeserving, threatening, and unwanted in the community. For minority parolees, Latinos and African Americans, the situation is even more devastating in that they are not only being marginalized for breaking the law, but for supposedly taking the few jobs available.

Politically, the typical male or female ex-prisoner has no ties to appointed or elected officials or to America's main institutions. Consequently, either because their right to vote has been taken away as a result of a criminal conviction or because they simply fail to exercise their vote, ex-prisoners are *strategically* forgotten or neglected by local, state, and federal politicians. As a general rule, politicians' main objective is to address the concerns of the "voting class," and thus the views and concerns of ex-prisoners are not likely to be addressed in a proper and efficient manner, as illustrated by the various legal barriers to reentry. In the case of minority ex-prisoners, Latinos, the situation is further complicated in that their friends and relatives cannot vote if they are not U.S. citizens.

Socially, ex-prisoners typically have no social support when they are released from prison. To the contrary, former prisoners are usually viewed as undeserving people who should not be entitled to voice their experiences, views, or concerns. Further, as people who have violated the law, community norms, or challenged the status quo, released prisoners are viewed and treated as third or fourth-class citizens. In the case of women and minority ex-prisoners, the post-prison experience is normally more consequential if they do not have friends or relatives to rely on for social support, like cultural understanding, appreciation, and, ultimately, reintegration. For instance, studies show that weak family ties or complete separation from their children creates a severe problem for reintegration and stability (Urbina, 2008).

Morally, male and female prisoners typically leave the prison system energized and motivated to start their new lives. However, for the typical offender, the prison experience is in fact disheartening, demoralizing, and damaging. Once released, inmates are scared and uncertain about having to interact with a judgmental society, and, for female and minority offenders, morally fragile to diverse and punitive gender, ethnic, or racial stereotypes. Even though the United States is often characterized as a sensitive, understanding, ethical, and moral society, the community is not very forgiving against those who are considered strangers, outsiders, different, or threatening (Álvarez & Urbina, 2014, 2018; Urbina & Álvarez, 2016, 2017). In a sense, ex-prisoners continue to pay, economically, politically, socially, or morally, for their criminal acts long after they are released from prison, as recently documented by Martha Escobar in *Captivity Beyond Prisons* (2016).

Evidently, having a population of ex-prisoners that is absolutely bankrupt carries high consequences in that it leads to the very same problem that we are arguably trying to solve: crime. In effect, studies show that recidivism is partially attributed to economic need as well as discriminatory policies and lack of community support (Cullen & Jonson, 2012; Cullen, Jonson, & Nagin, 2011; Petersilia, 2010; Urbina, 2008). Consider, for instance, the experience of one released female prisoner:

> I really tried to stay out of trouble, but its very difficult, you know. Like once you're into a routine and the people you're hanging about with and everything, and plus you're always getting hassled by the police . . . It was about

this time that I left home . . . and I was on the streets for a very long time . . . because I was homeless, I couldn't get a . . . job . . . but I still had . . . fines that I had to pay . . . So I am stuck in this rut. I've got to pay these fines or go to jail, and I've got to live as well. So I was committing more crimes, going back to court and getting more fines, and it was just a vicious circle. So the next thing I ended up back in prison again. (Maruna, 2001:71)

In sum, all inmates are older when they are released from prison. If inmates have served lengthy sentences, they might experience additional difficulties, like more severe health problems. More fundamentally, since the typical inmate leaves prison economically, politically, socially, and morally bankrupt, most offenders will return to prison.

Unfortunately, each time people return to prison, their situation becomes more devastating and consequential. For example, their chances of obtaining a legitimate job are further tarnished with an increase in apprehensions, prosecutions, convictions, and incarcerations. Of course, reentry also presents a critical situation for the prison system in various areas of daily prison life, like management, service delivery, and rehabilitation. For instance, reentry makes it difficult to maintain a reliable medical history, which is vital for community treatment. Still, while the majority of inmates wish to stay out of trouble and become productive members of society, their actual reality is closer to back to survival days than community integration (Urbina, 2008).

BUILDING BRIDGES BETWEEN PRISON AND SOCIETY

Understanding male and female offenders requires that we explore their lives by the totality of circumstances, experiences, events, and situations. This includes the investigation of not only life while incarcerated, but life before, during, and after incarceration (Urbina, 2008). In the context of the prison system, a central objective is to "rehabilitate" inmates for community reentry upon release, so that they can be productive members of society. However, too often, policymakers, politicians, social activists, and others with vested interest in "prison reform" concentrate on offenders who are entering prison and pay little attention to inmates who are about to be released, and essentially isolating inmates who are just released from prison, neglecting reintegration, public safety, and the conditions that originally led to criminal behavior and that will once again place people back in prison, resulting in an never-ending cycle.

As noted above, once inmates are released into the community, they are disconnected from conventional society. As such, without well-established bridges between prison and society, *the typical offender is prone to "fail" as a citizen,* reoffend, and end up in prison for a minor crime, or simply breaking parole conditions, with Latinos, African Americans, and Native Americans being prone to experience greater challenges (Díaz-Cotto, 1996; Oboler, 2009; Salinas, 2015; Urbina, 2008). In essence, as documented by Raymond Michalowski (1985:240),

Prisons in America exist as a kind of distorted mirror image of American society. Like the mirrors in a carnival funhouse, prisons exaggerate and expand some of the characteristics of the society they reflect. Yet, like funhouse mirrors, what they show is based in the very real object they are reflecting. The parallel between free society and prisons exists at both the organizational and the social level.

Exploring the female experience, Barbara Owen (1998:192) reports that

> Women in prison represent a very specific failure of conventional society—and public policy—to recognize the damage done to women through the oppression of patriarchy, economic marginalization, and the wider-reaching effects of such shortsighted and detrimental policies as the war on drugs and overreliance on incarceration as social control.

In all, the penal system, with its priority on security and control, places little emphasis on treatment and rehabilitation while inmates are incarcerated, with limited planning for community reentry upon release. Successful reintegration, though, involves proper planning prior to their release, as they are being released, and shortly after their release into the community. The focus should be immediately upon release and not after they have engaged in illegal behavior, and thus the challenge is trying to find ways to keep them in the community and not send them back to prison, especially for issues that can be addressed in the community. In effect, some of the most detrimental issues facing male and female prisoners are best addressed in the community and not behind bars. For instance, substance and alcohol abuse, domestic violence, employment skills, healthcare (like stress and depression), and parenting responsibilities are best addressed outside the correctional setting. However, under current penal policies, these problems are often deferred to the correctional system by a society unable, but mostly unwilling, to confront the problems of marginalized and neglected people, with the majority being Latinos, African Americans, women, and impoverished whites.

In sum, a well-established bridge between prison and society must be developed to avoid fear, chaos, ruptures, and recidivism. With a sharp increase of prison rates, the penal system is becoming a "way of life" for thousands of people in the United States, and for this very same reason the United States must realize that isolation and detachment is contributing to the very same problem we are trying to solve. Therefore, instead of neglecting, isolating, and marginalizing released prisoners, the criminal justice system, community agencies, and conventional society should work together, share resources, and exchange information to create a *road map* for inmates so that they have realistic established planning, goals, and continuity during reintegration.

Community Programs

The main objective of community-based programs is for ex-prisoners to resolve their legal and social issues without risking future arrest, prosecution, conviction, or incarceration, while keeping the community safe. In fact, considering that the typical male and female offender suffers from a series of complicated problems, including childhood abuse, addictions, and health issues, community-based programs are probably the single most essential element in the creation of proper and lasting bridges between prison and the community. Upon release, people typically end up in the same physical environment where they grow up, which is plagued with physical contamination, air pollution, drugs, guns, violence, and crime. This time, however, ex-prisoners are burdened with a criminal record and few social, political, and economic resources to rely on while they find a legal job to survive, while trying to meet the requirements of parole.

Unfortunately, even though community programs have proved to be an effective and beneficial mechanism for the reintegration of ex-prisoners into the community, these programs have not been a priority, and thus they have struggled to keep their doors opened because of limited funds, lack of volunteers, and social and political unwillingness to support these agencies. As agencies that are arguably helping criminals, community programs do not get proper recognition by the media, making it difficult to convince the community, policymakers, and criminal justice officials that reintegration is vital for controlling recidivism, fear, and community stability. In the current era of crime and punishment (Alexander, 2012; Salinas, 2015; Urbina & Álvarez, 2017), the biggest challenge facing community programs will continue to be lack of resources and resistance by the warriors of law and order. Community-based programs, though, must be made a priority in order to slow down the *cycle of crime, prison,* and *release.*

BREAKING STATE AND FEDERAL LEGAL BARRIERS FOR COMMUNITY REENTRY: RECOMMENDATIONS

Together, a well-planned and established bridge between the penal system and mainstream society is missing, and, by extension, there is a huge disconnect between prison and local communities, impacting not only reentry upon release but long-term community reintegration. To begin, there are numerous consequential legal barriers; that is, as reported by the Legal Action Center (2004:23):

> Without a job, it is impossible to provide for oneself and one's family. Without a driver's license, it is harder to find or keep a job. Without affordable housing or food stamps or federal monies to participate in alcohol or drug treatment, it is harder to lead a stable productive life. Without the right to vote, the ability to adopt or raise foster children, or access to a college loan, it is harder to become a fully engaged citizen in the mainstream society.

Therefore, along with the establishment of a well-planned bridge between prison and society to facilitate reentry upon release and ensure long-term community reintegration, the state and federal governments should amend existing laws to eliminate legal barriers so that laws will in fact protect public safety, while making sure that people with past criminal records successfully reintegrate. As recommended by the Legal Action Center (2004:22), the following principles are vital for the establishment of strategic reform:

1. Maximizing the chance that people with criminal records can successfully assume the responsibilities of independent, law-abiding citizens is a critical component of guaranteeing and reinforcing the community's legitimate interest in public safety.
2. An arrest alone should never bar access to rights, necessities, and public benefits. Doing so denies the presumption of innocence, the value of our legal system, to millions of Americans. Employers, housing authorities, and other decision-makers should not be permitted to consider arrest records.
3. A conviction should never bar access to a citizen's right to vote or to basic necessities such as food, clothing, housing, and education.
4. Eligibility for employment, housing, adoptive and foster parenting, or a driver's license should be based on the community's legitimate interest in public safety and the particulars of an indi-

vidual's history and circumstances. Blanket bans on entire categories of people, such as everyone convicted of a felony, are neither wise nor fair; they do not take into account such important factors as the nature of the circumstances of the conviction and what the person has done since the commission of the offense, including receiving an education, acquiring skills, completing community service, maintaining an employment history, or earning awards or other types of recognition.

5. States should enact legislation to provide for the automatic sealing or expungement of any arrest that never led to conviction, and of conviction records after an appropriate amount of time has elapsed. States also should issue certificates to qualified people with criminal records that acknowledge rehabilitation and lift automatic bars.

6. Given the potential for misuse, conviction information should not be publically accessible on the Internet. Access should be restricted to those agencies, such as law enforcement, that need to retrieve criminal records to perform their duties.

RECOMMENDATIONS FOR COMMUNITY REENTRY OF MALE AND FEMALE OFFENDERS

Exploring the experience of female offenders before, during, and after incarceration, Urbina (2008:203-204) notes the following recommendations, which are not politically appealing but they can serve as a significant step in breaking the *revolving door cycle of prison admissions and discharges,* which tends to get more vicious and consequential every time a female or male reenters the prison system.

1. As the prison population continues to increase, expansion of service delivery among existing programs and the development of additional programs are essential to avoid chaos, reduce medical and rehabilitation deficiencies, and secure a smooth transition from prison into the community.

2. Once released, community programs should be given the highest priority and authorities should be sensitive to the specific needs of the various populations being released from prison. Female offenders, for instance, need better delivery service because they are the ones with the greatest demand for basic healthcare, education, job-seeking skills, and pre-release planning. As for undocumented mothers, they also face the possibility of losing their children. Further, in the case of those who do not have the necessary documentation to obtain a social security number, they are further confronted with additional barriers for service delivery and legal employment.

3. Community programs often discriminate against indigent people through examinations, by withholding information about available resources, or negligence. Therefore, male and female offenders should be fully informed of the programs in their communities long before they are released from prison. Also, for those who are released on parole, parole officials should insure that people continue to receive infor-

mation regarding resources in the community.

4. A transition team, including correctional staff, community agencies, community organizers, and volunteers, could provide advice, counseling, services, and referrals.

5. Local governments, the media, and the community should advocate for a volunteer program in which people from the community would offer mentoring and one-on-one or group assistance to released prisoners.

6. The implementation of a realistic educational and employment program must be a priority, as a sound education and successful employment reentry strategy can increase public safety, can reduce spending on costly jails and prisons, reduce poverty for some of the most disadvantage citizens, and develop social and economic prosperity of racial and ethnic communities. Further, education and employment for reentry can also promote family stability and provide a more stable future for millions of children who have parents in jail or prison.

LIFE AFTER PRISON: STEPS TO MAKING IT OUTSIDE

The latest national data indicate that about two-thirds of released prisoners are rearrested within three years, illustrating the significance of joint reentry efforts and well-designed mechanisms. In effect, successful reentry upon release not only requires the elimination of legal barriers and the establishment of a well-designed bridge between prison and the community, but also strategic steps by the released prisoners themselves, if they are to make it on the outside. Imagine life after prison after being physically, socially, and politically disconnected from the community for years, often spending years in state prisons far from their hometown or in federal prisons in a different state. However, after years behind bars dreaming of freedom, inmates are normally unprepared for life after prison. As noted herein, along with a criminal record, the typical inmate has minimal education and work experience, shackled by addictions, chronic depression, or mental illness, hunted by the criminal stigma, under pressure to quickly find legal employment, and other pressing factors, like managing housing issues, drug or alcohol treatment needs, and family relationships (Urbina, 2008).

In fact, while inmates spend years behind bars waiting for the day of their release, *prisoners have little knowledge about the practicalities of street survival after prison.* To begin, seldom do prisoners realize that they are likely to have their parole revoked within the first 48 hours, and thus it is essential that they know, *through education while in prison,* and have the necessary steps in place before they are released. For instance, inmates must know that life after prison is not simply getting a job quickly upon release, and, of course, staying out of trouble. Inmates should *learn* that life after prison is more than simply rebuilding a new life, but seeking to break the cycle of crime, arrest, imprisonment, and release, while setting the foundation so that future generations will not follow the same path, the road to prison. As such, through education while incarcerated, inmates should learn the following 11 rules for making it outside after being released from jail or prison.

1. Support: Who Can Help?

In terms of supporting themselves financially, both men and women leave prison with no money and often with hundreds of dollars in debt, and thus they are unable to sustain themselves. As such, inmates should know that the single most important step is the one they start inside prison, a support group of people they can contact while in prison, people they can call, visit, or work with upon release. In fact, one of the biggest mistakes the majority of inmates make when leaving prison is not identifying or locating a safe support group. Prisoners need to know that they need to develop a network of people that do not have a criminal past. Sometimes the first thing inmates want to do is get laid, drunk, or high (Visher, Yahner, & La Vigne, 2010). However, inmates must learn that if they are serious about making it, they must give themselves time to resocialize, with a focus on a lifetime of freedom and not one to two days of excitement that will land them right back in prison.

In the context of building bridges between prison and conventional society, identifying friends and family who can help is essential to prevent recidivism. One recent study found that family members were a key housing resource for most men, sometimes providing cash, food, and emotional support (Visher et al., 2010). Further, lack of family ties can result not only in detachment from society, but create difficulties for inmates while they are incarcerated, and make it difficult to be reintegrated into the community upon release. In fact, inmates who come out of prison with a committed relationship, and those who form one soon after release are more likely to stay out of prison, revealing the significance of social support.

2. The First 48-Hours After Release

Since the majority of people who are released from prison have their parole revoked within 48-hours, inmates must learn about the significance of the first two days, the time when people are most vulnerable; when they are experiencing their weakest point. Inmates must realize that along with following the rules of their parole, they need to hang out with their support group. Prisoners should know that they need to have all of their faculties to do this, instead of being drunk, stoned, or preoccupied with other irrelevant matters. At this point, their *main* worry should be on the conditions of parole and any other requirements, staying away from "old" influences, and to avoid jeopardizing the reentry process.

3. Illegal Activities and Criminal Associations

Before leaving prison, inmates must be well aware that getting out of prison early may take months or years of work, counseling, treatment, and the cooperation of various programs, only to be thrown away by associating with people with a criminal past, associating with people who are engaged in illegal activities, or simply being in the wrong place. Prisoners must know that when they are on parole they cannot just watch themselves, but they have to be careful of others too and realize that parole is like defensive driving; they should not only follow the rules of the road, they also need to watch what the other drivers are doing to avoid an accident.

4. Dealing with Drug and Alcohol Addictions

Since many prisoners suffer from addictions and depression, inmates must learn the significance of attending, and the consequences of not attending Alcoholic Anonymous (A.A.) or Narcotics Anonymous (N.A.) after their release from prison. Of course, this includes all inmates with addictions, not only those who are released on parole. In fact, alcohol and drug addictions are among the most common elements for which people get involved in crime and, eventually, arrested, indicted, prosecuted, convicted, and sentenced to prison. As such, without proper treatment after prison, people are likely to get involved in crime and sent back to prison.

5. Confronting Life Situations Upon Release

Before leaving prison, inmates should also be educated on ways of confronting difficult and unexpected situations that might arise during the first few months after their release, especially during the first month, which is the most difficult time after release, as they have to walk away from temptations. In fact, the whole first year is very difficult, but the first 48-hours and the first month set the groundwork for successful community reintegration, then the focus is on doing what is effectively working, while making adjustments for leaving a criminal past behind and the enhancement of employment, family, and community stability.

6. Provincial or Federal Halfway Houses

Prisoners should also be familiar with provincial and federal halfway houses before they are release to reduce chaos, uncertainty, and ruptures, establishing continuity. A halfway house, for instance, can offer them a place to stay, food, and a little money to survive during the first few weeks. In effect,

tracking the experience of male ex-prisoners returning to Chicago, Cleveland, and Houston, researchers Christy Visher, Jennifer Yahner, and Nancy La Vigne (2010) found that housing was a major challenge and that housing stability diminished over time for many released male prisoners, resulting in recidivism, rearrests, and imprisonment.

7. Understanding the Nature of the Offense Committed

While the high majority of inmates probably understand that they in fact committed a crime, inmates do not necessarily understand the nature or significance of their behavior. Therefore, prisoners must fully understand the nature of their crime if they are to take responsibility, accountability, and wish to make it on the outside. In fact, inmates will never make it on the outside unless they understand the nature and consequences of their acts. Simply, if prisoners do not know *exactly why they did what they did*, there is a good chance it will happen again. Worse, not only are inmates doomed to fail, but they will be in and out of prison their entire life. The biggest problem, however, is that many prisoners are often too medicated to be educated on these issues. Yet, the mere fact of having inmates medicated, and, by extension, difficult for them to comprehend, indicates the *global importance* of treatment during incarceration.

8. The Prison Code: Honor Among Criminals

Prisoners must also learn that if they are living by the *criminal code* once they are released from prison they will not be out for very long, not only losing everything they gained but in a worse position than before.

Inmates must realize that they cannot follow the code on the outside and be *normal* law-abiding citizens. Prisoners need to fully understand that the code they live by to survive inside prison is the *same* thing that will send them back to prison, normally within the first three years.

9. Employment Upon Release

Before being released into the community, prisoners must also be educated on the realities of employment upon release. Under pressure, quite often when inmates get out of prison, they try to find employment fairly quickly. In truth, one of the biggest mistakes is trying to be *too normal,* because in fact they are not, yet, as illustrated herein. In fact, most of us have problems with just basic functions of everyday life as well as difficult or unexpected life situations that arise. To begin, many inmates face challenges seeking legal employment not only for the existence of a criminal record, but for lack of photo identification, a driver's license, a vehicle, a cell phone, a social security number, a physical address, an impressive resume, or references. Further, depending on the individual, it normally takes 6 to 12 months before inmates are ready to handle the stress, duties, and responsibilities of a full-time job. In all, combined with various other issues, a job can result in more stress, depression, and eventually lead to a breaking point if inmates try to move too quickly. Prisoners should learn that the focus must be on making themselves better, while participating in required programs and following the rules of parole and the halfway house, and cautiously progressing to a point where they can function in a day-to-day society. Eventually, the more people work, the more detached they will be from their criminal past and criminal associations, and the greater their chance for becoming socially and economi-

cally stable and thus taxpayers instead of a tax burden to society.

10. Education After Being Released

Over the years penal institutions have established educational programs for prisoners to enhance rehabilitation while incarcerated and better prepare inmates for reentry. Upon release, however, the educational component is abandoned by both inmates and the correctional system, impacting community reintegration and long-term economic, political, and social stability of inmates and the community at large. Therefore, both inmates and the penal system must realize and acknowledge that continued education after prison is, in a sense, the *secret* to making it on the outside, with the ultimate objective of breaking the cycle of crime, imprisonment, and release (see Urbina & Álvarez, Chapter 17, this volume).

11. Post-Release Monitoring, Counseling, and Mentoring

As a final step, both the penal system and prisoners must realize that *successful long-term reintegration involves post-release monitoring, counseling, and mentoring.* Specifically, because of changes in sentencing laws, more inmates are now serving full terms. As such, since some prisoners are being released with no parole, they have no official contact with state or federal authorities. Therefore, since no officers are monitoring their behavior, it is difficult to evaluate the *reintegration process,* determine the magnitude of specific legal barriers they are confronting, or provide a *needs-assessment* of their basic necessities. Achieving successful reintegration, then, requires well-planned and unintrusive post-release monitoring, counseling, and mentoring to help men and women address not only the issues mentioned herein, like addictions, traumas, and negative family and neighborhood influence in their lives, but to establish a *solid foundation* for the betterment and well-being of inmates and society at large.

In sum, these steps should constitute an educational blue book for the penal system and prisoners, where inmates are well-versed in these areas of survival before being released from prison. As for successful reentry, instead of neglecting prisoners, especially as they are about to be released, the penal system should expand the availability and quality of in-prison programming. Once released, the initial weeks after release from prison are a high-risk period for relapse and reoffending. Therefore, exiting prisoners need to have access to programs and service immediately upon release, continuing for several months to ensure that people can transform their desire for successful reentry and long-term reintegration into pro-social activities and behavior. Clearly, out-of-prison programming, including job training and substance abuse programs, for released prisoners can improve public safety and reduce spending not only on prisons but policing and the judicial system. In all, if we are in fact vested in stopping the cycle of crime, imprisonment, and release, reintegrating prisoners back into society should be a priority.

A TWENTY-FIRST CENTURY CHALLENGE

For the twenty-first century, critical questions remain to be answered, from a theoretical, research, and policy perspective. Likewise, the correctional system, the male and female offender population, and conventional society are likely to confront serious challenges. Globally speaking, though, the biggest challenge boils down to one question: How do we change the public opinion of Americans, particularly the "voting class," who, for example, recently elected people like Donald Trump, so that they can be more tolerant to a population that historically has been perceived and treated with *indifference* (Urbina & Álvarez, 2017)?

A question of such magnitude, of course, will not be resolved overnight in that it will require restructuring of the American society. What follows are a few recommendations that can serve as a "road map" for a more inclusive America. First, we must come to the realization that from whatever angle the situation is analyzed (cost-benefit, economically, politically, morally, ethically, or legally), we cannot continue to marginalize, discriminate, manipulate, subjugate, isolate, neglect, and silence male and female offenders. Second, we must acknowledge the "true" logic and utility of the prison system in the context of those who are being arrested, indicted, prosecuted, convicted, sentenced to prison, or placed on death row. In the words of one critic,

> What to do with those whom society cannot accommodate? Criminalize them. Outlaw their actions and creations. Declare them the enemy, then wage war. Emphasize the difference—the shade of skin, the accent in the speech or manner of clothes. Like the scapegoat of the Bible, place society's ills on them, then "stone them" in absolution. Its convenient. Its logical. It doesn't work. (Rodriguez, 1993:250)

Third, we need to be more sensitive to the experiences and realities of male and female offenders in the context of society as a whole. As reported by some investigators, ". . . the disturbing expansion of prisons and jails as a means of social control for the poor

... Now, all of these crises-the crises of class, the crises of race, the crises of prisons and the crises of education—are all interconnected . . . the have-nots are disproportionately black and brown" (Marable, 1999:41). Taken together, U.S. prisons are vast warehouses for the impoverished, the unemployed, the poorly educated, and, most particularly, for minorities. Fourth, the American society must acknowledge and accept responsibility for the implications and ramifications of neglecting the "undeserving" members of society or simply warehousing them in prison. In the same way that an alcoholic must accept the "problem and responsibility" before an effective treatment takes its course, we must acknowledge that the prison system yields very few benefits at the cost of many negative consequences. Fifth, in a highly judgmental and prejudicial society, prison-based education must be made a high priority. The fact that states like California are spending more money on corrections than education, and states like New York are sending more minorities to prison than to universities has long-term consequences (see Urbina & Álvarez, Chapter 17, this volume). Realistically, education is not only significant to compete in the job market, but it influences the level of ignorance in the general public, which in turn governs the level of stereotypes and fears about certain members of society—subsequently impacting elections and public policy. Sixth, male and female offenders must have better access to employment opportunities. As part of the restructuring process, policymakers must keep in mind not only the implications of low wages and highly advanced job requirements, but that jobs in the areas where the typical offender lives (who most likely lacks transportation) are scarce. As noted earlier, rearrests are tied to failures in economic support, including employment. It is ironic that the prison system is adopting some of the latest "safety technologies," yet advanced educational and vocational training for people in prison is minimal or nonexistent. In plain twenty-first century, how can it be possible that when it comes to quality and up-to-date technology, safety technologies stand on one end of the spectrum, and innovations that will prepare men and women for after release stand on the other end of the spectrum? Lastly, fueled by notions of colonialism, conquest, imperialism, slavery, stereotypes, hate, and threat perceptions, the history of race and ethnic relations in the United States continues to be vicious, vindictive, and bloody (Acuna, 2014; Almaguer, 2008; Bender, 2015; De León & Del Castillo, 2012; Urbina et al., 2014). Yet, "no single historical element has been more influential in unjustifiable behavior, beliefs, apathy, and feelings than 'indifference'" (Urbina, 2008:206). In this context, the educational system, starting in preschool, must play a more active role in advocating and developing more tolerance for indifference (Urbina & Wright, 2016), if we are to achieve tranquility, equality, and justice, along with an objective and balanced education.

CONCLUSION

Invariably, both male and female offenders are not only confronted with great uncertainty and confusion, they are economically, politically, socially, and morally bankrupt when they are released from prison. Morally, what will become of male and female inmates once they are released from prison? Will they be able to find legal employment with the skills they learned while incarcerated? Considering the wide range of problems facing prisoners, especially female offenders, will they be able to pay for their needs, like healthcare, and not return to illegal activities, like prostitution or narcotics trafficking? If inmates do not have the necessary skills, will they be able to acquire credentials and qualifications that will allow them to survive in a competitive job market? Will they be able to reunite with their children, partner, spouse, friends, or other loved ones? Will they be accepted by the community? Or, will they be met with looks of mistrust, disdain, rejection, or hostility? What is the probability that those released from prison will end up back in the correctional system?

Clearly, there is a big disconnect between prison and community reentry, hindering long-term community reintegration. If released prisoners cannot find legal employment, they are unable to obtain an education, they are not allowed to participate in community civic functions, they cannot find a mate for stability, and they cannot get help with basic necessities, what's left? What's left, especially for young Latino and African American men, is the *pharmacy* on the streets: Selling drugs or stealing.

In a sense, like offenders, the prison system as well as conventional society lack significant "rehabilitation." In effect, to promote and guarantee public safety, the federal government and all 50 states must adopt policies and practices that facilitate successful reintegration, judging people on their individual merits instead of racial, ethnic, or gender stereotypes, stigma, or prejudice. For the well-being of society as a whole, there seems to be increasing support in various states and Congress for the repeal of oppressive and counterproductive laws. In fact, a number of initiatives are currently underway that will help ex-convicts who have spent their time behind bars become independent and law-abiding citizens, thereby strengthening community safety and stability. Globally, instead of creating further isolation and detachment, the prison population, the correctional system, and conventional society should work together to create a more inclusive, understanding, and safe America. Above all, society must take steps towards the creation of a more tolerant and forgiving society, while advocating public safety and justice.

Section Fourth

LATINOS, GLOBALIZATION, AND SOCIAL CONTROL

Conquest was legal, colonialism was legal, slavery was legal, segregation was legal, the Holocaust was legal, preventing women and minorities from voting, among multiple other functions in everyday life, was legal, and signs declaring, "No dogs, no Niggers, no Mexicans allow" or "we serve whites only, no Spanish or Mexicans" were legal. Legality—or illegality—is a question of power, control, and dominance, not equality, legitimacy, or justice.

—Martin Guevara Urbina

Great spirits have always found violent opposition from mediocrities. The latter cannot understand it when a man does not thoughtlessly submit to hereditary prejudices but honestly and courageously uses his intelligence.

—Albert Einstein

Chapter 17

THE NEW FRONTIER: GLOBALIZATION, LATINOS, AND CRIMINAL JUSTICE

MARTIN GUEVARA URBINA AND SOFÍA ESPINOZA ÁLVAREZ

In the cabaret of globalization, the state shows itself as a table dancer that strips off everything until it is left with only the minimum indispensable garments: The repressive force.

–Subcomandante Marcos

Considering the wide usage of the term *globalization,* it appears, on the surface, that we are experiencing a transnational movement, in which essential elements are being tied together universally for the common good. Realistically, though, the concept of globalization dates back to antiquity through movements like expansionist wars, conquest, and colonialism. Communities around the globe have explored, fought, silenced, and killed in the name of linear social change, always moving forward, arguably. As existing barriers, boundaries, and borders are left behind, those who conquer either redefine or invent new barriers, boundaries, and borders. What has changed, as political, economic, and military leaders march along in the quest to reach every corner of the universe, are the dynamics of globalization, and sometimes taking new dimensions. The United States, though, has been the leader in the march for globalization and the undisputed champion when it comes to certain elements of the *modern globalization movement.* Beginning with the early days in the Americas (say, 1492 with the so-called discovery of America), the United States has fought ferociously to explore selected avenues, defining and redefining barriers and boundaries to achieve targeted objectives locally and abroad. Together, globalization appears to be an ideal avenue for the achievement of social change as well as the discovery of truth and reality. For some communities around the world, however, the truths of their everyday lives, in essence, their existence, are the unspoken and consequential realities in the *march for globalization.*

287

GLOBALIZATION: THE AMERICAN WAY

Normally, every New Year, every election, and every major political, financial, or social shift we claim, hope, and pray that the issues, concerns, and problems of the past will not be repeated. The unspoken element: hopefully, we have learned from the past. In academia, Spanish-born philosopher George Santayana's (1905:284) historical observation is often cited, "those who do not know history are condemned to repeat it." Ideologically, pragmatically, and symbolically, we advocate imperative concepts, like *universal* freedom, liberty, democracy, equality, justice, and peace. And, as a country that has historically conveyed the message of "America the beautiful," the United States has strategically used its media as well as political, financial, and educational institutions to advocate alluring, but, at times, illusive elements like morality, religiosity, diversity, tolerance, and culture.

Forcefully, though, two major movements seem to be in progress, with a unified objective, but, realistically, leading to two separate paths and outcomes. At one movement, possibly just as symbolic as pragmatic, Americans wished to enter and progress in the twenty-first century on the "right foot," *marching forward* to achieve public safety, national security, world order, global solidarity, unity, and peace. Ideally, the entire universe under a single flag: globalization at its best, *sin fronteras;* that is, without borders! Prize *trophies* include: Transnational technological innovations, like the World Wide Web, transnational economic treaties, such as NAFTA, and global military alliances among the superpowers, as in the post-9/11 war on terror. The other movement, involves the enforcement of existing *barriers,* the creation of additional barriers, boundaries, and borders, and the widening of gaps in significant areas, like race/ethnic rela-

tions, finance, politics, healthcare, education, and criminal justice policies and sanctions. This movement is also replete with lack of understanding for *difference* and *indifference,* lack of respect for the *stranger,* the *outsider,* and the *other,* and little (or no) tolerance for ideas, events, or situations that do not fit well with the status quo of mainstream America. This type of movement, unfortunately, not only counteracts the other, but it sets or reinforces the foundation for discontinuities and devastating ruptures in America's main institutions, while continuing to usher a legacy of hate, vindictiveness, ignorance, and hypocrisy—as illustrated during the 2015-2016 presidential elections, exacerbating with the election of Donald Trump and his administration.

Indeed, as Americans entered the twenty-first century, everything *seemed to indicate* that the United States would be *the country of the future,* with no, on the surface, known significant signs of major ruptures, discontinuities, or uncertainty. The September 11, 2001, terrorist attacks on the Pentagon and the World Trade Center, though, changed the world in its entirety, resulting in devastating ramifications for Americans. Then, we were "hit" with the 2007 economic crises, now referred to as the Great Recession (2007-2009), followed by one of the most unexpected and controversial presidential election in history, moving from a socalled united to a clearly "divided States of America." Worse, for some people in the United States and abroad (particularly Mexicans), their life drifted into a state of limbo, with globalization quickly defining and redefining new dynamics and dimensions.

This chapter, therefore, explores the influence of various crucial elements of the globalization movement, which, as in the past, significantly influence the minority experience, placing the Latino experience within a global context. The focus will be primarily (but not exclusively) on what the authors view as four of the most influential global elements shaping and reshaping the experience of *los de abajo,* or, in the words of Critical Race Theorist Derrick Bell (1992), the "Faces at the Bottom of the Well," in the United States and abroad, focusing not only on the Latino experience, but also equating the black and white experience to delineate race and ethnic variation in the globalization movement within an historical context. As such, seeking to better understand the experience of America's three largest race/ethnic groups, what follows is an exploration of the globalization of the *war on drugs,* the globalization of the *illegal alien* ideology, the globalization of the *national security* propaganda, and the globalization of *knowledge.*

THE GLOBALIZATION OF THE WAR ON DRUGS

One of the most essential examples of modern globalization is the transnational war on drugs that is currently being ferociously waged (Urbina & Álvarez, 2017; see also Álvarez, this volume). From a legal and historical standpoint, the drug movement predates what some people see as the advent of the war on drugs, with the Anti-Drug Abuse Acts of 1986 and 1988 simply marking the current era of the war on drugs spearheaded by the United States and Mexico. With elements of capitalism and appealing political rhetoric, anti-narcotics legislation quickly gained wide publicity in the media and was legitimized by high ranking government and law enforcement officials and, crucially, academia. In 1999, for example, the prestigious American Society of Criminology enlisted criminologists, sociologists, and other social scientists to contemplate how strategies of crime and delinquency prevention and evaluation could be effectively globalized in its call for academic papers, "Explaining and Preventing Crime: The Globalization of Knowledge," and in the subsequent publication of Professor David Farrington's presidential address under the same title.

The facilitated discourse marked a "point of no return" in the development of an increasingly callous and restrictive movement of punishment and social control that included order-maintenance policing, zero tolerance programs, public space zoning, juvenile transfers to adult court, and enhanced sentencing among other draconian, subjective, and poorly-designed measures (Urbina & Álvarez, 2017; see Álvarez, this volume). The *unspoken mentality,* "great timing to make drugs a global target," as such strategies had in fact been circulating in conservative think tanks, criminal justice circles, police associations, and court settings since the early 1970s, gaining momentum in the 1980s (Urbina & Álvarez, 2016). The academic discourse, simply, made explicit the expansionist logic, most notably, power, control, and expansion of the U.S. legal system, sending an overt and consequential signal to the international community that a new era of law and order was about to begin, which, eventually, resulting in a moral panic, especially in the United States and Mexico, while propagating race and ethnic stereotypes, fear, and uncertainty in the community.

In effect, drug prosecutions quickly increased to over 25 percent of all federal criminal cases and 44 percent of all federal prosecutions, with about 60 percent of all federal inmates being convicted on drug-related charges. Practically, state and federal drug policies have a far-reaching impact that is correlated with the disproportionate representation of minorities, Latinos and blacks, in jails and prisons throughout the United States (Alexander, 2012; Salinas, 2015; Urbina & Álvarez, 2016, 2017), and particularly the astronomical increase in the incarceration of female offenders, especially Latinas and African American women (Díaz-Cotto, 1996; Urbina, 2008). Together, soon after the escalation of such draconian measures, well-known scholar Elliott Currie (1993:10) characterized the war on drugs as an *American nightmare* and documents that "twenty years after the drug war began in earnest, we are far worse off than when we started." As we were approaching the twenty-first century, Currie (1993:31) reported, "the drug war has been overwhelmingly targeted at the communities of the poor and near-poor, especially the minority poor," further criminalizing, marginalizing, isolating, and silencing minorities and impoverished whites. Though, realistically, as reported by James Austin and John Irwin (2012), two leading authorities in the field of criminal justice, the law was not designed to be applied evenly nor applied according to the severity of crime. Michael Tonry (1995:4–5), a leading expert on corrections, notes that such policies ". . . were the foreseeable effects of deliberate policies spearheaded by the Reagan and Bush administrations and implemented by many states," and "crime controllers made no effort to minimize foreseeable racial disparities."

With additional restricted sanctions in place, the entire criminal justice system was transformed within a few years (Urbina & Álvarez, 2016, 2017; see Álvarez, this volume). Tonry (1995), for instance, documents that the prison population nearly tripled during the 1980s and by 1990 a quarter of young black males were in jail or prison, on probation or parole. In effect, the chance that a black male was in jail or prison was

seven times that of a white male. A 1990 analysis revealed that nationally 23 percent of black males aged 20–29 were under the control of the criminal justice system (Tonry, 1995). In California, 33 percent of black men aged 20 to 29 were under the control of the justice system in 1990 (Tonry, 1995). According to Jack Levin (1999), as a result of the war on drugs almost 30 percent of all young African American men were placed under the control of the criminal justice system, within a few years. As such, although African Americans made up approximately 12.3 percent of the U.S. population, they comprised nearly half of the population in U.S. prisons and jails, and, in later years, more than half of those sent to jails or prisons, quickly transforming the penal population from mostly white to mostly black and brown people (Alexander, 2012; Urbina & Álvarez, 2016, 2017). Similarly, for Latinos, from 1980 to 1993 the percentage of Latinos in prison rose from 7.7 percent to 14.3 percent (not including Latinos incarcerated in immigration facilities). During this same period, the number of inmates tripled from 163 to 529 per 100,000 Latino residents (Urbina & Álvarez, 2016, 2017; see also Álvarez, this volume).

Overall, almost one in three (32.2%) black men between the ages of 20–29 were either in prison, jail, on probation, or parole on any given day, and more than one in ten Latinos (12.3%) in the same age group were either in prison, jail, on probation, or parole on any given day during the same time frame, while for white men, the ratio was considerably lower: one in 15 (6.7%). Sixty years prior to that era, less than one-fourth of prison admissions were nonwhite. Eventually, nearly three-fourths were nonwhite, blacks and Latinos constituting almost 90 percent of all offenders sentenced to state prison for drug charges, with black women experiencing the greatest incarceration increase, rising by 78 percent from 1989 through 1994. An analysis of national trends not only reveals similar patterns in that the majority of new prison admissions were minority men, but the majority were impoverished and lacking a formal high school education (62%). Further, contrary to the popular imagination, the vast majority (73%) of inmates were admitted for either nonviolent crimes or no crimes at all. In fact, most of the crimes for which offenders were sent to correctional institutions (52.6%) failed into the "petty category" (Irwin & Austin, 1997:32), with less than five percent of the individuals being sent to prison for committing a crime that could be classified as very serious, clearly fueling the *criminal justice system's unspoken logic of power,* control, and expansion (Urbina & Álvarez, 2016). Further, Irwin and Austin (1997) note that not only was the prison quickly transformed, but that the Latino and African American communities were transformed in various other fundamental areas, like employment, education, and voting.

If incarceration rates continue (Urbina & Álvarez, 2016, 2017; see also Álvarez, this volume), an African American male born in 2001 has a one in three chance of going to prison during his lifetime, and a Latino born in 2001 has a one in six chance, while a white male has a one in 17 chance of going to prison. At the turn of the century, the Bureau of Justice Statistics also reported that the lifetime probability of going to prison among black women (5.6%) was almost as high as for white men (5.9), Latinas (2.2%), and white females (0.9%) having a much lower lifetime chance of going to prison (Bonczar, 2003). More recently, in *A Comprehensive Study of Female Offenders: Life Before, During, and After Incarceration* (2008) Martin Guevara Urbina reports that the biggest impact of the war on drugs has fallen on female offenders, many of them mothers of young children, who are being left behind to eventually become the "hidden victims of the war on drugs," and a seldom spoken reality of the globalization of the war on drugs.

Abroad, political rhetoric, academic slant, and a media propagated moral panic have been fueling the momentum of the transnational war on drugs, resulting in the passage of a sweeping anti-narcotics movement under Mexican President Felipe Calderon in 2006, leading to a much wider impact on the international nature of crime and punishment than never before, but, as in the United States, the biggest impact falling on the impoverished, uneducated, and powerless. Yet, the warriors of law and order appear to be more vested in the political economy of crime and punishment than improving the very conditions that set the foundation of social disorganization, like jobs, education, and healthcare—the unspoken realities of the dynamics of globalization.

In effect, as a mechanism of control and expansion, more than any other time in history criminality is becoming more and more transnational (as various other crime control policies, like anti-terrorism laws) and, by extension, are now contingent upon broader transnational arrangements (Sánchez, 2007). Richard Bennett (2004:6), for instance, highlights the significance of understanding "crime that transcends . . . borders and justice systems." Similarly, Urbina and Álvarez (2017) report that the globalization of the anti-narcotics movement has resulted in a global manifestation in the legal system; that is, responses to crime are not only becoming increasingly transnational but consequential in that years after the war on drugs started, crime rates have remained somewhat constant in the United States (see Álvarez, this volume), while increasing in Mexico. Yet, as documented by Michael Lynch in *Big Prisons, Big Dreams: Crime and the Failure of America's Penal System* (2007), bigger prisons have not resulted in lower crime rates.

However, the severe ramifications of the globalization of the anti-drugs movement have been devastating to countries around the globe, but most pressing in Columbia, Venezuela, and Mexico. Columbia, a country experiencing great financial, political, and social problems even before the international economic crises, was on the verge of war with Venezuela in 2008 and 2009, partly triggered by the war on drugs, prompting Venezuelan President Hugo Chávez to order his military forces to be prepared for war with Columbia. Worse, while Columbia and Venezuela, like several other Latin American countries, are spending millions and billions of dollars in military preparations for wars that might never happen, the highly charged language of Hugo Chávez and Colombian President Alvaro Uribe was overshadowing the more serious financial and social problems of their countries, like savage poverty, high unemployment rates, healthcare needs, and lack of educational preparation and limited opportunities. More globally, according to a report released by UNICEF on November 2009, nearly 200 million children under age of five have stunted growth because they do not have enough to eat, with approximately 1.02 billion hungry people worldwide (one in six people).

Internationally, the biggest impact of the globalization of the anti-narcotics movement has fallen on Mexico and its people. Spearheaded by the United States, the Merida Initiative ($1.4 billion) which was signed into law on June 30, 2008, fueled the *Mexican Drug War* and set the stage for Mexican President Felipe Calderon when he took office in 2006. In effect, in Mexico and, to a lesser degree the United States, we have witnessed the militarization of the police force, with President Calderon deploying over 45,000 soldiers nationwide, along with over 5,000 federal police officers. Since 2006, we have seen a dramatic increase in drug vio-lence, which has killed thousands of people (including federal police officers and soldiers), some journalists are either killed or disappeared, and we even seen the name of once America's and Mexico's most-wanted drug lord, Joaquin "El Chapo" Guzmán, on *Forbes* magazine's list of the 67 "Worlds' Most Powerful People." At number 41, Guzmán was considered more powerful than Venezuelan President Hugo Chávez (#67) and France's Nicolas Sarkozy (#56), and just below Iran's Supreme Leader Ayatollah Ali Khameni.

Unfortunately, seldom do we hear about the thousands of children being used in the drug trade or the thousands of women, many of them mothers of young children, going to prison for minor drug-related charges. To this end, walking through a Mexican federal prison, an overwhelming emotion overtook me, as I observed the *incarcerated children of the globalized anti-narcotics movement.* As I looked around to make a mental note, I turned around and asked: how is it possible that the most innocent and the weakest are behind bars and the ones most responsible are either designing policy to further expand, control, isolate, marginalize, and silence; preparing for multi-billion dollar wars that might never happen; or making the list of *Forbes* magazine? Again, as in the United States, instead of solving the conditions that led to crime in the first place, policymakers have been more concerned with draconian penal sanctions, with little probability of reducing crime. Normally, we hear about violence, corruption, torture, and, to a lesser extent, violations of international treaties and civil liberties, but seldom do we hear about diversion of resources for *los de abajo* ("the ones from below"), especially minorities, women, and children, a defined contradiction of U.S. propagated values.

In sum, an unspoken reality of globalization is the consequential impact of punitive policies that underlie the anti-narcotics movement on the disproportionate rate of arrests, prosecutions, convictions, sentencing, and imprisonment of minorities, particularly Latinos, blacks, and, more recently, Latinas and black women and children in the United States and abroad. Invariably, what symbolically and politically appeared like a smooth transition into the twenty-first century was in reality a rocky beginning even before the September 11, 2001, terrorist attacks. In this regard, Urbina and Álvarez (2017) report that due to significant changes in race and ethnic landscape, ethnic and race variation in formal punishment is highly probable to continue. Lastly, as the globalization of the anti-narcotics movement continues to gain momentum, academic investigators need to ensure that the war on drugs be analyzed in its totality, as illustrated by Michael Welch (2002, 2006, 2007). In effect, cross-national studies by Ruddell and Urbina (2004, 2007) suggest that adopting a global perspective not only allows us to apply a more holistic investigative approach, but it enables us to see essential gaps that need to be bridged, if we are to provide a universal explanation, and, hopefully, a solution to a global phenomenon.

THE GLOBALIZATION OF THE ILLEGAL ALIEN IDEOLOGY

The reification of the current immigration movement and its subsequent *illegal alien ideology* are pinnacle manifestations of globalization, connected to the anti-narcotics movement and rooted in American history (Álvarez & Urbina, 2018; see also Álvarez, this volume). In fact, there is an historical precedent to this linkage in that as early as the nineteenth century, drug problems and addicts were "identified with foreign groups and internal minorities who were already actively feared and the objects of elaborate and massive social and legal constraints" (Musto, 1973:122). From an historical standpoint, though, the main unspoken objective of *culture warriors* in the process of categorization, stigmatization, marginalization, and criminalization has been the creation and dissemination of a defined ideology against foreigners, with demonizing terminology, as *illegal alien* (signifying "criminal"), which is then used on different segments of society, like African Americans, Chinese, Japanese, Latinos, Middle Easterns, and, most recently, Mexicans, largely due to the highly polarized immigration debate, vividly illustrated by the April 2010 Arizona immigration law and more recently by Trump's proposed "big beautiful wall" (see Aguirre; Álvarez, this volume). As documented by David Garland (1990) and Jeffery Reiman and Paul Leighton (2017), the U.S. criminal justice system requires a *defined and effective ideology to fool enough people, enough of the time*. Chicano historian, Rodolfo Acuña in *Occupied America: A History of Chicanos* (2015) documents the historical origins and evolution of ethnic categorization, divides, manipulation, marginalization, and the silencing of Latinos through a *slavery-type* approach, mentality, and ideology, placing Latinos in a *slavery-type* status; that is, keeping Latinos financially, politically, socially, and emotionally *bankrupt*. In *Racial Fault Lines: The Historical Origins of White Supremacy in California* (2008), Tomas Almaguer documents the strategic orchestration of socialization, resocialization, *psychological intoxication,* marginalization, criminalization, and silencing through intimidation, stigmatization, deportation, vicious violence, and lynching of Mexican men, women, and children, solidifying the illegal alien ideology in the popular imagination. Historian David Gutiérrez in *Between Two Worlds: Mexican Immigrants in the United States* (1997) reports that the illegal alien ideology is a ready-made and highly effective weapon during rough economic cycles or political turmoil in the United States, like an atomic bomb, ready to be effectively used when deemed necessary. Once in orbit, the illegal alien ideology is highly propagated by the media and politicians vis-à-vis labels like *immigrants, wetbacks, the Mexican problem, they take our jobs, they don't pay taxes, they refuse to speak English,* or *they commit crime* and subsequently legitimized by high ranking government officials, academic racists, and warriors of language, culture, or law and order (see Álvarez, this volume), as recently documented by Álvarez and Urbina in *Immigration and the Law: Race, Citizenship, and Social Control* (2018).

Once the illegal alien ideology is legitimized, it then becomes institutionalized, functioning globally to categorize, divide, isolate, criminalize, and silence Latinos, most notably, Mexicans (Álvarez & Urbina, 2018; Urbina & Álvarez, 2016, 2017; see also Aguirre; Álvarez, this volume). Most recently, the latest global assault on illegal aliens was a direct manifestation of the *war on terror* (Álvarez & Urbina, 2018; Bosworth & Flavin, 2007; Welch, 2002). As quoted by the American Civil Liberties Union, "the war on terror has quickly turned into a war on immigrants," effectively globalizing the illegal alien ideology, with corresponding applicability and ramifications, as documented by Michael Welch (2006).

Beyond the cruelties against foreigners reported by scholars like Welch (2006) and contrary to the popular imagination, Robert J. Sampson of Harvard University illustrated in a 2006 article that Latino communities, some containing high concentrations of undocumented people, were safer than those of whites and blacks (Press, 2006), revealing

not only an unspoken reality, but a possible reality that clashes with the popular imagination, which is highly governed by the now globalized and institutionalized illegal alien ideology. As such, instead of being welcomed for possibly addressing community fear and safety concerns, Sampson received hate mail and was threatened by those in *disbelief.* Critically, just look at the thousands of anti-immigrants messages on the Worldwide Web, including the social media, particularly after Trump's anti-Mexican statements and policies.

In sum, the combined force of historical events like the September 11, 2001 terrorist attacks, the deployment of the military by President Calderon, and the highly proposed controversial wall along the 2,000-mile U.S.-Mexico border, the hundreds of laws passed, and the militarization of the southern border is simply the *ingredient* that anti-immigrant people were waiting for: the illegal alien ideology on a global scale. Symbolically and consequentially, like those who sought the return of blacks to Africa once slavery was outlawed and thus slavery's economic value diminished, the nativist wish to preserve both their socially constructed ideology and ethnic selectivity (Álvarez & Urbina, 2018; see also Berger & Luckmann, 1966; Levin, 2002; Reisler, 1997). Consider, for instance, Trump's idea of a "big beautiful wall" to keep Mexicans, other Latinos, Syrians, Muslims, and anyone trying to enter the country through Mexico. Even in established institutions which are supposed to serve as pillars of social change, people are confined to the limits of defined ideology (as discussed below). As such, renowned scholar Cornel West (2001) cites that people are confined to an institutionalized personality, a personality so accustomed to life within an institutional environment that life outside its boundaries seems daunting and beyond the limits of imagination.

THE GLOBALIZATION OF THE NATIONAL SECURITY PROPAGANDA

From a political and military standpoint, the single most notorious rupture in modern times was the September 11, 2001 terrorist attacks on U.S. territory, marking a new era as to how the United States and other governments organize to secure national security, sovereignty, power, and control. Pretending that the United States and, in a sense, the entire world was in devastating danger, the United States positioned itself as the undisputed champion of war and declared itself as the defender of the universe, propelling a signal of community fear and intimidation by the "devilish enemy," as often referenced by then President George W. Bush. While seeking to convey a notion that Americans are sensitive to universal freedom, democracy, civil liberties, and even casualties and cruelties of war, the United States and its allies repeatedly testified on national television that national security was now a global affair, with an urgent need to *react* to the act. In effect, being vigorously voiced by three of the most powerful people on the planet, former President George W. Bush, former Prime Minister of the United Kingdom Tony Blair, and former Prime Minister of Spain José Maria Aznar (leaders of three of the original countries who began exploration, conquest, colonialism, and imperialism), the national security propaganda quickly became a globalized movement, creating severe ramifications, anger, confusion, and uncertainty in the process.

Confusion, anger, and vindictiveness was then manifested in people drifting in two crucial directions: at the same time that people were calling for international alliances on various grounds and to quickly resolve the global political and military crises, others were calling for war and immediate design and implementation of dividing barriers in a country composed mostly of immigrants,

Native Americans being the only exception. Following the historical American approach of *action, immediate reaction,* people were quick to judge, blame, and convict, relying on the now globalized national security thesis, which continues to be highly charged with anger, prejudice, hypocrisy, and unfounded ideology. Dating back to the early days in the Americas with the vicious murdering of millions of Indians, lynching against African American slaves, and brutal violence against Mexicans during and after the Mexican-American War (see Baker, this volume), "People are inclined to personalize evil, to employ it, to stuff it into another human being. That way we can find the culprit, detect the enemy. This is psychologically tempting. It allows us to 'locate' evil, to see it, spit at it, hate it, blame it, perhaps even to kill it" (Groves, 1991:111). As for those already living in the United States, award-winning author Luis Rodríguez remarks in *Always Running* (1993:250),

> What to do with those whom society cannot accommodate? Criminalize them. Outlaw their actions and creations. Declare them the enemy, and then wage war. Emphasize the differences–the shade of skin, the accent in the speech or manner of clothes. Like the scapegoat of the Bible, place society's ills on them, then 'stone them' in absolution. It's convenient. It's logical. It doesn't work.

More precisely, 9/11 brought certain elements of national security and international relations out of the obscurity into the surface to be considered by law enforcement and military officials, debated by politicians and legal decision-makers, and to a feared and misinformed national and international community, converted into global propaganda under the pretext of national security. For warriors of law and order, particularly those vested in multibillion dollar profits, it was a matter of either now or never for a *justified war,* which in reality was a *terrorist invasion* by the United States and its allies. For U.S. high ranking government officials, 9/11 went far and beyond national security, to the very inner fiber of U.S. imperialism. The act and the manner in which it was executed was a slap on the face, a spit on the face to the most powerful country in the world, truly an unforgivable act to the United States, and subsequently sending a clear message to Saddam Hussein and others who dare to insult the United States, like Fidel Castro and Hugo Chávez in the past and today's Kim Jong-un.[27] Today, for instance, Trump wishes to declare war on various countries after terrorist tragedies, even if the presumed terrorist is a native of the country were the act occurred.

In essence, the September 11 attacks on American soil and the continuous attacks that followed, including those by the United States and its allies, are definite testaments of a terrifying and, in a sense, unjustified tragedies of the multiple deaths and killing horror that turns men, women, and children around the world into agonized victims and witnesses to the devastating destruction of their communities and homes, the death of their families and friends, the death of their innocence, the death of their dreams, the death of their religion, and the death of their God. Ultimately, 9/11 and its aftermath revived the catastrophic forces of evil, which has a human face, conveying the inevitable message that such human tragedies must not be allowed to happen anywhere in the world, not just in America. With minimal fighting occurring on U.S. soil, with the Mexican-American War (1846–1848), Pearl Harbor (1941), and 9/11 being a few isolated incidents, the attacks, as seen around the world through television screens, gave Americans a closer view of human suffering in our own land.

From a law and order standpoint, once the national security propaganda was *globalized* and *legitimized,* the militarization of the southern border and questionable law enforcement tactics in the United States and abroad were easier to rationalize and convey to a feared community experiencing a "moral panic." As such, thousands of people who were suspected of terrorist connections were held without charges and without procedural protections that could allow them to prove in neutral and fair hearings that terrorist ties did not exist, a practice that continues today, along with heavy surveillance. An explanation given for their detention was that they had violated immigration law, like overstaying their visas, with no violent crimes committed but yet subjected to unjustifiable treatment, as reported by Welch in *Scapegoats of September 11th: Hate Crimes and State Crimes in the War on Terror* (2006). For instance, instead of immediate release or deportation, thousands of people were incarcerated, a common strategy used in the past (Welch, 2002, 2007), as in the case of Pearl Harbor where *concentration camps* were actually established in the United States for Japanese Americans.

In sum, as documented by some scholars, the primary objective of the U.S. criminal justice system is not to prevent crime, reduce crime, or achieve universal justice and peace, rather its main goal is to create and propagate a visible and intimidating image of the presumed threat of deviance and crime in the United States (and abroad), especially by foreigners, *forgetting* that the United States is a country of immigrants, and, subsequently, reliance on militarism and globalized punishment (Álvarez & Urbina, 2018; Balko, 2013; Bosworth & Flavin, 2007; Dunn, 1996; Kil, 2011; Reiman & Leighton, 2017; Urbina & Álvarez, 2017). In effect, while people are quick to reference the multibillion dollar annual budget for the criminal justice system (police, judicial, corrections), which increased from $80 billion in 1982 to $260 billion in 2010 (Urbina & Álvarez, 2016), with the highest proportion going to payroll, revealing what French sociologist Emile Durkheim once observed, the usefulness of crime, people are subtle and silent about the actual realities of law and order, like the warehousing of Latinos and blacks, a new form of slavery, as illustrated by Michelle Alexander in *The New Jim Crow: Mass Incarceration in the Age of Colorblindness* (2012) and Urbina and Álvarez in *Ethnicity and Criminal Justice in the Era of Mass Incarceration: A Critical Reader on the Latino Experience* (2017). Lastly, transnational events, like 9/11, should not be utilized as avenues to isolate people and legitimize wars and the policing of the world, but interpreted and treated as *two-way avenues* by

the United States and the international community; that is, by being more inclusive and reaching out to people vis-à-vis two-way communication and understanding. Critically, while the United States has been experiencing tragedies across the country, from the Ferguson unrest (2014), to the Orlando nightclub shooting (2016), to the shooting of Dallas police officers (2016), along with thousands of police-involved shootings, the United States continues to hypocritically deploy the Geneva Conventions in its unsubstantiated critiques of supposed "human rights violations" in socialist countries, and to justify its invasions of Serbia, Somalia, Afghanistan, and Iraq. In fact, since the Declaration of Human Rights in 1948, the United States has signed, but not ratified various international statutes.

THE GLOBALIZATION OF KNOWLEDGE

Invariably, a *deeper* exploration of the intertwining dynamics of the globalization movement reveals that there has always been a gradual march and promotion for globalization, with corresponding dichotomies leading to opposing outcomes and unspoken motives, as illustrated by the globalization of the war on drugs, the illegal alien ideology, and the national security propaganda. Yet the biggest "splash" of globalization

> is taking place in the essence of human existence, *knowledge,* as the mind is an element that enables us to shift the winds of luck, reshape the forces of fate or destiny, and, ultimately, empower us to become *free* authors of our own lives, for the true art of human expression is the ability to express our dreams, thoughts, and emotions as we feel them or as they come to mind, as we search for universal equality, justice, peace, love, truth, and reality. (Urbina, 2014:232)

As such, we now venture into the dynamics of education and globalization, noting that the globalization of knowledge is in fact a modern form of revolution, orchestrated by the educational system and spearheaded by the criminal justice system.

Education and Globalization: Defining Barriers and Boundaries

The United States has always prided itself for (arguably) making education a priory at all levels for those who wish to venture into the world of learning, independent of race, ethnicity, gender, social class, culture, religion, or national origin, referring to landmark cases like *Brown v. the Board of Education* (1954) as illustrations of government sensitivity and effort to bridge centuries-old historical gaps. With the advent of this modern era of globalization, education has become of utmost importance to compete in a highly global and technological job market, forcing Americans to seek higher levels of learning, as noted by Marcelo Suarez-Orozco in *Learning in the Global Era: International Perspectives on Globalization and Education* (2007). For Latinos, though, a sound education and opportunity in the privileged world of academia has been more of an illusion than a reality, as documented by Acuña in *Sometimes There is no Other Side: Chicanos and the Myth of Equality* (1998) and Alfredo Mirandé in *The Stanford Law Chronicles: Doin' Time on the Farm* (2005). Again, more symbolic than pragmatic, the driving forces (to include the simultaneous interactions of historical structural and ideological factors) set the foundation for a dichotomous-global movement, leading to differing outcomes and, consequently, difficult to overcome, as illustrated by Urbina and Wright in *Latino Access to Higher Education: Ethnic Realities and New Directions for the Twenty-First Century* (2016).

In effect, the symbolism and hypocrisy of the system was set in orbit by the educational system itself (Acuña, 1998, 2011, 2013; Johnson, 2013; Mirandé, 2005; Moore, 2007; Zuberi & Bonilla-Silva, 2008; Urbina & Wright, 2016). As an historical reminder, people tend to forget that, as a community, Latinos, like blacks, Native Americans, and women, have been neglected by the educational system, but still expected to compete at the same level, while in search of the so-called American dream. Indeed, scholars, like American sociological theorist, William Graham Sumner, who taught the first sociology course in the United States and who began teaching at Yale University in 1876, was the major exponent of Social Darwinism in the United States, adopting a survival-of-the-fittest, dog-eat-dog approach to the social world and thus supporting human aggressiveness and competitiveness, even though the playing field was far from even.

Insensitive to long-term devastating consequences, the educational system has been everything, but inclusive in regards to minorities (Acuña, 1998, 2011; Aguirre & Martínez, 1993; Noboa, 2005; Ortego, 2007; Pizarro, 2005; Urbina & Wright, 2016), as recently reported by Gilberto Conchas in *Cracks in the Schoolyard: Confronting Latino Educational Inequality* (2016) and Michael Gottfried and Gilberto Conchas in *When School Policies Backfire* (2016). Worse, it has been the world of higher education that not only has contributed to significant race and ethnic variation in educational attainment, but it has "legitimized" and propagated race and ethnic stereotypes regarding educational potential and attainment. In 1890, for instance, the president of the American Economics Association warned his audience of scholars against the invasion of races of "the very lowest stage of degradation," further exacerbating the historical legacy of oppression. As if Social Darwinism needed additional dynamite, scholars at the highest educational levels aim to permanently eliminate possible competition from ethnic minorities. For example, we entered the twentieth century with scholars like Stanford University psychologist Lewis Madison Terman infusing the "academic imprimatur on racism, supporting the idea that Mexicans could not compete intellectually with Anglos" (Shorris, 1992:103; see also Terman, 1906; Urbina, 2003a). Combined with the introduction of the eugenics movement into the Unites States, the Binet-Simon scale (1916) for determining I.Q. gave nativist racism additional momentum. In 1921, Economics Professor Roy Garis of Vanderbilt University, in hearings before the United States Congress, stated that whites should not have to live in competition with "peons" who were trained by 400 years of Spanish oppression and tainted blood of the Mexican women. Soon after, U.S. Supreme Court

Justice Oliver Wendell Holmes, a strong proponent of eugenics, placed the Constitutional stamp of approval on forced sterilization in 1927. A few decades later, in the 1980s, John Tanton, an ophthalmologist by profession, complained of "hyperactive breeders" among Latinos. In 1995, Harvard's leading political scientist Samuel P. Huntington (2004:204) joined the debate by commenting about the growing Latino population and the inevitable "class of civilization," citing that "While Muslims pose the immediate problem to Europe, Mexicans pose the problem for the United States."

Then, as we were about to enter the twenty-first century, with the new wave of globalization quickly gaining momentum, scholars once again raced to unveil race and ethnic stereotypes and even offered the intellectual rationalization for twenty-first century racists in books like *The Bell Curve* by Richard Herrnstein and Charles Murray (1994), *Why Race Matters* by Michael Levin (1997), *The g Factor* by Arthur Jensen (1998), and *Race, Evolution, and Behavior* by J. Philippe Rushton (1999), with the ultraconservative and racist Pioneer Fund underwriting much of the research for the *Bell Curve* as well as *Race, Evolution, and Behavior*. Crucially, in twenty-first century America, Professor Huntington charged in 2004 that Mexican immigrants were the greatest threat to American national identity, having the potential to divide the nation into two peoples, Angelo versus Hispanic, two cultures, and two languages, English and Spanish. Clearly, as a colleague recently charged, "Donald Trump, we have been dealing with 'Donalds' for centuries."

These so-called *scientific discoveries* are then manifested in community sentiment and public policy (Urbina & Wright, 2016), as documented by Tukufu Zuberi and Eduardo Bonilla-Silva in *White Logic, White Methods: Racism and Methodology* (2008). In effect, the same "equal protection" argument utilized to pass civil rights legislation in the 1960s is now being used to dismantle past reform efforts, once again structured in ways that makes it difficult for minorities and women to escape their state of suppression, intimidation, and isolation, essentially, *bankruptcy.* Considering the significance of education in the globalization of knowledge, one of the most crucial assaults on the minority community, particularly Latinos and blacks, is the termination of affirmative action in some universities, under new propaganda that race and ethnic prejudice and discrimination no longer exist. Relying on conventional wisdom, the argument is that whites, not blacks or Latinos, are now the victims of discrimination, and that unqualified minorities are now entering the privileged world of universities because of affirmative action. In spite of the wide range of disparities that still exist in U.S. society, most of which show Latinos, blacks, and Native Americans with worse outcomes than whites in areas such as education, employment, income, home ownership, and health, a study by researchers at Tufts University and Harvard Business School shows that whites believe they are victims of racism more than blacks (Norton & Sommers, 2011). Figures show, though, that far more whites have entered the doors of the ten most elite institutions through "alumni preference" than the combined number of all Latinos and blacks entering through affirmative action (Acuña, 1998; Stein, 1995; Urbina & Wright, 2016).

Setting precedent in *educational jurisprudence,* the U.S. Supreme Court has ruled against affirmative action attempts to include race based criteria in university admissions, including law schools. As such, states are also passing legislation prohibiting hiring decisions, promotions, and admissions to state schools based on race, like the infamous 1978 *Regents of the University of California v. Bakke* decision, drastically impacting Latinos and blacks. For instance, the federal court-imposed ban on affirmative action at the University of Texas Law School quickly resulted in a 74 percent decline in Latino admissions and a 92 percent decline in African American admissions (Acuña, 1998).[28] Tied to the illegal alien ideology, Proposition 209 and Proposition 187, prohibiting school enrollment to undocumented students and eliminating the provision of all health services to undocumented immigrants, have had a dramatic impact not only on Latinos, but the entire minority community. Then, as an extra insult to both Mexicans and the fundamentals of education, since 2002, immigration authorities have been adding restrictions on commuter students who study in American universities, hurting thousands of Mexican students, a movement clearly tied to the illegal alien ideology and the national security propaganda.

Contrary to the popular imagination that Latinos, particularly unqualified minorities, are now taking whites' jobs, the truth and reality of Latinos continue to be under the shadows (Urbina, 2003a; Urbina et al., 2014; Urbina & Wright, 2016), with few escaping the *chains* of conquest, colonialism, and slavery (Urbina & Álvarez, 2016, 2017; Urbina & Smith, 2007; Urbina & Wright, 2016), which became heavier and heavier with the advent of the new era of globalization, especially the globalization of knowledge. In twenty-first century America, 2001, Latinos combined earned only 4.4 percent of the 40,744 doctorates nationwide, according to the National Science Foundation. Educational attainment data for 2009 show that Latinos hold less than five percent (838,000) of all professional and doctoral degrees (17,538,000). Reviewing educational attainment by race and ethnicity in 2010 for resident population 25 and older, for instance, Motel (2012) reports that Latino college graduates accounted for 3,588,593, in contrast to 43,924,341 for whites, 4,142,690 for blacks, 4,956,912 for Asians, and others (non-Latino) accounting for 1,059,929. In the privileged world of higher education, the minority proportion is even lower, especially within the ranks of full-time faculty members, with Latinos representing less than three percent of all full-time professors. Obviously, these figures directly contradict those in *The Shape of the River: Long-Term Consequences of Considering Race in College and University Admissions* by former Harvard University president, Derek Bok, and William Bowen (1998).

Yet, while the globalization march continues and thus making education the *survival weapon of the future* (Urbina & Wright, 2016; see also Suarez-Orozco, 2007; Suarez-Orozco & Qin-Hilliard, 2004), blatant attacks on ethnic minority education continue throughout the country, especially in the area of ethnic studies, Chicano Studies, Mexican American Studies, and bilingual education, along with the adoption of "English only" movements (Acuña, 1998, 2011, 2013; Stritikus, 2002; Urbina & Wright, 2016), as vividly documented by Acuña in *The Making of Chicana/o Studies: In the Trenches of Academe* (2011). To begin, the practice of school segregation of children of Latino ancestry was legal and common until the 1940s, when it was challenged in *Mendez v. Westminster School District of Orange County* (1947), a case that served as a precursor to the *Brown v. Board of Education* (1954). Then, over half a century after the passage of *Brown v. the Board of Education* by the U.S. Supreme Court, forcing schools across the country to be integrated, some communities are currently more segregated than in 1954, largely due to *white flight* (Rosen, 2000), leaving schools in the ghettos and barrios in a state of deterioration and crises. Towards the end of the twentieth century, award-winning author Jonathan Kozol, in *Savage Inequalities: Children in America's*

Schools (1992), illustrated the dynamics of economic variation in America's public school system, and highlighted the devastating effects it has on impoverished children, particularly minority children (Pizarro, 2005; Urbina & Wright, 2016). Then, as we progress in the twenty-first century, with multi-billion dollar military projects and a multi-billion dollar criminal justice enterprise (Urbina & Álvarez, 2016), the lack of education and its consequences on America's children (and adults) become more pressing (Conchas, 2016; Gottfried & Conchas, 2016; Kozol, 2006; Moore, 2007; Pizarro, 2005; Urbina & Wright, 2016; Valenzuela, 2016). In a 2007 report, Bob Balfanz of Johns Hopkins University defines America's public school system as *dropout factories,* in that one in ten high schools across the United States were not graduating more than 60 percent of the students, with the highest concentration of dropout factories in high-poverty areas, normally with a high proportion of minority students (Zuckerbrod, 2007). Realistically, a *better* America for the "lower-class," especially ethnic minorities has been more of an illusion than a reality (Acuña, 1998, 2011, 2013; Eitzen & Johnston, 2007; Urbina & Wright, 2016), further contributing to the devastating school-to-prison pipeline (see Álvarez, this volume).

Within the Latino community, there seems to be significant ethnic variation (Pizarro, 2005; Shorris, 1992; Urbina & Wright, 2016). According to a report issued May 22, 2002, by the Public Policy Institute of California, Mexican Americans earn far less than whites even after three generations because they receive less school than almost all other race and ethnic groups in the United States. For undocumented Latinos, the situation is even more detrimental in that they now find themselves at the mercy of consequential policies, which are rife with anti-immigrant sentiments and symbolism (Álvarez & Urbina, 2018; Aranda, 2006;

Cobas, Duany, & Feagin, 2009; Fox & Rivera-Salgado, 2004; Salinas, 2015), like the 1995 Proposition 187 in California, which denied public educational and health service to undocumented people, the 1996 Personal Responsibility Act, excluding immigrants and refugees from receiving basic assistance, and the April 2010 Arizona immigration law. More critical, without changes in the structure of America's main institutions, inequality will continue as people tend to quickly semi-consciously or consciously *react* to shifts in the status quo. For instance, studies have shown that the higher the educational level, the greater the income disparity between whites and nonwhites in U.S. society, with educated Latinos quickly facing the glass ceiling, not only in the educational system but in all main American institutions, as illustrated by Maria Chávez in *Everyday Injustice: Latino Professionals and Racism* (2011). As currently structured, rather than leveling the playing field, educational achievement maintains or even exacerbates inequality. These consequential statistics, though, are seldom mentioned in academic or public discussions.

Even under the best of circumstances, for those who manage to take part in the educational discourse, the negligence of *truthful teaching* (formal and informal), conscious, unconscious, or semi-unconscious, shaping and reshaping the pillars of knowledge, has been voiced even by renowned intellectuals. For Rene Descartes, "From my earliest years, I have accepted many false opinions as true," and Mark Twain remarked, "When I was fourteen my father was so ignorant I could hardly stand to have the old man around. But when I got to be twenty-one, I was astonished at how much he had learned in seven years," the point being that historical knowledge is grossly contaminated by historical, structural, and ideological subjectivity (Urbina, 2003a).

Historically, the U.S. educational paradigm has not been structured to teach people to fully explore and understand subjects under study in their totality, and thus evading the very essence of education. Worse, people are not only being taught selected, skewed, and manipulated information, but they are not being taught how to truly think independently, individually, or being allowed to explore the limits of imagination (Urbina, 2003b; Urbina & Wright, 2016). As noted by German-born theoretical physicists, Albert Einstein, "It is a miracle that curiosity survives formal education . . . Imagination is more important than knowledge." Yet in the midst of the globalization of knowledge, people are being trained more on memorization than analytical and critical reasoning, which would empower them to decipher the *highly skewed pages of historical knowledge,* making them aware of their potentialities (Urbina, 2003b) and, ultimately, getting them to see that imagination is an element that enables us to travel every corner of the universe, breaking all borders and boundaries. Nicely proclaimed by French poet Anatole France, "To know is nothing at all. To imagine is everything."

In sum, as a whole, education, much less objective education does not appear to be a top priority for state or federal officials (Acuña, 1998, 2011, 2013; Urbina & Wright, 2016), a situation that does not seem to be improving, but getting worse and critically devastating, as documented by Kozol in *The Shame of the Nation* (2006). As for ethnic minorities, ". . . the often hostile reaction and consternation of [people] to the entry of [minorities] into the privileged world of the academy is but a modern-day expression of the same historical patterns of social closures" (Urbina, 2011:125–126). As noted by renowned constitutional scholar Richard Delgado (2007), some issues just keep coming back in one form or another. Lastly, considering the rancorous, vicious, and vindictive forces confronting Latinos (as detailed in previous chapters), the essential question in twenty-first century America becomes: how long will it take to reduce the race and ethnic gap in the educational system? As question by Daniel Delgado in "'And You Need me to be the Token Mexican?': Examining Racial Hierarchies and the Complexities of Racial Identities for Middle Class Mexican Americans" (2014). Crucially, "scholars" at the highest echelons wish to slow down the educational process, to "domesticate" time and thus to domesticate Latinos, blacks, women, and poor whites.

Technology, Education, and Globalization: Staging the "Border"

A byproduct of education and thus intertwined with the forces of academy, modern technological advances, often shown as trophies of modernity, are serving as *launchers* for present-day globalization. However, technology is a two-sided sword in that it enables those who can afford it and those who can get required training to be active participants, giving those who actually take part in the globalization march a powerful tool to compete and survive in a modern world, but it excludes those who cannot afford technology and those who cannot obtain training, subsequently pushing people aside, without opportunity to ever be active participants in the globalization movement. Crucially, the implications and consequences of technology, like education, range from a single person to entire countries (Urbina, 2003a), making it uncertain as to how their lives will unfold in the future.

Globally, the teaching profession, itself a bastion of hypocrisy and mediocrity, has been in the forefront of a continuous assault against intellectual knowledge and discipline, creating significant race, ethnic, and gender variation in academic achievement, to include technological skills, and, by extension, success (Urbina, 2003a; Urbina & Wright, 2016; see also Noboa, 2005; Pizarro, 2005; Stritikus, 2002). Worse, the educational system has not only neglected and silenced ethnic minorities, but it has assisted in molding and legitimatizing punitive movements of the U.S. criminal justice system, which have resulted in thousands of Latinos under the control of the criminal and juvenile justice systems.

Historically, the "border" has been characterized as an element that does wonders, like national security, or as an entity that kills and destroys, like the termination of education for undocumented people, which, of course, might be perceived as a miracle by immigration hawks. In the context of the criminal justice system, University of Oxford Professor Mary Bosworth (2007) presents the prison as the *border* for Latinos, blacks, and impoverished whites in that once incarcerated, that's the end of the road, even upon release (Díaz-Cotto, 1996, 2006; Oboler, 2009; Urbina, 2008; see also Álvarez & Urbina, Chapter 16, this volume). Underneath it all, though, there is a much more crucial border for Latinos—beyond the river, beyond the high-tech fence that was being built along the 2,000-miles U.S.-Mexico border, beyond Trump's proposed "big beautiful wall," and beyond the prison—EDUCATION, that's the essential *BORDER,* a legal and subtle form of border within our communities, resulting in continued isolation, suppression, marginalization, intimidation, fear, political, financial, and social bankrupt-

cy, ignorance among society as a whole, and uncertainty. As the most powerful and consequential "border," this boundary shapes and reshapes the knowledge foundation for those who are not able to cross the border into the privileged world of formal education and even those who manage to cross the *educational border,* in that they are presented with subjective discourse; and ultimately the glass ceiling in their respected professions.

As such, in order for people to become active participants in *positive* globalization, especially the globalization of knowledge, the educational paradigm must be restructured to reach out and be more inclusive to actually improve lives and get people to become problem-solvers in modern society. This involves being intuitive and receptive of unconventional teaching methods, like problem-posing education (Urbina & Wright, 2016; see also Berger & Luckmann, 1966; Freire, 1997; Kuhn, 1996). As illustrated by Paulo Freire in *Pedagogy of the Oppressed* (1997:64), "In problem-posing education, people develop their powers to perceive critically *the way they exist* in the world *with which* and *in which* they find themselves; they come to see the world not as a static reality, but as a reality in process, in transformation." Ultimately, people must learn the essentials of being liberated and liberating so that eventually they can become the authors of their own lives. Above all, "Problem-posing education, as a humanist and liberating praxis, posits as fundamental that the people subjected to domination must fight for their emancipation" (Freire, 1997:67).

CONCLUSION

An exploration of the dynamics of globalization gives a positive, exciting, and promising adventure for some people, but a cruel, disheartening, demoralizing, and devastating experience for others. With elements of war versus peace, globalization (a two-edged sword), has been for centuries an effective avenue to explore new frontiers, conquer, expansion, and control. Today, in an already highly divided community, as seen during and after the 2015-2016 presidential elections, globalization is once again strategically being used to manipulate, subjugate, oppress, and marginalize Latinos, blacks, Native Americans, women, and poor whites: a new form of *revolution.* To some observers, "in its totality, the new era of globalization is being transformed into a modern form of colonialism" (Urbina et al., 2014:240), reestablishing a slavery-type status for some segments of society. As such, as the march for globalization continues, one must critically question the dynamics of social change in that the more ignorant and prejudiced people are, the more resistant they are to change, finding every possible excuse to justify and legitimize what in their mind is the inevitable reality. In essence, they would rather be blinded than accept the truth, on the face of analytical and rational thought or empirical facts, and if it was up to these people to infuse social change, blacks would still be in chains, women would still be perceived and treated as property, blacks, Indians, Latinos, and women would still not be able to vote, and there would still be signs saying, "We do not serve dogs, Niggers, or Mexicans."

As for the globalization of knowledge, once one begins to explore such movement in its totality, "the profound oceans of apathy and ignorance that surround even the most learned scholars in our fields of modern knowledge" become slightly visible (Urbina, 2003b:32). In effect, with the globalization of knowledge in full swing, the *pages of knowledge* continue to present subjective discourse, as noted by Urbina in "The Quest and Application of Historical Knowledge in Modern Times" (2003a:120), and thus "how is it possible to obtain generalizable, universal knowledge if such knowledge" is delimited by selected methodologies and ideologies to the exclusion of the truths and realities of other voices?

In the United States, arguably, *the country of the future,* education can no longer be approached as a *commodity of a privileged few, but as a basic necessity* to compete in a global and highly technological job market, to be able to ascertain, mobilize, and adopt in a transnational economy, and, in a sense, survive the upcoming challenges of globalization. Together, a *balanced educational model* is essential if the United States is to stay in the forefront of the globalization race, particularly the globalization of knowledge, and thus empower people to actually visualize the dynamics, truths, and unspoken realities of modernity, to include the globalization of the *war on drugs,* the globalization of the *illegal alien* ideology, and the globalization of the *national security* propaganda, in the context of the U.S. criminal justice system. At the end, people might realize that it is justice, equality, tolerance, understanding, love, and peace that are needed in this world, instead of border after border or war after war. Como dijo la gran revolucionaria Mejicana, Jovita Idar en 1911, "Hay que trabajar juntos en virtud de los lazos de sangre que nos unen."

Chapter 18

THE FUTURE OF LATINOS AND THE U.S. CRIMINAL JUSTICE SYSTEM

SOFÍA ESPINOZA ÁLVAREZ AND MARTIN GUEVARA URBINA

They came first for the Communists, and I didn't speak up because I wasn't a Communist. Then thjey came for the Jews, and I didn't speak up because I wasn't a Jew. Then they came for the trade unionists, and I didn't speak up because I wasn't a trade unionist. Then they came for me and by that time no one was left to speak up.

–Pastor Martin Niemoller

In this final chapter, we highlight the connectivity of various crucial elements discussed in previous chapters, provide propositions for bridging historical gaps, particularly in policing, and detail recommendations for future research. Ultimately, by seeking to analyze the Latino experience with the criminal justice system in its totality and placing it within a global context, we are better situated to vent into the future to better design and implement reforms that will yield positive social transformation in the American society and international community. As detailed throughout this book, the historical record clearly reveals that governance is a critical multifaceted everyday function, which has become redefined and, in a sense, more complicated with the advent of various antisocial control movements and the passage of thousands of criminal laws during the last four decades, starting with the RICO act in 1970 (Urbina & Álvarez, 2017; Urbina & Kreitzer, 2004), along with shifting demographic trends and corresponding elements of diversity, multiculturalism, and globalization (Urbina, 2014).

As a primary *formal* principle guiding social control and everyday life, renowned legal scholar Lawrence Friedman (1993:82), for instance, charged,

> laws and legal institutions are part of the system that keeps the structure [of inequality] in place, or allows it to change only in approved and patterned ways. . . . Law protects power and property; it safeguards wealth; and, by the same token, it perpetuates the subordinate status of the people on the bottom;

logically, illustrating the institutional parameters of formal social control, and by extension the significance, implications, and
ramifications of governing a multiethnic,
multiracial, and multicultural society in the
twenty-first century. Considering that law
enforcement officers are the front and most
visible agents of the law, we will focus on
policing in this chapter, a baseline analysis
which can then be used to explore the judicial and penal systems. Police officers are not
only influenced by the contemporary dynamics of criminal laws, but also the simultaneous interaction of historical, structural,
financial, political, and ideological forces
redefining and reshaping policing and by
extension the legal system and corrections
over the years. In effect, exploring policing
in its totality requires that law enforcement
be analyzed within a broader context—as the
police process does not end with local, state,
federal, or immigration law enforcement—
further complicating the dynamics and mission of the U.S. criminal justice system. As
reported herein, once individuals are detected and arrested, they must then confront the
complicated, lengthy, and often uncertain
judicial process, if they are indicted by a
grand jury or charged by the prosecutor. For
people indicted, prosecuted, convicted, and
sentenced to a correctional institution, they
must then experience the actual realities of
living behind bars in jails, state prisons, private prisons, federal facilities, immigration
detention centers, or military prisons. Ultimately, the majority of inmates are released
back into the community, where once again
they are likely to "encounter" the police,
particularly in the ghettos and barrios of
America.

The mere redefined role of the criminal
justice system, pressing shifts in demographic trends, and a highly diverse multicultural
community clearly show that the American
police in the twenty-first century must not
only be able and willing to effectively and
professionally serve our citizens, but be
reflective of the community it serves, if we are
going to live up to the democratic principles
of a modern society. More globally, with
continued shifts in both demographics and
law enforcement, as more Latinos join the
police force, the American police, including
Latino officers, police administrators, policymakers, and society at large, must be educated and sensitive to the various intertwining issues that influence the police, which
then impact other areas of social life. In this
context, what follows is a brief discussion of
how key elements of the machinery of justice
interact to achieve targeted objectives. As
advocated throughout this book, it will also
be noted that incorporating more Latinos
into the police force will be a challenging
process, but it will ultimately result in a more
effective and representative police force. In
addition, it will be proposed that leveling the
field in policing is an essential reform for
social equality, but the bigger challenge for
the new millennium is balancing the criminal justice system across the country and
achieving full representation in America's
main institutions. A research agenda for the
future will then be provided, and concluding
by placing policing within a broader context—for Latinos, who are projected as one of
the two largest groups in the country and
possibly the *upcoming majority* and subsequently not only the largest community to
"patrol," will be the population where Latino
officers will come from and, eventually,
where the majority of police officers will de-
rive to patrol the streets of the America of
tomorrow.

SCIENCE, LAW, AND THE AMERICAN IMAGINATION

Exploring the *Latino experience,* the authors of this volume unearth clear evidence that the combination of American science, law, and imagination has been used as a mechanism to manipulate, intimidate, oppress, control, and silence ethnic minorities, of course, under the notions of objective legal rationality, linear social change, and neutral scientific paradigms. In truth, though, as illustrated by Law Professor Peter Fitzpatrick in *The Mythology of Modern Law* (1992:x), "Law is autonomous yet socially contingent. It is identified with stability and order yet it changes and is historically responsive. Law is a sovereign imperative yet the expression of a popular spirit. Its quasi-religious transcendence stands in opposition to its mundane temporality, which cannot be reconciled by modernist explanations where reality is unified and truth indivisible." Invariably, contrary to the popular notion of equality and justice in law enforcement, judicial proceedings, and penal practices,

> Human experience indicates that whatever passes as 'good' (or in the name of progress) or 'evil' has something to do directly or indirectly with the identification, classification, formation, and implementation of a governing mechanism vis-à-vis labels like conservatives, liberals, underdogs, over dogs, middle dogs, and top dogs by way of hierarchy, superiority, inferiority, domination, subornation, and rule. (Urbina, 2003a:124)

As documented by the authors of this volume, American law itself is an audible reminder of the ideology of the historical racial supremacy, socially defined and enforced inferiority, and the rejection of equality and justice. In effect, beyond the confines of criminal behavior, the everyday life experience demonstrates that

anything that could undermine that group's dominance represents a threat. Antiracism, gay rights, feminism, and multiculturalism are all perceived as enemies of the status quo. Therefore, in places where these concepts are a part of the dominant discourse, it can be assumed that a certain segment of hetero-sexual White men will feel a great deal of strain as their traditional picture of the world and their place in it is threatened. (Blazak, 2004:212-213)

Functioning more as *a slaver than a liberator,* conventional science legitimizes criminalization, laws, the criminal justice system, and the ideology that upholds the machinery of law and order and everyday life, while creating a false consciousness in the imagination of society. In essence, "scientific paradigms mythicize history, truth and reality, and function as a cruel and brutal form of social control, consequently creating the glass ceiling that keeps the stranger, the outsider, the foreigner, the 'other' and those who are perceived as different and/or threatening in their place" (Urbina, 2003a:122). In retrospect, the false consciousness of the nature of crime, the political economy of crime, the dynamics of law and order, and the realities of social life distracts us from our own subordination, while inscribing immigrants as criminals, women as deviant for not conforming, progressive whites as traitors of the system, and young minorities as criminals.

The authors of this volume also demonstrate that globalization not only has altered the dynamics of crime that transcends international borders, but it has motivated justice systems to mobilize in transcending borders and boundaries, a movement that actually began several decades ago. In 1976, for instance, the Chicano cultural-nationalist journal *De Colores* dedicated a special issue to

Chicano (Mexican) prisoners, "Los Pintos the America" ("The Prisoners of America"), thereby relocating Latino prisoners to a hemispheric discursive space that would enable authors to explore the ramifications of the *internationalized* imprisonment of Latinos. The colorful cover design was a red, white, and blue watercolor of a perpendicular U.S. flag with the strips turning into prison bars, with a Chicano standing behind, exhibiting a minimalist pained facial expression, as he reaches through the steel prison bars to gaze back at the viewer. Critically, as noted by the editor, Anselmo Arellano, the ironies of ethnic minorities do not only apply to the already internationalized Latinos behind steel bars, but also to all Latinos who are being *held captive and enslaved by the tentacles of historically repressive institutions* in the United States and throughout the world. In the very essence of human existence, it is the refusal to accept to be labeled criminal, arrested, or imprisoned for contesting activities that are questionable, unjust, unethical, unconstitutional, or in violation of international law that leads to national and international repressive social control. Ultimately, it is the refusal to be stripped of statutory, constitutional, or international rights that gets a person arrested, lands a person in jail or prison, injured, or in the morgue.

The Criminal Justice Paradox: Governance, Equality, and Justice

In this new era of national and international governance, antisocial control movements, like the globalization of the *war on drugs,* the globalization of the *illegal alien* ideology, and the globalization of the *national security* propaganda (see Urbina & Álvarez, Chapter 17; this volume), have not only altered the dynamics of crime and punishment that transcend international borders and motivated the justice system to mobilize

in transcending borders and boundaries, but they have also fueled a criminal justice paradox with crucial questions for the future. To begin, with the United States. experiencing unprecedented shifts, like international political and military crises, fragile national and international relations, a fragmented political system, and economic instability and uncertainty, how will mainstream America respond to certain segments of society, particularly the poor, who traditionally have been used as scapegoats during difficult times? Therefore, those vested in social and criminal justice reform must be minded of a complex criminal justice paradox, as police administrators, for example, seek to maintain a balance between an effective police force and equality in the application of laws, while securing justice for individuals and communities.

Invariably, understanding the influence of globalization on law enforcement as well as the entire criminal justice system and, by extension, its impact on certain communities, particularly Latino and African American communities, requires that we not only consider historical forms of social control and contemporary imprisonment trends, analyzing the twists and turns of *criminalization and penalization over time* (De León, 2014; Urbina & Álvarez, 2016, 2017; see also Aguirre, this volume), but also the forces impacting the *role* and, in a sense, the very essence of policing, which could turn into a critical dilemma for police officers, especially minority officers, who might feel that they are being hired to wage war on their own communities. In fact, as noted earlier, two hundred years after the creation of the penal system, the United States is facing an unprecedented binge in criminalization and imprisonment, to the point that it now has the highest number of people under the control of the criminal justice system among "first-world" countries. Clearly, the time has come for us to reflect and ask long-delayed questions of governance, but also of equality, justice, and representation.

Criminal Justice Dilemmas: Questions for the Twenty-First Century

With various antisocial control movements in full-swing–and police officers in the frontline–law enforcement officers, police administrators, politicians, and the general public must be prepared to acknowledge and address a series of sensitive but critical questions. For police officers and administrators, the challenge is crucial in that they must be well-versed in legal issues, along with corresponding implications and ramifications, as police practices can positively or negatively impact entire communities, particularly Latino and black communities.

Among the various questions to consider as we patrol the streets of America, could the United States sustain its multibillion dollar criminal justice system, if one out of four black men of a certain age were not under some form of incarceration or police surveillance (see Álvarez, this volume)? As for ethnic minorities, could the criminal justice system survive and expand without the "new minority," Latinos, who are now the second largest group in the country, after whites? Beyond male-race variation, could the criminal justice system *survive and continue to grow* without the newly "targeted" population, female offenders, especially Latinas, black women, and poor white women? Ultimately, would the criminal justice system *survive, grow, and prosper* without the "intergenerational connection," minority offenders and their children, especially impoverished minority children? *"With thousands of people joining the workforce of the American criminal justice system primarily because of employment and job security"* (Urbina, 2014:230), would

the system, with an annual budget of 260 billion dollars (as of 2010), survive economically? Or, quite simply, what if young white women and men were being detected, arrested, indicted, prosecuted, convicted, placed on probation, sentenced to jail or prison, or executed at the same rate? Would politicians and law enforcement officials be advocating for more police if most patrolling and arrests were taking place in wealthy white communities, instead of poor communities, composed mostly of poor minorities? Would the American society support such practice by the police, the courts, and the penal system, if the largest pool of people were coming from white communities (rich or poor) and not from the barrios and ghettos of America? Would mainstream white America be asking for the aggressive implementation of existing criminal laws, the development of more laws, the hiring of more police officers, the creation of more jails and prisons, the privatization of corrections, and asking government and law enforcement officials to be more punitive on criminal defendants? Would the American media, mostly owned and controlled by white men, be promoting a punitive criminal justice system?

Socially and morally, since a high concentration of people arrested or incarcerated, with the high majority being uneducated, unemployed, and poor, are coming from Latino or African American neighborhoods, what will become of Latino and African American communities? What will become of young children, whose parents are already under the control of the criminal justice system? What will become of the overall Latino population, who are now not only one of the largest and fastest growing minority groups, but the group with the longest life expectancy, accounting for over 17 percent of the population? According to a 2010 government report, Latinos are expected to outlive whites by two years and blacks by more than seven years. Latinos born in 2006, for instance, could expect to live about 80 years and seven months, with life expectancy for whites being about 78 and almost 73 for blacks. What will be the fate of poor whites who are also victims of aggressive social control movements? What will become of the thousands of women arrested and sent to prison, with the majority of them being mothers of young children, as thousands of police officers are being added to the police force, with the *criminal justice control web getting wider and wider?* Notably, striving for positive transformation, while seeking to avoid a repressive criminal justice system, requires that criminal justice reformers analyze these issues in their totality, which in policing will ultimately influence police practices, the recruitment of new officers, the retention of officers, police training, and the community at large.

LATINOS AND THE AMERICAN POLICE: A CALL FOR CHANGE

Again, with pressing shifts in demographic trends, along with the various issues discussed herein, the need for equitable representation on the police force, the frontline agents of the law, becomes more apparent. More globally, if new recruits for departments will increase the rate of Latinos on the force across the country, there will be more of a Latino political presence, which will then positively influence the community and society at large. Having a political presence, for instance, may be particularly important as political influence may be used to encourage departments to address diversity issues, in addition to some of the questions raised above, in areas with a large Latino population as compared to those with fewer Latinos.

In all, obtaining a police force that is representative of the community is invaluable not only in the context of law enforcement, but also for assisting in the improvements of the judicial process and the penal system, a laudable goal as more Latinos enter the ranks of law enforcement. As reported by John Dempsey and Linda Forst (2011), the Latino officers' ability to relate to the highly diverse Latino community, especially as communicators in emergency situations, is essential to an all-inclusive operation of the department, police-community relations, and the well-being of the community as a whole. Of course, there are still numerous issues that Latino officers may experience once they become part of the force (Urbina & Álvarez, 2015, see also Vera Sanchez, this volume), illustrating the historical complexities of ethnicity inside the department and patrolling communities that are becoming more diverse and multicultural.

Assigning Latino officers to Latino neighborhoods would be a logical and effective choice for departments seeking to diversify their force, corresponding with the demographics of their respected communities. Yet, without strategic planning, such a choice may ignore the subtleties of ethnicity, as wide ethnic diversity may exist in large Latino neighborhoods, as ethnic minorities come from places like Mexico, Cuba, Puerto Rico, and other Central and South American countries, each of which have distinct cultural practices and use of the Spanish language. In short, there may be great ethnic diversity within the minority community, and residents may be quite different from the Latino officers that have been assigned to patrol their neighborhoods. In effect, considering the significance of communication in the criminal justice system (Urbina, 2004b), having Latino officers who do not speak

Spanish may further complicate their role, perceptions, and effectiveness within the community and police department, as the Latino community may feel that police officers, including Latino officers, are not being trained to truly meet community issues, and thus minority communities continue to be marginalized and neglected.

As for Latino officers, they may experience a type of double marginality, which is not so different from what some black officers confront. Consider, for example, the historic tense relationship between the police and the black community, and then black police officers entering the police force. The problems between the police and the black community are multifaceted, which may lead to calls for an increase in the number of black police in predominately white departments and for more black officers patroling black communities. According to Kenneth Bolton and Joe Feagin (2004), some of the black officers they interviewed felt they had to prove to the black community that they were not sell-outs, and that they were trying their best to actually help the African American community. Black officers also felt that they faced a double standard because of the expectations from the black community, and that they must work twice as hard as white officers to be accepted in the department.

In addition, once in the department, black officers faced various types of prejudice and discrimination ranging from only being allowed to patrol black neighborhoods, the inability to arrest white citizens, to inequities in evaluations, rewards, and discipline, while further complicating the relationship between black officers and the black community. For instance, even though there has been general support of black officers from black citizens, churches, and activist groups, largely due to the adversarial relationship between the police and some black commu-

nities, residents have had a difficult time reconciling the role of black police officers and the policing practices of the past in the United States. Bolton and Feagin (2004) conclude that some research has shown a declining impact of racism for black police officers; yet, in the interviews they conducted, the officers gave several examples of overt and covert racism they had experienced. Despite these negative occurrences, though, the officers ultimately had pride in their ability to do their job as well as being in a position of authority for the black community.

In the context of ethnic minorities-police relations, in many ways the experiences of Latino officers mirror those of black police officers. Similar to residents in black communities, some Latinos have had negative experiences with the police in the United States, and recent immigrants may have experienced corruption and abuse in their home countries. Once in the United States, these early experiences in their country of origin can engender a mistrust of the American police that can make police patrol in Latino communities difficult, and thus difficult to gain support and respect. Still, Latino officers fill a critical void as some Spanish-speaking community residents may feel more at ease when Latino, especially Spanish-speaking, officers show up, possibly sharing the same culture or country of origin. Then again, similar to the African American experience, this is where the double marginality may arise, as Latino officers may feel pressure to do their job differently or more aggressively simply because of their ethnicity. A conflicted situation, as newly immigrated Latinos, for example, may expect leniency from Mexican American police officers, resulting in role conflict for the officers (Dempsey & Forst, 2011; see also Durán, 2015).

Clearly, one of the most essential reasons for having a diverse police force is the hope that departments that reflect the community will be more sensitive and understanding of community needs and efficient in service delivery, resulting in fewer incidents of excessive force or brutality, while "controlling" for *overpolicing* and *underpolicing*. An investigation by Geoffrey Alpert and Roger Dunham (2004) on the use of force revealed a more intricate dynamic in the interactions between minority officers and minority citizens. The authors found that in the Miami Dade Police Department, black officers used force against black suspects more frequently than white or Latino officers (67% versus 40% and 41% respectively), while Latino officers used force against Latino suspects more frequently than white or black officers (35% versus 33% and 17% respectively). Although these results could be a product of patrol deployment and working with citizens of similar backgrounds, the findings suggest that minority officers respond differently to various ethnic groups, and that these officers may feel more comfortable using force against suspects from their own ethnic or racial group.

Together, while the experiences of Latino officers within police departments have not been as well documented as those of black police officers, the existing literature provides insight into the incorporation of ethnic minorities in police departments across the country, as documented by Urbina and Álvarez in *Latino Police Officers in the United States: An Examination of Emerging Trends and Issues* (2015). One particular study that surveyed more than 1,100 patrol officers in the Milwaukee Police Department found that Latino officers were more likely to report negative workplace experiences such as perceptions of bias, underestimating ability, and sexually offensive behavior (Barlow & Barlow, 2002). Further, both Latino and black officers perceived fewer opportunities for promotion and preferred assignments as

compared to whites, revealing continued historical perceptions of bias and lack of opportunity, resonating the remarks made by controversial Los Angeles Police Chief Daryl Gates in a 1978 press conference in which he charged that Latinos were not promoted because they were lazy (Skolnick & Fyfe, 1993).

Given the complicated dynamics of diversity and multiculturalism in the United States (Urbina, 2014), issues of ethnicity, race, and perception of bias can be further complicated within police departments as demographics continue to shift. Consider, for example, the position some Latino officers who appear "white" may find themselves in the course of their duties. These officers may be privy to conversations and comments about minority communities as well as Latino and black officers by white officers and citizens who may feel comfortable sharing their thoughts with them based on the officer's *white* appearance (Dempsey & Forst, 2011)– along with presumed political and ideological views.

Further, although minority officers may be recruited and assigned to patrol predominately minority communities, some officers may view these assignments as discriminatory and that they are not receiving the opportunity to work in other areas simply because of their ethnicity or race, possibly limiting their chances for promotion and recognition within the department and community as a whole. While being bilingual might be considered a positive attribute during the recruiting and hiring process, bilingual Latino officers may find themselves pulled away from their regular duties to serve as interpreters for others (Dempsey & Forst, 2011), a situation that might be considered as distracting by some police officers. Worse, these issues may take a serious emotional or psychological toll on some police officers, who might perceive themselves as the "tokens" or "working class" of the profession. In effect, Nnamdi Pole, Suzanne Best, Daniel Weiss, Thomas Metzler, Akiva Liberman, Jeffrey Fagan, and Charles Marmar (2001) studied 655 urban police officers to assess if there were any differences by gender, ethnicity, or race for duty-related symptoms of posttraumatic stress disorder (PTSD). The authors found that after controlling for relevant variables, Latino officers evidenced greater duty-related PTSD symptoms than either white or black officers (see also Pole, Best, Metzler, & Marmar, 2005).

With the various social movements of the 1950s and 1960s, some of these negative events have resulted in discrimination or affirmative action lawsuits, and, along the way, the creation of support groups for Latino officers. In this context, the National Latino Peace Officers Association (NLPOA) was founded in 1974 in the state of California with four main objectives: To recruit qualified Latino police officers, assist officers during their probationary period, encourage continued education, and provide assistance during the promotion process. Other prominent support groups include the Hispanic American Police Command Officers Association, The Hispanic National Law Enforcement Association, and the Federal Hispanic Law Enforcement Officers Association. Since these organizations have been playing vital roles in supporting Latino officers at various levels of law enforcement as well as implementing major changes in police departments around the country, these organizations can strategically be utilized in promoting police reform, from the hiring of Latino officers to egalitarian police practices to, ultimately, the creation of a new police force (Urbina & Álvarez, 2015).

Case in point: The NLPOA, along with a Japanese group, successfully challenged the height requirement of the California Highway Patrol, which opened the door for women and minorities that were kept out of law enforcement due to stature. Once established, these organizations can provide support and legal assistance when needed by women, minorities, and even whites. Well established organizations, though, are normally found in larger urban departments or in communities with sizeable populations of Latinos, leaving minority officers from smaller departments with a limited or no support network. As such, this type of limitation can be a crucial situation in small communities, as it can be difficult for Latino officers in small departments to make a stand and emphasize their ethnicity, which could result in hostile environments. Ultimately, these officers may find it easier to simply try and blend in, confirming to the established culture of the other officers, or the "good old boys" (see Vera Sanchez, this volume).

In sum, while Latinos have made great strides within law enforcement, from reflecting the composition of the community to entering the ranks of upper command and creating new policies, grave problems still persist, from the traditional issues of prejudice and discrimination to the emerging expectations and challenges based on their newly-acquired status, all of which demonstrate the dynamics of ethnicity inside (and outside) police departments as well as the judicial and penal systems in the United States. Currently, Latinos comprise a very small percentage of all sworn officers (Urbina & Álvarez, 2015); even though, for half a century, studies have described a lack of representation of Latinos in the police force and the corresponding challenges (Urbina & Álvarez, 2015; see also Durán, this volume). Evidently, despite their growing numbers in law enforcement, a wide gap remains to be bridged and there is still little empirical research on the impact of increased numbers of Latino officers on the police force (Urbina & Álvarez, 2015). While some researchers have found that the inclusion of Latino police officers can make a positive impact, others seem to view structural divisions in society and actual police institutions trumping ethnicity (Urbina & Álvarez, 2015; see also Durán; Vera Sanchez, this volume), clearly illustrating the need for equitable representation to eventually significantly influence departmental policies and community concerns–ultimately, creating a representative and modernized police to patrol a highly diverse and multicultural community in the twenty-first century; subsequently reforming the entire criminal justices system (policing, courts, and corrections).

LATINOS IN AMERICA'S MAIN INSTITUTIONS: BALANCING THE SYSTEM IN THE TWENTY-FIRST CENTURY

While equitable representation is a vital strategy, socially, morally, and constitutionally, for positive transformation in policing and, by extension, the entire criminal justice system (one of the most fundamental American institutions), *leveling the police field is only one chapter of the American story*. Realistically, bridging historical gaps, while avoiding disequilibrium, also calls for broad reform, starting with equitable representation in America's main institutions, to include the political system, the educational system, and the American media. As with law enforcement, with pressing shifts in demographic trends, balancing the overall American system must be made a priority in the twenty-first century for the United States to be adequately situated in a highly technological, competitive, and globalized world.

However, almost two decades into the twenty-first century, the story of ethnic minority hiring does not seem to significantly change across the United States, especially in institutions of critical importance for Latinos and other minorities (Chávez, 2011; Márquez, 2014; Urbina & Wright, 2016; Valencia, 2008). Consider, for instance, one of the most fundamental American institutions–the educational system–characterized by some critics as the most significant and influential, while at the same time, consequential institution (Urbina & Wright, 2016; see also Urbina & Álvarez, Chapter 17, this volume), as it impacts all other major institutions, beginning with the criminal justice system (Urbina & Wright, 2017). In 2013, over 80 percent of tenured professors at the nation's law schools were white, with Latino law student enrollments not only extremely low but slipping in the last few years (Falcón, 2013; Urbina & Wright, 2016), creating a detrimental situation not only for Latinos in the future but the entire American society, as there will be a very small pool of Latino graduates to fill the workforce, including the judicial system, if the current trends continue, especially in the coming decades when Latinos will be in high demand in the labor force to support an aging white population.

To be sure, historically, all decision-makers in the criminal justice system, as in all domains of life, were white men. Then, eventually, a slight *window* was forced open in which women, Latinos, blacks, and other ethnic/racial minorities could participate. In essence, after centuries of presumed social change, we would expect a certain level of equality, a balance, in the representation of those who operate the machinery of justice, particularly the judicial system which influences both policing and the penal system. In plain twenty-first century, though, reports show that the majority of "dominant [court] actors (judges, prosecutors) are white in contemporary United States" (Ulmer & Johnson, 2004:145; Urbina, 2005; Urbina & Kreitzer, 2004; Urbina & White, 2009). In effect, like African Americans, Latinos have been excluded from the most powerful positions in the legal and political system, like Supreme Court Justices, presidential cabinet positions, governors, legislators, judges, prosecutors, and defense attorneys. As reported by Law Professor Laura Gómez (2000), historically there has been a glass ceiling on Latinos' participation in the American legal system, impacting not only the judicial system, but also policing, corrections, and communities across the country. In fact, considering the state of Texas, in 2017, while Latinos constituted more than a quarter of Texas' voting-age population, just one Latina/o (Justice Eva Guzman) sits on the nine-member Texas Supreme Court, and only one Latina/o (Judge Elsa Alcala) sites on the nine-member Court of Criminal Appeals. Ironically, since 1945, 69 of the 76 justices to serve on the Texas Supreme Court have been white and only five were Latinos; and during the same period, 44 of 48 Court of Criminal Appeals judges were white, and only two were Latino. Nationally, Trump's cabinet does not include a single Latino, with only one Latina (Sonia Maria Sotomayor) sitting on the U.S. Supreme Court, the first and only Latina/o ever appointed to the Supreme Court.

As for law and order, revealing just how *white* one side of the criminal justice system is and how *dark* the other side of the legal spectrum is, with critical corresponding implications of an unbalanced system, one judge was quoted as saying: "You are reluctant to send white offenders to prisons that are largely black. It seems the prisons are becoming more and more black, and judges are leery because they have heard horror stories about things that happened, violence and whatnot" (Ulmer & Kramer, 1996:400).

Logically, the cited court official is most likely referring to white judges. Of course, as documented herein, extra-judicial discrimination takes place way before minority defendants even enter the judicial system. David Barlow and Melissa Barlow (2002: 338, 349), for instance, cite a police officer who admitted that he stops and questions blacks "because it is precisely what his supervisors want him to do," and some African American police officers also admitted that they practice racial profiling and actually see it as a "necessary and legitimate tool for police officers." Other examples of discrimination before trials begin include prosecutors who, aware of jurors' prejudice, conservative views, or conservative religious beliefs, are prone to prosecute Latinos and blacks from minor offenses to homicide cases, as documented by Urbina and Álvarez in *Ethnicity and Criminal Justice in the Era of Mass Incarceration: A Critical Reader on the Latino Experience* (2017) and in *Capital Punishment in America: Race and the Death Penalty Over Time* (2012). Once trials begin, there are subtle, but deadly, ways prosecutors and judges may ultimately affect the defendants' right to a fair and impartial jury, and, ultimately, the outcome of the trial, by, for example, allowing attorneys to make religious references during legal proceedings, including death penalty trials (Chávez & Miller, 2009).

Since police and judicial practices are highly institutionalized in the American culture, it's possible that minority representation in the legal system might not significantly alter *normalized* judicial and police behavior straightaway, but a strategized process must be put in place to bridge existing gaps and eventually secure a balanced system. It's been suggested that having minority attorneys could even work against minority defendants, especially in jury trials, in that juries continue to be predominately white and conservative; or, more precisely, it could result in a "backlash" by those who have been the deciders of social life for centuries, including life and death. A situation bluntly expressed by Paul Kaplan (2009b: 75), "courts talk like upper-class white men and subordinate those who do not." As a whole, Latino attorneys may be poorly situated to significantly influence the decision-making process if they do not hold positions of power across the entire judicial and political systems. In fact, to the extent that Latinos disproportionately represent what some scholars have characterized as "the working class" of the legal profession, or the "tokens," their presence may have minimal impact on the policymaking process or on the distribution of justice (Hagan, Huxter, & Parker, 1988; Urbina & Álvarez, 2017), not to mention

> *los muertos de hambre,* a phrase used by Mexicans to characterize people who are predators–human vultures and vendidos (sellouts or class traitors)–as these people are so starved for attention, recognition, and power that they snatch on scraps of garbage discarded by their glorified colonial masters as they battle to control the plantation. (Urbina, 2014: 278–279)

In our quest for equal representation in law enforcement and the legal system to maintain equilibrium in the criminal justice system, it's obvious that less is known about jurors' behavior, where juries' racial composition and unspoken beliefs have the potential to influence final decisions, as well as the process by which decisions are reached (Sommers, 2007), illustrating the influence of mainstream America on the judicial process; subsequently, impacting both policing and the penal system. For instance, one study analyzed 340 trials and found that the higher the number of whites to blacks on juries, the more likely blacks were to be sentenced to death, especially if the victim was white

(Bowers, Steiner, & Sandys, 2001), with similar findings reported in a non-felony study analyzing 317 juries in Texas comprised of whites and Latinos (Daudistel, Hosch, Holmes, & Graves, 1999). Another study found that the more whites on juries, the more conviction-prone were the juries, a trend that became more pressing if the defendant was Latino (Pérez, Hosch, Ponder, & Trejo, 1993). In effect, between 1983 and 2001, more than 50 black men were convicted by all-white juries, with cases showing a pattern of black juror exclusion by prosecutors, and all 50 African Americans were executed, with similar patterns found in the prosecution of Latinos (Urbina, 2011, 2012), as reported by Álvarez and Urbina in "Capital Punishment on Trial: Who Lives, Who Dies, Who Decides–A Question of Justice (2014)?"

Renowned constitutional scholar Richard Delgado charges that racism is really never eliminated, it simply transforms itself, always coming back in one way or another, making it extremely difficult to secure equal representation in policing as well as in America's main institutions. To be sure, racism has never really disappeared (Urbina & Álvarez, 2016, 2017). Ian Haney López, renowned constitutional law scholar specializing in the evolution of racism, recently published an eye-opening book, *Dog Whistle Politics: How Coded Racial Appeals Have Reinvented Racism and Wrecked the Middle Class* (2014), illustrating that since the civil rights movement, racism did not really vanish, it simply went underground, and surfaced through coded language and political policy. Strategically disguised to appear neutral and color-blind, these racial appeals then conveniently manipulate hostility toward nonwhites by aggressive and repeated blasts against immigrants as illegal aliens, welfare cheats, and criminals. Consider, for instance, the race-baited anger being fueled by Donald Trump, whom some critics have characterized as

America's Hitler, aggressively attacking Mexicans and Mexico the day he announced his candidacy for president and highly escalating his anti-Mexican verbal and policy attacks immediately after he was sworn in as President of the United States on January 20, 2017. In fact, his political campaign centered on a legacy of racial hate, making Mexicans and Mexico the focal target of this attacks. Individually, Trump's statements regarding the American identity of U.S.-born Federal Judge, Gonzalo Curiel, referring to him as a "Mexican judge," epitomizes racism. Broadly, such racist slurs against U.S-born Latinos dehumanize and dismiss Mexican professionals and the entire Latino community as foreigners who cannot do their job or be trusted. As noted above, Trump did not nominate a single Latino to his cabinet. When Press Secretary Sean Spicer was asked, "Your list of cabinet picks was the first since 1988 that doesn't include any Hispanics," he indicated that there are zero Latinos in the cabinet because Trump only wanted the "best and brightest." Of course, what's extremely dangerous is the fact that the flames Trump has been fanning since he began his presidential campaign have been spreading like wild fire, with immigration hawks, bigots, political pundits, and intellectual racists quickly exploiting Trump's anti-immigration paranoia, with several anti-immigration executive orders signed within his first week in the Oval Office.

In effect, in twenty-first century America, some politicians and legal decision-makers might seem concerned about the appearance of prejudice when defendants are rich Latinos or African Americans to avoid signs of racism, but such concerns may not be as consistent with other ethnic/racial minorities, especially if they are poor or negatively characterized by stereotypes, as in the case of Mexican immigrants and Middle-Easterners. For example, some government officials were not so concerned about hiding their prejudice against Asian Americans following the attacks on Pearl Harbor in 1941, Arab people in the wake of the September 11, 2001 terrorist attacks on the U.S., characterized by some scholars as *unleashing the cops* in minority communities (Welch, 2006, 2007, 2009), Latinos during the supposed "child migrant crisis" in 2014, or Trump's highly controversial travel ban, or what some critics are characterizing as a "Muslim ban," in that the ban included seven predominantly Muslim countries (Iran, Iraq, Libya, Somalia, Sudan, Syria and Yemen).

Taken together, in a call for justice in the very essence of democracy, *equal representation among those who operate the machinery of justice,* scholars have reported the utility of a balanced judicial system in a number of studies. A recent study showed that sentences were shorter for minorities in counties with proportionately more Latino and black lawyers (King, Johnson, & McGeever, 2010). Ryan King, Kecia Johnson, and Kelly McGeever (2010:26–27) further found that "more racial diversity in the bar results in less racial disparity in criminal sentencing," and conclude that "efforts to diversify the legal profession may have the ancillary benefit of minimizing unequal treatment across racial lines." For instance, the authors predict that states with more African Americans per capita in the legal profession would have less racial disparities in the prison system and in the application of the death penalty. In a nondeath penalty study, Geoff Ward, Amy Farrell, and Danielle Rousseau (2009: 757) found that "increasing racial and ethnic group representation in justice-related occupations is considered a potential remedy to racial inequality in justice administration, including sentencing disparity." In fact, Scott Phillips (2008:839) reports that positive results can already be found in some cases; that is, findings from his death sentencing study in Texas suggest that as "Hispanics wield more political power and are a greater presence within criminal justice," the more egalitarian the system will become.

In sum, regarding the criminal justice system, which includes law enforcement, in his writing on "democratic social control," John Braithwaite (2002:166–167) advocates a more equitable distribution of authority in processes of social control, as a mechanism for "enhancing the effectiveness, legitimacy, and ultimately the social justice of systems of social control" (Ward, Farrell, & Rousseau, 2009:768). Universally, this "control balance" in the operation of the American criminal justice system, starting with the frontline agents of the law, is in reality an essential element of liberty and democracy, if we are to in fact meet the Constitutional promise of equality under the law and equal justice in a free and democratic society. Beyond law enforcement, along with the courts and corrections, to the extent that Latinos disproportionately represent an extremely low percent in high-ranking positions, their presence may have minimal impact on the *leveling* of the overall American system, particularly the political, educational, and economic systems, which subsequently influence the police and the entire legal system. There-

fore, in a call for equality and justice in the very core of democracy, equal representation among those who operate America's institutions, from local police forces to the United States Supreme Court, truly yields for the establishment of a balanced American system. In all, we must advocate and be active participants for a more equitable social distribution across America, as *"equal representation must be present to maintain equilibrium in the . . . system"* (Márquez, 2014; Urbina, 2012:249).

Invariably, in the future, we have to ensure that Supreme Court Justice Sonia Maria Sotomayor, for example, does not become, in Rachel F. Moran's phrase, a "Society of One." With Latinos on their way to possibly become the upcoming majority, with expected resistance by the dominant segment of society, her appointment to an almost all-white environment not only raises the issue of a "Society of One" or, with changing demographics, a "Society of Few" in the near future, but it raises a troubling question in the midst of globalization: *"is this what some so-called progressives mean by a post-racial society in the new millennium"* (Urbina, 2014: 255)? In which case, moving beyond a post-racial America will be the challenge of our time.

DOCUMENTING THE LATINO EXPERIENCE: A RESEARCH AGENDA FOR THE FUTURE

As noted in previous chapters, few studies have delineated the significance, implications, and ramifications of shifting demographics, resulting in an incomplete story of the Latino experience and, by extension, the American experience. As documented in this book, historically the experience of ethnic minorities in the American criminal justice system has received minimal attention in research, publication, and discourse, and thus the

story of Latinos and the criminal and juvenile justice systems has been limited (Urbina, 2007; Urbina & Álvarez, 2017). As such, there is a great need for researchers to examine the ethnic experience in law enforcement, the judicial system, and the penal system, supplementing the existing foundation that will allow investigators to develop data sets that will enable empirical examinations of the minority experience across racial and ethnic groups to better separate the effects of race and ethnicity. As noted by Darrell Steffensmeier and Stephen Demuth (2001:169-170), "this finding that 'black-white' differences are suppressed or disappear when white and Hispanic defendants are combined together into a single group highlights the importance for clarity in delineating the white defendant group in 'racial' disparity studies."

Clearly, considering the significance of race/ethnic relations in the midst of the globalization of knowledge and the current political climate (under the Trump administration), perhaps more than ever, there has been a great need for researchers to examine the simultaneous interaction of historical and contemporary trends and issues (particularly structural, political, financial, and ideological forces) defining, shaping, and governing the functioning of the police, judicial system, and corrections; and subsequently the everyday experience of America's people, particularly immigrants and citizens of minority communities, if the United States is to actually engage in significant and *positive* social transformation, from policing to the legal system, from education to the political system, in the new millennium. Together, future criminal justice research should include not only greater focus on ethnic minorities (like Cubans, Mexican Americans, and Puerto Ricans) and racial minorities (like African Americans, Asian Americans, and Native Americans), but researchers must unearth the untold stories of ethnic/racial minorities, women, and poor whites, delineating for ethnic and race effects along the historical continuum. Similarly, researchers need to delineate the experience of the Latino workforce, in policing, judicial system, and corrections, while placing Latino employees within a broader context, if we are going to provide a *balance* to the existing literature and, more importantly, strive for

equal representation, equality, justice, and human dignity not only in the criminal justice system but in all American institutions.

Ultimately, if the United States is in fact going to be situated and reflective of a postracial society in the twenty-first century, social scientists must not only focus on the traditional "black-white" model of conducting research and publication, but criminal justice investigations must be objective and inclusive, including all ethnic and racial minorities, men and women, juveniles, and, considering the rapidly shifting demographics, must be made a *priority*–researching a variety of social, economic, political, and ideological issues currently confronting communities across the country, including Latino communities in both old and new destinations, to properly address currently pressing questions and thus effectively resolve emerging issues. Globally, for instance, scholars must analyze how recent state and federal laws and, by extension, police practices are affecting the lived experiences of ethnic and racial minorities, to include recent arrivals and those who have been in the United States for generations. As for specific issues impacting the present and future of both Latino employees and ethnic/racial minority citizens, how do recently enacted laws and policies (particularly those being targeted by the Trump administration) affect the educational prospects of Latinos, blacks, and poor whites (men and women)? What are the implications and consequences of legal uncertainties, and the contradicting realities dictated by federal, state, and local laws for the psychological state of immigrants and their children, including their health and family well-being? How are immigration bans and proposals for immigration reform being received by Latino professionals and ethnic minority immigrants in old and new destinations, and how do they affect police-community relations, civic engagement, political attitude, behavior, diversity, and multiculturalism?

After centuries of educational advancement, with the majority of the top colleges and universities in the world being housed in the United States, we have never taken the time to understand Latino communities, much less Latino professionals, the way we have taken time to understand whites. Symbolically and pragmatically, just as the neglecting or devaluing of ethnic research deprives Latino professionals (policing, courts, and corrections) and the Latino community of the dignity of voicing their truths and realities and of contributing to the *pages of history and knowledge,* failing to conduct an all-inclusive and objective analysis of the American criminal justice system and America's communities across the country "deprives society of hearing and understanding the everyday lives, experiences, concerns, and views of the forgotten and neglected voices" (Urbina, 2007:88), and therefore hindering our efforts as we strive for social change, understanding, tolerance, equality, justice, respect, and human dignity. Worse, this historical paradigm instills little hope for positive transformation, continuing with the historical legacy of brutality, manipulation, marginalization, oppression, prejudice, discrimination, power, control, and, ultimately, silencing of minorities and poor whites.

LATINOS IN THE NEW MILLENNIUM: THE BROWNING OF AMERICA

In these final sections, we situate both Latino professionals and the Latino community, *the emerging new face of the country,* within a broader social context, while seeking to better understand the universal significance and implications of the *browning* of America. As noted in the introductory chapter, contrary to the belief that Latinos are "new" to the United States, Latinos have been in the United States since 1565 in Florida and 1598 in New Mexico, many years before the Treaty of Guadalupe Hidalgo in 1848. Despite the long legacy of hate against Latinos, adults and juveniles, particularly undocumented people, or, to use the Texas' vernacular, *illegal aliens, immigrants, wetbacks,* or *the Mexican problem,* the Latino population will continue to grow. Today, Latinos live in every state and in every major city of the country, clearly indicating that Latinos are slowly *browning* the United States: notably, one of the two largest minority groups and possibly the *upcoming majority.*

Becoming the largest minority group in the United States as they entered the twenty-first century, Latinos began to significantly reshape American demographics, and, subsequently, social life; ultimately, redefining and reshaping the dynamics of America's main institutions in fundamental areas such as law, politics, social control, education, welfare, healthcare, housing, economics, and the American media. During the first decade of the twenty-first century, for instance, Latinos accounted for more than half of the U.S. population increase between 2000 and 2010 (MSNBC, 2011), and the Mexican American population grew by 7.2 million during the same decade, even though Mexican immigration to the United States declined by more than 60 percent between 2006 and 2010, from more than one million to 404,000 (Taylor, 2011). Further, while Mexican immigration has been significantly lower during the first decade of the twenty-first century than during the 1990s, the Mexican American population continued to increase, with Mexican births accounting for over 63 percent of the 11.2 million increase from 2000 to 2010 (Taylor, 2011). Overall, a decade into the twenty-first century, the La-tino population in the United States in-creased from 35.3 million in 2000 to 50.5 million in 2010, accounting for more than half of the nation's overall population growth during the decade, comprising 16.3 percent of the total U.S. population (one in six residents in the U.S. being Latino), 16.7 percent in 2011, over 17 percent in 2015, and its projected to increase to over 28 percent (about 119 million) by 2060, according to the latest projections from the U.S. Census Bureau (2014), and the overall minority pop-ulation is expected to increase to 56 percent of the total U.S. population by 2060 (Waz-waz, 2015). In fact, according to the U.S. Census Bureau, for children under the age of five, the United States is already a minority-majority nation, as in 2014 50.2 percent of about 20 million children under five years old were minorities, with children of Latino origin constituting the largest minority, 22 percent of the 19.9 million children under the age five. By 2020, more than half of the nation's children under the age of 18 are expected to be part of the ethnic or racial group (Wazwaz, 2015), and Latino children will become the largest youth population by mid-century, surpassing white children, indi-cating the significance of Latinos as commu-nity citizens, captives of the criminal justice system, or employees of the system in the coming decades.

The Changing Face of the United States: The America of Tomorrow

To more closely illustrate the recent eth-nic/race shifts in demographic trends, with corresponding influence on everyday social life, including the Latino experience with the criminal justice system, diversity, and multi-culturalism, while also illustrating the signifi-cance of the Latino population and subse-quently the need for Latino personnel (po-lice, courts, and corrections), we will utilize the state of Texas as an illustration. In Texas, the overall population grew to more than 25 million, with Latinos accounting for more than 65 percent of the state's growth since 2000. Actually, Texas' population increase accounted for nearly 25 percent of the na-tion's total population growth during the first decade of the twenty-first century (Ayala, 2011), adding more than 4.2 million Texas residents (an overall growth of 20.6%). While the non-Latino white population experienced the smallest increase (4.2%), the black population grew by 22 percent, and the Latino population increased by 42 per-cent (Jervis, 2011). In fact, for the first time in *recent* history, the Lone Star State is less than half non-Latino (Hispanic) white. The non-Latino white segment of the population dropped to 45 percent with Latinos consti-tuting about 38 percent of the total Texas population. As for ethnic demographics, with the Texas Anglo population already less than 50 percent, it is estimated that Mexican Americans will become the Texas majority by 2040 (Murdock, White, Hoque, Pecotte, You, & Balkan, 2003).

While the Latino population remains con-centrated in four population centers, Dallas-Fort Worth, Houston-Galveston, San An-tonio-Austin, and the Rio Grande Valley, Latinos now live in every major Texas city, with some cities undergoing significant de-mographic shifts. For example, in Harris County, where Houston is located, the La-tino population grew by nearly 50 percent (1.7 million), while the white population dropped from 1.4 million to 1.35 million, a six percent decline. In fact, in the first decade of the twenty-first century, historic white suburbs are now swelling with Latinos, as noted by Deacon Joe Rubio of the Houston Catholic Charities, "There is a sig-nificant spread from traditional barrios or neighborhoods to suburban areas and other areas where you wouldn't find them before" (Jervis, 2011:2).

Invariably, the recent demographic shifts are already having significant implications not only for the state of Texas, but the entire country as well as the global economy, highly influenced by the workforce. Steve Murdock, former Director of the Census Bureau, observes that "Texas growth is due to Hispanics. We're seeing this very marked slowdown in the Anglo population, and the marked increase of the non-Anglo population" (Ayala, 2011:1). Referencing historical trends, Murdock reports that realistically, "We're seeing the development of two population groups in Texas: aging Anglos and young minorities. We are seeing Hispanic growth not just deepen but become pervasive throughout the state" (Jervis, 2011:2). The implications are in fact pressing for long-term survival in that, for example,

> There are two populations . . . an older aging Anglo population who need a younger population to help pay for Social Security and a younger population, primarily minority, that needs assistance in getting the education they need to be competitive in what is increasingly a global economy. (Ayala, 2011:3)

Analyzing the Texas ethnic/racial transformation, which based on the 2010 Census, Texas youths increased by more than one million children under the age of 18 (95% being Latino), William Frey, a demographer for the Brookings Institute, reports that "the future of the state" is "a diverse one" and highly significant for the state, national, and global economy (Jervis, 2011:2). More explicitly, according to Murdock, "The Texas of today is the U.S. of tomorrow" (Jervis, 2011:2). In retrospect, in the midst of globalization, what are the *democratic* avenues for the productive survival of Texas, of the United States, of the world, if equal representation, equality, and justice are not made a high priority?

Universally, inequality remains largely tied to the larger question of the distribution of wealth in the United States and among the countries of the world. With the United States holding more than half of the world's wealth, a decade into the twenty-first century, whites accounted for less than 64 percent of the U.S. population in 2010; yet, they held almost 90 percent of all the wealth in the country in 2010: whites (88.4%), Latinos (4.0%), African Americans (2.7%), and people of other races the remaining 4.9 percent (Strachan, 2013), clearly illustrating that we are nowhere near a postracial society (Urbina, 2014). As for earnings in the workforce, based on 2011 American Community Survey Data, the racial divide is gravely pressing when one "maps" the earnings distribution per capita by age and race (white/nonwhite) for males. Evidently, the enormous gaps in the distribution of wealth and the wide earnings gap between white men and everyone else is a direct result of centuries of economic inequality in America's main institutions, which includes the underrepresentation of Latinos in the workforce, of course above pick and shovel jobs, with criminal justice being simply one of the many professions from which ethnic minorities have been excluded. According to a report by the Altarum Institute ("The Business Case for Racial Equality"), closing the earnings gap would actually increase total U.S. earnings by nearly $1 trillion (approximately 12%); that is, if the average income of minorities matched the income of whites. Reportedly, closing the gap would also benefit the whole economy in the future, as the GDP would be 16 percent higher in 2030 if minorities earned as much as whites, and 20 percent higher in 2050; again, revealing the global significance of equal representation, along with equitable pay, in the workforce.

Lastly, regarding equality in the criminal

justice system, which is tied to economics, toward the end of the twentieth century one critic charged, "American justice is rampant with inequity," concluding that "The wide gap between rhetoric and reality is disturbing . . . The whole legitimacy of the justice system is in question (Podgers, 1994:56-57), a critical situation for the poor people of America, both in and outside the criminal justice system, as documented by Jeffrey Reiman and Paul Leighton in *The Rich Get Richer and the Poor Get Prison* (2017). According to a study by Michael Norton and Dan Ariely (2011), the top 1 percent of Americans own approximately 40 percent of all the wealth in the United States (about 54 trillion in 2009), while the bottom 80 percent of Americans own about 7 percent of all the wealth in the country. Worse, citing census data, a report released on September 16, 2010, showed that one in seven Americans now live in poverty, with the overall poverty rate climbing to 14.3 percent (43.6 million people). While poverty increased among all ethnic and racial groups, the levels are much higher for Latinos and blacks; that is, the number of African Americans in poverty increased from 24.7 percent to 25.8 percent, for Latinos it increased from 23.2 percent to 25.3 percent, for whites the level increased from 8.6 percent to 9.4 percent, and child poverty rose from 19 percent to 20.7 percent. Individually, poverty is governed by national and international economic cycles, but also heavily influenced by the workforce, particularly unemployment, which is influenced by education and *opportunity* or lack of. Ultimately, these historical divides bring us back to a full circle, a call for equal representation in the workforce to bridge and prevent these pressing gaps, and what a better place to begin our journey than the criminal justice system—*equality before the law.*

A SEPARATE REALITY: HUMANIZING DIFFERENCE

Analyzing and documenting the ethnic realities of Latinos with the U.S. criminal justice system, the hiring of Latinos goes far beyond equal representation, demographic shifts, or public safety, as maintaining a balanced workforce is not only vital for the legitimate operation of the institution, but from everyday life to the governance of America's main institutions; in essence, the functioning of the entire country. As for social control, considering the various issues and questions raised herein, Americans need to come to the realization that unjustified social control, which has resulted in aggressive policing, mega-prosecutions, and mass incarceration, and society as a whole cannot be significantly improved by simply passing and enforcing more laws, as the United States is already the country with the most laws in the world, recently being characterized by some critics as a "police-state," particularly under President Trump. Globally, we need to be cautious of policies in all levels of government that promise an easy or questionable fix to complex situations. While some laws, policies, and executive orders might sound logical, effective, and politically appealing, such policies often led to severe ramifications, causing more uncertainty and chaos than they actually solve. Further, considering the historical twists and turns of diversity and multiculturalism, we need to be cautious about accepting the often cited "culture explanation" as a *last resort* approach to emerging or challenging problems within the American society.

Socially, instead of neglecting, marginalizing, and silencing certain segments of society, we should empower them with survival tools, like training, decent employment, and a solid education that will enable them to compete in a highly technological and competitive job market. In the context of criminal justice research, considering that various factors have defined and redefined the nature of crime, formal sanctions, and, more importantly, final outcomes, the dynamics of law enforcement practices, judicial proceedings, and penal operations need to be investigated by their totality, which involves the inclusion of Latinos. Beyond criminal justice, the world of academia needs to make an honest effort to include the voices that have traditionally been left out of academic books, educational lectures, and public discourse; this involves being inclusive in both research and publication by minority scholars, especially Latinos, and more so, Mexican Americans, who constitute the majority of the Latino population in the United States.

Universally, if the United States wishes to maintain its status as a democratic world leader, the ethnic gap, the racial gap, and the gender gap, particularly in America's main institutions, must be strategically addressed. Notably, in a highly globalized world, if the United States wishes to situate itself as the country of the future, as a "fully-democratic" society, and be on the forefront of positive globalization, including the globalization of knowledge, we must make sure to present an objective, inclusive, and universal truth and reality that is reflective of the American society. With Latinos on their way to possibly become the majority, their participation should not be viewed and treated as a one-way avenue, but as a two-way road, with Latinos being influenced by the forces of American institutions, but also ethnic minorities influencing the *future of America.* Finally, if we are to prioritize and truthfully develop and implement innovative and strategic mechanisms that will actually make a significant difference in achieving universal safety, equality, peace, and justice not only in the United States but throughout the world, it is time that the United States be more inclusive and reach out to all segments of the American society as well as other countries, with full representation in the criminal justice system being a highly visible starting point. Ultimately, in the name of unity and the betterment of society, Americans should seriously consider transformation that will actually improve lives.

A FINAL NOTE

In achieving equality, unity, solidarity, safety, and peace, one of the biggest challenges boils down to one question: "How do we change the public opinion of American citizens, particularly the 'voting class,' so that they can be more tolerant to a population that historically has been perceived and treated with 'indifference'" (Urbina, 2008: 204)? For instance, for centuries we have managed to resolve some of the most critical, consequential, and catastrophic events in the United States and abroad, and we have worked with diverse communities around the world for decades on various complicated issues. Yet some of the controversial issues currently facing the United States, like immigration, seem to be bringing out the worst of some people, creating fear, aggression, intimidation, retaliation, violence, and divided communities, as vividly illustrated since Trump declared his candidacy for president on June 16, 2015, escalating after his nomination and gravely exacerbating after his inauguration as President of the United States on January 20, 2017. Instead of promoting a message of intolerance, prejudice, hate, and vindictiveness, why not use this divided and antagonistic political climate to promote a universal message of understanding, unity, respect, and human dignity, illustrating our will and capacity to resolve and overcome conflictive and catastrophic events.

As for the future of U.S. Latinos and the American community, it is through the courage of crusaders for justice, activists, serious scholars, and other vested in equality for all that the pendulum of equality and justice begins to shift in a positive direction, while giving authority and a voice to those who have been historically silenced, to include Latinos, blacks, whites, Native Americans, and people of other races. Lastly, as we vent into the future we must be mindful that

Since our lives are socialized so that we accept the status quo as *la verdad y la realidad,* revolutionizing alternations to the existing social order will require that we open up and make a serious and honest effort to the cause, if we are to actually move *hacia un mejor futuro en un mundo moderno* (towards a better future in a modern world). However, as expected, any challenges to the existing order will be fought with great ferocity by those who wish to maintain the existing legacy of hypocrisy, hate, ignorance, dominance, and power. (Urbina, 2003a:127)

We look forward to seeing you in the "jungle" as our warriors meet and join the battle drum that calls for unity in the struggle for breaking the chains of modern slavery–like the butterflies flying the skies and the birds over the seas, all are welcomed for both ear and eye–promises of victory are high, for even if unattainable today, tomorrow still holds the torch and dream, like fire of paradise, glory of life, glory of eternity!

NOTES

1. Pérez notes only three cases where authorities brought legal action against Texas Rangers: *Hudson v. St. Louis Sw. Ry. Co. of Tex.*, 293 S.W. 811, 12 (1927); *Texas Breeders & Racing Ass'n v. Blanchard,* 81 F.2d 382, 383 (1936); *Vaughn v. State,* 166 S.W.2d 139, 140-41 (1942).
2. The riches earned in California were indeed significant; the value of the gold extracted from California mines in the initial decade of the gold rush totaled nearly $600 million, a value of more than $10 billion today.
3. See *Arizona v. Hicks,* 480 U.S. 321, 328 (1987), holding that merely looking at a turntable is not a "search."
4. Matthew S. Parrish, "The 'Plain Feel' Exception—A Fourth Amendment Rendition of the Princess and the Pea" (1993). *State v. Dickerson,* 481 N.W.2d 840 (Minn. 1992), cert. granted, 61 U.S.L.W. 3256 (U.S. 1992). In *Minnesota v. Dickerson,* 508 U.S. 366 (1993), the United States Supreme Court held that in the police may seize nonthreatening contraband detected through the sense of touch during a protective pat-down search of the sort permitted by *Terry v. Ohio* (1968), so long as the search stays within the bounds marked by *Terry.*
5. For a discussion of the judicial history, see Janet E. Mitchell (1991), "Note: The Selective Application of the Fourth Amendment: *United States v. Verdugo-Urquidez.*"
6. See Act of July 31, 1789, ch. 5,§24, i Stat. 29, 43 (repealed 1790).
7. A companion case involved Rodolfo Sifuentes, petitioner in No. 75-5387, who was arrested at the immigration checkpoint on U.S. Highway 77 near Sarita, Texas about 90 miles north of Brownsville (428 U.S. 543). The physical set up at the checkpoint is similar to the San Clemente checkpoint but it is operated somewhat differently in that all motorists are stopped for brief questioning, except for motorists that are recognized by the officers as local residents. Sifuentes approached the checkpoint without any visible passengers. However, when the agent approached the vehicle he saw four passengers, one in the front seat and three in the rear, slumped down in the seat. Further questioning revealed that while Sifuentes was a U.S. citizen, the four passengers were undocumented aliens. Sifuentes was indicted on four counts of transporting aliens under 8 U.S.C. 1324 (a)(2) and moved to suppress the evidence obtained, claiming that the stop was in violation of the Fourth Amendment. The motion was denied and he was convicted after a jury trial, but he appealed arguing that his conviction was the result of an illegal search.
8. His attorneys were Gustavo ("Gus") C. García, Carlos Cadena, John Herrera, and James DeAnda but only García and Cadena appeared before the Supreme Court.
9. In California each party is allotted ten peremptory challenges.
10. In the appeal, Hernández no longer pressed his objection to the exclusion of these two jurors.
11. In *Yick Wo v. Hopkins* (1886), the Supreme Court for the first time recognized that a law which is neutral on its face may entail purposeful discrimination because of the way it is

administered, in a case where a San Francisco ordinance prohibited the operation of a laundry except in a brick or stone building without the approval of the supervisors. The Board granted permits to all but one of the 80 non-Chinese applicants but to none of about 200 Chinese applicants.

12. Brief for the Mexican American Legal Defense and Education Fund and the Commonwealth of Puerto Rican Community Affairs in the United States, as Amici Curiae in Support of Petitioner. *Hernández v. New York* (1990/1991).

13. For a discussion of how even race-neutral practices and procedures result in underrepresentation of racial minorities, see King (1993).

14. The public correlates felonies with violent crime such as murder, robbery, and rape, but approximately 90 percent of criminal violations involve nonviolent crimes such as burglary and theft. Also, most defendants accused of property crimes or low-level drug dealing.

15. Deportable offenses include crimes of domestic violence and moral turpitude, independent of classification or sentence imposed by the trial court. Though, with some exceptions, a 1-year rule of thumb applies to other convictions; that is, if the sentence is one year or longer, the conviction will most likely result in deportation.

16. Guilty pleas tend to outnumber trials by more than five to one at the federal level and by about ten to one at the state and local levels, with most guilty pleas resulting from plea bargaining.

17. Major prior reforms include: Bail Reform Act of 1966 and the Bail Reform Act of 1984. Some states, including Wisconsin, have eliminated bail bonding for profit.

18. In some situations, delay is a major problem confronting the U.S. judiciary. Although trial juries or petit juries (Sixth Amendment) are considered fundamental to U.S. justice and liberty, not all people accused of violating criminal laws are entitled to a trial by jury–i.e., juveniles–and for petty offenses, unless the defendant is going to prison for more than six months. Studies indicate that judges are more likely to find guilt than juries. In federal courts, juries convict about 82 percent of the time in nondrug cases and about 87 percent of the time in drug related cases. Data from various states point in the same direction: juries convict approximately 2/3 of the time in criminal cases. Also, although most cases are disposed by a guilty plea, an important 2 to 10 percent of defendants are tried. Typically called the *jury trial penalty,* legal trials tend to reflect the philosophy: "He takes some of my time, I take some of his."

19. According to Western, while all men have a higher chance of going to prison today than they did 35 years ago, minorities, especially uneducated people, are being incarcerated at a highly disproportionate rate. For instance, in 1979, black men who dropped out of high school had about a 15 percent chance of ending up in prison by age 30–34, but it's nearly 70 percent today.

20. The first federal law addressing immigration was the 1864 *Act to Encourage Immigration.*

21. Between 1982 and 2001, total state corrections expenditures increased each year, rising from $15.0 billion to $53.5 billion (Kyckelhahn, 2012). Similarly, tracing the growth of state spending on corrections from 1986 to 2001, James Stephan (2004) reports an average annual increase of 6.2 for total state correctional spending and 6.4 percent specifically for prisons, with increases in the cost of adult incarceration outpacing those of education (4.2%) and health care (5.8%). Comparing state spending on prisons versus higher education, from 1987 to 2007 nationwide spending on corrections increased by 127 percent, while spending on higher education increased by 21 percent (Wade, 2010), with states spending four times more per capita to incarcerate than to educate (Prann, 2011). Between 1982 and 2010, spending on corrections represented between 1.9 percent and

3.3 percent of total expenditures by state government. In 2010, for instance, state expenditures totaled $1.9 trillion, with state spending on corrections standing at $48.5 billion. Between 1982 and 2010, spending on education varied between 29 percent and 33 percent and public welfare varied between 22 percent and 25 percent of total state expenditures (Kyckelhahn, 2012). From 1986 to 2012, spending from state funds for corrections increased by 427 percent, while total spending from state funds increased by 315 percent over the same time period.

22. The law gives the police powers to disperse suspected gang members from public space, while no crime has been committed until the police approach someone with an order to disperse. It is only after such demand is made that the law has been violated: the "failure to disperse on demand." The law is constituted as a two-step process that criminalizes the second step only after making invisible the first action by law enforcement, unjustified intrusion.

23. "The Yaquis are a famously fierce tribe, originally from northwestern Mexico, but now living partly in the U.S." (Shorris, 1992:420). Some of these individuals (or "Los Indios," as they call themselves) live in Arizona (Hayes, 1999a).

24. These southernmost islands in the West Indies, once under the British rule, now comprise a country named simply Trinidad and Tobago.

25. After a 20-month international legal and political dance between Mexico and the United States, 23-year old José Luis Del Toro was extradited to Florida for the November 7, 1997 murder of Sheila Bellush. Since the U.S. extradition treaty with Mexico requires states to waive the death penalty before Mexico sends a homicide defendant back for prosecution, Del Toro did not face the death penalty. Instead, prosecutors seek a life sentence. Del Toro, who was arrested in Mexico in November 1997 and returned on July 12, 1999, was convicted for first degree murder and burglary and was sentenced to life in prison on July 6, 2000.

26. Except for military people, Mexico abolished the sentence of death in 1929. And, while on the books, it has not been used in the military.

27. In 1961, U.S.-backed Cuban exiles launched the ill-fated Bay of Pigs invasion against Fidel Castro's communist government. A year later, the Soviet Union stationed missiles on the island, "shocking" the U.S. and forcefully insisted that they be removed, applying sanctions like the economic embargo that continues today.

28. As a result of the University of California Regents' 1995 decision to eliminate the race criteria, African American admissions at Berkeley's law school dropped from 75 in 1996 to 14 in 1997, while at UCLA's law school, African American admissions fell from 104 to 21 (Acuña, 1998).

REFERENCES

Abadinsky, H. (1997). *Probation and parole.* Upper Saddle: NJ Pearson Publishing.

Abadinsky, H. (2003). *Probation and parole.* Upper Saddle, NJ: Prentice Hall.

Abadinsky, H. (2009). *Probation and parole.* Upper Saddle, NJ: Prentice Hall.

Achor, S. (1978). *Mexican Americans in a Dallas barrio.* Tucson, AZ: University of Arizona Press.

Acosta, O. (1973). *The revolt of the cockroach people.* New York: Vintage.

Acuña, R. (1990). California commentary: Life behind bars is no way to build character. *Los Angeles Times,* February 12: B7.

Acuña, R. (1998). *Sometimes there is no other side: Chicanos and the myth of equality.* Notre Dame: University of Notre Dame Press.

Acuña, R. (2004). Defining America through immigration policy. *Choice,* 42: 1.

Acuña, R. (2005). Crocodile tears: Lynchings of Mexicans. *Hispanic Vista.* Available at: http://www.hispanicvista.com/HVC/Opinion/Guest_Columns/062005Acuna.htm.

Acuña, R. (2011). *The making of Chicana/o studies: In the trenches of academe.* Piscataway, NJ: Rutgers University Press.

Acuña, R. (2013). Los muertos de hambre: The war on Chicana/o studies–Unmasking the illusion of inclusion. Available at: http://mexmigration.blogspot.com/2013/11/acuna-on-war -against-chicanao-studies.html.

Acuña, R. (2015). *Occupied America: A history of Chicanos* (8th ed.). Upper Saddle River, NJ: Prentice Hall.

Adams, C. J., Robelen, E. W., & Shah, N. (2012). Civil rights data show retention disparities. Education Weekly. Available at: http://www.edweek.org/ew/articles/2012/03/07/23data _ep.h31.html.

Adelman, R., Reid, L. W., Markle, G., Weiss, S., & Jaret, C. (2017). Urban crime rates and the changing face of immigration: Evidence across four decades. *Journal of Ethnicity in Criminal Justice,* 15: 52–77.

Adler, R. (2006). But they claimed to be police, no la migra! The interaction of residency, status, class, and ethnicity in a (post-PATRIOT Act) New Jersey neighborhood. *American Behavioral Scientist,* 50: 48–69.

Agozino, B. (1997). *Black women and the criminal justice system: Towards the decolonization of victimization.* Brookfield, VT: Ashgate.

Aguirre, A. (2002). Propositions 187 and 227: A nativist response to Mexicans. In C. Hohm & S. Glynn (Eds.), *California's social problems* (2th ed.). Thousand Oaks, CA: Pine Forge Press.

Aguirre, A. (2004). Profiling Mexican American identity: Issues and concerns. *American Behavioral Scientist,* 47: 928–942.

Aguirre, A., & Baker, D. (1989). The execution of Mexican American prisoners in the Southwest. *Social Justice,* 16: 150–161.

Aguirre, A., & Baker, D. (1997). A descriptive profile of Mexican American executions in the Southwest. *The Social Science Journal,* 34: 389–402.

Aguirre, A., & Martínez, R. (1993). *Chicanos in higher education: Issues and dilemmas for the 21st century.* San Francisco, CA: Jossey-Bass.

Aguirre, A., & Simmers, J. (2009). Mexican border crossers: The Mexican body in immigration discourse. *Social Justice,* 35: 99–106.

Aguirre, A., & Turner, J. (2007). *American ethnicity: The dynamics and consequences of discrimination* (5th ed.). New York: McGraw-Hill.

Aguirre, A., & Turner, J. (2010). *American ethnicity: The dynamics and consequences of discrimination* (7th ed.). New York: McGraw-Hill.

Aguirre, A., Rodríguez, E., & Simmers, J. (2011). The cultural production of Mexican identity in the United States: An examination of the Mexican threat narrative. *Social Identities,* 17: 695–707.

Akram, S., & Johnson, K. (2002). Race, civil rights, and immigration law after September 11, 2001: The targeting of Arabs and Muslims. *New York University Annual Survey of American Law,* 58: 295–355.

Albert, M., & Obler, L. (1978). *The bilingual brain: Neuropsychological and neurolinguistic aspects of bilingualism.* New York: Academic Press.

Albonetti, C. (1991). An integration of theories to explain judicial discretion. *Social Problems,* 38: 247–266.

Alex, N. (1969). *Black in blue: A study of the Negro policeman.* New York: Appleton-Century-Crofts.

Alexander, M. (2012). *The new Jim Crow: Mass incarceration in the age of colorblindness.* New York: The New Press.

Alfieri, A. (2004). Color, identity, justice: Chicano trials. *Duke Law Journal,* 53: 1569–1617.

Allen, H., & Clubb, J. (2008a). *Executions in the United States, 1608–1940: The Espy File; Summary data of executions collected by M. Watt Espy between 1986 and 1996.* Inter-University Consortium for Political and Social Research.

Allen, H., & Clubb, J. (2008b). *Race, class, and the death penalty: Capital punishment in American history.* Albany: State University of New York Press.

Allen, J., Lewis, J., Litwack, L., & Als, H. (2000). *Without sanctuary: Lynching photography in America.* Santa Fe, NM: Twin Palms Publishers.

Almaguer, T. (1971). Toward the study of Chicano colonialism. *Aztlán: A Journal of Chicano Studies,* 2: 7–21.

Almaguer, T. (1994). *Racial fault lines: The historical origins of white supremacy in California.* Los Angeles, CA: University of California Press.

Almaguer, T. (2008). *Racial fault lines: The historical origins of white supremacy in California.* Berkeley: University of California Press.

Alpert, G., & Dunham, R. (2004). *Understanding police use of force: Officers, suspects, and reciprocity.* Cambridge: Cambridge University Press.

Álvarez, S. E., & Urbina, M. G. (2014). Capital punishment on trial: Who lives, who dies, who decides—A question of justice? *Criminal Law Bulletin,* 50: 263–298.

Álvarez, S. E., & Urbina, M. G. (Eds.). (2018). *Immigration and the law: Race, citizenship, and social control.* Tucson, AZ: University of Arizona Press.

Alvear, D. (2013). Hispanic population becoming the largest ethnic group in the state of California. Available at: http://nbclatino.com/2013/01/29/hispanic-population-becoming-the-largest-ethnic-group-in-the-state-of-california/.

Amar, A. (1994). Fourth Amendment first principles. *Harvard Law Review,* 107: 757–819.

Amar, A. (2002). Foreword. In J. Dressler (Ed.), *Encyclopedia of crime and justice.* New York: Macmillan Reference.

America's Voice. (2011). *The Dupnik rebellion: Pima's top cop says "no" to SB 1070.* Available at: http://americasvoiceonline.org/pages/Police_Speak_Out_Against_Arizona_Immigration _Law.

American Civil Liberties Union. (2010). Remembering Francisco Castaneda. Available at: http://www.aclu.org/blog/immigrants-rights-prisoners-rights/remembering-francisco castaneda.

American Civil Liberties Union. (2014). War comes home: The excessive militarization of American policing. Available at: https://www.aclu.org/sites/default/files/assets/jus14-war comeshome-report-web-rel1.pdf.

Amnesty International. (1998). *United States of America: Rights for all.* New York: Amnesty International Publications.

Amnesty International. (1999). Execution of foreign nationals. Available at: http://www .amnesty-usa.org/abolish/fnnat.html.

Amnesty International. (2003). *USA: Death by discrimination—The continuing role of race in capital cases.* Available at: http://www.amnesty.org/en/library/asset/AMR51/046/2003/en /bd8584ef-d712-11dd-b0cc-1f0860013475/amr510462003en.pdf.

Amnesty International. (2009). Jailed without justice: Immigration detention in the USA. Available at: http://www.amnestyusa.org/immigrantrights/page.do?id=1641031.

Amnesty International. (2011a). *Abolish the death penalty: The death penalty violates the rights of foreign nationals.* Available at: http://www.amnestyusa.org/abolish/factsheets/foreign _nationals.html.

Amnesty International. (2011b). *Texas denies World Court order and executes.* Available at: http://www.amnesty.org/en/library/asset/AMR51/063/2011/en/8f569254-ae0c-4780-b927- 4c5eca080541/amr510632011en.pdf.

Ampudia, R. (2010). *Mexicans on death row.* Houston: Arte Publico Press.

Anderson, G. (2005). *The conquest of Texas: Ethnic cleansing in the promised land, 1820–1875.* Norman: University of Oklahoma Press.

Andreas, P. (2003). *A tale of two borders: The U.S.-Mexico and U.S.-Canada lines after 9/11.* Working Papers, Comparative Immigration Studies, UC San Diego.

Appiah, K. A. (2000). Stereotypes and the shaping of identity. *California Law Review,* 88: 41–53.

Applegate, B., & Sitren, A. (2008). The jail and the community: Comparing jails in rural and urban contexts. *The Prison Journal,* 88: 252–269.

Aranda, E. (2006). *Emotional bridges to Puerto Rico: Migration, return migration, and the struggles of incorporation.* Lanham, MD: Rowman & Littlefield Publishers.

Archibold, R. (2010a). Arizona enacts stringent law on immigration. *Available at:* http: //www.nytimes.com/2010/04/24/us/politics/24immig.html.

Archibold, R. (2010b). Judge blocks Arizona's law on immigrants. *New York Times* (July 29): A1.

Ashar, S. (2002). Immigration enforcement and subordination: The consequences of racial profiling after September 11. *Connecticut Law Review,* 34: 1185–1199.

Atlanta Journal Constitution. (2006). House passes bill on illegals. Available at: http: //www.ajc.com/news/content/metro/stories/0324legillegal.html.

Austin, J., & Irwin, J. (2012). *It's about time: America's imprisonment binge* (4th ed.). Belmont: Wadsworth Publishing Company.

Ayala, E. (2011). Urban centers of Texas keep packing them in. *San Antonio Express News,* February 18. Available at: http://www.mysanantonio.com.

Bacon, D. (2009). *Illegal people: How globalization creates migration and criminalizes immigrants.* Boston, MA: Beacon Press.

Baker, D. V. (2016). *Women and capital punishment in the United States: An analytical history.* Jefferson, NC: McFarland.

Balderrama, F., & Rodríguez, R. (1995). *Decade of betrayal: Mexican repatriation in the 1930s.* Albuquerque: University of New Mexico Press.

Bales, K. (2004). *Disposable people: New slavery in the global economy.* Berkeley: University of California Press.

Bales, K. (Ed). (2005). *Understanding global slavery today: A reader.* Berkeley: University of California Press.

Balko, R. (2006). Overkill: The rise of paramilitary police raids in America. Available at: http://object.cato.org/sites/cato.org/files/pubs/pdf/balko_whitepaper_2006.pdf.

Balko, R. (2013). *Rise of the warrior cop: The militarization of America's police forces.* New York: PublicAffairs.

Barde, R., & Bobonis, G. (2006). Detention at Angel Island: First empirical evidence. *Social Science History,* 30: 103–36.

Barlow, D., & Barlow, M. (2002). Racial profiling: A survey of African American police officers. *Police Quarterly,* 5: 334–358.

Barnum, M. (2016). Exclusive–data show 3 of the biggest school districts hire more security officers than counselors. Available at: https://www.the74million.org/article/exclusive-data-shows-3-of-the-5-biggest-school-districts-hire-more-security-officers-than-counselors.

Barrera, M. (1979). *Race and class in the Southwest: A theory of racial inequality.* Notre Dame: University of Notre Dame Press.

Bartolomé, L., Macedo, D., Ríos, V., & Peguero, A. (2013). Latina/o students and the school-prison-pipeline. *Association of Mexican-American Educators,* 17: 1–105.

Battle, M. (2015). 12 heartbreaking facts about the school to prison pipeline that every person should know. Available at: http://www.teabreakfast.com/school-to-prison-pipeline-facts/.

Bayley, D., & Mendelsohn, H. (1968). *Minorities and the police: Confrontation in America.* New York, NY: Free Press.

Bean, F., & Bell-Rose, S. (Eds). (1999). *Immigration and opportunity: Race, ethnicity, and employment in the United States.* New York: Russell Sage Foundation Publications.

Beck, A. J., Karberg, J. C., & Harrison, P. M. (2002). *Prison and jail inmates at midyear 2001.* Washington, DC: U.S. Department of Justice, Bureau of Justice Statistics.

Beck, A., & Mumola, C. (1999). *Prisoners in 1998.* Washington, DC: Bureau of Justice Statistics.

Beck, A., & Shipley, B. (1989). Recidivism of Prisoners Released in 1988. Washington, DC: Bureau of Justice Statistics.

Beckett, K. (1997). *Making crime pay: Law and order in contemporary American politics.* New York: Oxford University Press.

Beckett, K., & Evans, H. (2015). Crimmigration at the local level: Criminal justice processes in the shadow of deportation. *Law & Society Review,* 49: 24–277.

Beckett, K., & Sasson, T. (2003). *The politics of injustice: Crime and punishment in America* (2nd ed.). Thousand Oaks, CA: Sage Publications.

Bejarano, C. (2005). *Que onda? Urban youth culture and border identity.* Tucson, AZ: University of Arizona Press.

Bell, D. (1992). *Faces at the bottom of the well: The permanence of racism.* New York: Basic Books.

Belvedere, K., Worrall, J., & Tibbetts, S. (2005). Explaining suspect resistance in police-citizen encounters. *Criminal Justice Review,* 30: 30–44.

Bender, S. W. (2003). *Greasers and gringos: Latinos, law, and the American imagination.* New York: New York University Press.

Bender, S. W. (2005). *Greasers and gringos: Latinos, law, and the American imagination.* New York: New York University Press.

Bender, S. W. (2014). Latina/o influence on U.S. politics: Reality and potential. In M. G. Urbina (Ed.), *Twenty-first century dynamics of multiculturalism: Beyond post-racial America.* Springfield, IL: Charles C Thomas.

Bender, S. W. (2015). *Mea culpa: Lessons on law and regret from U.S. history.* New York: New York University Press.

Benítez, H. (1994). Flawed strategies: The INS shift from border interdiction to internal enforcement actions. *La Raza Law Journal,* 7: 154–179.

Bennett, R. (2004). Comparative criminology and criminal justice research: The state of our knowledge. *Justice Quarterly,* 21: 1–22.

Berg, C. R. (2002). *Latino images in film: Stereotypes, subversion, and resistance.* Austin: University of Texas Press.

Berg, C. R. (2003). Colonialism and movies in Southern California, 1910–1934. *Aztlán: A Journal of Chicano Studies,* 28: 75–96.

Berg, C. R. (2014). The minority experience through the lens of the American media: Eight counter-stereotyping strategies from (of all places) TV ads. In M. G. Urbina (Ed.), *Twenty-first century dynamics of multiculturalism: Beyond post-racial America.* Springfield, IL: Charles C Thomas.

Berg, M., & DeLisi, M. (2006). The correctional melting pot: Race, ethnicity, citizenship, and prison violence. *Journal of Criminal Justice,* 34: 631–642.

Berger, P., & Luckmann, T. (1966). *The social construction of reality: A treatise in the sociology of knowledge.* New York: Anchor Books, Doubleday.

Bever, L. (2017). Hispanics 'are going further into the shadows' amid chilling immigration debate, police say. Available at: https://www.washingtonpost.com/news/post-nation/wp/2017/05/12/immigration-debate-might-be-having-a-chilling-effect-on-crime-reporting-in-hispanic-communities-police-say/?utm_term=.6031726a80b9.

Bhabha, H. K. (1996). Culture's in-between. In S. Hall & P. du Gay (Eds.), *Questions of cultural identity.* London: Sage Publications.

Binswanger, I., Krueger, P., & Steiner, J. (2009). Prevalence of chronic medical conditions among jail and prison inmates compared to the general population. *Journal of Epidemiology Community Health,* 63: 912–919.

Blalock, H. (1967). *Toward a theory of minority group relations.* New York: Wiley.

Blauner, R. (1969). Internal colonialism and ghetto revolt. *Social Problems,* 16: 373–408.

Blauner, R. (1972). *Racial oppression in America.* New York: Harper Collins

Blauner, R. (1987). Colonized and immigrant minorities. In R. Takaki (Ed.), *From different shores: Perspectives on race and ethnicity in America.* New York: Oxford University Press.

Blauner, R. (2000). *Still the big news: Racial oppression in America.* Philadelphia: Temple University Press.

Blazak, R. (2004). White boys to terrorist men: Target recruitment of Nazi skinheads. In P. Gerstenfeld & D. Grant (Eds), *Crimes of hate: Selected readings.* New York: Sage Publications.

Blevins, K., Listwan, S., Cullen, F., & Jonson, C. (2010). A general strain theory of prison violence and misconduct: An integrated model of inmate behavior. *Journal of Contemporary Criminal Justice,* 26: 148–166.

Blum, W. (1995). *Killing hope: U.S. military and CIA interventions since World War II.* Monroe, ME: Common Courage Press.

Bogardus, E. (1943). Gangs of Mexican-American youth. *Sociology and Social Research,* 28: 55–66.

Bok, D., & Bowen, W. (1998). *The shape of the river: Long-term consequences of considering race in college and university admissions.* Princeton: Princeton University Press.

Bolton, K. (2003). Shared perceptions: Black officers discuss continuing barriers in policing. *Policing: An International Journal of Police Strategies and Management,* 26: 386–399.

Bolton, K., & Feagin, J. (2004). *Black in blue: African-American police officers and racism.* New York: Routledge.

Bonczar, T. (2003). *Prevalence of imprisonment in the U.S. population, 1974–2001.* Bureau of Justice Statistics. Washington, DC: U.S. Department of Justice.

Bonczar, T., & Beck, A. J. (1997). *Lifetime likelihood of going to state or federal prison.* Washington, DC: U.S. Department of Justice, Bureau of Justice Statistics.

Bond-Maupin, L., & Maupin, J. (1998). Juvenile justice decision making in a rural Hispanic community. *Journal of Criminal Justice,* 26: 373–384.

Bonilla-Silva, E. (1997). Rethinking racism: Toward a structural interpretation. American *Sociological Review,* 62: 465–480.

Bonilla-Silva, E. (2001). *White supremacy and racism in the post-civil rights era.* Boulder, CO: Lynne Rienner Publishers.

Bonilla-Silva, E. (2006). *Racism without racists: Color-blind racism and the persistence of racial inequality in the United States* (2nd ed.). Lanham, MD: Rowman & Littlefield Publishers.

Bonta, J., & Andrews, D. (2007). *Risk-need-responsivity model for offender assessment and rehabilitation.* Ottawa, Canada: Public Safety Canada.

Bonta, J., & Andrews, D. (2016). *The psychology of criminal conduct* (6th ed.). New York: Routledge.

Bosworth, M. (2007). Identity, citizenship, and punishment. In M. Bosworth & J. Flavin (Eds.), *Race, gender, and punishment: From colonialism to the war on terror.* Piscataway, NJ: Rutgers University Press.

Bosworth, M., & Flavin, J. (Eds). (2007). *Race, gender, and punishment: From colonialism to the war on terror.* Piscataway, NJ: Rutgers University Press.

Bourgeois, P. (1995). *In search of respect: Selling crack in el barrio.* New York: Cambridge University Press.

Bowers, F. (2005). U.S.-Mexican border as a terror risk: Recent intelligence gives the most evidence yet of terrorist plans. Lawmakers push for tighter security. Available at: http://www.csmonitor.com/2005/0322/p01s01-uspo.html.

Bowers, W., Steiner, B., & Sandys, M. (2001). Death sentencing in black and white: An empirical analysis of jurors' race and jury racial composition. *University of Pennsylvania Journal of Constitutional Law,* 3: 171–275.

Boxer, P., Middlemass, K, & Delorenzo, T. (2009). Exposure to violent crime during incarceration: Effects on psychological adjustment following release. *Criminal Justice and Behavior,* 36: 793–807.

Brabeck, K., & Xu, Q. (2010). The impact of detention and deportation on Latino immigrant children and families: A quantitative exploration. *Hispanic Journal of Behavioral Sciences,* 32: 341–361.

Braga, A. (2008). Pulling levers, focused deterrence strategies and the prevention of gun homicide. *Journal of Criminal Justice,* 36: 332–343.

Braithwaite, J. (2002). Charles Title's control balance and criminological theory. In S. Cote (Ed.), *Criminological theories: Bridging the past to the future.* Thousand Oaks, CA: Sage.

Branaman, A. (2001). *Self and society.* Malden, MA: Blackwell.

Briggs, V. (1984). *Immigration policy and the American labor force.* Baltimore: John Hopkins University Press.

Brophy, A. (1972). *Foundlings on the frontier: Racial and religious conflict in Arizona territory, 1904–1905.* Tucson: University of Arizona Press.

Brotherton, D., & Barrios, L. (2004). *The almighty Latin king and queen nation: Street politics and the transformation of a New York City gang.* New York: Columbia University Press.

Brown, E., & Douglas-Gabriel, D. (2016). Since 1980, spending on prisons has grown three times as much as spending on public education. Available: https://www.washingtonpost.com/news/education/wp/2016/07/07/since-1980-spending-on-prisons-has-grown-three-times-faster-than-spending-on-public-education/.

Brown, R. (1969). The American vigilante tradition. In H. Graham & T. Gurr (Eds.), *Violence in America: Historical and comparative perspectives.* Washington: U.S. Government Printing Office.

Brown-Graham, A. (1999). Housing discrimination against Hispanics in private rental markets. *Popular Government,* Fall: 45–51.

Bull, G. (2014). Heavy police tactics a reality for immigrants, Latinos too. Available at: http://www.nbcnews.com/news/latino/heavy-police-tactics-reality-immigrants-latinos-too-n189551.

Bureau of Justice Statistics. (2004a). *Bulletin,* November. Washington, DC: U.S. Government Printing Office.

Bureau of Justice Statistics. (2004b). *Bulletin,* May. Washington, DC: U.S. Government Printing Office.

Bureau of Justice Statistics. (2007). *Contacts between police and the public: Findings from the 2005 national survey.* Washington, DC: U.S. Department of Justice

Burrell, W. B. (2005). Trends in probation and parole in the states. In *Book of the states, 2005 edition.* Lexington, KY: Council of State Governments, 595–600.

Bushway, S., & Piehl, A. (2001). Judging judicial discretion: Legal factors and racial discrimination in sentencing. *Law & Society Review,* 35: 733–764.

Bustamante, J. (1972). The wetback as deviant: An application of labeling theory. American *Journal of Sociology,* 77: 706–718.

Butcher, K., & Piehl, A. (2005). Why are immigrants' incarceration rates so low? Evidence on selective immigration, deterrence, and deportation. Available at: http://www.chicagofed.org/publications/workingpapers/wp2005_19.pdf.

Byxbe, F. R., Urbina, M. G., & Nicosia, P. (2011). Community oriented policing and partnerships: A recipe for success! *Police Forum,* 20: 4–16.

Cao, L., & Huang, B. (2000). Determinants of citizen complaints against police abuse of power. *Journal of Criminal Justice,* 28: 203–213.

Carrigan, W. (2006). *The making of a lynching culture: Violence and vigilantism in central Texas, 1836–1916.* Urbana, IL: University of Illinois Press.

Carrigan, W., & Webb, C. (2003). The lynching of persons of Mexican origin or descent in the US, 1848–1929. *Journal of Social History,* 37: 411–438.

Carroll, L., & Mondrick, M. (1976). Racial bias in the decision to grant parole. *Law and Society Review,* 11: 93–107.

Carson, E. A. (2014). *Prisoners in 2013.* Washington, DC: U.S. Department of Justice, Bureau of Justice Statistics.

Carson, E. A. (2015). *Prisoners in 2014.* Washington, DC: Bureau of Justice Statistics.

Carson, E. A. (2016). *Prisoners in 2015.* Washington, DC: U.S. Department of Justice, Bureau of Justice Statistics.

Carson, E. A., & Anderson, E. (2016). *Prisoners in 2015.* Washington, DC: U.S. Department of Justice, Bureau of Justice Statistics.

Carson, E. A., & Sabol, W. J. (2012). *Prisoners in 2011.* Washington, DC: U.S. Department of Justice, Bureau of Justice Statistics.

Carter, D. (1983). Hispanic interaction with the criminal justice system in Texas: Experiences, attitudes, and perceptions. *Journal of Criminal Justice,* 11: 213–227.

Carter, D. (1985). Hispanic perception of police performance: An empirical assessment. *Journal of Criminal Justice,* 13: 487–500.

Casanova, P. (1965). Internal colonialism and national development. *Studies in Comparative International Development,* 1: 27–37.

Cashmore, E. (2001). The experiences of ethnic minority officers in Britain: Under-recruitment and racial profiling in a performance culture. *Ethnic and Racial Studies,* 24: 642–659.

Cashmore, E. (2002). Behind the window dressing: Ethnic minority police perspectives on cultural diversity. *Journal of Ethnic and Migration Studies,* 28: 327–341.

Castañeda, J. (2007). *Ex Mex: From migrants to immigrants.* New York: The New Press.

Castells, M. (1997). *The power of identity.* Oxford: Blackwell Publishing.

Center for American Progress. (2011). *The 10 numbers you need to know about Alabama's anti-immigrant law.* Available at: http://www.americanprogress.org/issues/2011/11/top_10 _alabama_immigration.html.

Centers for Disease Control and Prevention. (2017). HIV among incarcerated populations. Available at: https://www.cdc.gov/hiv/group/correctional.html.

Chacón, J., & Davis, M. (2006). *No one is illegal: Fighting racism and state violence on the U.S.-Mexico border.* Chicago: Haymarket Books.

Chambliss, W. (1999). *Power, politics and crime.* Boulder: Westview Press.

Chambliss, W., & Seidman, R. (1971). *Law, order, and power.* Reading, MA: Addison-Wesley Publishing Company.

Champion, D. (2005). *Corrections in the United States: A contemporary perspective.* Upper Saddle, NJ: Prentice Hall.

Champion, D. (2008). *Probation, parole and community corrections.* Upper Saddle: NJ Pearson Publishing.

Chappell, B. (2010). Custom contestations: Lowriders and urban space. *City and Society,* 22: 25–47.

Chaudry, A., Capps, R., Pedroza, J., Casañeda, R., Santos, R., & Scott, M. (2010). *Facing our future: Children in the aftermath of immigration enforcement.* The Urban Institute. Available at: http://www.urban.org/UploadedPDF/412020_FacingOurFuture_final.pdf.

Chávez, H., & Miller, M. (2009). Religious reference in death sentence phases of trials: Two psychological theories that suggest judicial rulings and assumptions may affect jurors. *Lewis & Clark Law Review,* 13: 1037–1084.

Chávez, J. E., Englebrecht, C. M., López, A., Viramontez Anguiano, R. P., & Reyes, J. R. (2013). Collateral consequences: The impact of local immigration policies on Latino immigrant families in north central Indiana. In D. C. Brotherton, D. L. Stageman, & S. P. Leyro (Eds.), *Outside justice: Immigration and the criminalizing impact of changing policy and practice.* New York: Springer.

Chávez, L. R. (2013). *The Latino threat: Constructing immigration, citizens, and the nation.* Palo Alto, CA: Stanford University Press.

Chávez, M. (2011). *Everyday injustice: Latino professionals and racism.* Lanham: Rowman & Littlefield Publishers.

Chesney-Lind, M., & Pasko, L. (Eds). (2004). *Girls, women, and crime: Selected readings.* Thousand Oaks: Sage Publications.

Cheurprakobkit, S. (2000). Police-citizen contact and police performance attitudinal differences between Hispanics and non-Hispanics. *Journal of Criminal Justice,* 28: 325–336.

Cheurprakobkit, S., & Bartsch, R. (1999). Police work and the police profession: Assessing attitudes of city officials, Spanish-speaking Hispanics, and their English-speaking counterparts. *Journal of Criminal Justice,* 27: 87–100.

Chicago Daily Law Bulletin. (1992). Drano killer' executed in Utah. July 30: 1.

Chomsky, A. (2007). *"They take our jobs!" And 20 other myths about immigration.* Boston, MA: Beacon Press.

Chung, J. (2016). *Felony disenfranchisement: A primer.* Washington, DC: The Sentencing Project.

Clear, T. (1994). *Harm in American penology: Offenders, victims, and their communities.* Albany, NY: State University of New York Press.

Clear, T., & Cole, G. (2000). *American corrections.* Belmont, CA: Wadsworth Publishing Company.

Clear, T., & Dammer, H. (2000). *The offender in the community.* Belmont, CA: Wadsworth Publishing.

Cleere, J. (2006). *Outlaw tales of Arizona: True stories of Arizona's most famous robbers, rustlers, and bandits.* Guilford: The Globe Pequot Press.

Clemmer, D. (1940). *The prison community.* Boston: Christopher Publishing House.

Cobas, J., Duany, J., & Feagin, J. (2009). How the United States racializes Latinos: White hegemony and its consequences. Boulder, CO: Paradigm Publishers.

Cockcroft, J. (1986). *Outlaws in the promised land: Mexican immigrant workers and America's future.* New York: Grove Press.

Cohen, M., & Piquero, A. (2009). New evidence on the monetary value of saving a high risk youth. *Journal of Quantitative Criminology,* 25: 25–49.

Cohn, D., Talyor, P., López, M. H., Gallagher, C., Parker, K., & Maass, K. (2013). *Gun homicide rate down 49% since 1993 peak; public unaware.* Washington, DC: Pew Research Center.

Cole, D. (2001). Formalism, realism, and the war on drugs. *Suffolk University Law Review,* 35: 241–255.

Cole, D. (2003). *Enemy aliens: Double standards and constitutional freedoms in the war on terrorism.* New York: New Press.

Coleman, M., & Kocher, A. (2011). Detention, deportation, devolution and immigrant incapacitation in the US, post 9/11. *The Geographical Journal,* 177: 228–237.

Collica, K. (2013). *Female prisoners, AIDS, and peer programs: How female offenders transform their lives.* New York: Springer.

Colon, T. (2004). *Gang members in juvenile detention: A California story.* Presented at The Behavioral and Social Sciences Research Symposium, California State University, Chico.

Conchas, G. (2016). *Cracks in the schoolyard: Confronting Latino educational inequality.* New York: Texas College Press.

Conser, J., Russell, G., Paynich, R., & Gingerich, T. (2005). *Law enforcement in the United States.* Sudubury, MD: Jones and Bartlett Publishers.

Cooley, C. H. (1907). Social consciousness. *American Journal of Sociology,* 12: 675–687.

Corcoran, K. (2006). Mexican immigrants caught in backlash of terror anxiety. *San Jose Mercury News,* September 10: 4S.

Correia, D. (2010). Retribution will be their reward: New Mexico's las Gorras Blancas and the fight for Las Vegas land grant commons. *Radical History Review,* 108: 50–72.

Correia, M. (2010). Determinants of attitudes toward police of Latino immigrants and non-immigrants. *Journal of Criminal Justice,* 38: 99–107.

Cox, A. B., & Miles, T. J. (2013). Policing immigration. *The University of Chicago Law Review,* 80: 87–136.

Cox, O. (1945). Lynching and the status quo. *The Journal of Negro Education,* 14: 576–588.

Crawford, C. (2010). Minorities, space, and policing. In C. Crawford (Ed.), *Spatial policing: The influence of time, space, and geography on law enforcement practices.* Durham, North Carolina: Carolina Academic Press.

Cullen, F., & Jonson, C. (2012). *Correctional theory: Context and consequences.* Thousand Oaks, CA: Sage Publications.

Cullen, F., Jonson, C., & Nagin, D. (2011). Prisons do not reduce recidivism: The high cost of ignoring science. *The Prison Journal, 20:* 1–18.

Culver, J. H. (1992). Capital punishment, 1977–1990: Characteristics of the 143 executed. *Sociology and Social Research, 76:* 59–61.

Culver, L. (2004). The impact of new immigration patterns on the provision of police services in Midwestern communities. *Journal of Criminal Justice, 32:* 329–344.

Currie, E. (1985). *Confronting crime: An American challenge.* New York: Pantheon.

Currie, E. (1993). *Reckoning: Drugs, the cities, and the American future.* New York: Hill & Wang.

Daniels, R. (1990). *Coming to America: A history of immigration and ethnicity in American Life.* New York: Harper Collins Publishers.

Daudistel, H., Hosch, H., Holmes, M., & Graves, J. (1999). Effects of defendant ethnicity on juries' dispositions of felony cases. *Journal of Applied Social Psychology, 29:* 317–336.

Davis, G. (2007). In memoriam: Juan Bonilla Flores. Available at: http://www.americanlynching.com/flores.html.

De Angelis, J., & Kupchik, A. (2009). Ethnicity, trust, and acceptance of authority among police officers. *Journal of Criminal Justice, 37:* 273–279.

De Génova, N. (2004). The legal production of Mexican/migrant "illegality." *Latino Studies, 2:* 160–185.

De Génova, N., & Ramos-Zayas, A. (2003). *Latino crossings: Mexicans, Puerto Ricans, and the politics of race and citizenship.* New York: Routledge.

De León, A. (1983). *They called them greasers.* Austin: University of Texas Press.

De León, A. (1997). *The Tejano community, 1836–1900.* Dallas: Southern Methodist University Press.

De León, A. (2002). *Racial frontiers: Africans, Chinese, and Mexicans in Western America, 1848–1890.* Albuquerque: University of New Mexico Press.

De León, A. (2009). *Mexican Americans in Texas: A brief history* (3rd ed.). Wheeling: Harland Davidson.

De León, A. (2014). Defining Mexican Americans: Ethnic identity formation through time. In M. G. Urbina (Ed.), *Twenty-first century dynamics of multiculturalism: Beyond post-racial America.* Springfield, IL: Charles C Thomas.

De León, A., & Del Castillo, R. (2012). *North to Aztlán: A history of Mexican Americans in the United States* (2nd ed.). Hoboken, NJ: Wiley-Blackwell.

Death Penalty Information Center. (2001). *Federal death row prisoners.* Available at: http://www.deathpenaltyinfo.org/federal-death-row-prisoners#list.

Death Penalty Information Center. (2011). *Foreign nationals and the death penalty in the United States–consular rights, foreign nationals and the death penalty.* Available at: http://www.deathpenaltyinfo.org/article.php?did=198&scid=31#background.

Decker, S. H., & Smith, R. L. (1980). Police minority recruitment: A note on its effectiveness in improving black evaluations of the police. *Journal of Criminal Justice, 8:* 387–393.

Decker, S., & Van Winkle, B. (1996). *Life in the gang: Family, friends, and violence.* New York: Cambridge University Press.

Del Castillo, R. (1985). Tejanos and California Chicanos: Regional variations in Mexican American history. *Mexican Studies/Estudios Mexicanos, 1:* 134–139.

Del Puerto, L. (2011). Constitutional obstacle course: The challenges facing bill backers. *The Arizona Capitol Times,* 13 February: 1.

Delahunty, R. J., & Yoo, J. C. (2013). Dream on: The Obama administration's non enforcement of immigration laws, the DREAM act, and the take care clause. *Texas Law Review,* 91: 781–857.

Delgado, D. J. (2014). 'And you need me to be the token Mexican?': Examining racial hierarchies and the complexities of racial identities for middle class Mexican Americans. *Critical Sociology,* 1–20.

Delgado, D. J. (2018). Five myths about immigration: Immigrant discourse, locating white supremacy, and the racialization of Latino immigrants in the United States. In S. E. Álvarez & M. G. Urbina (Eds.), *Immigration and the law: Race, citizenship, and social control.* Tucson, AZ: University of Arizona Press.

Delgado, R. (2007). *The law unbound!: A Richard Delgado reader.* Boulder, CO: Paradigm Publishers.

Delgado, R. (2009). The law of the noose: A history of Latino lynching. *Harvard Civil Rights-Civil Liberties Law Review,* 44: 297–311.

Delgado, R. (Ed). (1995). *Critical race theory.* Philadelphia: Temple University Press.

Dempsey, J., & Forst, L. (2011). *Introduction to policing* (6th ed.). Clifton, NY: Delmar Cengage Learning.

Demuth, S. (2002). The effect of citizenship status on sentencing outcomes in drug cases. *Federal Sentencing Reporter,* 14: 271–275.

Demuth, S. (2003). Racial and ethnic differences in pretrial release decisions and outcomes: A comparison of Hispanic, Black, and White felony arrestees. *Criminology,* 41: 873–908.

Demuth, S., & Steffensmeier, D. (2004). The impact of gender and race-ethnicity in the pretrial release process. *Social Problems,* 51: 222–242.

Denzin, N. (1998). Reading the cinema of racial violence. *Perspectives on Social Problems,* 10: 31–60.

Díaz, J. (2011). Immigration policy, criminalization and the growth of the immigration industrial complex: Restriction, expulsion, and eradication of the undocumented in the U.S. *Western Criminological Review,* 12: 35–54.

Díaz, T. (2009). *No boundaries: Transnational Latino gangs and American law enforcement.* Ann Arbor, MI: The University of Michigan Press.

Díaz-Cotto, J. (1996). *Gender, ethnicity and the state: Latina and Latino prison politics.* Albany, NY: SUNY Press.

Díaz-Cotto, J. (2000). The criminal justice system and its impact on Latinas(os) in the United States. *The Justice Professional,* 13: 49–67.

Díaz-Cotto, J. (2006). *Chicana lives and criminal justice: Voices from el barrio.* Austin: University of Texas Press.

Dickey, W. (1993). Sentencing, parole, and community supervision. In L. Ohlin & F. Remington (Eds.), *Discretion in criminal justice: The tension individualization and uniformity.* New York: State University New York Press.

Dillon, S. 2009. Study finds high rates of imprisonment among dropouts. *The New York Times.* Available at: http://www.nytimes.com/2009/10/09/education/09dropout.html?_r=0.

Ditton, P., & Wilson, D. (1999). *Truth in sentencing in state prisons.* Washington, DC: US Department of Justice.

Dohan, D. (2003). *The price of poverty: Money, work, and culture in the Mexican American barrio.* Berkeley, CA: University of California Press.

Donald, M. (2005). Stuck in habeas hell; Bush breathes new life into Texas death-row inmate's case. *Texas Lawyer,* 21: 1.

Dooley, B. D., Seals, A., & Skarbek, D. (2014). The effect of prison gang membership on recidivism. *Journal of Criminal Justice,* 42: 267–275.

Dorfman, L., & Schiraldi, V. (2001). *Off balance: Youth, race and crime in the news.* Washington, DC: Building Blocks for Youth.

Doty, R. (2009). *The law into their own hands: Immigration and the politics of exceptionalism.* Tucson: University of Arizona Press.

Dow, D. (2005). *Executed on a technicality: Lethal injustice on America's death row.* Boston: Beacon Press.

Dowling, J. A., & India, J. X. (Eds.). (2013). *Governing immigration through crime: A reader.* Stanford: Stanford University Press.

Downs, K. (2016). Why aren't more people talking about Latinos killed by police? Available at: http://www.pbs.org/newshour/rundown/black-men-werent-unarmed-people-killed-police-last-week/.

Dray, P. (2002). *At the hands of persons unknown: The lynching of black America.* New York: Modern Library.

Drury, A., & DeLisi, M. (2010). The past is prologue: Prior adjustment to prison and institutional misconduct. *The Prison Journal,* 90: 331–352.

Dunbar, T., & Kravitz, L. (1976). *Hard traveling.* Pensacola: Ballinger Publishers.

Dunham, R., & Alpert, G. (1988). Neighborhood differences in attitudes toward policing: Evidence for a mixed-strategy model of policing in a multi-ethnic setting. *Journal of Criminal Law and Criminology,* 79: 1–18.

Dunn, T. (1996). *The militarization of the U.S.-Mexico border 1978–1992: Low-intensity conflict doctrine comes home.* Austin, TX: University of Texas Press.

Dunn, T. J. (2009). *Blockading the border and human rights: The El Paso operation that remade immigration enforcement.* Austin, TX: University of Texas Press.

Durán, R. (2009a). Legitimated oppression: Inner-city Mexican American experiences with police gang enforcement. *Journal of Contemporary Ethnography,* 38: 143–168.

Durán, R. (2009b). Over-inclusive gang enforcement and urban resistance: A comparison between two cities. *Social Justice: A Journal of Crime, Conflict and World Order,* 36: 82–101.

Durán, R. (2009c). The core ideals of the Mexican American gang. *Aztlan: A Journal of Chicano Studies,* 34: 99–134.

Durán, R. (2010). Racism, resistance, and repression: The creation of Denver gangs, 1924–1950. In A. Aldama, R. Rabaka, D. Maeda, & E. Facio (Eds.), *Enduring legacies: Ethnic histories and cultures of Colorado.* Boulder, CO: University of Colorado Press.

Durán, R. (2013). *Gang life in two cities: An insider's journey.* New York: Columbia University Press.

Durán, R. (2015). Mexican American law enforcement officers: Comparing the creation of change versus the reinforcement of structural hierarchies. In M. G. Urbina & S. E. Álvarez (Eds.), *Latino police officers in the United States: An examination of emerging trends and issues.* Springfield, IL: Charles C Thomas.

Durán, R., & Posadas, C. (2009). Qualitative analysis of juvenile arrests in Doña Ana County. Disproportionate Minority Contact (DMC). Technical Assistance and Resource Center (TARC). State of New Mexico. Blue Ribbon Panel.

Durán, R., & Posadas, C. (2010). Disproportionate minority contact in the land of enchantment: Juvenile injustice in a majority minority state. Unpublished paper.

Durán, R., & Posadas, C. (2013). Disproportionate minority contact in the land of enchantment: Juvenile justice disparities as a reflection of white-over-color ascendancy. *Journal of Ethnicity in Criminal Justice,* 11: 93–111.

Durand, J., Massey, D., & Parrado, E. (1999). The new era of Mexican migration to the United States. *The Journal of American History,* 86: 518–536.

Eith, C., & Durose, M. (2011). Contacts between police and the public, 2008. Available at: https://www.bjs.gov/content/pub/pdf/cpp08.pdf.

Eitzen, D., & Johnston, J. (2007). *Inequality: Social class and its consequences.* Boulder, CO: Paradigm Publishers.

Elion, V., & Megargee, E. (1978). Racial identity, length of incarceration, and parole decision-making. *Journal of Research in Crime and Delinquency,* 16: 233–245.

Elliot, B., & Verdeyen, V. (2002). *Game over: Strategies for redirecting inmate deception.* Lanham, MD: American Correctional Association.

Elliott, A., & Weiser, B. (2004). When prosecutors err, others pay the price. NYTimes.com. Available at: http://www.nytimes.com/2004/03/21/nyregion/21prosecute.html.

Engel, R., & Johnson, R. (2006). Toward a better understanding of racial and ethnic disparities in search and seizure rates. *Journal of Criminal Justice,* 34: 605–617.

Engen, R., & Gainey, R. (2001). Modeling the effects of legally relevant and extralegal factors under sentencing guidelines: The rules have changed. *Criminology,* 38: 1207–1230.

Equal Justice Initiative. (2010). *Illegal racial discrimination in jury selection: A continuing legacy.* Available at: http://eji.org/eji/files/EJI%20Race%20and%20Jury%20Report.pdf.

Eschbach, K., Hagan, J., & Rodríguez, N. (2003). Deaths during undocumented migration: Trends and policy implications in the new era of homeland security. *Defense of the Alien,* 26: 37–52.

Escobar, E. (1999). *Race, police, and the making of a political identity: Mexican Americans and the Los Angeles Police Department, 1900–1945.* Los Angeles, CA: University of California Press.

Escobar, M. (2016). *Captivity beyond prisons: Criminalization of experiences of Latina (im)migrants.* Austin: University of Texas Press.

Espino, R., Leal, D., & Meier, K. (Eds). (2008). *Latino politics: Identity, mobilization, and representation.* Charlottesville, VA: University of Virginia Press.

Espy, M., & Smykla, J. (2004). *Executions in the United States, 1608–2002: The Espy File* [Computer file]. 4th ICPS ed. Ann Arbor, MI: Inter-University Consortium for Political and Social Research [producer and distributor].

Estrada, L., García, F., Macías, R., & Maldonado, L. (1981). Chicanos in the United States: A history of exploitation and resistance. *Daedalus,* 110: 103–131.

Falcón, A. (2013). Opinion: Really, Yale appoints first tenured Latina faculty member? Available at: http://nbclatino.com/2013/01/16/opinion-yale-appoints-first-tenured-latina-faculty-member-the-first-really/.

Feagin, J. (2000). *Racist America: Roots, current realities, and future aspirations.* New York: Rutledge.

Feagin, J. (2006). *Systemic racism: A theory of oppression.* New York: Rutledge.

Feagin, J. R. (2012). *White party, white government: Race, class, and U.S. politics.* New York: Routledge.

Feagin, J., & Feagin, C. (2011). *Racial and ethnic groups.* Upper Saddle River: Prentice Hall.

Federal Bureau of Investigation. (2010). *Hate crime statistics, 2009.* U.S. Department of Justice. Available at: http://www2.fbi.gov/ucr/hc2009/data/table_01.html.

Federal Bureau of Investigation. (2014). Crime in the United States, by volume and rate per 100,000 inhabitants, 1995–2014. Available at: https://www.fbi.gov/about-us/cjis/ucr/crime-in-the-u.s/2014/crime-in-the-u.s.-2014/tables/table-1.

Federal Bureau of Investigation. (2015). FBI releases 2014 crime statistics. Available at: https://www.fbi.gov/news/pressrel/press-releases/fbi-releases-2014-crime-statistics.

Federal Bureau of Prisons. (2017). Inmate ethnicity. Available at: https://www.bop .gov/about/statistics/statistics_inmate_ethnicity.jsp.

Feeley, M., & Simon, J. (1992). The new penology: Notes on the emerging strategy of corrections and its implications. *Criminology,* 30: 449–474.

Feltz, R. (2008). A new migration policy: Producing felons for profit. *NACLA report on the Americas.* November/December: 26–30.

Fine, M., Freudenberg, N., Payne, Y., Perkins, T., Smith, K., & Wanzer, K. (2003). Anything can happen with police around': Urban youth evaluate strategies of surveillance in public places. *Journal of Social Issues,* 59: 141–58.

Fins, D. (2011). *Death penalty U.S.A.* A quarterly report by the Criminal Justice Project of the NAACP Legal Defense and Educational Fund. Available at: http://naacpldf.org/files /publications/DRUSA_Winter_2011.pdf.

Fiscella, K., Beletsky, L., & Wakeman, S. E. (2017). The inmate exception and reform of correctional health care. *American Journal of Public Health,* 107: 384–385.

Fitzpatrick, P. (1992). *The mythology of modern law.* New York: Routledge.

Fitzpatrick, T. (2001). New agenda for social policy and criminology: Globalization, urbanization and the emerging post-social security state. *Social Policy and Administration,* 35: 212–229.

Fleishman, M. (2003). Reciprocity unmasked: The role of the Mexican government in defense of its foreign nationals in United States death penalty cases. *Arizona Journal of International and Comparative Law,* 20: 359–407.

Florida Office of Program Policy Analysis and Government Accountability. (2007). *Corrections rehabilitative programs effective, but serve only a portion of the eligible population.* Tallahassee, FL: The Florida Legislature.

Forde-Mazrui, K. (1999). Jural districting: Selecting impartial juries through community representation. *Vanderbilt Law Review,* 52: 353–404.

Foucault, M. (1995). *Discipline and punish: The birth of the prison.* New York: Vintage Books.

Fountain, A. (2016). Stop ignoring the police killings of Latinos. Available at: http://america .aljazeera.com/opinions/2016/2/stop-ignoring-the-police-killings-of-latinos.html.

Fox, G. (1997). *Hispanic nation: Culture, politics, and the constructing of identity.* Tucson, AZ: University of Arizona Press.

Fox, J., & Rivera-Salgado, G. (Eds). (2004). *Indigenous Mexican migrants in the United States.* Boulder, CO: Lynne Rienner Publishers.

Freire, P. (1997). *Pedagogy of the oppressed.* New York: Continuum.

Fremon, C. (2005). *G-dog and the homeboys: Father Greg Boyle and the gangs of East Los Angeles.* Albuquerque, NM: University of New Mexico.

Friedman, L. (1984). *American law: An introduction.* New York: Norton.

Friedman, L. (1993). *Crime and punishment in American history.* New York: Basic Books.

Friedman, L. (2005). *A history of American law.* New York: Simon & Schuster.

Friedman, S. H., Collier, S., & Hall, R. C. W. (2016). PTSD behind bars: Incarcerated women and PTSD. In C. R. Martin, V. R. Preedy, & V. B. Patel (Eds.), *Comprehensive guide to post-traumatic stress disorders.* New York: Springer International Publishing.

Fussell, E. (2011). The deportation threat dynamic and victimization of Latino migrants: Wage theft and robbery. *The Sociological Quarterly,* 52: 593–615.

Fyfe, J. (1981). Race and extreme police–citizen violence. In R. McNeely & C. Pope (Eds.), *Race, crime, and criminal justice.* Beverly Hills, CA: Sage.

Fyfe, J. (1996). Training to reduce police-civilian violence. In W. Geller & H. Toch (Eds.), *Police violence: Understanding and controlling police abuse of force.* New Haven, CT: Yale University Press.

Gaes, G., Wallace, S., Gilman, E., Klein-Saffran, J., & Suppa, S. (2002). The influence of prison gang affiliation on violence and other prison misconduct. *The Prison Journal, 82:* 359–385.

Galindo, R., & Vigil, J. (2006). Are anti-immigrant statements racist or nativist? What difference does it make? *Latino Studies, 4:* 419–447.

García, J. (1980). *Operation Wetback: The mass deportation of Mexican undocumented workers in 1954.* Westport: Greenwood Press.

García, J. (1996). *Mexicans in the Midwest, 1900–1932.* Tucson: University of Arizona Press.

García, J. (2006). *Criminalizing unlawful presence: Selected issues.* Washington, DC: U.S. Library of Congress, Congressional Research Service.

García, M. (1981). *Desert immigrants: The Mexicans of El Paso, 1880–1920.* New Haven, CT: Yale University Press.

García, V., & Cao, L. (2005). Race and satisfaction with the police in a small city. *Journal of Criminal Justice, 33:* 191–199.

Garland, D. (1990). *Punishment and modern society.* Chicago: University of Chicago Press.

Garland, D. (2005). Penal excess and surplus meaning: Public torture lynchings in twentieth-century America. *Law & Society Review, 39:* 793–833.

Gelman, A., Fagan, J., & Kiss, A. (2007). An analysis of the New York City Police Department's "stop-and-frisk" policy in the context of claims of racial bias. *Journal of the American Statistical Association, 102:* 813–823.

Getlin, J. (2001). Racial profiling persists in N.J. *L.A. Times,* May 24: A16.

Giallombardo, R. (1966). Social roles in a prison for women. *Social Problems, 13:* 268–288.

Giardini, G. I., & Farrow, R. G. (1952). The paroling of capital offenders. *The Annals of the American Academy of Political and Social Sciences, 284:* 85–94.

Gibson, A. (1980). *The American Indian: Prehistory to the present.* Lexington: Heath.

Gibson, C., & Jung, K. (2006). *Historical census statistics on the foreign-born population of the United States: 1850–2000.* U.S. Census Bureau, Working Paper Series No. 56. Available at: http://www.census.gov/population/www/documentation/twps0081/tables/tab04.xls.

Gibson, D. (2010). Chicago police department may drop entrance exam in name of diversity. Available at: http://www.examiner.com/article/chicago-police-department-may-drop-entrance-exam-name-of-diversity.

Gilbreath, W. (2002). *Death on the gallows: The story of legal hangings in New Mexico, 1847–1923.* Silver City: High Lonesome Books.

Gilroy, P. (1993). *The black Atlantic: Modernity and double consciousness.* Cambridge, MA: Harvard University Press.

Giroux, H. (2013). Punishing youth and saturated violence in the era of casino capitalism. *Association of Mexican-American Educators Journal, 7:* 10–16.

Glaze, L., & Bonczar, T. (2010). *Probation and parole in the United States, 2009.* Washington, DC: U.S. Department of Justice, Bureau of Justice Statistics.

Glaze, L., & Bonczar, T. (2011). *Probation and parole in the United States, 2010.* Washington, DC: U.S. Department of Justice.

Glaze, L., & Kaeble, D. (2014). Correctional populations in the United States, 2013. Bureau of Justice Statistics Special Report, NCJ 248479. Washington, DC: United States Department of Justice, Office of Justice Programs, Bureau of Justice Statistics.

Glaze, L., & Palla, S. (2005). *Probation and parole in the United States, 2004.* Washington, DC: Bureau of Justice Statistics.

Glover, S. (2007). Racial profiling. In G. Barak (Ed.), *Battleground criminal justice.* Westport, CT: Greenwood Publishing Group, Inc.

Goffman, A. (2015). How we're priming some kids for college–and others for prison. Available at: http://www.ted.com/talks/alice_goffman_college_or_prison_two_destinies _one_blatant_injustice.

Golash-Boza, T. M. (2012a). *Immigration nation: Raids, detentions, and deportations in post-9/11 America.* New York: Routledge.

Golash-Boza, T. M. (2012b). *Due process denied: Detentions and deportations in the United States.* New York: Routledge.

Golash-Boza, T. M. (2015). *Deported: Policing immigrants, disposable labor and global capitalism.* New York: New York University Press.

Goldsmith, P., & Romero, M. (2008). "Aliens," "illegals" and other types of "Mexicanness": Examination of racial profiling in border policing. In A. Hattery, D. Embrick, & E. Smith (Eds.), *Globalization and America: Race, human rights, and inequality.* Lanham, MD: Rowman & Littlefield Publishers.

Goldsmith, P., Romero, M., Rubio-Goldsmith, R., Escobedo, M., & Khoury, L. (2009). Ethno racial profiling and state violence in a Southwest barrio. *Aztlán: A Journal of Chicano Studies,* 34: 93–123.

Goldstein, H. (1977). *Policing a free society.* Cambridge, MA: Ballinger Publishing.

Golub, A., Johnson, B., & Dunlap, E. (2007). The race/ethnicity disparity in misdemeanor marijuana arrests in New York City. *Criminal Public Policy,* 6: 131–164.

Gomberg-Muñoz, R. (2011). *Labor and legality: An ethnography of a Mexican immigrant network.* New York: Oxford University Press.

Gomberg-Muñoz, R. (2015). The punishment/el castigo: Undocumented Latinos and U.S. immigration processing. *Journal of Ethnic and Migration Studies,* 41: 1–18.

Gómez-Quiñones, J. (1990). *Chicano politics: Reality and promise, 1940–1990.* Albuquerque, NM: University of New Mexico Press.

Gómez, L. (2000). Race, colonialism and the criminal law: Mexicans and the American criminal justice system in territorial New Mexico. *Law and Society Review,* 34: 1129–1202.

Gómez, L. (2007). *Manifest destinies: The making of the Mexican American race.* New York: New York University Press.

Gonzales, A. (2014). *Reform without justice: Latino migrant politics and the homeland security state.* New York: Oxford University Press.

Gonzáles, M. (2009). *Mexicanos: A history of Mexicans in the United States.* Bloomington: Indiana University Press.

Gonzáles-Day, K. (2006). *Lynching in the West, 1850–1935.* Durham: Duke University Press.

González, J. (2000). *Harvest of empire: A history of Latinos in America.* New York: Viking.

Goode, E., & Ben-Yehuda, N. (1994). *Moral panics: The social construction of deviance.* Cambridge, MA.: Blackwell.

Goodman, D. J. (2013). More diversity in New York City's police dept., but blacks lag. Available at: http://www.nytimes.com/2013/12/27/nyregion/more-diversity-in-new-york-citys-police-but-blacks-lag.html?pagewanted=all&_r=0.

Gordon, C. (1991). Governmental rationality: An introduction. In G. Burchell, C. Gordon, & P. Miller (Eds.), *The Foucault effect: Studies in governmentality.* Chicago, IL: University of Chicago Press.

Gottfredson, D., & Ballard, K. (1966). Differences in parole decisions associated with decision-makers. *Journal of Research in Crime and Delinquency,* 3: 112–119.

Gottfried, M., & Conchas, G. (2016). *When school policies backfire.* Cambridge, MA: Harvard University Press.

Gould, L., Pate, M., & Sarver, M. (2011). Risk and revocation in community corrections: The role of gender. *Probation Journal,* 58: 250–264.

Grado, G. (2010). Culture war brewing over ethnic studies in Tucson schools. *The Arizona Capitol Times,* November 15: 1A.

Gratton, B., & Gutmann, M. (2000). Hispanics in the United States, 1850–1990, estimates of population size and national origin. *Historical Methods, 33:* 137–153.

Gray, K. M., Fields, M., & Maxwell, S. R. (2001). Examining probation violations: Who, what, and when. *Crime and Delinquency, 4:* 537–557.

Griffin, M., & Hepburn, J. (2006). The effect of gang affiliation on violent misconduct among inmates during the early years of confinement. *Criminal Justice and Behavior, 33:* 419–466.

Grogger, J., & Trejo, S. (2002). Falling behind or moving up? The intergenerational progress of Mexican Americans. Available at: http://www.ppic.org/publications/PPIC160/ppic160 .abstract.html.

Gross, S., O'Brien, B., Hu, C., & Kennedy, E. (2014). Rate of false conviction of criminal defendants who are sentenced to death. *Proceedings of the National Academy of Sciences, 111:* 7230–7235.

Groves, C. (1991). Us and them: Reflections on the dialectics of moral hate. In B. MacLean & D. Milovanovic (Eds.), *New directions in critical criminology.* Vancouver: Collective Press.

Gryll, S. (2011). Immigration detention reform; no band-aid desired. *Emory Law Journal, 60:* 1211–1256.

Guerin-Gonzáles, C. (1994). *Mexican workers and American dreams: Immigration, repatriation, and California farm labor, 1900–1939.* New Brunswick, NJ: Rutgers University Press.

Guerino, P., Harrison, P., & Sabol, W. (2011). *Prisoners in 2010.* Washington, DC: U.S. Department of Justice.

Gunther, G., & Sullivan, K. (1997). *Constitutional law* (13th ed.). New York: The Foundation Press.

Gutiérrez, D. (Ed). (1997). *Between two worlds: Mexican immigrants in the United States.* Wilmington: Jaguar Books.

Gutiérrez, R. (2004). Internal colonialism: An American theory of race. *Du Bois Review, 1:* 281–295.

Haarr, R. N. (1997). Patterns of interaction in a police bureau: Race and gender barriers to integration. *Justice Quarterly, 14:* 15–85.

Hagan, J. (1994). *Deciding to be legal: A Maya community in Houston.* Philadelphia: Temple University Press.

Hagan, J., & Palloni, A. (1999). Sociological criminology and the mythology of Hispanic immigration and crime. *Social Problems, 46:* 617–632.

Hagan, J., Huxter, M., & Parker, P. (1988). Class structure and legal practice: Inequality and mobility among Toronto lawyers. *Law & Society Review, 22:* 9–55.

Hall, K., Wiecek, W., & Finkelman, P. (1996). *American legal history: Cases and materials* (2nd ed.). New York: Oxford University Press.

Hall, S. (1980). Introduction to media studies at the Centre. In S. Hall, D. Hobson, A. Lowe, & P. Willis (Eds.), *Culture, media, language: Working papers in cultural studies, 1972–1979.* London: Hutchison.

Hall, S. (1997). The work of representation. In S. Hall (Ed.), *Representation: Cultural representations and signifying practices.* London: Sage Publications.

Halperin, R. (1997). Death penalty news. Available at: http://venus.soci.niu.edu/~archives /ABOLISH/ sep97/0226.html.

Hammer, M., & Rogan, R. (2002). Latino and Indochinese interpretive frames in negotiating conflict with law enforcement: A focus group analysis. *International Journal of Intercultural Relations, 26:* 551–575.

Hammett, T., Roberts, C., & Kennedy, S. (2001). Health-related issues in prisoner reentry. *Crime & Delinquency,* 47: 390–409.

Hardy, L. J., Getrich, C. M., Quezada, J. C., Guay, A., Michalowski, R. J., & Henley, E. (2012). A call for further research on the impact of state-level immigration policies on public health. *American Journal of Public Health,* 102: 1250–1253.

Harris, C., & Sadler, L. (1978). The plan of San Diego and the Mexican-United States war crisis of 1916: A reexamination. *The Hispanic American Historical Review,* 58: 381–408.

Harris, C., & Sadler, L. (2007). *The Texas Rangers and the Mexican Revolution: The bloodiest decade, 1910–1920.* Albuquerque, NM: University of New Mexico Press.

Harris, D. (1999). The stories, the statistics, and the law: Why "driving while black" matters. *Minnesota Law Review,* 84: 265–326.

Harris, D. (2003). *Profiles in injustice: Why racial profiling cannot work.* New York: The New Press.

Harrison, P., & Beck, A. (2002). *Prisoners in 2001.* Bureau of Justice Statistics. Washington, DC: U.S. Department of Justice.

Harrison, P., & Beck, A. (2005). *Prisoners in 2004.* Washington, DC: U.S. Department of Justice.

Harrison, P., & Beck, A. (2006). *Prisoners in 2005.* Washington, DC: U.S. Department of Justice.

Hartry, A. S. (2012). Gendering crimmigration: The intersection of gender, immigration, and the criminal justice system. *Berkley Journal of Gender, Law & Justice,* 27: 1–27.

Hassell, K. D., & Brandl, S. G. (2009). An examination of the workplace experiences of patrol officers: The role of race, sex, and sexual orientation. *Police Quarterly,* 12: 408–430.

Hassine, V. (2009). *Life without parole: Living in prison today* (5th ed.). New York: Oxford University Press.

Hawkins, D. (1981). Causal attribution and punishment for crime. *Deviant Behavior,* 1: 207–230.

Hayden, T. (2005). *Street wars.* New York: The New Press.

Hayes, K. W. (1999a). Personal communication with author via e-mail. May 7, 1999.

Hayes, K. W. (1999b). Personal communication with author via e-mail. May 27, 1999.

Heffernan, W., & Koenig, J. (2000). Introduction. In W. Heffernan & J. Koenig (Eds.), *From social justice to criminal justice: Poverty and the administration of criminal law.* New York: Oxford University Press.

Heizer, R., & Almquest, A. (1971). *The other Californians: Prejudice and discrimination under Spain, Mexico, and the United States to 1920.* Berkeley: University of California Press.

Herbst, L., & Walker, S. (2001). Language barriers in the delivery of police services: A study of police and Hispanic interactions in a Midwestern city. *Journal of Criminal Justice,* 29: 329–340.

Herman, E., & Chomsky, N. (2002). *Manufacturing consent: The political economy of the mass media.* New York: Pantheon Books.

Hernández, C. C. G. (2015). *Crimmigration law.* Chicago, IL: ABA Publishing.

Hernández, C., Haug, M., & Wagner, N. (1976). *Chicanos: Social and psychological perspectives.* St. Louis: C.V. Mosby.

Hernández, D. (2008). Pursuant to deportation: Latinos and immigrant detention. *Latino Studies,* 6: 35–63.

Hernández, J. (2010). Contemporary deportation raids and historical memory: Mexican expulsions in the nineteenth century. *Aztlan: A Journal of Chicano Studies,* 35: 115–142.

Hernández, J. (2012). *Mexican Americans colonization during the nineteenth century.* New York: Cambridge University Press.

Hernández, K. (2010). *Migra! A history of the U.S. Border Patrol.* Berkeley: University of California Press.

Herrnstein, R., & Murray, C. (1994). *The bell curve: Intelligence and class structure in American life.* New York: Free Press.

Heyman, J. (2001). Class and classification of the U.S.-Mexico border. *Human Organization,* 60: 128–140.

Heyman, J. (2002). U.S. immigration officers of Mexican ancestry as Mexican Americans, citizens, and immigration police. *Current Anthropology,* 43: 479–507.

Higgins, G., Vito, G., & Walsh, W. (2008). An understudied area of racial profiling. *Journal of Ethnicity in Criminal Justice,* 6: 23–39.

Hill, C., & Sadler, L. (1990). *Border and revolution: Clandestine activities of the Mexican Revolution.* Silver City: High Lonesome Books.

Hill, S., & Beger, R. (2009). A paramilitary policing juggernaut. *Social Justice,* 36: 25–40.

Hills, A. (2001). The inherent limits of military forces in peacekeeping operations. *International Peacekeeping,* 8: 79–98.

Hing, B. (2009). Institutional racism, ICE raids and immigration reform. Volume 197. UC Davis Legal Studies Research Paper Series.

Hinojosa-Smith, R. (1986). River of blood. *Texas Monthly,* 196.

Hinton, E. (2016). *From the war on poverty to the war on crime: The making of mass incarceration in America.* Cambridge, MA: Harvard University Press.

Hlawati, I. (2001). United States v. Montero-Camargo elimination of the race factor develops piecemeal: The Ninth Circuit approach. *University of Hawaii Law Review,* 23: 703–730.

Hochstetler, A., Murphy, D., & Simmons, R. (2004). Damaged goods: Exploring predictors of stress in prison inmates. *Crime & Delinquency,* 50: 436–457.

Hockenberry, S., Wachter, A., & Sladky, A. (2016). *Juvenile residential facility census, 2014: Selected findings.* Washington, DC: Office of Juvenile Justice and Delinquency Prevention.

Hofer, P. (1999). The effect of the federal sentencing guidelines on inter-judge disparity. *Journal of Criminal Law and Criminology,* 90: 239–321.

Holmes, M. (1998). Perceptions of abusive police practices in a U.S.-Mexico border community. *The Social Science Journal,* 35: 107–118.

Holmes, M. (2000). Minority threat and police brutality: Determinants of civil rights criminal complaints in U.S. municipalities. *Criminology,* 38: 343–367.

Holmes, M., & Smith, B. (2008). *Race and police brutality: Roots of an urban dilemma.* Albany, NY: State University of New York.

Houston Chronicle. (1993a). I am innocent, innocent. May 12: A1.

Houston Chronicle. (1993b). Mexican national's execution draws angry remarks, protests. March 26: A34.

Howard, S. E. (2010). Zoot to boot: The zoot suit as both culture and symbol. *Studies in Latin American Popular Culture,* 28: 112–131.

Howe, N. (2015). What's behind the decline in crime? Forbes. Available at: http://www.forbes.com/sites/neilhowe/2015/05/28/whats-behind-the-decline-in-crime/print/.

Huebner, B. (2013). The Missouri model: A critical state of the knowledge. In R. J. Bonnie, R. L. Johnson, B. M. Chemers, & J. Schuck (Eds.), *Reforming juvenile justice: A developmental approach.* Washington, DC: National Academies Press.

Huebner, B., Varano, S., & Bynum, T. (2007). Gangs, guns, and drugs: Recidivism among serious, young offenders. *Criminology & Public Policy,* 6: 187–222.

Huggins, D., Capeheart, L., & Newman, E. (2006). Deviants or scapegoats: An examination of pseudofamily groups and dyads in two Texas prisons. *The Prison Journal,* 86: 114–139.

Hughes, T., & Wilson, D. (2002). *Reentry trends in the United States: Inmates returning to the community after serving time in prison.* Washington, DC: U.S. Department of Justice.

Hughes, T., Wilson, D., & Beck, A. (2001). *Trends in state parole: 1990–2000.* Washington, DC: US Department of Justice, Office of Justice Programs, Bureau of Justice Statistics.

Human Rights Watch. (1998). *Shielded from justice: Police brutality and accountability in the United States.* Available at: http://www.hrw.org/legacy/reports98/police/index.htm.

Human Rights Watch. (2007). *Forced apart: Families separated and immigrants harmed by United States deportation policy.* Volume 19, number 3(G). New York: Human Rights Watch.

Human Rights Watch. (2009). *Forced apart (by the numbers): Non-citizens deported mostly for non-violent offenses.* Available at: http://www.hrw.org/en/reports/2009/04/15/forced-apart-numbers-0.

Human Rights Watch. (2015). *A price too high: US families torn apart by deportations for drug offense.* New York: Human Rights Watch. Available at: https://www.hrw.org/report/2015/06/16/price-too-high/us-families-torn-apart-deportations-drug-offenses.

Humes, K., Jones, N., & Ramirez, R. (2011). *Overview of race and Hispanic origin: 2010.* Washington, DC: U.S. Department of Commerce.

Huntington, S. (2004). The Hispanic challenge. *Foreign Policy,* March/April: 30–45.

Huspek, M., Martínez, R., & Jiménez, L. (1998). Violations of human and civil rights on the U.S.-Mexico border, 1995 to 1997: A Report. *Social Justice,* 25: 110–130.

Hutchinson Daily News. (1897). Condemned murderer escapes. July 12: 2.

Iber, J. (2000). *Hispanics in the Mormon Zion: 1912–1999.* College Station, TX: Texas A&M University Press.

ICE. (2008). Delegation of Immigration Authority Section 287(g) Immigration and Nationality Act. Available at: http://www.ice.gov/partners/287g/Section287_g.htm.

ICE. (2009). ICE identification of previously un-tracked detainee deaths highlights importance of detention reform. Available at: http://www.ice.gov/pi/nr/0908/090817washington.htm.

International Law Update. (2005). In death penalty case, where petitioner is appealing denial of Habeas Corpus, Eleventh Circuit denies stay where petitioner claims Vienna Convention violations but failed to raise issue on direct appeal. December 1.

Irlbeck, D. (2008). Latino police officers: Patterns of ethnic self-identity and Latino community attachment. *Police Quarterly,* 11: 468–495.

Irwin, J., & Austin, J. (1997). *It's about time: America's imprisonment binge* (2nd ed.). Belmont, CA: Wadsworth Publishing Company.

Jacobs, D., & O'Brien, R. (1998). The determinants of deadly force: A structural analysis of police violence. *American Journal of Sociology,* 103: 837–862.

James, D. (2004). *Profile of jail inmates, 2002.* Washington, DC: Bureau of Justice Statistics.

James, D., & Glaze, L. (2006). *Mental health problems of prison and jail inmates.* Washington DC: U.S. Department of Justice.

James, J. (1998). *Objective jail classification systems: A guide for jail administrators.* Washington DC: Department of Justice National Institute of Corrections.

Jaspin, E. (2007). *Buried in the bitter waters: The hidden history of racial cleansing in America.* New York: Basic Books.

Jensen, A. (1998). *The G factor: The science of mental ability.* Westport: Praeger.

Jervis, R. (2011). Hispanics guide huge growth in Texas. *USA Today.* February 23.

Johnson, B. (2003). *Revolution in Texas: How a forgotten rebellion and its bloody suppression turned Mexicans into Americans.* New Haven: Yale University Press.

Johnson, K. (1997). Some thoughts on the future of Latino legal scholarship. *Harvard Latino Law Review,* 2: 101–144.

Johnson, K. (2000). The case against race profiling in immigration enforcement. *Washington University Law Quarterly,* 78: 675–736.

Johnson, K. (2005). The forgotten 'repatriation' of persons of Mexican ancestry and lesson on the 'war on terror.' *Pace Law Review,* 26: 1–27.

Johnson, K. (2013). The keys to the nation's education future: The Latina/o struggle for educational equity. *Denver University Law Review,* 90: 1231–1249.

Johnson, K., & Lichter, D. (2008). Natural increase: A new source of population growth in emerging Hispanic destinations in the United States. *Population and Development Review,* 34: 327–346.

Johnson, M. (2015). How do Latino police feel about community relations? Available at: http://latinousa.org/2015/01/30/police-brutality-latinos/.

Johnson, W. W., & Jones, M. (1998). Probation, race, and the war on drugs: An empirical analysis of drug and non-drug felony probation outcomes. *Journal of Drug Issues,* 28: 985–1003.

Jonas, S., & Tactaquin, C. (2004). Latino immigrant rights in the shadow of the national security state: Responses to domestic preemptive strikes. *Social Justice,* 31: 67–91.

Jones-Brown, D. D., & King-Toler, E. (2011). The significance of race in contemporary urban policing policy. In K. Ismaili (Ed.), *U.S. criminal justice policy: A contemporary reader.* Sudbury, MA: Jones & Bartlett Learning.

Kaeble, D., & Bonczar, T. (2016). *Probation and parole in the United States, 2015.* Washington, DC: U.S. Department of Justice, Bureau of Justice Statistics.

Kaeble, D., & Glaze, L. (2016). *Correctional populations in the United States, 2015.* Washington, DC: U.S. Department of Justice, Bureau of Justice Statistics.

Kaiser Family Foundation. (2011). Medicaid's role for Hispanic Americans. Available at: https://kaiserfamilyfoundation.files.wordpress.com/2013/01/8189.pdf.

Kaiser Family Foundation. (2013). Health coverage for the Hispanic population today and under the Affordable Care Act. Available at: https://kaiserfamilyfoundation.files.wordpress.com/2013/04/84321.pdf.

Kaiser Family Foundation. (2014). Health coverage and care for the adult criminal justice-involved population. Available at: http://kff.org/uninsured/issue-brief/health-coverage-and-care-for-the-adult-criminal-justice-involved-population/.

Kane, R. (2002). The social ecology of police misconduct. *Criminology,* 40: 867–896.

Kaplan, P. (2009a). Looking through the gaps: A critical approach to the LAPD's Rampart Scandal. *Social Justice,* 36: 61–81.

Kaplan, P. (2009b). Nihilism and mistaken identity: (Self) hate crime in The Believer. *Journal of Criminal Justice and Popular Culture,* 16: 63–80.

Kappeler, V., & Potter, G. (2004). *The mythology of crime and criminal justice* (4th ed.). Prospect Heights: Waveland Press.

Kappeler, V., Blumberg, M., & Potter, G. (2000). *The mythology of crime and criminal justice* (3rd ed.). Prospect Heights: Waveland Press.

Karnik, N., Soller, M., Redlich, A., Silverman, M., Kraemer, H., Haapanen, R., & Steiner, H. (2010). Prevalence differences of psychiatric disorders among youth after nine months or more of incarceration by race/ethnicity and age. *Journal of Health Care for the Poor and Underserved,* 21: 237–250.

Katz, C., & Spohn, C. (1995). The effect of race and gender on bail outcomes: Test of an interactive model. *American Journal of Criminal Justice,* 19: 161–184.

Kaye, R. (2006). Border city fears influx of guns, drugs. Available at: http://www.cnn.com/CNN/Programs/anderson.cooper.360/blog/2006/05/border-cityfears-influx-of-guns-drugs.html.

Kennedy, E. (1979). Toward a new system of criminal sentencing: Law with order. *American Criminal Law Review,* 16: 353–382.

Kerstetter, W. (1996). Toward justice for all: Procedural justice and the review of citizen complaints. In W. Geller & H. Toch (Eds.), *Police violence: Understanding and controlling police abuse of force.* New Haven, CT: Yale University Press.

Keyes, D., Edwards, W., & Perske, R. (1999). Defendants with mental retardation executed in the United States since the death penalty was reinstated in 1976. Available at: http://www.essential.org/dpic/dpicmr.html.

Kil, S. (2011). Immigration and operations: The militarization (and medicalization) of the USA-Mexico border. In R. Frenkel, P. R. Frassinelli, & D. Watson (Eds.), *Traversing transnationalism: The horizons of literary and cultural studies.* Netherlands: Rodopi Press.

Kil, S., & Menjívar, C. (2006). The war on the border: Criminalizing immigrants and the militarizing of the US-Mexico border. In R. Martinez & A. Valenzuela (Eds.), *Immigration and crime: Race, ethnicity and violence.* New York: New York University Press.

Kilty, K., & de Haymes, M. (2000). Racism, nativism, and exclusion: Public policy, immigration, and the Latino experience in the United States. *Journal of Poverty,* 4: 1–25.

Kim, K., Becker-Cohen, M., & Serakos, M. (2015). *The processing and treatment of mentally ill persons in the criminal justice system.* Washington, DC: Urban Institute.

Kinder, K. (1982). *Victim: The other side of murder.* New York: Delacorte Press.

King, N. (1993). Racial jurymandering: Cancer or cure? A contemporary review of affirmative action in jury selection. *New York University Law Review,* 68: 707–776.

King, R., Johnson, K., & McGeever, K. (2010). Demography of the legal profession and racial disparities in sentencing. *Law & Society Review,* 44: 1–32.

Kleck, G. (1981). Racial discrimination in criminal sentencing: A critical evaluation of the evidence with additional data on the death penalty. *American Sociological Review,* 46: 783–805.

Klinger, D. A. (1997). Negotiating order in patrol work: An ecological theory of police response to deviance. *Criminology,* 35: 277–306.

Kong, L. (2010). Immigration, racial profiling, and white privilege: Community-based challenges and practices for adult educators. *New Directions for Adult and Continuing Education,* 125: 65–77.

Koscheski, M., Hensley, C., Wright, J., & Tewksbury, R. (2002). Consensual sexual behavior. In C. Hensley (Ed.), *Prison sex: Practice and policy.* Boulder, CO: Lynne Rienner Publishers.

Kozol, J. (1992). *Savage inequalities: Children in America's schools.* Logan, IA: Perfection Learning.

Kozol, J. (2006). *The shame of the nation: The restoration of apartheid schooling in America.* New York: Three Rivers Press.

Kraska, P. B., & Kappeler, V. E. (1997). Militarizing American police: The rise and normalization of paramilitary units. *Social Problems,* 44: 1–18.

Kraska, P., & Cubellis, L. (2004). Militarizing Mayberry and beyond: Making sense of American paramilitary policing. In S. Brandl & D. Barlow (Eds.), *The police in America: Classic and contemporary readings.* Belmont, CA: Wadsworth/Thompson.

Kretsedemas, P. (2008). Immigration enforcement and the complication of national sovereignty: Understanding local enforcement as an exercise in neoliberal governance. *American Quarterly,* 60: 553–573.

Kruttschnitt, C., Gartner, R., & Miller, A. (2000). Doing her own time? Women's responses to prison in the context of the old and the new penology. *Criminology,* 38: 681–718.

Kubrin, C. E., Zatz, M. S., & Martínez, R. (2012). *Punishing immigrants: Policy, politics, and injustice.* New York: New York University Press.

Kuhn, T. (1996). *The structure of scientific revolutions* (3rd ed.). Chicago: University of Chicago Press.

Kurland, P., & Lerner, R. (Eds). (2000). *The founders' Constitution.* Chicago: University of Chicago Press.

Kyckelhahn, T. (2012). *State corrections expenditures, FY 1982–2010.* Bureau of Justice Statistics. Washington, DC: U.S. Department of Justice.

LaBrie, C. (1999). Lack of uniformity in the deportation of criminal aliens. *New York University Review of Law and Society Change,* 25: 357–382.

Lacey, M., & Jacobs, A. (2009). Even as fears of flu ebb, Mexicans feel stigma. *New York Times,* May 5: 1.

Lanagan, P., & Levin, D. (2005). *Recidivism of prisoners released in 1994.* Washington, DC: Bureau of Justice Statistics Bulletin.

Lange, J., Johnson, M., & Voas, R. (2005). Testing the racial profiling hypothesis for seemingly disparate traffic stops on the New Jersey turnpike. *Justice Quarterly,* 22: 193–223.

Lasley, J. R., Larson, J., Kelso, C., & Brown, G. C. (2011). Assessing the long-term effects of officer race on police attitudes toward the community: A case for representative bureaucracy theory. *Police Practice and Research: An International Journal,* 12: 474–491.

Lazos Vargas, S. (2002). 'Latina/o-ization' of the Midwest: Cambio de colores (change of colores as agromaquilas expand into the heartland. *Berkeley La Raza Law Journal,* 13: 343–368.

Lee, C. (2007). Hispanics and the death penalty: Discriminatory charging practices in San Joaquin County, California. *Journal of Criminal Justice,* 35: 17–27.

Lee, F. (1997). Young and in fear of the police; parents teach children how to deal with officers' bias. *New York Times,* October 23: B1, 10.

Lee, J., Guilamo-Ramos, V., Munoz-Laboy, M., Lotz, K., & Bornheimer, L. (2016). Mechanisms of familial influence on reentry among formerly incarcerated Latino men. *Social Work,* 61: 199–207.

Lee, M., Martínez, R., & Rosenfeld, R. (2001). Does immigration increase homicide? Negative evidence from three border cities. *Sociological Quarterly,* 42: 559–580.

Legal Action Center. (2004). *After prison: Roadblocks to reentry.* Available at: http://www.lac.org/roadblocks-to-reentry/upload/lacreport/LAC_PrintReport.pdf.

Legislative Analyst's Office. (2017a). California's annual cost to incarcerate an inmate in prison. Available at: http://www.lao.ca.gov/PolicyAreas/CJ/6_cj_inmatecost.

Legislative Analyst's Office. (2017b). *Overview of inmate mental health programs.* Available at: http://www.lao.ca.gov/handouts/crimjust/2017/Overview-Inmate-Mental-Health-Programs-031617.pdf.

Leiber, M. J., & Peck, J. H. (2013). Probation violations and juvenile justice decision making: Implications for Blacks and Hispanics. *Youth Violence and Juvenile Justice,* 11: 60–78.

Leinen, S. (1984). *Black police, white society.* New York: New York University Press.

Levin, B. (2002). From slavery to hate crime laws: The emergence of race and status-based protection in American criminal law. *Journal of Social Issues,* 58: 227–245.

Levin, J. (1999). *Seeing social structure and change in everyday life.* Thousand Oaks: Pine Forge Press.

Levin, M. (1997). *Why race matters: Race differences and what they mean.* Westport: Praeger.

Levine, J. (1992). *Juries and politics.* Pacific Grove, CA: Brooks/Cole Publishing Company.

Lewin, T. (2010). Citing individualism, Arizona tries to reign in ethnic studies in school. *New York Times,* May 14: 13.

Leyva, Y. (2000). Justice delayed: Mexican Americans win stolen oil rights. *Common Dreams.org.* Available at: http://www.commondreams.org/views/081200-104.htm.

Lindner, C. (2007). Thatcher, Augustus and Hill: The path to statutory probation in the United States and England. *Federal Probation,* 71: 36–41.

Listwan, S., Colvin, M., Hanley, D., & Flannery, D. (2010). Victimization, social support, and psychological well-being. *Criminal Justice and Behavior,* 37: 1140–1159.

Lochner, T. (2007). Testimonials illustrate ICE raids: ACLU files request for information on "Return to Sender" Operation. *Contra Costa Times,* March 9: F4.

Locke, H. (1996). The color of law and the issue of color: Race and the abuse of police power. In W. Geller & H. Toch (Eds.), *Police violence: Understanding and controlling police abuse of force.* New Haven, CT: Yale University Press.

London, J. (2010). Immigration policy from 2010 to 2020. *Aztlán: A Journal of Chicano Studies,* 35: 177–183.

Looney, W. (1971). *The Texas Rangers in a turbulent era.* Unpublished master's thesis in history, Texas Tech University.

López, I. F. H. (2003). *Racism on trial: The Chicano fight for justice.* Cambridge: Belknap Press of Harvard University Press.

López, I. F. H. (2006). *White by law: The legal construction of race.* New York: New York University Press.

López, I. F. H. (2014). *Dog whistle politics: How coded racial appeals have reinvented racism and wrecked the middle class.* New York: Oxford University Press.

López, M., & Livingston, G. (2009). Hispanics and the criminal justice system: Low confidence, high exposure. Available at: http://pewhispanic.org/reports/report.php?ReportID =106.

Los Angeles Times. (1994). Unexpected friend on death row. January 2: A1.

Lugo, A. (2008). *Fragmented lives, assembled parts: Culture, capitalism, and conquest at the U.S.-Mexico border.* Austin: University of Texas Press.

Lum, R. (2007). Churches aiding targeted families: Movement grows nationwide to help immigrants at risk of deportation. *Oakland Tribune,* June 25. Available at: http://www.inside bayarea.com/timesstar/ci_6223660.

Lynch, M. (2007). *Big prison, big dreams: Crime and the failure of America's penal system.* New Brunswick, NJ: Rutgers University Press.

Lynch, M., & Groves, B. (1989). *Primer in radical criminology.* Albany, NY: Harrow & Heston Publishers.

Lytle, K. (2003). *Constructing the criminal alien: A historical framework for analyzing border vigilantes at the turn of the 21st century (Working Paper 83).* San Diego: University of California-San Diego Center for Comparative Immigration Studies.

Maciag, M. (2015). Where police don't mirror communities and why it matters. Available at: http://www.governing.com/topics/public-justice-safety/gov-police-department-diversity .html.

Macina, A. (2003). Avena and other Mexican nationals: The litmus for Lagrand and the future of consular rights in the United States. *California Western International Law Journal,* 34: 115–142.

MacKenzie, D. L. (2001). Corrections and sentencing in the 21st century: Evidence-based corrections and sentencing. *The Prison Journal,* 81: 299–312.

Maeve, M. (1999). The social construction of love and sexuality in a women's prison. *Advances in Nursing Science,* 21: 46–65.

Magaña, L. (2003). *Straddling the border: Immigration policy and the INS.* Austin: University of Texas Press.

Malavet, P. (2004). *America's colony: The political and cultural conflict between the United States and Puerto Rico.* New York: New York University Press.

MALDEF. (2008). *State and local anti-immigrant ordinances backfire.* Available at: www.maldef .orghttp://www.maldef.org/truthinimmigration/state_and_local_antiimmigrant_ordinances _backfire05092008/.

Mann, C. (1994). *Unequal justice: A question of color.* Bloomington, IN: Indiana University Press.

Marable, M. (1999). The politics of race. In *Conference summary: and action plan: Money, education, and prisons: Standing at the crossroads.* Milwaukee, WI: The Benedict Center.

Marchese, J. (2009). Managing gangs in a correctional facility: What wardens and superintendents need to know. *Corrections Today,* 71: 44–47.

Marger, M. (2009). *Race and ethnic relations: American and global perspectives.* Belmont, CA: Wadsworth.

Marin, M. (2015). The unarmed Latinos killed by police in 2015. Available at: http://aldia news.com/articles/politics/security/unarmed-latinos-killed-police-2015/40126.

Markert, J. (2010). The changing face of racial discrimination: Hispanics as the dominant minority in the USA–a new application of power-threat theory. *Critical Sociology,* 36: 307–327.

Márquez, B. (2014). *Democratizing Texas politics: Race, identity, and Mexican American empowerment, 1945–2002.* Austin: University of Texas Press.

Martínez, M. (2007). Deportations strand young US citizens. *Chicago Tribune,* April 30: C24.

Martínez, O. (1975). On the size of the Chicano population: New estimates, 1850–1900. *Aztlán: A Journal of Chicano Studies,* 6: 43–67.

Martínez, O. (2001). *Mexican-origin people in the United States: A topical history.* Tucson: University of Arizona Press.

Martínez, R. (2000). Immigration and urban violence: The link between immigrant Latinos and types of homicide. *Social Science Quarterly,* 81: 363–374.

Martínez, R. (2002). *Latino homicide: Immigration, violence, and community.* New York: Routledge.

Martínez, R. (2007). Incorporating Latinos and immigrants into policing research. *Criminology and Public Policy,* 6: 57–64.

Martínez, R., & Valenzuela, A. (2006). *Immigration and crime: Race, ethnicity, and violence.* New York: New York University Press.

Martínez, T. (1973). Advertising and racism: The case of the Mexican American. In O. Romano-V (Ed.), *Voices: Readings from El Grito.* Berkeley, CA: A Quinto Sol Book.

Martinot, S. (2003). The militarisation of the police. *Social Identities,* 9: 205–224.

Martinson, R. (1974). What works? Questions and answers about prison reform. *Public Interest,* 35: 22–54.

Maruna, S. (2001). *Making good: How ex-convicts reform and rebuild their lives.* Washington, DC: American Psychological Association.

Maruschak, L. M. (2008). *Medical problems of prisoners.* Washington, DC: Bureau of Justice Statistics.

Maruschak, L. M., Berzofsky, M., & Unangst, J. (2015). *Medical problems of state and federal prisoners and jail inmates, 2011–12.* Washington, DC: Bureau of Justice Statistics.

Maruschak, L., & Parks, E. (2012). *Probation and parole in the United States, 2011.* Washington, DC: U.S. Department of Justice, Office of Justice Programs.

Marx, K. (1852). The eighteenth brumaire of Louis Bonaparte. Available at: http://www .marxists.org/archive/marx/works/1852/18th-brumaire/ch01.htm.

Mason, K., & Fearn, N. (2009). Violence: Prevention and causes. In R. Ruddell & M. Thomas (Eds.), *Juvenile corrections.* Richmond, KY: Newgate Press.

Massey, D. (Ed). (2008). *New faces in new places: The changing geography of American immigration.* New York: Russell Sage Foundation.

Massey, D., Durand, J., & Malone, N. (2003). *Beyond smoke and mirrors: Mexican immigration in an era of economic integration.* New York: Russell Sage Foundation Publications.

Mata, A. (1998). Stereotyping by politicians: Immigrants bashing and nativist political movements. In C. Mann & M. Zatz (Eds.), *Images of color, images of crime.* Los Angeles: Roxbury.

Mauer, M. (2006). *Race to incarcerate.* New York: The Free Press.

Mauer, M., & Chesney-Lind, M. (2003). *Invisible punishment: The collateral consequences of mass imprisonment.* New York: The New Press.

Mauer, M., & McCalmont, V. (2013). *A lifetime of punishment: The impact of the felony drug ban on welfare benefits.* Washington, DC: The Sentencing Project.

Mazón, M. (1984). *The zoot suit riots: The psychology of symbolic annihilation.* Austin: University of Texas Press.

McCarthy, K. (2013). U.S. prison population declined for third consecutive year during 2012. Bureau of Justice Statistics. Available at: http://www.bjs.gov/content/pub/press/p12acpr.cfm.

McCay, R. (2011). *Mexican Americans and repatriation.* Texas State Historical Association. Available at: http://www.tshaonline.org/handbook/online/articles/pqmyk.

McCluskey, J., Perez McCluskey, C., & Enriquez, R. (2008). A comparison of Latino and white citizen satisfaction with the police. *Journal of Criminal Justice, 36*: 471–477.

McCormick, J. (1998). The wrongly condemned. *Newsweek, 132.*

McCrary, J., & Sangra, S. (2012). General equilibrium effects of prison on crime: Evidence from international comparisons. *Cato Papers on Public Policy, 2*: 165–193.

McKanna, C. (2007). *Race and homicide in nineteenth-century California.* Reno: University of Nevada Press.

McLemore, D. (2004). The forgotten carnage 89 years ago, Rangers singled out Hispanics, and thousands died. *Dallas Morning News,* November 28.

McMillen, N. (1989). *Black journey: Black Mississippians in the age of Jim Crow.* Urbana: University of Illinois Press.

MCSO. (2007). *Illegal aliens now banned from visiting sheriff's jails.* Maricopa County Sheriff's Office Media Office.

McWilliams, C. (1990). *North from Mexico: The Spanish-speaking people of the United States* (2nd ed.). New York: Praeger.

Mead, G. H. (1934). *Mind, self, and society.* Chicago: University of Chicago Press.

Meares, T. L., & Kahan, D. M. (1999). *Urgent times: Policing and rights in inner-city communities.* Boston: Beacon Press.

Meeks, E. (2007). *Border citizens: The making of Indians, Mexicans, and Anglos in Arizona.* Austin: University of Texas Press.

Meier, M., & Ribera, F. (1993). *Mexican Americans/American Mexicans: From conquistadors to Chicanos.* New York: Hill and Wang.

Menjívar, C., & Bejarano, C. (2004). Latino immigrants' perceptions of crime and police authorities in the United States: A case study from the Phoenix metropolitan area. *Ethnic and Racial Studies, 27*: 120–148.

Messier, F. (1999). Alien defendants in criminal proceedings: Justice shrugs. *American Criminal Law Review, 36*: 1395–1419.

Messinger, S., Berecochea, J., Rauma, D., & Berk, R. (1985). The foundations of parole in California. *Law and Society Review, 19*: 69–106.

Meyer, M. (1980). Police shootings at minorities: The case of Los Angeles. *Annals of the American Academy of Political and Social Science, 452*: 98–110.

Michalowski, R. (1985). *Order, law and crime.* New York: Random House.

Michalowski, R. (2007). Border militarization and migrant suffering: A case of transnational inquiry. *Social Justice,* 34: 60–72.

Miller, J. (2009). *21st century criminology: A reference handbook.* Thousand Oaks, CA: Sage.

Miller, T. (2005). Burring the boundaries between immigration and crime control after September 11th. *Boston Third World Law Journal,* 25: 81–123.

Miller, T., & Schivone, G. (2015). Gaza in Arizona: The secret militarization of the U.S.-Mexico border. Available at: http://www.salon.com/2015/02/01/gaza_in_arizona_the _secret_militarization_of_the_u_s_mexico_border_partner/.

Milovanovic, D., & Russell, K. (2001). *Petit apartheid in the U.S. criminal justice system: The dark figure of racism.* Durham, NC: Carolina Academic Press.

Minton, T. & Zeng, Z. (2016). *Jail inmates in 2015.* Washington, DC: Bureau of Justice Statistics.

Mirandé, A. (1978). Chicano sociology: A new paradigm for the social sciences. *Pacific Sociological Review,* 21: 293–312.

Mirandé, A. (1980). Fear of crime and fear of the police in a Chicano community. *Sociology and Social Research,* 64: 528–541.

Mirandé, A. (1985). *The Chicano experience: An alternative perspective.* Notre Dame, IN: University of Notre Dame Press.

Mirandé, A. (1987). *Gringo Justice.* Notre Dame, IN: University of Notre Dame.

Mirandé, A. (1989). *The Chicano experience: An alternative perspective.* Notre Dame, IN: University of Notre Dame Press.

Mirandé, A. (2005). *The Stanford law chronicles: Doin' time on the farm.* Notre Dame, IN: University of Notre Dame Press.

Mitchell, J. (1991). Note: The selective application of the Fourth Amendment: United States v. Verdugo-Urquidez. *Catholic University Law Review,* 41: 289.

Mitchell, O., & MacKenzie, D. L. (2004). *The relationship between race, ethnicity, and sentencing outcomes: A meta-analysis of sentencing research: Final report.* Submitted to the National Institute of Justice.

Mocho, J. (1997). *Murder and justice in frontier New Mexico, 1821–1846.* Albuquerque: University of New Mexico Press.

Mohl, R. (2003). Globalization, Latinization, and the nuevo new south. *Journal of American Ethnic History,* 22: 31–66.

Molina, N. (2010). Constructing Mexicans as deportable immigrants: Race, disease, and the meaning of "public charge." *Identities,* 17: 641–666.

Molina, N. (2014). *How race is made in America: Immigration citizenship and the historical power of racial scripts.* Berkeley: University of California Press.

Molvig, D. (2001). Overcoming the language barrier in court. *Wisconsin Layer,* 74, February.

Monge, J. (1997). *Puerto Rico: The trials of the oldest colony in the world.* New Haven, CT: Yale University Press.

Montgomery, C. (2002). *The Spanish redemption: Heritage, power, and loss of New Mexico's upper Rio Grande.* Los Angeles, CA: University of California.

Moore, C. (2009). The Immigration Oversight and Fairness Act: Ending the violation and abuse of migrant health. *Journal of Contemporary Law and Policy,* 26: 148–184.

Moore, J. (1970a). *Mexican Americans.* Englewood Cliffs, NJ: Prentice-Hall.

Moore, J. (1970b). Colonialism: The case of the Mexican Americans. *Social Problems,* 17: 463–472.

Moore, J. (1978). *Homeboys: Gangs, drugs, and prison in the barrios of Los Angeles.* Philadelphia, PA: Temple University Press.

Moore, W. L. (2007). *Reproducing racism: White space, elite law schools, and racial inequality.* Lanham, MD: Rowman & Littlefield Publishers.

Morales, A. (1972). *Ando sangrando: A study of Mexican American-police conflict.* La Puente, CA: Perspectiva Publications.

Morash, M., & Harr, R. N. (1995). Gender, workplace problems and stress in policing. *Justice Quarterly,* 12: 113–140.

Morgan, K. (1995). Factors influencing probation outcome. *Journal of Criminal Justice,* 22: 341–354.

Morgan, K. (2013). Issues in female inmate health: Results from a southeastern state. *Women & Criminal Justice,* 23: 121–142.

Morgan, K. (2016). *Probation, parole, and community corrections in theory and practice.* Durham, NC: Carolina Academic Press.

Morgan, K., & Smith, B. (2005). Victims, punishment, and parole: The effects of victim participation on parole hearings. *Criminology and Public Policy,* 4: 901–929.

Morín, J. (2009). *Latino/a rights and justice in the United States: Perspectives and approaches* (2nd ed.). Durham, NC: Carolina Academic Press.

Morín, J., & Del Valle, M. (1990). Racially motivated violence: International remedies for human rights violations in the United States. *International Review of Contemporary Law,* 1: 61–68.

Morris, A. (1996). Gender and ethnic differences in social constraints among a sample of New York City police officers. *Journal of Occupational Health Psychology,* 1: 224–235.

Motel, S. (2012). *Statistical portrait of Hispanics in the United States, 2010.* Washington, DC: Pew Research Center.

Motomura, H. (2010). The rights of others: Legal claims and immigration outside the law. *Duke Law Journal,* 59: 1723–1786.

MSNBC. (2011). New milestone: 1 in 6 US residents is Hispanic. March 24. Available at: http://www.msnbc.com.

Mucchetti, A. (2005). Driving while brown: A proposal for ending racial profiling in emerging Latino communities. *Harvard Latino Law Review,* 1: 1–32.

Mumola, C. J., & Beck, A. J. (1997). *Prisoners in 1996.* Washington, DC: U.S. Department of Justice, Bureau of Justice Statistics.

Muñoz, C. (1989). *Youth, identity, power: The Chicano movement.* New York: Verso.

Murdock, S., White, S., Hoque, M., Pecotte, B., You, X., & Balkan, J. (2003). *The new Texas challenge: Population change and the future of Texas.* College Station: Texas A&M University Press.

Murray, C., & Cox, L. (1979). *Beyond probation.* Beverly Hills, CA: Sage Publishing.

Musto, D. (1973). *The American disease: Origins of narcotics control.* London: Yale University Press.

Muzzatti, S. (2005). The police, the public, and the post-liberal politics of fear: Paramilitary policing post-9/11. In J. Hodgson & C. Orban (Eds.), *Public policing in the 21st Century: Issues and dilemmas in the U.S. and Canada.* New York: Criminal Justice Press.

Nadeau, J., & Barlow, J. (2012). Hispanic heritage runs deep in the USA. *USA Today,* October 11. Available at: http://www.usatoday.com/story/opinion/2012/10/11/hispanic-heritage-immigration-america/1627823/.

Naser, R., & La Vigne, N. (2006). Family support in the prisoner reentry process. *Journal of Offender Rehabilitation,* 43: 93–106.

Nasser, H. (2015). Police killings of Latinos spark less outrage than when victims are black. Available at: http://america.aljazeera.com/multimedia/2015/8/police-killings-of-latinos-spark-less-outrage.html.

National Center for Education Statistics. (2016). *Highlights from the U.S. PIAAC survey of incarcerated adults: Their skills, work experience, education, and training.* Available at: https://nces.ed.gov/pubs2016/2016040.pdf.

National Council of La Raza and The Urban Institute. (2007). *Paying the price: The impact of immigration raids on America's children.* Washington, DC: National Council of La Raza.

National Law Journal. (1998). Are 65 illegally on death row in U.S.? April 27: A16.

Nebraska Department of Corrections. (2016). *Culture survey.* Available at: http://www.corrections.nebraska.gov/pdf/NDCS%20Culture%20Study%20-%20Part%201.pdf.

NELP. (2006). *More harm than good: Responding to states' misguided efforts to regulate Immigration.* Available at: http://www.immigrantsolidarity.org/Documents/stateantiimmigrationlegislationguide.pdf.

NeMoyer, A., Goldstein, N. E. S., McKitten, R. L., Prelic, A., Ebbeck, J., Foster, E., & Burkard, C. (2014). Predictors of juvenile's noncompliance with probation requirements. *Law and Human Behavior,* 38: 580–591.

Neubauer, D. (2005). *America's courts and the criminal justice system* (8th ed.). Belmont, CA: Wadsworth.

Nevins, J. (2010). *Operation gatekeeper and beyond: The war on "illegals" and the remaking of the U.S.-Mexico boundary.* New York: Routledge.

New York Times. (1910). Why Rodriguez was burned. November 11: 1.

New York Times. (1985). Killer put to death in Texas. July 10: A11.

New York Times. (1993). Mexico fights to stop U.S. execution. January 26: A19.

New York Times. (1995). Ghoulish murderer is executed in Texas. December 12: A24.

New York Times. (2009). Traumatizing children to deep us 'safe.' Available at: http://theboard.blogs.nytimes.com/2009/01/14/traumatizing-children-to-keep-ussafe/?scp=1&sq=arpaio%20children%20mother&st=cse.

Newman, B. J., Johnston, C. D., Strickland, A. A., & Citrin, J. (2012). Immigration crackdown in the American workplace: Explaining variation in E-Verify policy adoption across the U.S. states. *State Politics & Policy Quarterly,* 12: 160–182.

Ngai, M. (2003). The strange career of the illegal alien: Immigration restriction and deportation policy in the United States, 1921–1965. *Law and History Review,* 21: 69–107.

Nieling, S., & Urbina, M. (2008). *Epilogue: Thoughts for the future. In M. Urbina, A comprehensive study of female offenders: Life before, during, and after incarceration.* Springfield, IL: Charles C Thomas.

Nieto-Phillips, J. (2004). *Language of blood: The making of Spanish-American identity in New Mexico, 1880s–1930s.* Albuquerque, NM: University of New Mexico.

Noboa, J. (2005). *Leaving Latinos out of history: Teaching U.S. history in Texas.* New York: Routledge.

Noonan, M. E. (2016a). *Mortality in state prisons, 2001–2014–statistical tables.* Washington, DC: Bureau of Justice Statistics.

Noonan, M. E. (2016b). *Mortality in local jails, 2000–2014–statistical tables.* Washington, DC: Bureau of Justice Statistics.

Norton, M., & Ariely, D. (2011). Building a better America–One wealth quintile at a time. *Perspectives on Psychological Science,* 6: 9–12.

Norton, M., & Sommers, S. (2011). Whites see racism as a zero-sum game that they are now losing. *Perspectives on Psychological Science,* 6: 215–218.

Nostrand, R. (1975). Mexican Americans circa 1850. *Annals of the Association of American Geographers,* 65: 378–390.

Nunnally, D. (2004). Hmong immigrants navigate perplexing legal system. *Milwaukee Journal Sentinel,* May 2: B1.

Oakland Tribune. (1921a). Mexico tries to save Ruiz boy. January 15: 3.

Oakland Tribune. (1921b). Third reprieve given to condemned youth. March 2: 1.

Oakland Tribune. (1921c). Ruiz, boy murderer, saved from gallows. July 5: 1.

Oboler, S. (Ed). (2006). *Latinos and citizenship: The dilemma of belonging.* New York: Palgrave Macmillan.

Oboler, S. (Ed). (2009). *Behind bars: Latino/as and prison in the United States.* New York: Palgrave Macmillan.

Office of Immigration Statistics. (2010). *Annual Report.* Available at: http://www.dhs.gov/xlibrary/assets/statistics/publications/enforcement_ar_2009.pdf.

Olguin, B. (2008). Toward a pinta/o human rights? New/old strategies for Chicana/o prisoner research and activism. *Latino Studies,* 6: 160–180.

Olivas, M. (2000). The chronicles, my grandfather's stories, and immigration law: The slave traders chronicle as racial history. In R. Delgado & J. Stephanic (Eds.), *Critical race theory: The cutting edge.* New Haven: Yale University Press.

Olivas, M. (2012). Obama's new immigration policy: Disappointment is in the details. *Chronicle of Higher Education.* Available at: http://www.chronicle.com/article/Obamas-New-immigration/132377.

Oliver, W., & Hilgenberg, J. (2006). *A history of crime and criminal justice in America.* Boston: Pearson.

Olson, D. E., & Lurigio, A. J. (2000). Predicting probation outcomes: Factors associated with probation rearrest, revocations, and technical violations during supervision. *Justice Research and Policy,* 1: 73–86.

Omi, M., & Winant, H. (1994). *Racial formation in the United States: From the 1960s to the 1990s* (2nd ed.). New York: Routledge.

Omi, M., & Winant, H. (2014). *Racial formation in the United States* (3rd ed.). Routledge.

Ortego, F. (2007). On war and remembrance: Hispanics and World War II. *La Prensa de San Antonio,* October 7.

Owen, B. (1998). *In the mix: Struggle and survival in a women's prison.* New York: State University of New York Press.

Padilla, F. (1987). *Puerto Rican Chicago.* Notre Dame, IN: University of Notre Dame Press.

Padilla, F. (1996). *The gang as an American enterprise.* New Brunswick, NJ: Rutgers University Press.

Pagán, E. (2003). *Murder at the sleepy lagoon: Zoot suits, race and riot in wartime L.A.* Chapel Hill, NC: University of North Carolina.

Parascandola, R., Fermino, J., & Gregorian, D. (2013). NYPD's stop and frisk blasted by judge, mayor Blumberg fights back. Available at: http://www.nydailynews.com/new-york /stop-frisk-violated-rights-judge-article-1.1424287.

Paredes, A. (1990). *George Washington Gomez: A mexicotexan novel.* Houston: Arte Publico Press.

Parenti, C. (2008). *Lockdown America: Police and prisons in the age of crises.* Brooklyn: Verso.

Parrish, M. (1993). The 'plain feel' exception–A Fourth Amendment rendition of the princess and the pea. *University of Cincinnati Law Review,* 62: 321.

Parvini, S. (2016). Family of teen fatally shot by undercover CHP officers files legal claim, saying he was unarmed. Available at: http://www.latimes.com/local/lanow/la-me-ln-chp-shooting-street-racing-20160719-snap-story.html.

Passel, J., Cohn, D., & López, M. (2011). *Hispanics account for more than half of nation's growth in past decade.* Washington, DC: Pew Research Center. Available at: www.pewhispanic.org.

Patt, Y. F., Hope, T. L., López, L. C., Zamora, H., & Salas, C. M. (2017). Hispanic exconvicts' perceptions of challenges and reintegration. *Journal of Offender Rehabilitation,* 56: 87–109.

PBS Perspective. (2016). Keeping kids safe: What youths, staff and family reported. Available at: http://pbstandards.org/cjcaresources/158/PbSPerspectiveJuly2016.pdf.

Perea, J. F. (1997). *Immigrants out! The new nativism and the anti-immigrant impulse in the United States.* New York: New York University Press.

Pérez McCluskey, C., & McCluskey, J. D. (2004). Diversity in policing: Latino representation in law enforcement. *Journal of Ethnicity in Criminal Justice,* 2: 67–81.

Pérez, A. (2006). Texas Rangers resurrected: Immigration proposals after September 11th. *The Scholar: St. Mary's Law Review on Minority Issues,* 8: 277–306.

Pérez, D., Hosch, H., Ponder, B., & Trejo, G. (1993). Ethnicity of defendants and jurors as influences on jury decisions. *Journal of Applied Social Psychology,* 23: 1249–1262.

Pérez, G. (2001). An upbeat west side story: Puerto Ricans and postwar racial politics in Chicago. *Centro Journal,* 13: 47–71.

Petersilia, J. (1985). Racial disparities in the criminal justice system: A summary. *Crime and Delinquency,* 31: 15–34.

Petersilia, J. (2004). What happens in prisoner reentry: Reviewing and questioning the evidence. *Federal Probation,* 68: 4–8.

Petersilia, J. (2010). A retrospective view of corrections reform in the Schwarzenegger administration. *Federal Sentencing Reporter,* 22: 148–153.

Petersilia, J. (2011). Beyond the prison bubble. Available at: http://www.uscourts.gov/viewer.aspx?doc=/uscourts/FederalCourts/PPS/Fedprob/2011-06/index.html.

Pew Center on the States. (2009). *One in 31: The long reach of American corrections.* Washington, DC: The Pew Charitable Trusts.

Pew Hispanic Center. (2009). *Hispanics and the criminal justice system: Low confidence, high exposure.* Available at: http://pewresearch.org/pubs/1182/hispanic-confidence-in-criminal-justice-system-low.

Pew Research Center. (2017). How Hispanic police officers view their jobs. Available at: http://www.pewresearch.org/fact-tank/2017/02/15/how-hispanic-police-officers-view-their-jobs/.

Pfaelzer, J. (2007). *Driven out: The forgotten war against Chinese Americans.* New York: Random House.

Phillips, A. (1917). A study of the after-career of 408 delinquent boys who were committed from the King County (Washington) juvenile court to the boys' parental school and the state training school during the five-year period 1911–1915. *Journal of the American Institute of Criminal Law and Criminology,* 8: 270–272.

Phillips, S. (2008). Racial disparities in the capital of capital punishment. *Houston Law Review,* 45: 807–840.

Phillips, S. (2009a). Legal disparities in the capital of capital punishment. *The Journal of Criminal Law & Criminology,* 99: 717–755.

Phillips, S. (2009b). Status disparities in the capital of capital punishment. *Law & Society Review,* 43: 807–837.

Phillips, S., Hagan, J., & Rodríguez, N. (2006). Brutal borders? Examining the treatment of deportees during arrest and detention. *Social Forces,* 85: 93–109.

Phillips, S., Rodríguez, N., & Hagan, J. (2002). Brutality at the border? Use of force in the arrest of immigrants in the United States. *International Journal of the Sociology of Law,* 30: 285–306.

Piquero, A., Jennings, W., & Farrington, D. (2013). The monetary costs of crime to middle adulthood: Findings from the Cambridge study in delinquent development. *Journal of Research in Crime and Delinquency,* 50: 53–74.

Piquero, N. L. (2003). A recidivism analysis of Maryland's community probation program. *Journal of Criminal Justice,* 31: 295–307.

Pittman, C. (1998). Interest points to death row's lack of equality. *St. Petersburg Times,* January 18: 1A.

Pizarro, M. (2005). *Chicanas and Chicanos in school: Racial profiling, identity battles, and empowerment.* Austin: University of Texas Press.

Platt, T., Frappier, J., Ray, G., Schauffler, R., Trujillo, L., & Cooper, L. (1982). *The iron fist and the velvet glove: An analysis of the U.S. police* (3rd ed.). San Francisco, CA: Synthex Press.

Podgers, J. (1994). Chasing the ideal: As more Americans find themselves priced out of the system, the struggle goes on to fulfill the promise of equal justice for all. *ABA Journal,* August: 56–61.

Pole, N., Best, S., Metzler, T., & Marmar, C. (2005). Why are Hispanics at greater risk of PTSD. *Cultural Diversity and Ethnic Minority Psychology,* 11: 144–161.

Pole, N., Best, S., Weiss, D., Metzler, T., Liberman, A., Fagan, J., & Marmar, C. (2001). Effects of gender and ethnicity on duty-related posttraumatic stress symptoms among urban police officers. *Journal of Nervous & Mental Disease,* 189: 442–448.

Pollock, J. (2010). *Ethical dilemmas and decisions in criminal justice* (6th ed.). Belmont, CA: Wadsworth.

Portes, A., & Rumbaut, R. (1990). *Immigrant America: A portrait.* Berkeley: University of California Press.

Portillos, E. (1998). Latinos, gangs, and drugs. In C. Mann & M. Zatz (Eds.), *Images of color, images of crime.* Los Angeles: Roxbury.

Posadas, C. (2007). Mexican immigrant women and their social networks in Phoenix metro, Arizona. Ph.D. dissertation, Arizona State University.

Potoc, M. (2011). Anti-Latino hate crimes spike in California in possible trend. *Southern Poverty Law Center,* August 12.

Press, E. (2006). Do immigrants make us safer? *The New York Times,* December 3.

Quinney, R. (1970). *The social reality of crime.* Boston: Little Brown & Company.

Quinney, R. (1974). *Critique of legal order; crime control in capitalist society.* Boston: Little Brown.

Quinney, R. (1977). *Class, state, and crime: On the theory and practice of criminal justice.* New York: Longman.

Radelet, M. (2010). Some examples of post-Furman botched executions. Death Penalty Information Center. Available at: http://www.deathpenaltyinfo.org/some-examples-post-furman-botched-executions#_ednref43.

Rah, J. (2001). Removal of aliens who drink and drive: Felony DWI as a crime of violence under 18 U.S.C. 16(b). *Fordham Law Review,* 70: 2109–2148.

Rakesh, K., Suro, R., & Tafoya, S. (2005). *Center the new Latino South: The context and consequences of rapid population growth.* Available at: http://pewhispanic.org/files/reports/50.pdf.

Ramírez, D., Hoopes, J., & Quinlan, T. (2003). Defining racial profiling in a post-September 11 world. *American Criminology Law Review,* 40: 1195–1233.

Ramírez, M. (2010). Revisiting the role of Latinos and immigrants in police research. In S. Rice & M. White (Eds.), *Race, ethnicity, and policing: New and essential readings.* New York: New York University Press.

Rantala, R. R., & Beck, A. J. (2016). *Survey of sexual violence in juvenile correctional facilities, 2007–12–Statistical tables.* Washington, DC: Bureau of Justice Systems.

Rantala, R. R., Rexroat, J., & Beck, A. J. (2014). *Survey of sexual violence in adult correctional facilities, 2009–2011. Statistical tables.* Washington, DC: Bureau of Justice Systems.

Rapaport, E. (2001). The Georgia immigration pardons: A case study in mass clemency. *Federal Sentencing Reporter,* 13: 184–187.

Reaves, B. (2015). *Local police departments, 2013: Personnel, policies, and practices.* Washington, DC: U.S. Department of Justice, Bureau of Justice Statistics.

Reclamation Project. (2014). *How white folks got so rich: The untold story of American white supremacy.* Unknown: RP Publishers.

Reid, D. (1973). *Eyewitness: I saw 189 men die in the electric chair.* Houston: Cordovan Press.

Reidy, T. J., & Sorensen, J. R. (2017). Prison homicides: A multidimensional comparison of perpetrators and victims. *Journal of Forensic Psychology Research and Practice,* 17: 99–116.

Reiman, J., & Leighton, P. (2017). *The rich get richer and the poor get prison* (11th ed.). New York: Routledge.

Reinarman, C. (2002). The social construction of drug scares. In P. Adler & P. Adler (Eds.), *Constructions of deviance: Social power, context, and interaction.* Belmont, CA: Wadsworth.

Reinventing Probation Council. (2000). *Transforming probation through leadership: The broken windows model.* New York: The Manhattan Institute.

Reisig, M. (1998). Rediscovering rehabilitation: Drug courts, community corrections and restorative justice. *Michigan Bar Journal,* 172: 172–176.

Reisler, M. (1997). Always the laborer, never the citizen: Anglo perceptions of the Mexican immigrant during the 1920s. In G. Gutierrez (Ed.), *Between two worlds: Mexican immigrants in the United States.* Wilmington, Delaware: Jaguar Books.

Reitzel, J., Rice, S., & Piquero, A. (2004). Lines and shadows: Perceptions of racial profiling and the Hispanic experience. *Journal of Criminal Justice,* 32: 607–616.

Rennison, C. (2002). *Hispanic victims of violent crime, 1993–2000.* U.S. Department of Justice. Available at: http://bjs.ojp.usdoj.gov/content/pub/pdf/hvvc00.pdf</URL>.

Reuters. (2010). Mexico says US border patrol officer killed teenager. Available at: http://www.reuters.com/article/idUSTRE65760020100608.

Rhodes, S. D., Mann, L., Simán, F. M., Song, E., Alonzo, J., Downs, M., Lawlor, E., Martinez, O., Sun, C. J., O'Brien, M. C., Reboussin, B. A., & Hall, M. A. (2015). The impact of local immigration enforcement on the health of immigrant Hispanics/Latinos in the United States. *American Journal of Public Health,* 105: 329–337.

Riccardi, N., & Gorman, A. (2010). Judge blocks key parts of Arizona immigration law. *Los Angeles Times,* July 29: A1.

Ríos, V. (2006). Racializing justice, disenfranchising lives: The hyper-criminalization of black and Latino male youth in the era of mass incarceration. *Souls,* 8: 40–54.

Ríos, V. (2011). *Punished: Policing the lives of black and Latino boys.* New York: New York University Press.

Robelo, D. (2014). The drug war = mass deportation: 250,000 deported for drug offenses in last 6 years. Available at: http://www.drugpolicy.org/blog/drug-war-mass-deportation-250000-deported-drug-offenses-last-6-years.

Roberts, D. (2001). Foreword: Race, vagueness, and the social meaning of order maintenance. *Journal of Criminology and Criminal Law,* 89: 775–836.

Robertson, C. (2011). Alabama wins in ruling on its immigration law. Available at: http://www.nytimes.com/2011/09/29/us/alabama-immigration-law-upheld.html?ref=opinion.

Robinson, M. (2002). *Justice blind? Ideals and realities of American criminal justice.* Upper Saddle River, NJ: Prentice-Hall.

Rodríguez, G. (2010). Fervor fueled by hate. *Los Angeles Times,* July 26: A15.

Rodríguez, L. (1993). *Always running: La vida loca: Gang days in L.A.* New York: Simon & Schuster.

Rodríguez, N., & Hagan, J. (2004). Fractured families and communities: Effects of immigration reform in Texas, Mexico, and El Salvador. *Latino Studies,* 2: 328–351.

Rodríguez, R. (1997). *Justice: A question of race.* Tempe, AZ: Bilingual Press.

Rojas, M. (2007). Remembering Josefa: Reading the Mexican female body in California Gold Rush chronicles. *Women's Studies Quarterly,* 35: 126–148.

Román, E. (2013). *Those damned immigrants: America's hysteria over undocumented immigration.* New York: New York University Press.

Romero, M. (2001). State violence, and the social and legal construction of Latino criminality: From el bandido to gang member. *Denver University Law Review,* 78: 1089–1127.

Romero, M. (2006). Racial profiling and immigration law enforcement: Rounding up of usual suspects in the Latino community. *Critical Sociology,* 32: 449–475.

Romero, M. (2008a). The inclusion of citizenship status in intersectionality: What immigration raids tell us about mixed-status families, the state and assimilation. *International Journal of Sociology of the Family,* 34: 131–152.

Romero, M. (2008b). Crossing the immigration and race border: A critical race theory approach to immigration studies. *Contemporary Justice Review,* 11: 23–37.

Romero, M., & Serag, M. (2005). Violation of Latino civil rights resulting from INS and local police's use of race, culture and class profiling: The case of the Chandler roundup in Arizona. *Cleveland Law Review,* 52: 75–96.

Romo, D. (2005). *Ringside seat to a revolution: An underground cultural history of El Paso and Juárez: 1893 to 1923.* El Paso, TX: Cinco Puntos Press.

Romo, R. (1983). *East Los Angeles: History of a barrio.* Austin, TX: University of Texas Press.

Romo, R. (1996). Mexican-American: Their civic and political incorporation. In S. Pedraza & R. Rumbaut (Eds.), *Origins and destinations: Immigration, race, and ethnicity in America.* Belmont, CA: Wadsworth Publishing Company.

Rosales, F. A. (1999). *Pobre raza!: Violence, justice, and mobilization among México lindo immigrants, 1900–1936.* Austin: University of Texas Press.

Rosas, G. (2010). Cholos, chuntaros, and the criminal abandonment of the new frontier. *Identities,* 17: 695–713.

Rosen, J. (2000). The lost promise of school integration. *New York Times,* April 2: A1, 5.

Rosenbaum, D. P. (2006). The limits of hot spots policing. In D. Weisburd & A. A. Braga (Eds.), *Police innovation: Contrasting perspectives.* New York: Cambridge University Press.

Rosenbaum, R. (1990). *Mexicano resistance in the Southwest: "The sacred right of self-preservation."* Austin: University of Texas Press.

Rosenbaum, R. (1998). *Mexicano resistance in the Southwest.* Dallas, TX: Southern Methodist University.

Rosenbaum, S. (1994). Keeping an eye on the INS: A case for civilian review of uncivil conduct. *La Raza Law Journal,* 7: 1–49.

Ross, J., & Richards, S. (2002). *Behind bars: Surviving prison.* Indianapolis, IN: Alpha books.

Roth, M. (2011). *Crime and punishment: A history of the criminal justice system.* Belmont, CA: Wadsworth.

Roy, B. (2009). *41 shots . . . and counting: What Amadou Diallo's story teaches us about policing, race, and justice?* Syracuse, NY: Syracuse University Press.

Ruddell, R. (2004). *America behind bars: Trends in imprisonment, 1950 to 2000.* New York: LFB Scholarly Publishing.

Ruddell, R., & Gottschall, S. (2011). Are all gangs equal security risks? An investigation of gang types and prison misconduct. *American Journal of Criminal Justice.* Available at: http://www.springerlink.com/content/78494m5037735052/.

Ruddell, R., & Urbina, M. G. (2004). Minority threat and punishment: A cross-national analysis. *Justice Quarterly,* 21: 903–931.

Ruddell, R., & Urbina, M. G. (2007). Weak nations, political repression, and punishment. *International Criminal Justice Review,* 17: 84–107.

Rudovsky, D. (2002). Breaking the pattern of racial profiling. *Trial,* 38: 29–36.

Ruiz, M., & Boucher, G. (1997). *Two badges: The lives of Mona Ruiz.* Houston, TX: Arte Público Press.

Ruiz, V. (1987). *Cannery women, cannery lives: Mexican women, unionization, and the California food processing industry, 1930–1950.* Albuquerque: University of New Mexico Press.

Ruiz, V. (1999). *From out of the shadows: Mexican women in twentieth-century America.* New York: Oxford University Press.

Rumbaut, R. (2008). The coming of the second generation: Immigration and ethnic mobility in southern California. *Annals of the American Academy of Political and Social Science,* 196: 196–236.

Rumbaut, R., Gonzales, R., Komaie, G., Morgan C., & Tafoya-Estrada, R. (2006). Immigration and incarceration: Patterns and predictors of imprisonment among first- and second generation young adults. In R. Martinez & A. Valenzuela (Eds.), *Immigration and crime: Race, ethnicity, and violence.* New York: New York University Press.

Rushton, J. (1999). *Race, evolution and behavior.* New Brunswick: Transaction Publishers.

Russell, K. (2001). Racial profiling: A status report of the legal, legislative, and empirical literature. *Rutgers Race & The Law Review,* 3: 61–81.

Sadowski-Smith, C. (2008). Unskilled labor migration and the illegality spiral: Chinese, European, and Mexican indocumentados in the United States, 1882–2007. *American Quarterly,* 60: 779–804.

Salinas, L. S. (2004). Deportations, removals and the 1996 Immigration Acts: A modern look at the ex post facto clause. *Boston University International Law Journal,* 22: 245–307.

Salinas, L. S. (2015). *U.S. Latinos and criminal injustice.* East Lansing, MI: Michigan State University Press.

Salinas, L. S. (2018). Always running: La Migra, detentions, deportations, and human rights. In S. E. Álvarez & M. G. Urbina (Eds.), *Immigration and the law: Race, citizenship, and social control.* Tucson, AZ: University of Arizona Press.

Salinas, M. (2002). Will all Hispanic men be suspect? *Seattle Post-Intelligencer,* July 30: B5.

Saltzburg, S., & Capra, D. (2010). *American criminal procedure: Cases and commentary* (9th ed.). Eagan, MN: West Publishing.

Samora, J., Bernal, J., & Peña, A. (1979). *Gunpowder justice: A reassessment of the Texas Rangers.* Notre Dame, IN: University of Notre Dame Press.

Sampson, R., & Lauritsen, J. (1997). Racial and ethnic disparities in crime and criminal justice in the United States. In M. Tonry (Ed.), *Ethnicity, crime, and immigration: Comparative and cross-national perspectives.* Chicago: University of Chicago Press.

San Antonio Express News. (1999). Death row: Death row history. Available at: http://express-news.com/news/deathrow/history.shtml.

San Diego Union-Tribune. (1985). Texas man put to death for slaying. July 9: A4, 8.

San Francisco Chronicle. (1993a). Mexico to fight California executions. August 5: A15.

San Francisco Chronicle. (1993b). Mexican officials visit San Quentin death row. August 7: B4.

Sanchez, J. O. (2016). *Religion and the Ku Klux Klan: Biblical appropriation in their literature and songs.* Jefferson, NC: McFarland.

Sánchez, L. (2007). The carceral contract: From domestic to global governance. In M. Bosworth & J. Flavin (Eds.), *Race, gender, and punishment: From colonialism to the war on terror.* Piscataway, NJ: Rutgers University Press.

Sandos, J. (1992). *Rebellion in the borderlands: Anarchism and the plan of San Diego, 1904–1923.* Norman: University of Oklahoma Press.

Santayana, G. (1905). *The life of reason.* London: Constable.

Santos, M. (2004). *About prison.* Belmont, CA: Thomson Wadsworth.

Saunders, M. (1995). California legal history: A review of Spanish and Mexican legal institutions. *Law Library Journal*, 87: 487–514.

Schiffman, H. (2000). Breard and beyond: The status of consular notification and access under the Vienna Convention. *Cardozo Journal of International and Comparative Law*, 8: 27–60.

Schlanger, M. (2003). Inmate litigation. *Harvard Law Review*, 116: 1557–1704.

Schmall, L. (2009). ICE effects: Federal worksite non-enforcement of U.S. immigration laws, 2007–2008. *University of San Francisco Law Review*, 44: 373–392.

Schmallenger, F., & Smykla, J. (2011). *Corrections in the 21st century*. New York, NY: McGraw-Hill Companies.

Schneider, J., & Schneider, P. (2008). The anthropology of crime and criminalization. *Annual Review of Anthropology*, 37: 351–373.

Schriro, D. (2009). *Immigration detention overview and recommendations*. Available at: http://www.ice.gov/doclib/about/offices/odpp/pdf/ice-detention-rpt.pdf.

Schuck, A., Lersch, K., & Verrill, S. (2004). The 'invisible' Hispanic?: The representation of Hispanics in criminal justice research. *Journal of Ethnicity in Criminal Justice*, 2: 5–22.

Schumacher-Matos, E. (2009). Demonization, Mexicans, and hate crimes. *SFGate.com*. Available at: http://articles.sfgate.com/2009-05-11/opinion/17199765_1_anti-immigrant-illegal immigrants-swine-flu.

Scott, D. W. (2014). Attitude is everything: Youth attitudes, gang involvement, and length of institutional gang membership. *Group Processes & Intergroup Relations*, 17: 780–798.

Scott, D. W., & Maxon, C. (2016). Gang organization and violence in youth correctional Facilities. *Journal of Criminological Research, Policy and Practice*, 2: 81–94.

Scott, J. (1974). The use of discretion in determining the severity of punishment for incarcerated offenders. *Journal of Criminal Law and Criminology*, 65: 214–224.

Scott-Hayward, C. (2011). *The fiscal crisis in corrections: Rethinking policies and practices*. New York: Vera Institute of Justice.

Sedlak, A., & McPherson, K. (2010a). *Conditions of confinement*. Washington, DC: Office of Juvenile Justice and Delinquency Prevention.

Sedlak, A., & McPherson, K. (2010b). *Youth's characteristics and backgrounds: Findings from the survey of youth in residential placement*. Washington, DC: Office of Juvenile Justice and Delinquency Prevention.

Sentencing Project. (2003). *Hispanic prisoners in the United States*. Washington, DC: Sentencing Project.

Sentencing Project. (2016). *Criminal justice facts: Trends in U.S. corrections*. Washington, DC: The Sentencing Institute.

Serpa, F. (2000). *The Personal Responsibility and Work Opportunity Reconciliation Act of 1996: An examination of its impact on legal immigrants and refugees in Rhode Island*. Rhode Island Advisory Committee to the U.S. Commission on Civil Rights Eastern Regional Office. Available at: http://www.eric.ed.gov/PDFS/ED448255.pdf.

Shahani, A., & Greene, J. (2009). Local democracy on ICE: Why state and local governments have no business in federal immigration law enforcement. A justice strategies report. Available at: http://www.justicestrategies.org/2009/localdemocracyicewhystateandlocal-governentshavenobusinessfederalimmigrationlawen.

Shammas, V. L. (2017). *Pains of imprisonment. In K. Kerley (Ed.), The encyclopedia of corrections*. New York: Wiley.

Sheridan, C. (2002). Contested citizenship: National identity and the Mexican immigration debates of the 1920s. *Journal of American Ethnic History*, 21: 3–35.

Sheridan, C. (2003). Another white race: Mexican Americans and the paradox of whiteness in jury selection. *Law and History Review*, 21: 109–144.

Shorris, E. (1992). *Latinos: A biography of the people.* New York: W.W. Norton & Company.

Shorris, E. (2001). *Latinos: A biography of the people* (revised ed.). New York: W.W. Norton & Company.

Simon, J. (1993). *Poor discipline parole and the social control of the underclass, 1980–1990.* Chicago, IL: University of Chicago Press.

Simon, J. (1997). Governing through crime. In L. Friedman & G. Fisher (Eds.), *The crime conundrum.* Oxford: Oxford University Press.

Simon, J. (2007). *Governing through crime: How the war on crime transformed American democracy and created a culture of fear.* New York: Oxford University Press.

Simon, J. (2014). *Mass incarceration on trial: A remarkable court decision and the future of prisons in America.* New York: The New Press.

Sims, B., & Jones, M. (1997). Predicting success or failure on probation: Factors associated with felony probation outcome. *Crime and Delinquency, 43:* 314–327.

Skolnick, J. (1975). *Justice without trial: Law enforcement in democratic society.* New York: Wiley & Sons.

Skolnick, J. (2011). *Justice without trial: Law enforcement in democratic society.* New Orleans, LA: Quid Pro Books.

Skolnick, J., & Caplovitz, A. (2001). Guns, drugs, and profiling: Ways to target guns and minimize racial profiling. *Arizona Law Review, 43:* 413–437.

Skolnick, J., & Fyfe, J. (1993). *Above the law: Police and the excessive use of force.* New York: Free Press.

Slater, E. (1995). Pizza thief gets 25 to life. *Los Angeles Times,* March 3.

Sloane, R. (2004). Measures necessary to ensure: The ICJ's provisional measures order in Avena and other Mexican nationals. *Leiden Journal of International Law, 17:* 673.

Slobogin, C. (2003). The poverty exception to the Fourth Amendment. *Florida Law Review, 55:* 391.

Smith, B. (1998). Children in custody: 20-year trends in juvenile detention, correctional, and shelter facilities. *Crime & Delinquency, 44:* 526–543.

Smith, B. (2003). The impact of police officer diversity on police-caused homicides. *Police Studies Journal, 31:* 147–162.

Smith, B., & Holmes, M. (2003). Community accountability, minority threat, and police brutality: An examination of civil rights criminal complaints. *Criminology, 41:* 1035–1064.

Snell, T. (2010). *Capital punishment, 2009–statistical tables.* Available at: http://bjs.ojp.usdoj.gov/index.cfm?ty=pbdetail&iid=2215.

Solis, C., Portillos, E. L., & Brunson, R. K. (2009). Latino youths' experiences with and perceptions of involuntary police encounters. *The Annals of the American Academy of Political and Social Science, 623:* 39–51.

Solomon, A., Kachnowski, V., & Bhati, A. (2005). *Does parole work? Analyzing the impact of post-prison supervision on rearrest outcomes.* Washington, DC: Urban Institute.

Sommers, S. (2007). Race and the decision making of juries. *Legal and Criminological Psychology, 12:* 171–187.

Soo-Jin Lee, S. (2005). Racializing drug design: Implications of pharmacogenomics for health disparities. *American Journal of Public Health, 95:* 2133–2138.

Sotomayor, E. (1982). Police abuse: The most volatile issue. *Perspectives: The Civil Rights Quarterly, 13:* 28–35.

Spickard, P. (2007). *Almost all aliens.* New York: Routledge.

Spohn, C. (2000). Thirty years of sentencing reform: The quest for a racially neutral sentencing process. *Criminal Justice, 3:* 427–501.

Spohn, C., & Holleran, D. (2000). The imprisonment penalty paid by young, unemployed black and Hispanic male offenders. *Criminology,* 38: 281–306.

Stannard, D. (1992). *American Holocaust: The conquest of the new world.* New York: Oxford University Press.

Stanton, S., & Brown, M. (2002). Massive hunt for girl's killer; authorities question several people in the case as tips pour in. *Sacramento Bee,* July 19: A1.

Staples, R. (1975). White racism, black crime and American justice: An application of the colonial model to explain crime and race. *Phylon,* 36: 14–22.

Starr, A., & Fernández, L. (2009). Legal control and resistance post-Seattle. *Social Justice,* 36: 41–60.

Starr, K. (2002). *California in war and peace.* Oxford: Oxford University Press.

Stavans, I. (1996). *Oscar "Zeta" Acosta: The uncollected works.* Houston: Arte Publico Press.

Steffensmeier, D., & Demuth, S. (2000). Ethnicity and sentencing outcomes in U.S. federal courts: Who is punished more harshly? *American Sociological Review,* 65: 705–729.

Steffensmeier, D., & Demuth, S. (2001). Ethnicity and judges' sentencing decisions: Hispanic-black-white comparisons. *Criminology,* 39: 145–178.

Steffensmeier, D., Ulmer, J., & Kramer, J. (1998). The interaction of race, gender, and age in criminal sentencing: The punishment cost of being young, black, and male. *Criminology,* 36: 763–797.

Stein, N. (1995). Questions and answers about affirmative action. *Social Justice: A Journal of Crime, Conflict, and World Order,* 22: 45–52.

Steiner, B., & Wooldredge, J. (2016). Examining the sources of correctional officer legitimacy. *Journal of Criminal Law and Criminology,* 105: 679–703.

Steiner, S. (1970). *La Raza: The Mexican Americans.* New York, NY: Harper and Row.

Steinmark, M. (2004). The case concerning Avena and other Mexican nationals (Mexico v. United States): A Mexican perspective on the fight for consular rights. *Law and Business Review of the Americas,* 10: 317.

Steinmetz, K. F., & Anderson, J. O. (2015). A probation profanation: Race, ethnicity, and probation in a midwestern state. *Race and Justice,* 6: 1–25.

Steinmetz, K. F., & Henderson, H. (2016a). Inequality on probation: An examination of differential probation outcomes. *Journal of Ethnicity in Criminal Justice,* 14: 1–20.

Steinmetz, K. F., & Henderson, H. (2016b). On the precipice of intersectionality: The influence of race, gender, and offense severity interactions on probation outcomes. *Criminal Justice Review,* 40: 361–377.

Stephan, J. (2004). *State prison expenditures, 2001.* Bureau of Justice Statistics. Washington, DC: U.S. Department of Justice.

Stephan, J., & Walsh, G. (2011). *Census of jail facilities, 2006.* Washington, DC: Bureau of Justice Statistics.

Stolzenberg, L., D'Alessio, S. J., & Eitle, D. (2013). Race and cumulative discrimination in the prosecution of criminal defendants. *Race and Justice,* 3: 275–299.

Stout, D. (2003). Legal immigrants can be held without bail, Court says. *New York Times,* April, 29.

Strachan, M. (2013). These 2 charts prove we're nowhere near a 'post-racial society.' Available at: http://www.huffingtonpost.com/2013/11/05/post-racial-society_n_4220366 .html.

Strauss, D. (1995). Affirmative action and the public interest. *The Supreme Court Review,* 1995: 1–43.

Stritikus, T. (2002). *Immigrant children and the politics of English-only.* New York: LFB Scholarly Publishing.

Strosnider, K. (2002). Anti-gang ordinances after City of Chicago v. Morales: The intersection of race, vagueness doctrine, and equal protection in the criminal law. *American Criminal Justice Review,* 39: 101–146.

Stumpf, J. P. (2006). The crimmigration crisis: Immigrants, crime, and sovereign power. *American University Law Review,* 56: 367–419.

Stumpf, J. P. (2013). The crimmigration crisis: Immigrants, crime, and sovereign power. In J. Dowling & J. X. Inda (Eds.), *Governing immigration through crime: A reader.* Stanford, CA: Stanford Social Sciences Press.

Stuntz, W., & Kahan, D. (2002). *Search and seizure. In J. Dressler (Ed.), Encyclopedia of crime and justice.* New York: Macmillan Reference.

Suárez-Orozco, M. (Ed.) (2007). *Learning in the global era: International perspectives on globalization and education.* Berkeley: University of California Press.

Suárez-Orozco, M., & Qin-Hilliard, D. (Eds). (2004). *Globalization: Culture and education in the new millennium.* Berkeley: University of California Press.

Substance Abuse and Mental Health Services Administration. (2011). *The TEDS report: Characteristics of probation and parole admissions aged 18 or older.* Rockville, MD: Substance Abuse and Mental Health Services Administration, Center for Behavioral Health Statistics and Quality.

Sufrin, C., Clarke, J., & Mullersman, K. (2016). *Pregnancy in prison statistics (PIPS): A multi-sector research collaboration.* Presentation at Johns Hopkins Health System, Baltimore, MD.

Sullivan, A. (2008). On thin ICE: Cracking down on the racial profiling of immigrants and implementing a compassionate enforcement policy. *Hastings Race and Poverty Law Journal,* 6: 101–144.

Sulzberger, A. G. (2010). Immigration law moves to center stage. Available at: http://www.nytimes.com/2010/10/03/us/politics/03nebgov.html?pagewanted=all&_r=0.

Swarns, R. (2003). Illegal aliens can be held indefinitely, Ashcroft says. *New York Times,* April 26.

Swavola, E., Riley, K., & Subramanian, R. (2016). *Overlooked: Women and jails in an era of Reform.* New York: Vera Institute of Justice.

Sykes, G. (1958). *Society of captives: A study of a maximum security prison.* Princeton, NJ: Princeton University Press.

Takaki, R. (1993). *A different mirror: A history of multicultural America.* Boston: Little Brown & Company.

Tapia, M. (2017). *The barrio gangs of San Antonio, 1915–2015.* Fort Worth, TX: Texas Christian University Press.

Taylor, P. (1931). Crime and the foreign born: The problem of the Mexican. In *Report on crime and the foreign born.* National Commission on Law Observance and Enforcement. Washington, DC: U.S. Government Printing Office.

Taylor, P. (2011). *The Mexican-American boom: Births overtake immigration.* Washington, DC: Pew Research Center. Available at: www.pewhispanic.org.

Teplin, L., Abram, K., McClelland, G., Mericle, A., Dulcan, M., & Washburn, J. (2006). *Psychiatric disorders of youth in detention.* Washington, DC: Office of Juvenile Justice and Delinquency Prevention.

Terman, L. (1906). Genius and stupidity: A study of some of the intellectual process of seven "bright" and seven "stupid" boys. *Pedagogical Seminary,* 13: 307–373.

Texas State Journal of Medicine. (1915–1916). Austin, TX: Texas Medical Association.

The Commonwealth Fund. (2015). Latinos have made coverage gains but millions are still uninsured. Available at: http://www.commonwealthfund.org/publications/blog/2015/apr/latinos-have-made-coverage-gains.

The Guardian. (2017). The counted: People killed by police in the U.S. Available at: https://www.theguardian.com/us-news/ng-interactive/2015/jun/01/the-counted-police-killings-us-database#.

The Upper Des Moines. (1868). Killing a Desperado. November 18: 1.

Theodore, N. (2013). Insecure communities: Latino perceptions of police involvement in immigration enforcement. Chicago, IL: Department of Urban Planning and Policy, University of Illinois at Chicago.

Thornton, R. (2005). *Guns, safety and proactive supervision.* Washington, DC: American Probation and Parole Association.

Tichenor, D. (2002). *Dividing lines: The politics of immigration control in America.* Princeton, NJ: Princeton University Press.

Time. (2006). Who we are. October 30: 44–45.

Tirman, J. (2015). *Dream chasers: Immigration and the American backlash.* Cambridge, MA: MIT Press.

Tolnay, S., & Beck, E. (1995). *A festival of violence: An analysis of southern lynchings, 1882–1930.* Urbana: University of Illinois Press.

Tonry, M. (1995). *Malign neglect: Race, crime, and punishment in America.* New York: Oxford University Press.

Tonry, M. (Ed). (2006). *The future of imprisonment.* New York: Oxford University Press.

Torréz, R. (1996). New Mexico and the Mexican American War. New Mexico Office of the State Historian. Available at: http://www.newmexicohistoryorg/filedetails.php?fileID=21394.

Tórrez, R. (2008). *Myth of the hanging tree: Stories of crime and punishment in territorial New Mexico.* Albuquerque: University of New Mexico Press.

Tovares, R. (2002). *Manufacturing the gang: Mexican American youth gangs on local television news.* Westport, CT: Greenwood.

Travis, J. (2005). *Prisoner reentry: The iron law of imprisonment. In R. Muraskin (Ed.), Key correctional issues.* Upper Saddle River, NJ: Pearson.

Trulson, C., & Marquart, J. (2002). Inmate racial integration: Achieving racial integration in the Texas prison system. *The Prison Journal, 82:* 498–525.

Tumin, M. (1964). Ethnic group. In J. Gould & W. Kolb (Eds.), *Dictionary of the social sciences.* New York: Free Press of Glencoe.

Turk, A. (1969). *Criminality and legal order.* Chicago: Rand-McNally.

Turner, S. F., Davis, L., Fain, T., Briathwaite, H., Lavery, T., Choinski, W., & Camp, G. (2015). A national picture of prison downsizing strategies. *Victims & Offenders, 10:* 401–419.

U.S. Bureau of Prisons. (2017). *Prison safety.* Available at: https://www.bop.gov/about/statistics/statistics_prison_safety.jsp.

U.S. Census Bureau. (2017). FFF: Hispanic heritage month 2016. Available at: https://www.census.gov/newsroom/facts-for-features/2016/cb16-ff16.html.

U.S. Commission on Civil Rights. (1970). Washington, DC: U.S. Government Printing Office.

U.S. Department of Education. (2016a). *State and local expenditures on corrections and education.* Available at: http://www2.ed.gov/rschstat/eval/other/expenditures-corrections-education/brief.pdf.

U.S. Department of Education. (2016b). *Key data highlights on equity and opportunity gaps in our nation's public schools.* Available at: http://www2.ed.gov/about/offices/list/ocr/docs/2013 - 14-first-look.pdf.

U.S. Department of Justice. (1998). *State court sentencing of convicted felons, 1994.* Washington, DC: Bureau of Justice Statistics.

Ulmer, J., & Johnson, B. (2004). Sentencing in context: A multilevel analysis. *Criminology,* 42: 137–177.

Ulmer, J., & Kramer, J. (1996). Court communities under sentencing guidelines: Dilemmas of formal rationality and sentencing disparity. *Criminology,* 34: 383–408.

Underwood, L. A., & Washington, A. (2016). Mental illness and juvenile offenders. *International Journal of Environmental Research and Public Health,* 13: 228–242.

United States Parole Commission. (2003). *History of the federal parole system.* Washington, DC: U.S. Department of Justice.

Urban Institute. (2016). The alarming lack of data on Latinos in the criminal justice system. Available at: http://apps.urban.org/features/latino-criminal-justice-data/.

Urbina, M. G. (2003a). The quest and application of historical knowledge in modern times: A critical view. *Criminal Justice Studies: A Critical Journal of Crime, Law and Society,* 16: 113–129.

Urbina, M. G. (2003b). Good teachers never die. *Hispanic Outlook,* 13: 31–32.

Urbina, M. G. (2004a). Language barriers in the Wisconsin court system: The Latino/a experience. *Journal of Ethnicity in Criminal Justice,* 2: 91–118.

Urbina, M. G. (2004b). A qualitative analysis of Latinos executed in the United States between 1975 and 1995: Who were they? *Social Justice: A Journal of Crime, Conflict & World Order,* 31: 242–267.

Urbina, M. G. (2005). Transferring juveniles to adult court in Wisconsin: Practitioners voice their views. *Criminal Justice Studies: A Critical Journal of Crime, Law and Society,* 18: 147–172.

Urbina, M. G. (2007). Latinas/os in the criminal and juvenile justice systems. *Critical Criminology: An International Journal,* 15: 41–99.

Urbina, M. G. (2008). *A comprehensive study of female offenders: Life before, during, and after incarceration.* Springfield, IL: Charles C Thomas.

Urbina, M. G. (2011). *Capital punishment and Latino offenders: Racial and ethnic differences in death sentences.* New York: LFB Scholarly Publishing.

Urbina, M. G. (2012). *Capital punishment in America: Race and the death penalty over time.* El Paso, TX: LFB Scholarly Publishing.

Urbina, M. G. (Ed.). (2014). *Twenty-first century dynamics of multiculturalism: Beyond post-racial America.* Springfield, IL: Charles C Thomas.

Urbina, M. G. (2016). Life after prison for Hispanics. In R. A. Gutierrez & T. Almaguer (Eds.), *The new Latino studies reader: A twenty-first-century perspective.* Berkeley: University of California Press.

Urbina, M. G., & Álvarez, S. E. (Eds.). (2015). *Latino police officers in the United States: An examination of emerging trends and issues.* Springfield, IL: Charles C Thomas.

Urbina, M. G., & Álvarez, S. E. (2016). Neoliberalism, criminal justice, and Latinos: The contours of neoliberal economic thought and policy on criminalization. *Latino Studies,* 14: 33–58.

Urbina, M. G., & Álvarez, S. E. (2017). *Ethnicity and criminal justice in the era of mass incarceration: A critical reader on the Latino experience.* Springfield, IL: Charles C Thomas.

Urbina, M. G., & Byxbe, F. (2011). Interacting forces in the judicial system: A case study in American criminal law. *International Journal of Humanities and Social Science,* 1: 141–154.

Urbina, M. G., & Kreitzer, S. (2004). The practical utility and ramifications of RICO: Thirty-two years after its implementation. *Criminal Justice Policy Review,* 15: 294–323.

Urbina, M. G., & Peña, I. A. (2018). Policing borders: Immigration, criminalization, and militarization in the era of social control profitability. In C. Crawford (Ed), *Spatial policing: The influence of time, space, and geography on law enforcement practices.* Durham, NC: Carolina Academic Press.

Urbina, M. G., & Smith, L. (2007). Colonialism and its impact on Mexicans' experience of punishment in the United States. In M. Bosworth & J. Flavin (Eds.), *Race, gender, and punishment: From colonialism to the war on terror.* Piscataway, NJ: Rutgers University Press.

Urbina, M. G., & White, W. (2009). Waiving juveniles to criminal court: Court officials express their thoughts. *Social Justice,* 36: 122–139.

Urbina, M. G., & Wright, C. R. (2016). *Latino access to higher education: Ethnic realities and new directions for the twenty-first century.* Springfield, IL: Charles C Thomas.

Urbina, M. G., Vela, J. E., & Sánchez, J. O. (2014). *Ethnic realities of Mexican Americans: From colonialism to 21st century globalization.* Springfield, IL: Charles C Thomas.

Valencia, R. R. (2008). *Chicano students and the courts: The Mexican American legal struggle for educational equality.* New York: New York University Press.

Valenzuela, A. (Ed.). (2016). *Growing critically conscious teachers: A social justice curriculum for educators of Latino/a youth.* New York: Teachers College Press.

Vallas, R. (2016). *Disabled behind bars: The mass incarceration of people with disabilities in America's jails and prisons.* Washington, DC: Center for American Progress.

Van Cleve, N. (2016). *Crooked county: Racism and injustice in America's largest criminal court.* Stanford, CA: Stanford University Press.

Vandiver, M. (1999). An apology does not assist the accused: Foreign nationals and the death penalty in the United States. *The Justice Professional,* 12: 223–245.

Vargas, J. (2001). U.S. border patrol abuses, undocumented Mexican workers, and international human rights. *San Diego International Law Review,* 2: 1–92.

Vásquez, S., Vivian, J., Chengalath, G., & Grimes, J. (2004). *Assaults within ADJC secure care facilities.* Phoenix, AZ: Arizona Department of Juvenile Corrections.

Vásquez, Y. (2011). Perpetuating the marginalization of Latinos: A collateral consequence of immigration law into the criminal justice system. *Howard Law Journal,* 54: 11–20.

Vázquez, R. (2000). The Hispanic death sentence in Texas. *LasCultras.com.* Available at: http://www.lasculturas.com/aa/aa061300a.htm.

Vera Sánchez, C., & Rosenbaum, D. (2011). Racialized policing: Officers' voices on policing Latino and African American neighborhoods. *The Journal of Ethnicity in Criminal Justice,* 9: 152–178.

Vicini, J. (2006). U.S. has most prisoners in world due to tough laws. Available at: http://news.yahoo.com/s/nm/20061209/tsnm/usaprisonersdc&printer=1.

Vidales, G., Day, K., & Powe, M. (2009). Police and immigration enforcement: Impacts on Latino(a) residents' perceptions of police. *Policing an International Journal of Police Strategies and Management,* 32: 631–653.

Vigil, E. (1999). *The crusade for justice: Chicano militancy and the government's war on dissent.* Madison, WI: University of Wisconsin Press.

Vigil, J. (2002). *A rainbow of gangs: Street cultures in the mega-city.* Austin, TX: University of Texas Press.

Vigil, J. (2007). *The projects: Gang and non-gang families in East Los Angeles.* Austin, TX: University of Texas.

Visher, C., & Travis, J. (2003). Transitions from prison to community: Understanding individual pathways. *Annual Review of Sociology,* 29: 89–113.

Visher, C., Yahner, J., La Vigne, N. (2010). *Life after prison: Tracking the experiences of male prisoners returning to Chicago, Cleveland, and Houston.* Urban Institute, Justice Policy Center.

Vito, G. (1987). Felony probation and recidivism. *Federal Probation,* 50: 17–25.

Wacquant, L. (2001). Deadly symbiosis: When ghetto and prison meet and mesh. In D. Garland (Ed.), *Mass incarceration: Social causes and consequences.* London: Sage.

Wacquant, L. (2009). *Punishing the poor: The neoliberal government of social insecurity.* Durham, NC: Duke University Press.

Wade, L. (2010). Comparing increases in U.S. corrections and higher education spending. Sociological Images. Available at: http://thesocietypages.org/socimages/2010/12/09 /comparing-increases-in-u-s-corrections-and-higher-education-spending/.

Walker, N., Senger, J., Villarruel, F., & Arboleda, A. (2004). *Lost opportunities: The realities of Latinos in the U.S. criminal justice system.* Washington, DC: National Council of La Raza.

Walker, S. (1998). *Popular justice: A history of American criminal justice* (2nd ed.). New York: Oxford University Press.

Walker, S. (2005). *Sense and nonsense about crime and drugs: A policy guide* (6th ed.). Belmont: Wadsworth.

Walker, S., Spohn, C., & DeLone, M. (2018). *The color of justice: Race, ethnicity, and crime in America* (6th ed.). Belmont, CA: Wadsworth.

Walmsley, R. (2009). *The world prison population list.* Essex, UK: International Centre for Prison Studies.

Walsh, J. (1995). Young and Latino in a cold war barrio: Survival, the search for identity, and the formation of street gangs in Denver, 1945–1955. (Master's Thesis, University of Colorado at Denver.)

Ward, D., & Kassebaum, G. (1964). *Women's prison: Sex and sexual structure.* Piscataway, NJ: Aldine.

Ward, G., Farrell, A., & Rousseau, D. (2009). Does racial balance in workforce representation yield equal justice? Race relations of sentencing in federal court organizations. *Law & Society Review,* 43: 757–806.

Warnshius, P. (1931). Crime and criminal justice among Mexicans in Illinois. In National Commission on Law Observance and Enforcement Report, *Crime and the foreign born.* Washington DC: Government Printing Office.

Warren, M. (1999). Foreign nationals and the death penalty in the United States. Available at: http://www.essential.org/dpic/foreignnatl.html.

Washington Post. (1993). Texas, California executions. August 25: A9.

Wazwaz, N. (2015). It's official: The U.S. is becoming a minority-majority nation. Available at: http://www.usnews.com/news/articles/2015/07/06/its-official-the-us-is-becoming-a-minority-majority-nation.

Weber, D. J. (Ed.). (2004). *Foreigners in their native land: Historical roots of the Mexican Americans.* Albuquerque, NM: University of New Mexico Press.

Weitz, M. (2010). *The Sleepy Lagoon murder case: Race discrimination and Mexican-American rights.* Lawrence, KS: University Press of Kansas.

Weitzer, R. (2000). White, black, or blue cops? Race and citizen assessments of police officers. *Journal of Criminal Justice,* 28: 313–324.

Weitzer, R., & Tuch, S. (2004). Race and perceptions of police misconduct. *Social Problems,* 51: 305–324.

Weitzer, R., Tuch, S. A., & Skogan, W. (2008). Police-community relations in a majority black city. *Journal of Research in Crime and Delinquency,* 45: 398–428.

Welch, M. (2002). *Detained: Immigration laws and the expanding I.N.S. jail complex.* Philadelphia: Temple University Press.

Welch, M. (2006). *Scapegoats of September 11th: Hate crimes and state crimes in the war on terror.* New Brunswick, NJ: Rutgers University Press.

Welch, M. (2007). Immigration lockdown before and after 9/11: Ethnic constructions and their consequences. In M. Bosworth & J. Flavin (Eds.), *Race, gender, and punishment: From colonialism to the war on terror.* Piscataway, NJ: Rutgers University Press.

Welch, M. (2009). *Crimes of power & states of impunity: The U.S. response to terror.* New Brunswick, NJ: Rutgers University Press.

West, C. (2001). *Race matters.* Boston, MA: Beacon Press.

West, H. (2010). *Prison inmates at midyear 2009–statistical tables.* Washington, DC: U.S. Department of Justice.

Western, B. (2002). The impact of incarceration on wage mobility and inequality. *American Sociological Review,* 67: 526–546.

Whitehead, J. (1991). The effectiveness of felony probation: Results from an eastern state. *Justice Quarterly,* 8: 525–543.

Whitehead, J. (2013). *A Government of wolves: The emerging American police state.* New York: SelectBooks.

Wickersham Commission. (1931). *Report on crime and the foreign born.* National Commission on Law Observance and Enforcement. Washington, DC: U.S. Government Printing Office.

Wilbanks, W. (1987). *The myth of a racist criminal justice system.* Monterrey, CA: Brooks/Cole.

Wilder, F. (2007). Detention archipelago: Jailing immigrants for profit. *NACLA report on the Americas.* May/June: 19–24.

Wilhelm, D., & Turner, N. (2002). *Is the budget crisis changing the way we look at sentencing and incarceration?* New York: Vera Institute of Justice.

Wilkins, V., & Williams, B. (2008). Black or blue: Racial profiling and representative bureaucracy. *Public Administration Review,* 68: 652–662.

Wilkins, V., & Williams, B. (2009). Representing blue: Representative bureaucracy and racial profiling in the Latino community. *Administration and Society,* 40: 775–798.

Wilkinson, D. (2004). *Guns, violence, and identity among African American and Latino youth.* New York: LFB Scholarly Publishing.

Wilson, J. Q. (1968). *Varieties of police behavior: The management of law & order in eight communities.* Cambridge: Harvard University Press.

Wilson, J. Q. (1983). *Thinking about crime.* New York, NY: Basic Books.

Wilson, M. (2004). *Crime and punishment in early Arizona.* Las Vegas: Rama Press.

Winterdyk, J., & Ruddell, R. (2010). Managing prison gangs: Results from a survey of U.S. prison systems. *Journal of Criminal Justice,* 38: 730–736.

Wolff, N., & Shi, J. (2009). Contextualization of physical and sexual assault in male prisons: Incidents and their aftermath. *Journal of Correctional Health Care,* 15: 58–77.

Woodward, K. (1997). *Concepts of identity and difference. In K. Woodward (Ed.), Identity and differences.* London: Sage Publications.

Wulf-Ludden, T. (2016). Pseudofamilies, misconduct, and the utility of general strain theory in a women's prison. *Women & Criminal Justice,* 26: 233–259.

Yinger, J. (1985). Ethnicity. *Annual Review of Sociology,* 11: 151–180.

Yosso, T. J. (2002). Critical race media literacy: Challenging deficit discourse about Chicanas/os. *Journal of Popular Film & Television,* 30: 52–62.

Young, L. (2005). Setting sail with the charming Betsy: Enforcing the International Court of Justice's Avena judgment in federal Habeas Corpus proceedings. *Minnesota Law Review,* 89: 890–915.

Zatz, M. (1984). Race, ethnicity, and determinate sentencing: A new dimension to an old controversy. *Criminology,* 22: 147–171.

Zatz, M., & Portillos, E. (2000). Voices from the barrio: Chicano/a gangs, families, and communities. *Criminology,* 38: 369–402.

Zayas, L. H., & Bradlee, M. H. (2014). Exiling children, creating orphans: When immigration policies hurt citizens. *Social Work,* 59: 167–175.

Zelinsky, W. (2001). *The enigma of ethnicity: Another American dilemma.* Iowa City: University of Iowa Press.

Zimbardo, P. G. (2008). *The Lucifer effect: Understanding how good people turn evil.* New York: Random House Trade Paperbacks.

Zimring, F. (2011). The consequences of fundamental conflict. University of California, Berkeley School of Law. Available at: http://www.law.berkeley.edu/institutes/csls/zimring chapter6.doc.

Zuberi, T., & Bonilla-Silva, E. (Eds). (2008). *White logic, white methods: Racism and methodology.* Lanham, MD: Rowman & Littlefield Publishers.

Zuckerbrod, N. (2007). 1 in 10 schools are 'dropout factories.' Available at: http://www.usa today.com/news/education/2007-10-30-dropout-factories_N.htm.

INDEX

Cases Cited

ABOUT THE EDITORS

Martin Guevara Urbina, PhD, a native of San Miguel de Allende, Guanajuato, Mexico, is a Mexican American author, writer, researcher, professor, and speaker who, as a sociologist and criminologist, has engaged in an intensive academic research, publication, and discourse agenda designed to provide readers with evidence-based information of ethnic and racial minorities in the United States, with an emphasis on the exploration of the Latino experience and a focus on the Mexican American experience.

Dr. Urbina is Professor of Criminal Justice in the Department of Natural & Behavioral Sciences at Sul Ross State University–Rio Grande College. Urbina has taught at New Mexico State University, Western Michigan University, University of Wisconsin–Milwaukee, Howard College, Southwest Texas Junior College, and Texas A&M University–Central Texas. Professor Urbina was awarded a *Certificate of Recognition for Outstanding Teaching* by Western Michigan University in 1999, and he was nominated for the *2002–2003 UWM Distinguished Undergraduate Teaching Award* by the University of Wisconsin–Milwaukee.

Professor Urbina is author, coauthor, or editor of over 60 scholarly publications on a wide range of topics, including several academic books: *Immigration and the Law: Race, Citizenship, and Social Control* (2018); *Hispanics in the U.S. Criminal Justice System: Ethnicity, Ideology, and Social Control* (2018); *Ethnicity and Criminal Justice in the Era of Mass Incarceration: A Critical Reader on the Latino Experience* (2017); *Latino Access to Higher Education: Ethnic Realities and New Directions for the Twenty-First Century* (2016); *Latino Police Officers in the United States: An Examination of Emerging Trends and Issues* (2015); *Twenty-First Century Dynamics of Multiculturalism: Beyond Post-Racial America* (2014); *Ethnic Realities of Mexican Americans: From Colonialism to 21st Century Globalization* (2014); *Capital Punishment in America: Race and the Death Penalty Over Time* (2012); *Hispanics in the U.S. Criminal Justice System: The New American Demography* (2012); *A Comprehensive Study of Female Offenders: Life Before, During, and After Incarceration* (2008); and *Capital Punishment and Latino Offenders: Racial and Ethnic Differences in Death Sentences* (2003, 2011). Currently, Dr. Urbina is working on three new academic books: *Latinos and the U.S. Legal System: Laws that Wound–A Call for a Balanced System; The Color of Justice–The Price of Injustice: Racism in the Age of Colorblindness;* and *Hispanic Soldiers: The Latino Legacy in the U.S. Armed Forces.*

His work has been published in national and international academic journals, to include *Justice Quarterly; Critical Criminology; Social Justice; Latino Studies; and Criminal*

393

Law Bulletin. Urbina's work has been cited (and/or contributed) in the popular media (newspapers, magazines, radio, television, and online news), including EFE News Agency (EFE is Spain's International News Agency, the largest newswire service in Spain, Latin America, and the Hispanic Media in the U.S. and the 4th largest newswire service worldwide); *El Periodico de Mexico; El Pais; El Universal (UNIÓN); Diario Las Americas; San Diego Union Tribune; El Nuevo Diario; El Nuevo Herald; La Prensa Latina; Viva Noticias; LA Times;* Terra; and Yahoo News. Urbina has made appearances in radio and television, including Zona Franca TV, Imagen Radio (air live to the entire country of Mexico and live stream worldwide), and Radio Bilingue (Línea Abierta, the first and only national live talk and call-in program in public broadcasting interconnecting Spanish-speaking audiences and newsmakers throughout the U.S. and Mexico). In the United States, Dr. Urbina appears frequently in primetime evening news for Telemundo, where he has discussed historical, existing, and emerging social, economic, political issues—like immigration, deportations, excessive/deadly force in policing, imprisonment of children, the school-to-prison pipeline, and national security.

Along with his academic endeavors, he is also writing other literary works: *An Adventure in Time: A Journey Without Boundaries* (fiction); *Mi Vida: Between the Wind and the Rain, I Looked up and Wept* (nonfiction); and *Kylor's Adventure Through the Rainforest: A Journey of Courage and Faith* (a children's book). Most recently, Dr. Urbina has also opted to venture into the world of poetry, with the illusion of writing a book of poems: *Cincuenta Poemas de Amor Para el Alma y el Corazon: Fifty Love Poems for the Soul and the Heart.*

During his spare time, Urbina loves evening walks. His biggest delight: *la lluvia* (rain)! For a complete list of Urbina's research and publications, visit his website (http://www.martinguevaraurbina.com) and his Author Page on Amazon (http://amazon.com/author/martin.guevara.urbina) for his books.

Sofía Espinoza Álvarez is an author, researcher, legist, social advocate, and philanthropist. She received a law degree from Universidad de León, San Miguel de Allende, Guanajuato, Mexico, and holds a Bachelor of Science (B.S.) degree in criminal justice (Texas, United States). Her areas of interest include Mexican and U.S. jurisprudence, philosophy of law, constitutional law, immigration law, law and society, and penology. She has maintained an active professional career and an intense research and publication agenda, publishing various academic books, book chapters, and journal articles. Her research has been published in national as well as leading, international peer-reviewed journals, including "Capital Punishment on Trial: Who Lives, Who Dies, Who Decides—A Question of Justice?" (*Criminal Law Bulletin,* 2014); and "Neoliberalism, Criminal Justice, and Latinos: The Contours of Neoliberal Economic Thought and Policy on Criminalization" (*Latino Studies,* 2016). Considering the dynamics of law enforcement in a highly charged political climate, Álvarez published a book analyzing critical issues confronting Latino officers, law enforcement in general, and society, entitled *Latino Police Officers in the United States: An Examination of Emerging Trends and Issues* (2015). In her book, *Ethnicity and Criminal Justice in the Era of Mass Incarceration: A Critical Reader on the Latino Experience*

(2017), Álvarez documents historical and contemporary forces shaping the Latino experience with the criminal justice system. Recently, she published a groundbreaking book, *Immigration and the Law: Race, Citizenship, and Social Control* (2018), where she and her coeditor bring together a group of renowned scholars from around the country to critically analyze one of the most crucial topics of our times, immigration and the law over time. In her new book, *Hispanics in the U.S. Criminal Justice System: Ethnicity, Ideology, and Social Control* (2018), Álvarez and her coauthor delineate the forces governing the Latino experience in policing, judicial system, and penal system.

Currently, she is researching the utility, implications, and ramifications of twenty-first century transnational social control movements, like the war on drugs and the war on terrorism; delineating the contours of U.S. and Mexican criminal laws. In her upcoming book, *Latinos and the U.S. Legal System: Laws that Wound–A Call for a Balanced System,* Álvarez and her coauthors will explore and delineate the ethnic realities of Latinos and the American legal system, illustrating the significance of fundamental issues like representation.

Vested in positive social transformation, since 2013, she has been working with migrant children, women, and men traveling to the U.S. through Mexico, seeing first-hand the global dynamics of immigration, and thus prompting her to start a non-profit organization–Empower Global Foundation (https://globalempower.org/). With a global mission, Empower Global is focused in empowering, habilitating, and creating awareness; seeking equality, justice, respect, and human dignity to vanquish universal consensus. The foundation endeavors rigorously in various activities of social projects and research, promoting an image of social and cultural integration, and striving for understanding, tolerance, and universal unity. "For the Progression of Humanity," Empower Global seeks to potentiate skills, empower communities, and generate proposals to benefit the most vulnerable, like migrant children, teenage mothers, elderly citizens, and indigent people.

In addition to her work as a legal scholar and academic endeavors in research, publication, and social activism, Álvarez is currently working and assisting people with immigration related issues, including visa requirements, and procedures for obtaining different types of visas for legal residence. Conjointly, she collaborates as a columnist for Univision and the Huffington Post where she presents her research on the ethnic realities of Latinos and the U.S. legal system, and illustrates the importance of key issues, such as representation. During her spare time, she is actively involved in various community activities–propagating an image of social and cultural inclusivity, empowerment, and unity. Visit her website (http://sofiaalva.com/), and her Author Page on Amazon (http://amazon.com/author/sofia.alvarez/) for her books.

CHARLES C THOMAS · PUBLISHER, LTD.

CRIMINAL JUSTICE TECHNOLOGY IN THE 21ST CENTURY
(3rd Edition)
by Laura J. Moriarty
Published 2017 • 296 pp. (7 x 10)
17 illustrations • 8 tables
$44.95 (paper) • $44.95 (ebook)

HIGH-RISK PATROL
(3rd Edition)
by Gerald W. Garner
Published 2016 • 290 pp. (7 x 10)
$44.95 (paper) • $44.95 (ebook)

FORENSIC ALCOHOL TEST EVIDENCE (FATE)
by John Brick
Published 2016 • 368 pp. (7 x 10)
16 illustrations • 32 tables
$59.95 (paper) • $59.95 (ebook)

FUNDAMENTALS OF PHYSICAL SURVEILLANCE
(3rd Edition)
by Raymond P. Siljander and Darin D. Fredrickson
Published 2016 • 300 pp. (7 x 10)
170 illustrations • 2 tables
$45.95 (paper) • $45.95 (ebook)

THE CONSEQUENCES OF DISASTERS
by Helen James and Douglas Paton
Published 2016 • 414 pp. (7 x 10)
82 illustrations • 57 tables
$62.95 (paper) • $62.95 (ebook)

HAIR AND JUSTICE
by Carmen M. Cusack
Published 2015 • 224 pp. (7 x 10)
$35.95 (paper) • $35.95 (ebook)

CRISIS NEGOTIATION FOR LAW ENFORCEMENT, CORRECTIONS, AND EMERGENCY SERVICES
by Arthur Slatkin
Published 2015 • 152 pp. (7 x 10)
10 illustrations
$32.95 (paper) • $32.95 (ebook)

ETHNICITY AND CRIMINAL JUSTICE IN THE ERA OF MASS INCARCERATION
by Martin Guevara Urbina and Sofia Espinoza Alvarez
2017 • 338 pp. (7 x 10)
2 tables

LAW ENFORCEMENT, POLICE UNIONS, AND THE FUTURE
by Ron DeLord and Ron York
Published 2017 • 272 pp. (7 x 10)
$42.95 (paper) • $42.95 (ebook)

TALKING ETHICS WITH COPS
by Neal Tyler
Published 2016 • 236 pp. (7 x 10)
$34.95 (paper) • $34.95 (ebook)

ADVANCED INTERVIEWING TECHNIQUES *(3rd Edition)*
by John R. Schafer and Joe Navarro
Published 2016 • 216 pp. (7 x 10)
$37.95 (paper) • $37.95 (ebook)

CRIME SCENE STAGING
by Arthur S. Chancellor and Grant D. Graham
Published 2016 • 368 pp. (7 x 10)
22 illustrations
$49.95 (paper) • $49.95 (ebook)

CHILD ABUSE INVESTIGATIONS
by Donald A. Hayden
Published 2016 • 368 pp. (7 x 10)
25 illustrations • 6 tables
$49.95 (paper) • $49.95 (ebook)

UNDERCOVER DISGUISE METHODS FOR INVESTIGATORS
by Arabella Mazzuki, Raymond P. Siljander and Simon Mitchell
Published 2015 • 226 pp. (7 x 10)
87 illustrations
$38.95 (paper) • $38.95 (ebook)

YOUTH GANGS *(4th Edition)*
by Robert J. Franzese, Herbert C. Covey and Scott Menard
Published 2016 • 380 pp. (7 x 10)
6 illustrations • 1 table
$63.95 (paper) • $63.95 (ebook)

LATINO POLICE OFFICERS IN THE UNITED STATES
by Martin Guevara Urbina and Sofia Espinoza Alvarez
Published 2015 • 290 pp. (7 x 10)
4 illustrations • 10 tables
$43.95 (paper) • $43.95 (ebook)

Find us on:
facebook
FACEBOOK.COM/CCTPUBLISHER

FREE SHIPPING ON ORDERS OVER $50! USE PROMO CODE: SHIP50
Available on retail purchases through our website only to domestic shipping addresses in the United States
TO ORDER: 1-800-258-8980 • books@ccthomas.com • www.ccthomas.com
Sign up for our eNewsletter at www.ccthomas.com for eOnly discounts!